Lecture Notes in Computer Science 14361

Founding Editors

Gerhard Goos
Juris Hartmanis

Editorial Board Members

The series Lecture Notes in Computer Science (LNCS), including its subseries Lecture Notes in Artificial Intelligence (LNAI) and Lecture Notes in Bioinformatics (LNBI), has established itself as a medium for the publication of new developments in computer science and information technology research, teaching, and education.

LNCS enjoys close cooperation with the computer science R & D community, the series counts many renowned academics among its volume editors and paper authors, and collaborates with prestigious societies. Its mission is to serve this international community by providing an invaluable service, mainly focused on the publication of conference and workshop proceedings and postproceedings. LNCS commenced publication in 1973.

George Bebis · Golnaz Ghiasi · Yi Fang ·
Andrei Sharf · Yue Dong · Chris Weaver ·
Zhicheng Leo · Joseph J. LaViola Jr. · Luv Kohli
Editors

Advances in Visual Computing

18th International Symposium, ISVC 2023
Lake Tahoe, NV, USA, October 16–18, 2023
Proceedings, Part I

Springer

Editors
George Bebis
University of Nevada Reno
Reno, NV, USA

Yi Fang
New York University
New York, NY, USA

Yue Dong
Microsoft Research
Beijing, China

Zhicheng Leo
University of Maryland
Collage Park, MD, USA

Luv Kohli
InnerOptic Technology
Hillsborough, NC, USA

Golnaz Ghiasi
Google Research
Mountain View, CA, USA

Andrei Sharf
Ben-Gurion University
Be'er Sheva, Israel

Chris Weaver
The University of Oklahoma
Norman, OK, USA

Joseph J. LaViola Jr.
University of Central Florida
Orlando, FL, USA

ISSN 0302-9743 ISSN 1611-3349 (electronic)
Lecture Notes in Computer Science
ISBN 978-3-031-47968-7 ISBN 978-3-031-47969-4 (eBook)
https://doi.org/10.1007/978-3-031-47969-4

This Springer imprint is published by the registered company Springer Nature Switzerland AG
The registered company address is: Gewerbestrasse 11, 6330 Cham, Switzerland

Paper in this product is recyclable.

Preface

It is with great pleasure that we welcome you to the proceedings of the 18th International Symposium on Visual Computing (ISVC 2023), which was held in Lake Tahoe (October 16–18, 2023). ISVC provides a common umbrella for the four main areas of visual computing including vision, graphics, visualization, and virtual reality. The goal is to provide a forum for researchers, scientists, engineers, and practitioners throughout the world to present their latest research findings, ideas, developments, and applications in the broader area of visual computing.

This year, the program consisted of seven keynote presentations, eleven oral sessions, one poster session, six special tracks, and three tutorials. We received close to 120 submissions for the main symposium from which we accepted 43 papers for oral presentation and 15 papers for poster presentation. A total of 25 papers were accepted for oral presentation in the special tracks from 34 submissions.

All papers were reviewed with an emphasis on the potential to contribute to the state of the art in the field. Selection criteria included accuracy and originality of ideas, clarity and significance of results, and presentation quality. The review process was quite rigorous, involving three independent double-blind reviews followed by several days of discussion. During the discussion period we tried to correct anomalies and errors that might have existed in the initial reviews. Despite our efforts, we recognize that some papers worthy of inclusion may have not been included in the program. We offer our sincere apologies to authors whose contributions might have been overlooked.

We wish to thank everybody who submitted their work to ISVC 2023 for review. It was because of their contributions that we succeeded in having a technical program of high scientific quality. In particular, we would like to thank the keynote speakers, the program chairs, the steering committee, the international Program Committee, the special track organizers, the tutorial organizers, the reviewers, the sponsors, and especially the authors who contributed their work to the symposium. We would like to express our appreciation to Springer for sponsoring the best paper award again this year.

We sincerely hope that ISVC 2023 offered participants opportunities for professional growth.

September 2023

George Bebis
Yue Dong
Yi Fang
Golnaz Ghiasi
Luv Kohli
Joseph J. LaViola Jr.
Zhicheng Leo
Andrei Sharf
Chris Weaver

Organization

Steering Committee

Bebis George (Chair)	University of Nevada, Reno, USA
Coquillart Sabine	Inria, France
Klosowski James	AT&T Labs Research, USA
Kuno Yoshinori	Saitama University, Japan
Lin Steve	Microsoft, China
Lindstrom Peter	Lawrence Livermore National Laboratory, USA
Moreland Kenneth	Oak Ridge National Laboratory, USA
Nefian Ara	NASA Ames Research Center, USA
Tafti Ahmad P.	University of Pittsburgh, USA

Area Chairs

Computer Vision

Fang Yi	New York University, USA
Golnaz Ghiasi	Google Brain, USA

Computer Graphics

Dong Yue	Microsoft, China
Sharf Andrei	Ben-Gurion University, Israel

Virtual Reality

Kohli Luv	InnerOptic Technology, Inc., USA
LaViola Joseph	University of Central Florida, USA

Visualization

Liu Zhicheng (Leo)	University of Maryland, USA
Weaver Chris	University of Oklahoma, USA

Publicity Chair

Ali Erol   Eksperta Software, Turkey

Tutorials and Special Tracks Chairs

Hand Emily   University of Nevada, Reno, USA
Tavakkoli Alireza   University of Nevada, Reno, USA

Awards Chairs

Sun Zehang   Apple, USA
Amayeh Gholamreza   Tesla, USA

Web Master

Isayas Berhe Adhanom   University of Nevada, Reno, USA

Program Committee

Nicoletta Adamo-Villani   Purdue University, USA
Emmanuel Agu   Worcester Polytechnic Institute, USA
Touqeer Ahmad   Blackmagic Design, USA
Kostas Alexis   Norwegian University of Science and Technology,
                                        Norway
Usman Alim   University of Calgary, Canada
Amol Ambardekar   Microsoft, USA
Soheyla Amirian   University of Georgia, USA
Mehdi Ammi   LIMSI-CNRS, France
Naga Surya Sandeep Angara   National Institute of Health, USA
Zahra Anvari   University of Texas at Arlington, USA
Mark Apperley   University of Waikato, New Zealand
Antonis Argyros   Foundation for Research and
                                        Technology – Hellas, Greece
Vijayan K. Asari   University of Dayton, USA
Aishwarya Asesh   Adobe, USA
Vassilis Athitsos   University of Texas at Arlington, USA
Melinos Averkiou   University of Cyprus, Cyprus

George Baciu	Hong Kong Polytechnic University, China
Abdul Bais	University of Regina, Canada
Nikos Bakalos	National Technical University of Athens, Greece
Peter Balazs	University of Szeged, Hungary
Selim Balcısoy	Sabancı University, Turkey
Reneta Barneva	SUNY Fredonia, USA
Paola Barra	Università di Napoli Parthenope, Italy
Ronen Barzel	Drawbridge Labs, UK
Anil Ufuk Batmaz	Concordia University, Canada
George Bebis	University of Nevada, Reno, USA
Jan Bender	RWTH Aachen University, Germany
Bedrich Benes	Purdue University, USA
Ayush Bhargava	Facebook, USA
Harsh Bhatia	Lawrence Livermore National Laboratory, USA
Sanjiv Bhatia	University of Missouri, St. Louis, USA
Ayan Biswas	Los Alamos National Laboratory, USA
Dibio Borges	Universidade de Brasília, Brazil
David Borland	University of North Carolina at Chapel Hill, USA
Nizar Bouguila	Concordia University, Canada
Thierry Bouwmans	University of La Rochelle, France
Jose Braz Pereira	EST Setúbal/IPS, Portugal
Valentin Brimkov	Buffalo State College, USA
Wolfgang Broll	Ilmenau University of Technology, Germany
Gerd Bruder	University of Central Florida, USA
Chris Bryan	Arizona State University, USA
Tolga Çapin	TED University, Turkey
Sek Chai	Latent AI, Inc., USA
Jian Chang	Bournemouth University, UK
Sotirios Chatzis	Cyprus University of Technology, Cyprus
Cunjian Chen	Michigan State University, USA
Zhonggui Chen	Xiamen University, China
Yi-Jen Chiang	New York University, USA
Isaac Cho	Utah State University, USA
Amit Chourasia	University of California at San Diego, USA
Tommy Dang	Texas Tech University, USA
Aritra Dasgupta	NYU, USA
Jeremie Dequidt	University of Lille, France
Daljit Singh Dhillon	Clemson University, USA
Sotirios Diamantas	Tarleton State University, Texas A&M System, USA
Alexandra Diehl	University of Konstanz, Germany
John Dingliana	Trinity College Dublin, Ireland

Ralf Dörner	RheinMain University of Applied Sciences, Germany
Yue Dong	Microsoft Research Asia, China
Gianfranco Doretto	West Virginia University, USA
Anastasios Doulamis	Technical University of Crete, Greece
Shengzhi Du	Tshwane University of Technology, South Africa
Meenal Dugar	Penn State University, USA
Soumya Dutta	Los Alamos National Laboratory, USA
Achim Ebert	University of Kaiserslautern, Germany
Parris Egbert	Brigham Young University, USA
Mohamed El Ansari	Moulay Ismail University, Morocco
El-Sayed M. El-Alfy	King Fahd University of Petroleum and Minerals, Saudi Arabia
Alireza Entezari	University of Florida, USA
Ali Erol	Sigun Information Technologies, UK
Mohammad Eslami	University of Pittsburgh, USA
Yi Fang	New York University, USA
Matteo Ferrara	University of Bologna, Italy
Nivan Ferreira	Universidade Federal de Pernambuco, Brazil
Francesco Ferrise	Politecnico di Milano, Italy
Robert Fisher	University of Edinburgh, UK
Gian Luca	Foresti University of Udine, Italy
Ioannis Fudos	University of Ioannina, Greece
Issei Fujishiro	Keio University, Japan
Radovan Fusek	VŠB-Technical University of Ostrava, Czechia
Marina Gavrilova	University of Calgary, Canada
Krzysztof Gdawiec	University of Silesia in Katowice, Poland
Golnaz Ghiasi	Google Research, USA
Daniela Giorgi	ISTI – CNR, Italy
Deeptha Girish	University of Cincinnati, USA
Wooi-Boon Goh	Nanyang Technological University, Singapore
Minglun Gong	University of Guelph, Canada
Laurent Grisoni	University of Lille, France
David Gustafson	Kansas State University, USA
Felix Hamza-Lup	Georgia Southern University, USA
Emily Hand	University of Nevada, Reno, USA
Brandon Haworth	University of Victoria, Canada
Subhashis Hazarika	SRI International, USA
Eric Hodgson	Miami University, USA
Jing Hua	Wayne State University, USA
Muhammad Hussain	King Saud University, Saudi Arabia
Ahmed Hussein	University of Guelph, Canada

Giuseppe Placidi	University of L'Aquila, Italy
Kevin Ponto	University of Wisconsin-Madison, USA
Jiju Poovvancheri	University of Victoria, Canada
Nicolas Pronost	Université Claude Bernard Lyon 1, France
Lei Qi	Iowa State University, USA
Hong Qin	Stony Brook University, USA
Christopher Rasmussen	University of Delaware, USA
Emma Regentova	University of Nevada, Las Vegas, USA
Guido Reina	University of Stuttgart, Germany
Erik Reinhard	InterDigital, France
Banafsheh Rekabdar	Portland State University, USA
Hongliang Ren	National University of Singapore, Singapore
Theresa-Marie Rhyne	Consultant, USA
Eraldo Ribeiro	Florida Institute of Technology, USA
Peter Rodgers	University of Kent, UK
Sudipta Roy	Jio Institute, India
Isaac Rudomin	Barcelona Supercomputing Center, Spain
Filip Sadlo	Heidelberg University, Germany
Punam Saha	University of Iowa, USA
Naohisa Sakamoto	Kobe University, Japan
Kristian Sandberg	Computational Solutions, Inc., USA
Nickolas S. Sapidis	University of Western Macedonia, Greece
Fabien Scalzo	Pepperdine University, USA
Thomas Schultz	University of Bonn, Germany
Andrei Sharf	Ben-Gurion University of the Negev, Israel
Puneet Sharma	UiT-The Arctic University of Norway, Norway
Timothy Shead	Sandia National Laboratories, USA
Mohamed Shehata	University of British Columbia, Canada
Gurjot Singh	Fairleigh Dickinson University, USA
Vineeta Singh	University of Cincinnati, USA
Alexei Skurikhin	Los Alamos National Laboratory, USA
Pavel Slavik	Czech Technical University in Prague, Czechia
Jack Snoeyink	University of North Carolina at Chapel Hill, USA
Fabio Solari	University of Genoa, Italy
Paolo Spagnolo	National Research Council, Italy
Jaya Sreevalsan-Nair	IIIT Bangalore, India
Chung-Yen Su	National Taiwan Normal University, Taiwan
Changming Sun	CSIRO, Australia
Guodao Sun	Zhejiang University of Technology, China
Zehang Sun	Apple Inc., USA
Carlo H. Séquin	University of California, Berkeley, USA
Ahmad Tafti	University of Pittsburgh, USA

Additional Reviewers

Aliniya, Parvaneh
Bhattacharya, Arindam
Chen, Ho-Lin
Golchin, Bahareh
Gong, Minglun
Iqbal, Hasan
Loizou, Marios
Mohamed, Abdallah

Nykl, Scott
Ramesh, Subhash
Randhawa, Zaigham
Sheibanifard, Armin
Shu, Ziyu
Wang, Meili
Zaveri, Ram
Zgaren, Ahmed

Keynote Talks

Machine Learning for Scientific Data Analysis and Visualization

Han-Wei Shan

The Ohio State University, USA

Abstract. In this talk, I will discuss our recent developments on using machine learning for scientific data analysis and visualization, with special focuses on visualization surrogates and compact representations for scientific data. I will first discuss how to construct visualization surrogates that can help streamline the visualization and analysis of large-scale ensemble simulations and facilitate the exploration of their immense input parameter space. Three different approaches for constructing such visualization surrogates: image space, object space, and hybrid image-object space approaches will be discussed. Then I will discuss how neural networks can be used to extract succinct representations from scientific data for rapid exploration and tracking of features. The use of geometric convolution to represent 3D particle data, and how regions of interest can be used as important measures for more efficient latent generation will be discussed.

Speaker Bio-Sketch: Han-Wei Shen is a Full Professor at The Ohio State University, and currently serves as the Editor-in-Chief of IEEE Transactions on Visualization and Computer Graphics. He is a member of IEEE VGTC Visualization Academy, and was the chair of the steering committee for IEEE SciVis conference from 2018-2020. His primary research interests are visualization, artificial intelligence, high performance computing, and computer graphics. Professor Shen is a winner of National Science Foundation's CAREER award and US Department of Energy's Early Career Principal Investigator Award. He received his BS degree from Department of Computer Science and Information Engineering at National Taiwan University in 1988, the MS degree in computer science from the State University of New York at Stony Brook in 1992, and the PhD degree in computer science from the University of Utah in 1998. From 1996 to 1999, he was a research scientist at NASA Ames Research Center in Mountain View California.

Estimating the Structure and Motion of Biomolecules at Atomic Resolutions

David Fleet

University of Toronto & Google DeepMind, Canada

Abstract. One of the foremost problems in structural biology concerns the inference of the atomic-resolution 3D structure of biomolecules from electron cryo-microscopy (cryo-EM). The problem, in a nutshell, is a form of multi-view 3D reconstruction, inferring the 3D electron density of a particle from large sets of images from an electron microscope. I'll outline the nature of the problem and several of the key algorithmic developments, with particular emphasis on the challenging case in which the imaged molecule exhibits a wide range of conformational variation (or non-rigidity). Through single particle cryo-EM, methods from computer vision and machine learning are reshaping structural biology and drug discovery. This is joint work with Ali Punjani.

Speaker Bio-Sketch: David Fleet is a Research Scientist at Google DeepMind (since 2020) and a Professor of Computer Science at the University of Toronto (since 2004). From 2012–2017 he served as Chair of the Department of Computer and Mathematical Sciences, University of Toronto Scarborough. Before joining the University of Toronto, he worked at Xerox PARC (1999–2004) and Queen's University (1991-1998). He received the PhD in Computer Science from the University of Toronto in 1991. He as awarded an Alfred P. Sloan Research Fellowship in 1996 for his research on visual neuroscience. He received research paper awards at ICCV 1999, CVPR 2001, UIST 2003, BMVC 2009, and NeurIPS 2022. In 2010, with Michael Black and Hedvig Sidenbladh he received the Koenderink Prize for fundamental contributions to computer vision that withstood the test of time. In 2022, with Ali Punjani, he received the Paper of the Year Award from the Journal of Structural Biology for work on cryo-EM. He served as Associate Editor of IEEE Trans PAMI (2000–2004), as Program Co-Chair for CVPR (2003) and ECCV (2014), and as Associate Editor-In-Chief for IEEE Trans PAMI (2005–2008). He was Senior Fellow of the Canadian Institute of Advanced Research (2005–2019), and currently holds a Canadian CIFAR AI Chair. His current research interests span computer vision, image processing machine learning and computational biology.

Curriculum Learning and Active Learning, for Visual Object Recognition when Data is Scarce

Daphna Weinshall

Hebrew University of Jerusalem, Israel

Abstract. Deep learning protocols typically involve the random sampling of training examples by way of SGD. We investigated alternative paradigms, based on the empirical observation that the value of data points changes with time and network proficiency. In this talk I will start with curriculum learning, where by strategically arranging the learning data to present simpler concepts before more complex ones, networks can accelerate their understanding of the easier concepts, resulting in faster convergence and enhanced overall performance. I will then discuss active learning, where one deals with the annotation of data within a predetermined annotation budget. The objective is to select the data instances for annotation that will yield the greatest improvement for the learner. Surprisingly, our findings challenge traditional active learning strategies, which typically assume a high budget. We demonstrate that when the budget is low, it is more beneficial to prioritize annotating a small number of examples that represent the easiest and most typical instances within the data. This stands in contrast to the conventional approach, which suggests selecting examples from the hardest and most atypical portion of the data distribution.

Speaker Bio-Sketch: Daphna Weinshall is a professor of Computer Science at the Hebrew University of Jerusalem, Israel. She acted as a visiting professor at MIT and NYU, and a visiting researcher at IBM Research NY, NECI Research Lab NJ, and Philips Research NY. Dr Weinshall served as an area chair on the program committees of NeurIPS, CVPR, ICCV, ECCV and IJCAI, and on the editorial boards of IEEE PAMI, CVIU and MVA. Additionally, she served as a panel chair or panel member on a number of prestigious grant evaluation committees, including the advance ERC Grants evaluation panel in computer science. Her undergraduate degree in mathematics and computer science is from Tel Aviv University, and she received her M.S. and Ph.D. in statistics (population genetics) from Tel Aviv University. Her recent work is focused on developing and expanding methodologies for deep learning in dynamical settings, including pioneering work on curriculum learning and active learning.

Have We Solved Image Correspondences?

Kwang Moo Yi

University of British Columbia, Canada

Abstract. Finding correspondence across images is a fundamental task in computer vision, which recently, as in many areas of computer vision, have been revolutionized by deep learning. In this talk, I will talk about the state of research in finding correspondence across images, and whether this long-standing problem is actually solved. I will follow the historical trend in how the correspondence problem was tackled in our community, focusing on its application to camera pose estimation with sparse correspondences. Specifically, I will discuss how point cloud networks and deep networks with specific architectural considerations have played a key role in initial breakthroughs, and how they have now become "transformer-ized". I will finally talk about the potential of using large-scale pre-trained models for the correspondence problem, and end with some thoughts on the future of correspondence research.

Speaker Bio-Sketch: Kwang Moo Yi is an assistant professor in the Department of Computer Science at the University of British Columbia (UBC), and a member of the Computer Vision Lab, CAIDA, and ICICS at UBC. Before, he was at the University of Victoria as an assistant professor. Prior to being a professor, he worked as a post-doctoral researcher at the Computer Vision Lab in École Polytechnique Fédérale de Lausanne (EPFL, Switzerland), working with Prof. Pascal Fua and Prof. Vincent Lepetit. He received his Ph.D. from Seoul National University under the supervision of Prof. Jin Young Choi. He also received his B.Sc. from the same University. He serves as area chair for top Computer Vision conferences (CVPR, ICCV, and ECCV), as well as Machine Learning (NeurIPS and AAAI). He is part of the organizing committee for CVPR 2023.

Visual Content Manipulation by Learning Generative Models

Jiebo Luo

University of Rochester, USA

Abstract. Visual content manipulation involves modifying or re-synthesizing an input image such that the output follows a guidance input, such as a target layout, semantic clues, or new attributes. However, even with the development of deep generative models, visual content manipulation is challenging because it typically requires transferring visual patterns in a non-rigid fashion. Moreover, unsupervised learning schemes are often required to learn models without image-guidance data pairs. I will focus on how to: 1) design model architectures and mechanisms for visual pattern transfer, 2) design unsupervised learning schemes for learning from unpaired data, and 3) improve the fidelity of the generated content. Specifically, I will present research results on a range of manipulation tasks including pose-guided transfer, example-guided image synthesis, semantic local editing, image completion, and structure-guided inpainting.

Speaker Bio-Sketch: Jiebo Luo is the Albert Arendt Hopeman Professor of Engineering and Professor of Computer Science at the University of Rochester. His research focuses on computer vision, NLP, machine learning, data mining, social media, computational social science, and digital health. He has authored nearly 600 papers and over 90 U.S. patents. Prof. Luo is also an active member of the research community: a Fellow of NAI, ACM, AAAI, IEEE, IAPR, and SPIE, Editor-in-Chief of the IEEE Transactions on Multimedia (2020–2022), as well as a member of the editorial boards of the IEEE Transactions on Pattern Analysis and Machine Intelligence (2006–2011), IEEE Transactions on Multimedia (2004–2009, 2013–2016), IEEE Transactions on Circuits and Systems for Video Technology (2010–2012), IEEE Transactions on Big Data (2018-), Pattern Recognition (2002–2020), ACM Transactions on Intelligent Systems and Technology (2015-present), and so on. In addition, he served as an organizing or program committee member for numerous technical conferences sponsored by IEEE, ACM, AAAI, ACL, IAPR, and SPIE, including most notably program co-chair of the 2010 ACM Multimedia Conference, 2012 IEEE Conference on Computer Vision and Pattern Recognition (CVPR), 2016 ACM Conference on Multimedia Retrieval (ICMR), and 2017 IEEE International Conference on Image Processing (ICIP).

Lights, Camera, Animation! Adaptive Simulation Methods for Training and Entertainment

Paul Kry

McGill University, Canada

Abstract. Physics-based simulations are a critical part of computer animation. This talk will provide a brief overview of new adaptive reduced methods that use rigid motion to speed up interactive and offline simulations of real-world phenomena. This includes merging rigid bodies at contacts, and rigidifying elastic bodies and shells when they are not deforming. The main challenge how to inexpensively identify when and where parts of a reduced system need more degrees of freedom. Applications and future directions will be discussed.

Speaker Bio-Sketch: Paul G. Kry received his B.Math. in computer science with electrical engineering electives in 1997 from the University of Waterloo, and his M.Sc. and Ph.D. in computer science from the University of British Columbia in 2000 and 2005. He spent time as a visitor at Rutgers during most of his Ph.D., and did postdoctoral work at Inria Rhône Alpes and the LNRS at Université René Descartes. He is currently an associate professor at McGill University. His research interests are in physically based animation, including deformation, contact, motion editing, and simulated control of locomotion, grasping, and balance. He co-chaired ACM/EG Symposium on Computer Animation in 2012, Graphics Interface in 2014, and served on numerous program committees, including ACM SIGGRAPH, ACM/EG Symposium on Computer Animation, Pacific Graphics, and Graphics Interface. He is currently an associate editor for Computer Graphics Forum, and for Computers and Graphics. He heads the Computer Animation and Interaction Capture Laboratory at McGill University. Paul Kry is currently the president of the Canadian Human Computer Communications Society, the organization which sponsors the annual Graphics Interface conference. Starting September 2016 Paul Kry served a 3-year term as a director at large on the ACM SIGGRAPH executive committee.

Beyond the Specs: A Computational and Human-Centered Approach to Wearability in AR/VR

Laura Trutoiu

Meta Reality Labs, USA

Abstract. In the rapidly evolving landscape of AR/VR, 'wearability' emerges as a potentially critical aspect that can shape the future of this technology and ensure broad adoption. This talk introduces a framework for 'wearability' in AR/VR. We will go outside of the usual technical specifications like field of view or latency to consider elements of user experience, comfort, and aesthetics, all tied to human factors considerations. Furthermore, the talk will touch on how bringing a computational data-driven approach to human factors like simulation and modeling can speed up development and insights. Drawing from my industry experiences, I'll advocate for bringing more multidisciplinary expertise and collaboration to the development of next-generation wearable, AR/VR technology. Finally, I'd like the audience to consider what would it take to make AR/VR fully inclusive and wearable for everyone?

Speaker Bio-Sketch: Laura Trutoiu currently leads a multidisciplinary team at Meta's Reality Labs, using her background in computer graphics and robotics to tackle complex system issues. Her work focuses on bringing a computational lens to human factors and design of AR/VR headsets. Her team integrates data science, user research, hardware design, and modeling to optimize the form factor of wearables, and bridge the digital and physical worlds. Previously, Laura was a Senior Computer Scientist at Magic Leap's Advanced Technology office in Seattle, where she prototyped next generation wearable spatial computers. She earned her PhD from the Robotics Institute at Carnegie Mellon University, and her research spanned several industry labs including Disney Research, Industrial Light and Magic, and Max Planck Institute for Biological Cybernetics. In the early days of Oculus Research, she developed the first proof of concept for face-to-face communication in head-mounted displays with realistic facial animations for avatars.

Contents – Part I

Video Analysis and Event Recognition

**ST: Innovations in Computer Vision & Machine Learning for
Critical & Civil Infrastructures**

ST: Generalization in Visual Machine Learning

Computer Graphics

Medical Image Analysis

Biometrics

Autonomous Anomaly Detection in Images

Contents – Part II

Applications

Object Detection and Recognition

Deep Learning

Posters

ST: Biomedical Image Analysis Techniques for Cancer Detection, Diagnosis and Management

Hybrid Region and Pixel-Level Adaptive Loss for Mass Segmentation on Whole Mammography Images

Parvaneh Aliniya$^{(\boxtimes)}$ ⓘ, Mircea Nicolescu ⓘ, Monica Nicolescu ⓘ, and George Bebis ⓘ

University of Nevada, Reno, NV 89557, USA
`aliniya@nevada.unr.edu`

Abstract. Breast cancer continues to be one of the most lethal cancer types, mainly affecting women. However, thanks to the utilization of deep learning approaches for breast cancer detection, there has been a considerable boost in the performance in the field. The loss function is a core element of any deep learning architecture with a significant influence on its performance. The loss function is particularly important for tasks such as breast mass segmentation. For this task, challenging properties of input images, such as pixel class imbalance, may result in instability of training or poor detection results due to the bias of the loss function toward correctly segmenting the majority class. Inspired by the success of sample-level loss functions, we propose a hybrid loss function incorporating both pixel-level and region-level losses, where the breast tissue density is used as a sample-level weighting signal. We refer to the proposed loss as Density-based Adaptive Sample-Level Prioritizing (Density-ASP) loss. Our motivation stems from the observation that mass segmentation becomes more challenging as breast density increases. This observation makes density a viable option for controlling the effect of region-level losses. To demonstrate the effectiveness of the proposed Density-ASP, we have conducted mass segmentation experiments using two publicly available datasets: INbreast and CBIS-DDSM. Our experimental results demonstrate that Density-ASP improves segmentation performance over the commonly used hybrid losses across multiple metrics.

1 Introduction

Despite significant progress in breast cancer screening over the last decades, breast cancer remains one of the most fatal cancer types among women [1]. Mammography is the most common screening tool for breast cancer detection, which has been shown to reduce mortality rate [4]. Automated breast cancer detection using mammography could help to reduce the cost of a second reader [2,3] while at the same time increasing the chance of early detection.

Powered by the well-proven effectiveness of deep learning, recent research work on abnormality detection has achieved promising results. However, these

G. Bebis et al. (Eds.): ISVC 2023, LNCS 14361, pp. 3–17, 2023.
https://doi.org/10.1007/978-3-031-47969-4_1

methods are still restricted by limitations, such as pixel class imbalance [5], which can adversely affect results in various tasks such as mass segmentation. These limitations have many times their root in the design of the loss function. In most cases, using a hybrid loss function – the weighted sum of different loss functions – has shown to be more beneficial compared to non-hybrid loss (using only one type of loss function). Although using the de-facto hybrid loss [5–7]–a weighted sum of Dice [8] and Binary Cross Entropy (BCE) [9] losses–has been shown to provide stability and robustness, the success of recent work on adaptive loss weighting strategies indicates that hybrid loss could be significantly improved by a sample-level design. Following the design of the ASP loss [10], which uses the mass ratio in the loss weighting strategy, we propose to employ the breast tissue density associated with each sample in the loss weighting strategy.

The rationale behind selecting breast tissue density as the sample-level signaling feature for hybrid loss stems from the observation that breast density (which represents the composition of fat, fibrous, and glandular tissue) is correlated with mass segmentation's difficulty. In the case of automatic detection from a single view, higher tissue density might be mistaken for an abnormality and increase the false positive rate. Therefore, the breast tissue density of each sample could provide valuable information during training. How to best leverage the information conveyed by each density category for training purposes is an important research question which we attempt to explore in this paper by introducing a region-level loss term in the hybrid loss. The benefit of the region-level loss term lies in the observation that comparison between the regions (rather than pixels) could result in the reduction of false positive and false negative rates by considering the dependencies between (via including surrounding pixels in the calculation of the loss) the pixels.

The Density-ASP loss function proposed in this paper consists of pixel-level and region-level losses. In this paper, loss functions such as Dice and BCE that consider pixels independently in the calculation of the loss are referred to as pixel-level losses. On the other hand, the loss functions that take the dependencies between the pixels into consideration are referred to as region-level losses. For the pixel-level loss term, we have combined Dice [5] and BCE [9]. The combination of these losses has been shown to help to address the issue of pixel class imbalance and increase training stability [6]. For the region-level loss term, we have combined Structural Similarity Index (SSIM) [11] and Region Mutual Information (RMI) [12]. It should be noted that the term hybrid applies to Density-ASP as well as each of the pixel-level and region-level terms (as they consist of two losses in their own categories). Instead of employing fixed weights [6,7] for each loss term, following the ASP loss methodology [10], we propose to use the ACR breast density category as an indicative signal for prioritizing the region-level loss term over the pixel-level loss term and vice versa. Therefore, the region-level loss is an adaptive loss term that will be prioritized for samples with higher density. Using AU-Net [6], which is a modern and effective variation of U-Net [14], as the baseline architecture, the Density-ASP loss has been evaluated on two benchmark datasets for mass segmentation: INbreast [15], and

CBIS-DDSM [16]. The results of our experiments illustrate that Density-ASP loss provides considerable performance improvements compared to commonly used hybrid losses.

The contributions of this paper are four-fold:

- Incorporating both pixel-level and region-level losses in the Density-ASP loss function.
- Employing breast tissue density as a prioritizing signal for adaptive sample-level prioritizing loss function for mass segmentation on whole mammograms.
- Evaluating Density-ASP on two benchmark datasets, INbreast and CBIS-DDSM.
- Quantitatively analyzing and comparing the findings of our experimental results for Density-ASP loss with the traditional hybrid loss for the baseline approach and state-of-the-art mass segmentation methods.

In the following sections, we first review related work in the field. The proposed method is then explained in detail. Our experimental results, analysis, and comparison with state-of-the-art methods are presented next. Finally, we provide our conclusions and discuss directions for future research.

2   Related Work

Recently, deep learning-based approaches have shown great promise in abnormality detection in medical images, with many studies achieving more accurate mass segmentation results compared to traditional approaches. In this section, we aim to briefly review the related work in deep learning-based approaches for breast mass segmentation, categorizing them into two groups: breast mass segmentation in whole mammograms and loss functions for binary segmentation of medical images.

2.1   Mass Segmentation on Whole Mammograms

The majority of breast mass segmentation approaches fall into one of the following categories based on the type of input they receive: region of interest (RoI) and whole mammogram. RoI-based mass segmentation approaches [17] have different properties, challenges, and strategies compared to methods using whole mammograms [6,7]; thus, in this section, the primary focus is on reviewing related work in the latter category.

Inspired by [18], one of the pioneer deep learning-based approaches for segmentation, Ronneberger et al. proposed U-Net [14], which is a fully convolutional symmetric encoder-decoder architecture that is instrumental for segmentation tasks with limited training data. This property of U-Net makes it specifically favorable for medical image segmentation where data scarcity is a relatively common limitation. U-Net combines low-level location information from the encoder with high-level semantic information from the decoder.

Thanks to the effectiveness of U-Net, a new wave of variations for different medical tasks has emerged [19–25], continuing to push the performance boundaries of medical image segmentation. In this context, the method proposed in [26] introduced a similar encoder-decoder architecture (leveraging dense blocks) where multi-scale information is utilized in the network. To enhance the performance of the network without additional parameters, atrous convolution [27] with various sample rates was used in the last encoder block. [28] is another U-Net-based approach based on the idea of utilizing a densely-connected network in the encoder and a CNN with attention gates in the decoder. Another line of research within the scope of multi-scale studies is [29], where the generator was designed as an improved version of U-Net. Before sending the segmentation results to the discriminator, multiscale results were created for three critics with different scales in the discriminator. Ravitha et al. [30], developed an approach employing the error of the outputs of intermediate layers relative to the ground truth labels as a supervision signal to boost model performance.

In [6], the authors introduced an attention-guided dense-up-sampling asymmetric encoder-decoder network (AU-Net) with an intermediate up-sampling block which includes a channel-wise attention mechanism designed to leverage the beneficial information presented in both low and high-level features. To mitigate the problem of relatively low performance of U-Net approach on small-size masses, [7] proposed to use a selective receptive field module with two parts, one for generating several receptive fields with different sizes and one for selecting the appropriate size of the receptive field. AU-Net has been chosen as the baseline model in this study.

2.2 Loss for Medical Image Segmentation

The choice of a suitable loss function, conveying the desired objectives of the task performed by a network, has a tremendous impact on the training process and overall performance of the network. Among the previously introduced losses for segmentation, while some consider the pixels independent entities, others seek to take regional information into consideration to capture the dependencies between the pixels. The first group is generally regarded as pixel-level losses, and the latter as region-level losses in the literature. Considering that both categories are relevant to this research, we provide a concise summary of related studies in both groups, starting with pixel-level approaches and emphasizing the ones proposed for the medical domain.

Binary segmentation could be considered as the classification of pixels into positive (foreground) and negative (background) classes. A common loss function for this task is the BCE loss [9] (Eq. 1) which penalizes the discrepancy between predicted and ground truth classes for all pixels. Weighted Binary Cross Entropy [31] and Balanced Cross Entropy [32] are two BCE variants that differentiate between the effect of false positives and false negatives through weighting coefficients. Focal loss [33] further improved BCE by changing the magnitude of the loss according to the hardness of the examples based on the confidence of the model. Dice loss [8] is suitable for addressing the pixel class imbalance problem

[34], formulated as the ratio of correctly classified pixels to the total number of positive pixels in the prediction and ground truth masks (Eq. 2). Tversky loss [35] provides a way to control the contribution of the false positive and the false negative terms in the Dice loss by weighting these terms.

All the aforementioned losses belong to the pixel-level category (i.e., they consider the pixels independently). While providing effective training signals for the network, they neglect to consider the relationship among pixels, which could provide a considerable boost, notably for cases with irregularity in shapes. Initially proposed for image quality assessment, SSIM [11] has been incorporated in the segmentation loss for medical image segmentation [13] and has inspired several region-level losses. SSL [36] and RMI [12] are two examples of region-level losses developed for segmentation. It should be noted that both of these losses consider a fixed-size window around each pixel as the region (a region is defined for each pixel) rather than a fixed location (a region is a fixed location in a grid) in the ground truth and the prediction as utilized in [37,38].

SSIM [11] uses luminance, contrast, and structure in measuring the differences between two regions. Inspired by the influence of the structural term in the SSIM, which has the potential to be customized for segmentation purposes, the authors of Structural Similarity Loss (SSL) [36] proposed to weight the cross-entropy of every two pixels based on the structural error (error between two image regions which indicates the degree of linear correlation) while ignoring pixels with low error and emphasizing on pixels with high error by thresholding the error rate. With the goal of maximizing the structural similarity between images, RMI [12] first converts the region around a center (pixel) to a multi-dimensional point (for a 3*3 region, it will be a 9D point) and then maximizes the MI between multidimensional distributions.

Several compound losses [33,35,39] have been proposed to reap the benefits of different losses by combining two or more of them. Combo loss [39] has been proposed to control the contribution of false positive and false negative by a weighting strategy in the BCE loss term where the total loss is a weighted sum of BCE and Dice loss. In adaptive sample-level prioritizing loss, we have proposed a novel approach to weight the loss terms (Dice and BCE) dynamically. This is performed in an adaptive manner by controlling the influence of each loss according to each sample using the ratio of the mass to image size as a weighting signal. It should be noted that ASP has three versions: quantile-based, cluster-based, and learning-based. In the quantile-based ASP, the images are groups based on the quantile to which the ratio of the mass belongs. In the cluster-based version, the category of an image is identified according to the K-means clustering of the ratios. Finally, the learning-based ASP is a parametrized version of the ASP loss.

We follow the same dynamic weighting strategy as ASP loss [10]. However, instead of utilizing the size of the mass, we opt to utilize the breast tissue density, which is mostly related to the difficulty of the segmentation. In addition, instead of solely using and weighting pixel-level losses, we introduce a combination of hybrid pixel-level and region-level losses.

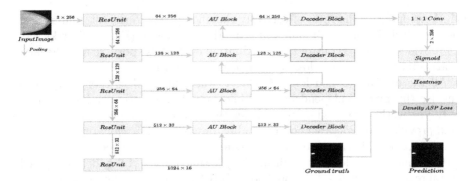

(a) The overall architecture of the proposed method.

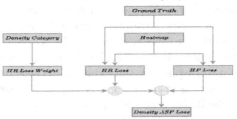

(b) Density-ASP Block.

Fig. 1. An overview of the proposed method.

3   Methodology

In this study, both hybrid pixel-level and region-level loss functions are utilized. Therefore, an overview of hybrid pixel-level L_{HP} and region-level L_{HR} losses are provided in the following sections.

3.1   Hybrid Pixel-Level Loss

The standard hybrid pixel-level loss, commonly used for mass segmentation in mammograms, is defined as a weighted sum of BCE and Dice loss, as shown below:

$$L_{BCE} = -\Big(ylog(\hat{y}) + (1-y)log(1-\hat{y})\Big) \tag{1}$$

$$L_{Dice} = 1 - \frac{\sum_{j=1}^{H \times W} \hat{y}_j y_j + \epsilon}{\sum_{j=1}^{H \times W} \hat{y}_j + \sum_{j=1}^{H \times W} y_j + \epsilon} \tag{2}$$

$$L_{HP} = \alpha L_{Dice} + \beta L_{BCE} \tag{3}$$

Here y and $\hat{y}$ represent the ground truth and the predicted segmentation masks, respectively. α and β (could be relative, for instance, formulated as $\beta = 1 - \alpha$) are the weighting parameters in the hybrid loss denoted as L_{HP} in

Eq. 3. While the cross entropy loss (Eq. 1) includes correctly classified positive and negative pixels, the Dice loss (Eq. 2) incorporates only correctly classified positive pixels, which makes it more suitable in the presence of considerable pixel class imbalance. The combination (Eq. 3) of the two losses has been shown to provide a better learning signal. In particular, it has been reported that adding BCE to the Dice loss helps to mitigate the unstable training associated with using only the Dice loss [33,34]. On the other hand, adding the Dice loss to BCE helps to improve the performance of the model on datasets with pixel class imbalance compared to using BCE alone.

3.2 Hybrid Region-Level Loss

Region-level losses aim to incorporate the context to which a pixel belongs in the loss calculation by representing each pixel with its own value and the neighboring pixels' values. In this paper, two of the region-level losses, SSIM and RMI, have been selected and are represented in the following:

$$L_{RMI}(Y_m; \hat{Y_m}) = \int_S \int_{\hat{S}} f(y, \hat{y}) \log\left(\frac{f(y, \hat{y})}{f(y)f(\hat{y})}\right) dy \, d\hat{y} \tag{4}$$

Here, Y_m and $\hat{Y_m}$ are the multi-dimensional points constructed using a centering pixel and the neighboring pixels in a surrounding square. S and $\hat{S}$ are the support sets corresponding to the ground truth and prediction masks, respectively. $f(y)$ and $f(\hat{y})$ represent the probability density functions for the ground truth and prediction masks, respectively. The $f(y, \hat{y})$ captures the joint PDF. The implementation details of the RMI loss are available in [12]. The second region-level loss used in this paper is SSIM-based loss in Eq. 5.

$$L_{SSIM}(Y_p; \hat{Y}_p) = 1 - \frac{(2\mu_{y_p}\mu_{\hat{y}_p} + C_1)(2\sigma_{y\hat{y}} + C_2)}{(\mu_{y_p}^2\mu_{\hat{y}_p}^2 + C_1)(\sigma_{\hat{y}}^2 + \sigma_{\hat{y}}^2 + C_2)} \tag{5}$$

Here, Y_p and $\hat{Y}_p$ represent patches in the ground truth and the prediction masks. μ and σ are the mean and variance for the corresponding patches, respectively. $\sigma_{y\hat{y}}$ is the covariance of the two patches. More details (including the selection of $C1$ and C_2) are available in [11] .Finally, the hybrid region-level loss is presented in Eq. 6.

$$L_{HR} = \eta L_{RMI} + \gamma L_{SSIM} \tag{6}$$

In the hybrid region-level loss L_{HR} (Eq. 6), L_{RMI} and L_{SSIM} are the RMI and SSIM losses, respectively. The hyperparameters η and γ represent the weighting coefficients.

3.3 Density-Adaptive Sample-Level Prioritizing Loss

While the aforementioned hybrid pixel-level loss is quite effective, we propose extending it by using an adaptive weighting strategy based on the idea of ASP

[10]. The resulting hybrid loss is a combination of region-level and pixel-level losses instead of using only pixel-level losses. We propose using breast tissue density as the sample-level signal for the extended hybrid loss's prioritizing strategy. In the following, the proposed framework for the Density-ASP loss is explained. Given a training set of N images and the corresponding segmentation masks, the baseline method learns a mapping between an input image to its segmented counterpart using the training data. In this study, AU-Net was selected as the baseline method; the architecture for AU-Net is presented in Fig. 1a. For the encoder and decoder, ResUnit and the basic decoder proposed in AU-Net have been used. The details of the AU block, basic decoder, and ResUnit encoder are presented in [6]. The Density-ASP loss requires the breast tissue density for each sample. The standard ACR density, which is available in both datasets, was used in this study. ACR breast density reflects the composition of the fat, fibrous, and glandular tissue in four categories.

There are noticeable differences in the appearance of the breast within different density categories in mammography images. Generally, the complexity of the texture increases as density increases. This provides meaningful distinguishing information for the loss function to prioritize the pixel-level or region-level terms in the loss function based on the density of each sample. The more complex the texture is (i.e., higher density category), the more important the contribution of the region-level term will be. Therefore, density is considered a determining factor in the weighting strategy.

In Fig. 1a, the prediction heatmap ($\hat{y}$ in the formulas) and ground truth segmentation masks are inputted to the Density-ASP module. The process of prioritizing loss is presented in Fig. 1b. Since there is no proven or intuitive connection between density and pixel-level term, the weight for this category remains fixed. However, the contribution of the region-level term will change in an adaptive manner, as shown in Eq. 7 and Fig. 1b. It should be noted that the weighting coefficients inside the pixel-level and region-level loss terms are not adaptive.

$$L^i_{Density-ASP} = p^i \theta^T L^i_{HR} + L^i_{HP} \tag{7}$$

$L^i_{Density-ASP}$ is the final Density-ASP loss for the ith sample. θ is the prioritizing vector consisting of the weights assigned to each density category, and p_i denotes a one-hot encoding of the density category to which the ith sample belongs. $p^i \theta^T$ will be the weight for the region-level loss term, which determines the importance of the region-level term according to the density category of ith sample.

4   Experimental Results

This section begins with a description of the datasets, and evaluation metrics. Subsequently, the experimental setting is presented, followed by a comprehensive analysis of the results on both datasets, including comparisons with the state-of-the-art approaches.

4.1 Datasets

We have conducted mass segmentation experiments using two publicly available datasets: INbreast and CBIS-DDSM. We have normalized the intensity of the images in both datasets and all images have been resized to 256×256. No data augmentation or image enhancement were considered in our experiments. To prevent overfitting, a randomly selected validation set was utilized for hyperparameter tuning. For the baseline approach, the batch size was set to four, the learning rate was initially set to $10-e4$, and a step decay policy with a decay factor of 0.5 was employed in all experiments. Irrespective of the abnormality type, all the images containing masses have been utilized in our experiments.

INbreast Dataset. The INbreast dataset contains 410 images associated with 150 cases, including various abnormality types. In the context of mass segmentation, only 107 of the images containing masses (the total number of masses across all of the images is 116) have been used in this study. A 5-fold cross-validation was employed, a commonly used setting for the measurement of the performance of methods on the INbreast dataset. The dataset was randomly divided into training (80%), validation (10%), and test (10%) sets.

CBIS-DDSM Dataset. From a total of 1944 cases in the CBIS-DDSM dataset, 1591 images containing masses were utilized in our experiments. The official split of the dataset (1231 and 360 images for train and test sets, respectively) was employed for the experimental results presented in this paper. 10% of the training data was randomly selected for the validation set. In a preprocessing stage for the CSIB-DDSM dataset, artifacts were removed, and images were cropped and resized.

4.2 Evaluation Metrics

Since mass segmentation in mammograms is characterized by a pixel class imbalance, we have selected several metrics to better illustrate the strengths and weaknesses of the proposed methods. Specifically, the Dice Similarity Coefficient (DSC), Relative Area Difference (ΔA), Sensitivity, and Accuracy have been selected due to the complementary information they provide. This combination of evaluation metrics highlights the performance of each method both on majority (background) and minority (masses) classes. It also reflects how accurately a method performs in terms of predicting the boundary of masses, which is crucial for mass classification.

4.3 Comparison with State-of-the-Art Methods

To assess the performance of Density-ASP loss, we have conducted a comprehensive comparison with three state-of-the-art mass segmentation approaches on whole mammograms: AU-Net (baseline), ARF-Net, and ASP. The official implementation of AU-Net, and the setting described in the AU-Net paper [6] (only the architecture was publicly available) were used in our experiments. ARF-Net is a state-of-the-art method for mass segmentation on whole mammograms. The method was implemented to the best of our understanding based on the original paper (i.e., the implementation of the approach or the trained models were not publicly available). For the ASP loss, we have used the same experimental setting and data split, so we have directly used the reported results in the original paper. The publicly available implementations of the RMI and SSIM were utilized. To ensure a fair comparison of the methods, no pre-training or data augmentation were used. The coefficients for density-based loss were $\theta = [0.5, 0.5, 0.85, 0.95]$ and $\theta = [0.25, 0.25, 0.85, 0.95]$ for the INbreast and CSIB-DDSM , respectively . η, γ, β were set to one; α was set to 2 and 2.5 for INbreast and CBIS-DDSM. These hyperparameters were selected through experimental evaluation.

Experimental Results Using INbreast. Table 1 summarizes our experimental results for all models trained on INbreast. The best results are highlighted using bold font. The Density-ASP loss achieved better performance across all of the metrics compared to the pixel-level hybrid losses. The improvement for the Density-ASP (over using hybrid pixel-level loss in the baseline method) is as follows: (DSC: $+9.27\%$, ΔA: -12.77%, Sensitivity: $+20.21\%$, Accuracy: $+0.19\ \%$), which is consistent across all metrics. The Density-ASP outperformed ARF-Net in DSC, ΔA, and sensitivity while the accuracy is 0.06% less. It should be noted that ARF-Net is designed to incorporate different sizes and, surpasses the baseline method in DSC, sensitivity, and accuracy. Better performance of the Density-ASP (in most metrics) compared to ARF-Net, indicates that improvement in the training that Density-ASP provides for the baseline method, not only closes the gap between AU-Net and ARF-Net in most of the metrics but also makes AU-Net outperform ARF-Net. In comparison with the ASP loss variations (as the best-performing version, cluster-based ASP was selected for comparison), Density-ASP performed better in terms of DSC, ΔA, and sensitivity. The accuracy of the cluster-based ASP variation is 0.13% higher than the Density-ASP. The results of the Density-ASP further validate the effectiveness of sample-level losses. Moreover, the fact that Density-ASP outperforms the ASP in most of the metrics indicates that introducing the region-level losses to the loss function with the density as a weighting signal is a promising approach for mass segmentation. We attribute this improvement to the utilization of density as the prioritizing signal, which helps to distinguish the contribution of the losses for each sample, leading to better segmentation.

The first four columns in Fig. 2 show some representative results for Density-ASP, AU-Net, ARF-Net, and all ASP variations for INbreast. These examples have been selected to include instances for each density category (mentioned at the top of the columns), demonstrating the segmentation capabilities of the methods across different density categories. The green and blue lines represent the contours of the ground truth and the prediction masks, respectively. It can be observed that the segmentation results for Density-ASP are more accurate compared to state-of-the-art methods across all the density categories.

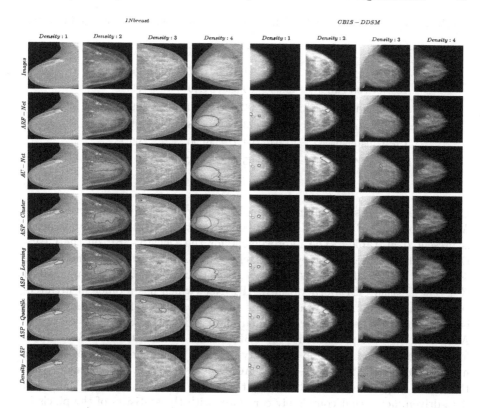

Fig. 2. Examples of the segmentation results for Density-ASP, AU-Net, ARF-Net, and ASP variations.

Table 1. Results for Density-ASP and state-of-the-art approaches for INbreast.

Method	DSC ↑	ΔA ↓	Sensitivity ↑	Accuracy ↑
ARF-Net	70.05	30.37	59.59	98.71
AU-Net (baseline)	65.32	23.68	57.95	98.46
ASP-Quantile-based	68.03	25.04	63.12	98.54
ASP-Learning-based	71.92	22.31	64.56	98.71
ASP-Cluster-based	74.18	19.28	67.21	**98.78**
Density-ASP	**74.59**	**10.91**	**78.16**	98.65

Table 2. Results for Density-ASP and state-of-the-art approaches for CBIS-DDSM.

Method	DSC ↑	ΔA ↓	Sensitivity ↑	Accuracy ↑
ARF-Net	48.82	11.47	47.27	99.43
AU-Net (baseline)	49.05	09.94	51.49	99.38
ASP-Quantile-based	**51.48**	**02.05**	52.00	99.43
ASP-Learning-based	51.33	23.17	45.38	**99.50**
ASP-Cluster-based	51.04	04.47	49.90	99.45
Density-ASP	50.64	05.96	**52.15**	99.41

Experimental Results Using CBIS-DDSM. The performance of Density-ASP loss on the CBIS-DDSM dataset compared to state-of-the-art approaches is presented in Table 2. The improvement for the Density-ASP on the CBIS-DDSM dataset (over using hybrid pixel-level loss in the baseline method) is as follows: (DSC: +1.59%, ΔA: −3.98%, Sensitivity: +0.66%, Accuracy: +0.03 %). The Density-ASP outperformed ARF-Net (which has a different architecture but used common hybrid loss) in all metrics except for accuracy, which is 0.02% lower. When compared to quantile-based ASP loss – a version of the ASP with the best performance on CBIS-DDSM– while Density-ASP outperformed quantile-based ASP in sensitivity (+0.15%), it under-performed in other metrics (DSC: −0.4%, ΔA: +3.91%, Accuracy: −0.03%). We speculate that the reason might be related to the fact that the mass ratio in ASP loss is a data-driven factor that completely correlates with the statistics of the pixels in the image. On the other hand, density is predefined and, in some cases, might not be aligned with the visual features, which might be a more common issue in the CBIS-DDSM dataset. The fact that Density-ASP improves in all of the metrics over the baseline method shows the effectiveness of using density and region-level losses for the CBIS-DDSM dataset. The last four columns in Fig. 2 show some representative examples where Density-ASP has better performance when compared to the previous methods in different density categories.

In general, the performance of the Density-ASP is better for the INbreast dataset. One observation is that in both datasets, there are examples that the density category of the image might not be perfectly aligned with visual features (for example, the 2nd column in Fig. 2), which could cause a higher weight for the term that does not match the initial idea of the Density-ASP. We speculate that the assigned density for the INbreast is more visually aligned with the images, resulting in better weighting for loss terms. Different distributions of each category in the datasets might also be a factor in the performance of the Density-ASP on two datasets.

5   Conclusion

We have proposed a new sample-level adaptive prioritizing loss that utilizes breast tissue density as a weighting signal. Moreover, we have proposed a hybrid loss function that includes region-level losses in the training. Finally, given the observed connection between the difficulty of mass identification and the breast tissue density category, this approach focuses on using the density for weighting of the region-level loss term to highlight the importance of the region-level term according to the density category for each sample adaptively. Our experimental results demonstrate improvements in all evaluation metrics on two benchmark datasets: INbreast and CBIS-DDSM. Customizing this category of losses for other domains or tasks is an appealing direction for future work. One other promising direction could be the extraction of texture descriptors [40], from the images themselves, as the assigned category in some cases may not correlate with the complexity of the texture in the image. This becomes more vital in medical imaging datasets where density information might not be available. In those cases, using data-driven, higher-level information could provide a way to use pixel-level and region-level losses in an adaptive manner.

References

1. Siegel, R.L., Miller, K.D., Fuchs, H.E., Jemal, A.: Cancer statistics 2022. CA: Cancer J. Clin. **72**(1), 7–33 (2022)
2. Batchu, S., Liu, F., Amireh, A., Waller, J., Umair, M.: A review of applications of machine learning in mammography and future challenges. Oncology **99**(8), 483–490 (2021)
3. McKinney, S.M., et al.: International evaluation of an AI system for breast cancer screening. Nature **577**(7788), 89–94 (2020)
4. Nyström, L., Andersson, I., Bjurstam, N., Frisell, J., Nordenskjöld, B., Rutqvist, L.E.: Long-term effects of mammography screening: updated overview of the Swedish randomised trials. Lancet **359**(9310), 909–919 (2002)
5. Malof, J.M., Mazurowski, M.A., Tourassi, G.D.: The effect of class imbalance on case selection for case-based classifiers: an empirical study in the context of medical decision support. Neural Netw. **25**, 141–145 (2012)
6. Sun, H., et al.: AUNet: attention-guided dense-upsampling networks for breast mass segmentation in whole mammograms. Phys. Med. Biol. **65**(5), 055005 (2020)
7. Xu, C., Qi, Y., Wang, Y., Lou, M., Pi, J., Ma, Y.: ARF-Net: an adaptive receptive field network for breast mass segmentation in whole mammograms and ultrasound images. Biomed. Signal Process. Control **71**, 103178 (2022)
8. Milletari, F., Nassir, N., Seyed-Ahmad, A.: V-net: fully convolutional neural networks for volumetric medical image segmentation. In 2016 Fourth International Conference on 3D Vision (3DV), pp. 565–571. IEEE (2016)
9. Yi-de, M., Qing, L., Zhi-Bai, Q.: Automated image segmentation using improved PCNN model based on cross-entropy. In: Proceedings of 2004 International Symposium on Intelligent Multimedia, Video and Speech Processing, pp. 743–746. IEEE (2004)
10. Liniya, P., Nicolescu, M., Nicolescu, M., Bebis, G.: ASP Loss: adaptive sample-level prioritizing loss for mass segmentation on whole mammography images. In: Iliadis, L., Papaleonidas, A., Angelov, P., Jayne, C. (eds.) ICANN 2023. LNCS, vol. 14255, pp. 102–114. Springer, Cham (2023). https://doi.org/10.1007/978-3-031-44210-0_9

11. Wang, Z., Bovik, A.C., Sheikh, H.R., Simoncelli, E.P.: Image quality assessment: from error visibility to structural similarity. IEEE Trans. Image Process. **13**(4), 600–612 (2004)
12. Zhao, S., Wang, Y., Yang, Z., Cai, D.: Region mutual information loss for semantic segmentation. In: Advances in Neural Information Processing Systems, vol. 32 (2019)
13. Huang, H., et al.: Unet 3+: a full-scale connected unet for medical image segmentation. In: ICASSP 2020–2020 IEEE International Conference on Acoustics, Speech and Signal Processing (ICASSP), pp. 1055–1059. IEEE (2020)
14. Ronneberger, O., Fischer, P., Brox, T.: U-Net: convolutional networks for biomedical image segmentation. In: Navab, N., Hornegger, J., Wells, W.M., Frangi, A.F. (eds.) MICCAI 2015. LNCS, vol. 9351, pp. 234–241. Springer, Cham (2015). https://doi.org/10.1007/978-3-319-24574-4_28
15. Moreira, I.C., Amaral, I., Domingues, I., Cardoso, A., Cardoso, M.J., Cardoso, J.S.: Inbreast: toward a full-field digital mammographic database. Acad. Radiol. **19**(2), 236–248 (2012)
16. Lee, R.S., Gimenez, F., Hoogi, A., Miyake, K.K., Gorovoy, M., Rubin, D.L.: A curated mammography data set for use in computer-aided detection and diagnosis research. Sci. Data **4**(1), 1–9 (2017)
17. Baccouche, A., Garcia-Zapirain, B., Castillo Olea, C., Elmaghraby, A.S.: Connected-UNets: a deep learning architecture for breast mass segmentation. NPJ Breast Cancer **7**(1), 151 (2021)
18. Long, J., Evan, S., Trevor, D.: Fully convolutional networks for semantic segmentation. In: Proceedings of the IEEE Conference on Computer Vision and Pattern Recognition, pp. 3431–3440. (2015)
19. Wu, S., Wang, Z., Liu, C., Zhu, C., Wu, S., Xiao, K.: Automatical segmentation of pelvic organs after hysterectomy by using dilated convolution u-net++. In: 2019 IEEE 19th International Conference on Software Quality, Reliability and Security Companion (QRS-C), pp. 362–367. IEEE (2019)
20. Zhang, J., Jin, Y., Xu, J., Xu, X., Zhang, Y.: Mdu-net: multi-scale densely connected u-net for biomedical image segmentation. arXiv preprint arXiv:1812.00352 (2018)
21. Zhou, Z., Rahman Siddiquee, M.M., Tajbakhsh, N., Liang, J.: UNet++: a nested u-net architecture for medical image segmentation. In: Stoyanov, D., et al. (eds.) DLMIA/ML-CDS -2018. LNCS, vol. 11045, pp. 3–11. Springer, Cham (2018). https://doi.org/10.1007/978-3-030-00889-5_1
22. Li, C., et al.: Attention unet++: a nested attention-aware u-net for liver CT image segmentation. In: 2020 IEEE International Conference on Image Processing (ICIP), pp. 345–349. IEEE (2020)
23. Cao, H., et al.: Swin-Unet: Unet-like pure transformer for medical image segmentation. In: Karlinsky, L., Michaeli, T., Nishino, K. (eds.) ECCV 2022. LNCS, vol. 13803, pp. 205–218. Springer, Cham (2022). https://doi.org/10.1007/978-3-031-25066-8_9
24. Oktay, O., et al.: Attention u-net: learning where to look for the pancreas. arXiv preprint arXiv:1804.03999 (2018)
25. Song, T., Meng, F., Rodriguez-Paton, A., Li, P., Zheng, P., Wang, X.: U-next: a novel convolution neural network with an aggregation u-net architecture for gallstone segmentation in CT images. IEEE Access **7**, 166823–166832 (2019)
26. Hai, J., Qiao, K., Chen, J., Tan, H., Xu, J., Zeng, L., Shi, D., Yan, B.: Fully convolutional densenet with multiscale context for automated breast tumor segmentation. Journal of healthcare engineering, (2019)

27. Chen, L.C., Papandreou, G., Kokkinos, I., Murphy, K., Yuille, A.L.: DeepLab: semantic image segmentation with deep convolutional nets, atrous convolution, and fully connected CRFs. IEEE Trans. Pattern Anal. Mach. Intell. **40**(4), 834–848 (2017)
28. Li, S., Dong, M., Du, G., Mu, X.: Attention dense-u-net for automatic breast mass segmentation in digital mammogram. IEEE Access **7**, 59037–59047 (2019)
29. Chen, J., Chen, L., Wang, S., Chen, P.: A novel multi-scale adversarial networks for precise segmentation of x-ray breast mass. IEEE Access **8**, 103772–103781 (2020)
30. Rajalakshmi, N.R., Vidhyapriya, R., Elango, N., Ramesh, N.: Deeply supervised u-net for mass segmentation in digital mammograms. Int. J. Imaging Syst. Technol. **31**(1), 59–71 (2021)
31. Pihur, V., Datta, S., Datta, S.: Weighted rank aggregation of cluster validation measures: a monte carlo cross-entropy approach. Bioinformatics **23**(13), 1607–1615 (2007)
32. Xie, S., Tu, Z.: Holistically-nested edge detection. In: Proceedings of the IEEE International Conference on Computer Vision, pp. 1395–1403, (2015)
33. Yeung, M., Sala, E., Schönlieb, C.B., Rundo, L.: Unified focal loss: generalising dice and cross entropy-based losses to handle class imbalanced medical image segmentation. Comput. Med. Imaging Graph. **95**, 102026 (2022)
34. Jadon, S.: A survey of loss functions for semantic segmentation. In: 2020 IEEE Conference on Computational Intelligence in Bioinformatics and Computational Biology (CIBCB), pp. 1–7. IEEE (2020)
35. Salehi, S.S.M., Erdogmus, D., Gholipour, A.: Tversky loss function for image segmentation using 3D fully convolutional deep networks. In: Wang, Q., Shi, Y., Suk, H.-I., Suzuki, K. (eds.) MLMI 2017. LNCS, vol. 10541, pp. 379–387. Springer, Cham (2017). https://doi.org/10.1007/978-3-319-67389-9_44
36. Zhao, S., Boxi, W., Wenqing, C., Yao, H., Deng, Cai.: Correlation maximized structural similarity loss for semantic segmentation. arXiv preprint arXiv:1910.08711 (2019)
37. Aliniya, P., Razzaghi, P.: Parametric and nonparametric context models: a unified approach to scene parsing. Pattern Recogn. **84**, 165–181 (2018)
38. Alinia, P., Parvin, R.: Similarity based context for nonparametric scene parsing. In: 2017 Iranian Conference on Electrical Engineering (ICEE), pp. 1509–1514. IEEE (2017)
39. Taghanaki, S.A., et al.: Combo loss: handling input and output imbalance in multiorgan segmentation. In: Computerized Medical Imaging and Graphics, vol. 75, pp. 24–33 (2019)
40. Simon, P., Uma, V.: Review of texture descriptors for texture classification. In: Satapathy, S.C., Bhateja, V., Raju, K.S., Janakiramaiah, B. (eds.) Data Engineering and Intelligent Computing. AISC, vol. 542, pp. 159–176. Springer, Singapore (2018). https://doi.org/10.1007/978-981-10-3223-3_15

Deep Learning Based GABA Edited-MRS Signal Reconstruction

Dikshant Sagar[1]([⊠]) [iD], Farnaz Mohammadi[2] [iD], Mohammad Pourhomayoun[1] [iD], Jooeun Joen[1] [iD], and Navid Amini[1] [iD]

[1] Department of Computer Science, California State University, Los Angeles, CA, USA
{dsagar2,mpourho,jjeon6,namini}@calstatela.edu
[2] Genentech Inc., South San Francisco, USA
mohammadi.farnaz@gene.com

Abstract. Magnetic Resonance Spectroscopy (MRS) is a non-invasive imaging technique based on nuclear magnetic resonance (NMR) principles. It analyzes the biochemical composition and metabolic processes of body tissues. Edited MRS Reconstruction converts raw MRS data into meaningful spectrum signals, providing valuable insights into cellular metabolism, organ function, and energy production. This process can help understand normal physiology, diagnose diseases, and monitor their progression. Additionally, it enables the extraction of metabolite concentrations, even when hidden by other biochemical compounds with higher concentrations (e.g., gamma-aminobutyric acid, glutamate, and glutamine). This study proposes a dual encoder head self-attention-based deep learning model to reconstruct the Edited MRS signal for acquiring GABA concentration and benchmark the model's performance on simulated raw MRS data from real GABA-edited ground truths. Our model achieves a 95% decrease in Mean Squared Error (MSE), a 70% decrease in Linewidth, a 450% increase in Signal to Noise Ratio (SNR), and a 42% increase in Peak Shape Score compared to the current existing method on the test set. We also illustrate our qualitative results, demonstrating our method's robust and accurate predictions compared to the ground truth. Our approach can help deliver rapid diagnosis and monitoring of neurological disorders, metabolic diseases, and certain types of cancers by providing refined and accurate data on metabolite concentrations.

Keywords: Magnetic Resonance Spectroscopy · Edited-MRS Reconstruction · Deep Learning · Machine Learning · Signal Processing

1 Introduction

Gamma-aminobutyric acid (GABA) is the principal inhibitory neurotransmitter in the human brain. GABAergic inhibition shapes and regulates patterns of neuronal activity, serving a key role in cortical information processing and plasticity [18]. GABA is present in the brain at millimolar (mM) concentrations

G. Bebis et al. (Eds.): ISVC 2023, LNCS 14361, pp. 18–29, 2023.
https://doi.org/10.1007/978-3-031-47969-4_2

and is, in principle, detectable by magnetic resonance spectroscopy (MRS). However, low-concentration metabolites, such as GABA, Glutathione (GSH), etc., are often overlapped by larger signals and cannot be reliably quantified; therefore, researchers and clinicians use spectral editing techniques to simplify the spectrum, selectively revealing signals from metabolites of interest and removing overlying signals of more concentrated metabolites [19]. MEscher-GArwood Point RESolved Spectroscopy (MEGA-PRESS) utilizes a sequence of radiofrequency (RF) pulses and gradients to selectively excite and manipulate specific resonances in the brain by employing a pair of editing pulses, often called "ON" and "OFF" pulses. These editing pulses are designed to selectively modulate the resonance of the target metabolite, such as GABA, glutamate, etc. Then, by taking the difference between the spectra obtained with the ON and OFF editing pulses, the MEGA-PRESS technique effectively isolates the resonance of the target metabolite from other overlapping signals [13]. This is also known as J-difference editing [11]. Another recent work, Hadamard Encoding and Reconstruction of MEGA-Edited Spectroscopy (HERMES) [4], uses a similar ON and OFF signal acquisition strategy to modulate the resonances of the target metabolites of interest. The acquired data is then processed using Hadamard reconstruction algorithms to separate and quantify the signals corresponding to each metabolite. These algorithms exploit the known encoding patterns and the acquired measurements to reconstruct the individual metabolite spectra. The above approaches, despite tackling important aspects of MRS editing, fall short in their reconstruction methodologies and deliver low signal-to-noise ratios (SNR). This can be attributed to MRS signals being weak and prone to noise, limiting the quality and accuracy of reconstructed spectra [14]. Low SNR can lead to reduced spectral resolution, difficulty in distinguishing overlapping peaks, and challenges in accurately quantifying metabolite concentrations [9]. As another shortcoming, current techniques fail to handle various artifacts that can affect MRS data, such as baseline distortions, chemical shift artifacts, and eddy current artifacts [6]. These artifacts can distort the spectral peaks, introduce false signals, and hinder accurate reconstruction. As such, mitigating and removing such artifacts and increasing the signal-to-noise ratio in MRS signal reconstruction remains a challenge. According to our literature review and based on our knowledge, no peer-reviewed work has been published where deep learning has been employed to tackle these specific challenges and developed a model capable of more efficient and accurate edited MRS reconstruction making our study the first of its kind. Hence, our contributions in this study are as follows:

- Aggregate and reconstruct raw MRS data from ground truth GABA-edited MRS scans.
- Create a Dualhead Self-Attention deep neural network to achieve state-of-the-art Edited-MRS signal reconstruction performance.
- Compare and evaluate our generated spectra with existing methods with custom and relevant evaluation metrics.

2 Methods

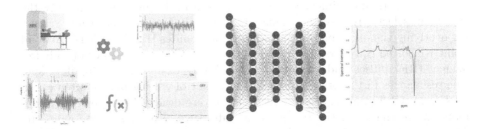

Fig. 1. Overall pipeline visualizing the entire process where it begins with clinicians acquiring MRS data. Subsequently, the ON and OFF Free Induction Decays (FIDs) are transformed into the frequency domain using Fast Fourier Transform. From there, the J-difference spectrum is computed based on the ON and OFF spectra. This J-difference spectrum, along with the ON and OFF FIDs, is then fed into our deep neural network. As a result, the Edited-MRS Reconstructed Signal is generated.

2.1 Dataset

The dataset used in this study has been sourced from the Harris Imaging Lab, University of Calgary [1], with 5000 simulated ground truth GABA-edited MRS signals with their raw MRS Free Induction Decay (FID) signals. For the dataset, the input raw MRS FID transients are generated using a transient maker that adds randomized noises to the ground truth signal that one can expect MRS scans to inherently have while acquisition such as random gaussian amplitude noise, random frequency noise and random phase noise. Then we repeat this process n times and stack them to have n number of different transients. Here, n has been fixed to 40, which is a standard number for real-world scenarios and also keeps our disk size resources in consideration. Now, we have 40 transient FIDs and one ground truth GABA-edited spectra each for 5000 data points. This final dataset is then divided into training and test sets randomly with a ratio of 80:20.

2.2 J-Difference Spectrum

J-difference editing is a magnetic resonance spectroscopy (MRS) technique that enables the selective detection and quantification of metabolites with coupled spin systems, such as J-coupled multiples. It offers a valuable means of investigating specific biochemical pathways or monitoring metabolite levels with diagnostic relevance [11]. In J-Difference editing, two distinct MRS experiments are performed with different editing pulses applied, in most cases called ON and OFF pulses for each transient. These editing pulses are designed to selectively invert or excite the specific coupled spin system of interest, taking advantage of the J-coupling interactions between the spins of the target metabolite and its neighboring nuclei [21]. The process of getting the spectrum at its core is very simple. First, the MRS FID signal acquisition is performed with the two ON and OFF pulses for each transient, and then the FIDs are converted into the frequency domain using Fast Fourier Transform (FFT) algorithm [16] for both pulses. Then the difference of these signals is taken to get the resulting J-Difference spectrum given by:

$$J\text{--}Difference\ Spectrum = FFT(FID_{OFF}) - FFT(FID_{ON}) \qquad (1)$$

In the standard Edited-MRS reconstruction procedures, an average of the J-difference spectrum of all the transients is taken to get the final Edited-MRS reconstructed signal [11,21]. However, in our case, we take our supervised deep neural network-based approach, explained in the next subsection, and the whole process is also visualized in Fig. 1.

2.3 Dual Branch Self-Attention Neural Network

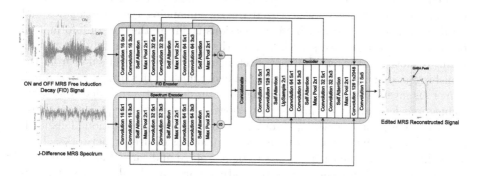

Fig. 2. Detailed architecture of our Dual Branch Self-Attention Neural Network.

To predict/reconstruct the target GABA-edited MRS spectra, we designed a dual-branch self-attention neural network based on an encoder-decoder architecture [3] with skip connections [7] between parallel spatial layers in the encoders and the decoder [20]. The architecture uses two encoders. The first one takes the MRS FIDs with ON and OFF pulses stacked channel-wise, which are in the time domain. The second one takes the J-Difference spectrum in the frequency domain. Both encoders are stacked with Convolutional [17] and max pool layers [15] that convolve and extract features between the transients and on the time/frequency axis, respectively. Also, we introduced Self-attention layers [24] after each convolutional block in the encoders, which are known to be helpful in extracting dependency information from sequential data. The self-attention is also known as scaled dot product attention and can be given by:

$$Attention = \frac{Softmax(QK^T)}{\sqrt{d_k}} \tag{2}$$

where Q and K are the query and key vectors, d_k is the dimensionality of the vectors, and $\sqrt{d_k}$ is the scaling factor and helps prevent extremely large dot products. Then, the final output of the attention layer is given by:

$$Output = Attention.V \tag{3}$$

where V is the value vector. In self-attention, Q, K, and V are all the same, which is the input to the attention layer. Self-attention mechanisms have proven to be highly effective in neural networks for signal-processing tasks [23, 25, 26, 28]. Unlike traditional convolutional or recurrent layers that rely on fixed local receptive fields, self-attention mechanisms enable capturing global dependencies and relationships within the input data. Self-attention allows the network to focus on the most relevant parts of the signal while considering the interactions between different elements [8]. By assigning weights to different elements based on their relevance and similarity, self-attention mechanisms emphasize the informative components and suppress irrelevant or noisy ones [24].

Our designed architecture also features skip connections, also known as residual connections, which play a crucial role in enhancing the performance and training of neural networks. These connections facilitate the flow of information by bypassing certain layers or blocks of the network and directly connecting them to subsequent layers. Further, deep neural networks often suffer from the vanishing gradient problem, where gradients diminish as they propagate through numerous layers, making it challenging to train deep networks effectively. Skip connections help alleviate this issue by allowing gradients to bypass several layers, providing a direct path for error signals during backpropagation. This facilitates better gradient flow, enabling easier training of deeper networks. They allow information from earlier layers to be preserved and carried forward to subsequent layers and also enable better feature reuse, as the downstream layers can access both the low-level and high-level features captured by earlier layers [7]. By leveraging skip connections, networks can more effectively capture and utilize a wide range of features, leading to improved representation learning and richer feature representations. By providing shortcut connections, the network can more quickly propagate important information across layers, reducing the number of iterations needed for the network to converge to an optimal solution. This can be particularly beneficial when dealing with complex or large-scale datasets [22].

Both the FID Encoder and the J-Difference Spectrum Encoder possess a similar architecture with 3 Convolutional-Self Attention Blocks. Each block has two convolutional layers, one self-attention layer, and one max pool player. The encodings from both encoders are concatenated on the channel axis and fed into the decoder, which contains 4 convolutional blocks. 3 of the blocks contain two convolutional layers, one self-attention layer, and one upsampling layer. The last output convolutional block only contains two convolutional layers, which generate the final Edited-MRS Signal in the frequency domain. Further details of the architecture design have been visualized in Fig. 2. The model was trained for 20 epochs, using the Adam optimizing algorithm with a decaying learning rate scheduler that reduced the learning rate by half after every 2 epochs starting from 0.001, and the batch size was 4 due to memory constraints. However, gradient accumulation was used with a step size of 4, making the effective batch size 16. The loss function used was a mean average error (MAE) [27] with custom loss weights, which forced the model to focus more on the central region where GABA peaks exist (2.8 ppm to 3.2 ppm).

2.4   Evaluation Metrics

In GABA-edited MRS reconstruction, we need to quantify some specific entities. For example, we want our model to look more closely at the section of the subspectra where GABA peaks are supposed to exist. Hence we evaluate the performance of the models on standard and custom metrics, which are as follows:

Mean Squared Error (MSE). MSE is a widely used metric in signal processing to assess the accuracy of a predictive model or an estimation algorithm when dealing with signal data. In signal processing, signals can represent various data types, such as audio, image, time series, or sensor data. MSE provides a quantitative measure of the discrepancy between the predicted or estimated signal and the true signal, making it a fundamental tool for evaluating the performance of signal processing algorithms [2]. Mathematically, the Mean Squared Error is calculated as follows:

$$\frac{1}{N}\sum_{i=1}^{N}(x_i - \hat{x}_i)^2 \tag{4}$$

where N is the number of signals in the data, x_i represents the true value of the signal at sample i, and $\hat{x}_i$ denotes the estimated or predicted value of the signal at sample i.

Signal to Noise Ratio (SNR). SNR is a key concept in signal processing that measures the quality and reliability of a signal in the presence of noise. In signal processing, noise refers to unwanted and random fluctuations that can corrupt or interfere with the desired signal. The SNR quantifies the relative strength of the signal compared to the background noise, providing a valuable metric for assessing signal quality [10]. Mathematically, the Signal-to-Noise Ratio is defined as:

$$SNR = \frac{SignalPower}{NoisePower} \tag{5}$$

In this work, we only calculate SNR for the region of interest, that is, the GABA peak that exists between 2.8 ppm and 3.2 ppm in the subspectra.

Linewidth. The linewidth, also known as the Full Width at Half Maximum (FWHM), is an important parameter used to characterize the spectral width or frequency resolution of a signal in signal processing and spectroscopy. It represents the range of frequencies or wavelengths over which the signal's intensity is above half of its maximum value. The linewidth provides valuable information about the bandwidth and sharpness of spectral features in a signal. Again, we only calculate FWHM for the region of interest, that is, the GABA peak that exists between 2.8 ppm and 3.2 ppm in the subspectra. This will assess the model's alignment of the subspectra and the reliability of the final quantification [12].

Peak Shape Score. We also a peak shape score to measure GABA peak shape similarity using Pearson correlation [5] between the predicted and original spectra to assess subtraction artifacts resulting from improper alignment of subspectra. The shape score is given by:

$$ShapeScore = 1 - PeakSimilarity \qquad (6)$$

*The final objective is to **minimize the MSE and the Linewidth** and **maximize SNR and Peak Shape Score**.*

Table 1. Performance comparison between various models on the test set.

Model/Approach	MSE ↓	SNR ↑	Linewidth ↓	Peak Shape Score ↑
Simple Average	0.0435	0.14	0.277	0.69
Spectrum Encoder Only (Base Model)	0.0735	0.02	0.204	0.74
Spectrum Encoder + Skip Connections	0.0581	0.20	0.148	0.81
Spectrum Encoder + Skip Connections + Self-Attention	0.0030	0.23	0.082	0.95
Spectrum Encoder + FID Encoder + Skip Connections	0.0023	0.71	0.082	0.96
Spectrum Encoder + FID Encoder + Skip Connections + Self-Attention (Final Model)	**0.0020**	**0.77**	**0.081**	**0.98**

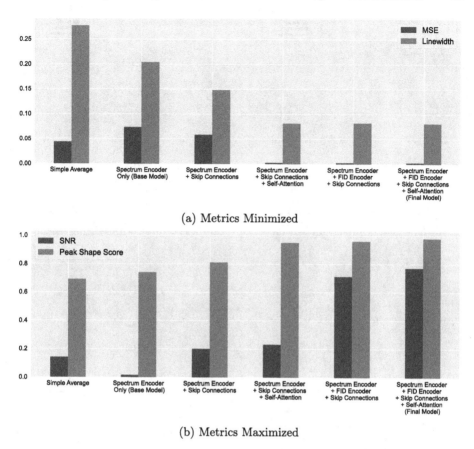

(a) Metrics Minimized

(b) Metrics Maximized

Fig. 3. Bar plots visualizing performance comparison between different models on different metrics.

3   Results and Discussion

This paper demonstrates how deep neural networks can enhance edited MRS signal reconstruction. We also illustrate how adding skip connections and self-attention mechanisms can enhance a deep neural network's capability to extract spatial and sequential interdependence features to perform much well in the end task. We also show how adding a parallel FID encoder branch improves our model's performance to perform the signal reconstruction. Table 1 displays the results of our ablation study on adding these architectural improvements to the base model, and from the performance metrics, we can conclude that our final model that incorporated the spectrum encoder, the FID encoder, skip connections, and the self-attention mechanism performs the best out of all the approaches and significantly much higher compared to the current method of choice, which is the simple average of the J-Difference spectrum. As there were no previous studies or other methods in this domain, we only compared the

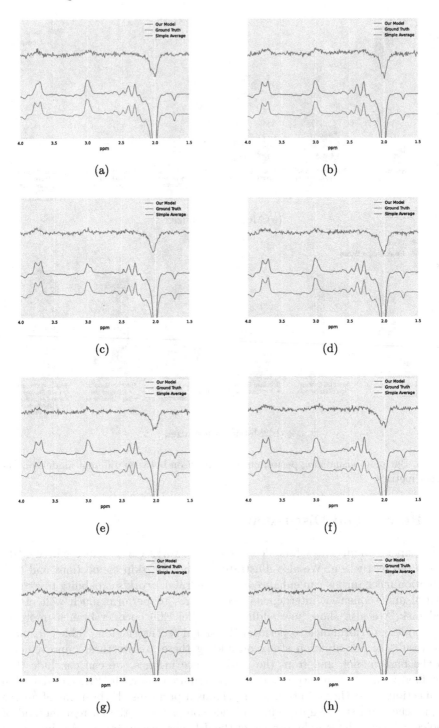

Fig. 4. This figure visualizes the qualitative output of the model on a few test samples comparing the ground truth signal (green), the signal generated from the simple average of the J-Difference Spectrum strategy (red), and the signal generated by our proposed model (blue). (Color figure online)

performance of our model on the Simple Average of the J-Difference spectrum method and the variants of our model using the metric described in Sect. 2.4. On the testing set, we observed that the simple average method achieved an MSE of 0.0435, SNR of 0.14, Linewidth of 0.277, and a peak shape score of 0.69. These metrics were comparable to other methods; however still subpar. Our first iteration of a deep learning model that consisted of only the spectrum encoder and a decoder performed worse in terms of MSE and SNR than the simple average method achieving 0.0735 and 0.02, respectively. However, it achieved better statistics in Linewidth and peak shape score, receiving 0.204 and 0.74. We observe that the model took a significant hit in terms of SNR. On the next iteration of our deep learning model, we added skip connections, essentially improving the transfer of spatial features deep within the network, and hence we achieved much better performance with an MSE of 0.0581, SNR of 0.20, Linewidth of 0.148, and peak shape score of 0.81. We especially improved on SNR from the previous interaction, as expected. Next, We additionally added a self-attention mechanism in the next iteration, and it further improved the performance in all metrics achieving an MSE of 0.0030, SNR of 0.23, Linewidth of 0.082, and peak shape score of 0.95. We observed the jump in performance was higher in MSE, Linewidth, and Peak shape scores. In the next iteration of our model, we introduced a second parallel encoder that encodes the FID signals of the transients, and for ablation purposes, we did not add self-attention in this version. This improved our model's performance by over 100% in terms of SNR by achieving 0.71 on the scale. The MSE was 0.0023, Linewidth was 0.082, and Peak shape score was 0.96. Our final model, which performed the best out of all versions, included the spectrum encoder, the FID encoder, skip connections, and the self-attention mechanisms. This model further improved our SNR by ∼ 9%, achieving a ratio of 0.77 and having the least MSE of 0.0020, Linewidth of 0.081, and a Peak shape score of 0.98. Figure 4 visualizes our qualitative results for multiple test data points depicting the ground truth spectrum, the spectrum generated by the currently available method of simple average of J-Difference spectrum, and the spectrum generated by our final model (Fig. 3). It clearly shows how close our generated output comes to the ground truth.

4   Conclusion

Edited-MRS reconstruction enables improved detection and quantification of specific metabolites in the brain or other tissues. By selectively manipulating certain metabolite signals, unwanted signals can be suppressed, allowing for clearer identification and measurement of the metabolites of interest. This capability is particularly valuable in studying neurochemical processes and investigating biomarkers related to various diseases and conditions. In this paper, we introduced a Dual branch Self-Attention deep neural network to achieve the task of Edited-MRS reconstruction and achieved state-of-the-art performance as compared to the previous method being used by clinicians, which included taking the simple average of the J-Difference spectrum. The utilization of Edited-MRS reconstruction techniques opens new avenues for advancing diagnostic and therapeutic approaches in various fields. By providing improved sensitivity and specificity in detecting and quantifying specific metabolites, Edited-MRS reconstruction holds promise for more accurate disease diagnosis, monitoring treatment response, and developing personalized treatment strategies. Our only limitation in this work was the unavailability of extensive in-vivo data. For future work, we want to work with clinicians to create a large benchmark dataset for the same task with high-quality in-vivo Edited-MRS data which we can further work on to tackle challenges with the reconstruction task that we might have missing or not encountered while working with simulated data, such as differences in acquisition techniques due to human errors, or differences due to distinct acquisition equipment.

References

1. https://cumming.ucalgary.ca/labs/harris-imaging/home
2. Allen, D.M.: Mean square error of prediction as a criterion for selecting variables. Technometrics **13**(3), 469–475 (1971)
3. Badrinarayanan, V., Kendall, A., Cipolla, R.: SegNet: a deep convolutional encoder-decoder architecture for image segmentation. IEEE Trans. Pattern Anal. Mach. Intell. **39**(12), 2481–2495 (2017)
4. Chan, K.L., Puts, N.A., Schär, M., Barker, P.B., Edden, R.A.: HERMES: Hadamard encoding and reconstruction of mega-edited spectroscopy. Magn. Reson. Med. **76**(1), 11–19 (2016)
5. Cohen, I., et al.: Pearson correlation coefficient. In: Noise reduction in speech processing. Springer Topics in Signal Processing, vol. 2, pp. 1–4. Springer, Heidelberg (2009). https://doi.org/10.1007/978-3-642-00296-0_5
6. Di Costanzo, A., et al.: Proton MR spectroscopy of the brain at 3 T: an update. Eur. Radiol. **17**, 1651–1662 (2007)
7. He, K., Zhang, X., Ren, S., Sun, J.: Deep residual learning for image recognition. In: Proceedings of the IEEE Conference on Computer Vision and Pattern Recognition, pp. 770–778 (2016)
8. Huang, S., Wang, D., Wu, X., Tang, A.: DSANet: dual self-attention network for multivariate time series forecasting. In: Proceedings of the 28th ACM International Conference on Information and Knowledge Management, pp. 2129–2132 (2019)
9. Iqbal, Z., Nguyen, D., Thomas, M.A., Jiang, S.: Deep learning can accelerate and quantify simulated localized correlated spectroscopy. Sci. Rep. **11**(1), 8727 (2021)
10. Johnson, D.H.: Signal-to-noise ratio. Scholarpedia **1**(12), 2088 (2006)
11. Kaiser, L., Young, K., Meyerhoff, D., Mueller, S., Matson, G.: A detailed analysis of localized J-difference GABA editing: theoretical and experimental study at 4 T. NMR Biomed. Int. J. Devoted Develop. Appl. Magn. Reson. In vivo **21**(1), 22–32 (2008)
12. Kumar Reddy, A.N., Sagar, D.K.: Half-width at half-maximum, full-width at half-maximum analysis for resolution of asymmetrically apodized optical systems with slit apertures. Pramana **84**, 117–126 (2015)
13. Mescher, M., Merkle, H., Kirsch, J., Garwood, M., Gruetter, R.: Simultaneous in vivo spectral editing and water suppression. NMR Biomed. Int. J. Devoted Develop. Appl. Magn. Reson. In Vivo **11**(6), 266–272 (1998)

14. Mikkelsen, M., Loo, R.S., Puts, N.A., Edden, R.A., Harris, A.D.: Designing GABA-edited magnetic resonance spectroscopy studies: considerations of scan duration, signal-to-noise ratio and sample size. J. Neurosci. Meth. **303**, 86–94 (2018)

15. Nagi, J., et al.: Max-pooling convolutional neural networks for vision-based hand gesture recognition. In: 2011 IEEE International Conference on Signal and Image Processing Applications (ICSIPA), pp. 342–347. IEEE (2011)

16. Nussbaumer, H.J., Nussbaumer, H.J.: The fast Fourier transform. In: Fast Fourier Transform and Convolution Algorithms. Springer Series in Information Sciences, vol. 2, pp. 80–111. Springer, Heidelberg (1981). https://doi.org/10.1007/978-3-642-81897-4_4

17. O'Shea, K., Nash, R.: An introduction to convolutional neural networks. arXiv preprint arXiv:1511.08458 (2015)

18. Petroff, O.A.: Book review: GABA and glutamate in the human brain. Neuroscientist **8**(6), 562–573 (2002)

19. Puts, N.A., Edden, R.A.: In vivo magnetic resonance spectroscopy of GABA: a methodological review. Prog. Nucl. Magn. Reson. Spectrosc. **60**, 29 (2012)

20. Ronneberger, O., Fischer, P., Brox, T.: U-Net: convolutional networks for biomedical image segmentation. In: Navab, N., Hornegger, J., Wells, W.M., Frangi, A.F. (eds.) MICCAI 2015. LNCS, vol. 9351, pp. 234–241. Springer, Cham (2015). https://doi.org/10.1007/978-3-319-24574-4_28

21. Saleh, M.G., et al.: Simultaneous edited MRS of GABA and glutathione. Neuroimage **142**, 576–582 (2016)

22. Szegedy, C., Ioffe, S., Vanhoucke, V., Alemi, A.: Inception-v4, inception-ResNet and the impact of residual connections on learning. In: Proceedings of the AAAI Conference on Artificial Intelligence, vol. 31 (2017)

23. Tao, W., et al.: EEG-based emotion recognition via channel-wise attention and self attention. IEEE Trans. Affect. Comput. (2020)

24. Vaswani, A., et al.: Attention is all you need. In: Advances in Neural Information Processing Systems, vol. 30 (2017)

25. Wang, Y., Yang, G., Li, S., Li, Y., He, L., Liu, D.: Arrhythmia classification algorithm based on multi-head self-attention mechanism. Biomed. Signal Process. Control **79**, 104206 (2023)

26. Wei, S., Qu, Q., Zeng, X., Liang, J., Shi, J., Zhang, X.: Self-attention Bi-LSTM networks for radar signal modulation recognition. IEEE Trans. Microw. Theory Tech. **69**(11), 5160–5172 (2021)

27. Willmott, C.J., Matsuura, K.: Advantages of the mean absolute error (MAE) over the root mean square error (RMSE) in assessing average model performance. Clim. Res. **30**(1), 79–82 (2005)

28. Yang, X., Zhao, J., Sun, Q., Lu, J., Ma, X.: An effective dual self-attention residual network for seizure prediction. IEEE Trans. Neural Syst. Rehabil. Eng. **29**, 1604–1613 (2021)

Investigating the Impact of Attention on Mammogram Classification

Marc Berghouse[✉] ⓘ, George Bebis ⓘ, and Alireza Tavakkoli ⓘ

University of Nevada, Reno, Reno, NV 89557, USA
{mberghouse,bebis,tavakkol}@unr.edu

Abstract. Attention, one of the most important features of modern CNNs, has been shown to improve the performance of mammogram classification, but our understanding of why attention offers improvements is rather limited. In this paper, we present the first comprehensive comparison of different combinations of baseline models and attention methods at multiple resolutions for whole mammogram image classification of masses and calcifications. Our findings indicate that attention generally helps to improve the baseline model scores, but the benefits are variable depending on the resolution and abnormality type. Furthermore, we find that pooling and overall model architecture (i.e., combination of baseline and attention) significantly impact mammogram classification scores. Specifically, scores are generally improved by architectural features that allow the model to retain as much information as possible while still focusing on relevant features. We also find that attention improves the correlation between model performance and LayerCAM activation in the region of interest. Our work provides insightful information to help guide the future construction of attention-based models for mammogram classification.

Keywords: Mammogram Classification · Attention · Deep Learning

1 Introduction

Attention has shown great promise in computer vision by guiding a model to focus on task-relevant local regions and channels [1]. In particular, it has been shown to increase performance in various classification [2], detection [3], and segmentation tasks [4]. Attention has also been shown to generally improve computer vision tasks in the field of medical imagery [2,5], where the region of interest often only comprises a small portion of the image.

Mammogram classification is an active area of research that has potentially life-saving con-sequences [6]. It has been extensively studied, and a wide variety of deep learning model architectures have been proposed for mammogram classification [7,8]. However, relatively little research has been performed on the impact of attention in mammogram classification. Although it is generally accepted that attention may improve model performance by focusing on relevant

G. Bebis et al. (Eds.): ISVC 2023, LNCS 14361, pp. 30–43, 2023.
https://doi.org/10.1007/978-3-031-47969-4_3

features [2,9], there have not been any rigorous studies that confirm this in the context of mammogram classification. Although many studies have shown that attention improves classification scores over the respective non-attention "baseline" models [10,11], none of them have compared combining different attention methods with various baseline models. Thus, it is unclear what attention models work best, and if attention generally leads to improvements in classification regardless of the baseline model. Furthermore, no research has been performed on the impact of mammogram resolution or abnormality type on attention performance. Therefore, we don't currently have sufficient understanding of how attention generally impacts whole image mammogram classification.

To better understand the impact of attention on whole image mammogram classification, we have performed extensive experiments with three baseline models and three attention methods (i.e., 12 distinct models in total). The rest of the paper is organized as follows: Section 2 data and methods, Sect. 2.1 data selection and preprocessing, Sect. 2.2 selection of models, Sect. 2.3 selection of attention models, Sect. 2.4 training and testing process, Sect. 3 results and discussion, Sect. 3.1 impact of attention on CNN performance, Sect. 3.2 impact of model architecture on performance differences, Sect. 3.3 impact of resolution on attention, Sect. 3.4 impact of abnormality type on attention, Sect. 3.5 relationship between model activation and AU-ROC, and Sect. 4 conclusions.

2 Data and Methods

2.1 Data Selection and Preprocessing

We used the CBIS-DDSM dataset [12] to analyze the impacts of attention on mammogram classification (benign or malignant). In order to understand how attention impacts model performance for different abnormality types, we trained and tested masses and calcifications separately. This dataset contains 1592 (1231 train, 361 test) images of masses and their respective segmented regions of interest and pathology, and 1513 (1227 train, 286 test) images of calcifications and their respective segmented regions of interest and pathology. Although CBIS-DDSM contains a relatively small amount of data, we chose this dataset because it uses an official train-test split, which we felt was appropriate for our rigorous analysis on the impacts of different attention methods.

Mammogram classification is highly dependent on image resolution where malignant masses or calcifications may be only a couple pixels wide [13]. To understand how the resolution of mammograms impacts attention methods, we tested models at resolutions of 500×300 and 1000×600 (height $\times$ width) pixels. Furthermore, we trained and tested separately on masses and calcifications.

Images were preprocessed according to standard methods in classification of whole-image mammograms with deep learning [14]. The images were normalized, segmented, cropped, flipped and enhanced with CLAHE. The preprocessed images were then resized to the target size for the respective experiment (either 500×300 or 1000×600 pixels). For training, we used brightness, rotation, contrast, and flipping augmentations.

2.2   Selection of Models

To understand how attention influences the classification of mammograms, we first selected three baseline models (Resnet50 [15], Densenet169 [16], Regnetx64 [17]). For each baseline model family, we trained and tested three different model sizes (eg. Resnet38, Resnet50, and Resnet101), and selected the particular model that performed the best. We chose Resnet50 and Densenet169 due to their high popularity for mammogram classification [18,19]. Regnetx64 is an architecture developed by Meta which represents a more state of the art version of Resnet50. Regnetx64 uses a quantized linear function to determine the width and depth of each stage in the network, which the authors claim result in significant improvements [17]. All of our baseline models (as well as the attention methods) come from the Huggingface PyTorch Image Models (TIMM) repository. For each of these baselines, we considered three different attention methods,yielding 12 different models in total.

2.3   Selection of Attention Methods

The main criteria for our choice of attention methods were modularity and popularity. Based on initial experiments, we identified three top performing attention methods that could be easily integrated with our baseline models: Squeeze and Excitation (SE), Efficient Channel Attention (ECA), and the Convolutional Bottleneck Attention Module (CBAM) [20–22]. SE and ECA utilize channel attention to appropriately weight task-relevant channels (Fig. 2b). ECA was developed to address the issue of dimensionality reduction for attention modules such as SE and CBAM, and it has been shown to outperform both of these attention methods [21]. CBAM uses both channel and spatial attention. For each baseline and attention combination, we performed ablation studies at low resolution to determine the best placement of the attention module within the baseline model.

2.4   Training and Testing Process

All models were trained with fine-tuning. Specifically, the last layer of each model was removed and replaced with a dropout layer, a fully connected (FC) layer with 1624, 1664, or 2048 input nodes (based on width of baseline network) and 64 output nodes, leaky ReLU activation with a slope of 0.1, another FC layer with 64 input nodes and 1 output node, and sigmoid activation in the final layer to produce a binary prediction (malignant or benign). We used pre-trained weights from Imagenet to initialize the models. Although some baseline+attention combinations had pre-trained weights in the TIMM repository, we used the respective baseline model weights to initialize all attention models to keep the comparison fair. For Resnet50, we trained and tested two different model weights, since we found that the standard Timm weights significantly under-performed when compared to the imagenet1k_V2 weights for Resnet50 found in the PyTorch library. We experimented with freezing certain parts of the models for fine-tuning, but found that it either resulted in no significant difference, or a slight decrease, in model scores. Therefore, no layers were frozen in our final experiments.

Hyperparameter tuning was done in a two step process. In the first step, we used Optuna to tune a large search space through Bayesian methods. These results narrowed the search space, then final tuning was done manually for each model. After manually tuning, we trained and tested each model within an approximate range of best hyperparameters over 40 times. We then used the top 30 scores for each model to calculate the results. The low resolution (500×300) models were primarily trained on a machine with an RTX 3070 (8 GB VRAM), and the high resolution (1000×600) models were all trained on a machine with an RTX 3090 (24 GB VRAM). We used a batch size of 10–16 (depending on VRAM constraints), the Adam optimizer, and cosine annealing with warm restarts for our scheduler.

3   Results and Discussion

3.1   Impact of Attention on CNN Performance

We have found that all attention methods generally improve baseline performance, but ECA and SE provide more consistent improvements than CBAM (Fig. 1a). By breaking the results down into model averages, we can observe CBAM yielded the largest performance increase for Densenet169, but it was the only attention method that decreased performance for Regnetx64 (Fig. 1b). Furthermore, all Densenet169 and Regnetx64 models generally outperform all Resnet50 models. We also found that all attention methods result in increased performance for Densenet169 and Resnet50, whereas only ECA and SE result in increased performance for Regnetx64, indicating that attention might be slightly less beneficial for Regnetx64. The only models that showed significant ($p < .05$) increases in AU-ROC over all model variations were Densenet169+CBAM and Densenet169+SE (Fig. 1b). Furthermore, the average differences between model AU-ROCs are relatively small. Thus, although choice of model architecture and attention module does matter, it should not have a large impact on results.

The number of trainable parameters is larger for Resnet50 and Regnetx64 than for Densenet169 (Table 1). Furthermore, the addition of CBAM and SE modules to Resnet50 and Regnetx64 leads to a larger increase in the number of parameters than when they are added to Densenet169. Thus, the poor performance of Resnet50, and Regnetx64+CBAM may be partially explained by the large number of parameters. Models with a large number of parameters have high complexity, and they are more likely to overfit than less complex models [23,24].

The poor performance of CBAM may be additionally explained by the fact that it has shown inconsistent performance, resulting in decreased scores compared to the baseline for some fine-grained tasks [25]. Since mammogram classification is a highly fine-grained task [26], it is possible that CBAM is helpful for a smaller range of models, abnormality types, and input image resolutions than the other attention methods are. We thus recommend that rigorous testing

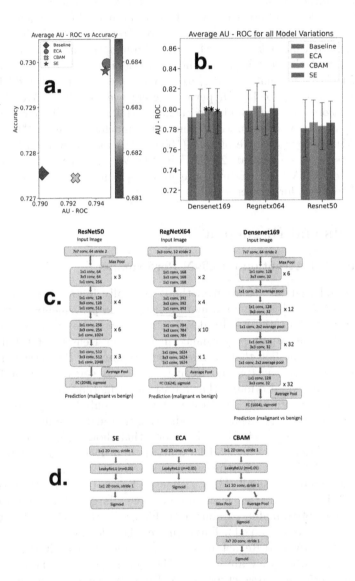

Fig. 1. Average results for all experiments, and architectures for baseline networks and attention methods. (a) Average AU-ROC vs accuracy with F1 colorbar. (b) Average AU-ROC for all model variations (network-specific breakdown of a). (c) Architecture comparison for Resnet50, Densenet169 and Regnetx64. (d) Architecture comparison for SE, ECA and CBAM attention modules. a&b show general increases in all scores due to attention. c&d are designed to highlight the differences between architectures used in this study, and are not a complete representation of the architectures.

be employed before using CBAM for mammogram classification (especially for calcifications).

In general, we found that CBAM was significantly harder to train than the baseline, SE, or ECA. CBAM took a significantly longer time to train than the other models, and the range of hyperparameters that produced good results was generally smaller (Table 1). However, the baseline models had the highest standard deviation between AU-ROC scores in different learning rate bins. Thus, attention results in less variation due to learning rate, which generally implies that models with attention will be less sensitive to hyperparameter choices. Similarly, Resnet50 was more difficult to train than Regnetx64 or Densenet169. Although Resnet50 trained faster than Densenet169, it was more prone to overfitting, and there was a smaller range of hyperparameters that would produce good results.

Table 1. This table contains various miscellaneous information that has been grouped together to save space. The first row gives the number of model parameters times 10^7. The second row gives the average run time for each model. The third row gives the standard deviation of AU - ROC for each model between groups of learning rates.

DN 169	RG 64	RN 50	CBAM DN 169	CBAM RG 64	CBAM RN 50	ECA DN 169	ECA RG 64	ECA RN 50	SE DN 169	SE RG 64	SE RN 50
1.26	2.47	2.36	1.28	4.36	6.39	1.26	2.47	2.36	1.28	4.36	6.39
20.12	14.53	10.05	19.64	28.26	21.40	18.55	15.19	12.84	20.00	16.04	13.83
.0042	.0066	.0069	.0043	.0060	.0038	.0045	.0045	.0048	.0036	.0041	.0050

Figure 2 shows the AU-ROC for each model variation trained separately on two different resolutions and for two different abnormality types. Based on this figure, the most significant increases in AU - ROC score due to attention were for Regnetx64 and Resnet50 for the 300×500 resolution masses, and Desnenet169 for the 600×1000 resolution masses and the 300×500 resolution calcifications. The best specific model performances were for Densnet169 with any attention method for the high resolution masses, and Regnetx64 with ECA for the high resolution masses. Figure 2 also reinforces the finding that ECA is the best attention method (greatest number of significant score increases compared to baseline), followed by SE then CBAM.

3.2   Impact of Model Architecture on Performance Differences

To further investigate these differences in performance, we analyzed the differences in model architecture between each baseline method (Fig. 1c). Densenet169 has a slower/more gradual increase in the number of feature maps (channels) than the other baseline networks do. Furthermore, all Densenet169 feature maps for each layer within a block are connected, meaning that no relevant information is lost within a block [16]. Densenet169 also ends up with less channels than

Resnet50 (1664 vs 2048). Regnetx64 has less changes in the number of channels than Resnet50, and also ends up with less channels (1624 vs 2048). Given the smaller growth rates of channel size and the similar final channel size for Densenet169 and Regnetx64, the relatively poor performance of Resnet50 might be due to its relatively wide architecture and/or bigger changes in number of channels between each layer. Although wide models may have a larger chance to overfit due to overparameterization, most research has shown increased performance for wider networks [27]. However, mammogram classification is an especially fine-grained task, so it's possible that a slightly larger tendency to overfit makes wider models perform worse in mammogram-related tasks. Furthermore, wide networks take significantly longer to train than thin networks. Thus, the poor performance of Resnet50 may be due to its relatively wide layers that potentially lead to overfitting, or the requirement of a longer training time than what was used in our experiments.

For the attention methods (Fig 1d.), we can see that the architectures of ECA and SE are relatively similar. The only difference is that SE has two 2D convolutional layers, and ECA only has one 1D convolutional layer. The first part of CBAM (channel attention) is nearly identical to the SE module. However, CBAM employs max and average pooling before sigmoid activation, which may restrict the predictive power of small features. After channel attention, the new feature map is passed to a spatial 7×7 2D convolutional filter followed by another sigmoid activation. This spatial convolution with a high kernel size further reinforces prediction of only the most salient features, reducing the input of small or less relevant features that may still be important for mammogram classification. Furthermore, spatial convolution has been shown to result in overfitting [28]. Thus, the relatively poor performance of CBAM may be partially due to its large spatial convolution since spatial convolution. However, we have also noted that CBAM was more difficult to train (due to larger training time and more sensitivity to hyperparameter choice), so we can't confidently conclude that the spatial convolution component of CBAM will always provide poor performance relative to other attention methods. Furthermore, we did some minor testing of CBAM with only the channel attention module, but this didn't result in a score increase over vanilla CBAM. More experimentation is needed to understand the exact shortcomings of CBAM (relative to SE and ECA), but we theorize that the explanation primarily lies with the max and average pooling, the large spatial convolution, or the difficulty in finding optimal hyperperameters for training.

Generally, our results seem to suggest that wider networks that use more pooling are likely to result in overfitting for mammogram classification. Although Densenet169 uses more pooling than any other architecture, the results are better than for Resnet50 because of the inter-connectedness of all feature maps, which ensures that small-but-important features are not lost. Thus, we posit that pooling is problematic insofar as it limits the amount of relevant information the model can use. If the underlying network architecture promotes strong connectivity between layers, then pooling does not seem to cause decreases in model performance for mammogram classification.

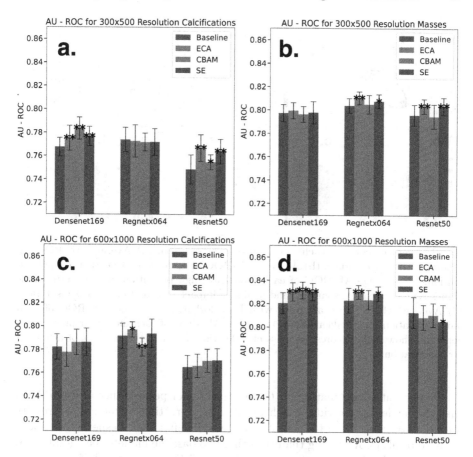

Fig. 2. Average AU-ROC for each model variation under each training/testing scenario for mammogram classification. One star indicates a significant ($p < .05$) difference from the baseline. Two stars indicate a very significant ($p < .01$) difference from the baseline. (a) Low resolution calcifications. (b) Low resolution masses. (c) High resolution calcifications. (d) High resolution masses. This figure generally shows improved performance due to attention, especially for ECA and SE.

3.3   Impact of Attention on Resolution

In addition to our general investigation of the impact of attention on mammogram classification, we also specifically investigated the impacts of attention on classification for different image resolutions. Our results indicate that attention has a greater impact at low resolution (Fig. 3a), although this is largely due to the much more significant increase in AU-ROC due to attention for Resnet50 at low resolution (Fig. 3b). Regnetx64, however, shows a slightly greater increase in AU - ROC when combined with ECA and SE at high resolution than it does at lower resolution (Fig. 3c).

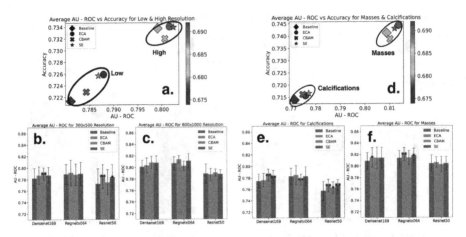

Fig. 3. Average scores of each model for each resolution. (a) Average AU-ROC vs. accuracy with F1 colorbar. (b) Average AU-ROC of each model variation for low resolution. (c) Average AU-ROC of each model for high resolution. a-c generally show higher scores at high resolution, and a higher impact of attention at low resolution. (d) Average AU-ROC vs. accuracy with F1 colorbar. (e) Average AU-ROC of each model variation for calcifications. (f) Average AU-ROC of each model for masses. d–f generally show higher scores for mass classification, and a higher impact of attention for calcifications.

One potential explanation for the relatively poor performance of Resnet50 is that the model is too wide, which resulted in overfitting. Although the results are not shown here due to lack of space, we did find that Resnet50 was more likely to result in overfitting than the other two baseline models. The addition of attention mechanisms helps to prevent this overfitting at low resolution. At high resolution, overfitting was generally less of an issue, so it's possible that attention is not able to provide much further improvement. However, like CBAM, it is also plausible that the "best" set of hyperparameters were not well determined for Resnet50 at high resolution, especially since the Resnet50 baseline showed the highest standard deviation of score based on choice of learning rate (Table 1). Although significant effort was made to ensure the best hyperparameters for each model were used, given the large number of models tested, it is conceivable that some were not trained in a way to produce the best possible scores.

Besides looking at how attention improves scores at different resolutions, we can also observe some general trends in the impact of resolution on mammogram classification. Clearly, classification scores are generally better at a higher resolution. Furthermore, there is much less variability for all model scores at high resolution. This has important implications for mammogram classification, since images are often heavily downsized to fit in various models [11,13].

3.4   Impact of Attention on Abnormality Type

We have also investigated the impact of attention on classification for different abnormality types. In general, we have found that SE and CBAM result in greater improvements in scores for calcifications than for masses (Fig. 3d). However CBAM also results in a large decrease in AU-ROC for calcifications when combined with Regnetx64. Thus, the performance of CBAM for calcifications is more reliant on baseline model architecture than for masses. ECA doesn't show any significant difference between scores for calcifications and masses. For Densenet169 and Resnet50, we found that attention results in greater score increases for the classification of calcifications than of masses (Figs. 3e and 3f). However, for Regnetx64, the opposite is true. One possible explanation for this trend is that Regnetx64 uses much less pooling than Densenet169 and Resnet50, meaning its architecture may be more favorable for small features such as calcifications. Thus, due to the constraints of resolution, attention is unable to offer as much of an impact in directing an already-good model to relevant features.

For calcification classification, the model scores may be significantly limited by the resolution of the image. Even at a resolution of 1000×600, some calcifications may only comprise a couple pixels. Consequently, Resnet50 and Densenet169, which both use a large amount of pooling, do not see much of a performance gain between low and high resolution (Fig 3). Regnetx64, which uses less pooling, sees much more significant increases in scores at high resolution. These results suggest that even at high resolution, too much pooling can result in a loss of relevant information. Densenet169, which uses the largest amount of pooling, shows a relatively small increase in scores for calcifications going from low to high resolution, but the largest increase in scores for masses going from low to high resolution (Fig. 2). The large amount of pooling may allow the model to focus on more relevant features for masses, but with calcifications, the pooling causes too much of a loss of information, even with the interconnectedness of the dense layers. This loss of information likely doesn't significantly impact Densenet169 at low resolution because the small features that would be lost to pooling have already been lost during downsizing.

3.5   Relationship Between Model Activation and AU-ROC

To investigate the impact of attention on mammogram classification at a deeper level, we considered the relation between class activation maps and AU-ROC. Specifically, we used LayerCAM [29] to calculate class activation maps for each test image and for each model variation. We then binarized the resulting heatmap and calculated the Jaccard index, or IOU, between the binarized heatmap and the respective mask for each image. We used a simple ascending search to determine the threshold for heatmap binarization that results in the highest IOU score. We found that ECA generally has the most consistent improvement in IOU score over the baseline (9/12 increases), then SE (7/12 increases), then CBAM (2/12 increases) (results not shown due to lack of space). We also observed that

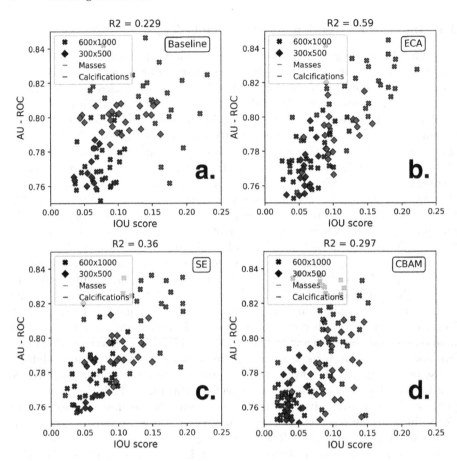

Fig. 4. Relationship between IOU and AU-ROC. Correlation coefficient (R2) is given at the top of each graph. (a) All baseline models. (b) All models with ECA. (c) All models with SE. (d) All models with CBAM. This figure generally shows that attention methods provide a stronger correlation between IOU and AU-ROC, which indicates that attention helps the models focus on task-relevent features.

IOU scores increase at higher resolution, and are higher for masses than for calcifications.

We further used scatter plots and linear regression to more precisely identify this relationship (Fig. 4). Our results indicate that all attention methods show more correlation between IOU and AU-ROC than the baseline models (Fig. 4a), but that this relationship is much more significant for ECA (Fig. 4b). This implies that attention generally causes a given model to focus on more relevant features in mammograms. Moreover, mass classification in high resolution mammograms provides the greatest IOU scores. Although not shown here due to a lack of space, the correlation between AU-ROC and IOU score increases at high resolution for all attention models. Thus, at higher resolutions, attention should theoretically provide a greater increase in scores. However, this is not what we have observed from resolution-averaged model performances (Fig. 3). Further investigation is required to determine the source of this contradiction.

4   Conclusions

Our work attempted to better understand how attention impacts mammogram classification. Our findings indicate that attention generally improves model performance. Furthermore, we found that ECA and SE significantly outperform CBAM. Between the baseline models, we found that Regnetx64 had the best performance, but may offer the lowest score increase due to attention. We also found that Densenet169 offers the highest increase due to attention, while Resnet50 gives the lowest scores. We theorize that differences in model architecture provide reasonable explanations for the differences we observed in model performance. Specifically, we found that wide architectures, and architectures with significant amounts of pooling, are more likely to overfit than thin models with less pooling. This impact was more noticeable for calcifications than for masses, which implies that the small features found in mammograms are often lost during pooling.

We have also presented evidence showing a correlation between IOU and AU-ROC scores. This correlation improves due to attention, with ECA showing the most significant correlation among the three attention methods examined. While others have used activation maps to show improvements due to attention, an IOU analysis providing an average score for all test images has not been presented. Our analysis shows that at a statistically relevant sample size, attention improves focus on task-relevant regions for mammogram classification. Future studies could leverage results from this study to develop a loss function that uses segmentation to make predictions for classification.

Our results could also be used to improve the design of future networks for mammogram classification and segmentation. Our findings indicate that model architecture and complexity are important considerations when designing networks for mammogram classification, as wide architectures and excessive pooling may result in overfitting. Furthermore, we have found that attention, especially ECA, results in significant performance increases for mammogram classification by helping the models to focus on task-relevant regions of the mammogram.

References

1. Guo, M.H., et al.: Attention mechanisms in computer vision: a survey. Comp. Visual Media **8**(5), 331–368 (2022)
2. Datta, S.K., Shaikh, M.A., Srihari, S.N., Gao, M.: Soft attention improves skin cancer classification performance. In: Reyes, M., et al. (eds.) IMIMIC/TDA4MedicalData -2021. LNCS, vol. 12929, pp. 13–23. Springer, Cham (2021). https://doi.org/10.1007/978-3-030-87444-5_2

3. Zhang, K., Wang, W., Lv, Z., Fan, Y., Song, Y.: Computer vision detection of foreign objects in coal processing using attention CNN. Eng. Appl. Artif. Intell. **102**, 104242 (2021)

4. Huang, Z., Wang, X., Huang, L., Huang, C., Wei, Y., Liu, W.: CCNet: criss-cross attention for semantic segmentation. In: 2019 IEEE/CVF International Conference on Computer Vision (ICCV), pp. 603–612, Seoul, Korea (South) (2019)

5. Anaya-Isaza, A., Mera-Jiménez, L., Zequera-Diaz, M.: An overview of deep learning in medical imaging. Inform. Med. Unlocked **26**, 100723 (2021)

6. Hassan, N.M., Hamad, S., Mahar, K.: Mammogram breast cancer CAD systems for mass detection and classification: a review. Multimed Tools Appl **81**, 20043–20075 (2022)

7. Altan, G.: Deep learning-based mammogram classification for breast cancer. Int. J. Intell. Syst. Appl. Eng. **8**(4), 171–176 (2020)

8. Shen, L., Margolies, L.R., Rothstein, J.H., et al.: Deep learning to improve breast cancer detection on screening mammography. Sci. Rep. **9**, 12495 (2019)

9. Azad, R., Asadi-Aghbolaghi, M., Fathy, M., Escalera, S.: Attention Deeplabv3+: multi-level context attention mechanism for skin lesion segmentation. In: Bartoli, A., Fusiello, A. (eds.) ECCV 2020. LNCS, vol. 12535, pp. 251–266. Springer, Cham (2020). https://doi.org/10.1007/978-3-030-66415-2_16

10. Lou, Q., Li, Y., Qian, Y., Lu, F., Ma, J.: Mammogram classification based on a novel convolutional neural network with efficient channel attention. Comput. Biol. Med. **150**, 106082 (2022)

11. Xu, C., Lou, M., Qi, Y., Wang, Y., Pi, J., Ma, Y.: Multi-Scale Attention-Guided Network for mammograms classification. Biomed. Signal Process. Control **68**, 102730 (2021)

12. Lee, R., et al.: A curated mammography data set for use in computer-aided detection and diagnosis research. Sci Data **4**, 170177 (2017)

13. Saunders, R.S., Jr., Baker, J.A., Delong, D.M., Johnson, J.P., Samei, E.: Does image quality matter? Impact of resolution and noise on mammographic task performance. Med. Phys. **34**(10), 3971–81 (2007)

14. Abdel-Nasser, M., Melendez, J., Moreno, A., Puig, D.: The impact of pixel resolution, integration scale, preprocessing, and feature normalization on texture analysis for mass classification in mammograms. Int. J. Optics **2016**, 1370259 (2016)

15. He, K., Zhang, X., Ren, S., Sun, J.: Deep residual learning for image recognition. In: Proceedings of the IEEE Conference on Computer Vision and Pattern Recognition, pp. 770–778 (2016)

16. Huang, G., Liu, Z., Van Der Maaten, L., Weinberger, K.Q.: Densely connected convolutional networks. In Proceedings of the IEEE Conference on Computer Vision and Pattern Recognition, pp. 4700–4708 (2017)

17. Radosavovic, I., Kosaraju, R.P., Girshick, R., He, K., Dollár, P.: Designing network design spaces. In: 2020 IEEE/CVF Conference on Computer Vision and Pattern Recognition (CVPR), pp. 10425–10433, Seattle, WA, USA (2020)

18. Chen, Y., Zhang, Q., Wu, Y., Liu, B., Wang, M., Lin, Y.: Fine-tuning resnet for breast cancer classification from mammography. In: Wu, C.Q., Chyu, M.-C., Lloret, J., Li, X. (eds.) ICHSE 2018. LNEE, vol. 536, pp. 83–96. Springer, Singapore (2019). https://doi.org/10.1007/978-981-13-6837-0_7

19. Al-Antari, M.A., Al-Masni, M.A., Kim, T.S.: Deep learning computer-aided diagnosis for breast lesion in digital mammogram. Adv. Exp. Med. Biol. **1213**, 59–72 (2020)

20. Hu, J., Shen, L., Sun, G.: Squeeze-and-excitation networks. In: 2018 IEEE/CVF Conference on Computer Vision and Pattern Recognition, pp. 7132–7141, Salt Lake City, UT, USA (2018)

21. Wang, Q., Wu, B., Zhu, P., Li, P., Zuo, W., Hu, Q.: ECA-Net: efficient channel attention for deep convolutional neural networks. In: 2020 IEEE/CVF Conference on Computer Vision and Pattern Recognition (CVPR), pp. 11531–11539, Seattle, WA, USA (2020)

22. Woo, S., Park, J., Lee, J.-Y., Kweon, I.S.: CBAM: convolutional block attention module. In: Ferrari, V., Hebert, M., Sminchisescu, C., Weiss, Y. (eds.) ECCV 2018. LNCS, vol. 11211, pp. 3–19. Springer, Cham (2018). https://doi.org/10.1007/978-3-030-01234-2_1

23. Kebria, P.M., et al.: Deep imitation learning: the impact of depth on policy performance. In: Cheng, L., Leung, A.C.S., Ozawa, S. (eds.) ICONIP 2018. LNCS, vol. 11301, pp. 172–181. Springer, Cham (2018). https://doi.org/10.1007/978-3-030-04167-0_16

24. Rice, L., Wong, E., Kolter, Z.: Overfitting in adversarially robust deep learning. In International Conference on Machine Learning, pp. 8093–8104, PMLR (2020)

25. Li, Z., Gu, T., Li, B., Xu, W., He, X., Hui, X.: ConvNeXt-based fine-grained image classification and bilinear attention mechanism model. Appl. Sci. **12**(18), 9016 (2022)

26. Hang, W., Liu, Z., Hannun, A.: GlimpseNet: attentional methods for full-image mammogram diagnosis. Proceedings (2017)

27. Doimo, D., Glielmo, A., Goldt, S., Laio, A.: Redundant representations help generalization in wide neural networks. Adv. Neural. Inf. Process. Syst. **35**, 19659–19672 (2020)

28. Yu, S., Jia, S., Xu, C.: Convolutional neural networks for hyperspectral image classification. Neurocomputing **219**, 88–98 (2017)

29. Jiang, P.T., Zhang, C.B., Hou, Q., Cheng, M.M., Wei, Y.: LayerCAM: exploring hierarchical class activation maps for localization. IEEE Trans. Image Process. **30**, 5875–5888 (2021)

ReFit: A Framework for Refinement of Weakly Supervised Semantic Segmentation Using Object Border Fitting for Medical Images

Bharath Srinivas Prabakaran[1], Erik Ostrowski[1(✉)], and Muhammad Shafique[2]

[1] Institute of Computer Engineering, Technische Universität Wien (TU Wien),
Vienna, Austria
{bharath.prabakaran,erik.ostrowski}@tuwien.ac.at
[2] eBrain Lab, Division of Engineering, New York University Abu Dhabi (NYUAD),
Abu Dhabi, United Arab Emirates
muhammad.shafique@nyu.edu

Abstract. Weakly Supervised Semantic Segmentation (WSSS) relying only on image-level supervision is a promising approach to deal with the need for Segmentation networks, especially for generating a large number of pixel-wise masks in a given dataset. However, most state-of-the-art image-level WSSS techniques lack an understanding of the geometric features embedded in the images since the network cannot derive any object boundary information from just image-level labels. We define a boundary here as the line separating an object and its background, or two different objects. To address this drawback, we are proposing our novel *ReFit* framework, which deploys state-of-the-art class activation maps combined with various post-processing techniques in order to achieve fine-grained higher-accuracy segmentation masks. To achieve this, we investigate a state-of-the-art unsupervised segmentation network that can be used to construct a boundary map, which enables *ReFit* to predict object locations with sharper boundaries. By applying our method to WSSS predictions, we achieved up to 10% improvement over the current state-of-the-art WSSS methods for medical imaging. The framework is open-source, to ensure that our results are reproducible, and accessible online at https://github.com/bharathprabakaran/ReFit.

Keywords: Weak Supervision · Semantic Segmentation · Masks · Medical Imaging Framework · CAM · Activation Maps · Boundary · Refinement

1 Introduction

State-of-the-art approaches for the semantic segmentation task require a deep learning model trained on a large amount of heavily annotated data, a task

B. S. Prabakaran and E. Ostrowski—Equal contribution.

referred to as Fully Supervised Semantic Segmentation (FSSS). The generation of pixel-wise masks for large datasets is a resource- and time-consuming process. For instance, one frame of the Cityscapes dataset, which contains thousands of pixel-wise frame annotations of street scenes from cities, requires more than an hour of manual user-driven annotation [1]. Furthermore, medical imaging and molecular biology fields require the knowledge of highly qualified and experienced individuals capable of interpreting and annotating the images. The interpretation of these individuals may vary based on their experience and know-how, further inducing a problem of varying masks, known as annotator bias. Therefore, to reduce the time and resources required for generating pixel-wise masks, a wide range of research works focus on developing approaches that focus on weaker kinds of supervision. This is where Weakly Supervised Semantic Segmentation (WSSS) can be highly beneficial.

WSSS approaches focus on generating masks with minimum supervision, such as image-level labels [2–4], bounding boxes [5,6], point annotations [7], and scribbles [8,9]. This work focuses on generating semantic segmentation masks for medical images using the most straightforward, and least-supervised, image-level labels. We limit the scope of our work to just using image-level labels since they are the most inexpensive form of annotation. To the best of our knowledge, the current state-of-the-art in image-level-based WSSS methods use class activation maps (CAMs) [10] to generate the pixel-level masks of an object from its image-level label. The central idea of CAMs is to use any model trained with classification loss to generate activation maps that highlight the image regions responsible for the prediction decision. This results mostly in a rough localization of the objects rather than precise pixel-wise masks. The most popular CAM approaches focus on adding regularization loss to improve the quality of the CAM prediction [11,12] or utilizing refinement methods that aim to enhance the CAM afterward [13,14]. For example, adversarial erasing [15] erases the most discriminative part of the CAM to force the model to consider different parts of an object. Chang et al. [11] use clustering to automatically sub-divide every class into sub-classes, implicitly generating distinctive classes for less discriminative parts of the CAM. Several other techniques focus on exploiting the ability of state-of-the-art classifiers to obtain viable object masks for the dataset [16–18]. However, these approaches are not primarily feasible for medical imaging use-cases, due to the classifier's inability to learn relevant information from the smaller and complex datasets. We propose to investigate the applicability of CAMs for automating the generation of pixel-wise segmentation masks for medical images given their image labels.

Although recognizing only the most discriminative parts of an object is enough to achieve a high classification accuracy, the activation map might leave out a sizeable portion of the object or include irrelevant background information, thus leading to an inaccurate mask. The most common approaches to acquiring a complete segmentation mask include adding more demanding conditions to the loss function, which improves the output CAM. This can be further refined, with respect to the initial CAM output, usually with pixel similarity calculations. Although more complex loss functions may succeed in covering the

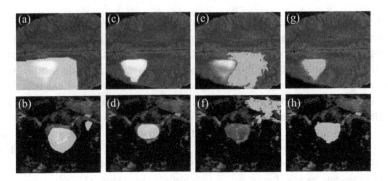

Fig. 1. Comparing the CAM's masks (a and b) and their ground truths (c and d) against the use of similarity-based clustering strategies when incorrect (e and f) and accurate (g and h) anchors are identified on the BRATS and Decathlon datasets.

complete object, their downside is that the highlighted area remains blurry and is still far from the sharp predictions achieved using FSSS. On the other hand, the refinement-based methods can predict sharp object borders, but they heavily rely on the quality of the initial predictions since they cannot spot parts of the object with a different color gradient than the rest. This could also lead to potential scenarios wherein a generated mask is inaccurate in certain instances when incorrect anchors are used to generate the masks with respect to an identified object. Figure 1 presents an overview of these differences with the help of illustrative examples from the BRATS [19] and Decathlon [20] datasets. As shown, the CAM prediction successfully generates a mask almost around the complete object but includes a lot of background pixels. In contrast, a similarity-based pixel clustering instance achieves sharper borders but may fail to capture the object due to changes in color gradients with respect to the background. It might also fail entirely in cases where wrong anchors are used due to a bad base prediction.

Therefore, state-of-the-art frameworks combine the two approaches to help alleviate each other's shortcomings to generate segmentation labels, known as *pseudo-labels*, to train an FSSS network, which proved to be the most accurate. For medical imaging datasets, state-of-the-art CAM models are not effective because the classifier fails to learn on them due to the smaller size and complexity of the dataset. Hence, we improve upon this strategy by extracting information obtained from saliency maps and their boundaries, to differentiate between the object and its surroundings through our novel BoundaryFit module that acts as an additional step between the initial CAM prediction and mask refinement.

As we have already discussed, the improved CAM output generally captures the complete object but still includes many background pixels in its predictions. These background pixels tend to deteriorate the quality of the refinement method, if they achieve higher logits/certainty than the actual target object. This may occur if the classifier fails to make confident predictions on the given dataset. Hence, our proposed BoundaryFit module aims to refine the borders

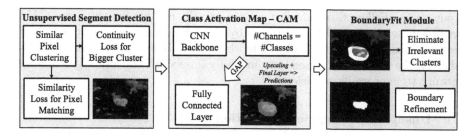

Fig. 2. Overview of our ReFit Framework, which starts with the unsupervised segmentation (USS) stage clustering the pixels of an image based on their similarity to the surrounding pixels; Next, we extract the edge map based on the input cluster, which determines a preliminary boundary of the target object; Finally, our BoundaryFit module conforms the two to obtain a fine-grained mask.

of the initial CAM prediction without relying on pixel similarities and instead focuses on Unsupervised Semantic Segmentation (USS) and saliency methods to generate a simplified *edge map* of the input image, which is the first step of our framework. Second, we use the edge map to determine the image's *response map* using GradCAM [21], which is a network used to obtain CAMs. Finally, we combine the two using our BoundaryFit module, which refines the object boundaries to obtain a fine-grained segmentation mask. We perform extensive experiments on three different medical imaging datasets, namely, the breast cancer ultrasound (BUSI) [22], the BRATS 2020 [19,23], and the Decathlon [20] datasets, to prove the effectiveness of the proposed framework and illustrate the benefits of our approach. To sum up, the key contributions of this work are:

1. Our novel ReFit framework can generate fine-grained segmentation masks of medical images using just image-level labels.
2. The BoundaryFit module, which can be incorporated into any conventional WSSS pipeline to obtain fine-grained segmentation masks.
3. We have illustrated the benefits and improvements of using ReFit on three real-world medical imaging datasets. The ReFit framework, including the BoundaryFit module, is open-source and accessible online[1].

2   Our ReFit Framework

Figure 2 presents an overview of our framework, which currently incorporates a generic CAM to obtain the necessary activation maps. First, an unsupervised segmentation (USS) network is used to cluster the image pixels into bigger groups based on the Quickshift [24] and SLIC [25] algorithms to create superpixels. Second, we use a trained classifier to generate a CAM, which acts as a preliminary segmentation mask, based on clusters from the USS, for each class in a given

---

[1] https://github.com/bharathprabakaran/ReFit.

input image. Followed by which our BoundaryFit module fits the fuzzy CAM prediction to the boundaries outlined by the USS map to generate a refined segmentation mask for each object in the image. If necessary, these pseudo-labels can be subsequently used to train a fully supervised semantic segmentation network to improve its precision.

2.1   Unsupervised Segment Detection

Our approach focuses on pre-refining the CAM prediction to the nearest edge inside the mask in order to reduce the model's identification of false-positive pixel predictions. To achieve this, we propose to generate a helpful edge map using a USS network to break down the image into simpler parts as a function for the input I as $I_{EM} = g_{USS}(I)$. The USS will cluster similar pixels together, removing unimportant details in the input image, leaving us with a less detailed image. The USS method we use for image simplification consists of two convolutional layers with ReLU, Batch Norm, a continuity loss, and a similarity loss. The continuity loss prevents the network from using an arbitrary number of pixel clusters and constrains them with a user-defined maximum value q. Meanwhile, the similarity loss encourages the network to only cluster pixels close to each other in the feature space.

For the ReFit framework, we used SLIC and Quickshift as the continuity loss and performed an extended hyperparameter search to generate suitable simplified images. On the one hand, clustering too many pixels into one group will merge the object with the background, while clustering too few pixels together will not simplify the image enough. Note that optimizing the hyper-parameters for a particular image would not work for a different image. Therefore our goal was to find hyperparameters that work well enough for all images.

To elaborate further, we iteratively cycle through all possible hyperparameter values in small step-sizes, while evaluating their results on the dataset to obtain the parameter value that offers the best results for a small sample of up to 100 random images. we have observed such a sample represents the dataset very well. The hyperparameter search could be mathematically optimized to find the optimal combination if an annotated dataset for validation is provided. But sufficient hyperparameters can be found by testing a few images and evaluating their performance. We can find better hyperparameters when using an annotated dataset for validation. But sufficient hyperparameters can be found by testing less than 100 images and evaluating their performance. The goal is to simplify the images as much as possible without losing the shape of the target objects. The use of other clustering algorithms is orthogonal to our approach and can easily be included in the framework.

2.2   Class Activation Map - CAM

Next, we start by training a conventional classifier model on the target dataset, which is subsequently used by a GradCAM [21] to extract the response map for each input edge map obtained from the USS stage. The generated segmentation masks for each class n in I_{EM} are considered together to be the initial response map, which is defined as $M_{CAM} := \{M_{CAM}^0, M_{CAM}^1, ..., M_{CAM}^n\}$. The original CAM predictions highlight the most discriminative object parts and a lot of background pixels around them, as illustrated in Fig. 1. For example, the initial response map from our CAM covers a significant portion of the image to ensure that the complete object is inside along with some background pixels. The next step, *i.e.,* the BoundaryFit module, is used to eliminate the irrelevant pixels and obtain a fine-grained segmentation mask of the object.

2.3   The BoundaryFit Module

Once we successfully generate the edge map, we can use it as an additional supervision source, which provides us with geometrical guidance for improved boundary detection. Hence, we can combine it with the initial response map from CAMs, which usually captures the complete object at the cost of adding many background pixels. Next, with a combination of the edge map obtained from the previous stage and a Floodfill algorithm [26], we successfully remove some irrelevant background pixels from the mask.

The Floodfill algorithm accomplishes this by starting from any negative pixel (x, y) in the initial response map and then turning all pixels belonging to the same cluster as (x, y) negative as well. Note that we define a cluster as the set of pixels inside an area closed by the boundaries in an edge map I_{EM}, including the pixels that demarcate the image borders. Since some pixel clusters also reach into the CAM prediction, only pixel clusters completely inside the CAM mask will remain positive. We define this step as follows:

$$
\begin{aligned}
h_{BF}(M_{CAM}, I_{EM}) &= (M_{CAM}(I_{EM}) \otimes I_{EM}) \\
&= M_{BF}
\end{aligned}
\tag{1}
$$

where $h_{BF}(\cdot)$ and $\otimes$ denote our BoundaryFit module and the combination process of edge map and CAM prediction, respectively, which provides us with the final segmentation mask (M_{BF}) that fits the estimated boundaries of the object.

3   Results and Discussion

The experiments are completed on a CentOS 7.9 Operating System executing on an Intel Core i7-8700 CPU with 16 GB RAM and 2 Nvidia GeForce GTX 1080 Ti GPUs. We executed our scripts using CUDA 11.5, Pytorch 3.7.4.3, torchvision 0.11.1, and Pytorch-lightning 1.5.1. We use the Dice Similarity Coefficient (DSC) metric, as shown by the state-of-the-art [14,27], to illustrate the benefits of using our approach to generate segmentation masks for the medical imaging datasets. We also consider the mean Intersection-over-Union (mIoU) ratio as an evaluation metric to analyze the framework's benefits. For all experiments, we evaluate the Dice Similarity Coefficient as:

Table 1. Comparison of GradCAM and ReFit (w/ GradCAM backbone) on BUSI.

Method	Avg. DCS	Avg. mIoU
Blank	64.1	47.2
GradCAM	65.5	48.5
ReFit	**67.2**	**50.6**

$$DSC = \frac{2|A \cdot B|}{|A| + |B|} \qquad (2)$$

where A and B are binary matrices denoting the ground truths and classification results, respectively, with each element corresponding to 1 for elements inside a group and 0 otherwise. We also evaluate the mean Intersection-over-Union (mIoU) ratio, which is used as the evaluation metric, and defined as

$$mIoU = \frac{1}{N} \sum_{i=1}^{N} \frac{p_{i,i}}{\sum_{j=1}^{N} p_{i,j} + \sum_{j=1}^{N} p_{j,i} - p_{i,i}} \qquad (3)$$

where N is the total number of classes, $p_{i,i}$ the number of pixels classified as class i when labelled as class i. $p_{i,j}$ and $p_{j,i}$ are the number of pixels classified as class i that were labelled as class j and vice-versa, respectively.

We have evaluated our framework on the following three different medical imaging datasets: (1) the breast cancer ultrasound dataset BUSI [22], (2) the Multimodal Brain Tumor Segmentation dataset BRATS 2020 [19,23,28], and (3) the Decathlon dataset [20]. For Decathlon, the dataset is divided in a 3 : 1 ratio for generating the training and validation sets, respectively; the subdivided dataset is already accessible as part of the code repository published in the WSS-CMER work. Every image contains either just the background or the background and the singular positive class. The base classifiers were trained on the training set and then evaluated on the validation set. The decathlon dataset contained the T2 and ADC phases for each image. We only used the ADC phase as discussed in the paper. For the BraTS dataset, the 3D images of the dataset were divided into slices and cropped. All slices were randomly subdivided into one of three sets to perform three-fold cross-validation. For training, the classifiers used a combination of two sets for training and were validated on the remaining set. For the BUSI dataset, since we do not train a model on the data, we directly evaluate the ImageNet pre-trained model on it. BUSI contains three classes, normal, benign, and malignant. We excluded the malignant class for evaluation since our method struggled to detect the malignant cases, as stated in the main article.

BUSI Dataset: We start by examining the results of GradCAM, built using a state-of-the-art classifier for the dataset, and compare them with the results from ReFit. Note, since learning the other classes proved too difficult with the

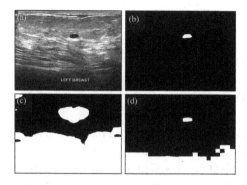

Fig. 3. (a) Image from the breast ultrasound dataset [22]; (b) ground truth; (c) Grad-CAM prediction; (d) ReFit prediction.

Table 2. Comparison of ReFit with state-of-the-art techniques on BRATS.

Method	Avg. DCS	Avg. mIoU
SEAM [14]	56.1	39.0
WSS-CMER [27]	59.7	42.6
Blank	64.6	47.7
GradCAM (w/ ResNet34)	67.3	50.7
GradCAM (w/ ResNet50)	68.5	52.1
ReFit (w/ ResNet34)	70.3	54.2
ReFit (w/ ResNet50)	**71.2**	**55.7**
FSSS	81.8	69.2

low amount of data, we have only evaluated the benign cases. We use an ImageNet [29] pre-trained GradCAM with a ResNet34 [30] backbone as a baseline, instead of a state-of-the-art CAM model for natural images, because the GradCAM achieved better results on the dataset. This is probably because the BUSI dataset is relatively small and does not contain enough data for a larger model to learn all the relevant information effectively. After generating the response maps with GradCAM, we have refined them using our BoundaryFit module to achieve the results presented in Table 1.

Conventional user-level evaluation of the BUSI images provides us with the understanding that the cancer objects in each image are relatively small compared to the background (see Fig. 3). Therefore, predicting a simple blank mask achieves an mIoU of 47.2%, while using GradCAM improves the results to 48.5%. However, with the ReFit framework, we improved the best prediction mask to the highest possible value. Similarly, the average DCS for ReFit is the highest among all three with a value of 67.2%. The state-of-the-art SEAM [14] and WSS-CMER [27] techniques are unable to learn sufficient information from this dataset to make predictions.

Table 3. Comparing ReFit and state-of-the-art techniques on Decathlon.

Method	Avg. DCS	Avg. mIoU
Blank	64.6	47.7
GradCAM (w/ ResNet101)	65.9	49.1
SEAM [14]	65.9	49.1
GradCAM (w/ ResNet18)	67.0	50.3
WSS-CMER [27]	71.3	55.4
GradCAM (w/ ResNet50)	76.1	61.4
GradCAM (w/ ResNet34)	78.0	63.9
ReFit (w/ ResNet34)	**79.4**	**65.8**
FSSS	86.8	76.7

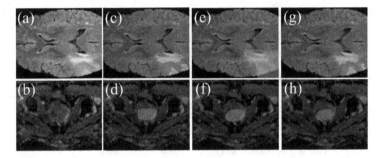

Fig. 4. Visual comparison of the BRATS and Decathlon dataset images (a and b, respectively); their ground truth segmentation masks (c and d); GradCAM predictions (e and f); and ReFit predictions (g and h).

BRATS 2020 Dataset: Next, we evaluate the effectiveness of our ReFit framework on the BRATS 2020 dataset and compare it with state-of-the-art techniques like SEAM and WSS-CMER. These results are shown in Table 2. Like with the BUSI dataset, we additionally evaluate the effectiveness of a GradCAM constructed using trained ResNet34 and ResNet50 classifiers as the baseline. As expected, our ReFit framework (with ResNet50) outperforms all other techniques to achieve average DCS and mIoU values of 71.2% and 55.7%, respectively. The FSSS evaluation is the result reached when using a traditional, fully supervised semantic segmentation network is trained on the provided ground-truth pixel-wise masks. This network acts as the upper bound, when compared to the use of other WSSS approach using pseudo-labels,, i.e., the goal of WSSS approaches is to reach or surpass the accuracy of FSSS. Like in the WSS-CMER [27] approach, we have combined all instances into one single 'positive' class. We have followed a similar approach for the Decathlon dataset, which is the next use-case.

Decathlon Dataset: Finally, we analyze the efficacy of the our framework on the Decathlon Prostate dataset and compare it with the state-of-the-art and simple GradCAMs built using various classifier variants. Out of all these approaches, the best outcome was achieved using a GradCAM built with a ResNet34 model, surpassing the state-of-the-art approaches. Hence, we evaluate the ReFit framework with a ResNet34-based GradCAM, which achieves the best outcome with a DCS score of 79.4%. We have illustrated the results of these experiments in Table 3.

Although we have illustrated that ReFit is successful in improving upon the current state-of-the-art, the literature on WSSS for medical imaging is not comprehensive and comparison partners are rather lacking. We are working with a set of very low-quality state-of-the-art predictions, trying to improve them to a certain degree. More investigation might be required into this to determine the actual benefits of using CAMs and the BoundaryFit module. Similarly, the BoundaryFit module works on the understanding that the object is clearly distinguishable from the background based on its boundaries; in unlikely scenarios where this is no longer the case, this could lead to potential problems.

Note, the state-of-the-art results for the last two datasets were extracted directly from [27], since we were unable to reproduce them at our end.

3.1   Ablation Studies

Figure 4 illustrates the visual comparison of the ReFit predictions for the BRATS and Decathlon datasets. As anticipated, the GradCAM over-estimates the object mask by including a significant number of background pixels for both datasets (Figs. 4(e) and (f)). And, by design, a significant portion of these pixels are eliminated by our BoundaryFit module to obtain a fine-grained segmentation mask (Figs. 4(g) and (h)).

4   Conclusion

In this paper, we have proposed the novel ReFit framework, which introduces a novel BoundaryFit module between CAM and the final FSSS model, to achieve finer segmentation masks, which can be used to improve the overall accuracy of the model. The BoundaryFit module provides additional saliency by utilizing unsupervised semantic segmentation models, which refine the CAM predictions to obtain higher-quality training labels for state-of-the-art FSSS models. The BoundaryFit module can be incorporated into any pre-existing WSSS framework to boost the quality of its predictions, as illustrated by three real-world medical imaging datasets. Finally, we showed that the predictions generated by ReFit achieve state-of-the-art performance, proving its effectiveness compared to other approaches by up to 10%. ReFit is open-source and is accessible online at https://github.com/bharathprabakaran/ReFit.

Acknowledgments. This work is part of the Moore4Medical project funded by the ECSEL Joint Undertaking under grant number H2020-ECSEL-2019-IA-876190. This work was also supported in parts by the NYUAD's Research Enhancement Fund (REF) Award on "eDLAuto: An Automated Framework for Energy-Efficient Embedded Deep Learning in Autonomous Systems", and by the NYUAD Center for Artificial Intelligence and Robotics (CAIR), funded by Tamkeen under the NYUAD Research Institute Award CG010.

References

1. Cordts, M. et al.: The cityscapes dataset for semantic urban scene understanding. In: Proceedings of the IEEE Conference on Computer Vision and Pattern Recognition, pp. 3213–3223 (2016)
2. Kolesnikov, A., Lampert, C.H.: Seed, expand and constrain: three principles for weakly-supervised image segmentation. In: Leibe, B., Matas, J., Sebe, N., Welling, M. (eds.) ECCV 2016. LNCS, vol. 9908, pp. 695–711. Springer, Cham (2016). https://doi.org/10.1007/978-3-319-46493-0_42
3. Pathak, D., Krahenbuhl, P., Darrell, T.: Constrained convolutional neural networks for weakly supervised segmentation. In: Proceedings of the IEEE International Conference on Computer Vision, pp. 1796–1804 (2015)
4. Pinheiro, P.O., Collobert, R.: From image-level to pixel-level labeling with convolutional networks. In: Proceedings of the IEEE Conference on Computer Vision and Pattern Recognition, pp. 1713–1721 (2015)
5. Khoreva, A., Benenson, R., Hosang, J., Hein, M., Schiele, B.: Simple does it: weakly supervised instance and semantic segmentation. In: Proceedings of the IEEE Conference on Computer Vision and Pattern Recognition, pp. 876–885 (2017)
6. Li, Q., Arnab, A., Torr, P.H.: Weakly-and semi-supervised panoptic segmentation. In: Proceedings of the European Conference on Computer Vision (ECCV), pp. 102–118 (2018)
7. Bearman, A., Russakovsky, O., Ferrari, V., Fei-Fei, L.: What's the point: semantic segmentation with point supervision. In: Leibe, B., Matas, J., Sebe, N., Welling, M. (eds.) ECCV 2016. LNCS, vol. 9911, pp. 549–565. Springer, Cham (2016). https://doi.org/10.1007/978-3-319-46478-7_34
8. Lin, D., Dai, J., Jia, J., He, K., Sun, J.: Scribblesup: scribble-supervised convolutional networks for semantic segmentation. In: Proceedings of the IEEE Conference on Computer Vision and Pattern Recognition, pp. 3159–3167 (2016)
9. Vernaza, P., Chandraker, M.: Learning random-walk label propagation for weakly-supervised semantic segmentation. In: Proceedings of the IEEE Conference on Computer Vision and Pattern Recognition, pp. 7158–7166 (2017)
10. Zhou, B., Khosla, A., Lapedriza, A., Oliva, A., Torralba, A.: Learning deep features for discriminative localization. In Proceedings of the IEEE Conference on Computer Vision and Pattern Recognition, pp. 2921–2929 (2016)
11. Chang, Y.T., Wang, Q., Hung, W.C., Piramuthu, R., Tsai, Y.H., Yang, M.H.: Weakly-supervised semantic segmentation via sub-category exploration. In: Proceedings of the IEEE/CVF Conference on Computer Vision and Pattern Recognition, pp. 8991–9000 (2020)
12. Jo, S., Yu, I.-J.: Puzzle-cam: improved localization via matching partial and full features. In: 2021 IEEE International Conference on Image Processing (ICIP), pp. 639–643. IEEE (2021)
13. Ahn, J., Kwak, S.: Learning pixel-level semantic affinity with image-level supervision for weakly supervised semantic segmentation. In: Proceedings of the IEEE Conference on Computer Vision and Pattern Recognition, pp. 4981–4990 (2018)

14. Wang, Y., Zhang, J., Kan, M., Shan, S., Chen, X.: Self-supervised equivariant attention mechanism for weakly supervised semantic segmentation. In: Proceedings of the IEEE/CVF Conference on Computer Vision and Pattern Recognition, pp. 12275–12284 (2020)

15. Wei, Y., Feng, J., Liang, X., Cheng, M.-M., Zhao, Y., Yan, S.: Object region mining with adversarial erasing: a simple classification to semantic segmentation approach. In: Proceedings of the IEEE Conference on Computer Vision and Pattern Recognition, pp. 1568–1576 (2017)

16. Xu, L., Ouyang, W., Bennamoun, M., Boussaid, F., Xu, D.: Multi-class token transformer for weakly supervised semantic segmentation. In: Proceedings of the IEEE/CVF Conference on Computer Vision and Pattern Recognition, pp. 4310–4319 (2022)

17. Zhou, T., Zhang, M., Zhao, F., Li, J.: Regional semantic contrast and aggregation for weakly supervised semantic segmentation. In: Proceedings of the IEEE/CVF Conference on Computer Vision and Pattern Recognition, pp. 4299–4309 (2022)

18. Ru, L., Zhan, Y., Yu, B., Du, B.: Learning affinity from attention: end-to-end weakly-supervised semantic segmentation with transformers. In: Proceedings of the IEEE/CVF Conference on Computer Vision and Pattern Recognition, pp. 16846–16855 (2022)

19. Menze, B.H., et al.: The multimodal brain tumor image segmentation benchmark (BRATS). IEEE Trans. Med. Imaging **34**(10), 1993–2024 (2014)

20. Antonelli, M., et al.: The medical segmentation decathlon. Nat. Commun. **13**(1), 1–13 (2022)

21. Selvaraju, R.R., Cogswell, M., Das, A., Vedantam, R., Parikh, D., Batra, D.: Grad-cam: Visual explanations from deep networks via gradient-based localization. In Proceedings of the IEEE International Conference on Computer Vision, pp. 618-626 (2017)

22. Al-Dhabyani, W., Gomaa, M., Khaled, H., Fahmy, A.: Dataset of breast ultrasound images. Data Brief **28**, 104863 (2020)

23. Bakas, S., et al.: Identifying the best machine learning algorithms for brain tumor segmentation, progression assessment, and overall survival prediction in the brats challenge arXiv preprint arXiv:1811.02629 (2018)

24. Zhu, Q., Wu, D., Xie, Y., Wang, L.: Quick shift segmentation guided single image haze removal algorithm. In: 2014 IEEE International Conference on Robotics and Biomimetics (ROBIO 2014), pp. 113–117. IEEE (2014)

25. Achanta, R., Shaji, A., Smith, K., Lucchi, A., Fua, P., Süsstrunk, S.: Slic super-pixels, Technical report (2010)

26. Fishkin, K.P., Barsky, B.A.: An analysis and algorithm for filling propagation. In: Magnenat-Thalmann, N., Thalmann, D. (eds.) Computer-Generated Images. Springer, Tokyo (1985). https://doi.org/10.1007/978-4-431-68033-8_6

27. Patel, G., Dolz, J.: Weakly supervised segmentation with cross-modality equivariant constraints. Med. Image Anal. **77**, 102374 (2022)

28. Bakas, S., et al.: Advancing the cancer genome atlas glioma MRI collections with expert segmentation labels and radiomic features. Sci. data **4**(1), 1–13 (2017)

29. Deng, J., Dong, W., Socher, R., Li, L. J., Li, K., Fei-Fei, L.: Imagenet: a large-scale hierarchical image database. In: 2009 IEEE Conference on Computer Vision and Pattern Recognition, pp. 248–255. IEEE (2009)

30. He, K., Zhang, X., Ren, S., Sun, J.: Deep residual learning for image recognition. In: Proceedings of the IEEE Conference on Computer Vision and Pattern Recognition, pp. 770–778 (2016)

A Data-Centric Approach for Pectoral Muscle Deep Learning Segmentation Enhancements in Mammography Images

Santiago V. Silva[✉], Cesar A. Sierra-Franco, Jan Hurtado,
Leonardo C. da Cruz, Victor de A. Thomaz, Greis Francy M. Silva-Calpa,
and Alberto B. Raposo

Department of Informatics and Tecgraf Institute, Pontifical Catholic University of
Rio de Janeiro, Rio de Janeiro, Brazil
{santiagosvs,casfranco,hurtado,lccruz,victorthomaz,greis,
abraposo}@tecgraf.puc-rio.br

Abstract. Deep learning-based segmentation has emerged as a powerful and effective technique for addressing diverse medical imaging tasks. Particularly, in mammography image analysis, segmenting the anatomical structures plays a significant role in computer-aided diagnosis assistance and positioning assessment. However, accurately identifying the pectoral muscle in the craniocaudal view presents challenges even for experienced radiologists due to its variable size, potential absence, and fibroglandular tissue overlaps. These challenges are further amplified when dealing with error-prone annotations, where mislabeled or inaccurately labeled data can lead to training the model on incorrect information. Consequently, this can cause the model to learn from these errors and produce underperforming or suboptimal results during inference. To address this, we propose a two-stage data-centric approach to enhance the accuracy of the deep-learning-based mammography segmentation model. In the first stage, we introduce a shape-based label analysis to automatically identify pectoral muscle labels with possible inconsistencies for a posterior manual review and correction. Then, in the second stage, we downsample the training dataset by removing outlier images with dubious annotations. The experimental results show the effectiveness of prioritizing training data quality and reliability. This approach significantly improved the model's ability to detect and accurately segment the pectoral muscle.

Keywords: Mammography Images · Deep Learning · Data-Centric AI

1 Introduction

Mammography is an X-ray imaging method used to analyze the breast's internal tissues for early cancer detection [1]. A mammography exam or mammogram usually includes two standard images representing top-bottom and side views of the breast, named craniocaudal (CC) and mediolateral oblique (MLO).

© The Author(s), under exclusive license to Springer Nature Switzerland AG 2023
G. Bebis et al. (Eds.): ISVC 2023, LNCS 14361, pp. 56–67, 2023.
https://doi.org/10.1007/978-3-031-47969-4_5

Both views allow the visualization of healthy tissues and potential abnormalities whose location can be inferred from reference structures, such as the pectoral muscle, the fibroglandular tissue, the fatty tissue, and the nipple. The location of the abnormalities and the spatial description of the reference structures play an essential role during the diagnosis and evaluation of mammogram adequacy. Providing a software assistant for the automated identification of the reference structures can both support medical interpretation and allow less experienced operators to collect data for further assessment. The identification of the structures of interest can be addressed as a semantic segmentation problem, where a pixel-level classification is performed to define the regions of the mammography image that correspond to a given structure. Deep learning models have shown superlative performance on the semantic segmentation task considering different domains, where mammography images are not the exception [9]. However, most of the approaches proposed in the literature focus on the MLO view only [2], where the reference structures are well-defined. The CC view segmentation is more challenging because the pectoral muscle is not always included, and its recognition can be difficult even for a clinical expert due to its possible overlap with the fibroglandular tissue, the different shapes and sizes that it can present in the mammogram projection, the presence of skin folds, the inclusion of brightness artifacts during acquisition, among others (See Fig. 1). The correct detection and segmentation of the pectoral muscle is very important because it defines the posterior region limits of the breast tissues. Based on the deep learning approach introduced in [9] for mammography image segmentation, we propose a data-centric methodology that aims to improve the segmentation of the pectoral muscle on CC view images. We introduce a set of efficient annotation correction and down-sampling strategies that are useful in refining the training dataset to reach a better performance on pectoral muscle detection and segmentation. Our experiments show how our methodology outperforms the results of the reference method by considering segmentation and classification metrics. The remainder of this paper is structured as follows. Section 2 presents some relevant work for our proposal. Section 3 introduces the details of the reference method for mammography image segmentation. Section 4 explains the proposed methodology. Section 5 shows the numerical and visual results. Finally, in Sect. 6, we present our conclusion and future work.

2   Related Work

Semantic segmentation techniques have been employed to actively identify structures of interest in mammography images. However, approaches to evaluating pectoral muscle focus only on the MLO view, neglecting the CC view. Yongze Guo et al. [6] applied a two-step process to segment the pectoral muscle in the MLO view. Initially, the authors employed a machine learning model to locate the image region containing the pectoral muscle. Subsequently, they utilized a generative adversarial network (GAN) to create an image of the segment of the pectoral muscle's shape. This approach enables accurate structure segmentation,

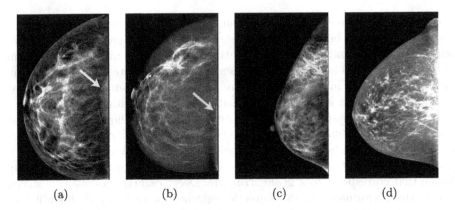

(a)   (b)   (c)   (d)

Fig. 1. Pectoral muscle segmentation difficulties. The red arrows are pointing the location of the pectoral. (a) A clearly visible pectoral muscle. (b) A thin projection of the pectoral muscle that can be difficult to differentiate from a skin fold or an acquisition artifact. (c) The fibroglandular tissue projection overlaps the pectoral muscle projection. (d) A bright acquisition artifact that can be confused with a pectoral muscle. (Color figure online)

even in cases of blurriness or obscuration. Dubrovina et al. [4] implemented a machine learning model to segment the fibro glanduralr tissue in MLO view without leaving the other main structures aside. Concerning the pectoral muscle, the authors emphasize that this structure is always located in the same area, and the model can detect it with relatively high accuracy. Using other techniques, the study by Rubio and Montiel [8] shows that a model-centric approach can contribute to finding a better model structure to segment the pectoral muscle. The authors compared the behavior and metrics of different combinations of two-stage segmentation architectures, one for feature extraction (VGG16 and ResNet50) and another for segmenting (FCN-8, U-Net, and PSPNet), using the mini-MIAS dataset, which is composed of digitized mammograms in MLO view. After experimenting with various combinations using the same dataset, they determined ResNet+PSPNet as the structure that yields the highest IoU results, and VGG+U-Net as the one that produces the lowest values on their dataset. Other computer vision methods include pixel-by-pixel classification using a Markov random field (MRF) modeling [5]. This modeling distributes intensities based on spatial information, aiding in the search for the curved triangular shape of the pectoral muscle in the MLO view and its semi-elliptical shape in the CC view. This method is limited to noise-free images, as it may fail on images with fibro glandural tissue overlap, making visualization of the muscle difficult. Santle Camilus et al. [3], implemented a pectoral segmentation area in MLO view using watershed transformation, which allows finding the contours by creating regions of interest and merging the regions that correspond to the pectoral muscle. Recently, Sierra-Franco et al. [9] introduced a large dataset and deep learning-based experiments for mammography image seg-

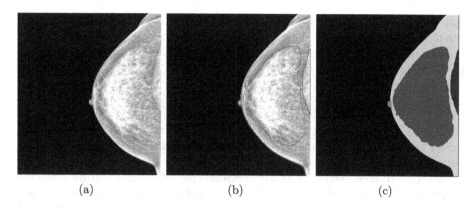

(a)   (b)   (c)

Fig. 2. Segmentation annotation on CC view mammography images. (a) Pre-processed image. (b) Polygon annotations. (c) Label map generated from the polygon annotations. The pectoral muscle is colored blue, the nipple is colored green, the fibro glandular tissue is colored magenta, the fat tissue is colored yellow, and the background (implicit class) is colored black. (Color figure online)

mentation, considering MLO and CC views. The authors define four structures of interest, including the pectoral muscle. We propose a data-centric approach for the improvement of the solution introduced in this work.

3   Mammography Segmentation

In this section, we explain some details about the reference work [9], where the authors present a private dataset for mammography image semantic segmentation on CC views and experimental results using different deep learning models.

3.1   Dataset

A collection of 5137 CC view mammography images was selected to construct the dataset, where four structures were considered for segmentation: nipple, pectoral muscle, fibro glandular tissue, and fatty tissue. All the collected images were annotated using a contour drawing tool by a team of annotators trained and supervised by clinical experts, generating a set of dense polygon annotations for the mentioned structures.

The polygons are rasterized and exported as label maps, where each pixel is assigned to a single class, i.e. the corresponding structure. The mammography image is normalized using the percentiles 2 and 98 as minimum and maximum values, then equalized using Contrast Limited Adaptive Histogram Equalization (CLAHE) [11] with kernel size being 1/8 of the height and width of the image, and finally re-scaled to the range [0, 255]. Figure 2 shows an example of the pre-processed image and its corresponding label map.

The annotated samples are split into the three standard subsets considered in a conventional supervised learning pipeline: training, validation, and test. The splitting process follows a random behavior with certain balancing regarding the fibro-glandular tissue density and avoiding data leakage. The distribution of samples resulted in 3737 samples for training ($\sim 70\%$), 943 samples for validation ($\sim 20\%$), and 457 samples for test ($\sim 10\%$).

3.2 Model Training

Although [9] presents multiple experiments considering different deep learning model architectures and training settings, we selected the best configuration as our reference. This configuration considers a Feature Pyramid Network (FPN) architecture [7] combined with an EfficienNetB3 model [10] as a feature extractor (backbone). The network input is a single-channel image with 384×384 size and intensity values in the range $[0, 1]$. The output of the network is a $384 \times 384 \times C$ per-pixel probability map, where C is the number of classes. This output considers an implicit background class defined for the non-annotated pixels. Because the segmentation task is modeled as a multi-class per-pixel classification problem, the final layer considers a softmax activation function. During training, the authors used a Jaccard loss function, batch size 4, learning rate 10^{-3}, and a maximum of 65 epochs with early stopping.

3.3 Drawbacks

The results of the selected model were reported using the metric Intersection over Union (IoU) on the test subset, reaching 0.85 for the mean IoU score and 0.79 for the pectoral muscle IoU score. Although the IoU of the pectoral muscle is promising and indicates that its segmentation is presenting a good performance, we noticed that the model tends to fail in challenging cases where the pectoral is not present, or the projected shape is very small and not clear. In Sect. 5, we present some numerical experiments confirming this behavior and demonstrating that pectoral muscle segmentation is still a difficult problem [5].

In addition to this model performance drawback, we also noticed some problems in the annotations of the pectoral muscle, such as multiple instances in the same image, unexpected segmentation shapes, and small segmentation shapes defined on images where the pectoral muscle was not included. These problems mainly occur due to annotator fatigue after an extensive repetitive annotation process or the lack of knowledge to identify the pectoral in a challenging case. Further, the annotation tool used in the study includes a feature that allows the user to estimate an initialization of the structures of interest using a pre-trained model. Thus, the annotator can forget to remove or correct noisy prediction shapes from this initialization.

4 Data-Centric Model Optimization

Knowing that data directly impacts the performance of machine learning models, correcting inconsistent annotation segmentations and noisy labels results in high-quality training sets. Efforts on the data are defined as Data-Centric AI, whose

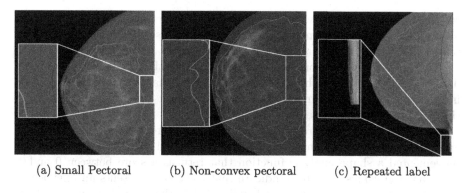

(a) Small Pectoral   (b) Non-convex pectoral   (c) Repeated label

Fig. 3. Errors in pectoral labels

purpose is to improve the information used for model training. To improve the pectoral muscle segmentation performance of the reference model [9], we propose a dataset refinement strategy divided into two stages.

In the first stage, we present methods for automatically identifying annotations with potential inconsistencies. Then, we review the selected annotations by checking and modifying them if needed. This review process is supervised by clinical experts, especially in challenging cases with difficult differentiation of the pectoral muscle. Finally, the reference model is re-trained on this new dataset following the same training hyperparameter configuration.

In the second stage, we perform numerical analysis on the modified training set using the corresponding trained model. Then, based on this analysis, we downsample the training dataset by removing the cases where the model fail and cannot learn effectively. As in the first stage, we re-train the reference model, obtaining the final optimized version.

4.1   Stage I: Annotation Correction

Annotation Selection. Based on our preliminary findings, we noticed three main problems in the pectoral muscle annotations. First, we found several small polygons segmenting a dubious region that, in most cases, was not part of the pectoral muscle. Second, we found several images presenting multiple polygons, which is unexpected because the pectoral muscle projection usually appears as a single compact shape. Third, we found multiple polygons with unexpected shapes, such as polygons presenting highly concave regions. The projection of the pectoral muscle tends to present a convex shape, so this annotation behavior is a probable annotation problem. Figure 3 illustrates these problems.

Since reviewing the entire dataset is a highly time-consuming task, we introduce some filter operations useful to select the annotations that can present any of the three described problems. To detect small annotations, we first rasterize the polygons in the corresponding image space, and then we count the number of pixels that are part of the rasterization. This amount allows us to quantify and approximate the polygon occupancy area in squared pixel units. Analyzing a subset of the full samples, we empirically defined a threshold area, i.e., 10^4, that allows us to differentiate small from large pectoral muscle annotations. Thus, we selected to review all the samples that were classified as small pectorals.

The polygon annotations are stored in a table that matches the polygon data with the mammography images. So, detecting images that present multiple instances of the pectoral muscle is simple. We select to review all the images that present more than one instance.

The pectoral muscle projection can present different sizes in the mammogram but generally presents a convex shape. Based on this assumption, we implemented a shape analysis function that returns a score between 0 and 1, such that the values close to 0 indicate that the shape presents an unexpected behavior, while the values close to 1 indicate that the shape is expected. As in the small pectoral muscle annotations selection, we define a threshold score, i.e., 0.22, to select the annotations to be reviewed.

For a given image, let us denote the rasterization of all its corresponding polygon instances as a binary image $\mathbf{P}$ and the shape analysis scoring function as s, which is a composed function defined as follows:

$$s(\mathbf{P}) = \min\{s_{\text{ecc}}(\mathbf{P}), s_{\text{sol}}(\mathbf{P}), s_{\text{top}}(\mathbf{P}), s_{\text{hau}}(\mathbf{P})\}, \tag{1}$$

where s_{ecc}, s_{sol}, s_{top}, and s_{hau} are inner scoring functions used to penalize different undesired behaviors of the analyzed shape.

s_{ecc} is a scoring function that uses the eccentricity of $\mathbf{P}$ to penalize rounded shapes. We expect elongated shapes to represent the pectoral muscle projection. The score is defined by the following Gaussian kernel:

$$s_{\text{ecc}}(\mathbf{P}) = 1 - \exp\left(-\frac{f_{\text{ecc}}(\mathbf{P})^2}{2\sigma_{\text{ecc}}^2}\right), \tag{2}$$

where $f_{\text{ecc}}(\mathbf{P})$ computes the eccentricity of a ellipse fitted to $\mathbf{P}$ and σ_{ecc} fixed to 0.3 is the standard deviation of the kernel.

Similarly, s_{sol} uses the solidity of $\mathbf{P}$ to penalize shapes whose area is different from the area of the corresponding Convex Hull (CH) shape, and is defined as follows:

$$s_{\text{sol}}(\mathbf{P}) = \exp\left(-\frac{|f_{\text{sol}}(\mathbf{P}) - 1|^2}{2\sigma_{\text{sol}}^2}\right), \tag{3}$$

where $f_{\text{sol}}(\mathbf{P})$ computes the solidity of $\mathbf{P}$ regarding its CH shape and σ_{sol} fixed to 0.1 is the standard deviation of the kernel.

Instead of penalizing the area dissimilarity between $\mathbf{P}$ and its CH shape, s_{hau} penalizes the distance between the corresponding contours, allowing us to detect highly concave regions. The score is also modeled as a Gaussian kernel:

$$s_{\text{hau}}(\mathbf{P}) = \exp\left(-\frac{d_{\text{hau}}(\mathcal{C}(\mathbf{P}), \mathcal{C}(\mathbf{P}_{\text{CH}}))^2}{2\sigma_{\text{hau}}^2}\right), \tag{4}$$

where d_{hau} computes the directed Hausdorff distance for a pair of contours, $\mathcal{C}$ computes the contours of a given binary image, $\mathbf{P}_{\text{CH}}$ is the CH image of $\mathbf{P}$, and σ_{hau} is the kernel standard deviation fixed to 0.012 times the width of the image.

Table 1. Total of modifications in reviewed images

Set	Total images	Pectoral Changes		
		>0%	>25%	>50%
Training	3737	476	125	11
Validation	943	105	31	4
Test	457	61	13	2
All	5137	642	169	17

Finally, s_{top} is a boolean scoring function that penalizes an unexpected topology of **P**. Thus, s_{top} returns one if **P** presents a single connected component without holes; otherwise, it returns zero. Using these filters, we selected 935 images from the entire dataset to review.

Annotation Review. Once the images that present a possible problematic annotation are selected, we review them by introducing corrections if needed. For this purpose, we adapted the annotation tool used in [9] to highlight the images that require review and to track the corrections for further assessment. We conducted the annotation review process with the support of clinical experts on those cases that present certain complexity in the differentiation of the pectoral muscle.

At the end of the review, we introduced annotation modifications in 642 images over the 935 reviewed images. To quantify the change degree of the modified annotations, we measure the percentage of pixels that are different in the rasterization of the new annotation regarding the rasterization of the old annotation. Table 1 shows the number of modifications in the training, validation, and test sets, distributed according to the change degree. This improved dataset is used to re-train the deep learning segmentation model.

4.2   Stage II: Downsampling

Using the model trained in the Stage I, we performed numerical analysis on the training set, evaluating if the pectoral muscle is detected correctly or not. This detection evaluation just considers if the pectoral muscle presence is defined correctly (more details about pectoral muscle detection can be found in Sect. 5). Then, we performed visual analysis on those cases that presented a wrong detection, where we noticed that in most of them the pectoral muscle was difficult to differentiate, even for the clinical experts. Further, the pectoral muscle delimitation can be mostly based on the clinical expert experience rather than explicit information included in the image.

Including these kinds of cases that present challenging situations can introduce noise in the training phase because some distortion can be added to the feature space. For this reason, we decided to exclude these cases from the training set and re-train the model over this downsampled set. We considered the following exclusion criteria for all the selected cases that presented a wrong pectoral muscle detection. First, we excluded all the images with possible missing pectoral muscle annotation, i.e., cases where the image presents a not annotated region similar to a pectoral muscle. Second, we excluded the images in which the pectoral muscle area is too bright, and it is difficult to differentiate the pectoral muscle. Some of these images present annotation, and others do not, generating inconsistent information that can disturb the model training. At the end of the filtering process, we excluded 469 samples from the full training set, obtaining better performance on pectoral muscle segmentation using the corresponding re-trained model.

5   Results

In this section, we validate the performance of the segmentation models trained on variations of the original mammography dataset, employing the strategies outlined in Sect. 4. Additionally, we detail the selected evaluation metrics, the evaluated training datasets and a comparative analysis of the results.

5.1   Evaluation Metrics

To evaluate the segmentation of the pectoral muscle and the other structures, we use the IoU score, a widely-used metric in segmentation tasks. The IoU measures the overlap between the model predicted structures and the ground-truth annotations. In addition to the IoU, we also compute classification metrics to assess the model's performance in detecting the pectoral muscle. We consider two classes: presence and absence of the pectoral muscle. The presence class is assigned if at least one pixel of the predicted mask belongs to the pectoral muscle structure. This approach allows us to calculate metrics such as accuracy, precision, recall, F1 score, and the confusion matrix specifically for the pectoral muscle detection task on the CC view. We define 3 classes for the pectoral muscle according to its size using K-Means, the algorithm labeled each image with the presence of pectoral muscle in its corresponding class (small, medium, large).

5.2   Evaluated Training Datasets

We created three different training sets using the two data enhancements stages described in Sect. 4: baseline, Stage I, and Stage II. The baseline training set consist of the original 3737 annotations without any improvements. The Stage I training set includes manually corrected annotations maintaining the same number of images as the original dataset. Lastly, the Stage II training set consist of 3268 images obtained through a downsampling approach, which eliminated complex images identified as outliers.

The mentioned training scenarios were evaluated over the same validation and test datasets, which comprised 943 and 457 samples, respectively. To minimize the influence of randomness on the model results, each set was trained six times, and the average of each metric result was computed.

Table 2. IoU Results on Validation set

Stage	Mean	Nipple	Fibro-tissue	Fatty-tissue	Pectoral			
					Global	Large	Medium	Small
Baseline	0.85	0.75	0.90	0.81	0.79	0.9	0.85	0.66
Stage I	0.86	**0.76**	0.90	0.80	0.82	0.89	0.83	0.6
Stage II	**0.87**	**0.76**	**0.92**	**0.85**	**0.84**	**0.9**	**0.87**	**0.7**

Table 3. IoU Results on Test set

Stage	Mean	Nipple	Fibro-tissue	Fatty-tissue	Pectoral			
					Global	Large	Medium	Small
Baseline	0.85	**0.77**	0.90	0.81	0.79	0.84	0.83	0.68
Stage I	0.86	0.76	**0.92**	0.84	0.80	0.83	0.82	0.70
Stage II	**0.87**	0.76	**0.92**	**0.85**	**0.84**	**0.86**	**0.84**	**0.73**

5.3 Intersection over Union Evaluation

Table 2 and Table 3 presents the average IoU results for each segmented structure on the validation and test sets, respectively. Additionally, we conducted a detailed analysis of the pectoral muscle based on its size. These results demonstrate the effectiveness of our approach to improve the model's performance across all mammography structures, particularly in the Stage II scenario. Moreover, We observed significant improvements in accurately delineating small pectoral muscles, effectively addressing cases that demand higher precision and finer details.

5.4 Classification Metrics for Pectoral Muscle Detection in CC View

The classification metrics are derived from the segmentation process, where the presence of a segmented pectoral muscle is considered a true positive case for classification. Tables 4 and 5 present the results of pectoral classification of the three selected models. Both tables show improved consistency in the classification metrics for the pectoral muscle detection task, attributed to data-enhancements in the training sets, particularly in the stage II dataset. The F1 metric exhibits an increase from 87% and 90% to 93% in both the validation and test sets. Notably, there is a significant reduction in the false positive rate of around 10%, making the model less prone to confusing the pectoral muscle with other artifacts such as skin folds or image glare.

Overall, our approach demonstrated improved segmentation performance across mammography structures, with enhancements in accurately delineating small pectoral muscles and reducing false positives predictions, as evidenced by the average IoU scores and the classification metrics (Fig. 4).

Table 4. Pectoral muscle classification results on Validation set

Stage	Acc	Prec	Rec	F1	TPR	TNR	FPR	FNR	n
Baseline	0.89	0.84	**0.96**	0.90	**0.96**	0,82	0.18	**0.04**	3737
Stage I	0.91	0.90	0.92	0.91	0.92	**0.93**	**0.07**	0.10	3737
Stage II	**0.93**	**0.91**	**0.96**	**0.93**	**0.96**	0.90	0.10	**0.04**	3268

Table 5. Pectoral muscle classification results on Test set

Stage	Acc	Prec	Rec	F1	TPR	TNR	FPR	FNR
Baseline	0.86	0.80	0.96	0.87	0.96	0.78	0.22	0.04
Stage I	0.90	0.83	**0.98**	0.90	**0.98**	0.83	0.17	**0.02**
Stage II	0.93	0.88	0.97	**0.93**	0.97	**0.88**	**0.12**	0.03

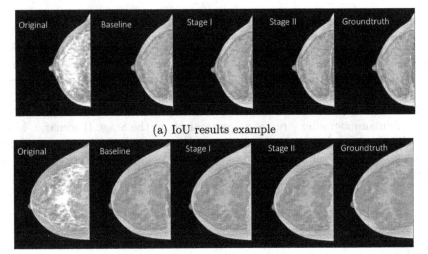

(a) IoU results example

(b) Pectoral Classification example

Fig. 4. Figure (a) demonstrates a progressive improvement in the segmentation of the pectoral muscle, with the Stage 2 model producing the closest segmentation to the original label. Figure (b) shows an example where the Baseline model incorrectly segmented a pectoral muscle with an atypical shape, and its corrected in the Stage I and Stage II models

6 Conclusion

This paper proposes a data-centric approach to enhance the accuracy of a deep-learning-based segmentation of anatomical structures in mammography images. Accurate segmentation of anatomical regions, such as the fibroglandular tissue, nipple, and pectoral muscle, plays a significant role in diagnosis and positioning assessment. However, due to mammography images' inherent complexity and variability, achieving high segmentation performance remains challenging, mainly for pectoral muscle detection in CC view. Our data-centric approach focuses on automatically detecting annotation inconsistencies and removing outliers in the training data, prioritizing quality and reliability. This process significantly improved IoU scores and classification metrics for the pectoral muscle detection task. Our results showcase a reduction of approximately 10% in false positive pectoral muscle detections on CC views compared to the baseline model.

References

1. Bick, U., Diekmann, F.: Digital mammography: what do we and what don't we know? Eur. Radiol. **17**, 1931–1942 (2007)
2. Bou, A.: Deep learning models for semantic segmentation of mammography screenings (2019)
3. Camilus, K.S., Govindan, V., Sathidevi, P.: Pectoral muscle identification in mammograms. J. Appl. Clin. Med. Phys. **12**(3), 215–230 (2011)
4. Dubrovina, A., Kisilev, P., Ginsburg, B., Hashoul, S., Kimmel, R.: Computational mammography using deep neural networks. Comput. Meth. Biomech. Biomed. Eng. Imaging Visual. **6**(3), 243–247 (2018)
5. Ge, M., Mainprize, J.G., Mawdsley, G.E., Yaffe, M.J.: Segmenting pectoralis muscle on digital mammograms by a Markov random field-maximum a posteriori model. J. Med. Imaging **1**(3), 034503–034503 (2014)
6. Guo, Y., Zhao, W., Li, S., Zhang, Y., Lu, Y.: Automatic segmentation of the pectoral muscle based on boundary identification and shape prediction. Phys. Med. Biol. **65**(4), 045016 (2020)
7. Lin, T.Y., Dollár, P., Girshick, R., He, K., Hariharan, B., Belongie, S.: Feature pyramid networks for object detection. In: Proceedings of the IEEE Conference on Computer Vision and Pattern Recognition, pp. 2117–2125 (2017)
8. Rubio, Y., Montiel, O.: Multicriteria evaluation of deep neural networks for semantic segmentation of mammographies. Axioms **10**(3), 180 (2021)
9. Sierra-Franco, C.A., Hurtado, J., Thomaz, V.D.A., da Cruz, L.C., Silva, S.V., Raposo, A.B.: Towards automated semantic segmentation in mammography images (2023)
10. Tan, M., Le, Q.: EfficientNet: rethinking model scaling for convolutional neural networks. In: International Conference on Machine Learning, pp. 6105–6114. PMLR (2019)
11. Zuiderveld, K.: Contrast Limited Adaptive Histogram Equalization, pp. 474–485. Academic Press Professional Inc, USA (1994)

Visualization

Visualizing Multimodal Time Series at Scale

Jiahang Huang[1], Andrew Ni[2], Jasmine Zhang[3], Hongyi Zhu[4], and Hui Zhang[1(✉)]

[1] University of Louisville, Louisville, KY, USA
`hui.zhang@louisville.edu`
[2] Amherst College, Amherst, MA, USA
[3] Carmel High School, Carmel, USA
[4] Eastlake High School, Sammamish, USA

Abstract. Today digital recording technology empowers us to understand real-world behaviors with high quality and high definition multimodal time series data. Making the presentation of these time series fit for analysis purpose, at the right scale and resolution, has become a leading data visualization challenge. In this paper, we present *TimeXplore*, a novel visual analysis tool to aid the exploration of time series at scale. *TimeXplore* allows one to query and navigate large volumes of time series and their aggregates in near real time, with a simple yet powerful interface. The visualization synchronized across modalities can provide still further capability for us to develop and verify our hypothesis in multimodal data analysis.

Keywords: Interactive visualization · Time series · Big Data

1 Introduction

Multimodal time series data, often comprising complex, high-dimensional information, are increasingly pervasive across various applications. These data introduce intricate relationships not only across time but also across diverse data modalities, which are crucial for characterizing system behaviors and identifying exceptional observations [20, 22]. Extracting insights from such data requires analysts to navigate, compare, and filter information from numerous sources, a challenging task given the data's volume and complexity [24]. However, effectively visualizing and exploring this complex multimodal longitudinal data presents several significant challenges:

Scale and Volume—The visual exploration of multimodal longitudinal data is essential for unraveling underlying structures, identifying patterns, and detecting anomalies within these intricate data streams. However, the colossal quantity of data involved poses a formidable challenge to existing time series visualization

G. Bebis et al. (Eds.): ISVC 2023, LNCS 14361, pp. 71–84, 2023.
https://doi.org/10.1007/978-3-031-47969-4_6

techniques. Moreover, the exploratory nature of data analysis often requires filtering, aggregation, and the fusion of multiple time series, adding to the complexity. The sheer scale and high data density inherent to multimodal longitudinal data make it inherently challenging to visualize and explore effectively.

Query Latency—To facilitate meaningful time-series exploration, the visualization tool must support low-latency interactions for querying and navigating subsets of the data. For example, consider a health monitoring system where a user wishes to examine a patient's heart rate over a specific time interval. The user may also want to view this data at varying temporal resolutions, such as per second, per minute, or per hour. The visualization tool must rapidly retrieve the data and update the visualization to deliver an immediate, responsive, and interactive user experience.

Human in the Loop—Analysis should be driven by end users who require data to be presented at scales and metrics aligned with their analytical expertise. Therefore, a fundamental design principle is to empower the tool to adapt to user-defined resolutions and metrics. This enables end users to review intermediate results and redirect the analysis as needed throughout the entire process.

Despite the growing importance of interactive exploration for large-scale time-series data, limited research has been conducted in this area, and there exists a pressing need for a scalable and responsive visualization tool. In this paper, we take the first step towards addressing these challenges by introducing a cloud-powered visual system that enables dynamic adjustments of aggregates along the longitudinal dimension, facilitating near real-time exploration of multimodal time series data.

2   Related Work

In the realm of multimodal time series data visualization, various approaches have been developed to extract insights from these complex datasets. TimeSearcher [9] introduces an exploratory tool [10], utilizing the concept of timebox, which empowers users to query time series data within specific time windows. However, it primarily focuses on analyzing time series data based on trends and patterns, making it suitable for scenarios where time series data within a timebox share similar scales. Challenges arise when visualizing diverse time series data without effective solutions like normalization or scaling, a limitation similarly observed in [5].

ThemeRiver [8] presents a unique approach, visualizing thematic variations within large document collections over time, providing insights into thematic changes alongside external events. Its 3D extension [13] enhances its capabilities by accommodating two attributes per variable in a data stream. However, ThemeRiver lacks support for dynamic queries or real-time interactions and faces scalability issues when dealing with numerous time series. DenseLines [15] takes a distinctive approach by revealing the density of time series data through discrete density representations, highlighting areas of interest in the data. Cuenca et al. [4] organize multiple time series into a hierarchical structure based on their proximity, which enables users to dynamically explore and compare temporal evolution patterns at different granularity levels through interaction. These methods emphasize the data sources dimension, reflecting major trends in many time series datasets over time.

Another perspective focuses on the time dimension, emphasizing the longitudinal features of time series data and their correlations. The Biometric Visual Dashboard [6] organizes multiple datasets spatially, enabling rapid analysis and trend interpretation. VisuExplore [16] targets time-oriented patient data, emphasizing chronic diseases and offering interactive features for data exploration. Falcon [21] utilizes quantitative values from time series similarity for interactive exploration within a visual environment. Robertson et al. [17] introduce trend visualization techniques using bubble charts, which showcase trends over time in three dimensions. It may have scalability limitations and require users to scan multiple frames for analysis. BinX [1] offers the ability to visualize time series data at different scales through linked visualizations, effective for dynamic exploration but also with scalability challenges for very large datasets. CareCruiser [7] provides visualization of time series data alongside event actions for comparison, with color-coded highlighting of interesting signals. It focuses on quantitative data and lacks explicit support for the exploration of multiple variables. ChronoLenses [23] employs a lens metaphor to support local exploration, allowing users to build pipelines of transformations on time series data. However, the method's scalability and computational complexity can pose challenges, particularly with extensive datasets.

While these approaches contribute valuable insights into multimodal data over time, they face challenges in handling the scale typical of large time series datasets. Moreover, navigating and exploring time series data, including their aggregates, in near real time demands intricate design and implementation. Our work strives to address these challenges, enhancing existing tools to enable intuitive exploration and user-driven analysis of time series data at scale.

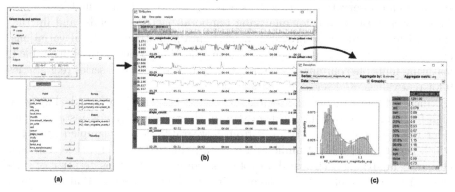

Fig. 1. Screen images of the three major display components in *TimeXplore*. (a) A multivariate time series builder. (b) A visualization window, synchronize and visualize multiple time series. (c) A descriptive summary panel showing data characteristics.

3   Overview Scenario

From the user' point, *TimeXplore* consists of three major display components: a time series builder to import data, a visualization window to present time series, and an analysis panel to define, generate and explore representations for various analysis and observations (see e.g., Fig. 1). The time series builder allows one to configure and import time series of interest from a cloud store, via a drag-and-drop interface (Fig. 1(a)). The selected time series data, of different types, are then presented in the visualization window of *TimeXplore*, channel by channel, allowing one to further search, view, and aggregate if needed (Fig. 1(b)). The descriptive summary window is the main tool that allows users to understand the statistical characteristics of the data sets being explored (Fig. 1(c)). The major contributions of this paper are summarized below:

- We propose a simple yet powerful interface that empowers users to query, navigate, and visualize multimodal time series data and their aggregates seamlessly. This user-friendly design enhances the accessibility and usability of our system, making it easier for analysts to interact with complex data.
- Our approach leverages cloud technology to enable the near real-time visualization and exploration of large-scale time series data. By performing aggregations in the cloud and retrieving only the necessary data, we ensure responsiveness and scalability without overwhelming the visualization with excessive data points.

4   Detail Methods and Implementation

4.1   Time Series Dataset

Time Series. A time series is a sequential collection of data points indexed based on their time order, often denoted as $X = x_1, x_2, ..., x_n$. Each x_i corresponds to an observation at time t_i, where $T = t_1, t_2, ..., t_n$ are the timestamps. Time series data is vital for analyzing temporal patterns, trends, and fluctuations within a system. It provides insights into global trends, local variations, and seasonality. Below is a sample multimodal time series dataset in Table 1, featuring multiple columns, each representing a recorded time series (e.g., Series 0 for real values, and series 1, 2, 3 for integers):

Such a table can become significantly large, especially when dealing with high-frequency sensory data collected from digital sources. For instance, consider the example of sensory data from a wearable device, sampled at 50 Hz, which results in roughly 4 million daily data points. Managing, processing, and efficiently analyzing such vast data volumes require careful consideration of storage and processing efficiency. Moreover, it's crucial to recognize that examining time series data at various granularities provides diverse insights. In healthcare, real-time monitoring of vital signs at a second-by-second granularity is vital for immediate anomaly detection and rapid responses. In contrast, daily step count analysis yields a holistic view of activity patterns over time.

Table 1. A sample multimodal time series dataset

Index	Series 0	Series 1	Series 2	Series 3
2020-04-05 22:10:00	1.024	1	1245	1
2020-04-05 22:11:00	1.206	2	1324	1
2020-04-05 22:12:00	1.234	3	1423	1
2020-04-05 22:13:00	1.345	3	1513	0
2020-04-05 22:14:00	1.456	4	1329	0

The central concerns revolve around handling near real-time queries and performing appropriate aggregations with large multimodal sensory data. To address these challenges, popular frameworks like Elasticsearch, Hadoop, and Spark have gained traction for large database analysis. Elasticsearch, in particular, excels in aggregating, searching, and processing indexed data and offers seamless integration [14,19].

Time Series in Elasticsearch. Given our demands for visualizing and analyzing large time series, especially the need for time series index processing and frequent aggregations, we've opted for Elasticsearch as our backend infrastructure. Elasticsearch's advanced features enable efficient handling of near real-time queries and vital aggregation operations for managing substantial multimodal sensory data. In Elasticsearch, Table 1 transforms into "documents" with each row representing a specific timestamp or index in the time series. The columns, signifying different time series, become "fields" and their values populate the respective document fields. This seamless transition streamlines the shift from tabular to Elasticsearch's document-oriented structure.

4.2 Exploiting Elasticsearch for Fast Search and Big Query

After completing the table/document transformation, the resulting documents can be efficiently organized and stored in an Elasticsearch index. This index acts as a repository for related documents, simplifying retrieval and search processes. Elasticsearch provides a user-friendly API for performing aggregation operations on indexed data. These operations are valuable for summarizing time series data. For instance, the date histogram aggregation method creates buckets based on a defined time interval and groups documents accordingly. Algorithm 1 demonstrates a sample query for calculating daily counts by summing values for "series 1" within specific days.

In *TimeXplore*, we utilize the Elasticsearch Python client to interact with Elasticsearch and send queries to the Elasticsearch cluster, consisting of multiple Elasticsearch instances collaborating to store and process data. The Python code efficiently handles query construction, including index, size, and aggregation parameters, and executes queries seamlessly. Algorithm 2 shows the Python code

Algorithm 1. Elasticsearch Aggregation Query. The request "GET /aggregation/search" is typically used to perform a search operation within Elasticsearch using the specified endpoint ("/aggregation/"). The query includes an aggregation named "daily_aggregation" that utilizes the "date_histogram" aggregation method. This method groups the data based on a specified time field, in this case, "local_time", with a fixed calendar interval of 1 day. Within the "daily_aggregation", another sub-aggregation named "total_num" is defined. This sub-aggregation calculates the sum of the "series 1" field, providing the total number for each day.

```
 1:  GET /aggregation/_search
 2:  {   "aggs": {
 3:        "daily_aggregation": {
 4:          "date_histogram": {
 5:            "field": "local time",
 6:            "fixed_interval": "1d"
 7:          },
 8:          "aggs": {
 9:            "total_num": {
10:              "sum": {
11:                "field": "series 1"
12:  }}}}}}
```

for the query in Algorithm 1. Furthermore, in *TimeXplore*, the data retrieval process intricately interfaces with the timebox, detailed in the subsequent section. This innovative design enables users to interact with the timebox, facilitating data retrieval based on selected date ranges, specific time intervals, and desired aggregation methods. The data retrieval operation smoothly runs in the background, ensuring a seamless user experience. Once data retrieval is successful, it seamlessly feeds into the visualization window, generating insightful visualizations.

4.3   Visualizing Time Series

Upon retrieving data, the subsequent step is data visualization through the dedicated visualization window. This window follows the principles of direct manipulation commonly utilized in interactive time-series visualizations [2,23], facilitating a responsive and intuitive user experience. The visualization window resembles a notebook, where each loaded data stream creates a separate tab for the overview of the multivariate time series. These tabs are labeled with a *Study_SubjectID* tag, which denotes the study name and subject ID, ensuring clear identification of the data. By organizing the visualizations in separate tabs, *TimeXplore* provides a structured and organized environment for data exploration and analysis. Users can easily switch between tabs to view different aspects of the data and gain comprehensive insights into the selected time series.

Visual exploration is pivotal for pattern recognition and insights [23]. *TimeXplore* optimizes this process with tailored interactive features. Its vertically stacked view permits users to display and compare multiple time series concur-

Algorithm 2. Perform Elasticsearch Query in Python. In this code, the 's.aggs.bucket()' method is used to define the date histogram bucket aggregation. It takes the name of the aggregation ('daily_aggregation'), the aggregation type ('date_histogram'), and additional settings such as the field to aggregate on ('local_time') and the interval ('1d' for 1 day). Inside the date histogram bucket aggregation, we use the s.aggs['daily_aggregation'].metric() method to define the sum metric aggregation. It takes the name of the aggregation ('total_num'), the aggregation type ('sum'), and the field to aggregate on ('series 1'). After executing the search and retrieving the results, we iterate over the date histogram buckets and extract the date and the sum for each bucket. When the aggregated results are retrieved, the next step is to visualize the data.

```
 1: Input: Elasticsearch client instance (es), index name (index)
 2: Output: Sum of series 1 (daily_counts)
 3:
 4: # Create a Search object targeting the desired index
 5: s = Search(using=es, index=index)
 6: # Define the date histogram bucket aggregation
 7: s.aggs.bucket('daily_aggregation', 'date_histogram', field='local_time', interval='1d')
 8: # Define the sum metric aggregation inside the date histogram bucket
 9: s.aggs['daily_aggregation'].metric('total_num', 'sum', field='series 1')
10: # Execute the search and retrieve the results
11: response = s.execute()
12: # Retrieve the aggregated sum
13: daily_counts = []
14: buckets = response.aggregations.daily_aggregation.buckets
15: for bucket in buckets do
16:     date = bucket.key_as_string
17:     value = bucket.total_num.value
18:     daily_counts.append((date, value))
19: end for
20: return daily_counts
```

rently, facilitating intuitive observation and relationship identification between variables. A timebox atop the visual panel empowers easy data navigation, enabling users to explore different segments effortlessly. Additionally, a Description panel furnishes users with descriptive statistics and supplementary insights, enriching data comprehension. Further elaboration on these features is provided in subsequent subsections.

Plotting Time Series. In *TimeXplore*, time series can be examined and explored within the visualization window, with each time series displayed in its independent horizontal channel. The time series, denoted as $X = x_1, x_2, ..., x_n$ collected from the time span $T = t_1, t_2, ..., t_n$, are rendered with Matplotlib [11] as line charts in default, allowing for the capture and reflection of the temporal structure, including the global trend and local fluctuations. Various draw styles are provided to facilitate different perspectives on the data (see Fig. 2a–2d). For example, the step line chart is suitable for expressing categorical data streams

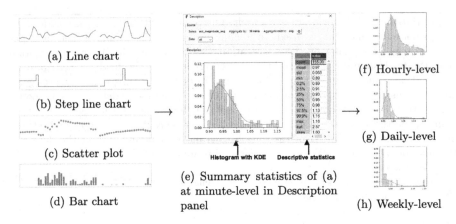

(a) Line chart

(b) Step line chart

(c) Scatter plot

(d) Bar chart

Histogram with KDE   Descriptive statistics

(e) Summary statistics of (a) at minute-level in Description panel

(f) Hourly-level

(g) Daily-level

(h) Weekly-level

Fig. 2. (a)–(d): various plotting styles for displaying time series. (e): histogram with summary description information in Description panel. Users can observe and understand the data distribution and get some critical values from these essential metrics listed in table. (f)–(h): different histograms updated across various time resolutions.

with step-wise changes, while the bar chart is effective for displaying discrete and aggregated data, providing a clear visualization of magnitude information.

Navigating Time Series with a Timebox Widget. To enhance the exploration of data segments, we have integrated a timebox feature. This interactive tool provides a data profile and allows users to navigate through various sections of the data with suggested time resolutions. Users can define a time span, denoted as $T_{s,e} = (t_s, t_e)$, where t_s represents the starting time and t_e the ending time. Interactions with the timebox involve stretching or dragging it to resize or relocate it. Upon releasing the timebox, the system calculates the updated time span and retrieves the corresponding data, which is then displayed to the user. This feature greatly aids users in pinpointing and exploring specific segments of interest within the data.

TimeXplore offers flexible time resolution adjustment, catering to various analytical needs. For automatic adjustment, the suggested time resolution r is determined using a calculation involving a fixed parameter k, which is defined by users as the maximum number of points shown on the screen, and a list of predefined resolution levels $\mathbf{s} = s_1, s_2, ..., s_l$. The calculation selects the appropriate time resolution r from the list $\mathbf{s}$ based on the condition that the time span divided by k falls within the range defined by s_{i-1} and s_i (as shown in Eq. 1). This ensures that the visualization adapts to the specific time span and provides users with an optimal level of granularity for exploring the data.

$$r \in s_i : s_{i-1} < \frac{(t_e - t_s)}{k} < s_i, i = 1, 2, ..., l \tag{1}$$

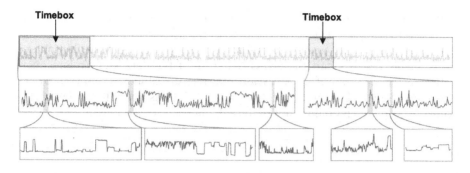

Fig. 3. Using timebox to adjust view windows.

For example, a list of pre-defined resolution levels could be $s=\{1\,\mathrm{s},\ 1\,\mathrm{min},$ $30\,\mathrm{min},\ 1\,\mathrm{h},\ 1\,\mathrm{day}\}$, which corresponds to integer time intervals as $\{1,\ 60,\ 1800,$ $3600,\ 14400\}$ s. Suppose the time span defined by the timebox (left) in Fig. 3 includes 0.6 million data points, and k is set to 10000. The calculated time interval is 0.6 million$/10000 = 60\,\mathrm{s}$. Since $1 < 60 <= 60$, the optimal granularity is determined to be $60\,\mathrm{s}$, i.e., $1\,\mathrm{min}$.

Alternatively, users have the option to manually define the time resolution by selecting a contextual menu item in each channel. Once the time resolution r is determined, the backend retrieves the data points corresponding to a total number of $\frac{(t_e - t_s)}{r} \times d$, where d represents the number of dimensions. This retrieved data is then used to update the visualization accordingly. Figure 3 shows the timebox. A profile of data streams at the initial time resolution is depicted in the background canvas, with values scaled into the range of $[0, 1]$, serving as a preview of the data to help users select the interested time span (see Fig. 3 (top)). It is worth noting that the original time resolution may make it difficult to identify behaviors due to dense data. However, by narrowing down the date range, users can obtain a zoom-in view of the time series with a higher sampling rate (see Fig. 3 middle and bottom rows).

Exploring Data Characteristics and Distributions. The Description panel in *TimeXplore* presents additional information about the data structure and distribution through a visual plot of a histogram with a kernel density estimation (KDE) curve. This plot is accompanied by summary statistics such as means, variances, and other relevant measures. By providing this information, users can gain insights into the underlying characteristics of the data.

An example is depicted in Fig. 2e, which illustrates a data stream with a positively skewed distribution and a tail in the positive direction. In this particular context, several critical values can be considered for identifying incipient outliers, including the upper quantile (75%), the top percentiles (such as 97.5% or 99.9%), and the Tukey Fences upper limit (TFU). These values serve as reference points for detecting unusual data points.

It's important to note that the visual plot and the summary statistics are updated automatically whenever the data is refreshed. This ensures that users have access to the most up-to-date information about the data distribution and gain valuable insights into the evolving nature of the data and explore unexpected patterns. Figure 2f–2h showcase multiple distributions observed in the same data segment but under different time resolutions, providing users with a comprehensive understanding of the data dynamics across different scales.

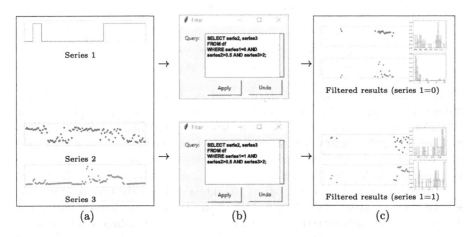

Fig. 4. Filtering panel supporting SQL-like queries. (a): Displaying all the data streams, where Time series 1 is shown as a binary type of data using a step line chart, while Time series 2 and 3 are displayed as continuous type data using scatter plots. The query is submitted in the filtering panel (b), and the resultant data segments are displayed in the channel (c). In this example, we use the query "SELECT * FROM df WHERE series 1 = 0" to preserve all the data segments where Time series 1 is 0. "df" is the name of the table that stores the data streams in the current visualization window. Furthermore, the statistical summary is automatically synchronized with the filtered data segments. From these results, we can observe that Time series 2 and 3 exhibit significant differences under different conditions.

Filtering Data with SQL-Like Queries. With *TimeXplore*, users are provided with the capability to leverage SQL-like queries, specifically the 'SELECT' statements, to filter multiple time series and focus on specific subsets of interest. These queries can be applied across multiple channels, empowering users to select observations that meet specific analysis criteria. The ability to filter out undesired data segments becomes particularly valuable in excluding noises, missingness, or invalid records from the recording.

Queris submitted by users are automatically parsed and validated. The time series in the current view window (often with aggregation applied) are then accessed and concatenated into one single table (i.e., data frame). This table is temporarily stored in a dedicated database, and the query is executed on this database using the SQLite3 library in Python. By applying these queries, data segments that do not meet the specified constraints are excluded from further computations and analysis. Additionally, these filtered data segments are not rendered in the visual channels, ensuring a clear and focused visualization. This allows users to effectively eliminate irrelevant data segments and concentrate on the most pertinent aspects of the data.

Figure 4 provides an example of the filtering functionality in *TimeXplore*. In this example, we use the filters to visualize and compare the different two groups of data with criteria specified in the query statements. By interactively applying filters, users can focus on portions of data that are of particular interest or relevance to analysis needs, and analyze the data more effectively. This enhances the overall user experience with *TimeXplore*.

5   Exploring UMAFall Dataset with *TimeXplore*

In this section, we present a use case of *TimeXplore* applied to the analysis of the UMAFall: Fall Detection Dataset. This dataset consists of mobility traces generated by a group of 19 experimental subjects who performed a set of predetermined Activities of Daily Life (ADL) and simulated falls [3,18]. Each activity and fall event in the dataset has a fixed duration of 15 s.

The UMAFall dataset captures data from various sensors, including accelerometer, gyroscope, and magnetometer sensors. The accelerometer measures linear acceleration, the gyroscope measures angular velocity, and the magnetometer measures the magnetic field. These sensors are commonly found in wearable devices and provide complementary information about the participants' motion and orientation. The sensor data is collected at a fixed frequency of 200 Hz, which means that 200 measurements are taken per second.

The UMAFall dataset also provides ground truth labels for each activity or event recorded in the dataset. It includes 11 types of Activities of Daily Life (ADL), such as walking, bending, hopping, jogging, etc. These ADLs represent common daily activities that individuals perform. Additionally, the dataset includes 3 types of emulated falls: forwards fall, backwards fall, and lateral fall. The ground truth labels can be used to develop sensor data based algorithms to detect specific activities and fall events. All these data are proprossed, normalized, and ingested into Elasticsearch indices to facilitate the exploration and visualization in *TimeXplore*.

Falls in these data sets exhibit distinct characteristics, due to their unique patterns and behavior and often involve rapid deceleration, which results in a sudden drop in acceleration magnitude or a negative spike in the signal. Falls can also generate high peak accelerations due to impact forces upon collision. Furthermore, falls are typically shorter in duration compared to other activities, featuring a rapid onset followed by a relatively brief period of intense acceleration or deceleration. Additionally, falls often involve changes in body orientation, such as tilting or rolling, which can be detected through the gyroscope sensor. Based

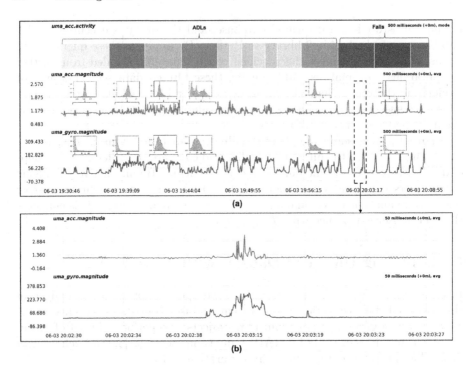

Fig. 5. Visualization of participant No. 14 in the UMAFall dataset with *TimeXplore*. (a) An overview of the data streams shows global trends and patterns with a 500 ms granularity. (b) By narrowing down to a specific time range with a finer granularity of 50 ms, we can observe detailed signal characteristics. Notable features such as rapid deceleration, high peak accelerations, and changes in body orientation become revealed at this scale.

on these characteristics, [12] presents a combined accelerometer and gyroscope detection schema. During a fall event, the acceleration signal decreases from 1 g to cross below the lower fall threshold of acceleration and, within 0.5 s, acceleration and angular velocity increase to cross above the upper fall threshold of acceleration and angular velocity almost simultaneously.

In this example, we specifically examine the data from participant *No.*14 to illustrate how *TimeXplore* can effectively explore and analyze sensor data to identify patterns and indicators of fall events. We first selected acceleration magnitude and angular velocity magnitude from the time series builder to load the full spectrum of data. Figure 5 gives a plot of the acceleration magnitude, angular velocity magnitude, and corresponding ground truth labels for this participant. The visualization provides an overview of the entire time span, displaying the data streams on a 500-ms scale (see Fig. 5 (a)). Additionally, from the real-time histogram presented in the description panel, we can see distinct patterns between various ADLs and fall events. To delve deeper into these patterns, we can zoom in to specific areas of interest in the visualization. For example, zooming into the right part of the graph with a finer granularity of 50 ms (see Fig. 5 (b)) will allow for a more detailed analysis of the characteristics exhibited during fall events, i.e., the rapid deceleration, the high peak of the accelerations, as well as changes in body orientation, as we mentioned earlier. These findings demonstrate the use of *TimeXplore* to effectively capture and visualize the distinct patterns present in the data at the right scale.

6   Conclusions and Future Work

In this paper, we introduced *TimeXplore*, a powerful visualization interface tailored for the exploration and analysis of multimodal time series data. Leveraging cutting-edge cloud-based indexing technology, *TimeXplore* provides an efficient and responsive platform for near real-time querying, searching, and exploration of extensive time series datasets. We showcase *TimeXplore's* capabilities using the UMAFall dataset, demonstrating its effectiveness in time series exploration and analysis. Given space constraints, we intend to validate its robustness and utility through comprehensive use case studies spanning diverse domains in future research. Future directions include the integration of visualization, continuous data, and machine learning algorithms to visualize data, report insights, and suggest new research directions in one data ecosystem.

Acknowledgements. This work was supported in part by National Science Foundation grant IIS-1651581 and DUE-1726532.

References

1. Berry, L., Munzner, T.: Binx: dynamic exploration of time series datasets across aggregation levels. In: IEEE Symposium on Information Visualization, pp. p2–p2. IEEE (2004)
2. Buono, P., Aris, A., Plaisant, C., Khella, A., Shneiderman, B.: Interactive pattern search in time series. Vis. Data Anal. **2005**(5669), 175–186 (2005)
3. Casilari, E., Santoyo-Ramón, J.A., Cano-García, J.M.: UMAFall: a multisensor dataset for the research on automatic fall detection. Procedia Comput. Sci. **110**, 32–39 (2017)
4. Cuenca, E., Sallaberry, A., Wang, F.Y., Poncelet, P.: Multistream: a multiresolution streamgraph approach to explore hierarchical time series. IEEE Trans. Visual Comput. Graph. **24**(12), 3160–3173 (2018)
5. Dachselt, R., Frisch, M., Weiland, M.: FacetZoom: a continuous multi-scale widget for navigating hierarchical metadata. In: Proceedings of the SIGCHI Conference on Human Factors in Computing Systems, pp. 1353–1356 (2008)
6. Faiola, A., Newlon, C.: Advancing critical care in the ICU: a human-centered biomedical data visualization systems. In: Robertson, M.M. (ed.) EHAWC 2011. LNCS, vol. 6779, pp. 119–128. Springer, Heidelberg (2011). https://doi.org/10.1007/978-3-642-21716-6_13
7. Gschwandtner, T., Aigner, W., Kaiser, K., Miksch, S., Seyfang, A.: CareCruiser: exploring and visualizing plans, events, and effects interactively. In: 2011 IEEE Pacific Visualization Symposium, pp. 43–50. IEEE (2011)

8. Havre, S., Hetzler, E., Whitney, P., Nowell, L.: Themeriver: visualizing thematic changes in large document collections. IEEE Trans. Visual Comput. Graph. **8**(1), 9–20 (2002). https://doi.org/10.1109/2945.981848

9. Hochheiser, H., Shneiderman, B.: Interactive exploration of time series data. In: Jantke, K.P., Shinohara, A. (eds.) DS 2001. LNCS (LNAI), vol. 2226, pp. 441–446. Springer, Heidelberg (2001). https://doi.org/10.1007/3-540-45650-3_38

10. Hochheiser, H., Shneiderman, B.: Dynamic query tools for time series data sets: timebox widgets for interactive exploration. Inf. Vis. **3**(1), 1–18 (2004)

11. Hunter, J.D.: Matplotlib: a 2d graphics environment. Comput. Sci. Eng. **9**(03), 90–95 (2007)

12. Huynh, Q.T., Nguyen, U.D., Irazabal, L.B., Ghassemian, N., Tran, B.Q.: Optimization of an accelerometer and gyroscope-based fall detection algorithm. J. Sens. 2015 (2015)

13. Imrich, P., Mueller, K., Imre, D., Zelenyuk, A., Zhu, W.: Interactive poster: 3d themeriver. In: IEEE Information Visualization Symposium, vol. 3. IEEE Computer Society Press Los Alamitos (2003)

14. Kumar, P., Kumar, P., Zaidi, N., Rathore, V.S.: Analysis and comparative exploration of elastic search, MongoDB and Hadoop big data processing. In: Pant, M., Ray, K., Sharma, T.K., Rawat, S., Bandyopadhyay, A. (eds.) Soft Computing: Theories and Applications. AISC, vol. 584, pp. 605–615. Springer, Singapore (2018). https://doi.org/10.1007/978-981-10-5699-4_57

15. Moritz, D., Fisher, D.: Visualizing a million time series with the density line chart. arXiv preprint arXiv:1808.06019 (2018)

16. Rind, A., et al.: Visual exploration of time-oriented patient data for chronic diseases: design study and evaluation. In: Holzinger, A., Simonic, K.-M. (eds.) USAB 2011. LNCS, vol. 7058, pp. 301–320. Springer, Heidelberg (2011). https://doi.org/10.1007/978-3-642-25364-5_22

17. Robertson, G., Fernandez, R., Fisher, D., Lee, B., Stasko, J.: Effectiveness of animation in trend visualization. IEEE Trans. Visual Comput. Graph. **14**(6), 1325–1332 (2008)

18. Santoyo-Ramón, J.A., Casilari, E., Cano-García, J.M.: Analysis of a smartphone-based architecture with multiple mobility sensors for fall detection with supervised learning. Sensors **18**(4), 1155 (2018)

19. Shah, N., Willick, D., Mago, V.: A framework for social media data analytics using Elasticsearch and Kibana. Wireless Netw., 1–9 (2018)

20. Song, D., Xia, N., Cheng, W., Chen, H., Tao, D.: Deep r-th root of rank supervised joint binary embedding for multivariate time series retrieval. In: Proceedings of the 24th ACM SIGKDD International Conference on Knowledge Discovery & Data Mining, pp. 2229–2238 (2018)

21. Steed, C.A., Halsey, W., Dehoff, R., Yoder, S.L., Paquit, V., Powers, S.: Falcon: visual analysis of large, irregularly sampled, and multivariate time series data in additive manufacturing. Comput. Graph. **63**, 50–64 (2017)

22. Weng, Y., Liu, L.: A collective anomaly detection approach for multidimensional streams in mobile service security. IEEE Access **7**, 49157–49168 (2019)

23. Zhao, J., Chevalier, F., Pietriga, E., Balakrishnan, R.: Exploratory analysis of time-series with chronolenses. IEEE Trans. Visual Comput. Graph. **17**(12), 2422–2431 (2011)

24. Zhao, Y., Wang, Y., Zhang, J., Fu, C.W., Xu, M., Moritz, D.: KD-Box: Line-segment-based KD-tree for interactive exploration of large-scale time-series data. IEEE Trans. Visual Comput. Graph. **28**(1), 890–900 (2021)

Hybrid Tree Visualizations for Analysis of Gerrymandering

Chenguang Xu[1]([✉])[ID], Sarah M. Brown[2][ID], Christan Grant[3][ID],
and Chris Weaver[4][ID]

[1] Oklahoma City University, Oklahoma City, OK 73106, USA
`shine.xu@okcu.edu`
[2] University of Rhode Island, Kingston, RI 02881, USA
`brownsarahm@uri.edu`
[3] University of Florida, Gainesville, FL 32611, USA
`christan@ufl.edu`
[4] University of Oklahoma, Norman, OK 73019, USA
`cweaver@ou.edu`

Abstract. In the United States, congressional redistricting follows a decennial Census. Gerrymandering can result from selection of district lines regardless of political parties. Understanding the relationships between the multiple dimensions in electoral data is a core goal of gerrymandering analysis. In this paper, we analyze patterns of gerrymandering in election data using a hybrid tree visualization technique that supports both overview and drill-down into a hierarchy of multidimensional relationships in that data. Visualization of hierarchical data is of major interest in information visualization. The technique utilizes a left-to-right node-link diagram to show overall hierarchical structure. Nodes in the diagram depict the levels in the dimensional hierarchy. Each node is rendered as an embedded view that shows its particular dimensional combination. Edges directly connect the contents of the embedded views to provide visual bridges that aid navigation and understanding of dimensional relationships. We demonstrate the utility of this hybrid technique is demonstrated through two use cases. This work aims to both ground and inspire the design of future visualizations for exploring gerrymandering.

Keywords: Tree visualization · Embedded views · Gerrymandering

1 Introduction

The redrawing of electoral district lines following each decennial United States Census can significantly impact the outcome of elections that follow. Gerrymandering is a phenomenon in which district lines are drawn to favor a political party or certain groups. The electoral data of interest in gerrymandering analysis is a multidimensional mix of quantitative, categorical, temporal, and hierarchical geographic data types. Each state has multiple district cycles, and each district

© The Author(s), under exclusive license to Springer Nature Switzerland AG 2023
G. Bebis et al. (Eds.): ISVC 2023, LNCS 14361, pp. 85–96, 2023.
https://doi.org/10.1007/978-3-031-47969-4_7

cycle involves multiple districts in that state. Gerrymandering analysis endeavors to understand such data by examining combinations of these dimensions including the various ways they may be meaningfully filtered, grouped, and aggregated. For this utility study, we mapped the data into a four-level hierarchy that progresses downward from election year to political party to redistricting cycle to district-level details. Exploring and analyzing these levels is critical to understanding the forms and effects of gerrymandering. Equipping gerrymandering analysts with the ability to drill down into different dimensional combinations of the data hierarchically is thus a key requirement for visual analysis tool design.

Visualization can help analysts to have insights, recall information, and communicate ideas about data. Hierarchical visualization techniques allow analysts to explore combinations of data dimensions by drilling down into those combinations visually. Multiple views facilitate identification of patterns within and comparison between such combinations. We integrate these two common approaches by embedding the views into the hierarchical visualization's nodes themselves. This approach offers a unified overview and drill-down for exploring different combinations of dimension. We enhance this integration by providing visual bridges that directly position and link the incoming edges from parent nodes and the outgoing edges to child nodes in relation to the corresponding visually encoded data in the embedded views. While we do not present usability results here, we hypothesize that this re-purposing of edges as a kind of visual linking [7] can improve interaction with and comprehension of the overall structure and the context of details in node-link styles of hierarchical visualizations. In this paper, we explore the potential of our integrated and enhanced technique for general application to multidimensional data through specific application to representative use cases in gerrymandering analysis. In particular, we demonstrate the technique's utility for analysis of key dimensional combinations in electoral data.

2   Related Work

This paper probes regions of the visualization design space that focus on mixed multidimensional data including hierarchical visualization and embedded views. The visualization design space has been extensively modeled and is increasingly populated. For sake of limited space we attempt only a cursory coverage here.

For general visualization design, Card and Mackinlay's framework offers guidance for the design of information visualizations with emphasis on the mapping between data and graphical context [5]. The visualization design space can be defined in terms of chart types and their combinations and enhancements [9,10]. Guidelines for multiple view designs consider cognitive aspects including the effort required for comparison, context switching, user's working memory, and learning [33]. Gleicher, et al. consider designs for visual comparison [16] and propose a framework to design multiple views for comparison tasks [15]. It is important to consider both spatial and data relationships in composite visualizations [20]. More specifically for gerrymandering analysis, visualization of geospatial network information typically involves composition of geographic and network representations [25].

Diverse composite visualizations exist for hierarchical data. Tuples and attributes in tabular data can be divided to form an aggregation hierarchy, such as in *breakdown visualization* that supports drill-down from overview to details across hierarchies through small multiple views [8]. A node-link diagram juxtaposed with heatmap views visualizes sequences of transactions in information hierarchies [4]. A phylogenetic tree visualization superimposed in a map links with geographic locations through a linear geographic axis [24]. TreeVersity2 [17] presents a space-filling visualization called StemView that nests bars at each level of an icicle plot. VEHICLE [23] embeds hierarchical stacked bar charts into a node-link diagram for exploring conflict event data, and uses a radial tree layout with glyphs as nodes to visualize hierarchical information. DimLift [14] utilizes dimensional bundling and applies multiple composition and interaction techniques to facilitate the exploration of hierarchical data.

Hierarchical visualization techniques are organized primarily in terms the variety of ways to represent nodes and edges to capture structural relationships and data details [27]. Common techniques, such as node-link diagrams and treemaps [29], can be combined to create hybrid techniques such as *elastic hierarchies* [35]. The navigability and comprehensibility of node-link techniques can be improved through techniques such as hierarchical edge bundling to reduce visual clutter amongst edges [19]. Aggregation of edges can also be calculated in data space as a precursor to their representation in visual space [13]. The hybrid hierarchical visualization technique described in this paper utilizes both data and visual aggregation. Each level of the hierarchy involves dimension-specific data filtering, grouping, aggregation, and other statistics to calculate the data to show in each node/embedded view. Each embedded view effectively provides a visual aggregation over a set of node siblings. Visual bridging helps to convey the correspondence between the individually visualized edges and the corresponding features in the embedded views as visual aggregates.

3   Gerrymandering

Gerrymandering refers to the political manipulation of district boundaries to advantage a political party or group. Redrawing district lines can have intended or unintended consequences, such as letting politicians choose their voters, packing partisans, splitting communities, diluting minority votes, etc. [22]. When states redraw their districts, they may consider and balance various criteria. Common criteria such as equal population, minority representation, contiguity, compactness, communities of interest, etc. can be reviewed to ensure fair redistricting.

There are a variety of alternative measures of continuity and compactness for comparing the redistricting maps drawn by independent redistricting commissions to those by state legislatures [12]. In addition to measures based on redistricting criteria, the seats-votes relationship was highlighted for assessing the swing ratio and partisan bias of redistricting plans [32]. Moreover, the measure of electoral competition has contributed to comparison of redistricting plans. A

Table 1. Precinct-Level data for the 2016 and 2020 elections in Oklahoma with congressional districts for the 2010 and 2020 redistricting cycles.

District 2010 Cycle	District 2020 Cycle	GEOID20	Party	Votes 2016	Votes 2020
2	2	40079000102	DEM	75	82
2	2	40079000102	REP	385	412
3	3	40113000113	DEM	17	14
3	3	40113000113	REP	37	40
3	3	40113000102	DEM	31	24
3	3	40113000102	REP	126	167

recent study suggests that independent redistrictors may not increase electoral competition to achieve political neutrality [18]. Most recently, DeFord, Eubank, and Rodden [11] introduced a measure, *partisan dislocation*, to indicate cracking and packing by considering a voter's geographic nearest neighbors.

Rather than developing measures, researchers use automated redistricting algorithms to generate redistricting plans and perform a comparative analysis to reveal gerrymandering. Two types of redistricting algorithms that are commonly used in the redistricting literature are partitioning algorithms and swapping algorithms [21]. Besides these two types of approaches, a divide and conquer redistricting algorithm [21] integrates partitioning and swapping elements. Automated districting simulations that are blind to partisanship and race are used to measure the unintentional gerrymandering that can emerge from patterns of the geographic distribution of voters with regard to their partisanship [6].

Gerrymandering statistics can be difficult to interpret. Non-experts in particular may shy away from quantitative metrics that are hard to fully comprehend [31]. Our work is motivated by calls to make gerrymandering statistics more visually interpretable and less confusing for both experts and non-experts [22].

4   Data Model in Gerrymandering

In order to visually explore and analyze the precinct data as shown in Table 1, we utilize the features of our visual hierarchy design for gerrymandering analysis. It shows the votes for each party per precinct in the state of Oklahoma in the 2016 and 2020 elections. The data includes congressional districts for two redistricting cycles. For example, the 2010 cycle for the congressional districts in Oklahoma starts on May 10, 2011 and ends on Dec 31, 2021, whereas the 2020 cycle is from Nov 22, 2021 to Jun 30, 2031 [1]. We compare statistics between the two major parties. For example, the party with a higher voting share percentage (VSP) in a district, which is calculated by Eq. (1) given $i \in precincts$ and $j \in parties$, wins the election for a House seat in the U.S. Congress.

$$VSP(votes|party = j) = \frac{\sum_i votes_i \wedge party = j}{\sum_i votes_i}. \tag{1}$$

Relationship $R(\{votes, party\})$ indicates the relationship between the votes variable and the party variable as shown in Eq. (2). Here we use voting share percentage as the aggregate measure over precincts, and apply a relationship to it, such as $VSP(votes|party = Dem) > VSP(votes|party = Rep)$.

$$R(\{votes, party\}) : VSP(votes|party = a) > VSP(votes|party = b). \quad (2)$$

The relationship can be greater than ($>$) or smaller than ($<$), and we exclude the possibility of a tie ($=$) in a two-party contest.

In the gerrymandering analysis, the *state relationship* $R_{state}(\{votes, party\})$ indicates which party has a higher voting share percentage in the state level data, while a *district relationship* $R_{district}(\{votes, party\})$ is the relationship in the district-level. Congressional districts are divisions of a state. Seeing the relationship in each district could provide an important perspective on disparate results from elections. Given these relationships, a distance function can be applied to measure if two relationships $R_{state}(\{votes, party\})$ and $R_{district}(\{votes, party\})$ are the same or reversed:

$$d(R_{state}(\{votes, party\}), R_{district}(\{votes, party\})) = \begin{cases} 0 & \text{if same relationship} \\ 1 & \text{if reverse relationship} \end{cases}$$
$$(3)$$

For example, if $R_{state}(\{votes, party\})$ is the *state relationship* that Republicans have a higher voting share percentage and $R_{district}(\{votes, party\})$ is a *district relationship* that has lower voting share percentage for Republicans in a specific district, the distance between the two relationships is 1. Using a distance function alone can not reveal if a districting plan of a state is gerrymandered. One approach to assess gerrymandering is to examine all districts' distances. We propose a summary function S, defined in Eq. 4, using relationship distance d and $|D|$ as the number of the unique distinct values in a redistricting plan. The value of S indicates what proportion of the districts do not follow the state relationship. If we compare the summary of district distances with the voting share percentage of the minority party at the state level, the disparity suggests that the districting plan is gerrymandered. For example, the minority party has a 40% voting share percentage at the state level, but the sum of the distances is 0.6 in a state with five districts. The sum indicates that the minority party should win the majority of the seats (3 out of 5). The different outcomes (i.e., 40% vs 60%) may be caused by gerrymandering.

$$S(votes, party, D) = \frac{1}{|D|} \sum_{\forall D_i \in D} d(R_{state}(\{votes, party\}), R_{D_i}(\{votes, party\}))$$
$$(4)$$

For the relationship, we apply the winning margin as shown in Eq. 5 in the study of gerrymandering. The winning margin helps to examine the competitiveness of federal elections. By comparing the competitiveness of different redistricting plans, analysts can find additional support for the hypothesis that a redistricting plan is a partisan gerrymander.

$$VoteMargin = |VSP(votes|party = a) - VSP(votes|party = b)| \quad (5)$$

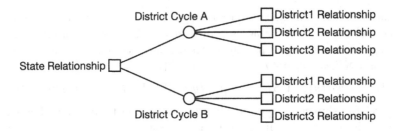

Fig. 1. The hierarchical view design for the gerrymandering analysis.

5   Visual Design

Our visualization technique is designed for visualizing relationships in hierarchical data structures that embed complex node information. To explore relationships, a node-link diagram is used to represent overall hierarchical structure.

The hierarchical structure is organized into a three-level tree structure as shown in Fig. 1. The state relationship $R_{state}(\{votes, party\})$ maps to the node in the first level of the tree structure, and the $R_{district}(\{votes, party\})$ district relationships map to the nodes in the third level. The different *district cycles* are the nodes in the middle level of the tree, and they are connected to the state relationship and their own district relationships. To differentiate the relationship levels from the district cycle level in the node-link diagram, we use different shapes to encode their nodes. For example, circle nodes represent district cycles, and square nodes represent relationships in Fig. 1. There are two reasons why we choose a node-link diagram over other hierarchical visualization techniques [28] like treemaps [29], Sunburst [30], or icicle plots [34] as a base representation. First, the non-leaf nodes for district cycle components are more expressive in a node-link diagram than in treemaps that strongly emphasize leaf nodes over all other nodes. Second, node-link diagrams have more flexible layouts than space-filling methods [26]. For example, it is easy to adjust the widths of each level in a node-link diagram to make room for embedded views.

We embed multiple views into nodes in our tree visualizations, and each view shows a different dimensional combination that relates to the nodes. The visualizations provide the visual bridging that analysts can follow from the view of the parents to the view of the children. The visual bridging also indicates the relationship between the nodes in the host tree visualization and the visual objects in the embedded view.

Color is a powerful visual channel to guide attention. We try to pick better color schemes for different components in our hybrid visualization system. First, we consider the well-known colors in our application domain which is political science. The color blue is associated with the Democratic Party, and the red represents the Republican Party. The political colors are reserved for the embedded charts that convey political parties' information. Next, we select a yellow-green sequential color palette to encode the *distance* and summary distance values in both tree nodes and relevant elements in the embedded view. The color green

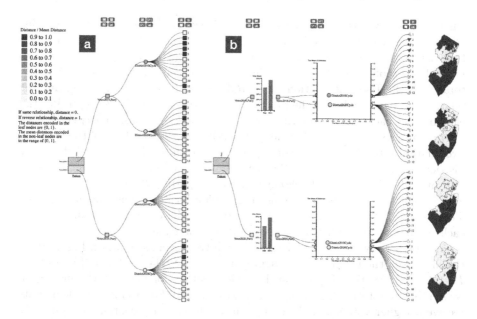

Fig. 2. An example demonstrating the design of the visualization for evaluating the efficiency gap. (Note that here we root the tree one level higher to add a summary of the state relationships.) The user first visualizes an initial tree visualization (a). Later, the user selects three views to embed into the tree visualization (b): a bar chart comparing vote shares between two parties, a scatterplot showing summary statistics, and a map view providing more context for districts in New Jersey.

and yellow are visually distinguishable from the predefined political colors. The yellow-green sequential color palette is more easily distinguishable between low distance values and high distance values than the green only sequential color palette, especially when the distances in the leaf nodes are either 0 or 1. Last but not least, we exclude the predefined colors above and use other colors based on different hue channels for the charts in the hybrid visualization.

6 Analysis Examples

In this section, we describe how the visualization technique can be applied to the electoral precinct data of the U.S. presidency from *Dave's Redistricting App* [2] and congressional redistricting data from *All About Redistricting* [1]. For our analysis, we applied the 2016 and 2020 presidential vote share data at the precinct level. The election data was disaggregated to 2020 census blocks following the method described by Amos, et al. [3].

6.1 Evaluating the Efficiency Gap

This use case was inspired by an evaluation of the efficiency gap [31]. The relationship between seats and votes in the two-party system [32] could indicate the efficiency gap. We inspect changes of the efficiency gap before and after the redistricting plan. We start by looking at the structure of the hierarchical data. Our tree visualization has four levels, as shown in Fig. 2(a). Looking at the heatmap view of the root node, we observe that there are two relationships in the electoral data set. The first relationship is $R(\{Votes2016, Party\})$, representing the relationship extracted from the precinct-level votes data of the 2016 presidential election and each party's information. The second relationship $R(\{Votes2020, Party\})$ applies to the 2020 presidential election. In the first level of the tree, the two relationships are split into corresponding branches. The next level shows the district cycles, in which we see that the congressional districts for each election year are split into 2010 and 2020 cycles. By comparing these two cycles, we can gain insight into how the new redistricting plan has an impact on the election. The last level shows the leaf nodes that present the congressional districts for each combination of a district cycle and an election year.

We further investigate the details in each tree level as shown in Fig. 2(b). In the first level, the mean distance aggregated for the relationship $R(\{Votes2020, Party\})$ is 0.208. By clicking the show view button for views in the first level, we see that the state relationship $R_{state}(\{Votes2020, Party\})$ is that Democrats receive a higher vote share than Republicans in the presidential election (58% vs 42%). At the district cycle level, a scatterplot shows the statistics calculated for the two districting cycles. We find that the mean distance in the 2020 district cycle is 0.167. Comparing this number to the vote share for Republicans, it is obvious that the discrepancy between overall statewide support (42%) for Republicans and the proportion of their winning districts (16.7%) indicates partisan bias and hence supports a contention of gerrymandering. In addition, we see that the 2020 district cycle has a lower mean distance than the 2010 district cycle. This shows that partisan bias is higher under the new districting plan.

To understand the disparity and examine the congressional district lines, we inspect individual districts in the leaf nodes. We observe that the distances for District 2, 3, and 4 in the 2010 cycle are equal to 1, which represents a reverse district relationship compared to the state relationship. In contrast, the districts whose distance is 1 in the 2020 district cycle are District 2 and District 4. Since District 3 is no longer showing the reverse relationship, we investigate several aspects of gerrymandering. One crucial aspect relating to gerrymandering is whether the congressional district lines of the flipping district are drawn differently in the new districting plan. The embedded map view clearly shows that the congressional district lines for District 3 are quite different between the two district cycles. Another aspect is to check the degree of partisanship. Switching to a strip plot at the leaf level, we find that the vote shares for the two parties in District 3 are extremely close in the 2010 cycle (50.1% Republican versus 49.9% for Democrat), while the vote shares in the 2020 cycle are much further apart (58.1% Democrat versus 41.9% Republican). Meanwhile, the vote shares for the Democratic party in the adjoining districts including Districts 2 and 4, decreased in the 2020 cycle, whereas the vote shares for the Republican party increased. This indicates possible gerrymandering tactics like cracking and packing. In this

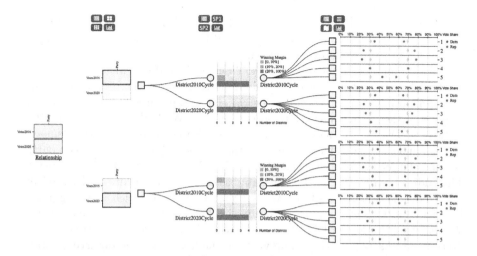

Fig. 3. Example of the hybrid tree visualization to assess electoral competition. (Note that here we root the tree one level higher to add a summary of the state relationships.) The user selects a heatmap view in the first level, a grouped bar chart in the district cycle level to explore changes in competitiveness between the two districting cycles, and a strip plot in the leaf level to show vote details for districts in Oklahoma.

case, the Republican voters may have been cracked from District 3 into District 2 and 4; consequently, those votes are diluted. Concomitantly, the Democratic voters from District 2 and 4 might have been packed into District 3.

Through this exploration, we gained an understanding of how district lines are drawn and what consequences may affect future elections. This use case validates the effectiveness of the visualization to identify potential gerrymandering, and suggests further exploration. Our visualization supports smooth navigation and drill-down into each level of the hierarchy. The features of the visualization thus facilitate visual identification and comparison for gerrymandering analysis.

6.2   Assessing Electoral Competition

In the second use case, we demonstrate how we utilize our visualization to investigate the redistricting plan that appears to impact electoral competition.

Figure 3 shows the hybrid tree visualization for the presidential election in Oklahoma. In this case, the root level and the first level are not connected by lines; instead, the two duplicated and highlighted views in the first level implicitly represent the parent-child relationships with the root node. The mean distances of the internal nodes and the distances of the leaf nodes are all 0, as indicated by their respective fill colors. This clearly indicates that the district relationships are compatible with the state relationship in which the Republican party always wins every district in Oklahoma.

Since we are particularly interested in the recent election, we track the lower branch which presents the relationship $R(\{Votes2020, Party\})$. When we look at the bar chart at the district cycle level, we find that one highly competitive district (i.e., a winning margin of 0% to 10%) in the 2010 cycle becomes less competitive in the 2020 cycle; the number of moderately competitive districts (i.e., a winning margin of 10% to 20%) changes from 0 to 1 after redistricting.

To delve more deeply into these changes, we more closely examine individual districts' voting shares. We embed a strip plot in the leaf level, and examine the changes of the voting shares for the two parties. We find that the competition is close in District 5 in the 2010 cycle (i.e., Republican 52.9% vs. Democrat 47.1%), and that the difference between the shares of the votes for the two parties becomes larger in the 2020 cycle (i.e., 59.5% Republican vs. 40.5% Democrat). This indicates that District 5 is probably safer and more secure for Republicans after redistricting. In addition, we find that District 3, which is a neighbor of District 5, shrinks its winning margin in the 2020 district cycle. We assume that the district lines for both districts were redrawn in the new redistricting plan. To confirm this, we switch to map views in the leaf nodes and observe a notable difference in the border between the two districts.

Our findings in Oklahoma are a strong sign that gerrymandering can occur even without overturning elections. We conclude that Districts 3 and 5 were likely gerrymandered to protect Republican candidates, especially in District 5. The embedded views show different facets of data for their respective purposes, and visual bridging enables an understanding of the relationships between them. More generally, flexible view choice allows for alternative designs that scale to accommodate two or more parties and few or many districts, such as by adding visual links from district nodes to map regions in Fig. 2(b). Overall, our hybrid tree visualization technique aids in exploring hierarchical structure in gerrymandering and gaining a deeper understanding of the underlying information.

7   Conclusion

In this paper we introduce a hybrid tree visualization technique to explore hierarchical structure in the gerrymandering domain. Through two use cases, we demonstrate that the technique allows users to gain insights about gerrymandering of congressional districts. The use cases indicate that the hybrid visualizations enhance not only the exploration of the hierarchical structure but also the understanding of the complex relationships within and between the underlying data dimensions. We plan to continue this work on utility assessment presented here with usability studies of the two visualizations and others in realistic application by expert and casual analysts in the gerrymandering domain.

References

1. All About Redistricting. https://redistricting.lls.edu
2. Dave's Redistricting App. https://davesredistricting.org
3. Amos, B., McDonald, M.P., Watkins, R.: When boundaries collide: constructing a national database of demographic and voting statistics. Public Opin. Q. **81**(S1), 385–400 (2017)

4. Burch, M., Beck, F., Diehl, S.: Timeline trees: visualizing sequences of transactions in information hierarchies. In: Proceedings of the Working Conference on Advanced Visual Interfaces, pp. 75–82 (2008)
5. Card, S.K., Mackinlay, J.: The structure of the information visualization design space. In: Proceedings of the Visualization Conference, Information Visualization Symposium and Parallel Rendering Symposium, VIZ 1997, pp. 92–99. IEEE (1997)
6. Chen, J., Rodden, J.: Unintentional gerrymandering: political geography and electoral bias in legislatures. Q. J. Polit. Sci. **8**(3), 239–269 (2013)
7. Collins, C., Carpendale, S.: Vislink: revealing relationships amongst visualizations. IEEE Trans. Visual Comput. Graph. **13**(6), 1192–1199 (2007)
8. Conklin, N., Prabhakar, S., North, C.: Multiple foci drill-down through tuple and attribute aggregation polyarchies in tabular data. In: Proceedings of the IEEE Symposium on Information Visualization, pp. 131–134. IEEE (2002)
9. Crisan, A., Fisher, S.E., Gardy, J.L., Munzner, T.: GEViTRec: data reconnaissance through recommendation using a domain-specific visualization prevalence design space. IEEE Trans. Visual Comput. Graph. **28**(12), 4855–4872 (2021)
10. Crisan, A., Gardy, J.L., Munzner, T.: A systematic method for surveying data visualizations and a resulting genomic epidemiology visualization typology: GEViT. Bioinformatics **35**(10), 1668–1676 (2019)
11. DeFord, D.R., Eubank, N., Rodden, J.: Partisan dislocation: a precinct-level measure of representation and gerrymandering. Polit. Anal. **30**(3), 403–425 (2021)
12. Edwards, B., Crespin, M., Williamson, R.D., Palmer, M.: Institutional control of redistricting and the geography of representation. J. Polit. **79**(2), 722–726 (2017)
13. Elmqvist, N., Fekete, J.D.: Hierarchical aggregation for information visualization: overview, techniques, and design guidelines. IEEE Trans. Visual Comput. Graph. **16**(3), 439–454 (2009)
14. Garrison, L., Müller, J., Schreiber, S., Oeltze-Jafra, S., Hauser, H., Bruckner, S.: DimLift: interactive hierarchical data exploration through dimensional bundling. IEEE Trans. Visual Comput. Graph. **27**(6), 2908–2922 (2021)
15. Gleicher, M.: Considerations for visualizing comparison. IEEE Trans. Visual Comput. Graph. **24**(1), 413–423 (2017)
16. Gleicher, M., Albers, D., Walker, R., Jusufi, I., Hansen, C.D., Roberts, J.C.: Visual comparison for information visualization. Inf. Vis. **10**(4), 289–309 (2011)
17. Guerra-Gomez, J., Pack, M.L., Plaisant, C., Shneiderman, B.: Visualizing change over time using dynamic hierarchies: TreeVersity2 and the StemView. IEEE Trans. Visual Comput. Graph. **19**(12), 2566–2575 (2013)
18. Henderson, J.A., Hamel, B.T., Goldzimer, A.M.: Gerrymandering incumbency: does nonpartisan redistricting increase electoral competition? J. Polit. **80**(3), 1011–1016 (2018)
19. Holten, D.: Hierarchical edge bundles: visualization of adjacency relations in hierarchical data. IEEE Trans. Visual Comput. Graph. **12**(5), 741–748 (2006)
20. Javed, W., Elmqvist, N.: Exploring the design space of composite visualization. In: Proceedings of the 2012 IEEE Pacific Visualization Symposium, pp. 1–8. IEEE, Songdo, South Korea (2012)
21. Levin, H.A., Friedler, S.A.: Automated congressional redistricting. J. Exp. Algorithmics (JEA) **24**, 1–24 (2019)
22. Levitt, J.: A citizen's guide to redistricting. Available at SSRN 1647221 (2008)
23. Mayer, B., Lawonn, K., Donnay, K., Preim, B., Meuschke, M.: VEHICLE: validation and exploration of the hierarchical integration of conflict event data. Comput. Graph. Forum **40**(3), 1–12 (2021)

24. Parks, D.H., Beiko, R.G.: Quantitative visualizations of hierarchically organized data in a geographic context. In: 2009 17th International Conference on Geoinformatics, pp. 1–6. IEEE (2009)
25. Schöttler, S., Yang, Y., Pfister, H., Bach, B.: Visualizing and interacting with geospatial networks: a survey and design space. Comput. Graph. Forum **40**(6), 5–33 (2021)
26. Schulz, H.J., Schumann, H.: Visualizing graphs-a generalized view. In: Tenth International Conference on Information Visualisation, pp. 166–173. IEEE (2006)
27. Schulz, H.J.: Treevis. net: a tree visualization reference. IEEE Comput. Graph. Appl. **31**(6), 11–15 (2011)
28. Schulz, H.J., Hadlak, S., Schumann, H.: The design space of implicit hierarchy visualization: a survey. IEEE Trans. Visual Comput. Graph. **17**(4), 393–411 (2010)
29. Shneiderman, B.: Tree visualization with tree-maps: 2-d space-filling approach. ACM Trans. Graph. (TOG) **11**(1), 92–99 (1992)
30. Stasko, J., Zhang, E.: Focus+ context display and navigation techniques for enhancing radial, space-filling hierarchy visualizations. In: Proceedings of the IEEE Symposium on Information Visualization 2000, pp. 57–65. IEEE (2000)
31. Stephanopoulos, N.O., McGhee, E.M.: Partisan gerrymandering and the efficiency gap. Univ. Chicago Law Rev. **82**, 831 (2015)
32. Tufte, E.R.: The relationship between seats and votes in two-party systems. Am. Polit. Sci. Rev. **67**(2), 540–554 (1973)
33. Wang Baldonado, M.Q., Woodruff, A., Kuchinsky, A.: Guidelines for using multiple views in information visualization. In: Proceedings of the Working Conference on Advanced Visual Interfaces, Palermo, Italy, pp. 110–119 (2000)
34. Woodburn, L., Yang, Y., Marriott, K.: Interactive visualisation of hierarchical quantitative data: an evaluation. In: 2019 IEEE Visualization Conference (VIS), pp. 96–100. IEEE (2019)
35. Zhao, S., McGuffin, M.J., Chignell, M.H.: Elastic hierarchies: combining treemaps and node-link diagrams. In: Proceedings of the IEEE Symposium on Information Visualization, 2005, INFOVIS 2005, pp. 57–64. IEEE (2005)

ArcheryVis: A Tool for Analyzing and Visualizing Archery Performance Data

Zhiyuan Cheng[1], Zeyuan Li[1], Zhepeng Luo[2], Mayleen Liu[1],
Jonathan D'Alonzo[1], and Chaoli Wang[1(✉)]

[1] University of Notre Dame, Notre Dame, IN 46556, USA
{zcheng6,zli28,mliu5,jdalonzo,chaoli.wang}@nd.edu
[2] Columbia University, New York, NY 10027, USA
zl3092@columbia.edu

Abstract. We present ArcheryVis, a tool for analyzing and visualizing archery performance data collected from two elementary school trainees over a year. The goals are to digitally archive their training target papers, automatically detect and calibrate shots, and analyze their performance via a visual interface. We achieve automatic shot detection using a deep neural network, compute scores and relevant statistical measures, and design coordinated multiple views for interactive user exploration. Experimental results demonstrate the effectiveness of ArcheryVis.

Keywords: Archery performance · Shot detection · Visual interface

1 Introduction

Archery is a popular sport enjoyed by people around the world. While it may not be as widely practiced as some mainstream sports, its popularity has grown steadily and holds a significant place in recreational and competitive circles. Our motivation for developing a tool that analyzes and visualizes archery performance data stemmed from a real scenario with two elementary school trainees (a boy and a girl). They began weekly training at a local archery shop/club in the third grade. Alternatively, they practiced with target papers for one week and 3D animal targets for another week. Later on, they also received additional training sessions over weekends. Over one year, they each completed 36 target papers, totaling 72 papers (63 25"×25" and 9 17"×17"). These papers are bulky, making them inconvenient to store long-term. More importantly, it is challenging for the trainees and their trainer to analyze their performance over time, let alone make a comparison between them. As they continued their training, more target papers collected only exacerbated the challenges of post hoc analysis.

In response, we present ArcheryVis, which outlines the following steps to streamline the process of archiving, analyzing, and visualizing archery performance data. First, instead of carrying target papers around, it is much more convenient to take photos of target papers on-site via smartphones for digital recording. With raw data stored as digital images, we want to develop a solution that automatically "scans" each image to detect landmarks (i.e., the rings, center, and shots) from which we can reliably calibrate shots, compute scores, and gather relevant statistical measures. After that, we have the necessary information to "reconstruct" the target papers on the screen for performance analysis. We design and develop a set of coordinated multiple views to support effective visual exploration and comparison of the archery performance data.

2   Related Work

2.1   Archery Performance Analysis

High-performance shooting in archery is the ability to accurately shoot an arrow at a given target. Researchers have long explored various physiological, psychological, biomechanical, and kinematic factors contributing to archery performance. Vendrame et al. [15] conducted a systematic review (41 studies spanning 35 years) of archery performance assessment. The investigation of the influence of a wide range of physiological and kinematic parameters revealed that high-performance archers maximize postural stability and develop personal strategies for muscular activation and time management.

An early work by Landers et al. [9] examined the physical, psychological, and perceptual/visual variables using an overall hierarchical regression model and identified seven important variables related to elite archers' shooting performance. Soylu et al. [13] recorded surface electromyography (EMG) signals of musculus flexor digitorum superficialis and extensor digitorum of archers during archery shooting to compare the repeatability of EMG linear envelopes of archery groups. Tinazci [14] investigated the relationships between physiological and mechanical dynamics during arrow releasing in archery with the quality of the arrow shot, involving four elite male archers. Kim et al. [7] explored the mental, skill, and fitness factors affecting archery performance. They met with experts and conducted a confirmatory factor analysis and the analytic hierarchy process to identify the most important factors. Quan and Lee [12] studied the relationship between aiming patterns and scores. The aiming pattern was defined using averaged acceleration data measured from accelerometers attached to the body. They employed regression analysis with dynamic time warping to explore the effective way to raise scores in archery shooting. Kim et al. [6] performed a meta-analysis study to investigate the effectiveness of psychological skills training interventions for archers in Korea. Their study revealed that psychological skills training for archers is effective, and the player level and training period are crucial factors.

Recent works also explore machine learning and visualization techniques for archery performance analysis. Muazu Musa et al. [11] leveraged artificial neural network and k-nearest neighbor classification techniques to forecast and scout high-performance archers. The machine learning techniques were trained on physical fitness and motor skill parameters, including hand grip, vertical jump, standing broad jump, static balance, upper muscle strength, and core muscle strength. Kawaguchi et al. [5] proposed a system to easily search differences in multiple trial motions of the same archer. The time-series data was collected using the angular velocity sensor attached to the bow. Dynamic time warping was utilized to determine the similarity of multiple shots.

Unlike all the above works, we only collected archery data directly related to target performance, excluding any contributing factors. This is similar to Kolayis et al. [8], which manually assesses target performance in archery, focusing on the error distributions using the one-sided ANOVA and chi-squared tests. The differences are that our ArcheryVis detects shots automatically and emphasizes the analytical capability via visualization, which is not presented in prior research to our best knowledge.

2.2 Archery Scoring Apps

Even though visualization research on archery performance data is scarce, several archery scoring apps are available for training or competition, including MyTargets Archery, Archery Companion, iArchery, and Archer's ToolBox. MyTargets Archery allows users to store and manage their equipment, noting their bows, arrows, sight marks, and relevant information. A sight mark is a reference point that archers use to adjust the position of their sight's pins or reticles when aiming at different distances. Scoresheets are available for different rounds with color coding to the target. Archery Companion lets users track scores and sight marks and choose the round they shoot. The scoresheet only shows the arrow values and end score. With iArchery, users can log their round scores, sight marks for specific equipment, and personal bests. They can select the round, bow type, and date shot in the scoresheet. Finally, Archer's ToolBox provides similar functions as other apps. Besides, this app allows users to send scores to their club for verification.

All these apps are designed for manual scoring and training journals. Our ArcheryVis aims to detect shots and calculate scores from raw image input automatically. It goes beyond scoresheets by reconstructing the results for "in-place" visual analysis. Moreover, it supports visual comparison across trainees, a missing feature in these apps.

3   Data Collection, Processing, and Analysis

3.1   Data Collection

We asked the two elementary school trainees to take a photo of their respective completed target paper using a smartphone after each training session. The photo was taken so that the camera's view was approximately perpendicular to the target paper, and the target's center (i.e., the bullseye) was nearly at the center of the camera's image plane. Each photo was taken under a similar indoor lighting condition and was cropped using the smartphone's built-in camera app. The collected digital images were uploaded to a shared Google folder each time for subsequent processing and analysis.

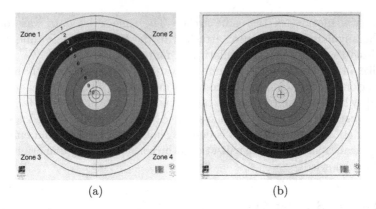

(a)   (b)

Fig. 1. (a) and (b) show detected rings and the center of an archery target paper. (Color figure online)

3.2 Ring and Center Detection

We apply the popular Hough transform [3] to detect the rings due to its robustness in detecting geometric shapes even in the presence of noise. It transforms points in the image space to a parameter space, where the geometric shape's parameters (such as slope and intercept for lines or center and radius for circles) can be more easily detected. Figure 1 (a) shows an example of the ring detection result. We can see that the detected rings (shown in red) overlap well with the ring boundary pixels on the image. Some ring pixels have slight offsets (e.g., the bottom part of Fig. 1 (a)) as they are distorted. This is due to two reasons. First, the target paper was not placed perfectly flat when the photo was taken. Second, the camera's view was not exactly perpendicular to the target paper.

We do not rely on the Hough transform for center detection because it is a small cross on the target paper (refer to Fig. 1 (a)). Instead, we get the bounding box of the outmost ring and treat its center as the center of the target. Figure 1 (b) shows the bounding box and its center (shown in blue).

3.3 Shot Detection and Calibration

We treat shot detection as an image segmentation problem and apply a 2D fully convolutional network (FCN) [10] to obtain segmented results where pixel blobs corresponding to foreground shots are separated from the background image. FCNs allow for efficient and accurate pixel-level predictions, making them valuable in applications requiring precise spatial understanding or object segmentation. Previously, Hu et al. [4] leveraged an FCN to automatically detect and segment ants from surveillance videos to explore their movement patterns.

Unlike convolutional neural networks (CNNs) that are mainly used for classification, FCNs are designed to produce dense pixel-wise predictions by preserving spatial information. An FCN typically follows an encoder-decoder architecture.

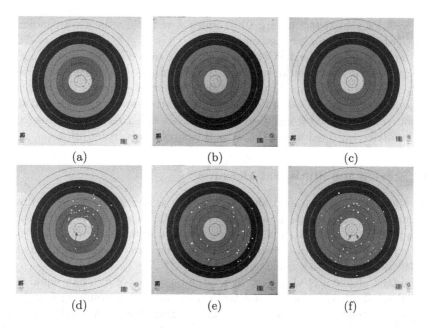

Fig. 2. (a) to (c) show target papers for training, testing, and inference. (d) to (f) show respective shot detection results. False negatives are highlighted in arrows.

The encoder extracts hierarchical features from the input image through convolutional layers. The decoder performs upsampling operations to recover the spatial dimensions lost during encoding. The final output of an FCN is a dense prediction map with the same spatial dimensions as the input image. Each pixel in the output map represents a class label or a probability distribution over classes, depending on the specific segmentation task.

In our scenario, the original FCN [10] suffers from a loss of resolution due to downsampling. We tackle this problem by adding additional upsampling blocks to the end of each layer so that different feature levels are extracted and integrated towards the final prediction. We use the first 20 images of the 72-image collection for network training. Each image is resized to 2048 × 2048 pixels and manually labeled to obtain ground-truth results. We perform data augmentation via random cropping and rotation, producing 6000 small block samples (256×256 pixels each). These blocks are divided into training, validation, and testing sets with 70%, 20%, and 10% split. The network is trained using the Adam optimizer with a learning rate of 10^{-3}. We set 20 epochs for training with early stopping.

Figure 2 shows our shot detection results. Sampled training, testing, and inference results are displayed in (d) to (f), where the pixel-wise predictions (i.e., shot blobs) are displayed in white. We can see that training, testing, and inference achieve satisfactory results with minor errors. Only a few false negatives (highlighted in arrows) are presented in any of these cases. We also provide the original images in (a) to (c) to confirm no false positives. The overall precision and recall for shot detection are 100% and above 96%, respectively, indicating our FCN-based solution's effectiveness.

After shot detection via FCN, the centroid of each detected foreground blob is treated as the shot positions. Occasionally, ambiguity is taken care of where two or more blobs overlap. Note that each photo has a slightly different zoom level and crop range. To calibrate the results, we transform each detected shot's position via scaling and translation so that the shots across different images can be accurately registered under the same set of reference center+rings.

3.4   Scoring and Statistical Measures

With shot positions identified and calibrated, it is straightforward to score the accumulated points, which is the primary indicator of archery performance. As shown in Fig. 1 (a), the two innermost rings, known as the "inner ring" and "outer ring," equal 10 points each. The remaining nine rings are valued sequentially from 9 to 1, working from the inside out.

Similar to Kolayis et al. [8], we divide the target paper into four equal quadrants along the horizontal (x) and vertical (y) axes. The resulting four zones, respectively, represent the upper-left, upper-right, lower-left, and lower-right parts of the target (refer to Fig. 1 (a)). The zone-level analysis allows us to spot if a trainee has a preferred zone to shoot or if the shots are balanced across zones.

A report [1] by Archery Analytics GmbH outlines various analysis techniques used with autonomous spotters developed by them. The covered statistics include the number of arrows, number of points, point per arrow, group center, the shift of the arrow group, horizontal and vertical dispersions, scatter ellipse, and arrow grouping indicator. Similarly, we provide the following statistical measures for downstream visualization:

- count: the number of shots considered
- score: the total points of all shots considered
- mean: the average point of all shots considered
- standard deviation: the average amount of variability of all shots considered
- horizontal dispersion: the spread (in pixels) of the shots along the x-axis
- vertical dispersion: the spread (in pixels) of the shots along the y-axis

4   Visual Interface and Interaction

Figure 3 shows a screenshot of the ArcheryVis visual interface, developed using D3 [2]. The interface has controls on the left, the primary target view in the middle with the statistics view on its top, and two other views on the right (top-right: attribute view, bottom-right: temporal view). The controls allow users to choose the trainee(s) and filter shots in the views based on the point range, zone, and date (range). The target view reconstructs the shots. The shots of the

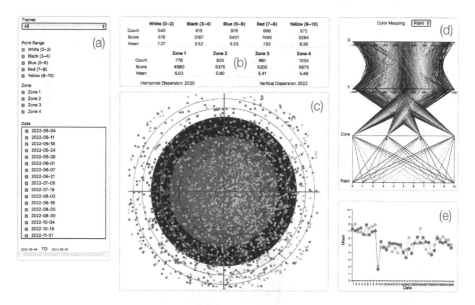

Fig. 3. The ArcheryVis interface consists of (a) multiple controls and (b) statistics, (c) target, (d) attribute, and (e) temporal views. The visualization here considers all shots by both trainees.

boy and girl are drawn in cyan and pink colors for differentiation. Mousing over a shot displays a tooltip showing its relevant information (name, x-coordinate, y-coordinate, date, and point). The statistics view displays the count, score, and mean across point ranges and zones of displayed or highlighted shots in tabular form. It also reports horizontal and vertical dispersions. The attribute view displays shot data using parallel coordinates along four dimensions: x-coordinate, y-coordinate, zone, and point. Users can color each shot (displayed as a polyline) in this view based on a chosen dimension. They can also brush one or more dimensions for filtering. Finally, the temporal view plots the performance over dates using the mean value. Mousing over a date displays a tooltip with relevant information (date, count, score, mean, and standard deviation) and highlights the corresponding shots in the target view.

5   Results and Discussion

5.1   Brushing and Filtering

The four views of ArcheryVis are dynamically linked to support a comprehensive visualization and comparison of the archery performance data. Two brushing examples are given in Fig. 4. In (a) and (b), we brush the temporal view, highlighting the shots in the target view. In (c) and (d), we brush the attribute view, and the selected shots that meet query conditions are shown in the target view. (d) also shows mousing over a shot displaying the tooltip.

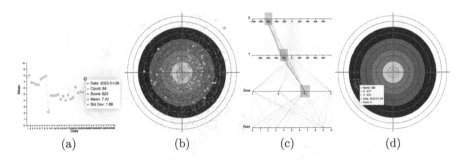

(a)   (b)   (c)   (d)

Fig. 4. Two examples of brushing and linking. Brushing (a) the temporal view links to (b) the target view. Brushing (c) the attribute view links to (d) the target view.

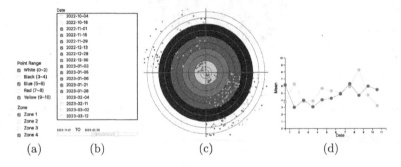

(a)   (b)   (c)   (d)

Fig. 5. An example of filtering using controls of (a) point range and zone, and (b) date (range). (c) and (d) show the resulting target and temporal views.

In Fig. 5, we show an example of filtering. Only the white, blue, and yellow ranges are selected for the point range. For the zone, only Zones 1 and 4 are selected. We select a range from November 2022 to January 2023 for the date. The resulting target and temporal views are shown in (c) and (d). In Fig. 6, we show another filtering example. Only the black, blue, and red ranges are selected for the point range. For the zone, only Zones 2 and 3 are selected. The resulting statistics, target, and attribute views are shown in (b) to (d).

5.2   Trainee Comparison

Figure 7 shows the target views of the two trainees accumulated over the 36 dates. Interestingly, the boy shot more arrows in Zones 2 and 4 (the right half of the target), whereas the girl shot more arrows in Zones 1 and 3 (the left half). The statistics view reports 678 shots for the boy in Zones 1 and 3 (mean: 5.93) and 1191 in Zones 2 and 4 (mean: 5.64). For the girl, there are 1061 shots in Zones 1 and 3 (mean: 5.52) and 769 in Zones 2 and 4 (mean: 5.63). This disparity could be explained by how the trainees hold the bow. The boy is right-handed, and he holds the bow with his left hand and shoots more at the right half of the target. The girl is left-handed and does the opposite. Both trainees'

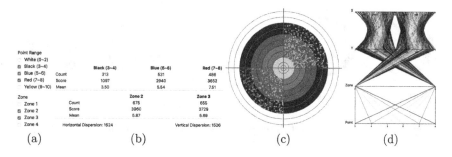

Fig. 6. Another filtering example using controls of (a) point range and zone. (b) to (d) show the resulting statistics, target, and attribute views.

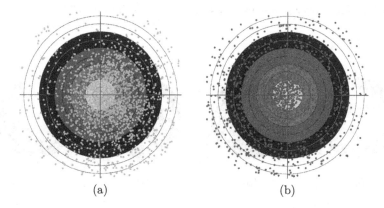

Fig. 7. The target views of (a) the boy and (b) the girl accumulated over the 36 dates.

performance is slightly better on the half of the target, where fewer arrows are shot. If we examine the top/bottom halves of the target, both achieve a better performance on the top half of the target (the means of top and bottom are 5.98 and 5.56 for the boy and 5.82 and 5.33 for the girl). Zone-wise, both have the best performance in Zone 1 (294 shots for the boy with a mean of 6.21 and 484 shots for the girl with a mean of 5.89).

In Fig. 8, the temporal view shows the best and worst dates for the two trainees, highlighted in (a) to (d). The best dates were 5/11/2022 (mean: 8.02) for the boy and 6/1/2022 (mean: 7.90) for the girl. The worst dates for both were 7/19/2022 (mean: 2.11 for the boy; mean: 1.67 for the girl). This was the first time they shot 20 yards instead of 10 yards from the target. The left ellipse in the temporal view shows that this change has the most significant negative impact on their performance (the mean drops stunningly from 7.92 to 2.11 for the boy and 7.05 to 1.67 for the girl). The right ellipse highlights another dip in their performance. This was due to their first use of sight, which aids in aligning the bow and arrow with the target. It took them a few sessions to adjust. As beginners, conditions, such as shooting distance and sight usage,

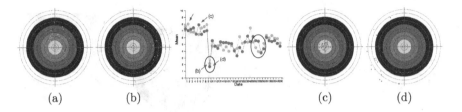

Fig. 8. The best and worst dates of the boy (a and b) and the girl (c and d).

highly influence their performance. Finally, with the Pearson linear coefficient of 0.6478, the performances of these two trainees have a moderately positive correlation. Their overall means across all dates are similar: 5.74 for the boy and 5.57 for the girl.

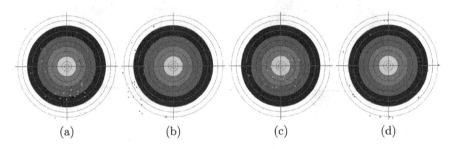

Fig. 9. Standard deviation and horizontal and vertical dispersions are unreliable performance indicators.

5.3   Statistical Measure as Performance Indicator

As expected, the mean is a reliable performance indicator, but this is not true for other statistical measures. A large standard deviation may indicate bad performance. For example, Fig. 9 (a) shows the boy's target paper of 2/11/2023. With a standard deviation of 2.43, this is the boy's second-worst date (mean: 3.69). However, a small standard deviation does not necessarily indicate good performance. For example, Fig. 9 (b) shows the girl's target paper of 7/19/2022. With a standard deviation of 1.71, this is the girl's worst date (mean: 1.67).

Horizontal and vertical dispersions are the spreads of the shots along the x and y-axes, respectively. A large/small difference between them does not imply bad/good performance, as these measures are highly susceptible to outliers. Figure 9 (c) shows the boy's target paper on 7/5/2022. The horizontal and vertical dispersions are, respectively, 1342 and 665 (the difference is 677). This, however, is the boy's second-best date (mean: 7.92). In contrast, Fig. 9 (b) shows the girl's target paper on 12/13/2022. The horizontal and vertical dispersions are 1866 and 1855 (the difference is 11). This, however, is the girl's second-worst date (mean: 3.30).

5.4 Empirical Evaluation

We initially evaluated ArcheryVis with the two trainees and their trainer. We walked through the visual interface and interaction as a group, introducing the available functions. Then, they started their free exploration, each taking 10~15 min. Overall, all of them were satisfied with the functions provided by ArcheryVis. In particular, the tool helped them identify some previously unknown findings (e.g., the preference of left/right side of the target in association with right/left-handedness), which we reported in Sect. 5.2. They viewed this version of ArcheryVis as a promising start and would like to use it in practice.

5.5 Limitations

ArcheryVis focuses on automatic shot detection and scoring as well as the analytical aspects of the tool via visual interface and interaction. It does not study varied contributing factors related to archery performance, as discussed in Sect. 2. Also, it does not record the shooting order on the same target paper, which precludes the in-depth chronological performance study within the same training session. Furthermore, we do not investigate how the paper size and shooting distance affect the performance. Even though the data collected are rather limited, ArcheryVis does offer new capabilities not available in current archery scoring apps.

6 Conclusions and Future Work

We have presented ArcheryVis, a tool for analyzing and visualizing archery performance data. Our primary contributions lie in automating shot detection and enabling visual exploration and comparative study of archery trainees. Experimental results demonstrate that ArcheryVis achieves its intended goals.

In the future, we would like to pursue the following directions. First, we will further evaluate ArcheryVis with the trainer and trainees to identify potential improvements. Second, we will collect more information, including the shooting order and distance, to better help the trainer and trainees analyze archery performance data. Third, we will refine our process to support the continued use of the developed tool. The local archery shop/club could provide such a service so that trainees can conveniently review their data, and the trainer can access the digital data of all the trainees for scalable visual analysis. We need to address the scalability issue with many trainees and a sizable training data record. Finally, besides the current web-based visual interface, we will develop an app version of the tool for wide dissemination.

Acknowledgements. This research was supported in part by the U.S. National Science Foundation through grants DUE-1833129, IIS-1955395, IIS-2101696, and OAC-2104158. The authors thank Tram Trinh and Janet Meng, who contributed to the project's development, and the anonymous reviewers for their comments.

References

1. Archery Analytics: Data Analysis in Archery - A guideline by Archery Analytics GmbH (2020)
2. Bostock, M., Heer, J.: D3.js - Data-Driven Documents. https://d3js.org
3. Duda, R.O., Hart, P.E.: Use of the Hough transformation to detect lines and curves in pictures. Commun. ACM **15**(1), 11–15 (1972)
4. Hu, T., et al.: AntVis: a web-based visual analytics tool for exploring ant movement data. Visual Inf. **40**(1), 58–70 (2020)
5. Kawaguchi, M., Mitake, H., Hasegawa, S.: Archery shots visualization by clustering and comparing from angular velocities of bows. In: Proceedings of International Conference on Augmented Humans, pp. 21:1–21:10 (2020)
6. Kim, E.J., Kang, H.W., Park, S.M.: The effects of psychological skills training for archery players in Korea: Research synthesis using meta-analysis. Int. J. Environ. Res. Pub. Health **18**(5), 2272:1–2272:11 (2021)
7. Kim, H.B., Kim, S.H., So, W.Y.: The relative importance of performance factors in Korean archery. J. Strength Conditioning Res. **29**(5), 1121–1129 (2015)
8. Kolayis, İE., Çilli, M., Ertan, H., Knicker, J.A.: Assessment of target performance in archery. Procedia. Soc. Behav. Sci. **152**, 451–456 (2014)
9. Landers, D.M., Boutcher, S.H., Wang, M.Q.: A psychobiological study of archery performance. Res. Q. Exerc. Sport **57**, 236–244 (1986)
10. Long, J., Shelhamer, E., Darrell, T.: Fully convolutional networks for semantic segmentation. In: Proceedings of IEEE Conference on Computer Vision and Pattern Recognition, pp. 3431–3440 (2015)
11. Muazu Musa, R., Abdul Majeed, A.P.P., Taha, Z., Abdullah, M.R., Husin Musawi Maliki, A.B., Azura Kosni, N.: The application of artificial neural network and k-nearest neighbour classification models in the scouting of high-performance archers from a selected fitness and motor skill performance parameters. Sci. Sports **34**(4), e241–e249 (2019)
12. Quan, C., Lee, S.: Relationship between aiming patterns and scores in archery shooting. Korean J. Sport Biomech. **26**(4), 353–360 (2016)
13. Soylu, A.R., Ertan, H., Korkusuz, F.: Archery performance level and repeatability of event-related EMG. Hum. Mov. Sci. **25**(6), 767–774 (2006)
14. Tinazci, C.: Shooting dynamics in archery: a multidimensional analysis from drawing to releasing in male archers. Procedia Eng. **13**, 290–296 (2011)
15. Vendrame, E., et al.: Performance assessment in archery: a systematic review. Sports Biomech. (2022). Accepted

Spiro: Order-Preserving Visualization in High Performance Computing Monitoring

Tommy Dang[(⊠)], Ngan V. T. Nguyen, Jie Li, Alan Sill, and Yong Chen

Texas Tech University, Lubbock, TX 79409, USA
{tommy.dang,ngan.v.t.nguyen,jie.li,alan.sill,yong.chen}@ttu.edu

Abstract. As High-Performance Computing (HPC) is moving closer to entering the exascale era, monitoring HPC systems is becoming increasingly important and continuously more complex. The innovations in interactive visualization provide tremendous assistance in presenting complex HPC data to be more comprehensible and promote the roles of humans in the analysis process. With the larger number of system components in the monitoring tasks, representing them in order requires a scalable mechanism for handling multiple visual elements and simultaneously preserving the context of ordering. In this paper, we propose a novel method for utilizing the spiral layout for order-preserving visualization in HPC monitoring, called *Spiro*. To demonstrate the effectiveness and usefulness of *Spiro*, we present the case studies of the application to a real-world temporal, multivariate HPC dataset.

Keywords: High-Performance Computing Center · RESTful API · Time-Series Data Analysis · Spiral Layout · Multivariate Clustering · Multidimensional Data Visualization

1 Introduction

The advancement in High-Performance Computing (HPC) towards scale and computing ability brings an important question: How and to what extent can we effectively monitor such a complex system? Having an intuitive, interactive interface for monitoring system components is of utmost importance due to the massive number of elements that the system administrators need to examine. Here, visualization is essential to help make sense of observations and aid the exploratory task alongside the analysis.

For a typical monitoring interface, one often comes across the task of observing variables behave in a specific manner, commonly with a built-in function for ordering visual elements. Order arrangement of visual elements is often coupled with a linear scale [15]. However, with a system comprised of hundreds to thousands of nodes (which will be represented as one element each), plotting all data

G. Bebis et al. (Eds.): ISVC 2023, LNCS 14361, pp. 109–120, 2023.
https://doi.org/10.1007/978-3-031-47969-4_9

points along the linear axis for an overview is challenging because of limited screen display and potentially cluttering views, leading to difficulty in conveying the system information as a whole.

We propose a new technique for monitoring HPC system components, called *Spiro*, which utilizes the spiral layout for order-preserving visualization and supports interactive behaviors with animation. This opens up discussions regarding using a spiral structure to represent non-periodical data, which the structure originated with. We validate the usability of *Spiro* via an extensive case study with real-world HPC datasets comprised of temporal measurements of computer health metrics. The contribution of this work can be laid out as follows:

- An interactive visualization for monitoring HPC system components data, called *Spiro*, which: 1) provides a compact view ensuring order-preserving logic within system components, 2) shows trajectories and distribution over time, and 3) allows quick observation on changes via animations.
- Demonstration of the approach by applying it to real data acquired from an HPC center. The case study is incorporated with clustering: K-means and leader algorithms

The rest of this paper is organized as follows: Sect. 2 summarizes existing work that is close to our paper. Section 4 describes the design rationale and tasks analysis. Section 5 shows the findings through case studies with the real HPC data. Section 6 concludes our paper with outlook for future work direction.

2   Related Work

2.1   Spiral Layout in Visualization

Since first introduced and formalized as the *Spiral Visualization* by Carlis and Konstan [3], the spiral layout has been employed as the visualization technique for representing periodic serial data. Weber et al. [21] explored how to convey information demonstrated by such visualization and discovered that a spiral chart is able to show periodic patterns better than a line chart. In an extensive study on visualization morphing to teach users an unfamiliar visualization method by analogy to a familiar visualization, Ruchikachorn and Mueller [15] paired linear chart as the source and spiral chart as the target. The authors found that although the spiral chart was the easiest concept to understand compared to parallel coordinates, hyperbox, and treemap, scale stretching, and time direction are two aspects that needed the help of animation for comprehension. The use of spiral layout has been applied for various domains, from food consumption, neuron cell firing frequencies, and sound [3], music [5], a fast word-cloud algorithm for text visualization [10]. The spiral structure demonstrates the ability to aid users in effectively identifying recurrent patterns and cycles in time-series data [12].

2.2   Monitoring with Spiral Layout

Prior work has focused on leveraging the strength of visualization on the monitoring task. From a security perspective, Bertini et al. [2] presented SpiralView, a visualization tool supporting system administrators in the routine activity of network monitoring. The tool is built around the main spiral visualization, where groups of interest can be highlighted, and users can see how they associate with the network resources. VanDaniker [20] demonstrated the effectiveness of spiral layout in representing transportation community monitoring in numerous observations: congestion and road work activity, collisions, flight delays, uptime, and downtime of traffic detector. The spiral layout also proves its usefulness in healthcare applications, such as in the monitoring of elderly people [11] or upper limb activity [4]. Recently, Lohfink et al. [13] proposed a novel combination of spiral charts with anomaly detection for real-world sensor data monitoring. The interactive visualization has color as the encoding for measurement data and anomaly score as line thickness.

3   Monitoring Tasks

Monitoring an HPC system is a challenging task because of the increasing scale and complexity of HPC data. The substantial size of system components hinders the process of plotting them on screen, with the corresponding massive number of visual elements that need to be displayed, leading to visual complexity [14]. With the level of exploration in visualization formulated by Shneiderman [17]: overview first, zoom and filter, then details on demand, overview is the primary and fundamental task. In particular, with monitored computer health metrics, having the components presented in a specific order would help tremendously in understanding the overall patterns and spotting the differences or inconsistencies between different metrics.

Spiro implements low-level visual analysis tasks that largely capture the monitoring and exploratory tasks [1,8,18] as follows:

- **T1**: Present an overview of the monitoring data over time. The approach should support a straightforward interface representing the multivariate temporal data, emphasizing the order of computing health metrics. The main focus of this task was to communicate with the audience through visual representation, with different structures based on various modes.
- **T2**: Retrieve and display details-on-demand on items of interest. For an in-depth analysis, it is important to have detailed information based on additional interaction while keeping the details available for further investigation.
- **T3**: Highlight patterns from the observation of a variable. This task intends to explore the temporal behavior of a chosen criterion, such as detecting high usage of CPU consumption for an extended amount of time.
- **T4**: Find correlations between groups of variables. This task aims to consider characteristics in multivariate data and domain knowledge. For example, correspondence between CPU1 temperature and CPU2 temperature, knowing that CPU1 is the main unit and CPU2 is the secondary unit in most cases.

- **T5**: Provide temporal dynamic shifts for identifying changes. Due to the dynamic nature of the data, it is important to observe the change over time. This task aims to pinpoint the detail-oriented aspect of identifying the ever-changing monitoring status of the system.
- **T6**: Cluster elements based on HPC criteria. This task stems from the need to group similar compute servers based on their characteristics, supporting the usage behavior analysis, load balancing, and efficient scheduling.

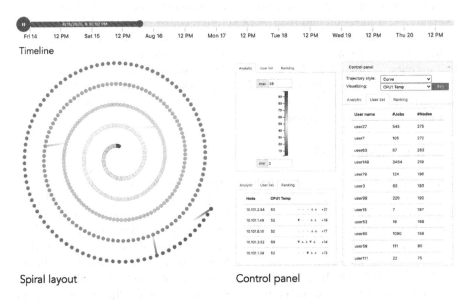

Fig. 1. Main components of our *Spiro* interface: (top) timeline controller, (left) spiral layout of 467 nodes ranked and colored by CPU temperatures in the HPC system, and (right) control panel.

4 *Spiro* Design

4.1 Design Rationales

In this section, we present the visual encodings, layout, and interactivity in design rationales for *Spiro*. One of the most important questions to be addressed here is how to visually represent the data, considering the constraints in data complexity, space arrangement in visual display, and preserving the context in ordering elements. Ordering arrangement often comes in the form of a linear scale [15]; however, considering the hundreds or thousands of nodes, a linear scale presents several scenarios: For a limited displaying screen, either we present all visual elements in a single view or having users switch between a different, consecutive chunk of ordered nodes with interactions, such as scrolling. To preserve the order of nodes along the linear scale, the former case comes with reducing element size such that all nodes fit along an extended line, leading to difficulty in legibility and element selection, while the latter hinders the observation of the system as a whole. Both sides of the trade-off do not scale well with the increasing number of system components.

We propose *Spiro* with order-preserving visualization of system components in a spiral structure. Our design choices are further backed by the result of a visualization design utilizing a spiral layout to "visually represent as many people as possible" by Dörk et al. [7]. In *Spiro*, we also use animations to show the changes in ranking two consecutive time steps. Animation in the spiral layout has been used to visualize multidimensional query results by Sawant and Healey [16], where animations are used to highlight the similarities and differences between queries. Here, the animation design emphasizes the most significant changes between two snapshots in a row.

To satisfy the visual analysis tasks above, considering the aforementioned limitations and the specialty of HPC data, *Spiro* proposes the following design decisions:

- **D1**: Present the computing nodes in a spiral layout, with specific order-preserving context (Task **T1**).
- **D2**: Recording a node's trajectory (historical rankings) between different positions along the spiral to provide temporal distribution (Task **T3**). This trajectory can be characterized by a curve moving through all the visited positions or a heatmap showing the density of frequent visits.
- **D3**: Provide interactions: click on elements for details-on-demand (Task **T2**), mouse-over for element's trajectory (Task **T3**), take snapshot for later comparison (Task **T4**).
- **D4**: Incorporate animation to provide the movements: Dynamic timeline slider, continue/pause button, and comet tails of the nodes with significant changes (Task **T5**)
- **D5**: Provide selections for exploring different data attributes while keeping the visual structure consistent (Task **T4**).
- **D6**: Apply corresponding colors for indicating clustering on individual elements, having the same visual structure for consistency (Task **T6**)

4.2 Visual Encoding

The systematic health metrics are applied across all compute servers in HPC systems to monitor the node status, corresponding to different values for different nodes at different timestamps. Considering these characteristics along with order-preserving context, the main structure of *Spiro* is designed to have compute nodes ordered along with a spiral layout, and each presents the value of a measurement at a particular time point. Figure 1 shows the overview and visual component of *Spiro*, including the timeline, spiral layout, and control panel. On the top is the timeline, which also acts as a time slider and toggle for running or pausing captures. The time elapsed is indicated by the mark made by a horizontal, blue bar down the timeline, where the current timestamp is superimposed.

Time will run automatically by default, and the corresponding monitoring status will be updated on the spiral layout.

The most important component of *Spiro* is the spiral layout, in which compute servers are represented by nodes ordered along with the structure. The color of the node indicates the value of the metric it is presenting in an ascending order starting from the center of the spiral. The color scale is consistent across multiple criteria to reduce the cognitive load for users in terms of visual encoding, also helping to detect the correlation between different variables by comparing the corresponding snapshots. Between two different timestamps, *Spiro* presents the change in rankings/values via comet tails (of the top five computing nodes) on the updated layout for all nodes. The animation offers the trends of the most significant changes in values, helping users capture the immediate, major discrepancies in monitoring status. The details for these changes can be found in the tab "Ranking" in the control panel. On the spiral layout, five nodes are moving outward, moving to the higher values, confirmed by all increasing trends in the ranking (Plus 21, Plus18, Plus17, Plus14, Plus12). The green and red indicators indicate the trends of these nodes in the latest five timestamps.

The control panel in Fig. 1 contains the ranking criteria drop-down, visualization styles, and detailed table. There are three tabs for presenting color legend,

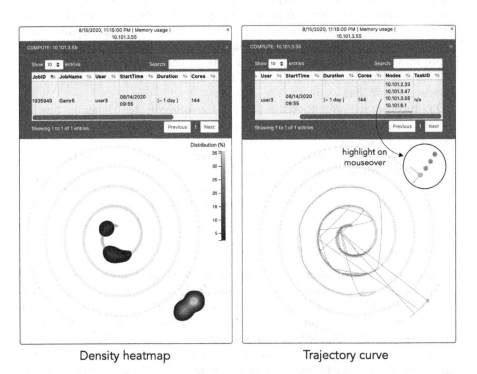

Density heatmap   Trajectory curve

Fig. 2. Two Memory usage snapshots of the same computing node, upon two visual representations describing its trajectory between different positions along the spiral: Density heatmap and trajectory curve of the selected computing node over one hour.

details into major changes upon selected criteria, and user selection for an in-depth view into usage behavior per user (user names have been redacted due to privacy). Figure 2 presents the two visual representations of a node's trajectory between different positions along the spiral to provide temporal distribution. The trajectory appears upon mousing over the corresponding node. While the heatmap provides the density of the order positions that a node's value is put in, the curve demonstrates the connection between every two consecutive positions. This presents a trade-off: The lines in the curve visualization are not able to present the frequent positions visited as sharply as the heatmap but give the idea of the actual trajectory. The heatmap is an intuitive example of highlighting the high-frequency positions while maybe overlooking the level of detail. In the heatmap of Fig. 2, we can notice that this computing node (10.101.3.55) constantly had high memory usage while running job *Gamr5* of *user3*. With the observation from the presentations of different computer health metrics, we can further analyze the usage behavior pattern [22], such as identifying whether the jobs allocated on these nodes are data-intensive or computing-intensive.

Spiro provides two ordering options for the spiral layout: by ranking (which is demonstrated throughout this paper) and by absolute value, as shown in Fig. 3. For these design alternatives, with ordering by ranking, all nodes are visualized with their corresponding color coding for values, hence the relative position among the nodes and better view of node value distribution; while in absolute value, the position of a node is the mapping 1-1 to its value, hence many nodes can have the same positions and overlap to each other.

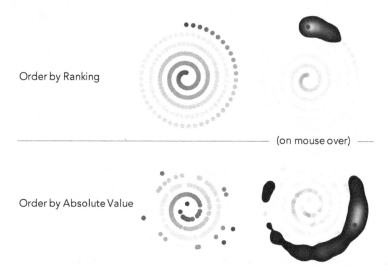

Fig. 3. Two ordering arrangements for *Spiro* layout: by ranking and by absolute values of the computer metrics, such as Power consumption.

5   Case Studies

5.1   Clustering on Compute Servers

Job clustering is an essential task in monitoring the HPC system. Based on the behavior observed on each group of computing nodes, we can categorize the trend of resource consumption and make the corresponding updates on job scheduling and load balancing. In this work, we present the approaches for grouping computing statuses (each cluster represents the major operating status of computers in the HPC center over the observed period) based on multivariate health metrics using clustering methods, including K-means and Leader algorithms [6,9]. The flexibility of *Spiro* layout allows new metaphors on the structure; here, we present the clustering result using *Spiro*. Figure 4 illustrates an example of applying K-means clustering algorithm with L2 normalization using Euclidean distance (of multivariate health metrics) for the computer statuses on August 18, 2020, at 9:30:00AM. On the left is the spiral layout, having each node as a radar chart, with nine axes spread as nine metrics. A close-up view of the arrangement of these metrics is presented in the bottom right corner of Fig. 4.

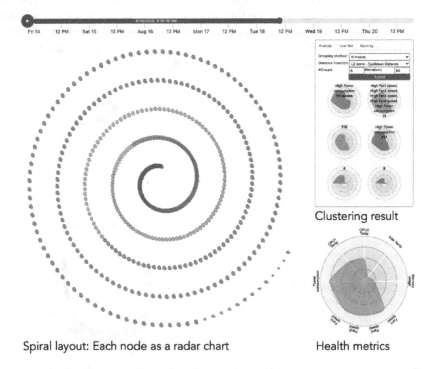

Fig. 4. Clustering result by K-means algorithm with six clusters. The framework automatically detects the cluster with high indicators for every metric. *Left:* Spiral layout for visualizing metric clusters. *Right:* The six clusters (top) and arrangement of health metrics via radar chart (bottom).

Spiro automatically identifies the clusters with notable characteristics, such as the orange cluster exhibiting high Fan speed for all four fan components and high power consumption. Meanwhile, the blue and red clusters both have high power consumption, as indicated, but experience different behaviors in memory usage, hence the two separate groups. The spiral layout showcases the majority of nodes in red, which are in high demand of power consumption (217 of 467 nodes); therefore, users can capture the status of the majority status of nodes when combining the spiral layout with the clustering result. *Spiro* provides the flexibility to demonstrate different scenarios using the same structure.

5.2   Exploring Usage Behavior

In this section, we will focus on the temporal behavior of *Memory usage*, one of the eight indicators in the health metrics of this HPC system. Figure 5 presents snapshots of memory usage captured at the same time in three consecutive days. The color of a node corresponds to the percentage of total memory usage, with the color scale shown on the right of Fig. 5. In most cases, most nodes are in blue to green, indicating the lower values in percentage, simultaneously with a few nodes in orange for higher usage (toward the end of the spiral layout). However, in the middle snapshot, the highest nodes are red, which has never occurred before, showing an unusual event. At this point, all the nodes in the outer rim of the spiral turned into yellow-red colors, showing higher usage than the other time points. The animation incorporated with this snapshot also shows the same outward-going orientation of the node's memory usage, demonstrating the same direction of usage rising over time.

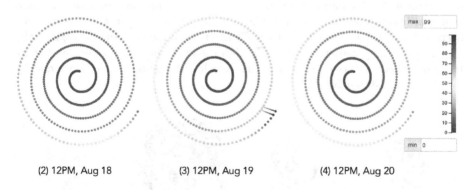

(2) 12PM, Aug 18   (3) 12PM, Aug 19   (4) 12PM, Aug 20

Fig. 5. Snapshots of memory usage at the same time every day, from August 18 to August 20. The middle snapshot shows an unusual event with noticeably increased usage of high-order nodes in red. (Color figure online)

Figure 6 presents the trajectories of two health metrics of one node throughout the observation interval. From the heatmap representation, the distribution for CPU1 Temperature focuses around the second rim of the spiral, meaning that the temperature never went too high. However, the memory usage distribution concentrates solely on the high percentage, signifying that this node utilizes abundant memory. From these two observations, we can see that while this node does not consume plenty of CPU (inferred from low CPU temperature), it occupies a significant amount of memory. One possibility for this behavior is that this node runs data-intensive jobs [22].

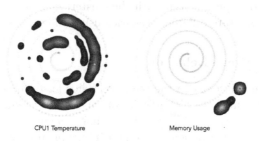

Fig. 6. CPU1 temperature and Memory usage of node 10.101.2.1.

Figure 7 presents four heatmaps of corresponding health metrics: CPU1 Temperature, CPU2 Temperature, Memory Usage, and Power consumption for one user. CPU2 can be considered as a backup resource to help carry the computation load with CPU1; here, the range of CPU2 temperature stays at a very low-value extent, associated with the low values in CPU1. From the observation of values in the lower range of CPU1 and CPU2 temperature, this user does not use many computing resources, hence the low temperature. The indicators can also confirm this for insignificant use in power consumption. Onto the memory usage, although the area having a high density of values is in the lower range, overall visualization shows high usage occurrences in memory (at approximately top 15 positions), leading to relatively high use of memory resources. Similar to the case in Sect. 5.2, the behavior of this user has the tendency to correspond to a series of data-intensive jobs.

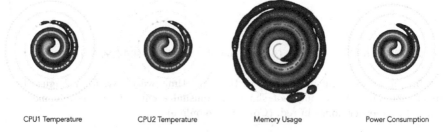

Fig. 7. CPU1 Temperature, CPU2 Temperature, Memory Usage and Power consumption of user. The user's name has been redacted due to privacy reasons.

6   Conclusion and Future Work

Visualizing a large number of HPC system components while preserving the context of node order is a challenging task. This paper presents a novel visualization technique for representing computing nodes while keeping order-preserving context. The case study demonstrated the usefulness and effectiveness of this technique in different scenarios: exploring health metrics as individuals or as components of a computing node, understanding user behavior over time, and comparing different users, taking into account the difference between the data-intensive jobs and computing-intensive jobs. Future work aims to incorporate the interactive features and expand the test cases with a rigorous user study.

Acknowledgments. The authors acknowledge the High-Performance Computing Center (HPCC) at Texas Tech University [19] in Lubbock for providing HPC resources and data that have contributed to the research results reported within this paper. This research is partly supported by the National Science Foundation under grant CNS-1362134, OAC-1835892, and through the IUCRC-CAC (Cloud and Autonomic Computing) Dell Inc. membership contribution.

References

1. Amar, R., Eagan, J., Stasko, J.: Low-level components of analytic activity in information visualization. In: IEEE Symposium on Information Visualization, 2005. INFOVIS 2005, pp. 111–117. IEEE (2005)
2. Bertini, E., Hertzog, P., Lalanne, D.: SpiralView: towards security policies assessment through visual correlation of network resources with evolution of alarms. In: 2007 IEEE Symposium on Visual Analytics Science and Technology, pp. 139–146. IEEE (2007)
3. Carlis, J.V., Konstan, J.A.: Interactive visualization of serial periodic data. In: Proceedings of the 11th Annual ACM Symposium on User Interface Software and Technology, pp. 29–38 (1998)
4. Chadwell, A., Kenney, L., Granat, M., Thies, S., Head, J.S., Galpin, A.: Visualisation of upper limb activity using spirals: a new approach to the assessment of daily prosthesis usage. Prosthet. Orthot. Int. **42**(1), 37–44 (2018)
5. Chew, E., Chen, Y.C.: Mapping midi to the spiral array: disambiguating pitch spellings. In: Bhargava, H.K., Ye, N. (eds.) Computational Modeling and Problem Solving in the Networked World. Operations Research/Computer Science Interfaces Series, vol. 21, pp. 259–275. Springer, Boston (2003). https://doi.org/10.1007/978-1-4615-1043-7_13
6. Dang, T.N., Wilkinson, L.: ScagExplorer: exploring scatterplots by their scagnostics. In: 2014 IEEE Pacific Visualization Symposium, pp. 73–80. IEEE (2014)
7. Dörk, M., Gruen, D., Williamson, C., Carpendale, S.: A visual backchannel for large-scale events. IEEE Trans. Visual Comput. Graph. **16**(6), 1129–1138 (2010)
8. Filipov, V., Schetinger, V., Raminger, K., Soursos, N., Zapke, S., Miksch, S.: Gone full circle: a radial approach to visualize event-based networks in digital humanities. Visual Inform. **5**(1), 45–60 (2021)
9. Hartigan, J.A.: Clustering Algorithms. Wiley, Hoboken (1975)

10. Herold, E., Pöckelmann, M., Berg, C., Ritter, J., Hall, M.M.: Stable word-clouds for visualising text-changes over time. In: Doucet, A., Isaac, A., Golub, K., Aalberg, T., Jatowt, A. (eds.) TPDL 2019. LNCS, vol. 11799, pp. 224–237. Springer, Cham (2019). https://doi.org/10.1007/978-3-030-30760-8_20
11. Juarez, J.M., Ochotorena, J.M., Campos, M., Combi, C.: Spatiotemporal data visualisation for homecare monitoring of elderly people. Artif. Intell. Med. **65**(2), 97–111 (2015)
12. Larsen, J.E., Cuttone, A., Jørgensen, S.L.: QS spiral: visualizing periodic quantified self data. In: CHI 2013 Workshop on Personal Informatics in the Wild: Hacking Habits for Health & Happiness (2013)
13. Lohfink, A.P., Anton, S.D.D., Schotten, H.D., Leitte, H., Garth, C.: Security in process: visually supported triage analysis in industrial process data. IEEE Trans. Visual Comput. Graphics **26**(4), 1638–1649 (2020)
14. Monroe, M., Lan, R., Lee, H., Plaisant, C., Shneiderman, B.: Temporal event sequence simplification. IEEE Trans. Visual Comput. Graphics **19**(12), 2227–2236 (2013)
15. Ruchikachorn, P., Mueller, K.: Learning visualizations by analogy: promoting visual literacy through visualization morphing. IEEE Trans. Visual Comput. Graph. **21**(9), 1028–1044 (2015)
16. Sawant, A.P., Healey, C.G.: Visualizing multidimensional query results using animation. In: Visualization and Data Analysis 2008, vol. 6809, p. 680904. International Society for Optics and Photonics (2008)
17. Shneiderman, B.: The eyes have it: a task by data type taxonomy for information visualizations. In: Proceedings 1996 IEEE Symposium on Visual Languages, pp. 336–343 (1996). https://doi.org/10.1109/VL.1996.545307
18. Shneiderman, B.: The eyes have it: a task by data type taxonomy for information visualizations. In: Proceedings 1996 IEEE Symposium on Visual Languages, pp. 336–343 (1996)
19. TTU: High performance computing center (HPCC) at Texas tech university. website (2020). https://www.depts.ttu.edu/hpcc/. Accessed 6 July 2020
20. VanDaniker, M.: Leverage of spiral graph for transportation system data visualization. Transp. Res. Rec. **2165**(1), 79–88 (2010)
21. Weber, M., Alexa, M., Müller, W.: Visualizing time-series on spirals. In: Infovis, vol. 1, pp. 7–14 (2001)
22. Zhang, H., You, H., Hadri, B., Fahey, M.: HPC usage behavior analysis and performance estimation with machine learning techniques. In: Proceedings of the International Conference on Parallel and Distributed Processing Techniques and Applications (PDPTA), p. 1. The Steering Committee of The World Congress in Computer Science, Computer Engineering and Applied Computing (WorldComp) (2012)

From Faces to Volumes - Measuring Volumetric Asymmetry in 3D Facial Palsy Scans

Tim Büchner[1]([✉]) [iD], Sven Sickert[1][iD], Gerd Fabian Volk[2][iD],
Orlando Guntinas-Lichius[2][iD], and Joachim Denzler[1][iD]

[1] Computer Vision Group, Friedrich Schiller University Jena, 07743 Jena, Germany
`{tim.buechner,sven.sickert,joachim.denzler}@uni-jena.de`
[2] Department of Otorhinolaryngology, Jena University Hospital,
07747 Jena, Germany
`{Fabian.Volk,orlando.guntinas}@med.uni-jena.de`

Abstract. The research of facial palsy, a unilateral palsy of the facial nerve, is a complex field of study with many different causes and symptoms. Even modern approaches to evaluate the facial palsy state rely mainly on stills and 2D videos of the face and rarely on 3D information. Many of these analysis and visualization methods require manual intervention, which is time-consuming and error-prone. Moreover, existing approaches depend on alignment algorithms or Euclidean measurements and consider only static facial expressions. Volumetric changes by muscle movement are essential for facial palsy analysis but require manual extraction. Our proposed method extracts an estimated unilateral volumetric description for dynamic expressions from 3D scans. Accurate positioning of 3D landmarks, problematic for facial palsy, is automated by adapting existing methods. Additionally, we visualize the primary areas of volumetric disparity by projecting them onto the face. Our approach substantially minimizes human intervention simplifying the clinical routine and interaction with 3D scans. The proposed pipeline can potentially more effectively analyze and monitor patient treatment progress.

Keywords: Facial Volumes · Facial Palsy · Radial Curves · Emotions

1 Introduction

Advancements in imaging techniques provide novel insights across various disciplines, particularly in the medical field. Especially in the area of facial palsy, a unilateral palsy of the facial nerve [25], 3D scans offer new capabilities to analyze the treatment progress. The limiting scope of 2D images cannot capture the full extent of the palsy, and, therefore, 3D models could bridge this gap [15,25]. Obtaining volumetric information can be an indicator for facial changes [4,21],

Supported by Deutsche Forschungsgemeinschaft (DFG - German Research Foundation) project 427899908 BRIDGING THE GAP: MIMICS AND MUSCLES (DE 735/15-1 and GU 463/12-1).

as facial muscle contractions, in reality, lead to 3D volume shifts of facial soft tissues, i.e., the muscle, fat tissue, and overlying skin.

Many methods for processing 3D data involve human interaction [15,23], making them time-consuming and prone to errors. Our work aims to develop an automated method for estimating unilateral facial volumes from generated meshes. We visualize the disparities in a patient's 3D scan to guide the medical professional's decision-making process for treatment during the clinical routine. First, we provide a method to reliably place 3D facial landmarks for patients with facial palsy and reduce the runtime of exiting methods by 96.6% [18]. Next, we extract radial curves from the 3D scan, starting at the nose tip [2–4,24]. These curves offer a detailed and structured description of the face surface for lateral comparisons. Our approach minimizes human intervention is fully automatic after parameter selection, and is available as open-source software[1].

2   Related Work

Existing methods for assessing facial palsy [9,20,26] rely on 2D images, either by using landmarks [12,14] or neural networks [20] to estimate existing palsy grading. However, many critical facial features cannot be captured by 2D images, such as the depth of the face or the volume differences between the face sides. Additionally, head rotation contributes to difficulties in analyzing 2D images.

3D morphable models are a common way to describe 3D face scans [11,13,19]. These incorporate landmarks as the primary reference points during the fitting [11] or leverage a symmetric template model acquired from healthy faces [13,19]. However, facial palsy patients have a wide range of asymmetry during facial movements, so these methods are unsuitable for this task. The fitting process eliminates detailed information on the face surface, which we require for understanding small volume changes. Consequently, we refrain from using 3D morphable models for lateral comparisons giving up semantic knowledge for a more comprehensive description of the face surface. Current methods for tracking volume changes in the mid and lower face rely on sparse features [21]. Their findings indicate that subtle facial expressions lead to measurable volume changes, which we aim to capture using a dense representation.

Some 3D palsy assessment methods require manual interaction [15,16,22,23], while others attempt automation [4,24] but focus only on face surface analysis. Utilizing radial curves [3,4] shows potential for detailed anatomical descriptions. Initially aligned using landmarks, the curves remain on the original face scan surface, retaining their features and overcoming template-based limitations. Radial properties enable structured face surface descriptions divided into distinct regions. Existing facial palsy approaches demonstrated this [4]. Nonetheless, the one-to-one mapping between curve points eliminates the influence of each side on the other. We overcome limitations by generating lateral face meshes using radial curves and revealing volume disparities between both facial sides.

---

[1] https://github.com/cvjena/corc.

3 Data Acquisition

We investigate volumetric changes in patients with facial palsy. Facial muscle contractions lead to 3D volume shifts of facial soft tissues, i.e., the muscle, fat tissue, and overlying skin [21]. We used the 3dMD face system (3dMD LCC, Georgia, USA) to capture these movement exercises, generating a 3D facial mesh using multiple 2D images and infrared structured light. This setup ensures that the mesh faces towards the z-axis, and the face remains close to the coordinate system's center. The patients follow an instruction tutorial and are asked to maintain a neutral expression for 3 s, followed by 3 s of smiling.

We recorded patients suffering from postparalytic facial syndrome at their treatment's beginning and end. Our data contains only patients with unilateral chronic synkinetic facial palsy with symptoms persisting for over six months. A common symptom in flaccid facial palsy is muscle atrophy, the affected side has a lower volume than the healthy side [25]. Volume changes are expected due to the imbalance on the affected and the contralateral side in the synkinetic patients.

4 Methods

Our goal is to achieve a fully automatic analysis of volumetric changes caused by facial tissue shifts during muscle contractions. Furthermore, we want to visualize the local volumetric differences between the face sides. First, we extract 3D landmarks from the 3D scan by adapting existing methods to patients with facial palsy [18]. Second, we obtain radial curves from the 3D scan using these landmarks [4]. Third, we develop a volumetric description of the face sides based on the radial curves. Lastly, we employ the lateral properties of radial curves to produce a disparity heatmap and compare it to the volumetric results. Our method also applies to point clouds, as we use only the vertices of the 3D mesh.

4.1 3D Landmark Extraction for Facial Palsy Patients

The structured semantic representation of 3D facial features is crucial for many processing steps. Either by landmarks or 3D morphable models (3DMM) [11, 13,18], these representations are the basis for further analysis. Models estimating these descriptors train on healthy faces, thus, unsuitable for patients with facial palsy and necessitate manual intervention [15,23]. As 3DMMs modify the template surface for fitting [11], they are unsuitable for volume analysis. We opt for a multi-view consensus 3D landmark extraction method introduced by [18] and adapt it to patients with facial palsy. They use several virtual camera views ($n = 96$) around the face to estimate 2D landmarks. Utilizing the intrinsic and extrinsic camera parameters, the 2D landmarks are projected onto the 3D mesh.

We aim for a fast, automatic approach to support medical practitioners during the clinical routine. The original implementation takes 30 s to extract the landmarks for one single scan on an Nvidia GeForce GTX 3070 [18]. Hence, processing a six-second video (at 30 frames per second) would take around 5400 s

Fig. 1. Virtual camera locations to approximate 3D landmarks using [18]: The camera positions are on a sphere around the face to generate lateral views.

(90 min). Instead of using 96 random camera locations, we achieve suitable landmarks with only eight fixed camera locations. We focus on lateral views of the face[2], depicted in Fig. 1, to minimize unknown symmetry biases in the learned model. The 3D facial landmarks, as seen in Fig. 2, for a patient with facial palsy fit accordingly for both sides of the face. As patients often have unilateral palsy, only one side of the face is affected, and we view both face sides independently of each other. Thus we assume that neither the healthy nor palsy side introduces a bias to the landmark estimation for the other side. Our fixed camera locations are: *yaw* angles of -40, -20, 20, and $40°$ and *pitch* angles of -30 and $30°$. The pre-trained model uses the virtual cameras RGB and depth images as input [18]. Additionally, we remove rendering pipeline overhead, reduce unnecessary memory access and cache misses, and use new CUDA features. We greatly reduce the computation time for a single surface scan to one second, thus, reducing the processing time for a six-second video to 180 s.

4.2 Radial Curves

In a set $\mathcal{X} \in \mathbb{R}^{k \times 3}$ with k points, either a point cloud or the vertices of a mesh, radial curves are a structured description of the scanned surface [2–4,24]. Radial curves, emitting from a common start point and limited by a maximal distance r, are surface descriptors defined by a tensor $\Gamma \in \mathbb{R}^{n \times m \times 3}$ with n curves with m curve points. In the case of faces, the nose tip is the start point, and the chin limits the distance [2,4,24], as depicted in Fig. 2. To extract the curve group Γ alignment is crucial, thus, we normalize $\mathcal{X}$ with $\bar{\mathcal{X}} = (\mathcal{X} - T) \cdot R_H^{-1}$. The translation vector $T \in \mathbb{R}^3$ is the nose tip, and $R_H \in \mathbb{R}^{3 \times 3}$ is the head pose obtained from the eye and mouth landmarks [6]. Each radial curve γ_α resides on a plane p_α, defined by normal d_α^n and vector along it d_α, rotated through the nose tip with an angle $\alpha = \frac{360°}{n}$. For lateral descriptions, n has to be an even

---

[2] All shown individuals agreed to have their images published in terms with the GDPR.

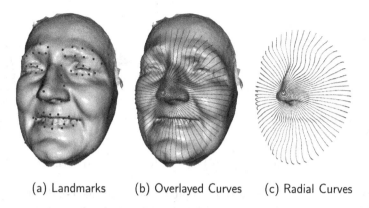

(a) Landmarks   (b) Overlayed Curves   (c) Radial Curves

Fig. 2. We highlight the extracted landmarks (a) and the resulting radial curves Γ (b) on the face scan of a patient with facial palsy. In (c), the curves Γ_{left} describe the left (blue) and right Γ_{right} (red) sides of the face. (Color figure online)

number and greater equals than four [4,24]. All points in $\bar{\mathcal{X}}$ that lie around the plane p_α with maximal distance δ are selected [4,24]:

$$S_\alpha = \left\{ x_i \in \bar{\mathcal{X}} \,\middle|\, |x_i^T d_\alpha^n| < \delta \wedge x_i^T \cdot d_\alpha > 0 \right\}. \tag{1}$$

With the 3dMD camera system, we use $\delta = 0.8$ mm. A temporary projection of S_α onto the plane p_α simplifies ordering and fitting, as seen in Fig. 3a. We sort the points by distance to the nose tip [24] and afterward for a correct surface description with a graph traversal algorithm [4]. A 2D spline approximates the curve γ_α in the ordered points $\bar{S}_\alpha$. We equidistantly sample m point between the nose tip and the most distant point, shown in Fig. 3d. Lastly, we project the spline points back into the original 3D coordinate system. After computing all n curves, we obtain Γ. Aligning the curve tensor to the scan is only necessary for visualization and is done with $\Gamma := \Gamma \cdot R_H + T$, as seen in Fig. 2.

4.3 Lateral Face Mesh Generation

The tensor Γ represents a structured face surface. The pointwise difference between the lateral curve pairs (γ_α and $\gamma_{360-\alpha}$) computes asymmetry [4]. However, this approach neglects the overall state of each face, especially volume information, which is measurable even for small movements [21]. We overcome this limitation by estimating unilateral facial volume based on a watertight mesh of Γ. A watertight mesh is a 2-manifold mesh [7], where every edge is part of precisely two faces [8]. Despite receiving a mesh surface, we create a new volumetric mesh to ensure watertight properties and support point cloud scanners. As we already have a face surface descriptor Γ, we do need general surface reconstruction algorithms [1,10]. The left tensor Γ_{left} includes all curves γ_α with $\alpha \in [0, 180]$ and the right tensor Γ_{right} all curves γ_α with $\alpha \in [180, 360]$. Please

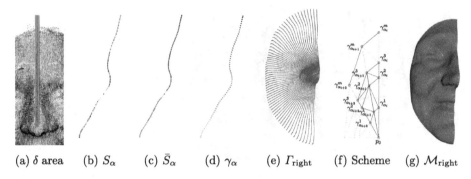

(a) δ area   (b) S_α (c) $\bar{S}_\alpha$ (d) γ_α (e) Γ_{right} (f) Scheme   (g) $\mathcal{M}_{\text{right}}$

Fig. 3. We visualize each curve extraction process step and the resulting triangulation $\mathcal{M}_{\text{left}}$ of the left facial surface scan. The color coding of S_α, $\bar{S}_\alpha$, and the γ_α indicate the order of the points.

note, that curve γ_0 and γ_{360} are identical and the views are from the patient's point of view.

Γ_{left} and Γ_{right} construct the closed lateral face surfaces $\mathcal{M}_{\text{left}}$ and $\mathcal{M}_{\text{right}}$, as seen in Fig. 3g. The borders of $\mathcal{M}_{\text{left}}$ and $\mathcal{M}_{\text{right}}$ are connected with an underlying sphere mesh, as seen in Fig. 4b, and a side mesh along the vertical face center, as seen in Fig. 4c. All steps are watertight, and we apply the combined mesh for the volume approximations. A tetrahedron volume can be computed using each triangle, with the origin as the fourth point. We obtain a correct volume by ensuring that the triangle winding order is counter-clockwise [8].

Radial Curve Mesh Generation. The generation algorithm is based on the radial curves tensor Γ_{left} and Γ_{right}, see Fig. 3e. As each curve γ lies on the scan surface of the face, the generated also mesh represents the face surface, see Fig. 3g. The degree of detail is adjustable by the number of points m and the number of curves n. Each curve starts at the same point p_0, which is the nose tip of the face. The equidistantly sampled points ensure that points between adjacent curves describe similar perimeter locations. Between two adjacent curves γ_{α_i} and $\gamma_{\alpha_{i+1}}$, we create a triangulation pattern shown in Fig. 3f. The triangulation $\mathcal{M}$ includes all points, and the mesh is without holes and watertight. Our approach relies only on the extracted radial curve tensors Γ_{left} and Γ_{right} without any hyperparameters The outer edges of $\mathcal{M}_{\text{left}}$ and $\mathcal{M}_{\text{right}}$ connect to the underlying sphere and side meshes, linking every edge precisely to two faces.

Underlying Sphere Mesh. Several approaches are possible to close the volume below the face mesh to enable volume calculations. First, we require a south pole point S as a reference point. We use the endpoint $E1$ of the curve γ_{180} and the endpoint $E2$ of the curve γ_0 as orientation. Additionally, we use the nose tip C as a third reference point, shown in Fig. 4a. S is the perpendicular intersection of the centerline and the line connecting $E1$ and $E2$ with the distance r, the

(a) Construction of the arc   (b) Triangulated underlying   (c) Mesh using constrained
segments   sphere mesh   Delaunay triangulation

Fig. 4. The side mesh (b) fills the gap between the facial and underlying sphere mesh (a). The inner edges of the radial curves (a) serve as orientation.

same value as for the radial curve extraction, to C. The case of $E1$, $E2$, and C being co-linear cannot occur since these points reference anatomical facial structures and would otherwise indicate a severe facial deformity or a severe error during previous extraction steps. We could use the south pole point S and the boundary points of the face to form simple triangles. However, different facial shapes (e.g., a deep eye socket or mouth being open) will lead to self-intersections [8]. A spherical approach prevents trivial self-intersections, even though theoretically possible but unlikely in practice, as the sphere is convex, and the head will fit inside the sphere. For each radial curve γ_α, we calculate the arc on the corresponding sphere using the corresponding endpoint and S, ensuring alignment with the outer edges of the surface mesh. We triangulate sphere segments like the facial mesh, as depicted in Fig. 4b. Consequently, the underlying sphere is closed and directly connected to the scan surface mesh.

Face Side Mesh. The final component is the face side closing the facial and sphere mesh gap. A triangulation scheme as in Fig. 3f is not feasible due to the different point densities. However, we can use a constrained Delaunay triangulation to fill the gap [5,17]. We use the curves γ_0 and γ_{180} of the curve tensor Γ and sphere meshes boundary edges to constrain the triangulation, as depicted in Fig. 4a. The face side mesh is useable for both the left and right sides of the face. This operation guarantees a watertight mesh, as the boundary edges constrain the triangulation. Therefore, we obtain three watertight meshes, the facial mesh $\mathcal{M}_{\text{left}}$ and $\mathcal{M}_{\text{right}}$, the underlying sphere- and the face side mesh.

4.4   Volume Estimation for Lateral Face Sides

We create a 2-manifold mesh from the radial curve tensor Γ_{left} and Γ_{right}, as described in Subsect. 4.3. Please note that self-intersections are possible but unlikely in practice. The meshes are watertight and closed, allowing us to estimate the patient's lateral face volume; examples are shown in Fig. 6. Summing up the signed tetrahedrons' volumes yields the total volume of the mesh [8]:

$$V = \sum_{i=1}^{n} \frac{1}{6} \cdot (p_i^{(1)} \times p_i^{(2)} \cdot p_i^{(3)}), \qquad (2)$$

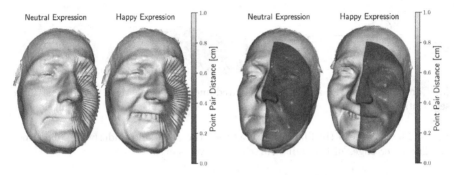

(a) Vector field visualization $\mathcal{V}$ between tensors Γ_{left} and $\bar{\Gamma}_{\text{left}}$.

(b) Projection of the volumetric difference onto the facial surface

Fig. 5. Both visualizations show the disparities (maximum 1 cm) between the left and right sides of the face between the *neutral* and *happy* expressions.

where $p_i^{(1)}$, $p_i^{(2)}$ and $p_i^{(3)}$ are the vertices of the triangle i. We assume all tetrahedrons share the same origin $[0,0,0]^T$ as a fourth point. Overlapping tetrahedron bodies cancel each other out due to the triangle's counter-clockwise winding order, thus providing a correct volume estimation. As before, the degree of detail is adjustable by the number of points m and the number of curves n. We observed that the relative difference among the face sides is not affected significantly. We chose $n = 64$ curves and $m = 64$ spline points in our analysis to balance accuracy and computation time. The calculations are conducted in the original coordinate system, resulting in real-world values measured in millimeters.

4.5   Volumetric Difference Visualization

Volume estimation provides crucial information about the disparities between the left and right sides of the face. Additionally, identifying the specific locations of volumetric differences can aid doctors in optimizing the treatment of facial palsy patients. We assume the left side is the palsy side, and the right is the healthy side. Mirroring the curve tensor Γ_{right} along the vertical centerline, defined by γ_0 and γ_{180}, yields $\bar{\Gamma}_{\text{left}}$, which describes the left side without palsy. As the curve tensors and face scan align, we can directly compare the points of Γ_{left} and $\bar{\Gamma}_{\text{left}}$. Due to the equidistant spline sampling, this pointwise correspondence enables us to indicate where the palsy and contralateral sides differ.

For a 3D visualization, we create a vector field $\mathcal{V}$ between pairwise points from Γ_{left} to $\bar{\Gamma}_{\text{left}}$. The vector length measures the side disparities. As the radial curves γ_α lie on the face's surface, the vectors also originate on the surface. For the visualization, we use a sequential colormap (Imola) without dark shades to reduce interference with shadows introduced by the render engine, as depicted in Fig. 5a. We set the upper limit of the color range to 1 cm to ensure comparable visualizations between the different time steps. This visualization aids doctors in identifying the affected areas of the palsy side.

Additionally, we project the volumetric differences onto the facial surface, see Fig. 5b. This visualization is more intuitive for doctors, who can more easily identify the affected areas without interpreting a vector field or interacting with the 3D renderer. We use the identical color mapping used for the vector field visualization. The projection requires computing the intersection between $\mathcal{V}$ and the facial surface mesh $\mathcal{M}_{\text{left}}$. The vertex colors are then assigned to the corresponding vector length color range value. This approach is similar to [25], indicating the differences between time steps but does not require registration of the facial surface meshes. For example, Fig. 5b shows that the chin area is affected more than the cheek area.

5 Volume Analysis During Dynamic Movements

Lastly, we are interested in the dynamic analysis of the facial volume during an instructed movement. Thus, we analyzed patients' volumetric changes and locations mimicking facial expressions. During dynamic movements, temporal noise might occur from the 3dMD camera system (3dMD LCC, Georgia, USA), which propagates to the 3D landmarks and radial curves. Thus, we apply a sliding window of 5 frames to the 3D landmarks to reduce the impact on subsequent processing steps. The radial curve range is set to $r = 85$ mm, the distance between the nose tip and the chin. Patients were instructed to mimic a *happy* facial expression following a *neutral* phase that lasted about three seconds. We visualize the time progression in Fig. 6. The top row displays four face scans, the lateral meshes, and the projected volumetric differences of a patient during selected time steps. The second row illustrates the volume of the left (blue) and right (red) sides of the face, as well as the absolute volume difference between the two sides (black). The third row shows the averaged one-to-one pointwise distance of $\mathcal{V}$ between the affected and contralateral sides [4].

The initial difference might be due to inherent facial asymmetries, muscle atrophy or compensatory hypertrophy, a mixture of both, or inaccuracy in the method. However, as it remains constant during the neutral phase, we assume our method is stable throughout dynamic movements. During the movement phase, the volume difference increases, indicating increasing facial asymmetry for both measurement methods. However, the volumetric analysis enables insight into the impact of both faces sides. The palsy side mesh (left/blue) decreases in volume, whereas the healthy side (right/red) experiences an increase in volume. A change is expected as the facial muscles contract [21]. The volume reduction on the palsy side could be due to tissue pulled towards the healthy side. The facial muscles of both sides form a more extensive interwoven network. Suppose one side (the healthy contralateral side) is contracting stronger. In that case, this automatically pulls over the facial soft tissue (that we observe as volume change) from the palsy side to the healthy side, as the contraction on the healthy side is not counterbalanced by a symmetric activity on the palsy side.

Our method exhibits similar behavior to the pointwise distance [4], indicating that it measures the same asymmetry. However, pointwise distance cannot reveal

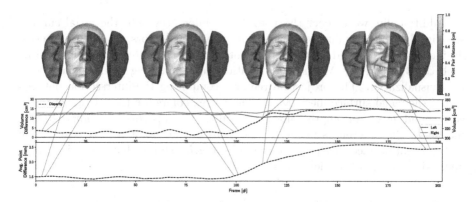

Fig. 6. We measure the volumetric changes from a `neutral` to a `happy` facial expression. The palsy side (blue) decreases while the healthy side (red) increases in volume, indicating a shift from the palsy side to the healthy side. (Color figure online)

the palsy side's impact on the healthy side, making volumetric analysis more suitable for assessing this effect. Based on pointwise disparities, our proposed visualization effectively illustrates the volumetric differences between the healthy and palsy sides.

6   Conclusions and Future Work

We introduced a method for calculating volumetric facial disparities, improving on existing approaches and providing insights into the palsy side's impact. In addition, our approach also offers visualization of volumetric differences, enhancing facial asymmetry understanding. Moreover, we can analyze dynamic changes during a single movement, extending the method's usefulness.

As our approach is automatic and requires minimal parameter tuning (number of radial curves n, spline points m, and δ based on the sensor), we do not rely on any assumptions and estimations about facial symmetry. The joint visualization, see Fig. 6, of the volume differences, the facial expression, and the difference heatmap helps to understand the behavior of the facial muscles during a single movement. The projected volumetric differences between the meshes, see Fig. 5b, can be used to identify the affected areas of the face in a single image. Visualizations guide treatment decisions during the clinical routine, and our approach can help doctors better understand facial asymmetry. This insight is significant for treating facial palsy, as the muscle contractions create facial expressions. Our work offers a combined tool to analyze facial volume changes during dynamic movements bridging the gap between static and dynamic analysis based on 3D data. We open up future medical research to define instance exercises that address counter-actions to volume shifts towards the healthy side.

Our approach's effectiveness depends on 3D scan quality and intermediate facial landmark estimation. Our future work aims to join 3D morphable models with radial curves, enabling the automatic identification of affected facial regions.

References

1. Bernardini, F., Mittleman, J., Rushmeier, H., Silva, C., Taubin, G.: The ball-pivoting algorithm for surface reconstruction. IEEE Trans. Vis. Comput. Graph. **5**(4), 349–359 (1999). https://doi.org/10.1109/2945.817351
2. Berretti, S., Del Bimbo, A., Pala, P., Mata, F.J.S.: Face recognition by SVMS classification of 2D and 3D radial geodesics. In: 2008 IEEE International Conference on Multimedia and Expo, pp. 93–96. IEEE, Hannover, Germany (2008). https://doi.org/10.1109/ICME.2008.4607379
3. Bowman, A.W., Katina, S., Smith, J., Brown, D.: Anatomical curve identification. Comput. Stat. Data Anal. **86**, 52–64 (2015). https://doi.org/10.1016/j.csda.2014.12.007
4. Büchner, T., Sickert, S., Volk, G.F., Guntinas-Lichius, O., Denzler, J.: Automatic objective severity grading of peripheral facial palsy using 3D radial curves extracted from point clouds. In: Challenges of Trustable AI and Added-Value on Health, pp. 179–183 (2022). https://doi.org/10.3233/SHTI220433
5. Delaunay, B.N.: Sur la sphère vide. Bulletin de l'Académie des Sciences de l'URSS. VII. Série **1934**(6), 793–800 (1934)
6. Derkach, D., Ruiz, A., Sukno, F.M.: Head pose estimation based on 3-D facial landmarks localization and regression. In: 2017 12th IEEE International Conference on Automatic Face & Gesture Recognition (FG 2017), pp. 820–827. IEEE (2017)
7. Edelsbrunner, H.: Surface reconstruction by wrapping finite sets in space. In: Aronov, B., Basu, S., Pach, J., Sharir, M. (eds.) Discrete and Computational Geometry. Algorithms and Combinatorics, vol. 25, pp. 379–404. Springer, Heidelberg (2003). https://doi.org/10.1007/978-3-642-55566-4_17
8. Giblin, P.: Graphs, Surfaces and Homology. 3 edn. Cambridge University Press, Cambridge (2010). https://doi.org/10.1017/CBO9780511779534
9. Haase, D., Minnigerode, L., Volk, G.F., Denzler, J., Guntinas-Lichius, O.: Automated and objective action coding of facial expressions in patients with acute facial palsy. Eur. Arch. Otorhinolaryngol. **272**(5), 1259–1267 (2015). https://doi.org/10.1007/s00405-014-3385-8
10. Kazhdan, M., Bolitho, M., Hoppe, H.: Poisson surface reconstruction. In: The Eurographics Association (2006). https://doi.org/10.2312/SGP/SGP06/061-070
11. Li, T., Bolkart, T., Black, M.J., Li, H., Romero, J.: Learning a model of facial shape and expression from 4D scans. ACM Trans. Graph. **36**(6), 1–17 (2017). https://doi.org/10.1145/3130800.3130813
12. Lou, J., Yu, H., Wang, F.Y.: A review on automated facial nerve function assessment from visual face capture. IEEE Trans. Neural Syst. Rehabil. Eng. **28**(2), 488–497 (2020). https://doi.org/10.1109/TNSRE.2019.2961244
13. Lugaresi, C., et al.: MediaPipe: a framework for building perception pipelines (2019). https://doi.org/10.48550/arXiv.1906.08172
14. Miller, M.Q., Hadlock, T.A., Fortier, E., Guarin, D.L.: The auto-eFACE: machine learning-enhanced program yields automated facial palsy assessment tool. Plast. Reconstr. Surg. **147**(2), 467–474 (2021). https://doi.org/10.1097/PRS.0000000000007572
15. Özsoy, U., Sekerci, R., Hizay, A., Yildirim, Y., Uysal, H.: Assessment of reproducibility and reliability of facial expressions using 3D handheld scanner. J. Craniomaxillofac. Surg. Official Publication Euro. Assoc. Craniomaxillofac. Surg. **47**(6), 895–901 (2019). https://doi.org/10.1016/j.jcms.2019.03.022

16. Patel, A., Islam, S.M.S., Murray, K., Goonewardene, M.S.: Facial asymmetry assessment in adults using three-dimensional surface imaging. Prog. Orthod. **16**(1), 36 (2015). https://doi.org/10.1186/s40510-015-0106-9

17. Paul Chew, L.: Constrained Delaunay triangulations. Algorithmica **4**(1), 97–108 (1989). https://doi.org/10.1007/BF01553881

18. Paulsen, R.R., Juhl, K.A., Haspang, T.M., Hansen, T., Ganz, M., Einarsson, G.: Multi-view consensus CNN for 3D facial landmark placement. arXiv:1910.06007 [cs], vol. 11361, pp. 706–719 (2019). https://doi.org/10.1007/978-3-030-20887-5_44

19. Paysan, P., Knothe, R., Amberg, B., Romdhani, S., Vetter, T.: A 3D face model for pose and illumination invariant face recognition. In: 2009 Sixth IEEE International Conference on Advanced Video and Signal Based Surveillance, pp. 296–301. IEEE, Genova, Italy (2009). https://doi.org/10.1109/AVSS.2009.58

20. Raj, A., Mothes, O., Sickert, S., Volk, G.F., Guntinas-Lichius, O., Denzler, J.: Automatic and objective facial palsy grading index prediction using deep feature regression. In: Papież, B.W., Namburete, A.I.L., Yaqub, M., Noble, J.A. (eds.) MIUA 2020. CCIS, vol. 1248, pp. 253–266. Springer, Cham (2020). https://doi.org/10.1007/978-3-030-52791-4_20

21. Rawlani, R., Qureshi, H., Rawlani, V., Turin, S.Y., Mustoe, T.A.: Volumetric changes of the mid and lower face with animation and the standardization of three-dimensional facial imaging. Plast. Reconstr. Surg. **143**(1), 76–85 (2019). https://doi.org/10.1097/PRS.0000000000005082

22. Sarhan, F.R., et al.: Quantified analysis of facial movement: a reference for clinical applications. Clin. Anat. p. ca.23999 (2023). https://doi.org/10.1002/ca.23999

23. ten Harkel, T.C., Vinayahalingam, S., Ingels, K.J.A.O., Bergé, S.J., Maal, T.J.J., Speksnijder, C.M.: Reliability and agreement of 3D anthropometric measurements in facial palsy patients using a low-cost 4D imaging system. IEEE Trans. Neural Syst. Rehabil. Eng. **28**(8), 1817–1824 (2020). https://doi.org/10.1109/TNSRE.2020.3007532

24. Thümmel, M., Sickert, S., Denzler, J.: Facial behavior analysis using 4D curvature statistics for presentation attack detection. In: 2021 IEEE International Workshop on Biometrics and Forensics (IWBF), pp. 1–6 (2021). https://doi.org/10.1109/IWBF50991.2021.9465080

25. Volk, G.F., et al.: Long-term home-based surface electrostimulation is useful to prevent atrophy in denervated facial muscles. In: Vienna Workshop on Functional Electrical Stimulation (FESWS) (2019)

26. Zhuang, Y., et al.: Video-based facial weakness analysis. IEEE Trans. Biomed. Eng. **68**(9), 2698–2705 (2021). https://doi.org/10.1109/TBME.2021.3049739

Video Analysis and Event Recognition

Comparison of Autoencoder Models for Unsupervised Representation Learning of Skeleton Sequences

Thura Zaw, Jiaxin Zhou[✉], and Takashi Komuro[✉]

Graduate School of Science and Engineering, Saitama University, Saitama 338-8570, Japan
thu.r.z.973@ms.saitama-u.ac.jp, jx.shou1@gmail.com,
komuro@mail.saitama-u.ac.jp

Abstract. This study comprehensively explores the performance of six distinct feature extraction models on two widely used skeleton datasets, UCLA and NTU 60, with a focus on establishing the superiority of hybrid transformer architectures. The models include autoencoder, convolutional autoencoder, temporal autoencoder (GRU autoencoder), transformer, convolutional transformer, and transformer with a convolutional encoder, representing diverse approaches in skeleton data analysis. The primary objective is to compare the models' effectiveness in extracting meaningful features from the skeleton datasets. Rigorous evaluations and comparisons are conducted using quantitative measures and visualizations to assess each model's discriminative power in capturing relevant information. The findings demonstrate that the transformer model consistently outperforms all other models on both datasets, showcasing its unique capability in extracting meaningful and discriminative features from skeleton data. Additionally, the study investigates hybrid models, combining transformer architectures with other feature extraction techniques, revealing their potential to surpass individual model capabilities. These findings can guide future studies in selecting appropriate models for similar tasks and promoting the development of more accurate and robust action recognition systems based on skeleton data.

Keywords: Human Action Recognition (HAR) · Autoencoder · Transformer · Convolution · Features extraction

1 Introduction

Unsupervised action recognition offers a promising solution to the limitations of traditional supervised approaches by learning meaningful representations directly from unlabeled skeleton data. By tapping into the inherent structure and temporal dynamics of human motion [3, 8], unsupervised methods extract discriminative features without extensive manual annotations. Deep learning models have emerged as powerful tools for feature extraction in unsupervised skeleton action recognition. These models capture essential patterns and dependencies within the skeleton data, facilitating effective

G. Bebis et al. (Eds.): ISVC 2023, LNCS 14361, pp. 135–146, 2023.
https://doi.org/10.1007/978-3-031-47969-4_11

representation learning. The skeleton image representation models, ConvNets and Skele-Motion, which convert skeleton input sequences into images to enhance their usability with Convolutional Neural Networks (CNNs) [2, 4, 5]. J. Tu, H. Liu and F. Meng, et al., introduces a novel LSTM autoencoder network (LSTM-AE) for spatial-temporal data augmentation in skeleton-based human action recognition [14], which effectively preserves temporal information, eliminates irrelevant details, and achieves superior performance compared to state-of-the-art methods on large-scale datasets like NTU 60 [22]. A change direction patterns (CDPs) and 3D pose features in a unified deep structure using a convolutional autoencoder with attention mechanisms, effectively extracting discriminative spatiotemporal relationships of whole body joints for 3D action recognition across multiple datasets [15].

While autoencoder-based models leverage image recognition principles, transforming the skeleton sequences into 2D images to extract relevant features, other models focus on the temporal analysis of individual frames. Chiara et al. introduces the Spatial-Temporal Transformer network (ST-TR) that employs a Spatial Self-Attention module (SSA) for intra-frame interactions and a Temporal Self-Attention module (TSA) for inter-frame correlations in a two-stream network [19]. By incorporating recurrent connections and self-attention mechanisms, these models excel at capturing long-term dependencies and spatial relationships. Overall, the unsupervised approach in skeleton action recognition offers a compelling alternative to supervised methods [6, 7], enabling effective and efficient recognition of human actions without heavy reliance on annotated data. The exploration of diverse deep learning architectures enhances the capabilities of unsupervised methods, paving the way for more accurate and robust action recognition in challenging scenarios where labeled data is scarce or expensive to acquire.

The purpose of the study is to compare the performance of different models for un-supervised skeleton action recognition. By evaluating the performance of various models, including autoencoder, convolutional autoencoder, GRU autoencoder, transformer, convolutional transformer, and transformer with convolutional encoder, the goal is to identify the most effective approach for recognizing and understanding human actions based on skeleton data.

This task contributes by providing a comprehensive comparison of multiple models for unsupervised skeleton action recognition. It evaluates the performance of different architectures, including autoencoders, convolutional autoencoders, GRU autoencoder, transformers, convolutional transformers, and transformer with convolutional encoder, allowing for an informed selection of the most suitable model. By assessing the performance of each model, this task contributes to understanding the strengths and weaknesses of different approaches in unsupervised skeleton action recognition. It provides insights into which models are more effective in capturing and representing the essential features and temporal dynamics of human actions from skeleton data.

2 Related Work

Human action recognition encompasses various approaches, including unimodal and multimodal analysis with different data modalities [1, 9]. Joint Trajectory Maps (JTM) represent spatial-temporal information in 3D skeleton sequences as 2D images, enabling the use of Convolutional Neural Networks (ConvNets) and achieving state-of-the-art results [2]. Deep learning models, such as two-stream Convolutional Neural Networks, 3D Convolutional Neural Networks, and LSTM networks, have been explored extensively for gesture recognition [13]. Innovative approaches have been proposed to improve human action recognition. SkeleMotion captures temporal dynamics by encoding magnitude and orientation values of skeleton joints, achieving superior performance on the NTU RGB+D 120 dataset [4]. Skeleton optical spectra encode spatial-temporal information into color texture images, effectively learning discriminative features without extensive parameter training [5]. Joint distance maps (JDMs) encode spatial-temporal information into color texture images, enabling effective action and interaction recognition [10]. Residual networks, such as Deep Residual Networks (ResNets), have been investigated for human action recognition using skeletal data obtained from depth sensors, achieving state-of-the-art performance with reduced computational requirements [11].

For cases with multiple data modalities, a two-stream framework combining CNN and RNN has been adopted [12]. Verma et al. propose a technique combining RGB and skeleton information using ConvNets and LSTM for human activity recognition, achieving satisfactory results on multimodal datasets [12]. Tomas et al. focus on combining RGBD color information and motion information from skeletal joints, achieving improved recognition accuracy using a combined deep architecture of CNN and Stacked Autoencoders [13]. Juanhui, T et al. introduces a novel LSTM autoencoder network (LSTM-AE) for spatial-temporal data augmentation in skeleton-based human action recognition, combining the temporal preservation of LSTM with autoencoder's ability to eliminate irrelevant information, resulting in improved performance compared to state-of-the-art methods on large datasets like NTU RGB+D and Smart Home, and easy integration with RNN-based action recognition models [14]. Khezerlou et al. presents the 3DPo-CDP descriptor, a unified deep structure combining change direction patterns (CDPs) and 3D pose features transformed into images, processed through a convolutional autoencoder with weighted multi-scale channel and spatial attention modules, and augmented with wavelet representation to achieve effective 3D action recognition across multiple challenging datasets [15].

Temporal sequence models play a crucial role in skeleton-based action recognition. Sparse-Transformer Based Siamese Network (TBSN) leverages temporal characteristics and achieves superior performance on few-shot video classification tasks [16]. Independently recurrent neural networks (IndRNNs) address gradient vanishing and exploding problems, providing a solution for temporal modeling [17]. Hierarchical Transformer and Spatial-Temporal Transformer networks effectively capture spatial and temporal structures in skeleton sequences, achieving state-of-the-art performance on multiple datasets [18, 19]. The structure-asymmetrical autoencoder framework for unsupervised representation learning captures spatiotemporal representations, outperforming generative learning methods [20].

3 Methods

3.1 Proposed Methods

Juanhui et al. proposes an LSTM autoencoder network for spatial-temporal data augmentation in skeleton-based human action recognition, which preserves temporal information, eliminates irrelevant details, and utilizes a regularized cross-entropy loss for improved representation learning, outperforming state-of-the-art methods on largescale datasets and offering easy integration with existing RNN-based action recognition models [14]. Khezerlou et al., propose convolutional autoencoder with multi-scale attention modules for 3D skeleton-based action recognition [15]. Like these two proposed models, we exploit autoencoder convolutional autoencoder, and temporal (GRU) autoencoder in our experiments. The convolutional autoencoder allows us to capture spatial features effectively, while the temporal autoencoder (GRU autoencoder) enables us to model the temporal dynamics of the actions. Cheng et al., proposes a novel unsupervised learning framework called Hierarchical Transformer for skeleton-based human action recognition. This framework utilizes hierarchically aggregated self-attention modules to effectively capture both spatial and temporal structures in skeleton sequences [18]. Zhou et al. proposes a novel framework for unsupervised representation learning using a structure-asymmetrical auto-encoder in which a 2D-CNN-based encoder and RNN-based decoder learns separable spatiotemporal representations in a low-dimensional feature space under the supervision of salient skeleton motion cues [20].

In this study, we tackle the challenging task of unsupervised skeleton action recognition, where we aim to understand and recognize human actions based solely on skeletal data, representing spatial coordinates or joint angles over time. To enhance the recognition performance, we propose a novel approach by combining two different models, resulting in what we refer to as hybrid models. Specifically, we explore the combination of convolutional networks with autoencoders to leverage the strengths of both architectures. The convolutional autoencoder allows us to capture spatial features effectively, while the temporal autoencoder (GRU autoencoder) enables us to model the temporal dynamics of the actions. Additionally, we investigate the combination of transformer architectures with convolutional networks to further improve the recognition accuracy. The transformer excels in capturing long-range dependencies and relationships within the skeletal data, while the convolutional encoder complements this by extracting spatial information. Our experiments involve training and testing six different models: autoencoder, convolutional autoencoder, temporal autoencoder (GRU), transformer, convolutional transformer, and transformer with convolutional encoder. Through these combinations, we demonstrate promising results, showcasing the potential of hybrid models in advancing the field of unsupervised skeleton action recognition.

Convolutional Transformer. The convolutional transformer model combines the strengths of convolutional layers and the transformer architecture. It consists of convolutional layers for capturing spatial patterns and a transformer-based encoder-decoder structure for sequence reconstruction. The convolutional layers extract spatial information, while the transformer components capture long-range dependencies and temporal dynamics. By minimizing the mean squared error loss, the model achieves accurate sequence reconstruction, leading to improved skeleton action recognition.

Transformer with Convolutional Encoder. The Convolutional Transformer Autoencoder is a hybrid model that combines the strengths of convolutional layers and the Transformer architecture for sequence-to-sequence reconstruction tasks. The input sequence is first passed through a series of convolutional layers to extract spatial patterns and reduce the dimensionality of the data. The resulting feature maps are then reshaped, and positional encoding is applied to introduce positional information. The encoded sequence is passed through the Convolutional Encoder, which employs several convolutional layers to further extract hierarchical representations. This model can serve as a feature extractor for the skeleton temporal dataset. The Convolutional Encoder part captures local temporal patterns, while the Transformer Decoder part captures global dependencies in the skeleton sequences (Fig. 1).

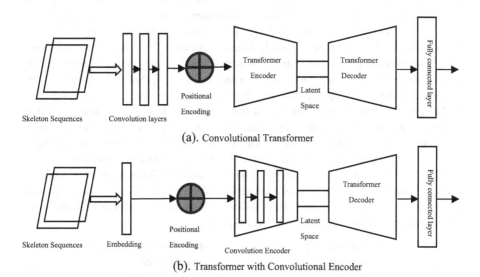

(a). Convolutional Transformer

(b). Transformer with Convolutional Encoder

Fig. 1. Overview of Hybrid Transformer Models

4 Experiments

In our experimental setup, we employed two distinct datasets: the UCLA Skeleton Dataset and the NTU 60 Skeleton Dataset. These datasets were utilized to train and evaluate the performance of our models. The UCLA Skeleton Dataset offered a diverse range of human skeletal data, capturing various poses and motion patterns, while the NTU 60 Skeleton Dataset provided a large-scale collection of 3D skeletal data from multiple camera views, encompassing a wide range of activities and subjects.

During the training process, we set the number of epochs to 100, allowing the model to iteratively learn and optimize its parameters. The learning rate was set to 0.0001, controlling the step size during gradient descent optimization. To update the model's parameters, we employed the Adam optimizer, which efficiently adapts the learning rate based on the gradient's past and current behavior. By utilizing these training configurations and leveraging the rich information present in the UCLA and NTU 60 skeleton datasets, we aimed to train our Convolutional Transformer Autoencoder to effectively learn skeletal representations and reconstruct accurate motion sequences.

4.1 Datasets

NW-UCLA Skeleton Dataset. The Multiview 3D event dataset captured at UCLA and created by Jiang Wang and Xiaohan Nie [21] consists of synchronized RGB, depth, and human skeleton data from three Kinect cameras. This dataset encompasses 10 action categories performed by 10 actors and includes data from multiple viewpoints. Additionally, the dataset features a total of 20 joints, providing detailed information about the skeletal representation of human motion. To ensure consistency and improve the model's performance, we normalize the skeleton data. This normalization process involves scaling the coordinates of the joints within each skeleton sequence. We compute the minimum and maximum values for the x, y, and z coordinates across all frames and joints. Using these values, we rescale each coordinate to a range of $[-1, 1]$. Since the original skeleton sequences have varying lengths, we perform down sampling to create sequences of fixed length. We extract a fixed number of frames from each sequence, ensuring that all sequences have the same length. In our case, we down sampled the sequences to a length of 15 frames. This step helps standardize the input size for the model and facilitates batch processing during training. Finally, we convert the processed data into feature-label pairs. The features consist of the down sampled and normalized skeleton sequences, while the labels are one-hot encoded vectors representing the activity class of each sequence. These pairs are used for training, validation, and testing our Convolutional Transformer Autoencoder model on the UCLA Skeleton dataset.

NTU-60 Skeleton Dataset. The dataset consists of skeletal data captured from depth sensors, providing information about human motion in a three-dimensional space [22]. It includes a total of 60 action classes, covering a diverse range of human activities. These action classes encompass various actions such as walking, sitting, waving, jumping, and more. In terms of joint representation, the NTU 60 A skeleton dataset captures skeletal data from 25 joints. To preprocess the NTU-60 skeleton dataset, the following steps were taken. To ensure uniform sequence lengths, a padding step was performed. If a sequence was shorter than the desired length, zeros were appended to the sequence until the desired length was reached. This step aimed to standardize the sequence length across the dataset. The subsequences were then extracted from the padded sequences using a method called Dynamic Key Frames. In the case of training, frames were chosen based on joint movement/activity scores. The frames with the highest scores, up to a maximum of 30 frames or the desired number of segments, were selected. For validation and testing, multiple segments with the highest joint movement/activity scores were chosen, and each segment was added to the dataset multiple times. By performing these preprocessing steps, the NTU-60 skeleton dataset was transformed into subsequences that captured Dynamic Key Frames. These subsequences contained frames with noticeable changes in joint positions, providing valuable information for further analysis and model training.

4.2   Results Analysis and Comparisons

In the "Analysis and Comparison" section, a comprehensive evaluation was conducted on the UCLA and NTU 60 skeleton datasets using six models: Autoencoder, Convolutional Autoencoder, Temporal Autoencoder (GRU Autoencoder), Transformer, and the hybrid models: Convolutional Autoencoder and Transformer with Convolutional Encoder. In our study, we employed the KNN classifier [23] to classify actions in skeleton datasets. To accomplish this, we trained the KNN classifier using the extracted features from the training dataset, obtained through various unsupervised learning models. For the UCLA dataset, which consisted of 10 action classes, and the NTU-60 dataset, which had 60 action classes, we ensured that the training data accurately represented the action diversity present in each dataset. This allowed us to assess the classification accuracy and effectiveness of the KNN classifier in correctly assigning action labels to previously unseen skeleton sequences (Table 1).

Table 1.   Accuracy Comparison of different models on testing datasets

No	Model	UCLA Dataset	NTU 60 Dataset	
		Classification Accuracy (%)	Cross View Classification Accuracy (%)	Cross Subject Classification Accuracy (%)
1	Autoencoder	57%	25%	30%
2	Convolutional Autoencoder	36%	38%	37%
3	Temporal Autoencoder (GRU)	63%	21%	27%
4	Transformer	48%	79%	77%
5	Convolutional Transformer	60%	61.5%	39%
6	Transformer with Convolutional Encoder	**73%**	**88.3%**	**88%**

The hybrid Transformer model stood out as the most efficient and effective one with 73% based on the results obtained. The Convolutional Transformer demonstrated superior performance in various aspects, such as reconstruction accuracy, capturing important motion dynamics, and accurate classification of actions. And the ordinary autoencoder is still on the margin of reasonable practice. Furthermore, the analysis revealed that the hybrid models, specifically the Convolutional Autoencoder and Transformer with Convolutional Encoder, showcased promising results in skeleton action recognition. These hybrid models, which combine the strengths of both Convolutional Neural Networks (CNNs) and Transformers, exhibited improved performance compared to the other individual models. This finding highlights the advantages of leveraging the combined power of both convolutional and transformer-based architectures in capturing spatial and temporal features from the skeleton data, leading to enhanced action recognition capabilities.

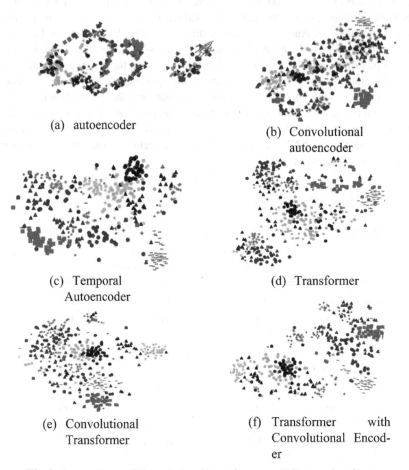

(a) autoencoder

(b) Convolutional autoencoder

(c) Temporal Autoencoder

(d) Transformer

(e) Convolutional Transformer

(f) Transformer with Convolutional Encoder

Fig. 2. Latent Space of Convolutional Transformer on UCLA testing dataset

We show the t-SNE visualization result of learned representation in Fig. 2, where n-dimensional vectors are represented as 2-Dimensional latent space. Same actions were clustered together in the feature space. Depending on the learning models, the clustering tendency may differ. According to the results as shown in Fig. 2(e) and (f), the 10 different color dots are well clustered in hybrid models in which each color dot represents a single action.

The input and output of respective models are visualized in skeleton structures as shown in Fig. 3. It is clear that inputs and outputs have high rate of similarity by visual comparisons. This means models can learn clearly on respective skeleton data sequences.

To visualize and analyze the classification results, we utilized the confusion matrix, a powerful tool that displays the predicted labels against the true labels. The confusion

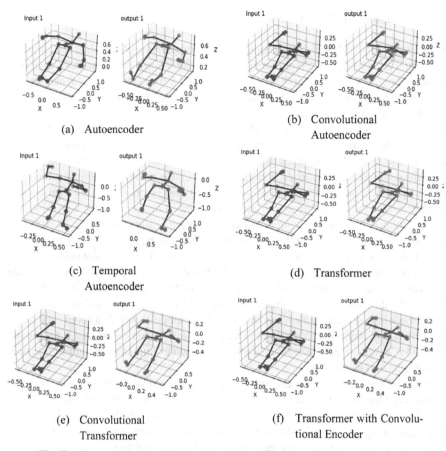

(a) Autoencoder

(b) Convolutional Autoencoder

(c) Temporal Autoencoder

(d) Transformer

(e) Convolutional Transformer

(f) Transformer with Convolutional Encoder

Fig. 3. Input and output of Convolutional Transformer on UCLA testing dataset

matrix provided a comprehensive overview of the classification performance, highlighting any potential misclassifications or patterns in the predictions. The visualization of the confusion matrix offered a clear representation of how well the KNN classifier was able to differentiate and classify actions in the tested datasets. These findings contribute to a deeper understanding of the effectiveness of the KNN classifier in action recognition tasks and provide valuable information for further improvements and optimizations in skeleton-based action recognition systems. The results from the evaluation emphasize the effectiveness and superiority of the hybrid models, particularly the Convolutional Transformer, in skeleton action recognition. The findings provide valuable insights into the potential of utilizing hybrid architectures for improved performance in this domain, enabling more accurate and efficient analysis of human actions based on skeletal data.

5   Conclusion and Future Works

In conclusion, we conducted a comprehensive comparison of six different models, including Autoencoder, Convolutional Autoencoder, Temporal Autoencoder (GRU Autoencoder), Transformer, and the hybrid models: Convolutional Autoencoder and Transformer with Convolutional Encoder. Our evaluation focused on their performance in skeleton action recognition using the UCLA and NTU 60 skeleton datasets. Based on the analysis of the results, the hybrid models emerged as the superior performers among the evaluated models. Specifically, the Convolutional Transformer model exhibited the most efficient and effective performance across various evaluation metrics. This model demonstrated exceptional reconstruction accuracy, robust capturing of motion dynamics, and accurate classification of actions. Furthermore, the hybrid models, particularly the Convolutional Autoencoder and Transformer with Convolutional Encoder, outperformed the individual models in skeleton action recognition. The findings from our comparison highlight the significance of employing hybrid models in skeleton action recognition tasks. Leveraging the complementary abilities of convolutional and transformer-based architectures, the hybrid models demonstrated superior performance by effectively capturing both spatial and temporal features inherent in skeletal data.

Overall, the comparison of these six models revealed the promising potential of hybrid models in skeleton action recognition. These models provide a robust and accurate approach to analyze and understand human actions based on skeletal data, paving the way for advancements in various applications such as human-computer interaction, surveillance, and healthcare.

As future work, there are several promising directions to explore based on the findings of this study. One avenue is to develop a novel model by combining the advantages of each individual model evaluated in this study. This hybrid model could potentially achieve even higher accuracy and robustness in skeleton action recognition tasks. Additionally, extending the experiments to different datasets and data modalities holds great potential for further research. Testing the models on diverse datasets enables a comprehensive evaluation of their generalization capabilities and performance across various scenarios. Furthermore, investigating the transferability of the models to different domains or tasks would be valuable. Training the models on different datasets, particularly those involving different action categories or varying contexts, can provide insights into their adaptability and scalability. This exploration would contribute to the development of more versatile and robust models for real-world applications. In summary, future work could involve the development of a hybrid model that combines the strengths of different models, exploring different datasets and data modalities, and assessing the transferability of the models to new domains. These directions offer exciting opportunities to advance the field of skeleton action recognition and enhance its practical applications.

References

1. Vrigkas, M., Nikou, C., Kakadiaris, I.A.: A review of human activity recognition methods. Front. Robot. AI **2**, 28 (2015)
2. Wang, P., Li, W., Li, C., Hou, Y.: Action recognition based on joint trajectory maps with convolutional neural networks. Knowl.-Based Syst. **158**, 43–53 (2018)

3. Yuanyuan, S., Yunan, L., Xiaolong, F., Kaibin, M., Qiguang, M.: Review of dynamic gesture recognition. Virtual Reality Intell. Hardw. **3**(3), 183–206 (2021)
4. Caetano, C., Sena, J., Bremond, F., Dos Santos, J.A., Schwartz, W.R.: SkeleMotion: a new representation of skeleton joint sequences based on motion information for 3D action recognition. In: 16th IEEE International Conference on Advanced Video and Signal Based Surveillance (AVSS), pp. 1–8. IEEE (2019)
5. Hou, Y., Li, Z., Wang, P., Li, W.: Skeleton optical spectra-based action recognition using convolutional neural networks. IEEE Trans. Circ. Syst. Video Technol. **28**(3), 807–811 (2016)
6. Zhang, H., Hou, Y., Wang, P., Guo, Z., Li., W.: SAR-NAS: skeleton-based action recognition via neural architecture searching. J. Vis. Commun. Image Represent. 73, 102942 (2020)
7. Zhao, X., et al.: Structured streaming skeleton – a new feature for online human gesture recognition. ACM Trans. Multimedia Comput. Commun. Appl. **11**(1), Article 22 (2014). 18 pages
8. Bloom, V., Makris, D., Argyriou, V.: G3D: a gaming action dataset and real time action recognition evaluation framework. In: IEEE Computer Society Conference on Computer Vision and Pattern Recognition Workshops, pp. 7–12 (2012)
9. Chen, C., Jafari R., Kehtarnavaz, N.: UTD-MHAD: a multimodal dataset for human action recognition utilizing a depth camera and a wearable inertial sensor. In: IEEE International Conference on Image Processing (ICIP), Quebec City, QC, Canada, pp. 168–172 (2015)
10. Li, C., Hou, Y., Wang P., Li, W.: Joint distance maps based action recognition with convolutional neural networks. IEEE Sig. Process. Lett. **24**(5), 624–628 (2017)
11. Pham, H., Khoudour, L., Crouzil, A., Zegers, P., Velastin, S.A.: Exploiting deep residual networks for human action recognition from skeletal data. Comput. Vis. Image Underst. **170**, 51–66 (2018)
12. Verma, P., Sah, A., Srivastava, R.: Deep learning-based multi-modal approach using RGB and skeleton sequences for human activity recognition. Multimedia Syst. **26**(6), 671–685 (2020)
13. Tomas, A., Biswas, K.: Human activity recognition using combined deep architectures. In: IEEE 2nd International Conference on Signal and Image Processing (ICSIP), pp. 41–45. IEEE (2017)
14. Juanhui, T., Hong, L., Fanyang, M., Mengyuan, L., Runwei, D.: Spatial-temporal data augmentation based on LSTM autoencoder network for skeleton-based human action recognition. In: 25th IEEE International Conference on Image Processing (ICIP), Athens, Greece, pp. 3478–3482 (2018)
15. Khezerlou, F., Baradarani, A., Balafar, M.A.: A convolutional autoencoder model with weighted multi-scale attention modules for 3D skeleton-based action recognition. J. Vis. Commun. Image Represent. **92**, 103781 (2023)
16. He, J., Gao, S.: TBSN: sparse-transformer based Siamese network for few-shot action recognition. In: 2021 2nd Information Communication Technologies Conference (ICTC), pp. 47–53. IEEE (2021)
17. Li, S., Li, W., Cook, C., Gao, Y.: Deep independently recurrent neural network (INDRNN). arXiv preprint arXiv:1910.06251 (2019)
18. Cheng, Y.B., Chen, X., Chen, J., Wei, P., Zhang, D., Lin, L.: Hierarchical transformer: Unsupervised representation learning for skeleton-based human action recognition. In: 2021 IEEE International Conference on Multimedia and Expo (ICME), pp. 1–6. IEEE (2021)
19. Plizzari, C., Cannici, M., Matteucci, M.: Skeleton-based action recognition via spatial and temporal transformer networks. Comput. Vis. Image Underst. **208**, 103219 (2021)
20. Zhou, J., Komuro, T.: An asymmetrical-structure auto-encoder for unsupervised representation learning of skeleton sequences. Comput. Vis. Image Underst. **222**, 103491 (2022)
21. Northwestern-UCLA Multiview Action 3D Skeleton Dataset Homepage. https://wangjiangb. github.io/my_data.html. Accessed 28 June 2023

22. Action Recognition Datasets: "NTU RGB+D" Dataset (NTU-60 Dataset) Homepage. https://rose1.ntu.edu.sg/dataset/actionRecognition. Accessed 30 June 2023
23. Paramasivam, K., Sindha, M.M.R., Balakrishnan, S.B.: KNN-based machine learning classifier used on deep learned spatial motion features for human action recognition. Entropy **25**, 844 (2023). https://doi.org/10.3390/e25060844

Local and Global Context Reasoning for Spatio-Temporal Action Localization

Ryuhei Ando[✉], Yasunori Babazaki, and Katsuhiko Takahashi

NEC Visual Intelligence Research Laboratories, Kawasaki, Japan
{ryu-ando,y_babazaki,katsuhiko.takahashi}@nec.com

Abstract. Localizing persons and recognizing their actions from videos is an essential task in video understanding. Recent advances have been made by reasoning the relationships between the actor and another actor, as well as between the actor and the environment. However, reasoning the relationships globally over the image is not always the efficient way, and there are cases that locally searching for the relative clues is more suitable. In this paper, we move one step further and model the relationship between an actor and the actor's relevant surrounding context. We developed a pipeline that observes over the full image to collect context information globally and around the actor to collect context information locally. This is achieved by implementing a Near-Actor Relation Network (NARN) that focuses on reasoning the context information locally. Two key components of our NARN enable the effective accumulation of the local context information: pose encoding, which encodes the human pose information as an additional feature, and spatial attention, which discriminates the relative context information from the others. Our pipeline accumulates the global and local relation information and gathers them for the final action classification. Experimental results on the JHMDB21 and AVA datasets demonstate that our proposed pipeline outperforms a baseline approach that only reasons about the global context. Visualization of the learned attention map indicates that our pipeline is able to focus on spatial areas that contains relative context information for each action.

Keywords: Action Detection · Video Understanding · Context Reasoning

1 Introduction

Action detection or spatial-temporal action localization aims at localizing persons and recognizing their actions from videos. Since this is an essential task in video understanding, it has drawn enormous research attention over recent years [5,7,8,13,20]. In contrast to object detection which can be done solely based on the visual appearance of each actor, action identification using just visual appearance is difficult in many cases. Even for the human eye, it is difficult to understand what actions are being performed by the actor if the information is

© The Author(s), under exclusive license to Springer Nature Switzerland AG 2023
G. Bebis et al. (Eds.): ISVC 2023, LNCS 14361, pp. 147–159, 2023.
https://doi.org/10.1007/978-3-031-47969-4_12

limited, e.g. if an image is cropped by the actor's bounding box. Therefore, many works have investigated the usage of other clues for recognizing actions by reasoning about the actors' interactions with surrounding context, which includes the environment, other people, and objects. Recent works [13,16,17] on reasoning the relationship between the actor and the environment, as well as reasoning between the actor and another actor, have successfully boosted the performance of action detection. The conventional approach for action detection is depicted in Fig. 1(a). Most of these methods utilize full images for reasoning the relationship between the actor and the environment.

However, observing the full image globally for reasoning about the actors' interactions with the surrounding context is not always the most efficient way, and locally searching for those clues is more suitable for solving the task. Since a context that has a relationship with the actor is most likely to be near the actor, it is simpler and more efficient to search near the actor for the clue to infer the action than to search over the whole image. Of course, there are also situations where we are not able to find either relevant object or the environment around the actor, in which case looking over the entire image is required. For example, actions like swinging baseball bat needs to recognize the baseball bat that the actor is holding, which is likely to be placed near the actor. In this situation, it is more efficient to look around the actor rather than the whole image to recognize the baseball bat. On the other hand, there are actions like throwing a ball, which needs to recognize the ball. This ball can be either near the actor or far from the actor if the ball is already thrown. Thus, combining both approach is vital for efficient action detection.

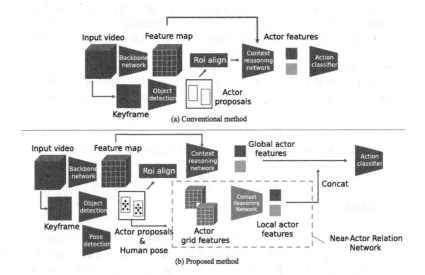

Fig. 1. (a) conventional method of action detection with context reasoning. (b) proposed method of local context reasoning with Near-Actor Relation Network

In this paper, we propose an hybrid action detection pipeline that observes over the full image for global context information and the surrounding of the bounding box for local context information. We implemented a Near-Actor Relation Network (NARN) that focuses on reasoning the context information placed near the actor. Our pipeline expands the detected person bounding box and create a feature map for each actor to search for context information near the actor. Motivated by the recent work that utilizes human pose information for action recognition [2,14], we utilize the human pose as support feature as pose information contains dense spatial information of the actor which can be used as the clue for reasoning the relative context more precisely. We also gather the context information that is related to the actor and exclude the information that is not, by introducing a masking architecture to discriminate between the two. The proposed pipeline is depicted in Fig. 1(b). Our NARN is implemented along the ACAR-Net (Actor Context Relation Network), which is a typical model that collects the context information globally with state-of-the-art performance in action detection. In contrast, our NARN is responsible for gathering the local context information.

We conducted experiments on the JHMDB21 dataset [9] as well as the Atomic Visual Actions (AVA) dataset [8] for spatio-temporal action localization. Our proposed method with NARN outperformed the baseline approach, which only utilizes the global context information. We also visualize the attention map produced by the NARN.

Our contributions are as follows:

- We propose to model a hybrid approach of reasoning about local and global context information for spatio-temporal action localization. Context information located near the actor was not treated properly by the previous methods, which is important for achieving high accuracy.
- We developed a Near-Actor Relation Network for collecting the local context information. This is realized by the two main operations in this module, which is pose encoding and spatial attention.
- We evaluated our hybrid pipeline on the JHMDB21 and AVA datasets. From the experiment, we confirmed a gain of our hybrid pipeline over the baseline methods.

2 Related Works

Action Recognition. Research on action recognition can be categorized into three types: action classification, temporal localization, and spatio-temporal action localization. Early works mainly focused on classifying a short video clip into an action class. For the backbone network architecture, 3D-CNN [5,18], a two-stream network [6,15], and 2D-CNN [12] have been the three dominant models. As the research on classifying short video clips progresses, the research focus has shifted to understanding longer videos. This requires not only recognizing the category, but also locating the start and end time of the action instance. Many works [3,21] have relied on temporal proposals and classification approaches by extending object detection frameworks to the 1D temporal dimension. More recently, with the advancements in transformer architectures, there has been greater focus placed on transformer backbones [1,4,7].

Spatial-Temporal Action Detection. A more detailed grasp of the actions in video requires an understanding of not only time but also space, which is known as spatial-temporal action localization. This task can be considered as a finer version of object detection, since the action instances need to be localized in both space and time. Many approaches for spatio-temporal action localization employ state-of-the-art object detectors on 3D-CNN video features [8,11,22]. Several researches shows that taking temporal information into account properly is effective [13,16,20].

Context Reasoning for Action Recognition. Rather than temporal information, incorporating context information such as interaction with human, objects, and the surrounding scene has gathered attention. Most of the time, recognizing the action of an actor depends on the actor's relationship with other actors and objects, so this is a straight-forward process. Sun *et al.* [16] proposed Actor-Centric Relation Network, which computes and accumulates relation information from the actor and global scene features, and then generates relation features for action classification. Girdhar *et al.* [7] proposed the Action Transformer Network for encoding the pairwise relationship between actors using the Transformer-style architecture. Tang *et al.* [17] proposed the Asynchronous Interaction Aggregation Network, which leverages three kinds of interactions by aggregating different types of interaction with an Interaction Aggregation structure. Pan *et al.* [13] proposed the Actor-Context-Actor Relation Network for improving spatio-temporal action localization by explicitly reasoning about higher-order relations between actors and context. However, in these approaches, the image is searched globally for reasoning about the actors' interaction with the context. In contrast, our proposed method looks around the detected actor's bounding box for useful context information, which we define as the local context. Since, utilizing the local context information is not always possible, we combine the conventional global context feature with the local context feature to obtain the final prediction.

3   Proposed Method

In this section we describe our method for reasoning about the actors' interaction with the surrounding context in both globally and locally. Our pipeline aims at modeling and aggregating global and local actor-context relations for achieving accurate action detection.

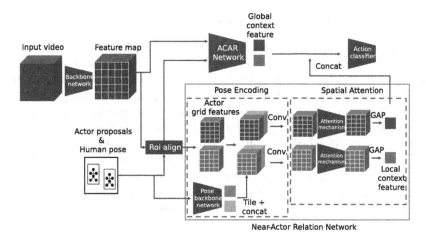

Fig. 2. Overall pipeline. Videos are processed with a backbone network to produce spatio-temporal feature maps. For each actor proposal, we extract features from the feature maps by RoiAlign operation. Actor features and feature maps are then processed to compute global context features by ACAR. Given the actor proposal, feature map, and pose, the Near-Actor Relation Network encodes pose information and computes the local relation between the actor and surrounding context.

3.1 Overall Pipeline

We first introduce our overall pipeline for action detection, where the local actor-context relation modeling module is the essential component. The overall scheme of the proposed pipeline is presented in Fig. 2. The pipeline takes a video clip as an input and estimates the action labels of all persons in the video. The framework of the following state-of-the-art methods is built on an off-the-shelf person detector and a video backbone network, and the ACAR module (Actor-Context-Actor Relation module) further processes the person and context features for the final action prediction.

Technically, the pipeline focuses on predicting the action labels of the person detected by the person detector on the center frame (i.e., key frame) of the input video clip. The input video clip is first sent to the video backbone network to extract the spatial-temporal feature. Then, the feature is spatially cropped by the bounding box of the detected person (actor) by the RoIAlign operation with a 7×7 spatial output and squeezed temporally by the average pooling operation. Finally, the MaxPool operation is applied to produce N actor feature $A^i \in \mathbb{R}^C$, which $0 < i < N$. The output of the video backbone results in a video feature map $X \in \mathbb{R}^{C \times H \times W}$, where C, H, and W are the channel, height, and width respectively. The ACAR module utilizes the video feature map and actor feature to calculate the actor-context-actor relation feature $F_g \in \mathbb{R}^d$, which we call it a global context feature.

3.2   Near-Actor Relation Network

The proposed Near-Actor Context Relation Network (NARN) is described in Fig 2. The NARN module is positioned next to the ACAR module in our pipeline. Our module takes the actor grid feature map $A_g^i \in \mathbb{R}^{C \times H \times W}$ and human pose $P^i \in \mathbb{R}^{J \times 2}$, where J is the number of joints in the pose (17 in this paper) taken as inputs. The output is the local context feature. This module encodes the local context feature information by obtaining the actor feature before the MaxPool operation is applied, which we call the actor grid feature. We assume that the relevant context information often lies near the actor, therefore we reason about those context relation using the actor grid feature. As mentioned earlier, the NARN module has two main operations: pose encoding and spatial masking. These two operations are described in detail in the following subsections.

Pose Encoding. We utilize the pose encoding operation to encode the human pose information as additional information for context reasoning. The pose information is also expected to give the model a clue as to what spatial area it should focus on.

This operation takes the actor grid feature map and human pose as input and outputs the pose-actor grid feature. The actor grid feature map is obtained by spatially cropping by the bounding box of the detected actor using the RoIAlign operation with a 14×20 spatial output and is then squeezed temporally by the average pooling operation to calculate actor grid feature map $A_g^i \in \mathbb{R}^{C \times H_g \times W_g}$, where H_g, W_g are the height and width of the actor grid feature map. To capture the local context that lies near the actor, we expand and add offsets to the bounding box. Specifically, the bounding box for each actor is expanded by the ratio r for the height direction and width direction. We set r to 1.2 in this paper. Then, an offset is added to the bounding boxes in the height or width direction to create a square bounding box. For example, if the width is shorter than the height, an offset is added to the width direction to make the width and height the same. After, the bounding boxes is clipped by the image size to make sure the box is inside the image region. In constrast to actor feature A^i, the MaxPool operation is not applied for creating actor grid feature map A_g^i so as to retain the spatial information. The human pose P^i is processed to pose backbone network to produce the human pose feature $P'^i \in \mathbb{R}^C$.

For the Actor-Centric Relation Network(ACRN) in the ACAR module, we developed a similar architecture for encoding local context relations by combining the human pose features P'^i with the actor grid feature map A^i. Specifically, the module copies each human pose feature $P'^i \in \mathbb{R}^C$ to each spatial location of the actor grid feature map $A_g^i \in \mathbb{R}^{C \times H \times W}$ and concatenates towards the channel dimension. The feature is further processed to convolution layers to reduce the channel dimensions, resulting in pose-actor grid features $F \in \mathbb{R}^{C \times H_g \times W_g}$.

Spatial Attention. We employ the spatial masking operation to create a contrast between the relevant context information and the others. Inspired by the recent attention mechanism, we developed a similar architecture to create an attention map that operates as a mask to discriminate the relevant context information. The scheme of this operation is depicted in Fig. 3.

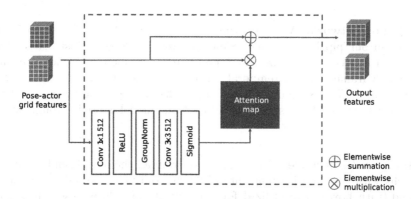

Fig. 3. Spatial attention operation to compute an attention map that indicates the local position of relevant context information. The attention map has the same spatial shape as the input features.

This operation takes the pose-actor grid features $F \in \mathbb{R}^{C \times H_g \times W_g}$ as input and outputs the feature map that has the same size as the input. Our idea here is to take advantage of the attention mechanism and filter the relevant features in the feature map that are important to infer the actor's action.

The attention is obtained by calculating an attention location to an attention map. To generate an attention map, we simply build a top layer based on a convolution layer and normalization layer.

4   Experiments on JHMDB21

The JHMDB21 dataset [9] contains 928 videos with 21 actions. The videos are temporally trimmed to clips and have three training/validation splits. This dataset includes one human actor with one action on each video clip. We utilized the first split of the training/validation splits in this paper. We report the frame-level mean average precision with an intersection-over-union (IOU) threshold of 0.5.

4.1   Implementation Details

Person and Pose Detector. For person detection on JHMDB21, we used the human detection results generated by the Yolov5 object detector [10], specifically the Yolov5x model. The model is pre-trained with the COCO dataset, and fine-tuned on the JHMDB21 training split dataset. We used the HRNet [19] as a pose detector. For the pose backbone network, we used GCN-based model similar to [23] to convert the keypoint coordinate to vector. Keypoint coordinate is normalized in a person-wise manner to account for translation with its neck joint.

Backbone Network. We used the SlowFast network [5] as the backbone network in our pipeline, which is SlowFast ResNet-50 8×8 instatiation pre-trained on Kinetics400 dataset. The inputs are 64-frame clips, where we sample $T = 8$ frames with a temporal stride $\tau = 8$ for the slow pathway and $\alpha T = 32(\alpha = 4, T = 8)$ frames for the fast pathway. Frames are repeated if the clip has less than 64 frames. The same backbone model is used throughout the paper.

Training and Inference. For training, we train all the models end-to-end for 6 epochs with the base learning rate of 0.0008 and used the batch size of 16. Ground-truth boxes were utilized for training. As in [13], we use softmax for pose actions and sigmoid for others before binary cross-entropy loss for training. For inference, we used the detected person boxes with detection scores greater than 0.7 for action classification.

4.2   Comparison on JHMDB21

We compare our pipeline with the baseline methods on the validation set of JHMDB21. We used the ResNet50 backbone here for feature extraction. The results are listed in Table 1. All the experiments were trained and inferenced at our environment. We conducted two types of setting on validation dataset, which is oracle and inference setting. We used the ground-truth bounding box as a person proposal when oracle, and bounding box generated by object detection model when inference. Under the oracle setting, our method achieved 83.10 mAP, which is a better performance than the result of the comparison method (ACAR). Note that the ACAR utilized in this experiment only includes the higher-order relation reasoning operator module and does not include the actor-context feature bank module, since the source code provided by [13] did not include the module. Under the inference setting, our method acheived 68.29 mAP, which is also a better performance than ACAR.

4.3   Ablation Study

We conducted ablation experiments to investigate the effect of different components in our pipeline on the JHMDB21 dataset. To validate the design of the proposed method, we ablated the impacts of different components of our NARN module as shown in Table 2. After removing both the pose encoding and spatial attention operation, it achieved 82.84 mAP. This result is still better than the result with onlty global features in Table 2, indicating that merging local context information with global context information has a positive effect on action

Table 1. Results on JHMDB21 dataset (pretrained on Kinetics400). Input indicates the input data type to the model (V and P refer to visual frame and pose, respectively). Data row indicates the person bounding box used for validation set (oracle and inference respectively refer to the ground truth bounding box and inferred bounding box computed by the object detection model).

Model	Input	Data	Val mAP
ResNet50	V	Oracle	79.84
ACAR (HR^{2}O)	V	Oracle	82.17
ACAR (HR^{2}O) + NARN (Ours)	V + P	Oracle	**83.10**
ResNet50	V	Inference	65.37
ACAR (HR^{2}O)	V	Inference	67.29
ACAR (HR^{2}O) + NARN (Ours)	V + P	Inference	**68.29**

detection. Adding the pose encoding and spatial attention operations, also has a positive effect on both the oracle and inference setting. As seen in the table, we see that by adding both components at the same time achieves the best accuracy in both the oracle and inference setting.

Table 2. Ablation study on proposed method. Checkmark indicates on/off of the options in the model. Global only indicates the model with only glabal features. Other rows are the same as Table 1.

Global only	Pose encoding	Spatial attention	Input	Data	Val mAP
✓			V	Oracle	82.17
			V	Oracle	82.84
		✓	V	Oracle	82.96
	✓		V + P	Oracle	82.89
	✓	✓	V + P	Oracle	**83.10**
✓			V	Inference	67.29
			V	Inference	67.93
		✓	V	Inference	67.97
	✓		V + P	Inference	68.15
	✓	✓	V + P	Inference	**68.29**

4.4 Qualitative Results

Our NARN generates an attention map that indicates the local position of relevant context information. We visualize the attention map to check the effect of this module for capturing the local context information. The visualization results are shown in Fig. 4. We can observe that the attended regions usually include the actor, actor's body parts, and objects being interacted by the actor. We can see that NARN successfully gathers the local information as intended.

    (a) Kick ball (0.9949)   (b) Pour (0.9457)   (c) Swing baseball (0.9839)

    (d) Golf (0.9930)   (e) Shoot bow (1.0)

Fig. 4. Visualization results of the attention map in our Near-Actor Relation Network (NARN). Heat maps illustrate the attended regions by the model. Red region indicates the high attended area and blue region indicates the low attended area. (Color figure online)

5   Experiments on AVA

The Atomic Visual Actions(AVA) dataset [8] is a video dataset built for spatio-temporal action detection. The dataset consists of 430 videos, 299 for train and the remaining 131 for test. In this dataset, box annotations and their corresponding action labels are provided on keyframes, which are defined with a temporal stride of 1 s over a 15-minutes video. This dataset includes multiple human actors with multiple actions on each video clip. We use the AVA version 2.2 benchmark.

5.1   Implementation Details

We used a similar setting to that in [13] for training. Specifically, we train the model end-to-end for 6 epochs with a base learning rate of 0.064 at batch size 32. For person detection on keyframes, we used the human detection boxes provided by Pan *et al.* [13].

5.2 Comparison on AVA

We compare our pipeline with the baseline method on the AVA v2.2 dataset. The results of the comparison are shown in Table 3. All the experiments were trained and inferenced at our environment. Our method achieved 27.40 mAP, which is a better performance than the comparison method.

Table 3. Results on AVA dataset (pretrained on Kinetics400)

Model	Input	Val mAP
ACAR (HR^2O)	V	27.19
ACAR (HR^2O) + NARN (Ours)	V + P	27.40

6 Conclusion

In this paper, we proposed the Near-Actor Relation Network (NARN), to determine the relevant local context elements characterizing an actor's action in videos. With this module, we built a pipeline that can aggregate the actor's global context information and local context information simultaneously. We evaluated the accuracy of NARN and the whole pipeline for action detection and demonstated its effectiveness. Future work will include more precise context reasoning for the situations where the relevant context information is occluded.

References

1. Arnab, A., Dehghani, M., Heigold, G., Sun, C., Lučić, M., Schmid, C.: ViViT: a video vision transformer. In: Proceedings of the International Conference on Computer Vision (ICCV), pp. 6836–6846 (2021)
2. Choutas, V., Weinzaepfel, P., Revaud, J., Schmid, C.: PoTion: pose motion representation for action recognition. In: Proceedings of the Conference on Computer Vision and Pattern Recognition (CVPR), pp. 7024–7033 (2018)
3. Dai, X., Singh, B., Zhang, G., Davis, L.S., Qiu Chen, Y.: Temporal context network for activity localization in videos. In: Proceedings of the International Conference on Computer Vision (ICCV), pp. 5793–5802 (2017)
4. Fan, H., et al.: Multiscale vision transformers. In: Proceedings of the International Conference on Computer Vision (ICCV), pp. 6824–6835 (2021)
5. Feichtenhofer, C., Fan, H., Malik, J., He, K.: Slowfast networks for video recognition. In: Proceedings of the International Conference on Computer Vision (ICCV), pp. 6202–6211 (2019)
6. Feichtenhofer, C., Pinz, A., Zisserman, A.: Convolutional two-stream network fusion for video action recognition. In: Proceedings of the Conference on Computer Vision and Pattern Recognition (CVPR), pp. 1933–1941 (2016)

7. Girdhar, R., Carreira, J., Doersch, C., Zisserman, A.: Video action transformer network. In: Proceedings of the Conference on Computer Vision and Pattern Recognition (CVPR), pp. 244–253 (2019)

8. Gu, C., et al.: AVA: a video dataset of spatio-temporally localized atomic visual actions. In: Proceedings of the Conference on Computer Vision and Pattern Recognition (CVPR), pp. 6047–6056 (2018)

9. Jhuang, H., Gall, J., Zuffi, S., Schmid, C., Black, M.J.: Towards understanding action recognition. In: Proceedings of the International Conference on Computer Vision (ICCV), pp. 3192–3199 (2013)

10. Jocher, G.: YOLOv5 by Ultralytics (2020). https://doi.org/10.5281/zenodo.3908559, https://github.com/ultralytics/yolov5. Accessed July 2023

11. Li, D., Qiu, Z., Dai, Q., Yao, T., Mei, T.: Recurrent tubelet proposal and recognition networks for action detection. In: Proceedings of the European Conference on Computer Vision (ECCV), pp. 303–318 (2018)

12. Lin, J., Gan, C., Han, S.: TSM: temporal shift module for efficient video understanding. In: Proceedings of the International Conference on Computer Vision (CVPR), pp. 7083–7093 (2019)

13. Pan, J., Chen, S., Shou, M.Z., Liu, Y., Shao, J., Li, H.: Actor-context-actor relation network for spatio-temporal action localization. In: Proceedings of the IEEE/CVF Conference on Computer Vision and Pattern Recognition (CVPR), pp. 464–474 (2021)

14. Rajasegaran, J., Pavlakos, G., Kanazawa, A., Feichtenhofer, C., Malik, J.: On the benefits of 3D pose and tracking for human action recognition. In: Proceedings of the Conference on Computer Vision and Pattern Recognition (CVPR), pp. 640–649 (2023)

15. Simonyan, K., Zisserman, A.: Two-stream convolutional networks for action recognition in videos. In: Advances in Neural Information Processing Systems (NeurIPS), vol. 27 (2014)

16. Sun, C., Shrivastava, A., Vondrick, C., Murphy, K., Sukthankar, R., Schmid, C.: Actor-centric relation network. In: Proceedings of the European Conference on Computer Vision (ECCV), pp. 318–334 (2018)

17. Tang, J., Xia, J., Mu, X., Pang, B., Lu, C.: Asynchronous interaction aggregation for action detection. In: Vedaldi, A., Bischof, H., Brox, T., Frahm, J.-M. (eds.) ECCV 2020. LNCS, vol. 12360, pp. 71–87. Springer, Cham (2020). https://doi.org/10.1007/978-3-030-58555-6_5

18. Tran, D., Bourdev, L., Fergus, R., Torresani, L., Paluri, M.: Learning spatiotemporal features with 3D convolutional networks. In: Proceedings of the International Conference on Computer Vision (ICCV), pp. 4489–4497 (2015)

19. Wang, J., Sun, K., Cheng, T., Jiang, B., Deng, C., Zhao, Y., Liu, D., Mu, Y., Tan, M., Wang, X., et al.: Deep high-resolution representation learning for visual recognition. IEEE Trans. Pattern Anal. Mach. Intell. (PAMI) 43(10), 3349–3364 (2020)

20. Wu, C.Y., Feichtenhofer, C., Fan, H., He, K., Krahenbuhl, P., Girshick, R.: Long-term feature banks for detailed video understanding. In: Proceedings of the Conference on Computer Vision and Pattern Recognition (CVPR), pp. 284–293 (2019)

21. Xu, H., Das, A., Saenko, K.: R-C3D: Region convolutional 3D network for temporal activity detection. In: Proceedings of the International Conference on Computer Vision (CVPR), pp. 5783–5792 (2017)

22. Yang, X., Yang, X., Liu, M.Y., Xiao, F., Davis, L.S., Kautz, J.: STEP: spatio-temporal progressive learning for video action detection. In: Proceedings of the Conference on Computer Vision and Pattern Recognition (CVPR), pp. 264–272 (2019)

23. Zhou, H., et al.: Composer: compositional reasoning of group activity in videos with keypoint-only modality. In: Avidan, S., Brostow, G., Cissé, M., Farinella, G.M., Hassner, T. (eds.) ECCV 2022. LNCS, vol. 13695, pp. 249–266. Springer, Cham (2022). https://doi.org/10.1007/978-3-031-19833-5_15

Zero-Shot Video Moment Retrieval Using BLIP-Based Models

Jobin Idiculla Wattasseril[(✉)] [iD], Sumit Shekhar [iD], Jürgen Döllner [iD],
and Matthias Trapp [iD]

Hasso Plattner Institute, Digital Engineering Faculty, University of Potsdam,
Potsdam, Germany
{jobin.wattasseril,sumit.shekhar,matthias.trapp}@hpi.uni-potsdam.de,
doellner@uni-potsdam.de

Abstract. Video Moment Retrieval (VMR) is a challenging task at the intersection of vision and language, with the goal to retrieve relevant moments from videos corresponding to natural language queries. State-of-the-art approaches for VMR often rely on large amounts of training data including frame-level saliency annotations, weakly supervised pre-training on speech captions, and signals from additional modalities such as audio, which can be limiting in practical scenarios. Moreover, most of these approaches make use of pre-trained spatio-temporal backbones for aggregating temporal features across multiple frames, which incurs significant training and inference costs. To address these limitations, we propose a zero-shot approach with sparse frame-sampling strategies that does not rely on additional modalities and performs well with feature extraction from just individual frames. Our approach uses Bootstrapped Language-Image Pre-training based models (BLIP/BLIP-2), which have been shown to be effective for various downstream vision-language tasks, even in zero-shot settings. We show that such models can be easily repurposed as effective, off-the-shelf feature extractors for VMR. On the QVHighlights benchmark for VMR, our approach outperforms both zero-shot approaches and supervised approaches (without saliency score annotations) by at least 25% and 21% respectively, on all metrics. Further, we also show that our approach is comparable to state-of-the-art supervised approaches trained on saliency score annotations and additional modalities, with a gap of at most 7% across all metrics.

Keywords: Video moment retrieval · Temporal sentence grounding · Video grounding · Natural language video localization · Zero-shot · Vision-Language Pre-trained models · BLIP

1 Introduction

Due to the temporally linear nature of videos, it is often inefficient to locate specific parts-of-interest within videos, e.g., moments when particular objects, persons, or events appear. This problem becomes more severe as videos become

G. Bebis et al. (Eds.): ISVC 2023, LNCS 14361, pp. 160–171, 2023.
https://doi.org/10.1007/978-3-031-47969-4_13

longer and more complex, granular actions occur within short windows of time. Additionally, with the increased rate at which videos are being produced and consumed, there is a need for fast and accurate video retrieval techniques, that can be easily integrated into existing service-based computing environments. The task of localizing and retrieving parts/moments from videos that are described by user-provided natural language queries is referred to as Video Moment Retrieval (VMR) [27], and has important applications in video summarization [9,20], video editing [10,23], and surveillance analysis [3,21].

Current state-of-the-art VMR approaches [11,16,17] rely on a combination of (*i*) weak supervision in the form of Automatic Speech Recognition (ASR) pre-training, (*ii*) saliency score annotations, and (*iii*) training on additional modalities such as audio. These approaches have shown promising results on benchmark datasets, but they suffer from several limitations each. For example, ASR pre-training requires access to a large amount of labeled speech data, which may not be available for all domains. Saliency score annotations are expensive to collect and may not generalize to other datasets or domains. Audio signals may not always be available or reliable, particularly in edited videos or videos with noisy environments. Additionally, in order to model the spatio-temporal dependencies between video frames, existing state-of-the-art approaches use pre-trained spatio-temporal backbones [1,6,24] for temporal feature extraction at the clip-level (extracting and aggregating features from a group of frames). Though such models have shown to exhibit improved performance for downstream tasks, they have the downside of incurring higher training and inference costs than frame-level feature extraction (extracting features from individual frames) [24].

To address these limitations, we propose a zero-shot approach for VMR that does not require weakly supervised pre-training or training on additional modalities and performs feature extraction at the frame-level. We achieve this by (*i*) employing sparse frame sampling strategies, (*ii*) using off-the-shelf Vision-Language Pre-trained (VLP) models [5] as pre-trained feature extractors to compute frame and query embeddings, and (*iii*) performing moment-query matching with simple merging strategies. Specifically, we use a class of VLP models, termed Bootstrapped Language-Image Pre-training (BLIP)-based models [13,14] for encoding frames and input queries, and for computing image-text similarities. These models have exhibited excellent performance on a range of downstream vision-language tasks, and we show that they can be effectively repurposed for VMR.

The main contributions of this paper are as follows: (*i*) We propose a zero-shot approach for VMR that performs efficient frame-level feature extraction using off-the-shelf BLIP-based models and does not require weakly supervised pre-training or training on additional modalities (Fig. 1). (*ii*) We show that our approach beats a vast majority of existing zero-shot and supervised approaches, while being extremely competitive with the state-of-the-art, by evaluating the QVHighlights benchmark dataset for VMR. (*iii*) We conduct a performance analysis based on the length of moments and show that our approach exhibits superior performance compared to the previously best-reported model on retrieving short moments.

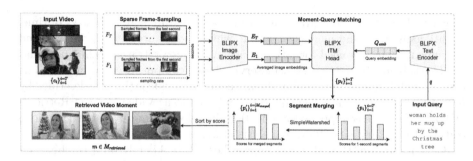

Fig. 1. Overview of our full pipeline. From the input video, frames are sparsely sampled and passed through the BLIPX Image Encoder to get image embeddings for each 1-s segment. The input query is passed to the BLIPX Text Encoder to obtain a query embedding. Scores are generated for each 1-s segment by passing the image embeddings and the query embedding to the BLIPX ITM Head. The segments are then merged, and sorted based on scores to retrieve the top moments.

2   Related Work

Video Moment Retrieval (VMR). Most VMR approaches can be non-exclusively categorized into the following: (i) proposal-based methods, where candidate moments are first proposed, and then ranked by some scoring mechanism [8,28], (ii) proposal-free methods, where the start and end boundaries of moments are directly predicted, without the intermediate step of generating and ranking proposal candidates [7,15], (iii) reinforcement-learning based methods, where VMR is formulated as a sequence decision-making problem, and then solved using deep reinforcement learning techniques [26], and (iv) weakly supervised methods, where instead of using annotations of the starting/ending timestamps of moments, only the video-query pairs are used for training [2,19]. Zhang et al. [27] gives a comprehensive survey of the topic, with regard to the proposed approaches, evaluation methodology, and benchmark datasets.

Zero-Shot VMR with VLP Models. Using VLP models for performing zero-shot VMR has gained some attention lately, with Nam et al. [18] using an off-the-shelf object detector to perform zero-shot VMR training on text corpora and unlabeled video collections. Wang et al. [22] utilize a pre-trained Contrastive LanguageImage Pre-training (CLIP) model along with a prompt learning framework to perform zero-shot VMR. Lei et al. [11] provides a zero-shot baseline for VMR using the CLIP model, which was improved upon by Diwan et al. [4] by using an off-the-shelf video captioning model and shot detection based moment proposals, in conjunction with the CLIP model.

BLIP-Based Models. Li et al. [14] proposed the original BLIP model, introducing a novel VLP framework that enables multi-task pre-training and a new dataset bootstrapping method for learning from noisy image-text pairs, so as to be able to filter out noisy captions from web texts and to generate synthetic captions for web images. Additionally, the model makes use of a custom ITM loss during its training and has a dedicated ITM head (fully connected layer) in its architecture, that can capture the fine-grained alignment between the vision and language modalities. In their subsequent work, Li et al. [13] improve upon this with the BLIP-2 model, extending their dataset bootstrapping technique to learn from frozen unimodal models and Large Language Models (LLMs), achieving state-of-the-art performance on multiple downstream vision-language tasks. The BLIP and BLIP-2 models have been shown to outperform even task-specific fine-tuned models in zero-shot settings, on text-video retrieval tasks.

3 Method

We define the task of VMR as follows: Let q be a given natural language query, and let $v = \{c_1, \ldots, c_{N_v}\}$ be an input video of duration T seconds, comprising of a sequence of N_v segments, ordered in time with corresponding temporal intervals $\{(s_1, e_1), \ldots, (s_{N_v}, e_{N_v})\}$, $0 \le s_u < e_u \le T$, $\forall\, u \in \{1, \ldots, N_v\}$. Then, VMR aims to find the temporal intervals of one or more contiguous subsequences of segments, that semantically correspond to q. Each such subsequence is defined as a moment m, i.e., $m = \{c_i, c_{i+1}, \ldots, c_j\}$ for some $1 \le i \le j \le N_v$, and the temporal interval corresponding to m is defined as (s_i, e_j). For our approach, we treat v as a sequence of 1–s segments, i.e., $v = \{c_1, \ldots, c_T\}$.

Using the categorization of approaches described in Sect. 2, our approach is (i) proposal-free, i.e., every 1–s segment of the input video is treated equivalently as a potential moment; and (ii) zero-shot, i.e., does not require task-specific training. The zero-shot baselines by Lei et al. [11] and Diwan et al. [4] are the closest to our approach, with key differences being that our approach uses the BLIP family of models [13,14] instead of CLIP for encoding images and text, and for ITM, while also not requiring the generation of candidate moment proposals.

Figure 1 shows the overall pipeline of our approach, which can be condensed into the following steps: (i) Computing image and text embeddings, (ii) Sparse frame sampling strategies, (iii) and Moment-query matching. We describe each of these steps in detail in the following subsections. Throughout this section, we use the term *BLIPX* to refer to both, the BLIP and BLIP-2 models interchangeably, as our approach remains consistent across both models.

3.1 Computing Image and Text Embeddings

The first step involves splitting the input video v of length T seconds into smaller, non-overlapping chunks of maximum length T_{chunk}. This is done to avoid Graphics Processing Unit (GPU) out-of-memory errors while computing the image embeddings as a batch, thereby allowing our method to scale to videos of arbitrary length. It is to be noted that these chunks are processed independently of each other, allowing our approach to be applied on a rolling basis without needing to process the entire video beforehand. Hence, our method is capable of consuming video streams without any modification. The value for T_{chunk} can be chosen according to available GPU memory. In our experimental setup, we choose $T_{chunk} = 120$ s. Processing on a chunk-by-chunk basis, we sample a set of s frames, $F_i = \{f_{i,1}, \ldots, f_{i,s}\}$, from every 1–s segment $c_i \in v$, according to one of the sparse frame sampling strategies described in Sect. 3.2.

As described in Sect. 2, the BLIP and BLIP-2 models incorporate mechanisms for enhanced image-text matching and exhibit strong performance for multiple downstream vision-language tasks even in zero-shot settings. We therefore use the pre-trained BLIP/BLIP-2 model encoders for encoding images and texts, and the ITM head for computing image-text similarities.

For every 1–s segment c_i, we pre-process the sampled frames F_i as described in Li et al. [14], and embed them using the BLIPX image encoder, to obtain corresponding image embeddings. Finally, for each c_i, we average these embeddings across all sampled frames for the segment, to obtain a single representative image embedding:

$$E_i = \sum_{j=1}^{s} BLIPX_{Img}(f_{i,j}) \qquad i \in \{1, \ldots, T\} \qquad (1)$$

where E_i is the representative image embedding for c_i, $BLIPX_{Img}$ is the BLIPX image encoder, and $f_{i,j} \in F_i$ with $j \in \{1, \ldots, s\}$. Averaging the embeddings across the sampled frames allows for a simple way to aggregate information sampled from multiple parts of each second. We note that our approach performs frame-level feature extraction at $s = 1$, and clip-level feature extraction for $s > 1$.

For the input query q, we follow the text pre-processing steps as performed by Li et al. [14], after which q is embedded using the BLIPX text encoder, to obtain the corresponding text embedding:

$$Q_{emb} = BLIPX_{Text}(q) \qquad (2)$$

where Q_{emb} is the query embedding and $BLIPX_{Text}$ denotes the BLIPX text encoder.

3.2   Sparse Frame-Sampling Strategies

Generating image embeddings for all of the frames in a video is both redundant and computationally expensive. To mitigate this and make the steps described in the previous section tractable, we employ sparse frame sampling strategies. As described in the previous section, we sample a fixed number of frames from every second of the video, which we denote the *sampling rate* $s \in \{1, \ldots, FPS\}$. The number of frames in a second is determined by the video's frame rate, frames per second (FPS). Assuming a 1–s segment c_i as input, we describe two sparse frame-sampling strategies as follows.

Uniform Sampling. In this strategy, we uniformly sample s frames from the segment. For example, for a video with $s = 2$, we pick the first and middle frames. More generally, for a 1-s segment $c_i = \{f_{i,1}, \ldots, f_{i,FPS}\}$, with frame rate FPS and sampling rate s, the set of sampled frames F_i is given by:

$$F_i = \left\{ f_{i,1+(k-1)\cdot\lceil \frac{FPS}{s} \rceil} \mid k \in \{1, \ldots, s\} \right\} \qquad (3)$$

Sharpness Sampling. Consecutive video frames in a second of footage, are often redundant and might include motion blur. This strategy aims to mitigate this by sampling frames after sorting them in order of least motion blur (or equivalently highest sharpness). For this, we use a simple and fast Laplacian-based sharpness metric: for a given frame, we first convolve it with the Laplacian operator, after which we compute the variance of the convolved image, which we define as the sharpness of the image. Being a second-order derivative operator, this variance will be lower for frames with higher blur, and vice-versa:

$$S(f) = \text{Var}\left[\Delta(f)\right] \tag{4}$$

where $S(f)$ is the sharpness value of a given input frame f, and $\Delta(f) = \frac{\partial^2 f}{\partial x^2} + \frac{\partial^2 f}{\partial y^2}$ is the second-order derivative of f. After computing $S(f)$ for every frame f in $c_i = \{f_{i,1}, \ldots, f_{i,FPS}\}$, we sample the top s frames according to the highest sharpness, to obtain the set of sampled frames F_i:

$$F_i = \underset{\substack{I \subset W : |I| = s \\ W = \{1, \ldots, FPS\}}}{\arg\max} \sum_{u \in I} S(f_{i,u}) \tag{5}$$

3.3 Moment-Query Matching

After obtaining the query embedding Q_{emb} and the representative image embeddings E_i for every c_i, $i \in \{1, \ldots, T\}$ in Sect. 3.1, we use the ITM head (discussed in Sect. 2) of the BLIPX model to compute the similarity between the query embedding and each 1–s segment's representative image embedding. This enables every c_i to have a query-matching score p_i associated with it:

$$p_i = BLIPX_{ITM}(Q_{emb}, E_i) \qquad i \in \{1, \ldots, T\} \tag{6}$$

where $BLIPX_{ITM}$ is the ITM head of the BLIPX model.

After obtaining a query-matching score for every c_i, we merge 1–s segments that may be associated with the same moment. Diwan et al. [4] introduced the SimpleWatershed algorithm as a post-processing step to merge consecutive video segments satisfying a similarity *score threshold* γ. We adapt it directly as a merging strategy as follows: For every contiguous subsequence of 1-s segments $c_i, c_{i+1}, \ldots, c_j$ in the video, with respective scores $p_i, \ldots, p_j$, we merge the segments into a single segment if $p_k \geq \gamma$, $\forall\ i \leq k \leq j$, to form the set of all such merged segments, M_{merged}.

The score p_i' for the ith merged segment in M_{merged} is set to be the maximum of the scores of the individual 1–s segments within it prior to merging. For a given value of k, we then fetch the top k moments from M_{merged} sorted by the highest scores:

$$M_{retrieved} = \underset{\substack{I \subset W : |I| = k \\ W = \{1, \ldots, |M_{merged}|\}}}{\arg\max} \sum_{u \in I} p_u' \tag{7}$$

where $M_{retrieved}$ is the set of retrieved moments for the input query. In our experiments, we set k to some very high value, so as to include all the segments in M_{merged}.

4   Experiments

Dataset. We evaluate our approach using the QVHighlights dataset [11], which is a benchmark dataset for VMR. The dataset consists of annotated examples, with each example consisting of a YouTube video, a natural language query, and moment timestamps associated with the query. Additionally, for each video, there are saliency/highlightness score annotations on a 5-point Likert scale for every 2-s clip within the video. The *train-val-test* split percentage of the dataset is 70% − 15% − 15%. Of the original 1550 videos in the *val* set, only 1434 videos are currently available (defined as the *val-filt* set in Diwan et al. [4]) due to videos being de-listed or made private on YouTube, or download errors. Diwan et al. [4] evaluated the Moment-DETR model proposed by Lei et al. [11] on the *test, val,* and *val-filt* sets and observed that it resulted in approximately the same evaluation metric results. To ensure fair comparison, we report metrics in the following manner: if a model's performance is reported on the *val-filt* set in Diwan et al. [4], we use it directly; in cases where this is not available, we first create *sub-train* and *sub-val* datasets by randomly splitting the *train* set in an 85% − 15% split percentage, and then train such models using the *sub-train* set for training and the *sub-val* set for validation, while finally reporting on the *val-filt* set. In cases where such training was not possible due to computational limitations, we report their performance on the *test* set, following the assumption as Diwan et al. [4], that metrics reported on the *val-filt* and *test* sets can be interchanged for analysis.

Fig. 2. Sample predictions by our approach on QVHighlights *val-filt* set. Text boxes represent input queries, and images correspond to representative frames (ordered temporally) from the top retrieved moment predicted by our model.

Evaluation Metrics. Following the approaches of Lei et al. [11] and Diwan et al. [4], we use Mean Average Precision (mAP) with Intersection over Union (IoU) thresholds 0.5 and 0.75, as well as average mAP over IoU thresholds in the range [0.5 : 0.05 : 0.95], for evaluating moment retrieval with multiple moments, and Recall@1 (R1) with IoU thresholds 0.5 and 0.7 for evaluating single moment retrieval.

Hyperparameter Tuning. Since our approach is zero-shot and does not use the *train* set for training or fine-tuning, we use a random subset of it as a validation set, and tune the following hyperparameters (discussed in Sect. 3.2): sampling strategies - Uniform and Sharpness; sampling rate s with range [1 : 1 : 8]; and score threshold γ with ranges [0.1 : 0.1 : 0.9], [0.01 : 0.01 : 0.1] and [0.001 : 0.001 : 0.01]. We report the following sets of tuned parameters: For BLIP: {sampling strategy = Sharpness, $s = 1$, $\gamma = 0.01$}; for BLIP-2: {sampling strategy = Uniform, $s = 1$, $\gamma = 0.002$}.

Baseline Comparison. We compare our approach against existing baselines for Moment Retrieval (MR) listed in Lei et al. [11] and Diwan et al. [4], while also including the current state-of-the-art. Using the same terminology as Diwan et al. [4], we categorize the baselines into three categories: (i) Zero-shot: models which are not explicitly trained on the QVHighlights dataset; (ii) VMR-Supervised: models which are trained on the QVHighlights dataset excluding saliency score annotations; and (iii) VMR-Supervised + Saliency: models which are trained on the QVHighlights dataset including saliency score annotations.

5   Results and Discussion

Main results. We present the main results of our experiments in Table 1. We report our best approaches using both the BLIP and BLIP-2 models, denoted as "Sharpness + BLIP + SimpleWatershed" and "Uniform + BLIP-2 + SimpleWatershed" in the table, respectively. As discussed in the previous section, we categorize existing baselines into Zero-shot, VMR-Supervised and VMR-Supervised + Saliency, and compare our approach against these, on either the *val-filt* set or the *test* set (marked with an "*" in Table 1) of the QVHighlights dataset. Figure 2 shows qualitative examples predicted by our approach.

When comparing with zero-shot approaches, we observe that our approaches outperform existing approaches from Lei et al. [11] and Diwan et al. [4]. Our approaches improve upon the previous best zero-shot performance by at least 25% on all metrics. It is worth noting that while the zero-shot approaches by Lei et al. [11] and Diwan et al. [4] employ frame-level feature extraction similar to ours, usage of BLIPX embeddings in our approach performs significantly better than CLIP embeddings used in their work. We hypothesize that this is because BLIPX has been trained on less noisy image-text pairs and uses a dedicated ITM head (as discussed in Sect. 2), contributing to better image-text alignment than CLIP. Additionally, we note that our approach achieves superior performance to that of Diwan et al. [4], despite not requiring the additional step of generating moment proposals before frame-sampling.

Table 1. Results using Recall@1 and mAP metrics (higher is better) on QVHighlights *val-filt* set (rows without an "*") or *test* set (rows with an "*"). Bold values indicate the best-performing approach within each category. Models trained on an additional audio modality are denoted by "+ Audio". The "w/PT" suffix denotes models incorporating weakly-supervised pre-training on ASR captions.

Category	Method	R1		mAP		
		@0.5	@0.7	@0.5	@0.75	avg
Zero-shot	CLIP + Watershed (Lei et al. (2021) [11])	16.88	5.19	18.11	7.00	7.67
	ShotDetect + CLIP + SimpleWatershed (Diwan et al. (2022) [4])	48.33	30.96	46.94	25.75	27.96
	Sharpness + BLIP + SimpleWatershed (Ours)	**60.81**	43.86	**58.73**	37.98	37.83
	Uniform + BLIP-2 + SimpleWatershed (Ours)	60.32	**44.77**	58.36	**38.98**	**38.92**
VMR-Supervised	MCN* (Hendricks et al. (2017) [8])	11.41	2.72	24.94	8.22	10.67
	CAL* (Escorcia et al. (2017) [25])	25.49	11.54	23.40	7.65	9.89
	XML* (Lei et al. (2020) [12])	41.83	**30.35**	44.63	**31.73**	**32.14**
	Moment-DETR w/o saliency loss (Lei et al. (2021) [11])	**45.03**	25.81	**48.42**	21.91	24.68
VMR-Supervised + Saliency	XML+* (Lei et al. (2021) [11])	46.69	33.46	47.89	34.67	34.90
	Moment-DETR* (Lei et al. (2021) [11])	52.89	33.02	54.82	29.40	30.73
	Moment-DETR w/PT (Lei et al. (2021) [11])	59.74	41.10	59.90	35.42	36.19
	UMT + Audio (Liu et al. (2022) [16])	58.51	41.28	55.20	36.21	35.96
	UMT + Audio w/PT* (Liu et al. (2022) [16])	60.83	43.26	57.33	39.12	38.08
	QD-DETR (Moon et al. (2023) [17])	60.60	43.31	60.74	39.10	39.14
	QD-DETR + Audio (Moon et al. (2023) [17])	**61.09**	**44.91**	**61.66**	**40.42**	**40.24**

On comparison to VMR-Supervised approaches, our approach outperforms all models, by at least 21% on all metrics. We note that all of these supervised approaches make use of either additional modalities (e.g., optical flow features in Moment Context Network (MCN) model [8]) or clip-level feature extraction (e.g., stacked/average-pooled frame features in Clip Alignment with Language (CAL) model [25]; Inflated 3D Convnet (I3D) features [1] in Crossmodal Moment Localization (XML) [12] model; SlowFast features [6] in Moment-DETR [11] model) for capturing spatio-temporal context. This suggests that a frame-level feature extraction approach such as ours, which uses no task-specific supervised data, can be a surprisingly strong baseline for VMR, even outperforming supervised approaches that make use of additional modalities or more computationally intensive spatio-temporal backbones.

In the VMR-Supervised + Saliency category, we observe that our approach performs better than some of the earlier approaches such as XML+ [11] and Moment-DETR (without ASR pre-training) [11] on all metrics. As noted by Diwan et al. [4], pre-training on ASR captions provides a significant jump in performance across all metrics (c.f. in Table 1: Moment-DETR vs. Moment-DETR w/PT; UMT + Audio vs. UMT + Audio w/PT). Despite this advantage, our approach outperforms Moment-DETR [11] with ASR pre-training on all metrics except mAP@0.5. We also note that the best performing approaches include an additional audio modality, contributing to improved performance across all metrics (c.f. in Table 1: QD-DETR vs. QD-DETR + Audio). We observe that our approach is competitive with such approaches, despite not making use of an audio modality or saliency score annotations: comparing with the current state-of-the-art, (QD-DETR + Audio in Table 1), our approach has a gap of at most 7% across all metrics.

Table 2. Results with respect to moment length using avg. mAP metric (higher is better) on QVHighlights *val-filt* set. Bold values indicate the best-performing approach across all categories. Models trained on an additional audio modality are denoted by "+ Audio". The "w/PT" suffix denotes models incorporating weakly-supervised pre-training on ASR captions.

Category	Method	Long	Medium	Short
Zero-shot	ShotDetect + CLIP (Diwan et al. (2022) [4])	27.49	26.15	7.08
	ShotDetect + CLIP + SimpleWatershed (Diwan et al. (2022) [4])	33.19	28.44	4.90
	Sharpness + BLIP + SimpleWatershed (Ours)	41.85	39.56	10.62
	Uniform + BLIP-2 + SimpleWatershed (Ours)	45.10	39.26	**11.04**
VMR-Supervised	Moment-DETR w/o saliency loss (Lei et al. (2021) [11])	31.38	25.29	2.63
VMR-Supervised + Saliency	Moment-DETR (Lei et al. (2021) [11])	41.11	32.30	3.28
	Moment-DETR w/PT (Lei et al. (2021) [11])	45.18	37.53	3.50
	UMT + Audio (Liu et al. (2022) [16])	43.40	41.44	4.69
	QD-DETR (Moon et al. (2023) [17])	42.73	**42.36**	7.63
	QD-DETR + Audio (Moon et al. (2023) [17])	**47.84**	41.87	6.98

Performance Analysis by Moment Length. Diwan et al. [4] do a performance comparison of various approaches on the average mAP metric, after segregating the *val-filt* set into three categories based on the duration of ground truth moments: Long moments, which are greater than 30 s; Middle moments, which are between 10 and 30 s; and Short moments, which are less than 10 s. Extending this comparative study, we include our approach along with the current state-of-the-art and report our findings in Table 2. We support Diwan etal.'s [4] claim of the poor performance of all approaches on short moments, observing that this pattern holds true for even recent and state-of-the-art supervised approaches. Further, we observe that while supervised approaches still dominate in the categories of Medium and Long moments, our approach improves on the state-of-the-art performance in Short moments (QD-DETR in Table 2) by more than 44%.

6 Conclusions and Future Work

In this paper, we have proposed an efficient zero-shot approach for VMR that performs frame-level feature extraction using off-the-shelf BLIP-based models without requiring any weakly supervised pre-training or training on additional modalities. Our approach outperforms existing zero-shot and supervised approaches and is highly competitive with the state-of-the-art on the QVHighlights benchmark dataset. Furthermore, we have shown that our approach exhibits superior performance compared to the previously best-reported model on retrieving short moments. For future work, we would like to explore the incorporation of saliency score-like information into our model in a zero-shot manner to improve its performance on retrieving long moments. Furthermore, adapting weakly supervised pre-training for BLIP-based models on additional modalities such as audio and/or text, as well as other content-aware frame sampling strategies, to enhance the performance of our approach, represent promising directions for future research.

Acknowledgments. This work was partially funded by the Research School on "Service-Oriented Systems Engineering" of the Hasso Plattner Institute.

References

1. Carreira, J., Zisserman, A.: Quo vadis, action recognition? A new model and the kinetics dataset. In: CVPR 2017, pp. 4724–4733. IEEE Computer Society (2017). https://doi.org/10.1109/CVPR.2017.502
2. Chen, J., Luo, W., Zhang, W., Ma, L.: Explore inter-contrast between videos via composition for weakly supervised temporal sentence grounding. In: AAAI 2022, pp. 267–275. AAAI Press (2022). https://ojs.aaai.org/index.php/AAAI/article/view/19902
3. Choe, T.E., Lee, M.W., Guo, F., Taylor, G., Yu, L., Haering, N.: Semantic video event search for surveillance video. In: ICCV Workshops 2011, pp. 1963–1970. IEEE (2011)
4. Diwan, A., Peng, P., Mooney, R.J.: Zero-shot video moment retrieval with off-the-shelf models. CoRR abs/2211.02178 (2022). https://doi.org/10.48550/arXiv.2211.02178
5. Du, Y., Liu, Z., Li, J., Zhao, W.X.: A survey of vision-language pre-trained models. In: IJCAI 2022, pp. 5436–5443. ijcai.org (2022). https://doi.org/10.24963/ijcai.2022/762
6. Feichtenhofer, C., Fan, H., Malik, J., He, K.: Slowfast networks for video recognition. In: ICCV 2019, pp. 6201–6210. IEEE (2019). https://doi.org/10.1109/ICCV.2019.00630
7. Hao, J., Sun, H., Ren, P., Wang, J., Qi, Q., Liao, J.: Can shuffling video benefit temporal bias problem: a novel training framework for temporal grounding. In: Avidan, S., Brostow, G., Cissé, M., Farinella, G.M., Hassner, T. (eds.) ECCV 2022. LNCS, vol. 13696, pp. 130–147. Springer, Cham (2022). https://doi.org/10.1007/978-3-031-20059-5_8
8. Hendricks, L.A., Wang, O., Shechtman, E., Sivic, J., Darrell, T., Russell, B.C.: Localizing moments in video with natural language. In: ICCV 2017, pp. 5804–5813. IEEE Computer Society (2017). https://doi.org/10.1109/ICCV.2017.618
9. Huang, J., Worring, M.: Query-controllable video summarization. In: ICMR 2020, pp. 242–250. ACM (2020). https://doi.org/10.1145/3372278.3390695
10. Leake, M., Davis, A., Truong, A., Agrawala, M.: Computational video editing for dialogue-driven scenes. ACM Trans. Graph. **36**(4), 130:1–130:14 (2017). https://doi.org/10.1145/3072959.3073653
11. Lei, J., Berg, T.L., Bansal, M.: QVHighlights: detecting moments and highlights in videos via natural language queries. CoRR abs/2107.09609 (2021). arxiv.org/abs/2107.09609
12. Lei, J., Yu, L., Berg, T.L., Bansal, M.: TVR: a large-scale dataset for video-subtitle moment retrieval. In: Vedaldi, A., Bischof, H., Brox, T., Frahm, J.-M. (eds.) ECCV 2020. LNCS, vol. 12366, pp. 447–463. Springer, Cham (2020). https://doi.org/10.1007/978-3-030-58589-1_27
13. Li, J., Li, D., Savarese, S., Hoi, S.C.H.: BLIP-2: bootstrapping language-image pre-training with frozen image encoders and large language models. CoRR abs/2301.12597 (2023). https://doi.org/10.48550/arXiv.2301.12597
14. Li, J., Li, D., Xiong, C., Hoi, S.C.H.: BLIP: bootstrapping language-image pre-training for unified vision-language understanding and generation. In: ICML 2022,

vol. 162, pp. 12888–12900. PMLR (2022). https://proceedings.mlr.press/v162/li22n.html

15. Liu, D., et al.: Context-aware biaffine localizing network for temporal sentence grounding. In: CVPR 2021, pp. 11235–11244. Computer Vision Foundation/IEEE (2021). https://doi.org/10.1109/CVPR46437.2021.01108

16. Liu, Y., Li, S., Wu, Y., Chen, C.W., Shan, Y., Qie, X.: UMT: unified multimodal transformers for joint video moment retrieval and highlight detection. In: CVPR 2022, pp. 3032–3041. IEEE (2022). https://doi.org/10.1109/CVPR52688.2022.00305

17. Moon, W., Hyun, S., Park, S., Park, D., Heo, J.P.: Query-dependent video representation for moment retrieval and highlight detection. In: CVPR 2023, pp. 23023–23033 (2023)

18. Nam, J., Ahn, D., Kang, D., Ha, S.J., Choi, J.: Zero-shot natural language video localization. In: ICCV 2021, pp. 1450–1459. IEEE (2021). https://doi.org/10.1109/ICCV48922.2021.00150

19. Song, Y., Wang, J., Ma, L., Yu, Z., Yu, J.: Weakly-supervised multi-level attentional reconstruction network for grounding textual queries in videos. CoRR abs/2003.07048 (2020). arxiv.org/abs/2003.07048

20. Tang, K., Bao, Y., Zhao, Z., Zhu, L., Lin, Y., Peng, Y.: AutoHighlight: automatic highlights detection and segmentation in soccer matches. In: IEEE BigData 2018, pp. 4619–4624. IEEE (2018). https://doi.org/10.1109/BigData.2018.8621906

21. Tellex, S., Kollar, T., Shaw, G., Roy, N., Roy, D.: Grounding spatial language for video search. In: ICMI-MLMI 2010, pp. 31:1–31:8. ACM (2010). https://doi.org/10.1145/1891903.1891944

22. Wang, G., Wu, X., Liu, Z., Yan, J.: Prompt-based zero-shot video moment retrieval. In: MM 2022, pp. 413–421. ACM (2022). https://doi.org/10.1145/3503161.3548004

23. Wang, M., Yang, G.W., Hu, S.M., Yau, S.T., Shamir, A., et al.: Write-a-video: computational video montage from themed text. ACM Trans. Graph. **38**(6), 177–1 (2019)

24. Xie, S., Sun, C., Huang, J., Tu, Z., Murphy, K.: Rethinking spatiotemporal feature learning: speed-accuracy trade-offs in video classification. In: Ferrari, V., Hebert, M., Sminchisescu, C., Weiss, Y. (eds.) ECCV 2018. LNCS, vol. 11219, pp. 318–335. Springer, Cham (2018). https://doi.org/10.1007/978-3-030-01267-0_19

25. Xu, M., et al.: Boundary-sensitive pre-training for temporal localization in videos. In: ICCV 2021, pp. 7200–7210. IEEE (2021). https://doi.org/10.1109/ICCV48922.2021.00713

26. Zeng, Y., Cao, D., Lu, S., Zhang, H., Xu, J., Qin, Z.: Moment is important: language-based video moment retrieval via adversarial learning. ACM Trans. Multim. Comput. Commun. Appl. **18**(2), 56:1–56:21 (2022). https://doi.org/10.1145/3478025

27. Zhang, H., Sun, A., Jing, W., Zhou, J.T.: The elements of temporal sentence grounding in videos: a survey and future directions. CoRR abs/2201.08071 (2022). arxiv.org/abs/2201.08071

28. Zhang, S., Peng, H., Fu, J., Luo, J.: Learning 2D temporal adjacent networks for moment localization with natural language. In: AAAI 2020, pp. 12870–12877. AAAI Press (2020). https://ojs.aaai.org/index.php/AAAI/article/view/6984

Self-supervised Representation Learning for Fine Grained Human Hand Action Recognition in Industrial Assembly Lines

Fabian Sturm[1,2]([✉]), Rahul Sathiyababu[1], Harshitha Allipilli[1],
Elke Hergenroether[2], and Melanie Siegel[2]

[1] Bosch Rexroth AG, Lise-Meitner-Straße 4, 89081 Ulm, Germany
`fabian.sturm@bosch.com`
[2] University of Applied Sciences Darmstadt, Schöefferstraße 3,
64295 Darmstadt, Germany

Abstract. Humans are still indispensable on industrial assembly lines, but in the event of an error, they need support from intelligent systems. In addition to the objects to be observed, it is equally important to understand the fine-grained hand movements of a human to be able to track the entire process. However, these deep learning based hand action recognition methods are very label intensive, which cannot be offered by all industrial companies due to the associated costs. This work therefore presents a self-supervised learning approach for industrial assembly processes that allows a spatio-temporal transformer architecture to be pre-trained on a variety of information from real-world video footage of daily life. Subsequently, this deep learning model is adapted to the industrial assembly task at hand using only a few labels. It is shown which known real-world datasets are best suited for representation learning of these hand actions in a regression task, and to what extent they optimize the subsequent supervised trained classification task.

Keywords: Self-Supervised Learning · Human Action Recognition · Industrial Vision

1 Introduction

Due to the rising costs of maintaining high-tech systems and the increasing technological demands on operators, many manufacturing companies are recognizing the importance of keeping humans at the center of their production processes. This is particularly true in the field of factory automation, where production costs need to be economical and flexible enough to produce multiple product variants. Despite the advancements in automation technology, it has been found that 70% of assembly lines worldwide are still operated exclusively by humans. This highlights the essential role that human operators play in the production process, as they are able to handle a wide range of products cost-effectively

G. Bebis et al. (Eds.): ISVC 2023, LNCS 14361, pp. 172–184, 2023.
https://doi.org/10.1007/978-3-031-47969-4_14

and adapt to new or optimized processes with ease. However, human operators are not without their limitations. They can make mistakes, especially at the beginning of a learning process or when performing repetitive tasks. Moreover, the psychological consequences of performing the same task every day can be detrimental to their well-being. To address these challenges, this work focuses on assembly assistance systems based on deep learning vision applications that can assist assemblers based on their movements in the assembly process.

However, traditional supervised deep learning approaches require significant amounts of data and labels, [25,26] which can be challenging for industrial companies to provide. These companies may not have the necessary resources or expertise to record, clean, and label their processes for deep learning applications. Additionally, the employees with the necessary domain knowledge may be scarce and only available for a short period of time. Moreover, the data may rarely leave the factory premises, making it difficult to share with others.

Self-supervised representation learning approaches reduce the resource-intensive task of data labeling and allow deep-learning models to be pre-trained on a similar task from, for example, the non-industrial world, which can then be used to adapt them to the industrial use case using only a small amount of labeled data [1,9]. This allows the respective industrial domain expert to incorporate his knowledge into the deep learning model in the shortest possible time, and the industrial company to support its employees with this knowledge. In this work, a self-supervised learning approach for a two-towered spatio-temporal transformer encoder architecture is investigated. This model learns the representation of hand movements from various daily videos based on hand skeleton data. The learned representation results from sequences that are partially masked. The model reconstructs these masked regions, similar to the approach of the BERT model [3]. Subsequently, the suitability for a transfer of the weights to an industrial use case is checked and evaluated on the basis of values such as the amount of labeled data, training time and performance on a test data set. The main contributions are as follows:

- The presentation of an efficient approach of masked auto encoding in spatio-temporal transformer encoder architectures
- To show how daily real world data can be used to fine-tune the trained models for industrial applications
- Extensive experiments on challenging video benchmarks and achieve comparable or better results with improved state-of-the-art methods

For this purpose, different self-supervised learning approaches based on masked autoencoders (MAE) are presented in Sect. 2. Subsequently, the model architecture and the masking method used is described in Sect. 3. This model architecture is first supervised trained on an industrial dataset to create a ground truth. Subsequently, the same model is pretrained self-supervised with a masking approach on different presented real world datasets before it is tested for its usability for fine-tuning on an industrial dataset in Sect. 4. Thereby, it is also analyzed to what extent this method optimizes the learning process in Sect. 5. Finally, it is concluded with an outlook in Sect. 6.

2   Related Work

Generative self-supervised learning is a method to provide knowledge to a model that should recognize patterns in unlabeled data based on observation. Through this observation, it is additionally possible to use previously unrecognized patterns in addition to the obvious patterns recognized by a labeler who has domain knowledge in a supervised learning approach. This observation and learning is usually done by an autoencoder which converts an input into a latent representation which is then converted back into the structure of the input with the help of a decoder. The resulting deviation is then taken as a measurement value to check the performance of the model [17]. In order to train the autoencoder for better generalizability, a masking method for the input data can be applied to create a denoising autoencoder [7,24]. In the following sections, an overview of different methods of the most promising masked self-supervised learning methods investigated for this industrial use case are introduced which are, related to skeleton based data where the focus relies on images, video data, and multivariate time series data.

MAE in Image and Video Data. The idea of MAEs is relatively simple and has been successfully applied in the field of natural language processing (NLP) for quite some time. The most popular NLP approach that is trained with this method is the BERT Model [3]. Some part of the language data, up to 15%, is made unrecognizable and is to be reconstructed by the model. This way, the model learns the correct context of the data and can afterward be fine-tuned to different tasks from the same domain with fewer labels compared to a supervised approach. However, this masking procedure has also been used in image processing for quite some time under the term denoising autoencoders [23]. One of the more popular recent work from [7] used as autoencoder a Vision Transformer (ViT) [4] architecture and found that significantly more masking compared to the BERT approach with 15% can be applied to images, about 75% depending on the depth of the model and the mask strategies, proving that MAEs can also be used as scalable vision learners. They also proved that random masking can produce a significantly better result on images than, for example, block masking or grid masking. In this way, they have revolutionized the method of self-supervised learning by not only reaching the state of the art for image pretraining, but also bridges the gap between visual and linguistic MAE pretraining [2]. Similar findings were reported at the same time by [28] during the investigation of multiple masking strategies like square, block-wise, and random masking, with achieving the best performance with random masking. Their presented SimMIM model also confirms that direct prediction of pixels as in MAE does not perform worse than other methods with complex design, such as tokenization, clustering, or discretization. [5] extended these pixelwise masking approaches for images by applying random masking on videos and proofed that with randomly masked spatio-temporal information, not only the fine-tuning results can be improved, but also the amount of masking can be increased by up to 90% by starting to reach good results in the downstream task with masking ratios higher than 70%. The VideoMAE model also proved that masking is very well applicable for representation learning of videos [20]. They used a tube masking approach and proved that with this masking method already a relatively small amount of data is sufficient for training and not a very large data set is required as previously assumed.

MAE in Multivariate Time Series and Skeleton Based Data. Similar approaches like the previous ones for masking has also been used for multivariate time series data, showing that this method of representation learning can also be used for very dense types of data [29]. [29] used a transformer encoder architecture similar to BERT that was used with the same random masking approach [3]. What was interesting here is that the same samples could be used multiple times for pre-training purposes, as long as they were masked at different locations. MTSMAE introduced by [19] added to the traditional ViT embedding approaches a patch embedding layer [21] in the direction of time after the embedding. They also show that a high masking level in such dense data can lose more information, greatly reduce the redundancy of the data, and reduce the overall understanding of the model about the low-level information. Consequently, a too high masking ratio, such as 95%, also means that a large amount of data is lost. The data that the model can learn is limited, which can affect the model's understanding of the data. Therefore, they chose a masking ratio of 85% and achieved the best results for the representation learning and subsequent downstream classification task. [27] introduced SkeletonMAE a masked autoencoder approach which considers 3D skeleton data. They investigated random and fixed masked images as well as joint masking methods and a new spatio-temporal masking method for skeletal data introduced at both the joint plane and the image level, with the proper combination of masking ratios in both spatial and temporal dimensions. The approach achieved the best results of fixed masking accuracy of 85.4% and random masking accuracy of 86.6% in the downstream task with a fixed masking ratio in the temporal domain by 40% and the spatial domain by 50% and random masking ratio with 50% in spatial and 40% and 50% in temporal. These ratio parameters matched the findings from [19] and can be used as general state-of-the-art values for such a masking method.

3 Proposed Method

In the following section, the feature extraction of the hand skeleton information to save resources is explained in more detail before the encoder model architecture to be trained is presented. Subsequently, the masking method for learning the representation is discussed.

3.1 Model Architecture

Preextraction of Hand Skeleton Data. An approach for keypoint extraction is used that is inspired by Google's MediaPipe Hands solution architecture.

The model consists of a palm recognition module followed by a hand feature detector that provides 21 2.5D coordinates for various landmarks. These vertices serve as key features for the subsequent transformer model. The process begins with a palm detector network optimized for real-time mobile use [30]. Instead of detecting the entire hand with fingers, the model first identifies the palms through bounding boxes to ensure stability. An encoder-decoder feature extractor, similar to a feature pyramid network [13], recognizes the palm at different scales. To balance the imbalance between background and palm detection during training, the focal loss [14] is used [30]. When a palm is detected, an image section is generated that includes the entire hand for further analysis. This image section is then fed into a convolutional neural network that identifies the 21 landmarks of the hand with 2.5D coordinates. These coordinates include x and y values, and a z value with a relative depth to the wrist, and a probability of hand presence and handedness information. To optimize subsequent frames, the detected landmarks are used to calculate a new crop area, keeping the hand within this region. Subsequent frames are cropped accordingly, avoiding redundant detection by the single-shot detector, except when the probability of hand presence falls below a certain threshold [30]. By reducing the number of compute cycles required during inferencing, the convolutional neural network operates on smaller cropped images, and the single-shot detector only scans the entire image when necessary due to lost hand detection, see Fig. 1.

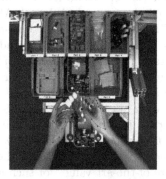

Fig. 1. Hand Skeleton Detector in Industrial Environment

ConvGTN. The hand keypoint extractor skeleton output serves as the foundation for the subsequent part of the architecture. This section focuses on classifying the temporal and sequential correlations within the extracted time series of keypoints. To achieve this, a specialized gated transformer network [15] is employed, specifically adapted for this use case, see Fig. 2. Previously, the network from [15] demonstrated remarkable performance on 13 multivariate time series classification tasks, including human action recognition tasks similar to the one in this work. The adapted architecture revolves around a two-tower transformer with batch normalization [10] instead of layer normalization like in the traditional approach from [22], where each tower's encoder captures attention in both temporal and spatial-channel dimensions at each time step. As activation function, in the feed forward block of the encoders the Gaussian Error Linear Units (GELU) is used [8]. Additional parameters for the encoders are QUERY = 32, VALUE = 32, KEY = 4, with N = 4 layers and D_HIDDEN = 512 hidden layers. To merge the encoded features from the two towers, an adaptive weighted concatenation acts as a gate before the last fully connected layers. This gate dynamically determines which tower contributes more crucial features to the classification process during backpropagation. The output of both encoders is additionally supplemented beforehand by a linear layer with 128 input features and the respective output features of each tower 126 keypoints or 100 frames to come to the original input dimension and to equalize it with the input signal of [126, 100]. To enhance the model's predictive capabilities, an additional Conv1D layer with a kernel size of 3 is introduced. This extra convolution facilitates better correlation detection between the hand keypoints represented as [21 * 3 * 2] [keypoints per hand, xyz coordinates, hands], embedded temporally within the model. It leads to improved gradients in the temporal tower for each time step of the input data represented as [128, 126, 100] [batch size, features, sequence length]. The Conv1D layer is succeeded by a linear layer with 128 input and 128 output features and a learnable positional encoding layer [11]. The full amount of trainable parameters in this model are 1,743,684 and has with these settings way fewer parameters than the initial setup from [15] with more than 18Mio parameters.

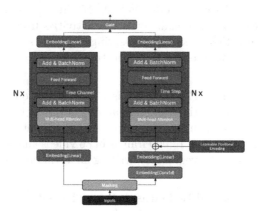

Fig. 2. ConvGTN Model Architecture

3.2   Masking Method

As masking method, random masking is used. The reason for this are the results of [27] and [5] which turned out to be a promising method due to the similar structure of the data which is skeleton based video data. Before splitting the information for both towers, the sequential input is masked temporally and spatially with a masking ratio of 50%. This prevents the model from recognizing spatial masking too easily by so-called tubes, and from recognizing temporal patterns too easily by masked frames [7]. The training procedure is to mask first the sequences, see Fig. 2, send the full sequence with the masked areas into the model so that the model reconstructs the sequence as a regression task and back propagate and calculate the loss with a mean squared error only on the masked areas to prevent the model to learn the structure of the sequence by heart and only focus on the disturbed areas.

4   Experiments

The following section presents the datasets selected for pre-training based on the findings from [18] and the Industrial Hand Assembly Dataset V1 for the downstream task, as well as the model training environment and training time, before the experiments are discussed in more detail.

4.1   Datasets

20bn-Something-Something V2. The 20bn-something-something V2 dataset [6,16] is a large-scale video dataset which is widely used as a benchmark for action recognition tasks. It contains 220,847 video clips with a duration of 2 to 6 s, each showing short human actions or activities from various sources. It covers 174 different action classes, representing a diverse set of everyday human activities, interactions with objects, and gestures.

EGTEA Gaze. The EGTEA Gaze dataset [12] focuses on gaze estimation in the context of object interactions and human-object interactions in an egocentric vision setup. The dataset contains data from 61 participants interacting with 28 different objects. It consists of 14,000 frames in 86 videos and covers 32 activities, like pouring liquids, cutting vegetables, writing on a whiteboard, and using tools.

Industrial Hand Assembly Dataset V1. The Industrial Hand Assembly Dataset V1 [18] consists of industrial hand assembly recordings which are available as videos or already pre extracted hand skeleton data in 12 fine-grained hand action classes. The dataset includes 459,180 frames in its basic version and in another available version, 2,295,900 frames after applying spatial augmentation. One of its essential characteristic is the presence of occlusions, hand-object interactions, and a diverse set of fine-grained human hand actions specifically tailored for industrial assembly tasks.

4.2   Model Training Environment

The model architecture was implemented using PyTorch and integrated with Google's MediaPipe Hands framework. Training and tuning of hyperparameters were performed on the STANDARD_NC6 instance of Microsoft Azure, which is equipped with 6 vCPUs and 56 GiB of memory. For the final training of the model, a GPU corresponding to half a K80 card with 12 GiB of memory was used, along with a maximum of 24 data disks and 1 NCiS. Training time ranged from 20 h and 09 min to 50 min for the pre-trained model and up to 1 h and 45 min for the fine-tuned model, depending on the amount of data used, see the last column in Table 2 and the last column in Table 3.

4.3   Self-supervised Pretraining and Downstream Task

To verify that the model architecture and random masking works as desired, the model is first trained on all datasets separate and once combined using the random masking method as described. The reconstruction performance of the action sequences of the model is checked using the respective measurement values, root mean squared error (RMSE), mean squared error (MSE) and R2 score as well as the training time. Furthermore, the respective performance of the model is visualized in a test plot in which the representability of hand movements is demonstrated. These trained models are afterward fine-tuned on the Industrial Hand Action Dataset V1 by applying the complete self-supervised trained model to a classifier consisting of a flatten layer, a linear layer with 126 × 100 input features and the set of classes as output features, followed by a final SoftMax layer. With this additional classifier, the model has 1,882,284 trainable parameters. Since the datasets from Sect. 4.1 have different sizes, different BATCH_SIZEs had to be used in the self-supervised training phase, see first entries in each column in Table 1. The small amount of data was compensated during masking, as in [29], by masking a sample several times per iteration and using it for training, so that the model saw a sample several times in different executions, see ITERMASK cell in Table 1. Thus, as expected, a consistent improvement was observed even if significantly fewer data was available as, for example, in the 20bn-something-something V2 dataset which was trained with a BATCH_SIZE of 128. Also for the downstream task, due to the different amount of data, different hyperparameters have to be applied for the training to stabilize the model and to detect the corresponding patterns in the data, see second entries in column EPOCHS, BATCH, and LR in Table 1.

Table 1. Hyperparameters for Self-Supervised Learning | Downstream Task

Model	Dataset	EPOCHS	BATCH	LR	RANDMASK	ITERMASK
CGTN	20bn-sth-sth	300 | 80	128 | 32	2e−5 | 1e−5	50%	1
CGTN	IHADV1	300 | 80	16 | 32	2e−4 | 1e−5	50%	5
CGTN	EGTEA	300 | 80	16 | 32	2e−4 | 1e−5	50%	5
CGTN	ALL_DATA	300 | 80	128 | 32	2e−4 | 1e−5	50%	1

5   Results and Analysis

In the following section, the results of the self-supervised pre-training and the fine-tuning of the downstream task based on it are presented before an analysis of the training process takes place.

5.1   Results Self-supervised Learning

As seen in Table 2, the best result was obtained with all datasets combined. It took with more than 20 h the longest training time but with an R2 Score of 50.7% and a way lower MSE and RMSE of 0.0001 and 0.01 only the standalone 20bn-sth-sth dataset could keep up with these good results to some extent. It can also be seen in Table 2 that the more data are available and the more variance the data obtain, the better the representation result becomes. An example of the very good representation results can be seen in Fig. 3 where the red and blue dots are the true sequence and the green and yellow dots depending on the hand's, left or right, are the predicted ones during picking up a bigger part. This shows that after the self-supervised representation learning, the model is able to recreate very accurate sequences from scratch.

Table 2. Results of Pretraining using Self-supervised Learning

Model	Dataset	RSME	MSE	R2	Training Time
CGTN	20bn-sth-sth	0.03	0.0009	45.3%	15:07:53.10
CGTN	IHADV1	0.316	0.1	40.4%	02:03:30.20
CGTN	EGTEA	0.264	0.07	30.7%	00:50:15.13
CGTN	ALL_DATA	0.01	0.0001	50.7%	20:09:15.13

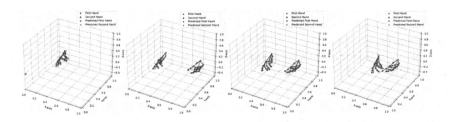

Fig. 3. Predicted Representation of Hand Action

5.2   Results Downstream Task

The downstream task shows a similar picture regarding the amount of data as the previous self-supervised comparison, with a maximum training time of 1:45:18 h. The 20bn-sth-sth dataset, as well as all data sets together, showed significantly

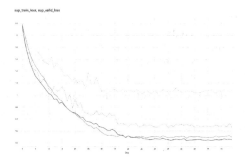

Fig. 4. Train-Val Loss Curve

Table 3. Results of Downstream Task

Model	Pretrained Dataset	Finetune	Test Accuracy by Labeld Data 80% | 60% | 40% | 20% | 10%
CGTN	NO_DATA	IHADV1	94.32% | 92.12% | 90.50% | 69.43% | 52.14%
CGTN	20bn-sth-sth	IHADV1	93.70% | 90.30% | 85.70% | 79.22% | 65.60%
CGTN	IHADV1	IHADV1	94.30% | 90.20% | 78.30% | 75.20% | 68.10%
CGTN	EGTEA	IHADV1	72.40% | 68.60% | 63.10% | 61.80% | 58.40%
CGTN	ALL_DATA	IHADV1	95.63% | 92.64% | 93.15% | 83.13% | 68.49%

better results with many labels. Both data sets achieved an accuracy of over 95% with 80% labeled data and with fewer labels. As expected, accuracy in classification decreases with fewer labels, but the results are still within a very good range with an achieved accuracy up to 93.15% with only 40% of the labels, see Table 3. To compare how self-supervised pretraining improves the results, the first row presents the results of fully supervised training of the model. As in the other experiments, the number of labels in the IHADV1 dataset was reduced piece by piece for this purpose. Although the results show that very good comparable measurements are produced even without pretraining in the high label range, Fig. 4 clearly shows that pretraining leads to better generalizability of the model. This is visible in the smaller gap between the training curve which is the normal line and the validation loss which is the dotted line in comparison of the golden and the blue line. In addition, the results in the low-label range which should be the target for these experiments in Table 3 are clearly worse compared to the pretrained data.

5.3   Analysis

The results demonstrated clearly that more data with more variance in the self-supervised masking produces significantly better results, generalizability, and performance in the self-supervised method as well as in the subsequent down-stream task. It has also been shown that a break-even point is reached with a small amount of labels, such as 40% in this case, producing very high test accuracy results. The improvement with more and high variation data, as in the case of all datasets combined, but also the 20bn-sth-sth dataset, was additionally recognized during training when looking at the weights through the gate. It was recognized that the more data available to the gate, the better the tower could be balanced, leading to a better final result. When fewer data was available, only one tower was optimized, since the gate is designed for only one tower in the end. This shows that using a large set of unlabeled data under these conditions is necessary for the robustness of similar models, but this needs to be further investigated in later experiments.

6   Conclusion and Outlook

In this work, it was shown that it is possible to pre-train a spatio-temporal deep learning model without labels using data from everyday life and then fine-tune it efficiently with only a few labels. This approach resulted from the high costs of labels for a company, which had to be prevented. Furthermore, with this approach it is possible to train scalable models in a self-supervised way and use them afterward in an industrial application for quality monitoring like in this case human assembly recognition. In future experiments, it will be tested how stable the model reacts to further assembly steps, if catastrophic forgetting is experienced at some point and how the self-supervised pre-training process can be optimized.

References

1. Autoencoders, S.D.: Learning useful representations in a deep network with a local denoising criterion, Pascal Vincent, Hugo Larochelle, Isabelle Lajoie, Yoshua Bengio and Pierre-Antoine Manzagol. J. Mach. Learn. Res. ll, 3371–3408 (2010)
2. Cao, S., Xu, P., Clifton, D.A.: How to understand masked autoencoders. arXiv preprint arXiv:2202.03670 (2022)
3. Devlin, J., Chang, M., Lee, K., Toutanova, K.: BERT: pre-training of deep bidirectional transformers for language understanding. In: Burstein, J., Doran, C., Solorio, T. (eds.) Proceedings of the 2019 Conference of the North American Chapter of the Association for Computational Linguistics: Human Language Technologies, NAACL-HLT 2019, Minneapolis, MN, USA, 2–7 June 2019, Volume 1 (Long and Short Papers), pp. 4171–4186. Association for Computational Linguistics (2019). https://doi.org/10.18653/v1/n19-1423
4. Dosovitskiy, A., et al.: An image is worth 16×16 words: transformers for image recognition at scale (2021)
5. Feichtenhofer, C., Li, Y., He, K., et al.: Masked autoencoders as spatiotemporal learners. Adv. Neural. Inf. Process. Syst. **35**, 35946–35958 (2022)
6. Goyal, R., et al.: The "something something" video database for learning and evaluating visual common sense (2017). https://doi.org/10.48550/ARXIV.1706.04261, https://arxiv.org/abs/1706.04261
7. He, K., Chen, X., Xie, S., Li, Y., Dollár, P., Girshick, R.: Masked autoencoders are scalable vision learners. In: Proceedings of the IEEE/CVF Conference on Computer Vision and Pattern Recognition, pp. 16000–16009 (2022)

8. Hendrycks, D., Gimpel, K.: Gaussian error linear units (GELUS). arXiv preprint arXiv:1606.08415 (2016)
9. Hinton, G.E., Osindero, S., Teh, Y.W.: A fast learning algorithm for deep belief nets. Neural Comput. **18**(7), 1527–1554 (2006)
10. Ioffe, S., Szegedy, C.: Batch normalization: accelerating deep network training by reducing internal covariate shift. In: Bach, F.R., Blei, D.M. (eds.) Proceedings of the 32nd International Conference on Machine Learning, ICML 2015, Lille, France, 6–11 July 2015. JMLR Workshop and Conference Proceedings, vol. 37, pp. 448–456. JMLR.org (2015). https://proceedings.mlr.press/v37/ioffe15.html
11. Li, Y., Si, S., Li, G., Hsieh, C.J., Bengio, S.: Learnable fourier features for multi-dimensional spatial positional encoding (2021)
12. Li, Y., Liu, M., Rehg, J.M.: In the eye of the beholder: gaze and actions in first person video (2020). https://doi.org/10.48550/ARXIV.2006.00626, https://arxiv.org/abs/2006.00626
13. Lin, T., Dollár, P., Girshick, R.B., He, K., Hariharan, B., Belongie, S.J.: Feature pyramid networks for object detection. CoRR abs/1612.03144 (2016). http://arxiv.org/abs/1612.03144
14. Lin, T., Goyal, P., Girshick, R.B., He, K., Dollár, P.: Focal loss for dense object detection. CoRR abs/1708.02002 (2017). http://arxiv.org/abs/1708.02002
15. Liu, M., Ren, S., Ma, S., Jiao, J., Chen, Y., Wang, Z., Song, W.: Gated transformer networks for multivariate time series classification. CoRR abs/2103.14438 (2021). https://arxiv.org/abs/2103.14438
16. Mahdisoltani, F., Berger, G., Gharbieh, W., Fleet, D.J., Memisevic, R.: Fine-grained video classification and captioning. CoRR abs/1804.09235 (2018). http://arxiv.org/abs/1804.09235
17. Ng, A.: Sparse autoencoder (NA). https://www.stanford.edu/class/cs294a/sparseAutoencoder.pdf
18. Sturm, F., Hergenroether, E., Reinhardt, J., Vojnovikj, P.S., Siegel, M.: Challenges of the creation of a dataset for vision based human hand action recognition in industrial assembly. In: Arai, K. (ed.) SAI 2023. LNNS, vol. 711, pp. 1079–1098. Springer, Cham (2023). https://doi.org/10.1007/978-3-031-37717-4_70
19. Tang, P., Zhang, X.: MTSMAE: masked autoencoders for multivariate time-series forecasting. In: 2022 IEEE 34th International Conference on Tools with Artificial Intelligence (ICTAI), pp. 982–989. IEEE (2022)
20. Tong, Z., Song, Y., Wang, J., Wang, L.: VideoMAE: masked autoencoders are data-efficient learners for self-supervised video pre-training. Adv. Neural. Inf. Process. Syst. **35**, 10078–10093 (2022)
21. Trockman, A., Kolter, J.Z.: Patches are all you need? Trans. Mach. Learn. Res. **2023** (2022)
22. Vaswani, A., et al.: Attention is all you need. Adv. Neural Inf. Process. Syst. **30** (2017)
23. Vincent, P., Larochelle, H., Bengio, Y., Manzagol, P.A.: Extracting and composing robust features with denoising autoencoders. In: Proceedings of the 25th International Conference on Machine Learning, pp. 1096–1103 (2008). https://doi.org/10.1145/1390156.1390294
24. Vincent, P., Larochelle, H., Lajoie, I., Bengio, Y., Manzagol, P.A., Bottou, L.: Stacked denoising autoencoders: learning useful representations in a deep network with a local denoising criterion. J. Mach. Learn. Res. **11**(12) (2010)
25. Vondrick, C., Pirsiavash, H., Torralba, A.: Anticipating visual representations from unlabeled video. In: Proceedings of the IEEE Conference on Computer Vision and Pattern Recognition, pp. 98–106 (2016)

26. Vondrick, C., Shrivastava, A., Fathi, A., Guadarrama, S., Murphy, K.: Tracking emerges by colorizing videos. In: Proceedings of the European Conference on Computer Vision (ECCV), pp. 391–408 (2018)

27. Wu, W., Hua, Y., Wu, S., Chen, C., Lu, A., et al.: SkeletonMAE: spatial-temporal masked autoencoders for self-supervised skeleton action recognition. arXiv preprint arXiv:2209.02399 (2022)

28. Xie, Z., et al.: SimMIM: a simple framework for masked image modeling. In: 2022 IEEE/CVF Conference on Computer Vision and Pattern Recognition (CVPR), pp. 9643–9653 (2021)

29. Zerveas, G., Jayaraman, S., Patel, D., Bhamidipaty, A., Eickhoff, C.: A transformer-based framework for multivariate time series representation learning. In: Proceedings of the 27th ACM SIGKDD Conference on Knowledge Discovery & Data Mining, pp. 2114–2124 (2021)

30. Zhang, F., et al.: MediaPipe hands: on-device real-time hand tracking. CoRR abs/2006.10214 (2020). https://arxiv.org/abs/2006.10214

ST: Innovations in Computer Vision & Machine Learning for Critical & Civil Infrastructures

Pretext Tasks in Bridge Defect Segmentation Within a ViT-Adapter Framework

Matthieu Pâques[1]([☒]), Didier Law-Hine[2]([☒])[iD], Otmane Alami Hamedane[2], Thanh-Tung Nguyen[3], Viet-Vu Tran[3], and Nicolas Allezard[1]

[1] Université Paris-Saclay, CEA, List, 91120 Palaiseau, France
{matthieu.paques,nicolas.allezard}@cea.fr
[2] Socotec Monitoring, 9 rue Léon Blum, 91120 Palaiseau, France
didier.lawhine@socotec.com
[3] Socotec Vietnam, 17/575 Kim Ma, Ngoc Khanh, Ba Dinh, Hanoi, Vietnam

Abstract. Computer vision-based systems hold great potential for assisting experts during visual inspections of civil infrastructures. They can enhance efficiency and objectivity in detecting and characterizing anomalies, thereby supporting maintenance obligations. Here, we report on the image semantic segmentation of multiple bridge defects (Crack, Corrosion, Rebar Corrosion and Spallation) within a Vision Transformers (ViT)-Adapter framework. ViTs have shown outstanding performance on a variety of tasks provided they are correctly pre-trained. By capitalizing on publicly available datasets with self-supervised pre-training methods (DINO, iBOT, SupMAE), segmenter models were efficiently trained for each defect category with minimal annotation efforts. Self-supervised pre-training on a medium-scale specific dataset was found to outperform supervised pre-training on both a massive generalist dataset (SA-1B) and a small specific dataset. More specifically, SupMAE exhibited a propensity for preparing the segmenter to handle "stuff" defects (Crack, Corrosion, and Spallation), while DINO demonstrated better performance for "thing" defects (Rebar Corrosion).

Keywords: Computer Vision · Semantic Segmentation · Vision Transformers · Bridge Defect · Visual Inspection · Self-Supervised Pre-training · Stuff vs Thing classes

1 Introduction

Bridge defects are pervasive in the field of civil engineering, necessitating strict inspection and maintenance protocols to safeguard infrastructure and uphold public safety. Enhancing the efficiency of bridge inspections can be achieved through the implementation of deep learning algorithms capable of detecting and localizing different type of defects in bridge images [21,22].

For example, the detection of spallation has been achieved with a dataset comprising three levels of severity using a comparative analysis of multiple

G. Bebis et al. (Eds.): ISVC 2023, LNCS 14361, pp. 187–198, 2023.
https://doi.org/10.1007/978-3-031-47969-4_15

Convolutional Neural Networks (ConvNets) [24]. For the purpose of crack segmentation, a feature silencing module has been integrated into a ConvNet [5]. The detection of rebar corrosion has been investigated employing a model with Ground Penetrating Radar images as inputs [2].

Deep neural networks require a substantial amount of data to effectively generalize, taking into account the diversity of objects and varying weather conditions. For this purpose, the utilization of pre-training on a pretext task has demonstrated its effectiveness. Notably, leveraging Vision Transformers (ViT) on a large-scale dataset consistently yields remarkable outcomes [10,18].

Finding a dataset closely aligned with structural defect segmentation remains a decisive yet challenging endeavor. In this regard, self-supervised methods offer a promising approach, as they have the capability to learn informative image representations without the need for explicit annotations. These methods prioritize proximity to the target task, enhancing their suitability for addressing the challenges in structural defect segmentation. Instance discrimination-based pre-training tasks, common in the state-of-the-art, extract global information suitable for classification but differ from the local-level focus of segmentation [7,8,12]. Dense pre-training tasks like reconstruction, on the other hand, yield performance gains in segmentation-related studies [13,16].

Structural defects disrupt from most object detection studies as they mostly belong to "stuff" objects (e.g. "grass", "wall") by opposition to "thing" objects i.e. countable, with specific volume or shape (e.g. "car", "dog"). The distinction between "stuff" and "thing" objects has already been identified (e.g. COCO stuff [6]) but the topic remains largely unexplored regarding what pre-training to choose depending on the nature of the object.

In this work, we utilize a substantial database, referred to as the Sofia database, which comprises inspection data carried out on bridges spanning from 1996 to 2021. This database contains a comprehensive collection of 139,455 images, encompassing diverse types of structural defects on various bridge components [19]. According to the available classification labels the defect are approximately distributed in 31% Crack, 12% Corrosion, 7% Rebar corrosion and 10% Spallation, the remaining percentage being other defects. We first build a subdataset for segmentation and develop a defect segmenter targeting those four above-mentioned classes. An active-learning based pipeline is developed to streamline the labeling process, incorporating pre-trained models from publicly available datasets. Subsequently, supervised and self-supervised pre-training methods are being investigated for model training optimization, with a particular attention paid to the nature of the object to segment in the downstream task. The overarching aim is to leverage the entire pool of public and private data and models to enhance the accuracy and effectiveness of the defect segmenter.

2   Methods

2.1   ViT-Adapter Model

ViT models excel at capturing global information, making them suitable for tasks involving global context analysis like classification. However, dense tasks such as segmentation require local information extraction for achieving accurate pixel-level predictions, which is a specific advantage of convolution layers absent in conventional ViTs. Additionally, conventional ViTs lack the benefits of learning multi-scale representations because of their columnar architecture. To overcome these limitations, a ViT Adapter architecture was introduced [9], incorporating a parallel convolution module that extracts four features at varying resolutions, enabling the integration of multi-scale information into ViT.

In this work, we opt for a lightweight segmenter head on top of the ViT-Adapter backbone model. To generate a segmentation mask from the multi-scale features, we employ the Feature Pyramid Network (FPN) approach [17]. The FPN process involves reducing the depth of the features by half using a kernel convolution (3,3). The features are upsampled to achieve the same resolution and then combined through summation. A dense layer is then employed to decrease the number of channels and match the number of classes for prediction.

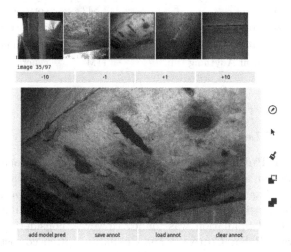

Fig. 1. Segmentation tool. Pixano [1] is adapted to construct a segmentation dataset.

2.2   Datasets

The purpose of our experiments involved searching for available specialized datasets on structural defects and generalist datasets designed to accommodate diverse domains. Additionally, segmentation datasets targeting the four aforementioned structural defects were created. All the datasets used in this work are listed in Table 1. The Pixano annotation tool [1] was adapted to build our segmentation subdatasets (Fig. 1). The tool incorporates active learning by providing initial annotations from pre-trained models, which are subsequently reviewed and corrected by a human operator if needed. This iterative process minimizes the need for manual annotation for a significant portion of image pixels, and the model weights are regularly updated through re-training on the newly annotated data. The whole process results in a segmentation dataset composed of 5,792 images with mask for the 4 considered defects (Table 1). Train and validation subdatasets are obtained by splitting with ratio 66% and 33%.

Table 1. List of the datasets used in the study with their associated pre-training purposes : Supervised Learning (SL) or Self/Semi Supervised Learning (SSL).

Name	Source	Nb images	Domain	Purpose
Crack-Public	Concrete Crack Conglomerate [3]	10,995	crack	SL
Corr-Public	Corrosion Condition State [4]	440	corrosion	SL
RebCorr-Public	Rebar Corrosion [11]	2,622	rebar corrosion	SL
Sofia	private [19]	139,455	13 defects	SSL
Crack-Sofia	private	1,714	crack	SL
Corr-Sofia	private	1,542	corrosion	SL
RebCorr-Sofia	private	1,068	rebar corrosion	SL
Spall-Sofia	private	1,468	spallation	SL
SA-1B	Segment Anything [14]	11M	generalist	SL

2.3 Supervised Learning (SL) Pre-training

Pre-training on Public Datasets. A straightforward approach entails supervised pre-training on a source dataset that closely aligns with the target dataset, encompassing similar types of images and classes. We compile a list of available datasets suitable for this pre-training purpose (Table 1). No available public data for the defect label Spallation was found. However, considering the semantic closeness between Rebar Corrosion and Spallation (often consists on a visible rebar inside a spallation), the RebCorr-Public dataset [11] was also used as a pretext task to pretrain on Spallation.

SAM. The Segment Anything Model (SAM) has recently been introduced [14] as a foundation model for segmentation, which utilizes a ViT backbone and a transformer decoder. Notably, the SAM training process involves the use of the SA-1B dataset, distinguished by its massive scale (11 million images, 1 billion masks) and the adoption of segmentation by a prompt methodology. The prompt, represented as points or bounding boxes, serves to indicate the object to be segmented. The decoder component takes both the prompt and the image representation from the backbone as input. For our study, we select the SAM ViT/b16 model (106M parameters) instead of the SAM ViT/h16 model (683M parameters) as the baseline for comparison with the ViT-s8-Adapter model for self/semi-supervised tasks (28M parameters). We retrieve the weights of the ViT/b16 model from [14] to initialize a ViT/b16 Adapter backbone.

2.4 Self- And Semi-Supervised Learning (SSL) Pre-training

DINO. DINO [8] is a self-supervised learning method that utilizes a master-student framework. The student and master models receive augmented versions of the original image, with the student receiving both global and local views. The objective is to increase the similarity between the master and student representations using a cross-entropy loss function. To prevent undesirable trivial solutions, DINO employs sharpening and centering techniques. Sharpening involves using a softmax activation with a temperature below unity to amplify differences in representation dimensions, while centering subtracts the average representation term by term to avoid dominant dimensions.

SupMAE. The Masked Autoencoder (MAE) [13] approach employs a self-supervised technique where the input image is partitioned into patches, a subset of which is removed, and the backbone model is trained using the remaining visible patches. A semi-supervised variant called SupMAE is proposed [16], which boosts training efficiency by introducing a parallel classification task alongside the reconstruction task. Considering the presence of classification data in the Sofia dataset [19], which includes information on defects and bridge components, SupMAE is chosen over MAE for this study. Multi-scale models require a fixed 2D grid to assemble the features of the different scales. To adapt Sup-MAE to multi-scale models, we replace the patches to be masked with a masking token instead of removing them from the input sequence. While this alteration does lead to the loss of one of the method's advantages, namely the reduction in the model's input size and its associated computational cost, our implementation of SupMAE in the ViT-Adapter architecture still manages to effectively reduce computational expenses. Before each ViT block is employed, the hidden patches are eliminated, and at the end of each block, empty patches (zeros) are reintroduced to facilitate the assembly of ViT and Adapter representations.

iBOT. The iBOT method [26] adapts the DINO framework to add a supplementary Masked Image Modeling loss (MIM loss). In DINO, the similarity loss is specifically applied to the class token of the cropped images, while the MIM loss enforces similarity on the patch tokens, allowing the model to learn information more locally. The application of a secondary loss on the patch tokens has shown to be advantageous for dense tasks [15,20]. The iBOT method matches DINO on global task such as classification (ImageNet: +0.4% top1 accuracy) while outperforming it on dense tasks such as segmentation or detection on few public datasets (ADE20K: +3.8% mIoU, COCO: +1.1% AP).

2.5   Training Parameters

For the segmentation, we use the AdamW optimizer with a learning rate of 0.001 and the Recall Cross Entropy loss [23]. The model is trained for 60 epochs with a batchsize of 4 running on 4 P5000 16Go gpus. The images are resized to (512,512) pixels and augmented by color jittering, random crop and horizontal flip. The model performance is assessed every epoch using the accuracy (Acc) and the mean intersection over union (mIoU). We use the mIoU as the reference metrics to fairly measure both classes performances (background and defect). The selected model corresponds to the best model according to the mIoU on the validation set. For the self-supervised experiments, we use the optimizer, the learning rate, the losses, the image size and the batchsize suggested in the original papers and we set a number of 100 epochs. To match the computational resources required, we run the experiments on 8 A100 80Go gpus. Unless explicitly stated, the ViT-Adapter backbone and/or the FPN segmenter are trained from scratch.

We apply the different pre-training methods on the whole backbone (ViT/s8 + Adapter). A comparison with DINO method applied to different parts of the backbone (any, ViT part and whole) reveals the advantages of pre-training the entire backbone rather than the ViT alone (Table 2). We admit an unfavorable bias towards the SAM [14] implementation, since only ViT weights are retrieved (training on a 11M images dataset would be too costly). However, the larger number of parameters of the ViT/b16 (106M vs 28M) should compensate for the partial backbone pre-training.

Table 2. Comparison of the segmenter ViT/s8 Adapter performance with different parts of the backbone pre-trained. Pre-training dataset: Sofia. Segmentation dataset: Crack-Sofia.

Pre-training	Pre-trained backbone	Acc	mIoU
None	None	97.68	60.03
DINO	ViT/s8	98.09	62.16
DINO	ViT/s8 Adapter	**98.25**	**63.90**

3   Results and Discussion

Table 3 summarizes the performance obtained for the four considered defects on the validation datasets (Sofia segmentation subdatasets) from the different listed pre-training methods : supervised (SL), self/semi-supervised (SSL), or a combination of both (best SSL then SL).

Figure 2 depicts the successful segmentation of the structural defect in a challenging environment (i.e. presence of a corroded cable with rebar corrosion). Conversely, Fig. 3 showcases less satisfactory results. These failures in detection

Table 3. Comparison between pre-training methods: Supervised (SL), Self/Semi-Supervised (SSL). Segmenters are pre-trained on the pre-training dataset(s), then are trained and validated on the Sofia segmentation subdatasets. (bold) best, (underline) best SSL, (*) weights retrieved from the authors.

Training dataset	Pre-training method	Pre-training dataset	Acc.	mIoU
Crack-Sofia	SL	Crack-Public [3]	98.06	62.63
	SL* (SAM)	SA-1B [14]	98.04	63.01
	SSL (DINO)	Sofia	98.25	63.90
	SSL (SupMAE)	Sofia	98.31	64.78
	SSL (iBOT)	Sofia	98.20	63.84
	SL* (SAM) then SL	SA-1B then Crack-Public	**98.45**	65.48
	best SSL then SL	Sofia then Crack-Public	98.35	**65.95**
Corr-Sofia	SL	Corr-Public [4]	6.06	69.12
	SL* (SAM)	SA-1B [14]	97.47	75.96
	SSL (DINO)	Sofia	97.57	76.90
	SSL (SupMAE)	Sofia	97.84	77.86
	SSL (iBOT)	Sofia	97.56	76.37
	SL* (SAM) then SL	SA-1B then Corr-Public	97.77	77.52
	best SSL then SL	Sofia then Corr-Public	**97.82**	**78.25**
RebCorr-Sofia	SL	RebCorr-Public [11]	99.49	67.78
	SL* (SAM)	SA-1B [14]	99.61	68.48
	SSL (DINO)	Sofia	99.68	74.76
	SSL (SupMAE)	Sofia	99.47	68.92
	SSL (iBOT)	Sofia	99.67	73.56
	SL* (SAM) then SL	SA-B then RebCorr-Public	**99.74**	75.13
	best SSL then SL	Sofia then RebCorr-Public	99.70	**75.29**
Spall-Sofia	SL	RebCorr-Public [11]	94.91	66.52
	SL* (SAM)	SA-1B [14]	96.97	74.68
	SSL (DINO)	Sofia	97.24	76.63
	SSL (SupMAE)	Sofia	97.29	76.92
	SSL (iBOT)	Sofia	97.32	76.78
	SL* (SAM) then SL	SA-1B then RebCorr-Public	96.95	74.48
	best SSL then SL	Sofia then RebCorr-Public	**97.38**	**77.89**

seem to primarily occur in out-of-distribution scenarios, such as those involving very large cracks or unseen concrete wall pattern.

A significant finding from our experiment is the importance of pre-training on a large and close-to-target-domain dataset. Across all classes, SSL pre-training on the full Sofia dataset (139k images of various structural defects) consistently yields superior performance compared to SL pre-training on a massive generalist dataset (SA-1B, 11M images) or a small specific dataset ("Defect"-Public, few hundreds of images).

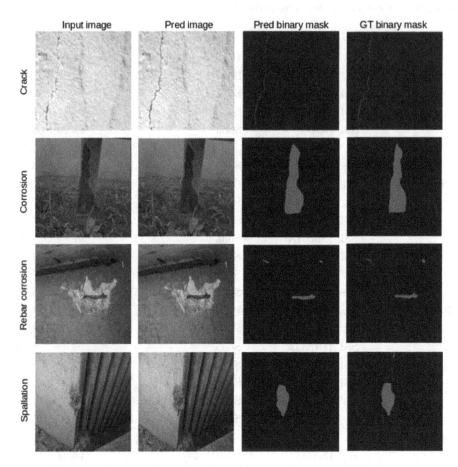

Fig. 2. Segmentation predictions on the Sofia specialized subdatasets. Pre-training: best SSL then SL. From left to right: input image, image with prediction, prediction binary mask and ground truth binary mask.

When comparing the two SL pre-training methods, SAM (SA-1B) exhibits remarkable generalization ability, outperforming close-to-target-domain datasets for the four defects. The superiority of SAM becomes more pronounced when dealing with a small specialized dataset (Corrosion) or one that is far from the target domain (Spallation) (SAM vs. specialized: Corrosion: +6.84% mIoU, Spallation: +8.18% mIoU). Combining SAM with SL pre-training gives a significant gain over SAM pre-training for all defects but Spallation. The existing well-learned representation by SAM could be adversely affected by the domain gap between RebCorr-Public [11] and Spall-Sofia.

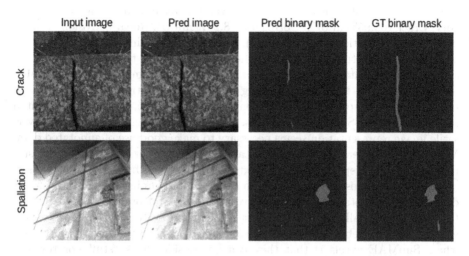

Fig. 3. Examples of poor segmentation predictions on the Sofia specialized subdatasets. Pre-training: best SSL then SL. From left to right: input image, image with prediction, prediction binary mask and ground truth binary mask.

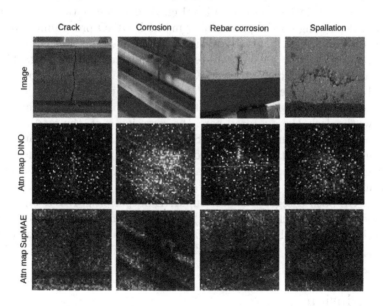

Fig. 4. Sum of the attention maps of the ViT/s8 after backbone pre-training on the full Sofia dataset. 6 attention heads, one color per head.

Combining the best self-supervised pre-training with supervised pre-training (best SSL then SL) yields the most favorable results for each defect category: Crack (65.95% mIoU), Corrosion (78.25% mIoU), Rebar corrosion (75.29% mIoU), and Spallation (77.89% mIoU). Interestingly, adding the SL pre-training after the SSL pre-training induces a net gain compared to SSL alone even for a very small SL dataset (e.g. Corrosion: Corr-Sofia 440 images, +0.39% mIoU). We also observe a large gain of doing a prior SSL pre-training before the SL pre-training on a specific dataset, even when the specific dataset is substantial (e.g. Crack: Crack-Sofia 10,995 images, +2.32%). We conclude a strong and versatile image representation seems necessary to make good use of annotated data. Moreover, the general image representation learned under SSL method can still be fine-tuned for a specific task with extra labeled images from a specific dataset.

Lastly, upon closer examination on the SSL pre-training methods, SupMAE demonstrates a notable ability to serve as a successful pretext task for Crack, Corrosion, and Spallation with the best mIoU. However, it yields the least favorable results for Rebar Corrosion. A common characteristic among the classes where SupMAE excels is that they can be considered as "stuff" or textural objects. In SupMAE, the understanding of texture is favored by the reconstruction task in the pixel dimension. Conversely, with iBOT, the reconstruction is executed in a latent dimension which does not bring much advantage for texture detection. Rebar corrosion exhibits characteristics similar to a "thing" object, possessing a distinct shape (thin and long) and color (dark brown). In this scenario, DINO appears to be the most effective pre-training method. Upon examining the attention maps of ViT (Fig. 4), one can notice a difference of behaviour depending on the pre-training method. DINO pre-training, based on instance discrimination, tends to identify a single object per image, resulting in one dominant object or region activated on the attention maps (e.g. third column, second row: the rebar corrosion). On the other hand, the dense pretext task of SupMAE enables the model aware of multiple objects resulting in different objects or regions being activated on the attention maps (e.g. second column, third row: the deck, the guardrail bars, the corrosion spot, the road).

To validate the stronger ability of SupMAE than DINO to prepare a model for "stuff" object detection, we use two ViT/b16 pre-trained with each method and trained with a linear segmenter head on the ADE20k dataset [25] containing 115 "thing" classes (clock, person, table, ...) and 35 "stuff" classes (wall, sky, floor, ...). On both category classes, SupMAE outperforms DINO but the gain is stronger for "stuff" classes (+4.31%) than for "thing" classes (+3.63%) confirming the superior ability of SupMAE to extract textural information ("stuff": $mIoU_{supmae} = 47.24$ %, $mIoU_{dino} = 42.93$ %, "thing": $mIoU_{supmae} = 35.41$ %, $mIoU_{dino} = 31.78$%).

4   Conclusion

To the best of our knowledge, this is the first time that a ViT-Adapter architecture has been applied to bridge defect segmentation, coupled with state-of-the-art self-supervised pre-training methods (DINO, SupMAE, iBOT). Experiments were conducted targeting four critical types of bridge defects: Crack, Corrosion, Rebar Corrosion, and Spallation. After identifying the pre-training as a strategic feature for ViT model performance, our study mainly focuses on pre-training methods and the nature of pre-training datasets (specific or generalist). Importantly, we find out that self-supervised pre-training on a medium scale but specific dataset (Sofia) gave better results than both supervised pre-training on a small specific dataset and supervised learning on a massive generalist dataset (SA-1B). We also noted that the combination of self-supervised pre-training and supervised pre-training on a specific dataset yielded the best overall results, highlighting that labeled data have a stronger impact on performance once the model has already acquired a robust representation of images.

Finally, the superiority of SupMAE for "stuff" defects (Corrosion, Crack and Spallation) and conversely the superiority of DINO on "thing" defects (Rebar Corrosion) pointed the predisposition of each method regarding whether the object to segment could be considered more as a "stuff" or a "thing". A qualitative analysis of the attention maps highlighted a tendency to focus on the most salient object ("thing") for DINO, while SupMAE induces attention for a more diverse range of object including background and textural object ("stuff"). This finding is reinforced by our experiment also on the benchmark dataset ADE20k, prompting further investigation into which self-supervised pre-training method best aligns with "stuff" or "thing" objects.

References

1. Pixano homepage. https://pixano.cea.fr/. Accessed 17 July 2023
2. Ahmed, H., La, H.M., Tran, K.: Rebar detection and localization for bridge deck inspection and evaluation using deep residual networks. Autom. Constr. **120**, 103393 (2020)
3. Bianchi, E., Hebdon, M.: Concrete crack conglomerate dataset. University Libraries, Virginia Tech. Dataset (2021)
4. Bianchi, E., Hebdon, M.: Corrosion condition state semantic segmentation dataset. University Libraries, Virginia Tech. Dataset (2021)
5. Billah, U.H., La, H.M., Tavakkoli, A.: Deep learning-based feature silencing for accurate concrete crack detection. Sensors **20**(16), 4403 (2020)
6. Caesar, H., Uijlings, J., Ferrari, V.: Coco-stuff: thing and stuff classes in context. In: Proceedings of the IEEE Conference on Computer Vision and Pattern Recognition, pp. 1209–1218 (2018)
7. Caron, M., Misra, I., Mairal, J., Goyal, P., Bojanowski, P., Joulin, A.: Unsupervised learning of visual features by contrasting cluster assignments. In: Advances in Neural Information Processing Systems, vol. 33, pp. 9912–9924 (2020)
8. Caron, M., et al.: Emerging properties in self-supervised vision transformers. In: Proceedings of the IEEE/CVF International Conference on Computer Vision, pp. 9650–9660 (2021)
9. Chen, Z., et al.: Vision transformer adapter for dense predictions. arXiv preprint arXiv:2205.08534 (2022)
10. Dosovitskiy, A., et al.: An image is worth 16×16 words: transformers for image recognition at scale. arXiv preprint arXiv:2010.11929 (2020)

11. Foucher, P., Decor, G., Bock, F., Charbonnier, P., Heitz, F.: Evaluating of a deep learning method for detecting exposed bars from images. In: NSG2021 2nd Conference on Geophysics for Infrastructure Planning, Monitoring and BIM, vol. 2021, pp. 1–5. European Association of Geoscientists & Engineers (2021)

12. Grill, J.B., et al.: Bootstrap your own latent a new approach to self-supervised learning. In: Advances in Neural Information Processing Systems, vol. 33, pp. 21271–21284 (2020)

13. He, K., Chen, X., Xie, S., Li, Y., Dollár, P., Girshick, R.: Masked autoencoders are scalable vision learners. In: Proceedings of the IEEE/CVF Conference on Computer Vision and Pattern Recognition, pp. 16000–16009 (2022)

14. Kirillov, A., et al.: Segment anything. arXiv preprint arXiv:2304.02643 (2023)

15. Li, C., et al.: Efficient self-supervised vision transformers for representation learning. arXiv preprint arXiv:2106.09785 (2021)

16. Liang, F., Li, Y., Marculescu, D.: SupMAE: supervised masked autoencoders are efficient vision learners. arXiv preprint arXiv:2205.14540 (2022)

17. Lin, T.Y., Dollár, P., Girshick, R., He, K., Hariharan, B., Belongie, S.: Feature pyramid networks for object detection. In: Proceedings of the IEEE Conference on Computer Vision and Pattern Recognition, pp. 2117–2125 (2017)

18. Minderer, M., et al.: Revisiting the calibration of modern neural networks. In: Advances in Neural Information Processing Systems, vol. 34, pp. 15682–15694 (2021)

19. Pâques, M., Law-Hine, D., Alami Hamedane, O., Magnaval, G., Allezard, N.: Automatic multi-label classification of bridge components and defects based on inspection photographs (2023). in press

20. Rabarisoa, J., Belissen, V., Chabot, F., Pham, Q.C.: Self-supervised pre-training of vision transformers for dense prediction tasks. arXiv preprint arXiv:2205.15173 (2022)

21. Savino, P., Tondolo, F.: Civil infrastructure defect assessment using pixel-wise segmentation based on deep learning. J. Civ. Struct. Heal. Monit. **13**(1), 35–48 (2023)

22. Spencer, B.F., Jr., Hoskere, V., Narazaki, Y.: Advances in computer vision-based civil infrastructure inspection and monitoring. Engineering **5**(2), 199–222 (2019)

23. Tian, J., Mithun, N.C., Seymour, Z., Chiu, H.P., Kira, Z.: Striking the right balance: recall loss for semantic segmentation. In: 2022 International Conference on Robotics and Automation (ICRA), pp. 5063–5069. IEEE (2022)

24. Yasmin, T., Le, C., La, H.M.: Deep architecture based spalling severity detection system using encoder-decoder networks. In: Bebis, G., et al. (eds.) ISVC 2022. LNCS, vol. 13599, pp. 332–343. Springer, Cham (2022). https://doi.org/10.1007/978-3-031-20716-7_26

25. Zhou, B., Zhao, H., Puig, X., Fidler, S., Barriuso, A., Torralba, A.: Scene parsing through ade20k dataset. In: Proceedings of the IEEE Conference on Computer Vision and Pattern Recognition, pp. 633–641 (2017)

26. Zhou, J., et al.: iBOT: Image BERT pre-training with online tokenizer. arXiv preprint arXiv:2111.07832 (2021)

A Few-Shot Attention Recurrent Residual U-Net for Crack Segmentation

Iason Katsamenis[1](✉) , Eftychios Protopapadakis[2] , Nikolaos Bakalos[1] ,
Andreas Varvarigos[3] , Anastasios Doulamis[1] , Nikolaos Doulamis[1] ,
and Athanasios Voulodimos[1]

[1] National Technical University of Athens, 9th Iroon Polytechniou str., 15773
Athens, Greece
{iasonkatsamenis,bakalosnik,thanosv}@mail.ntua.gr,
{adoulam,ndoulam}@cs.ntua.gr
[2] University of Macedonia, 156th Egnatia str., 54636 Thessaloniki, Greece
eftprot@uom.edu.gr
[3] Imperial College London, South Kensington Campus, London SW7 2BT, UK
andreas.varvarigos20@imperial.ac.uk

Abstract. Recent studies indicate that deep learning plays a crucial role in the automated visual inspection of road infrastructures. However, current learning schemes are static, implying no dynamic adaptation to users' feedback. To address this drawback, we present a few-shot learning paradigm for the automated segmentation of road cracks, which is based on a U-Net architecture with recurrent residual and attention modules (R2AU-Net). The retraining strategy dynamically fine-tunes the weights of the U-Net as a few new rectified samples are being fed into the classifier. Extensive experiments show that the proposed few-shot R2AU-Net framework outperforms other state-of-the-art networks in terms of Dice and IoU metrics, on a new dataset, named CrackMap, which is made publicly available at https://github.com/ikatsamenis/CrackMap.

Keywords: Semantic segmentation · U-Net · Attention · Recurrent residual convolutional unit · Road cracks

1 Introduction

The development of cracks on the road surface is a frequently occurring defect and can constitute a safety hazard for road users. Cracking in its various types (longitudinal, oblique, alligator cracks, etc.) affects the traffic flow and safety, resulting in poor performance of the road infrastructure, accidents, as well as increased CO_2 emissions, fuel costs, and time delays. Indicatively, for 2006, the comprehensive cost of traffic crashes where road conditions contributed to crash

This work has received funding from the European Union's Horizon 2020 Research and Innovation Programme under grant agreement No 955356 (Improved Robotic Platform to perform Maintenance and Upgrading Roadworks: The HERON Approach).

occurrence or severity, in the United States alone, is estimated at \$217.5 billion, which corresponds to 43.6% of the total crash costs [26]. More recent evidence highlights that approximately \$400 billion is invested globally each year in pavement construction and maintenance [23]. Therefore, the adoption of effective monitoring strategies can lead to enormous economic, social, and environmental benefits to the community.

Recently, there has been a great research interest in the automatic visual inspection of road distress, by analyzing visual data [20]. Generally, deteriorated pavement produces rough surfaces, which entails that various image processing methods such as thresholding [18], edge detection [28], and mathematical morphology [22] can be used to localize crack regions. The core idea behind these approaches is that cracked regions tend to demonstrate non-uniformity, while on the other hand, the color and textural characteristics of the non-deteriorated road surface are more consistent and smoother. However, even though such techniques are computationally efficient, they are susceptible to image noise and fail to generalize the differentiation between the defect and the surface background [9,12].

Current developments in deep learning and artificial intelligence technology have led Convolutional Neural Networks (CNNs) to be an effective tool for the automatic visual inspection of road infrastructures [1,16,19]. The main asset of such deep architectures, compared to the aforementioned conventional image processing methods, is the fact that they leverage throughout the learning procedure annotated ground truth data [8]. Thereby, these algorithms demonstrate high identification accuracy by effectively learning the essential features needed to classify a given pixel as defective or not [3,10].

Usually, Fully Convolutional Networks (FCNs), or their variants U-Nets, are considered for providing a precise pixel-based segmentation of damaged areas from RGB images of road infrastructures [12,14,21]. This is mainly due to the fact that FCNs have emerged as powerful segmentation tools, especially for performing accurate pixel-based classification tasks for challenging problems (e.g., biomedical imaging problems with data expressed either in 2D or 3D [5,24], as well as crack segmentation [6]). To enhance the performance of the original U-Net, numerous elements have been introduced, such as residual convolutional units [2,27] and attention gates instead of the typical skip connection [11,17].

1.1   Current Limitations and Our Contribution

Inspired by the above research work, we present R2AU-Net, which is a deep U-Net structure with recurrent residual and attention modules (see Fig. 1). Compared to the standard U-Net, R2AU-Net incorporates recurrent residual convolutional layers (R2CL) that ensure better feature representation for the segmentation task and attention gates to highlight salient features that are passed through the skip connections [2,17].

Still, however, the most crucial hindrance of the aforementioned typical deep learning frameworks is that they treat the segmentation task as a static procedure. More specifically, they leverage knowledge derived from labeled data, but,

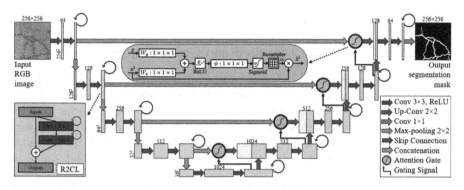

Fig. 1. The proposed U-Net architecture with recurrent residual and attention modules for road crack segmentation.

nevertheless, it is not possible to further refine their outputs by exploiting user interaction, especially in cases where the deep network underperforms [24]. To this end, we introduce a few-shot refinement scheme which is a semi-supervised learning paradigm, based on the R2AU-Net, that is able to adapt the model's behavior and weights according to user's feedback, to further increase the segmentation performance (see Fig. 2).

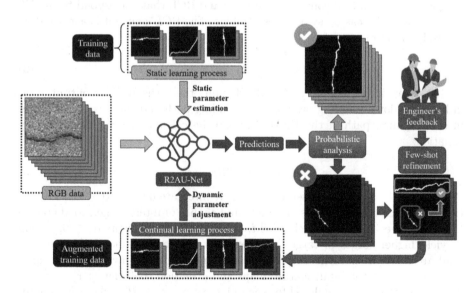

Fig. 2. A schematic representation of the proposed few-shot retraining strategy.

2   Proposed Architecture

2.1   R2AU-Net Architecture for Road Crack Segmentation

In this section, we present R2AU-Net, whose architecture is illustrated in Fig. 1 and is a combination of Recurrent Residual U-Net [2] and Attention U-Net [17]. It is emphasized that the model was designed for segmenting cracks in RGB images and, hence, provides meticulous information on a variety of metrics and properties that are critical for the automated and robotic-driven maintenance processes, such as geometry, type, orientation, length, density, and shape of cracks.

In particular, the operations within the Recurrent Convolutional Layers (RCL) in R2CL (see Fig. 1) are carried out based on the discrete time steps which are expressed according to the RCNN [13]. Suppose we have an input at layer l within an R2CL block, and a pixel located at (i, j) within an input on the feature map k in the RCL. We denote $\mathcal{Y}_{ijk}^l(t)$ the output of the model at time step t, which can be expressed as:

$$\mathcal{Y}_{ijk}^l(t) = (w_k^\varrho)^T \cdot x_l^{\varrho(i,j)}(t) + (w_k^r)^T \cdot x_l^{r(i,j)}(t-1) + \beta_k \tag{1}$$

where $x_l^{\varrho(i,j)}(t)$ and $x_l^{r(i,j)}(t-1)$ represent respectively the inputs to the standard convolution layers and l^{th} RCL. In parallel, w_k^ϱ and w_k^r denote respectively the weights of the standard convolutional layer and RCL that correspond to the kth feature map, whereas β_k symbolizes the bias. The RCL's output is activated by the ReLU function ϱ as follows:

$$\mathcal{R}(x_l, w_l) = \varrho(\mathcal{Y}_{ijk}^l(t)) = max(0, \mathcal{Y}_{ijk}^l(t)) \tag{2}$$

Let x_l an input sample of the R2CL unit, then, the R2CL's output x_{l+1}, in both the downsampling layer in the encoding path and the upsampling layer in the decoding path of the R2AU-Net, can be calculated using the following equation:

$$x_{l+1} = x_l + \mathcal{R}(x_l, w_l) \tag{3}$$

In parallel, as one can observe in Fig. 1 we integrate into R2AU-Net an attention gate mechanism to focus on points and shapes of interest (i.e., road cracks) [17]. More specifically, for each pixel i, the attention coefficients $\alpha_i \in [0, 1]$ tend to yield higher values in target crack regions and lower values in background road areas. We obtain the output of the attention gate in layer l by multiplying element-wise the input feature maps and attention coefficients: $\hat{x}_i^l = x_i^l \cdot \alpha_i^l$. Attention values are calculated for each pixel vector $x_i^l \in \mathbb{R}^{F_l}$, where F_l denotes the number of feature maps in layer l. Also, a gating vector $g_i \in \mathbb{R}^{F_g}$ is utilized in order to determine the focus area per pixel. To achieve greater performance the attention coefficient is derived by leveraging the additive attention:

$$Q_\alpha^l = \psi^T(\varrho(W_x^T x_i^l + W_g^T g_i + \beta_g)) + \beta_\psi, \quad a_i^l = \sigma(Q_\alpha^l) \tag{4}$$

where σ corresponds to the sigmoid activation function, $W_x \in \mathbb{R}^{F_l \times F_{int}}$ and $W_g \in \mathbb{R}^{F_g \times F_{int}}$ are linear transformations that are calculated by utilizing channel-wise $1 \times 1 \times 1$ convolutions for the input tensors, and, lastly, $\beta_g \in \mathbb{R}^{F_{int}}$ and $\beta_\psi \in \mathbb{R}$ denote the bias.

2.2 Few-Shot Learning for Segmentation Refinement

As shown in Fig. 2, we hereby propose a dynamic rectification scheme that leverages expert users' feedback on a small part of the data in order to improve the overall performance of the aforementioned R2AU-Net. The proposed retraining strategy dynamically updates the weights of the model, so that (a) the refined incoming samples are trusted as much as possible, while simultaneously (b) a minimal degradation of the already gained knowledge is achieved. To this end, let us denote p_{ij} the soft label value of a pixel that is located in position (i, j) of a given image. Then, for each input n we calculate the average image confidence score I_n, defined as:

$$I_n = \frac{1}{\sum_{\forall i,j} \zeta_{ij}} \cdot \sum_{i=1}^{R} \sum_{j=1}^{C} \zeta_{ij} \cdot p_{ij} \tag{5}$$

where C and R correspond to the image's columns and rows respectively. In parallel, $\zeta_{ij} \in \{0, 1\}$ equals 1 when $p_{ij} > \vartheta$ and 0 otherwise, where ϑ is the detection acceptance threshold, which is set to 0.5. As such, the confidence score considers only the cracked regions over the image n, provided by the deep classifier. Subsequently, we rank the images according to I_n scores. The 5% of the lower ranked images are provided to an engineering expert, who rectifies the model's segmentation outputs. Lastly, the refined few-shot annotated data are fed back to the network for updating the model's weights.

3 Experimental Setup and Results

3.1 Dataset Description

For the training procedure five datasets, consisting of 4,717 images in total, that depict crack defects, were utilized (see Table 1). During the data preprocessing step, the RGB data were resized to a resolution of 256×256 pixels. Lastly, 80% of the data was used for training the models (3,774 images), while the rest 20% was used for validation (943 images).

For the data collection process of the CrackMap dataset that constitutes the test dataset for the current study, a GoPro HERO9 Black was used. The images were captured on various streets in South Greece during late August, between 11:00 AM and 4:00 PM. The weather during this period was hot and dry, with clear skies, ensuring no presence of water tracks on the road surface. During the data acquisition process, the optical sensor was mounted on an inspection vehicle (see Fig. 3a). It is emphasized that the acquired data are RGB images with an

Table 1. Utilized datasets for training and evaluation tasks.

Set	Name	Number of RGB samples
Train and Validation	CFD	118
	CRACK500	3,363
	Cracktree200	206
	DeepCrack	521
	GAPS384	509
	Total	**4,717**
Test	**CrackMap**	**120 − 6**

aspect ratio of 4:3 and, in particular, with a pixel resolution of 5,184×3,888 (see Fig. 3b). Moreover, the RGB sensor was set to shoot at a high frame rate and, more specifically, at 50 frames per second in order to ensure sufficient data acquisition regarding both the positive (road surface with cracks) and negative (non-deteriorated road surface) events.

(a) Vehicle-mounted sensor

(b) Acquired RGB data

Fig. 3. Experimental setup for acquiring RGB road images.

It is also highlighted that in order to deal with the severe class imbalance problem from the acquired RGB data, image patches with a resolution of 256×256 were manually extracted and then annotated. The individual patches encompass one or multiple road cracks and were segmented as well as verified by engineer experts, within the framework of the H2020 HERON project [7]. As presented in Table 1, the CrackMap dataset contains 120 annotated images with a resolution of 256×256. We evaluate the comparative models that perform the crack segmentation task on the CrackMap data, minus the 6 extracted images that correspond to the 5% of the lower ranked images and were eventually utilized for the refinement process (see Sect. 2.2). CrackMap has been made available to the scientific community, for verifying the results and further research, at https://github.com/ikatsamenis/CrackMap.

3.2 Comparative Algorithms and Training Configuration

The validation of the proposed methodology for the crack segmentation task is based on examining its performance against other state-of-the-art approaches that perform crack recognition and precise localization in a different way. In particular, we compare the proposed static and dynamically refined R2AU-Net models on the CrackMap dataset (minus the 6 extracted images) with the following segmentation algorithms: (i) U-Net [21], (ii) V-Net [15], (iii) ResU-Net [27], (iv) R2U-Net [2], (v) Attention U-Net [17], and (vi) ResUNet-a [4].

The aforementioned deep models were developed using Keras and TensorFlow libraries in Python. In parallel, they were trained and evaluated on an NVIDIA Tesla T4 GPU provided by Google Colab. We trained the neural networks for 100 epochs with early stopping criteria set to 10 epochs in order to avoid overfitting, using mini-batches of size 8. The training processes started from scratch by randomly initializing the networks' weights. The models are trained end-to-end using the Adam algorithm to optimize the dice loss function, in order to deal with class imbalance problems. It is noted in parallel that the optimizer is set to its default parameters ($\beta_1 = 0.9$ and $\beta_2 = 0.999$), with an initial learning rate of 10^{-3} that is decayed by a factor of 10 each time there was no improvement in the validation loss, for 5 consecutive epochs. Lastly, for the rectification mechanism, we fine-tune the proposed R2AU-Net by retraining it for 5 epochs, with a learning rate reduced by a factor of 10, to avoid damaging its weights.

3.3 Experiments and Comparisons

Figure 4 depicts a visual comparison of the output masks generated by our method and the aforementioned comparative models. For a quantitative analysis of the experimental results, the performance of the implemented models is evaluated in terms of the Dice coefficient and IoU metric. In particular, we compute the aforementioned metrics for every RGB image of the CrackMap dataset (minus the 6 extracted images) and, thereby, we report the average values across all 114 images of the test set with a confidence level of 95%. As can be observed in Table 2 the proposed R2AU-Net outperforms the various state-of-the-art algorithms by at least 1.69% and 1.89% in terms of Dice and IoU scores respectively.

In parallel, Fig. 5 illustrates indicative segmentation outputs of the R2AU-Net before and after applying the proposed few-shot rectification mechanism. As shown in Table 2, the rectified R2AU-Net model demonstrated increased performance of 4.63% and 5.83% in terms of Dice and IoU respectively, after the few-shot refinement procedure. To investigate whether this improvement is statistically significant, we exploit the Wilcoxon signed-rank test on the obtained scores of the two models, which is a nonparametric statistical test that compares two paired groups [25]. The obtained p-values for both metrics are lower than .001 and, thus, we can reject the null hypothesis, which entails that there is a statistically significant difference in the comparative results of the R2AU-Net, before and after the proposed few-shot refinement process.

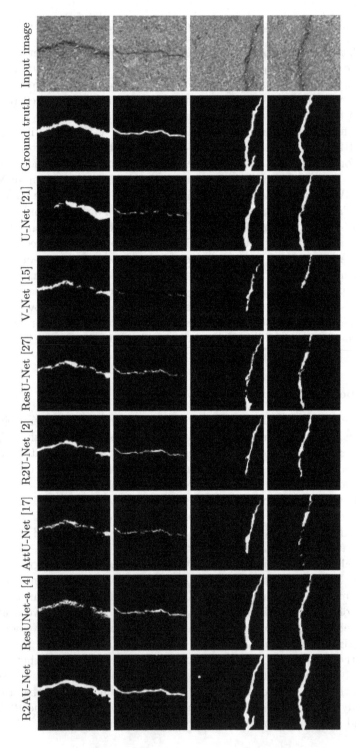

Fig. 4. Visual comparison of the static deep models' segmentation outputs.

Table 2. Performance evaluation and comparisons.

Model	Avg. Dice	Avg. IoU
U-Net [21]	49.73% ± 3.75%	35.54% ± 3.36%
V-Net [15]	38.04% ± 4.65%	26.57% ± 3.68%
ResU-Net [27]	60.37% ± 2.50%	44.53% ± 2.48%
R2U-Net [2]	70.74% ± 1.59%	55.39% ± 1.84%
AttU-Net [17]	52.64% ± 3.70%	38.06% ± 3.21%
ResUNet-a [4]	63.28% ± 2.47%	47.60% ± 2.49%
R2AU-Net	**72.43% ± 1.36%**	**57.28% ± 1.61%**
FS R2AU-Net	**77.06% ± 1.17%**	**63.11% ± 1.50%**

Lastly, we assess the computational complexity of the algorithms under comparison. It is noted that no dedicated hardware accelerators were employed for any of the compared models and to ensure fairness, all testing procedures were executed on the same GPU. The static models demonstrated similar processing times, with R2AU-Net presenting an average of 0.174±0.006 s per image and 0.156±0.005 s after the dynamic refinement process. Thus, the few-shot learning framework retained and improved the resource-effective characteristics of the original model, which indicates that this scheme is computationally efficient, which is a crucial asset in real-time monitoring applications.

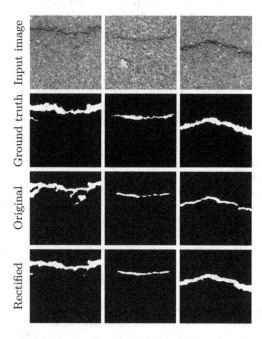

Fig. 5. Output masks produced by the original R2AU-Net against the proposed rectified few-shot learning paradigm.

4   Conclusions

This paper presents a few-shot learning strategy for road crack segmentation. The proposed scheme is based on R2AU-Net which exploits recurrent residual and attention mechanisms to capture richer global context information and local semantic features. Furthermore, the adopted few-shot refinement process, through which the network weights are dynamically updated as a few incoming rectified samples are fed into the algorithm, led to state-of-the-art performance on a new publicly available dataset. Lastly, future work can focus on leveraging multisensor data and fusion techniques to further improve the segmentation capabilities of the proposed system.

References

1. Ahmed, T.U., et al.: An integrated CNN-RNN framework to assess road crack. In: 2019 22nd International Conference on Computer and Information Technology (ICCIT), pp. 1–6 (2019)
2. Alom, M.Z., et al.: Recurrent residual convolutional neural network based on U-Net (R2U-Net) for medical image segmentation. arXiv preprint:1802.06955 (2018)
3. Billah, U.H., Tavakkoli, A., La, H.M.: Concrete crack pixel classification using an encoder decoder based deep learning architecture. In: Bebis, G., et al. (eds.) ISVC 2019. LNCS, vol. 11844, pp. 593–604. Springer, Cham (2019). https://doi.org/10.1007/978-3-030-33720-9_46
4. Diakogiannis, F.I., et al.: ResUNet-a: a deep learning framework for semantic segmentation of remotely sensed data. ISPRS J. Photogramm. Remote. Sens. **162**, 94–114 (2020)
5. Huang, H., et al.: UNet 3+: a full-scale connected UNet for medical image segmentation. In: 2020 IEEE International Conference on Acoustics, Speech and Signal Processing (ICASSP), pp. 1055–1059 (2020)
6. Jenkins, M.D., et al.: A deep convolutional neural network for semantic pixel-wise segmentation of road and pavement surface cracks. In: 2018 26th European Signal Processing Conference (EUSIPCO), pp. 2120–2124. IEEE (2018)
7. Katsamenis, I., et al.: Robotic maintenance of road infrastructures: the heron project. In: Proceedings of the 15th International Conference on PErvasive Technologies Related to Assistive Environments, pp. 628–635. PETRA 2022, Association for Computing Machinery, New York, NY, USA (2022)
8. Katsamenis, I., et al.: Simultaneous precise localization and classification of metal rust defects for robotic-driven maintenance and prefabrication using residual attention u-net. Autom. Constr. **137**, 104182 (2022)
9. Katsamenis, I., Protopapadakis, E., Doulamis, A., Doulamis, N., Voulodimos, A.: Pixel-level corrosion detection on metal constructions by fusion of deep learning semantic and contour segmentation. In: Bebis, G., et al. (eds.) ISVC 2020. LNCS, vol. 12509, pp. 160–169. Springer, Cham (2020). https://doi.org/10.1007/978-3-030-64556-4_13
10. Katsamenis, I., et al.: Deep transformer networks for precise pothole segmentation tasks. In: Proceedings of the 16th International Conference on PErvasive Technologies Related to Assistive Environments, pp. 596–602 (2023)

11. König, J., et al.: A convolutional neural network for pavement surface crack segmentation using residual connections and attention gating. In: 2019 IEEE International Conference on Image Processing (ICIP), pp. 1460–1464 (2019)
12. Lau, S.L., et al.: Automated pavement crack segmentation using U-Net-based convolutional neural network. IEEE Access **8**, 114892–114899 (2020)
13. Liang, M., Hu, X.: Recurrent convolutional neural network for object recognition. In: Proceedings of the IEEE Conference on Computer Vision and Pattern Recognition, pp. 3367–3375 (2015)
14. Long, J., Shelhamer, E., Darrell, T.: Fully convolutional networks for semantic segmentation. In: Proceedings of the IEEE Conference on Computer Vision and Pattern Recognition, pp. 3431–3440 (2015)
15. Milletari, F., Navab, N., Ahmadi, S.A.: V-Net: fully convolutional neural networks for volumetric medical image segmentation. In: 2016 Fourth International Conference on 3D Vision (3DV), pp. 565–571. IEEE (2016)
16. Ogawa, N., et al.: Distress level classification of road infrastructures via CNN generating attention map. In: 2020 IEEE 2nd Global Conference on Life Sciences and Technologies (LifeTech), pp. 97–98 (2020)
17. Oktay, O., et al.: Attention U-Net: learning where to look for the pancreas. arXiv preprint:1804.03999 (2018)
18. Oliveira, H., Correia, P.L.: Automatic road crack segmentation using entropy and image dynamic thresholding. In: 2009 17th European Signal Processing Conference, pp. 622–626 (2009)
19. Pandey, A.K., et al.: Convolution neural networks for pothole detection of critical road infrastructure. Comp. Electr. Eng. **99**, 107725 (2022)
20. Protopapadakis, E., Katsamenis, I., Doulamis, A.: Multi-label deep learning models for continuous monitoring of road infrastructures. In: Proceedings of the 13th ACM International Conference on PErvasive Technologies Related to Assistive Environments, pp. 1–7 (2020)
21. Ronneberger, O., Fischer, P., Brox, T.: U-Net: convolutional networks for biomedical image segmentation. In: Navab, N., Hornegger, J., Wells, W.M., Frangi, A.F. (eds.) MICCAI 2015. LNCS, vol. 9351, pp. 234–241. Springer, Cham (2015). https://doi.org/10.1007/978-3-319-24574-4_28
22. Tanaka, N., Uematsu, K.: A crack detection method in road surface images using morphology. MVA **98**, 17–19 (1998)
23. Torres-Machí, C., et al.: Sustainable pavement management: integrating economic, technical, and environmental aspects in decision making. Transp. Res. Rec. **2523**(1), 56–63 (2015)
24. Voulodimos, A., et al.: A few-shot U-Net deep learning model for COVID-19 infected area segmentation in CT images. Sensors **21**(6) (2021)
25. Wilcoxon, F.: Individual comparisons by ranking methods. In: Kotz, S., Johnson, N.L. (eds.) Breakthroughs in Statistics. Springer Series in Statistics. Springer, New York (1992). https://doi.org/10.1007/978-1-4612-4380-9_16
26. Zaloshnja, E., Miller, T.R.: Cost of crashes related to road conditions, united states, 2006. In: Annals of Advances in Automotive Medicine/Annual Scientific Conference, vol. 53, p. 141. Association for the Advancement of Automotive Medicine (2009)
27. Zhang, Z., Liu, Q., Wang, Y.: Road extraction by deep residual U-Net. IEEE Geosci. Remote Sens. Lett. **15**(5), 749–753 (2018)
28. Zhao, H., Qin, G., Wang, X.: Improvement of canny algorithm based on pavement edge detection. In: 2010 3rd International Congress on Image and Signal Processing, vol. 2, pp. 964–967 (2010)

Efficient Resource Provisioning in Critical Infrastructures Based on Multi-Agent Rollout Enabled by Deep Q-Learning

Polyzois Soumplis[1,2]([⊠]), Panagiotis Kokkinos[2,3], and Emmanouel Varvarigos[1,2]

[1] School of Electrical and Computer Engineering, National Technical University of Athens, Athens, Greece
soumplis@mail.ntua.gr
[2] Institute of Communication and Computer Systems, Athens, Greece
[3] Department of Digital Systems, University of Peloponnese, Sparta, Greece

Abstract. Next-generation smart environments, an integral part of our modern lives, integrate computing and networking technologies to enrich our experiences. Harnessing cutting-edge technologies like the Internet of Things, Artificial Intelligence, and Edge Computing, they function under the control of critical infrastructures often processing complex computer vision tasks such as object recognition and image segmentation in real-time. These infrastructures manage vast volumes of data with intensive computational demands. In response to these challenges, infrastructures have evolved to distributed that consists of resources of different capabilities and different operators. Within these environments, the security and communication among different domains are fundamental. Each domain potentially has different levels of security requirements and may use various protocols for communication. As data travels across these domains, it is exposed to a variety of threats, including data breaches, cyberattacks, and unauthorized access. In such a environment, where multiple domains co-exist, each with its own unique resources and security specifications, communication constraints across them further complicate the resource allocation process. This complexity is further increased by the diverse computing and networking constraints imposed by applications. In this work, we propose a multi-Agent Deep Reinforcement Learning mechanism that operates based on multi-Agent Rollout and deep Q-learning in order to serve the different applications' requirements. The proposed optimization mechanism considers multiple objectives during the resource allocation process and tries to fulfill the specific constraints set by the demands and the broader objectives set by the infrastructure operator. Through rigorous evaluations, we showcase the effectiveness and efficiency of our proposed mechanisms in accommodating the heterogeneous and stringent workload requirements, whilst optimizing the use of infrastructure resources. Our simulation experiments confirm that the proposed mechanism can substantially enhance the efficiency of resource allocation in critical infrastructures.

Keywords: critical infrastructure · multi-Agent Rollout · Deep Q-Learning · Reinforcement Learning

G. Bebis et al. (Eds.): ISVC 2023, LNCS 14361, pp. 210–223, 2023.
https://doi.org/10.1007/978-3-031-47969-4_17

1   Introduction

In our digital era, we are witnessing the advent of smart environments such as smart grids, smart cities, autonomous 5G/6G and optical networks, intelligent supply chain networks and smart utility networks. These facilitate essential services our society relies on, in sectors like energy production and distribution, transportation systems, water and waste management, and public health services. The respective environments and services are based on complex systems with high and heterogeneous requirements that make use of computing and networking resources. As a result, these resources are recognized as critical infrastructures [1], since their interruption, degradation, or destruction can impact national security, economy, public health, and safety.

In today's interconnected world, computing and networking critical infrastructures typically function as large-scale distributed systems to meet the massive and stringent requirements of emerging applications, including advanced computer vision tasks like real-time object recognition and intricate image analysis. These systems are composed of resources that belong to various domains and are managed by different operators, raising significant security challenges [2]. The different operators, can have diverse security policies. This can potentially lead to vulnerabilities, providing opportunities for malicious actors to exploit. Enabling different levels of communication across the different domains is of paramount importance during the resource allocation process.

When optimizing the performance of the application executions and the utilization of such an environment, it is important to consider the cross-domain and the interoperability requirements that stem from the heterogeneous nature of the constituent systems [3]. This can result to multiple optimization parameters/constraints that must be taken into consideration during the optimization process. As the multi and conflicting objectives need to be addressed simultaneously and also in real time, it leads to numerous possible decisions, rendering the optimal selection, a challenging task.

The resource allocation complexity increases further when security constraints related to the critical infrastructures need to be taken into account as they limit or prohibit the exchange of information with the optimization mechanisms due to security, privacy and operational integrity reasons. In such environments, the data becomes especially sensitive. Misuse can pose significant risks both to users and infrastructure operators, potentially enabling exploitation of vulnerabilities. This necessitates the need for optimization mechanisms that operate in a decentralized manner and ensure the careful and selective dissemination of information among different providers and operators, aiming to safeguard the infrastructure's security while ensuring its smooth operation.

With the growing trend of modularity and scalability in computational tasks, applications are effectively implemented as microservices. This is particularly relevant for computer vision tasks, where the sheer volume of data makes it challenging to transport all the information while it can also vary with time. This approach allows for a more flexible deployment and scalability, ensuring that tasks are independently developed, deployed, and scaled based on demand. When integrated into critical infrastructures, these microservices dynamically adapt to the workload changes and ensure optimal performance. In this work, we present a multi-agent Rollout enabled by Deep Q-Learning mechanism to enable the efficient resource allocation in critical infrastructures.

A multi-agent approach seems the most prominent solution, with different agents cooperating/competing over time to fulfill conflicting objectives, like minimizing communication delay and processing costs, or maximizing resource utilization, all set by the workloads and infrastructure operators. Initially, we model the respective problem as a Markov Decision Process (MDP) problem. As the complexity can be quite high given the increased space-action space, we employ the multi-Agent Rollout [4] and the multi-Agent Deep Q-learning technique to optimize the resource allocation performance and support various levels of cooperation, thereby enhancing the infrastructure's security.

The rest of this paper is organized as follows. In Sect. 2, we report on related work. In Sect. 3, we present the infrastructure under consideration and introduce the resource allocation mechanisms. In Sect. 4, we evaluate the efficiency of these mechanisms and finally in Sect. 5, we conclude our work.

2 Related Work

The challenge of resource allocation, especially regarding virtualized resources, has been a prominent area of research in the realm of cloud computing. Recognizing the complexity of executing processes across multi-layered infrastructures, the respective computational workloads are segmented into a multitude of tasks, each carrying distinct networking and processing requirements. This particular approach facilitates scalable execution across an extensive spectrum of computational resources.

In [5], the authors conducted an analysis of the positioning of virtual machines (VMs) on physical systems within a cloud data environment. They followed a graph-based model of the infrastructure, where nodes correspond to VMs and links to the network interaction between them. The primary objective was to minimize the peak utilization across the links, to optimally use network resources and minimize congestion. To do so, they proposed a first-fit heuristic algorithm to allocate as many communicating VMs on identical physical systems as possible reducing at the same time the communication overheads. Authors in [6] developed "Foggy", an architectural framework based on open-source tools that handles requests from end users in a multi-level heterogeneous fog/edge environment. The requests arrive in a FIFO queue, and at each stage, the available nodes are ranked by their processing power and their networking towards the end user, in order to extract the best match.

Multi-Agent systems have also been proposed to support the operation of critical infrastructures. In [7] the authors present multi-Agent mechanisms to safeguard various domains such as e-commerce, e-health systems, network-based Intrusion Detection Systems, telematic and transport systems, and environmental monitoring. The efficacy of such systems depends on the agents' ability to monitor, communicate and generate decisions, ensuring also the confidentiality and integrity of the data stored and communicated. In [8] the authors design and implement a multi-Agent system intended for the intelligent operation of a distributed smart grid at distribution level. In [9], the authors propose a control strategy for defense in Cyber-Physical Systems, with a focus on protecting Critical Infrastructure. Their controller identifies optimal decisions to address system vulnerabilities, modelling the respective problem as a multi-Agent, general sum game model. The problem is solved using a reinforcement learning mechanism. Authors in

[10] proposed a dynamic resource scheduling scheme for critical smart-healthcare tasks in a near/far edge-cloud infrastructure. Their model consists of a multi-Agent system with four kinds of agents, named personal agent, master personal agent, fog node agent, and master fog node agent. The scheduling strategy relies on effective prioritization of the tasks according to their criticality and on balancing network load.

Reinforcement learning is a technique that is also being used in the context of network and computing resource provisioning. Authors in [11] present a deep reinforcement learning approach, based on state-action-reward-state-action (SARSA), for addressing the problem of task off-loading and resource allocation in Multiple access Edge Computing (MEC) environments. They model user requests as a sequence of sub-tasks, which can be executed by either the nearest edge server, the adjacent edge server, or the central cloud. The proposed solution aims to minimize service delay and energy consumption by dynamically making offloading decisions and allocating resources based on the current state of the infrastructure. [12] presents a solution for the microservice coordination problem in mobile edge computing environments, where mobile users (e.g., autonomous vehicles) offload computation to the edge clouds. The authors aim to minimize a weighted combination of delay and migration costs by determining the optimal deployment locations for microservices. They first propose an offline algorithm able to derive the optimal objective and then use a Q-learning-based reinforcement learning approach. [13] proposes a deep reinforcement learning solution for microservice deployment in heterogenous edge-cloud environments, with microservices considered as a service chain, in which their execution must be performed in a pre-specified order. Simulations are conducted with a combination of real and synthetic data, with the objective of minimizing the average waiting time of the microservices.

Neural networks have also been used to facilitate the deployment of applications and tackle the uncertainties of the network efficiently. In [14] authors employ Deep Reinforcement learning and a heuristic mechanism that operate sequentially and enhance the resource allocation efficiency given the expansive search space. Authors in [15] developed AREL3P, a Reinforcement Learning based solution that adapts the allocation of the resources to the predictions made for the application requirements by an ML mechanism. In [16] authors proposed a Double Deep Q-Learning VNF placement algorithm (DDQN-VNFPA) that employs a two-fold approach: first determining the optimal solution from a large solution space using DDQN, and then strategically placing/releasing application resources via a threshold-based policy. Other works [17, 18] also consider Deep Reinforcement Learning combined with Graph Neural Network (GNN) techniques to enable the topology aware resource allocation.

3 Workload Management in Critical Infrastructures

3.1 Infrastructure Model

In our work, we consider a critical infrastructure based on distributed computing resources that are interconnected with a variety of communication technologies including both wireless and wired networks that span across the different network domains (access, metro core). Computing resources initially came in the form of datacenters that offer abundant resources at low cost and high security levels during execution process.

As datacenters are placed in relatively small number of locations around the world, their applicability in the execution of time-sensitive workloads is limited, due to the need to transfer the application data in faraway locations that results in increased communication latency and over usage of the networking resources. To address this issue, edge computing resources are progressively being utilized to service applications requiring low latency, as these are strategically placed closer to data generation sources and across various locations. Edge resources can vary both in size and capabilities, with the most common being micro-datacenters (mDC's), modular data centers in shipping containers, specialized computing devices (FPGA, GPU) and IoT devices (e.g., Arduino, Raspberry Pi, NVIDIA Jetson). These can be placed on providers' premises (e.g., the Central Office - CO), or on other large and small premises (e.g., stadiums, malls, businesses, houses). This diversity of resources, while beneficial in terms of flexibility and adaptability, introduces a considerable degree of complexity to the management mechanism, while increasing the vulnerability of the infrastructure as a whole.

Figure 1 illustrates the infrastructure model we consider in our work, where computing resources belong to various domains, each adhering to different security protocols and serving various applications. Inter-domain communication is also governed by specific security constraints to maintain the data integrity and confidentiality of the domains, introducing limitations in the information exchanged. This poses another challenge for the resource allocation mechanisms and their ability to efficiently allocate resources.

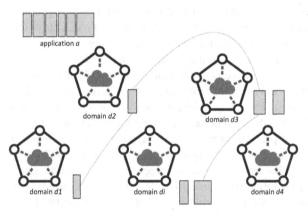

Fig. 1. A critical, computing and networking, infrastructure composed of multiple domains, where distributed applications are executed.

This shift in the architecture design has altered the way applications are build and are executed. Applications are now broken down into a sequence of tasks, enabling greater flexibility, scalability, and efficiency. Tasks can be processed in parallel and scaled individually according to demand, which helps to better utilize resources and increase overall system performance. This is especially important in multi-domain critical infrastructures, where handling large volumes of data and maintaining reliable performance are crucial. For instance, a workload execution might include tasks such as firewall enforcement, load balancing, wide area network (WAN) optimization, and intrusion prevention. Each task is capable of being executed at various nodes of the critical infrastructure and is characterized by its discrete computing and storage requirements. Constraints exist among tasks of the same application, particularly regarding their network requirements, such as the necessary bandwidth for communication or an upper limit on the latency between two tasks, to ensure their proper and timely execution. This environment necessitates the development of innovative resource allocation mechanisms that are operate efficiently under the constraints imposed by both the critical infrastructure and the applications.

3.2 Problem Formulation

We denote the computing and networking critical infrastructure as a fully connected directed graph $G = (V, E)$. The graph is composed of a set of nodes V which correspond to the nodes equipped with computing (CPU, RAM) and storage resources and to nodes where the data is generated. Links E represent the connectivity and the communication characteristics among the corresponding nodes and they embody parameters such as transmission latency, available bandwidth and security constraints among different nodes. Each node $v \in V$ has its own set of resources under control and its profile is represented by the tuple $\tau_v = [c_v, r_v, s_v, o_v, n_v]$, where c_v corresponds to the processing capacity of the node v quantified in CPU units. This indicates the computational power of the node and determines how much processing load it can handle. Respectively, r_v is the node's RAM capacity measured in RAM units and s_v is the node's storage capacity measured in storage units. Also, each node is characterized by monetary costs o_v, which is the node's operating cost and n_v is the node's networking cost coefficient. Operational cost relates to the expenses made for purchasing, deploying, and operating the respective computing/storage systems. Networking cost coefficient results from the usage of the communication link between two nodes. If more than one connected task is executed in the same node, the respective communication latency is assumed to be equal to zero. Finally, each node is associated with a specific domain $d_v \in D$. As a result, a collection of communicating domains $C = \{C_d : d \in D\}$ exists, where each C_d represents the domains with which the communication is allowed.

Each application demand $a \in A$, is generated at a node of the infrastructure π_a and is described by a chain of tasks w_a each one specific resource requirements represented by the tuple $\tau_{t,a} = [\varepsilon_{a,t}, \rho_{a,t}, \mu_{a,t}, \theta_{a,t,t'}]$, where $\varepsilon_{a,t}$ is the task's CPU demand, $\rho_{\alpha,t}$ is its memory demand and $\mu_{a,t}$ is the size of the data that need to be processed. The latency limit among two consecutive tasks t, t' of the application is described as $\theta_{a,t,t'}$ and describes the maximum acceptable delay between the nodes v, v' where these tasks will be placed. Hence, each application is described by the tuple $a = (\pi_a, w_a)$.

3.3 Deterministic Markov Decision Process Model

For the purpose of effectively allocating resources for applications' workloads A over the critical infrastructure G we initially model the respective problem as a finite horizon deterministic Markov Decision Process. The MDP model of the resource allocation problem represents a discrete-time dynamic system and is defined by the tuple (X, U, R). The state space $X = (T, W)$ is composed of two components: (i) the resource status of the nodes T, which is the set of tuples τ_v of the infrastructure nodes v, $T = \bigcup_{v \in V} \tau_v$, and (ii) the task status W, which represents the applications that need to be served over the infrastructure, $W = \bigcup_{a \in A} w_a$. This results in a state space of size $N = 3 \cdot |V| + \sum_{a \in A} [|T_A| \cdot (1 + 3 \cdot |A|)]$. The action space U contains all possible actions that can be taken from a given state, with each action at state k, $u_k \in U$ corresponding to the assignment of a task of an application to one of the infrastructure nodes V. It is worth mentioning that constraints exist during the resource allocation process and consequently not all possible actions can be valid for a given state. For a given state x_k, a feasible action u_k (assigning a task to a node) must satisfy the following constraints; (i) Capacity Constraint: For each candidate node $v \in V$, the capacity (CPU,RAM, Storage) required by a task should not exceed its remaining in state x_k, $CPU\_r(x_k) \leq CPU(v, x_k)$, $RAM\_r(x_k) \leq RAM(v, x_k)$, $Str\_r(x_k) \leq Str(v, x_k)$, (ii) Latency Constraint: The latency between two nodes that serve communicating tasks should be less than or equal to the acceptable latency limit. $l_{v,v'} \leq \theta_{a,t,t'}$.

These constraints collectively determine the possible actions (task assignments) at any given state. R is the reward function, given by the function $g_k(x_k, u_k)$. This function provides scalar feedback that signifies the effect of the action, from state x_k to state x_{k+1} in the resource allocation process and is defined as a weighted sum of two components (i) the negative CPU cost, and (ii) the negative task latency. The aim is to maximize through the reward an objective function that consists of the (i) nodes operational cost, and (ii) applications latency, while minimization (iii) the utilization of the activated infrastructure resources. The total cost of a control sequence J is additive in nature as the tasks of the different applications are served. Assuming that A applications need to be served, the total cost of a control sequence is $J(x_o; x_{o,1}, \ldots, x_{o,I}, \ldots, x_{N,I}) = g_N(x_N) + \sum_{k=0}^{N-1} g_k(x_k, u_k)$, where $g_k(x_k, u_k)$ denotes the cost when the system is in state x_k and control function u_k is applied and $g_N(x_N)$ represents the terminal cost when all the applications are served.

The one that minimalizes the cost is $J^*(x_o) = \min_{u_k \in U_k(x_k)} J(x_o; x_1, \ldots, x_k, \ldots, x_N)$ is the optimal value function at the initial state x_o. It is the set of actions for the different states that maximizes the total rewards can be tracked through the use of Dynamic Programming (DP). To do so, the DP algorithm, constructs the optimal solution starting from $J_N^*(x_N)$) and proceeding to $J_{N-1}^*(x_{N-1})$) up to $J_0^*(x_0)$). The optimal solution is identified using a forward algorithm that constructs the optimal control sequence $(u_0^*, u_1^*, \ldots, u_{N-1}^*)$ and state trajectory $(x_1^*, x_2^*, \ldots, x_N^*)$ for the given initial state x_0.

3.4 Multi-Agent Rollout Enabled by Deep Q-Learning

The complexity of resource allocation over the critical infrastructure escalates with the increasing number of nodes and the diverse workloads. Given this intricacy, we adopt the multi-agent Rollout approach. Multiple Rollout Agents either collaborate or compete to address the de-mands of the assigned workloads. These agents utilize multiple DQN agents operating across different domains. Their cooperation is governed by the communication constraints established by the infrastructure, ensuring they effectively approximate the costs associated with various resource allocation decisions.

The Rollout process works as follows: each Rollout agent $l \in L$ is assigned with an application demand. To provision the required resources, it starts from its current state $x_{l,k}$

and generates a sequence of actions with depth h, and calculates the total acquired reward $\sum_{n=k}^{k+h} g_n(x_{l,n}, u_{l,n})$. After reaching state $x_{l,k+h}$ it consults a fast sub-optimal policy to evaluate the future cost $\widetilde{J}_k$ ($f_{l,k+h}(x_{l,k+h}, u_{l,k+h})$) that corresponds to the approximated cost of the actions that are expected to be taken from the remaining agents. The agent operates sequentially, in a given order (Fig. 2) and explores all possible placements across the different possible domains and their nodes. As the search space can be large, the algorithm prunes nodes that do not meet certain conditions. Such conditions are: (i) the minimum latency requirements among the tasks of the applications and (ii) the CPU, RAM and storage capacity, (iii) security constraints. By serving the application demands sequentially and applying a multi-agent approach instead of all-agents-at-once the state-space is significantly reduced from $O(|U|^{|A|})$ to $O(|U| \cdot |A|)$.

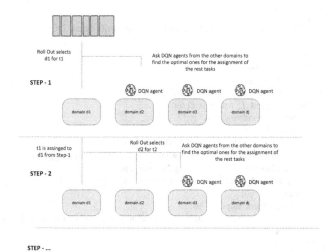

Fig. 2. The Multi-Agent Rollout Process Facilitated by Deep Q-Network (DQN) Agents.

The operation of the Rollout is also based on the approximation of future costs $\tilde{J}_{k+1}$ that is the decisions that will be made by the other agents. In order to approximate the cost-to-go cost given a state, a multi-Agent Deep Q-Learning (DQL) approach [19] is used. This algorithm leverages the power of deep neural networks to approximate the Q-function and exploit the structure of the Markov Decision Process problem. It enhances the traditional Q-Learning by enabling it to handle the high-dimensional state space. Each agent maintains a Q-table, where individual entries $Q(x_{l,k}, u_{l,k})$ correspond to Q-values associated with specific state-action pairs. Q-values are updated following the Bellman equation: $Q(x_{l,k}, u_{l,k}) = Q(x_{l,k}, u_{l,k}) + a \cdot [g(x_{l,k}, u_{l,k}) + \gamma \cdot max(Q(x_{l,k'}, u_{l,k'})) - Q(x_{l,k}, u_{l,k})]$, where α is the learning rate and γ is the discount factor that quantifies the relative importance of future rewards.

DQN agents are trained to estimate Q-values by tuning neural network weights to minimize the difference between predicted and target values, using accumulated experience. In a multi-domain critical infrastructure multiple DQN agents can be deployed, each one j_d associated with a specific domain $d \in D$ and is independently trained to handle the allocation of resources for tasks within its assigned domain. As these agents are operating autonomously, a mechanism for inter-agent communication is also introduced to ensure a global optimization level. Agents exchange parameters of their Q-function approximations that is the weights and biases of their neural networks. Let's denote the parameters of the Q-function approximation for agent j_d at time t as $\theta_{j_d}(t)$. At time t, each DQN agent j_d for each domain $d \in D$, shares its current parameters $\theta_{j_d}(t)$, with the agents $j \in C_d$ with which communication is possible . Upon receiving these parameters, each agent j updates its own parameters using a combination of its current and the received parameters and calculated the weighted average of the two sets of parameters, $\theta_{j_{d1}}(t) = \eta \cdot \theta_{j_{d1}}(t) + (1-\eta) \cdot \theta_{j_{di}}(t)$ for all $j_{di} \in C_d$, where η is a parameter that represents the degree of trust among agents (Table 1).

Table 1. The pseudocode of the training of the multi-agent DQN network.

1. Initialize: θ_{j_d}, ε, c
2. **For** each episode **do**:
3.   Initialize state $x_{j,0}$
4.   **For** each time step within the episode **do**:
5.   **For** each agent j_d with d in D **do**:
6.   Initialize window size h
7.   **For** each h **do**:
8.   Select action $u_{j,k}$ based on current state $x_{j,k}$ and ε
9.   Take action $u_{j,k}$, observe new state $x_{j,k+1}$ and reward $g(x_{j,k}, u_{j,k})$
10.   Update target Q-value using Bellman equation
11.   Update θ_{j_d} based on observed reward and target Q-value
12.   **End For**
13.   **If** mod(time step, c) ==0:
14.   Exchange θ_{j_d} with communicating agents and update accordingly
15.   **End If**
16.   **End For**
17.   **If** all workloads are assigned:
18.   Continue to next episode
19.   **End If**
20.   **End For**

4 Simulation Experiments

4.1 Experimental Setup

To examine the performance of the proposed mechanisms we performed a number of simulation experiments. The mechanisms were developed in Python and the PyTorch library was leveraged for the design and implementation of the Deep Q-Network of the different agents. Consequently, an artificial neural network was presumed as a function approximator for the Q values, featuring an input layer, a hidden layer, and an output layer. The input layer consists of units equivalent to the number of elements in the state vector. The hidden layer comprises 64 units, and the output layer has units corresponding to the number of actions available. The activation function for the hidden layer is the Rectified Linear Unit (ReLU), which imparts non-linearity to the model, facilitating the handling of complex relationships between states and actions. As for the parameters of the DQN network, we selected $\varepsilon = 0.9$, $\gamma = 0.5$, and $\eta = 0.5$. These parameters ensure an optimal balance between exploration and exploitation during the learning process, as well as a suitable learning rate.

We assumed a critical infrastructure consisting of 100 nodes that are equipped with different size resources in terms of CPU, RAM, and storage. Their values were derived from the uniform distributions within the closed intervals of [5,50], [8,128], and [4,256] units respectively. The monetary cost associated with using the resources for a specific duration was assumed to lie within the intervals of [6, 7] latency units (l.u.) for 70% of the nodes, [3, 4] l.u. for 20% of the nodes, and [1, 2] l.u. for the remaining 10% of nodes. The delay for these respective categories was assumed to be within [1–3], [3–5] and [5–10] l.u. so as to capture the different type of resources that are available in a critical infrastructure that incorporates cloud and edge resources. As for the communication delay between infrastructure nodes, it was assumed to be within [1, 5] l.u. Edge resources were assigned a delay of [3, 4] l.u. and cloud resources a delay of [7, 8] l.u., measured from the data generation points [20].

Additionally, we introduced a variable number of application demands, each of which requests [1, 4] tasks and the requirements of each task lie in the range of [1–5] CPU cores, [4–64] GB RAM, and [16–64] GB storage. The task latency demand within an application was assumed to lie within the range [1, 3] l.u. We trained the multi-agent Deep Q-Learning algorithm across such application demands, adjusting and optimizing as necessary to achieve the best possible performance. Training was conducted over 500 episodes, allowing the algorithm to learn and adapt based on the vast array of state-action pairs encountered.

4.2 Evaluation Results

We examined the performance in the achieved weighted cost (equal values of the weighting coefficients) for the different methods by varying the number of applications demands from 200 to 1000. We considered the multi-Agent Rollout mechanism which operates without a width limit h, the multi-Agent Deep Q-Network, and we also incorporated a greedy best-fit heuristic, which acts as the baseline for scenario for our experiments. The results are presented in Fig. 3a. Note that while the use of data for training the models is certainly important, the key aspect in evaluating the effectiveness of our method is assessing the performance of the rollout process.

As we can see the multi-Agent rollout mechanism yields the lowest costs, taking advantage of both the lookahead window and the future cost approximation. This superior performance can be attributed to the consideration of the future decisions made by the different agents in the current state, which results in an improved resource allocation. The multi-Agent DQN networks also outperforms the best-fit heuristic, thanks to its ability to leverage past experiences and new knowledge to make more informed decisions. By exploiting the training data, it learns about the costs and rewards associated with different actions in various states, and thus the multi-Agent DQN mechanism is able to identify and select the actions that are most likely to minimize the overall cost. On the

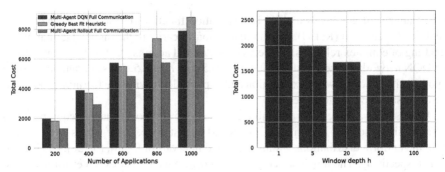

Fig. 3. **a)** The performance of the proposed mechanism for a varying number of application workloads, **b)** The effect of the window depth (h) in the performance of the Multi-Agent Rollout Mechanism.

other hand, while the best-fit heuristic is relatively straightforward and computationally efficient, showcased the worst performance as it is less capable of adapting to and managing the complexities and uncertainties of the resource allocation task especially the latency constraints among the unserved tasks of an application. This greedy heuristic assigns tasks to resources based solely on immediate availability, neglecting to consider the long-term consequences of these assignments.

Next, we examined the performance of the multi-Agent Rollout mechanism by adjusting the depth windows h. This adjustment allowed us to examine the tradeoff between performance and execution time. As the depth decreases, we reduce the number of actions evaluated at a given state, thus examining only h actions and decreasing execution time by a factor equal to $(|U| - h)/|U|$. The results presented in Fig. 3b and correspond to 200 application demands. As anticipated, the multi-Agent Rollout mechanism demonstrated reduced performance with smaller window sizes. But leveraging future cost approximation, it made decisions that improved the performance relative to the greedy baseline scenario. Interestingly, even with a window with half the size of the action space, the rollout mechanism achieved a performance level close to the optimal one. This suggests that the depth window h can be a useful tool for fast decisions.

Finally, we evaluated the impact of agent communication on the Loss function of the multi-agent DQN network for a critical infrastructure that consist of 100 nodes and needs to host 200 application demands. Effective communication is of critical importance for efficient resource allocation and is limited in critical infrastructures. Communication allows agents to share critical information regarding their states, actions, and rewards at specific time periods in order to enable a better update of the weights of the neural network. Thus, communication can potentially enhance the global performance of the multi-agent system by aligning the agents' individual objectives with the system's overall objective.

As it is depicted in Fig. 4a, the loss function is larger when there is limited communication among agents and improves as the level of communication among agents increases. In all cases the loss decreases with time due to the training. These different communication scenarios were then integrated in the multi-Agent Rollout mechanism in order to evaluate its performance among different communication levels. As our

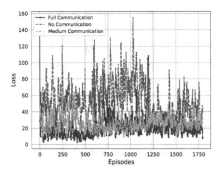 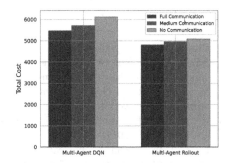

Fig. 4. **a)** The average loss function of the multi-Agent DQN mechanism for different levels of communication among agents, **b)** The effect of the different levels of communication in the performance of the multi-Agent DQN and the multi-Agent Rollout mechanism.

experiments indicate (Fig. 4b), even in the absence of communication among agents, the deviation in the performance of the rollout mechanism remains minimal. This showcases that the multi-Agent rollout mechanism is able to provide good solutions even in absence of communication among agents and showcases the resiliency of our mechanism, despite varying levels of inter-agent communication.

5 Conclusions

The problem of the efficient resource allocation over critical infrastructures is of paramount importance given a diverse computing and networking resources characterized by different resource types, varying communication latencies, constraints, and costs of usage. In this work, to address the complex nature of this task, we proposed a Multi-Agent Rollout mechanism that leverages multi-Agent Deep Q-Learning to perform the resource allocation. Our simulation results that the multi-Agent DQN and the multi-Agent Rollout mechanism significantly outperform the traditional greedy best-fit heuristics in the context of resource allocation. The superiority of these approaches lies in their ability to consider both immediate and future rewards made by other agents, making more informed decisions and leading to optimized resource utilization and cost reduction. Additionally, we analyzed various parameters that could influence the performance of the multi-Agent Rollout mechanism, such as the window size. We demonstrated that performance and execution time are inversely related, and interest-ingly, the mechanism exhibited robust performance even with smaller window sizes and maintained resilience under communication limitations. In conclusion, the pro-posed resource allocation mechanisms provide significant benefits in the management of complex critical infrastructures, offering efficient, cost-effective solutions that can handle a wide range of constraints imposed by the infrastructure and application work-loads.

Acknowledgement. The work presented is supported by the EU Horizon 2020 research and innovation program under grant agreement No. 101017171 in the context of the MARSAL project and by the Hellenic Foundation for Research and Innovation (H.F.R.I.) under the "2nd Call for H.F.R.I. Research Projects to support Faculty Members & Researchers" (Project Number: 04596).

References

1. Chen, T.M.: Smart grids, smart cities need better networks. IEEE Netw. **24**(2), 2–3 (2010)
2. Milanović, J.V., Zhu, W.: Modeling of interconnected critical infrastructure systems using complex network theory. IEEE Trans. Smart Grid **9**(5), 4637–4648 (2018)
3. Varga, P., et al.: Making system of systems interoperable – the core components of the arrowhead framework. J. Netw. Comput. Appl. **81**, 85–95 (2017). ISSN 1084-8045
4. Bertsekas, D.P.: Multiagent rollout algorithms and reinforcement learning. CoRR abs/1910.00120 (2019)
5. Li, X., Lian, Z., Qin, X., Jie, W.: Topology-aware resource allocation for IoT services in clouds. IEEE Access **6**, 77880–77889 (2018)
6. Santoro, D., Zozin, D., Pizzolli, D., De Pellegrini, F., Cretti, S.: Foggy: a platform for workload orchestration in a fog computing environment. In: 2017 IEEE International Conference on Cloud Computing Technology and Science (CloudCom) (2017)
7. Zubair, B.A.: Multi-agent systems for protecting critical infrastructures: a survey. J. Netw. Comput. Appl. **35**(3), 1151–1161 (2012)
8. Pipattanasomporn, M., Feroze, H., Rahman, S.: Multi-agent systems in a distributed smart grid: design and implementation. In: 2009 IEEE/PES Power Systems Conference and Exposition, Seattle, WA, USA, pp. 1–8 (2009)
9. Panfili, M., Giuseppi, A., Fiaschetti, A., Al-Jibreen, H.B., Pietrabissa, A., Priscoli, F.D.: A game-theoretical approach to cyber-security of critical infrastructures based on multi-agent reinforcement learning. In: 2018 26th Mediterranean Conference on Control and Automation (MED), Zadar, Croatia, pp. 460–465 (2018)
10. Mutlag, A.A., et al.: Multi-agent systems in fog-cloud computing for critical healthcare task management model (CHTM) used for ECG monitoring. Sensors **21**, 6923 (2021)
11. Alfakih, T., Hassan, M.M., Gumaei, A., Savaglio, C., Fortino, G.: Task offloading and resource allocation for mobile edge computing by deep reinforcement learning based on SARSA. IEEE Access **8**, 54074–54084 (2020)
12. Wang, Y., Zhang, W., Deng, H., Li, X.: Efficient resource allocation for security-aware task offloading in MEC system using DVS. Electronics 11(19), 3032 (2022)
13. Chen, L., et al.: IoT microservice deployment in edge-cloud hybrid environment using reinforcement learning. In: IEEE Internet of Things Journal, vol. 8, no. 16, pp. 12610–12622 (2021)
14. Quang, P.T.A., Hadjadj-Aoul, Y., Outtagarts, A.: A deep reinforcement learning approach for VNF forwarding graph embedding. IEEE Trans. Netw. Serv. Manage. **16**(4), 1318–1331 (2019)
15. Bunyakitanon, M., Vasilakos, X., Nejabati, R., Simeonidou, D.: End-to-end performance-based autonomous VNF placement with adopted reinforcement learning. IEEE Trans. Cogn. Commun. Netw. **6**(2), 534–547 (2020)
16. Pei, J., Hong, P., Pan, M., Liu, J., Zhou, J.: Optimal VNF placement via deep reinforcement learning in SDN/NFV-enabled networks. IEEE J. Sel. Areas Commun. **38**(2), 263–278 (2020)
17. Sun, P., Lan, J., Li, J., Guo, Z., Hu, Y.: Combining deep reinforcement learning with graph neural networks for optimal VNF placement. IEEE Commun. Lett. **25**(1), 176–180 (2021)
18. Jalodia, N., Henna, S., Davy, A.: Deep reinforcement learning for topology-aware VNF resource prediction in NFV environments. In: 2019 IEEE Conference on Network Function Virtualization and Software Defined Networks (NFV-SDN), Dallas, TX, USA, pp. 1–5 (2019)

19. Hester, T., et al.: Deep Q-learning from demonstrations. In: Proceedings of the AAAI Conference on Artificial Intelligence, vol. 32, no. 1 (2018)
20. Pallewatta, S., Kostakos, V., Buyya, R.: Microservices-based IoT application placement within heterogeneous and resource constrained fog computing environments. In: 12th IEEE/ACM International Conference on Utility and Cloud Computing, pp. 71–81 (2019)

Video-Based Recognition of Aquatic Invasive Species Larvae Using Attention-LSTM Transformer

Shaif Chowdhury[1]([✉]), Sadia Nasrin Tisha[1], Monica E. McGarrity[2], and Greg Hamerly[1]

[1] Baylor University, Waco, TX 76706,, USA
shaif_chowdhury1@baylor.edu
[2] Texas Parks and Wildlife Department, Austin, USA
https://tpwd.texas.gov/
https://www.baylor.edu

Abstract. Aquatic species like zebra and quagga mussels are invasive in United States waterways and cause ecological and economic damage. Due to the time-consuming nature of conventional early detection methods, there is a need for automated systems to detect and classify invasive and non-invasive species using a video-based system without any human supervision. We present a video classification model for rapidly recognizing invasive and non-invasive mussel larvae from plankton or water sample videos.

Many recent video recognition models are transformer-based and use a combination of spatial and temporal attention, often with large-scale pre-training. We present a model with a CNN-based patch encoder and transformer blocks consisting of temporal attention with LSTM that is end-to-end trainable and effective without pre-training. Based on detailed experiments, the Attention-LSTM model significantly improves over state-of-the-art video classification models, classifying invasive and non-invasive larvae with 99% balanced accuracy. Our code is available at https://anonymous.4open.science/r/AttLSTM-10CF/.

Keywords: Recognition · Video Recognition · Attention-LSTM · Transformer · Aquatic Invasive Species · Dreissenid · Quagga Mussel · Zebra Mussel

1 Introduction

Zebra and Quagga mussels are native to Eurasia but have become widely introduced and invasive into North American waters causing ecological disruption [24]. These organisms fight for resources causing the extinction of other freshwater mussels [26]. Dreissenid mussels spread rapidly, forming large colonies and restricting water flow and impeding power generation from water systems, clogging pipes, and other machinery [8]. In the United States, dreissenid cause

G. Bebis et al. (Eds.): ISVC 2023, LNCS 14361, pp. 224–235, 2023.
https://doi.org/10.1007/978-3-031-47969-4_18

several hundred million in damages to power plants, water systems, and industrial water intakes annually. Dreissenid mussels are relatively easy to detect, but they spread quickly laying millions of eggs a year. Once adult zebra mussels have established a presence in a water body, with reproducing adults present, eradicating or controlling their growth is populations is not possible and impacts on water infrastructure are imminent. That means it is imperative to monitor the presence of such invasive species at the larval stage [17]. The conventional methods of detecting veliger presence are to collect plankton or water samples and then examine the selection using cross-polarized light microscopy [17] or environmental DNA [27]. Both of these methods are costly, time-consuming, and require human experts. For this reason, it is vital to develop an automated procedure to visually monitor the veliger of invasive species from water sample videos (Fig. 1).

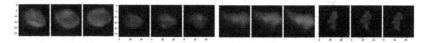

Fig. 1. Example of invasive dreissenid and non-invasive species larvae in our dataset. There are four different organisms in this image, with the first six columns containing images of two different invasive larvae (three for each organism) and the following six containing images of two different non-invasive larvae.

This research aims to classify invasive dreissenid and non-invasive larvae from videos of water samples. We track objects in the video across frames and then extract a cropped image for each tracked object from each frame in which it appears. Every object has a sequence of images that must be classified as invasive or non-invasive. A set of invasive and non-invasive images are shown in Fig. 6. Previously invasive species recognition [6] has been done using a VGG-based CNN and an autoencoder-based feature fusion strategy. Invasive organisms often have very distinguishable movement compared to non-invasive larvae [25], which makes it crucial to model both spatial features and temporal relations between different frames. This paper introduces an Attention-LSTM-based model for end-to-end video-based classification of invasive and non-invasive organisms.

1.1   Attention-LSTM

Recognition is a fundamental challenge in computer vision, both in image and video recognition. Based on the success of transformers in natural language processing [32], many transformer-based architectures have been proposed for image and video recognition [1, 10, 21]. The Video Vision Transformer has shown to be effective at classifying videos in multiple video recognition datasets [1] using a space-time attention transformer.

But transformer-based models are generally more effective when large datasets are available for pre-training [10, 32]. On the other hand, LSTMs have been known to be very efficient in modeling sequential information [9, 15]. CNN-based architectures have also proven to be good at extracting spacial features

[9,11]. Another recent development is the Sequencer [30] architecture by Tatsunami et al. that used Bi-directional Long-Short-Term Memory (LSTM) for image classification. The authors have conducted detailed experiments showing that the Sequencer outperforms Vision Transformers with comparable parameters on ImageNet1k. This indicates that the recurrence mechanism of LSTM can model long-range sequences in the same way self-attention layers can (Fig. 3).

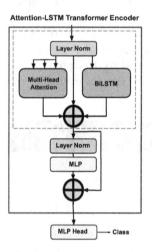

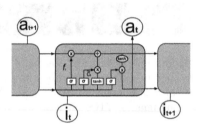

Fig. 2. The Attention-LSTM transformer.

Fig. 3. An LSTM unit.

Our architecture is based on a novel Attention-LSTM transformer block combining bi-directional LSTM and multi-head attention layers. The introduction of the LSTM layer and self-attention are efficient for modeling fine-grained features in the video. We propose a hybrid model for video classification that extracts features from the video frames using a ConvNet. We use transformer blocks to encode the spatial features, consisting of layers of multi-head attention and Bi-LSTM. The sequential output of multi-head attention and Bi-LSTM are combined and passed to a feed-forward network. Then, we perform layer normalization similar to the Vision Transformer Encoder. To perform classification, we attach a global average pooling layer at the end of transformer blocks and pass the output to a linear classifier with a softmax activation function. We test our model on classifying invasive larvae from water sample videos and compare it with state-of-the-art video classification models.

2   Related Work

Invasive dreissenids mussels have been spreading in the United States for decades, but application of machine learning in this area has been limited. Tracking invasive species [7] is generally done manually using a microscope with cross-polarized light [17]. Due to the rapid spreading of invasive dreissenid larvae [28], it is necessary to use a video-based recognition system to check for Zebra and Quagga mussel larvae early and often [22]. Our invasive species recognition is based on video samples collected from the Colorado River, Davis Dam (AZ) [31].

Since the introduction of ConvNets [20] there has been a lot of research work on classifying underwater images. Many of these underwater object recognition frameworks are based on popular CNN models like AlexNet [20], ResNet [16] etc. But the classification of dreissenid veligers has some unique challenges due to microscopic size and features that are hard to distinguish even by human annotators. And dreissenid veligers can also be rare, depending on the season. As a result, there needs to be more data imbalance in recognizing invasive larvae. Our dataset is created from a video of water samples, where invasive and non-invasive larvae often have different types of movement. So, we have decided to treat this problem as a video classification problem using cropped frames taken from the video. The annotation is done by experts inspecting the tracked objects on the video and the cropped images. In the next section, we will look at recent video classification approaches and provide the background for our video recognition framework that achieves state-of-the-art in our Quagga mussel dataset.

Since the success of ConvNets [14,20] in widespread Computer Vision problems like Image classification [20], Object Detection [13] and Segmentation [2], there has been growing interest in applying them to Video recognition. Due to the massive growth of online video-based data, several large video datasets have emerged, like Kinetics [18], Moments-in-time [23] etc. Unlike images, videos require modeling spatial features and temporal relations between other frames [33]. This makes it challenging to apply traditional CNN-based frameworks for Video classification.

More recently, transformer-based networks [32] have achieved state of the art in several key areas of machine learning, including text summarizing [12], image classification [10], segmentation [4], detection [5] etc. Transformers are based on two main ideas: 1. Self Attention mechanism to model long-term dependencies between sequences. and 2. Pre-training on a large dataset and then fine-tuning on a smaller dataset, which significantly improves the accuracy for fine-tuned tasks [19]. Generally, transformer-based video recognition frameworks feed frame-level patches to the transformer with temporal attention or use a combination of spatiotemporal attention, often using CNN to create patches [1,3].

The recently introduced Vision Transformer (ViT) by Dosovitskiy et al. [10] creates multiple patches from 2D images, performs linear projections to get 1D tokens, and then utilizes transformer blocks with a final MLP layer for classification. Transformer-based video recognition frameworks generally use a similar approach to create patches from every video frame and use a space-time attention-based transformer [1]. Gedas Bertasius et al. [3] have compared the different types of attention like Space Attention, Joint Space-Time Attention, and Axial Attention for video recognition in their Timesformer model, etc.

It is generally well-understood how much attention layers contribute to ViT's success. But, LSTM-based model Sequencer [30] has tried token mixing in vision architectures using only LSTM and achieved state of the art on ImageNet classification benchmark. One attractive property of LSTM is that it learns to map an input sequence of variable length into a fixed-dimensional vector representation. Standard LSTMs are generally better at classifying sequential features than an MLP [29], especially with long-range sequences. At the base level, a video representation framework must encode the spatial features and understand the temporal relation between frames. So, to model the material connection between different frames, we use transformer blocks consisting of multi-head attention followed by an LSTM layer.

In this paper, we develop a video recognition framework for classifying invasive species. Our model is based on frame-level patches fed to an attention-LSTM-based transformer. We propose a variant of our model that is convolution-free and faster to train while achieving comparable accuracy. We compare the performance of our model with space-time transformer-based architecture ViVIT [1] and Long-term Recurrent CNN [9].

3   Proposed Method

In this section, we introduce the Attention-LSTM model as shown in Fig. 2. Firstly, we discuss the Vision transformer architecture and preliminary background on LSTM, introduce the Attention-LSTM model and its components, and based on that, we develop several architectures for video classification.

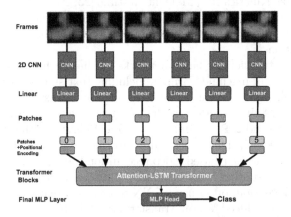

Fig. 4. Model Overview: We extract features from video frames using a Convolution Neural network, add positional encoding to the flattened patches and feed them to the Attention-LSTM transformer. We add a final MLP layer to classify from the resulting sequence.

The original transformer introduced by Vaswani et al. [32] received input as a 1D sequence of tokens. For 2D images, Vision transformer (VIT) [10] creates N patches of 2D tokens, flattens the tokens, and then employs a trainable linear projection to get tokens of D dimensions. Along with that, standard 1D positional encoding is added to the tokens. These tokens are passed through transformer encoders consisting of alternating layers of multi-headed self-attention, layer normalization, and MLP blocks. The MLP contains two layers with a GELU non-linearity.

If we consider z_l as a sequence of tokens given as input to the transformer, then the behavior of the transformer is described by the following equations: $y^l = \mathrm{MSA}(\mathrm{LN}(z^l)) + z^l$ and $z^{(l+1)} = \mathrm{MLP}(\mathrm{LN}(y^l)) + y^l$

Here MSA is multi-headed self-attention, LN is layer normalization, and MLP is a multi-layer perceptron. In case multiple transformer layers $z^{(l+1)}$ can be used as an input to the next transformer block.

We can think of a video as temporally ordered sequence of image frames like $(x_1, x_2, x_3, \dots)$ and $x_1 \in \mathbb{R}^{(H \times W \times C)}$, where (H, W) is the resolution of the images and C is the number of channels. Our model would use input in the form of $V \in \mathbb{R}^{(H \times W \times C \times F)}$, where F is the number of frames. We would create F 1D patches with positional encoding and pass them to the Attention-LSTM-based transformer. Figure 4 provides an overview of the model.

LSTM
LSTMs excel in sequential data tasks like speech recognition, image, and video captioning. Before Transformers, LSTMs were NLP leaders. They're also crucial in video recognition, with Convolutional LSTMs predicting frames. LSTMs use hidden units for memory, employing three gates: input gate i_t, forget gate f_t, and output gate o_t. The forget gate f_t decides what information to discard from the cell state. The input gate i_t combines values to update and candidates to add. The output gate o_t determines the unit's output. This structure enables LSTMs to retain long-term dependencies. While CNNs are great at processing spatial features, LSTM models are great at retaining temporal association. So, for sequential data, the LSTM recurrence mechanism helps achieve better performance from Transformers.

Multi-head Attention
MultiHead Attention is crucial in the Vision Transformer model, excelling in various Computer Vision tasks. It enables the model to focus on different patches and grasp frame relationships. The process involves projecting input into query (Q), key (K), and value (V) transformations, using a parameter d_k for key dimension. The attention score is then computed according to this equation: [32]:

$$\mathrm{Attention}(Q, K, V) = \mathrm{Softmax}\left(\frac{Q \cdot K^T}{\sqrt{d_k}}\right) \cdot V$$

here, T denotes transpose. Output is computed by multiplying Attention scores with value V, maintaining input shape. It's replicated for longer sequences, attending to parts differently.

3.1 Model Architecture

This section will provide details of the Attention-LSTM model architecture, which has two main components: the Patch Encoder and the Attention-LSTM transformer block.

Patch Encoder:
The Vision Transformer feeds the transformer's linear projections of flattened patches along with positional encoding. In our case, we create patches from every

temporal video frame. The goal here is to develop compact features that capture the visual information for every frame. For transformer-based video recognition, several architectures have proposed 2D CNN [3,10] or 3D CNN [1] based models for patch encoding. Due to the rapid development of deep learning, CNNs [20] had great success in large-scale image recognition problems making it the best candidate for feature extraction. So, for patch encoding, we apply a ConvNet for every frame. We add temporal positional encoding to flattened feature vectors and feed them to the Attention-LSTM transformer.

For video processing, we decompose each frame into N non-overlapping patches, each of size $A \times B$, such that the N patches span the entire frame. In case the number of frames in a video is larger than N, we uniformly randomly select N frames, maintaining their increasing temporal order. We apply ConvNet to create features from these patches, where each patch x is given by $x_t = \text{ConvNet}(f_i)$, where f_i is of size $(A, B, 3)$. We flatten these patches into vectors $x_t \in \mathbb{R}^{(A \times B \times 3)}$. Here, $t \in \{1, \ldots, N\}$ denotes the temporal location of the frame. We linearly map each patch $x(t)$ into a flattened embedding vector z. Finally, the sequence of tokens going to the transformer encoder is as follows:

$$z = [z_{cls}, x_1, x_2, \ldots, x_N] + p \tag{1}$$

where the projections $x_1, x_2, \ldots$ are created by a convolutional operation. An optional learned classification token z_{cls} is prepended to this sequence, similar to the BERT Transformer. A learnable positional embedding, p is added to the tokens to retain positional information.

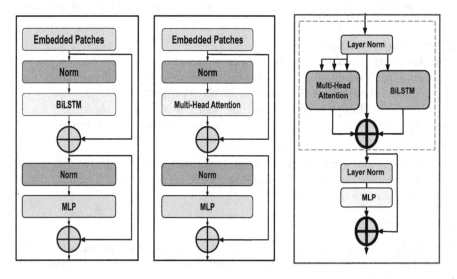

Fig. 5. 1. Sequencer, 2. Transformer, and 3. Attention-LSTM Block. 1. A Sequencer Block consists of a BiLSTM layer. 2. In contrast Transformer block consists of Multi-Head attention. 3. Attention-LSTM combines MultiHead Attention and LSTM layer.

3.2   Attention-LSTM Layer

In the last few years, several different variants of transformers have appeared. The sequencer model has replaced attention with Bi-LSTM. This paper tries to combine the strength of LSTM and attention to create a practical transformer module for long-range fine-grained features. So, we propose a new architecture combining a BiLSTM with multi-head attention and concatenating the results with a residual connection. Like Vision Transformer, MLP block is applied at the end of the transformer and residual connections, layer normalization after every transformer block. Incorporating an attention mechanism with LSTM makes our model highly effective-a comparison between different diagrams is shown in Fig. 5.

The tokens (z) created by the patch encoder are passed through layers of multi-headed self-attention (MSA), BiLSTM, layer normalization (LN), and multi-layer perceptron (MLP):

$$y^l = \text{MSA}(\text{LN}(z^l)) + z^l + \text{BiLSTM}(\text{LN}(z^l)) \tag{2}$$
$$z^{(l+1)} = \text{MLP}(\text{LN}(y^l)) + y^l \tag{3}$$

Like ViT, multiple transformer layers $z^{(l+1)}$ can be used to input the next transformer block. At the end of transformer blocks, we merge the patches using a global average pooling layer and perform the final classification using a softmax activation. We used a cross-entropy loss function with softmax activation in the final layer.

Table 1. Model Details: Details of the Transformer model variants, the number of transformer layers, transformer heads, and the number of parameters for an image of size $(28, 28, 3)$.

Model Type	Parameters	Layers	Heads	Patch size
Att-LSTM-S (2D CNN)	$47k$	2	2	32
Att-LSTM-S (Linear)	$183k$	2	2	32
Att-LSTM-S (2D CNN)	$446k$	2	2	64
Att-LSTM-S (Linear)	$292k$	2	2	64

3.3   Model Variations

In this section, we present several different model variants and evaluate them on different datasets. We have used model variants depending on the size of the dataset.

ConvNet-Based: Our base model is based on one convolution layer, followed by linear projections for patch creation. We used a filter size of (3×3) and a stride size of 1, then created flattened patches with linear projections and added learnable positional embedding.

Linear Projections: Here we use linear projections on flattened frames to create patches and add positional encoding for every temporal step.

We create several variations of our model for training on different datasets by changing the number of transformer layers and attention heads. We use a similar naming convention to that of Vision Transformer. We consider Attention-LSTM-Small ($L = 2, H = 2$), Attention-LSTM-Base ($L = 6, H = 6$) with patch size of 32 & 64 and present the number of parameters for each of them in Table 1. Here the number of layers is given by L, and the number of heads in the attention layer is provided by H.

4   Invasive Species Dataset

Our dataset is processed from videos of water streams. We have used a Kalman Filter-based proprietary algorithm for tracking and cropping larvae images from videos. So a set of frames is available for every organism. The dataset has two types of objects: Invasive and non-invasive. It contains cropped images of 6,905 organisms, with 1,220 invasive organisms (quagga mussels) and 5,685 non-invasive organisms. There are a total of 221,702 images across two organisms. The dataset is imbalanced towards non-invasive species as it takes around 85 percent. So, along with accuracy, we report F1 Score for invasive species as evaluation criteria. Every organism has a minimum of 6 to a maximum of 42 frames. In our classification model, we used six frames with a size of ($28 \times 28 \times 3$). We used 70% of the data for training and validation and 30% as a test.

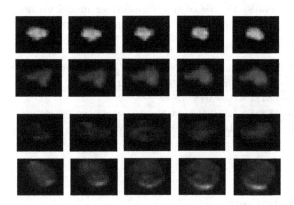

Fig. 6. These are five images of the same organism plotted in each row. The first two rows are from non-invasive organisms, and the next two are from dreissenid veligers. Notice the movement of dreissenid veligers as they progress through the water. This shows the importance of taking motion cues of invasive species into account while modeling fine-grained features of the organisms.

5   Empirical Evaluation

We train models with patch sizes of 64, 32. We train all models with the Adam optimizer and cross-entropy loss with a batch size 32. The Adam optimizer is applied with an initial learning rate of 0.001 and an exponential decay rate of 0.9, which we found especially useful for training larger datasets.

We evaluate the Attention-LSTM model primarily on our quagga mussel dataset, test it with three different backbone architectures, and present the detailed results in Table 2. We offer the results with different variants, like Attention-LSTM-Small, and Attention-LSTM-Base, with varying sizes of patch and backbone structures. We report the test accuracy for the invasive species dataset and compare the results with ViVIT and LRCN models and a single image VGG CNN.

The results demonstrate that Attention-LSTM-based video recognition achieved 99% accuracy in classifying invasive and non-invasive images. Attention-LSTM improves the accuracy significantly compared to other video recognition frameworks like ViVIT, LRCN, or VGG-based single image CNN, while also being faster to train.

Table 2. Comparison with state of the art on invasive larvae dataset. Results are based on ten experiments with 100 training epochs, using H and L for transformer head and layer size. Training time per epoch is labeled as Time. VGG CNN relies on a single image, while accuracy for organisms is calculated via majority voting. All the other models are based on the first five images of an organism. The F1 score is the key metric for estimating invasive species' presence and prevalence. The results show that Attention-LSTM significantly improves and outperforms other video recognition models across comparable parameter bands.

Method	Patch Size	H	L	Time	F1 Score(Invasive)	Accuracy
Att-LSTM-S (Linear)	32	2	2	1 s	$99.18 \pm 0.84\%$	$99.71 \pm 0.30\%$
Att-LSTM-S (2D CNN)	32	2	2	2 s	$99.15 \pm 1.5\%$	$99.51 \pm 0.87\%$
Att-LSTM-B (Linear)	64	2	2	1 s	$98.72 \pm 1.95\%$	$99.34 \pm 1.22\%$
Att-LSTM-B (2D CNN)	64	2	2	4 s	$98.56 \pm 2.71\%$	$99.51 \pm 0.87\%$
Att-LSTM-S (Linear)	32	6	6	1 s	$99.65 \pm 0.37\%$	$99.87 \pm 0.13\%$
Att-LSTM-S (2D CNN)	32	6	6	4 s	$99.75 \pm 0.2\%$	$99.32 \pm 1.89\%$
Att-LSTM-B (Linear)	64	6	6	3 s	$98.28 \pm 3.83\%$	$99.27 \pm 1.53\%$
Att-LSTM-B (2D CNN)	64	6	6	4 s	$99.46 \pm 0.93\%$	$99.86 \pm 0.33\%$
ViVIT	32	2	2	1 s	$92.39 \pm 1.64\%$	$97.33 \pm 0.54\%$
ViVIT	32	6	6	3 s	$92.78 \pm 3.52\%$	$97.48 \pm 1.5\%$
ViVIT	64	2	2	2 s	$93.57 \pm 1.28\%$	$97.75 \pm 0.44\%$
ViVIT	64	6	6	3 s	$94.75 \pm 1.35\%$	$98.18 \pm 0.43\%$
LRCN	-	-	-	3 s	$89.26 \pm 2.57\%$	$96.19 \pm 0.77\%$
VGG CNN	-	-	-	-	$90.8 \pm 0.21\ \%$	$93.6 \pm 0.11\ \%$

6   Conclusion

Invasive species have a detrimental impact on the aquatic environment, leading to infrastructural damage. We present an Attention-LSTM-based transformer for video-based, end-to-end recognition of aquatic invasive species larvae. The combination of LSTM and Multi-Head Attention allows our model to recognize more fine-grained features from videos. We achieves a remarkable 99% F1 score in accurately identifying invasive larvae from water sample videos. Future efforts will focus on categorizing dreissenid veligers based on their life stage and providing recommendations to address them effectively. These methods show significant potential for enhancing the effectiveness of early detection programs for invasive dreissenid mussels.

References

1. Arnab, A., Dehghani, M., Heigold, G., Sun, C., Lučić, M., Schmid, C.: Vivit: a video vision transformer. In: CVPR, pp. 6836–6846 (2021)
2. Badrinarayanan, V., Kendall, A., Cipolla, R.: Segnet: a deep convolutional encoder-decoder architecture for image segmentation. IEEE Trans. Pattern Anal. Mach. Intell. **39**(12), 2481–2495 (2017)
3. Bertasius, G., Wang, H., Torresani, L.: Is space-time attention all you need for video understanding? In: ICML, vol. 2, p. 4 (2021)
4. Chen, J., et al.: Transunet: transformers make strong encoders for medical image segmentation. arXiv preprint arXiv:2102.04306 (2021)
5. Chen, Z., et al.: Vision transformer adapter for dense predictions. arXiv preprint arXiv:2205.08534 (2022)
6. Chowdhury, S., Hamerly, G.: Recognition of aquatic invasive species larvae using autoencoder-based feature averaging. In: Bebis, G., et al. (eds.) ISVC 2022. LNCS, vol. 13598, pp. 145–161. Springer, Cham (2022). https://doi.org/10.1007/978-3-031-20713-6_11
7. Churchill, C.J., Baldys, S.: USGS zebra mussel monitoring program for north Texas. US Department of the Interior, US Geological Survey (2012)
8. Connelly, N.A., ONeill, C.R., Knuth, B.A., Brown, T.L.: Economic impacts of zebra mussels on drinking water treatment and electric power generation facilities. Environ. Manag. **40**(1), 105–112 (2007)
9. Donahue, J., et al.: Long-term recurrent convolutional networks for visual recognition and description. In: CVPR, pp. 2625–2634 (2015)
10. Dosovitskiy, A., et al.: An image is worth 16x16 words: transformers for image recognition at scale. In: ICLR (2020)
11. Gao, Z., Tan, C., Wu, L., Li, S.Z.: Simvp: simpler yet better video prediction. In: CVPR, pp. 3170–3180 (2022)
12. Guo, M., et al.: Longt5: efficient text-to-text transformer for long sequences. arXiv preprint arXiv:2112.07916 (2021)
13. He, K., Gkioxari, G., Dollár, P., Girshick, R.: Mask R-CNN. In: Proceedings of the IEEE International Conference on Computer Vision, pp. 2961–2969 (2017)
14. He, K., Zhang, X., Ren, S., Sun, J.: Deep residual learning for image recognition. In: Proceedings of the IEEE Conference on Computer Vision and Pattern Recognition, pp. 770–778 (2016)

15. Hochreiter, S., Schmidhuber, J.: Long short-term memory. Neural Comput. **9**(8), 1735–1780 (1997)

16. Jiang, Z., Zhao, C., Wang, H.: Classification of underwater target based on S-ResNet and modified DCGAN models. Sensors **22**(6), 2293 (2022)

17. Johnson, L.E.: Enhanced early detection and enumeration of zebra mussel (dreissena spp.) veligers using cross-polarized light microscopy. Hydrobiologia **312**, 139–146 (1995)

18. Kay, W., et al.: The kinetics human action video dataset. arXiv preprint arXiv:1705.06950 (2017)

19. Khan, S., Naseer, M., Hayat, M., Zamir, S.W., Khan, F.S., Shah, M.: Transformers in vision: a survey. ACM Comput. Surv. (CSUR) **54**(10s), 1–41 (2022)

20. Krizhevsky, A., Sutskever, I., Hinton, G.E.: Imagenet classification with deep convolutional neural networks. Commun. ACM **60**(6), 84–90 (2017)

21. Liu, Z., et al.: Swin transformer: hierarchical vision transformer using shifted windows. In: CVPR, pp. 10012–10022 (2021)

22. Lucy, F., Muckle-Jeffs, E.: History of the zebra mussel/ICAIS conference series. Aquatic Invasions (2010)

23. Monfort, M., et al.: Moments in time dataset: one million videos for event understanding. IEEE Trans. Pattern Anal. Mach. Intell. **42**(2), 502–508 (2019)

24. Nalepa, T.F., Schloesser, D.W.: Quagga and Zebra Mussels: Biology, Impacts, and Control. CRC Press, Boca Raton (2013)

25. Nichols, S.J., Black, M.: Identification of larvae: the zebra mussel (dreissena polymorpha), quagga mussel (dreissena rosteriformis bugensis), and Asian clam (corbicula fluminea). Can. J. Zool. **72**(3), 406–417 (1994)

26. Schloesser, D.W., Metcalfe-Smith, J.L., Kovalak, W.P., Longton, G.D., Smithee, R.D.: Extirpation of freshwater mussels (bivalvia: Unionidae) following the invasion of dreissenid mussels in an interconnecting river of the laurentian great lakes. Am. Midl. Nat. **155**(2), 307–320 (2006)

27. Sepulveda, A.J., Amberg, J.J., Hanson, E.: Using environmental DNA to extend the window of early detection for dreissenid mussels. Manag. Biol. Invasions **10**(2) (2019)

28. Stokstad, E.: Feared quagga mussel turns up in western united states (2007)

29. Sutskever, I., Vinyals, O., Le, Q.V.: Sequence to sequence learning with neural networks. In: Advances in Neural Information Processing Systems, vol. 27 (2014)

30. Tatsunami, Y., Taki, M.: Sequencer: deep LSTM for image classification. arXiv preprint arXiv:2205.01972 (2022)

31. Turner, K., Wong, W.H., Gerstenberger, S., Miller, J.M.: Interagency monitoring action plan (I-MAP) for quagga mussels in lake mead, Nevada-Arizona, USA. Aquat. Invasions **6**(2), 195 (2011)

32. Vaswani, A., et al.: Attention is all you need. In: Advances in Neural Information Processing Systems, vol. 30 (2017)

33. Xie, S., Sun, C., Huang, J., Tu, Z., Murphy, K.: Rethinking spatiotemporal feature learning: speed-accuracy trade-offs in video classification. In: Proceedings of the European Conference on Computer Vision (ECCV), pp. 305–321 (2018)

ST: Generalization in Visual Machine Learning

Latent Space Navigation for Face Privacy: A Case Study on the MNIST Dataset

Muhammad Shaheryar$^{(\boxtimes)}$ ⓘ, Lamyanba Laishram ⓘ, Jong Taek Lee ⓘ,
and Soon Ki Jung$^{(\boxtimes)}$ ⓘ

School of Computer Science and Engineering, Kyungpook National University,
Daegu, Republic of Korea
{shaheryar,yanbalaishram,jongtaeklee,skjung}@knu.ac.kr

Abstract. Preserving privacy in facial recognition systems while maintaining high accuracy is a challenging problem. In this research, we propose a novel method for achieving image privacy with latent space navigation and synthetic data generation. Our approach aims to generate synthetic samples that are ambiguous to recognize for humans while still being correctly classified by the classifier. To demonstrate the effectiveness of our method, we conduct experiments on the MNIST dataset, chosen for its interpretability and low dimensionality. We create latent spaces with different dimensions (10-D, 30-D, and 50-D) through an encoder-decoder architecture, enabling controlled sampling close to class boundaries. Our optimization technique ensures privacy protection by producing diverse and confusing images that the MNIST digit classifier can correctly identify. The results of our study serve as a foundation for future research in privacy-preserving facial recognition systems, offering a promising direction to safeguard user privacy without compromising classifier accuracy.

Keywords: Latent space walk · Face perturbation · Autoencoder

1 Introduction

It is no secret that the remarkable advancements in artificial intelligence have revolutionized numerous industries, unlocking unprecedented opportunities and potential. However, the nature of deep learning models processing copious amounts of sensitive data has sparked concerns regarding the privacy of sensitive data. On the subject of facial recognition, we can effortlessly recognize how their application has positively impacted various fields abstractly, the security and user authentication landscapes. However, their extensive deployment raises certain concerns about the privacy of individuals. Thus, the golden intersection where aspects such as the accuracy of the model and protection of privacy coexist amiably has yet to be discovered.

In order to protect people's privacy while using facial recognition technology, a variety of methods and procedures have been developed. By altering or

G. Bebis et al. (Eds.): ISVC 2023, LNCS 14361, pp. 239–250, 2023.
https://doi.org/10.1007/978-3-031-47969-4_19

obscuring the original face characteristics to prevent direct identification, these strategies seek to secure sensitive facial data. Synthetic data creation plays a critical role in privacy-preserving face recognition. Concerning human identification of face recognition systems, the objective is to develop synthetic face samples that are aesthetically realistic to the human eye yet unidentifiable as specific persons. Techniques like perturbations, randomizations, and generative models are used to generate differences in the synthetic data, making it difficult for humans to distinguish the identities of the people.

One approach to addressing the concern involves making use of Variational Autoencoders (VAEs) [9], which offer a method of transforming facial images from the pixel space to the latent space, where they can be represented by meaningful and abstract features. Within this latent space, facial attributes are captured and go beyond the pixel-space boundary. This transformative process enhances the model by providing yet another layer of abstraction and by enabling us to gain more insight into the underlying attributes of the facial data. Latent space exploration has emerged as a powerful technique in the domains of machine learning and computer vision. Researchers can gain insightful information, previously perceived as impossible, by traversing the dimensions of the latent space within a generative model. Such a novel technique will enable us to greatly surpass the boundaries of traditional analysis and open doors for critical tasks, including data augmentation, synthesis, and interpolation. For instance, images with desired attributes are being generated by enabling controlled manipulation of latent codes using techniques of conditional generative adversarial networks (cGANs) [13]. Other examples include latent space interpolation techniques such as spherical interpolation and morphing, which have been employed to produce seamless transitions between varying images, enabling applications of face morphing and style transfer [1].

Moreover, latent space exploration has also positively affected unsupervised representation learning. By leveraging the latent space, researchers can extract useful factors of variation in the data, enabling the discovery of interpretable and semantically useful latent dimensions [6]. The growing focus on data privacy and the potential misuse of biometric data have sparked increased interest in face recognition systems that prioritize privacy protection. Latent space exploration has emerged as an auspicious approach to address this issue by allowing functional privacy preservation mechanisms. In recent times, significant progress has been made in the field, leading to the creation of methods that utilize latent space exploration to generate facial image representations that prioritize privacy. For example, variational autoencoders (VAEs)-based methods have been suggested to unveil facial attributes in the latent space, enabling selective modification while preserving privacy [14]. Studies have also investigated the utilization of adversarial training frameworks to produce privacy-conscious facial images that maintain accurate classification by face recognition models [15]. With all these, various other privacy mechanisms have also been used by privacy-preserving face recognition methods to ensure safety. For example, adding noise to the latent space or the training process to protect privacy during recognition [7]. The visualization of the latent space of deep learning models holds certain significance for comprehending the learned representations and their potential uses. This understanding will breathe new life and open up possibilities for various applications, such as image generation, data augmentation, and style transfer.

In our research, we tackle this challenge by introducing a novel approach that integrates latent space navigation and ambiguous data generation to attain privacy-preserving recognition. While there are approaches that replace faces with avatars or masks, our method offers a different approach to privacy preservation. Rather than entirely obscuring a face, we aim to generate synthetic images that are still correctly classified by a classifier, maintaining classifier accuracy.

2   Related Work

GANSpace [5] is a framework presented by Hrknen et al, that allows for exploring and controlling the latent space of Generative Adversarial Networks (GANs). This enables disentangled feature manipulation and generation, although it should be noted that the framework is currently limited to GAN architectures and may not be applicable to other generative models.

StyleGAN2 [8] is a high-quality image synthesis model with improved disentanglement and control over the latent space, leading to better image manipulation. Large model size and computational requirements might hinder its use on resource-constrained devices.

Image2StyleGAN++ [2] is another method for image manipulation in StyleGAN2 that allows direct editing in the latent space, enabling intuitive and semantic image control, but it needs access to pre-trained StyleGAN2 models, which might be resource-intensive for training and inference.

Boutros et al. [4] explore the use of privacy-friendly synthetic data as an alternative to authentic biometric data in face recognition. The paper provides a comprehensive taxonomy of use cases for synthetic face data and discusses recent advancements in face recognition models developed using synthetic data. It also addresses the challenges and future prospects of leveraging synthetic data to overcome legal, ethical, and data-hungry model limitations in the field of face recognition".

Klys et al. [10] introduce the Conditional Subspace VAE (CSVAE), a VAE-based generative model that facilitates unsupervised learning of features correlated to binary labels in the data. The CSVAE employs mutual information minimization to create a low-dimensional latent subspace associated with each label, allowing for easy interpretation and independent manipulation. The authors demonstrate the efficacy of their model on attribute manipulation tasks using the Toronto Face and CelebA datasets.

Leeb et al. [11] explain the latent response framework, utilizing tools to visualize and understand representations learned by variational autoencoders. By intervening in the latent space, it quantifies the impact on semantic information, revealing geometric and causal structures, especially useful for disentangled representations. Although limited by scalability for large generative models, latent responses offer promise for understanding real datasets, facilitating the development of better-performing and interpretable models without relying on ground truth labels.

3   Methodology

This study explores the MNIST dataset through an autoencoder-based analysis. We implement a three-layer encoder and decoder, varying the latent space dimensions (10, 30, and 50). The encoder compresses input images (28 × 28 pixels) into a lower-dimensional representation, while the decoder reconstructs them. Training utilizes Adam optimizer and binary cross-entropy loss over 10 epochs. We derive a latent space representation, sample random points for interpolation, reconstruct images, and subsequently classify them using a pre-trained classifier. The workflow of our method is depicted in Fig. 1.

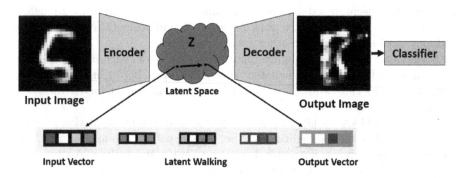

Fig. 1. Workflow of our architecture for MNIST Dataset.

This process showcases the utility of our method in handling the MNIST dataset and its potential impact on classification tasks. Once trained, the encoder is utilized to obtain the latent space representation of the entire training set. To visualize this high-dimensional latent space, we apply t-SNE (t-distributed stochastic neighbor embedding) [12] facilitating intuitive visualization. The resulting 2D scatter plot reveals how the autoencoder has learned to cluster similar digit samples together, providing insights into the structure and quality of the latent space representation learned from the MNIST dataset. The visual analysis offers a valuable understanding of the autoencoder's performance in capturing meaningful features and grouping similar digits in the latent space.

Figure 2 illustrates a 2D latent space representation with circular decision boundaries. Two circles represent class boundaries, with centers marked as blue and red dots. It shows the separation of data points in the latent space and the presence of class-specific structures. Arrows emanating from each point signify random directions in the latent space. The concept demonstrated in the visualization is related to "latent space walk" or "latent space interpolation." In the visualization, the circular decision boundaries represent clusters of data points, each corresponding to a specific class or category. The centers of these circles serve as representative points for each class. When we perform a "latent space walk," we move smoothly and continuously between these centers or points in the latent space. This movement allows us to explore the manifold of the data, generating new data samples by interpolating between existing points.

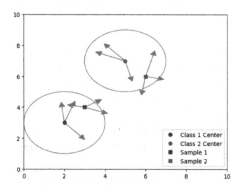

Fig. 2. 2D Latent space representation with class boundaries.

To traverse the latent space and generate new latent codes, we employ vector arithmetic, adding or subtracting specific vectors to move in various directions, typically aligned with data variations. This technique enables the creation of novel latent codes, which can then be decoded to produce fresh data samples. This latent space walk allows for smooth exploration of data variations, with the manipulation of latent codes granting control over the generation of new data samples.

Let I be the input image, and let E be the encoder and D be the decoder. Then we can represent the encoded latent space of I as $z = E(I)$, where z is a vector of length 10, 30, or 50. Let C be the classifier that can recognize the digit in I. Let $C(z)$ be the output of the classifier for the latent representation z. We want to anonymize I by perturbing z such that $C(z') = C(z)$, and $z' = z + \epsilon d$, where ϵ is a small positive value, and d is a vector that maximizes the loss of $C(z')$ with respect to z. Specifically, we want to find the direction d in the latent space that maximizes the loss of the classifier and then move z along that direction by a small amount ϵ to obtain the anonymized latent z'.

To find the direction d, we compute the gradient of the loss of $C(z')$ with respect to z using backpropagation: $d = \nabla L(C(z'), C(z))$, where ∇ denotes the gradient with respect to z. This gradient represents the direction in which the perturbations should be applied to z in order to maximize the loss of the classifier $C(z')$ while maintaining the classifier's output for the original samples $C(z)$ constant.

Once we have obtained the anonymized latent representation z', we generate the anonymized image I' using the decoder D. We then verify if $C(I')$ still recognizes I' as the original digit I. If $C(I')$ correctly classifies I' as the same digit as I, then we can say that the anonymization is successful.

To add some noise to the anonymized latent representation z', we can randomly perturb its values by a small amount using a Gaussian distribution with mean 0 and variance σ^2. This can be done by adding a vector n $N(0, \sigma^2)$ to z'. The step by step process of our work is summarized below:

WORKING STEPS:

1. Mapping in Latent Space: The encoder maps the input images I from the MNIST dataset to their corresponding 10, 30, and 50-dimensional latent space representations z. The encoder function is denoted as the $E(I)$, which computes z from I, and the decoder function is denoted as the $D(z)$, which reconstructs the images I' from z.

   The training objective is to minimize the reconstruction loss $L(I, I')$ between the original images I and their reconstructions I' using mean squared error (MSE) [3]: $L(I, I') = ||I - I'||^2$

2. Class of Interest: Let C be the set of all possible digit classes in the MNIST dataset, and C_i be the class of interest (e.g., $C_i = 5$).

3. Random Sample Selection: To pick a random sample z from class C_i, we randomly select an index j from the set of latent space representations z_i of class C_i: $z = z_i j$

4. Computed Direction for Anonymization: The computed direction in the latent space that maximizes anonymization for the chosen sample z is represented as d. This direction is obtained through the gradient of the classifier loss with respect to the sample: $d = \nabla L(C(z)$.

5. Anonymized Sample Generation: To obtain the anonymized sample z', we move the original sample z in the direction d by an amount controlled by the anonymization parameter ϵ: $z' = z + \epsilon d$

6. Anonymized Image Reconstruction: The decoder D is used to reconstruct the anonymized image I' from the anonymized sample z': $I' = D(z')$.

7. Classification Check: We use the trained classifier function C to predict the class label of the anonymized image I': $label = C(I')$

8. Recognizability Assessment: If the predicted label is equal to the class of interest C_i (i.e., $label = C_i$), then the anonymized image is still recognizable as the class of interest. Otherwise, it is misclassified.

The value of ϵ is very crucial in the method since it is applied in the generated anonymous samples in the computed space in order to check their recognizability. The optimal value of ϵ is derived by repetitively checking it with the samples and is highlighted when it shows a perfect equilibrium between anonymity and perceptibility.

An encoder-decoder design can be educated on face images to get a low-dimensional depiction. Given a certain person's face image as the course of interest, the computed directions in the unexposed area can be utilized to perturb the depiction, producing an anonymized variation of the face while maintaining essential attributes. The anonymized face can then be deciphered to rebuild an anonymized image, and its recognizability can be analyzed by a classifier to ensure privacy while enabling recognition within a particular limit of resemblance. The anonymization process can retain essential attributes by operating in the latent space, along with patterns that allow downstream tasks, such as classification or generation, while also covering sensitive details in the original data. The epsilon specification enables fine-grained control over the degree of anonymization. This individuals to personalize the degree of privacy based on particular demands and compromises. The technique can be effortlessly incorporated into existing encoder-decoder models, making it suitable for numerous styles and enabling easy adaptation to various domains, such as face recognition, where high-dimensional data prevails.

4   Experimental Result

The t-SNE visualization in Fig. 3 shows how well the high-dimensional MNIST dataset can be condensed into representations of lesser dimensions (10D, 30D, and 50D). Different colors denote the associated class labels for each data point, which represents a sample of hand-written digits. The multiple clusters seen in the plot demonstrate the intrinsic separability of various digit classes in the condensed latent space, demonstrating that the dataset's important patterns and structures are captured by the t-SNE algorithm. To better comprehend the underlying structure of the dataset and to aid in the analysis and interpretation of MNIST data, this visualization offers insightful information about the distribution of digit classes and their relationships.

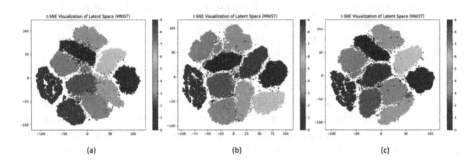

(a)   (b)   (c)

Fig. 3. Latent space visualization of MNIST Dataset. (a) 10D, (b) 30D, and (c) 50D latent space.

Figure 4 illustrates how the value of epsilon affects the accuracy of our classifier during the synthetic sample generation. The increase in ϵ value is met with perturbations to the generated samples which gradually makes it more difficult for the classifier to recognize it. We can observe a sharp decline in the accuracy of our classifier at the significant point of epsilon = 2.5 where it begins to hallucinate and halts correctly identifying the values. This critical value of epsilon indicates the boundary where the synthetic samples achieve the desired objective of being accurately classified by the classifier but confound human recognition, making certain that privacy is secured during facial recognition tasks.

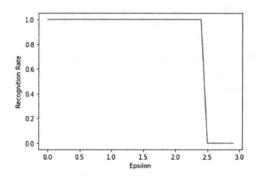

Fig. 4. Impact of epsilon value on classifier accuracy during synthetic sample generation.

In Fig. 5, the top row showcases the synthetic samples generated for digit class 0 using three different latent representations: 10-D, 30-D, and 50-D. Alongside each set of synthetic samples, the corresponding classification results are displayed. Considering different dimensions of the latent space, these visualizations help us garner an understanding of how effective the samples are, for the classification of digit class 0.

The objective of this research work was to achieve a facial recognition system where privacy is not regarded as in-efficacious. The samples that were generated by our method attain the fine spot between being detectable by a classifier and simultaneously being imperceptible to humans. Making use of such synthetic data is ever so fruitful since it enables us to establish a robust and secure system that upholds privacy protection.

In Figs. 6 and 8, we showcase the diverse sets of synthetic samples obtained by adding varying values of epsilon ϵ to the generation process. Epsilon ϵ serves as a perturbation factor, introducing controlled noise to the generated samples. As we observe these figures, we can notice the progressive transformation of the synthetic digits as ϵ increases.

At low ϵ values, the samples closely resemble the original MNIST dataset of digits, allowing the classifier to identify them correctly. However, as we start increasing the value of ϵ, the samples begin exhibiting subtle deformations which cause the classifier to struggle and begin to classify them incorrectly. Thus as we continue to increase the ϵ value, we reach a point where the value of ϵ causes the classifier to constantly output inaccurately.

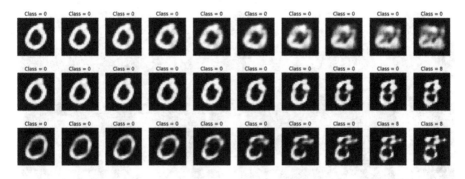

Fig. 5. Synthetic samples and classification results for digit class 0.

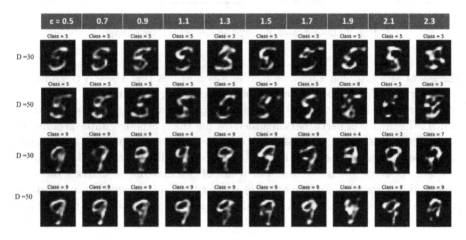

Fig. 6. Progressive transformation of synthetic samples with varying epsilon values for digit class 5 and 9.

These visualizations help us paint us picture of how greatly the value of ϵ impacts the quality of the synthetic data and allow us to understand the boundary at which the classifier is able to predict accurately.

In our research, we achieved a remarkable classifier accuracy of 98.68% in accurately classifying samples that had alterations to deceive the human eye. We applied a technique of synthetic data generation to produce the samples which involved, using a simple SoftMax loss function on a pre-trained classifier. Our classifier demonstrated great performance despite the ambiguity of the generated digits which carves a potential pathway to utilize our method to generate privacy-focused samples that exhibit high accuracy.

We performed an experiment using face images and the latent space of Style-GAN as a means of performing interpolations as shown in Fig. 7. The goal was to generate synthetic samples that appeared realistic to the human eye but had the potential to deceive face recognition systems. The process involved navigation of

Input Image   Latent Walking   ⟶   Final Image

Fig. 7. Latent walking experiment on the face image.

the latent space to generate new face representations that showed resemblance to the original faces, despite any perturbations being introduced.

To achieve this, we applied our approach, manipulating the latent value to control the degree of perturbation added during the synthetic sample generation. By selecting and trying out different values, we reached a point of equilibrium where we maximized the capability of the visually realistic synthetic face samples to evade the recognition systems. The result of this experiment demonstrates the potential implications for privacy and security in face recognition applications since realistic yet fake faces can be used to trick standard methods of recognition.

5   Future Work

In our study, we presented our initial research on privacy-preserving approaches with latent space exploration using the MNIST dataset. Our experimental results demonstrate the efficiency of our approach in generating classifier-oriented samples that humans struggle to recognize. We also observed that by experimenting with various epsilon values, we can transform the samples in a way where the classifier is tricked into misclassifying it.

In the future, we intend to expand our research by introducing real-face images as they are far more complex and carry high dimensionality. We aim to utilize the functionalities of any trained auto-encoder that would perform latent walks and generate samples that could trick the face recognizers but remain clear for humans. This is certain to carve the pathway for a privacy-oriented future where face recognition systems have functionalities to safeguard privacy.

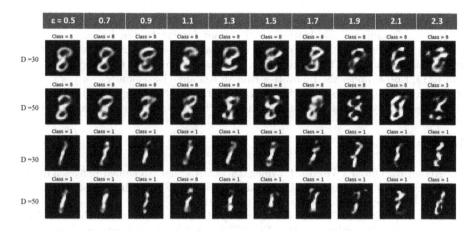

Fig. 8. Progressive transformation of synthetic samples with varying epsilon values for digit class 8 and 1.

6 Conclusion

In this study, we effectively used an autoencoder-based approach to explore the latent space using the MNIST dataset. The t-SNE visualization demonstrated the autoencoder's powerful feature extraction capabilities and confirmed its capacity to group like digits together. We explored "latent space walking" and showed how adaptable it is to navigate the data distribution in the latent space and produce new data samples. We were able to achieve anonymization while maintaining key features for recognition tasks by perturbing the latent representations of MNIST images. The created anonymized samples were realistic yet unrecognizably anonymous, providing a potential approach to protecting privacy. The effectiveness of the methodology in finding a balance between privacy preservation and recognition accuracy was consistently demonstrated by our experimental results spanning 10-D, 30-D, and 50-D latent spaces. We also demonstrate the effectiveness of our approach with face images. The novelty in our work lies in the application of the latent space navigation technique for privacy preservation in facial recognition. While the concept of latent walks might seem basic, it's the adaptation and optimization of this technique for privacy preservation in the context of facial recognition that makes our approach novel. In conclusion, we believe that our research introduces new pathways for the development of technologies that are conscious of privacy. The findings of our research have a diverse array of real-world applications and are bound to replace the existing architectures of face recognition as concerns regarding privacy continue to grow.

Acknowledgements. This study was supported by the BK21 FOUR project (AI-driven Convergence Software Education Research Program) funded by the Ministry of Education, School of Computer Science and Engineering, Kyungpook National

University, Korea (4199990214394) and by Institute of Information & communications Technology Planning & Evaluation (IITP) grant funded by the Korea government (MSIT) (No. 2019-0-00203, Development of 5G-based Predictive Visual Security Technology for Preemptive Threat Response) and also by the MSIT(Ministry of Science and ICT), Korea, under the Innovative Human Resource Development for Local Intellectualization support program (IITP-2022-RS-2022-00156389) supervised by the IITP (Institute for Information & communications Technology Planning & Evaluation).

References

1. Abdal, R., Qin, Y., Wonka, P.: Image2StyleGAN: how to embed images into the StyleGAN latent space? In: Proceedings of the IEEE/CVF International Conference on Computer Vision, pp. 4432–4441 (2019)
2. Abdal, R., Qin, Y., Wonka, P.: Image2StyleGAN++: how to edit the embedded images? In: Proceedings of the IEEE/CVF Conference on Computer Vision and Pattern Recognition, pp. 8296–8305 (2020)
3. Allen, D.M.: Mean square error of prediction as a criterion for selecting variables. Technometrics **13**(3), 469–475 (1971)
4. Boutros, F., Struc, V., Fierrez, J., Damer, N.: Synthetic data for face recognition: current state and future prospects. Image Vis. Comput. 104688 (2023)
5. Härkönen, E., Hertzmann, A., Lehtinen, J., Paris, S.: GANSpace: discovering interpretable GAN controls. In: Advances in Neural Information Processing Systems, vol. 33, pp. 9841–9850 (2020)
6. Higgins, I., et al.: Beta-VAE: learning basic visual concepts with a constrained variational framework. In: International Conference on Learning Representations (2016)
7. Ji, J., et al.: Privacy-preserving face recognition with learnable privacy budgets in frequency domain. In: Avidan, S., Brostow, G., Cissé, M., Farinella, G.M., Hassner, T. (eds.) ECCV 2022. LNCS, vol. 13672, pp. 475–491. Springer, Cham (2022). https://doi.org/10.1007/978-3-031-19775-8_28
8. Karras, T., Laine, S., Aittala, M., Hellsten, J., Lehtinen, J., Aila, T.: Analyzing and improving the image quality of StyleGAN. In: Proceedings of the IEEE/CVF Conference on Computer Vision and Pattern Recognition, pp. 8110–8119 (2020)
9. Kingma, D.P., Welling, M.: An introduction to variational autoencoders. Found. Trendsö Mach. Learn. **12**(4), 307–392 (2019)
10. Klys, J., Snell, J., Zemel, R.: Learning latent subspaces in variational autoencoders. In: Advances in Neural Information Processing Systems, vol. 31 (2018)
11. Leeb, F., Bauer, S., Besserve, M., Schölkopf, B.: Exploring the latent space of autoencoders with interventional assays. In: Advances in Neural Information Processing Systems, vol. 35, pp. 21562–21574 (2022)
12. Van der Maaten, L., Hinton, G.: Visualizing data using t-SNE. J. Mach. Learn. Res. **9**(11) (2008)
13. Park, T., Liu, M.Y., Wang, T.C., Zhu, J.Y.: Semantic image synthesis with spatially-adaptive normalization. In: Proceedings of the IEEE/CVF Conference on Computer Vision and Pattern Recognition, pp. 2337–2346 (2019)
14. Tang, D., Zhou, S., Jiang, H., Chen, H., Liu, Y.: Gender-adversarial networks for face privacy preserving. IEEE Internet Things J. **9**(18), 17568–17576 (2022)
15. Yang, J., Zhang, W., Liu, J., Wu, J., Yang, J.: Generating de-identification facial images based on the attention models and adversarial examples. Alex. Eng. J. **61**(11), 8417–8429 (2022)

Domain Generalization for Foreground Segmentation Using Federated Learning

Islam Osman$^{(\boxtimes)}$ (ID), Islam Abdelfattah (ID), and Mohamed S. Shehata (ID)

Department of Computer Science, The University of British Columbia, Kelowna,
Canada
islam.osman@gmail.com

Abstract. Foreground segmentation is one of the main applications in computer vision, as it separates an object in an image from its background. State-of-the-art models are achieving great metrics in terms of object segmentation tasks. However, when these models are subject to domain shift, their performance massively degrades. This is due to poor generalization. Domain generalization can be achieved by training the model using multiple datasets from different domains. However, most of the existing foreground segmentation models are unable to learn effectively from multiple datasets. If the training of multiple datasets is done simultaneously, the model cannot learn the different distributions, as each distribution requires its own set of parameters. Moreover, if the training is done sequentially, the models will struggle to perform well on all datasets due to a problem called catastrophic forgetting. This paper proposes a deep learning model and a novel training procedure to learn from multiple domains while overcoming the mentioned problems effectively. The proposed model is an encoder with a multi-head decoder that combines shared and isolated parameters for different domains. The proposed training procedure is similar to federated learning, where client models are created such that each client learns from a specific domain. After that, the main model learns the knowledge gained by each client using knowledge distillation with regularization to prevent the main network from forgetting the previously gained knowledge. Experiments demonstrate the effectiveness of our proposed work in comparison with state-of-the-art models.

Keywords: Foreground segmentation · Domain generalization · Knowledge distillation · Federated learning · Deep learning

1 Introduction

Foreground segmentation separates objects from the rest of the image by isolating the pixels containing that object and copying them into another binary image with values for the isolated pixels only in an operation called masking. This process is applied on a video frame-by-frame. As many computer vision applications depend on Foreground Segmentation, There has been a lot of research

G. Bebis et al. (Eds.): ISVC 2023, LNCS 14361, pp. 251–263, 2023.
https://doi.org/10.1007/978-3-031-47969-4_20

done on the topic, and many great models that were able to perform the task of segmentation with high accuracy and performance, like REFNet [1] and STCN [2]. However, when these models are subject to domain shift, the performance of these models degrades. This is a result of poor domain generalization. To improve the domain generalization of these models, they need to be trained using multi-domain datasets. When these models are trained using multiple datasets, they face another set of problems. The first problem is the inability to learn the different distributions if the training on multiple datasets is simultaneously (a.k.a. joint training). The second problem appears if the models are trained using multiple datasets sequentially. This problem is known as catastrophic forgetting. In sequential training, the model's parameters are only up to date with the recent domain (dataset) and lose learned information from the previous domains.

Recently, many research works have addressed the problems in domain generalization in different research areas. Examples of these research areas are 1) multi-task learning, where a model is trained to perform multiple tasks such as image classification and object detection simultaneously. 2) domain adaptation, where a model is trained to be able to shift to new domains using zero or few labeled images. 3) Continual learning to allow a model to learn effectively from multiple datasets for the same task (e.g., multiple image classification datasets). This paper proposes a novel approach that can learn effectively from single or multiple datasets and adapt to new domains using a few labeled images. This novel approach combines deep learning architectural design, continual learning, and federated learning. Federated learning [3] is a decentralized learning technique used for privacy and real-time updates for multi-user/multi-device platforms. It works by training multiple models on different user data with different data distributions and then transferring that knowledge as learned parameters to the main central model to update it.

To overcome the problem mentioned problems in achieving domain generalization, we propose a Knowledge Distillation Network (KDNet) that has multi-head outputs and is trained using a novel technique that combines federated learning with continual learning to learn from multiple datasets. The architecture of KDNet is an encoder with a multi-head decoder that combines shared and isolated parameters for different domains. The proposed training technique is similar to federated learning, where client models are created such that each client learns from a specific domain. After that, the main (server) model learns the knowledge gained by each client using knowledge distillation with a continual learning-based regularization to prevent the main network from forgetting the previously gained knowledge.

To the best of our knowledge, this is the first time federated learning has been introduced in foreground segmentation to achieve domain generalization. The main contributions of this paper are summarized as follows:

- Proposing a novel deep-learning model and training technique to effectively learn from single or multiple datasets. Hence, achieves state-of-the-art performance on multiple datasets by a noticeable gap of 14.1%.

– The proposed training technique allows the model to adapt to new domains using as few as one labeled image.

The rest of the paper is organized as follows: Sect. 2 provides an overview of the state-of-the-art models in foreground segmentation and their types and an overview of federated learning and some of its techniques. The proposed work architecture and model design are discussed in Sect. 3. The experiments in Sect. 4 show the performance of the proposed work against other state-of-the-art foreground segmentation models in single and multi-domain contexts. Finally, Sect. 5 shows the conclusion and future work.

2   Related Work

Foreground segmentation models are showing outstanding performance nowadays for the segmentation task. Foreground segmentation models could be categorized into statistical-based models and deep-learning-based models. Statistical-based foreground segmentation models depend mainly on the change in the pixel intensity of the background of any image and also depend on the reasons behind this change to be able to separate the objects from the background. Furthermore, Statistical methods also depend on motion vectors to separate the object pixels from the foreground. Optical flow is a widely used statistical method that depends on motion vectors. Optical flow depends on processing a sequence of images to approximate the 3-D velocities of surface points. Then, these vectors could be used for various tasks, including object segmentation. Optical flow has been used for foreground segmentation as seen in [4] and [5]. Statistical models struggle to isolate the background when environmental challenges exist in the image, like illumination change, moving camera, and dynamic background.

Recently, deep neural networks have been used for the task of foreground segmentation, and they have been showing a significant improvement in the task of foreground segmentation. Deep-learning networks are divided into convolutional neural networks (CNN) and transformers. One of the earlier CNN models that used an encoder-decoder type neural network is FgSegNet [6]. Several models use neural network-based architectures like CascadeCNN [7], which is based on a multi-resolution convolutional neural network (CNN) with a cascaded architecture. RANet+ [8], which is Ranking Attention Network, uses an encoder-decoder framework to learn pixel-level similarity and segmentation in an end-to-end manner. The most recent model, STCN [2], uses a Space-Time Correspondence Network and negative squared Euclidean distance to compute affinities. On the other hand, transformer-based models like TransBlast [9] are also being used and showing promising results. TransBlast is trained using self-supervised learning to leverage the limited data and learn a strong object representation while using the augmented subspace loss function. However, all these models suffer from catastrophic forgetting when subject to domain shifts. This paper proposes a federated learning technique to mitigate the effect of catastrophic forgetting and achieve domain generalization, even though federated learning is being used mainly for domain generalization on multiple mobile devices.

Federated learning is a machine learning technique that enables multiple devices to train a central model without sharing their data. In federated learning, the model is trained locally on each device using the data on that device, and the updated weights are shared with a central server. The central server then updates its weights using the aggregated updates from all the devices and releases the updated model to the devices. This process is repeated to keep the model up to date with new data. Different settings for federated learning have been used in networking, and IoT, like Cross-silo [10] and Cross-device [11]. Cross-silo federated learning refers to the collaborative training of machine learning models across multiple organizational silos, where each silo represents a distinct entity with its private dataset. This approach enables the pooling of data while ensuring data privacy and security. In contrast, cross-device federated learning involves training models directly on decentralized devices, such as smartphones or IoT devices, without the need for data transfer to a central server. The focus is leveraging diverse devices' computational power while preserving user privacy. Both approaches contribute to privacy-preserving machine learning, but their distinction lies in the data distribution and collaboration mechanisms employed. It has been found that Cross-silo is the best setting for the proposed solution in this paper, as the main focus is not on data privacy but on domain generalization.

3   Proposed Work

The proposed work comprises two main components: 1) model architecture consisting of an encoder with a multi-head decoder. 2) training technique that combines federated learning with continual learning.

3.1   Model Architecture

The proposed model is an encoder-decoder architecture. The encoder is ResNet50, and the decoder is three blocks. Each decoder block consists of three convolutional layers. Each convolutional layer is followed by a normalization layer, and an up-sampling layer follows each decoder block. The number of filters of all convolutional layers in each block is the same but differs from one block to another. Such that convolution layers in the first block have 256 filters, in the second block have 128 filters, and in the last block have 64 filters. This size of all filters in all decoder blocks is 3×3. After the three blocks, a multi-head is added to produce the outputs for different domains. The head is defined as two convolutional layers. The first one has $3 \times 3 \times 64$ filters followed by a batch normalization layer. The second convolutional layer has a $1 \times 1 \times 1$ filter with a sigmoid activation function. This architecture is for the main model (server), while the client's model is the same but has a single head.

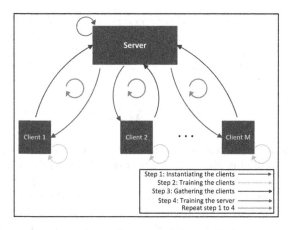

Fig. 1. Training procedure of KDNet.

3.2 Training Technique

As shown in Fig. 1, the training procedure is a repeated cycle of four main steps: 1) instantiating the clients, 2) training the clients, 3) gathering the clients, and 4) training the main model (server).

Instantiating the Client: In this step, all clients are instantiated from the server (i.e., a clone of the shared weights of the server is sent to the client). The clients initialize their network parameters with the cloned weights of the server. It is important to mention that only the encoder and decoder parameters are copied to the client (i.e., the heads' parameters are not copied). After that, a head is initialized with random weights added at the end of the client network.

Training the Clients: The clients' training is straightforward. Each client is trained on its local dataset using supervised learning. The goal is that each client successfully learns to segment the foreground objects in the local dataset.

Gathering the Clients: The server gathers only the trained client networks (i.e., the local dataset of each client is not included)

Training the Server: This is the most significant step where the server network learns the knowledge gained by all client networks. The server uses a large unlabeled dataset. Then, for each batch in this dataset, only one client will process this batch to produce the output mask. The clients are selected in a round-robin order (i.e., client[1], client[2], ..., client[M], client[1], ..., etc.). After that, the server applies the knowledge distillation loss function to learn to produce an output similar to the client's output. However, the server should learn from each client without affecting the knowledge gained by other clients. Hence, each client updates only one head of the server. Also, a term in the loss function is added to regularize the updates of shared parameters between clients (i.e., the encoder and decoder parameters). This term minimizes the distance between the output of other clients after the update and before the current client's update. The loss function used is defined as follows:

$$\mathcal{L}^i = \ell(y^i, y_n^i) + \frac{1}{M} \sum_{j \neq i}^{M} \ell(y_o^j, y_n^j) \tag{1}$$

the $\mathcal{L}^i$ is the loss function for updating the server with the ith client. The first loss term is reducing the distance between the server's output of ith after the update y_n^i and the output of the ith client y^i. The second term is reducing the distance between the output of all other heads of the server before y_o^j, and after y_n^j, the update and M represents the number of clients. The second term acts as a regularization term to force the network to update the parameters in a way that does not cause a huge change in the output of other heads. As shown in the loss function, the ground truth (label) of the batches in the dataset is not used.

4   Experiments

To evaluate KDNet, Three experiments are conducted. The first experiment is traditional foreground segmentation, where the model is trained using datasets individually (separated training). This experiment compares the results of KDNet with other foreground segmentation models. The second experiment tests the model generalization by training using multiple datasets (multiple domains). In this experiment, there are two training methods, namely joint and fine-tuning (sequential). Joint training means multiple datasets are combined to form one large dataset. Then, the model is trained using this large dataset. In sequential training, the model is trained using the dataset one after the other. After the model is trained using the last dataset, the models are evaluated using all datasets. The last experiment is few-shot learning. In this experiment, we test the ability of the model to adapt to new domains using a few labeled images.

4.1   Datasets

Densely Annotated VIdeo Segmentation 2016 (DAVIS16) [12] is a video object segmentation dataset. DAVIS consists of 50 videos. Each video has several frames ranging from 50 to 104. In each video, a single object is annotated, which is the object of interest in this video.

SegTrackV2 [13] is a video multiple objects segmentation dataset. The number of videos in the dataset is 14, and the number of frames ranged from 21 to 279 in each video. In this dataset, each frame has multiple ground-truth corresponding to each object in the video.

ChangeDetection.Net (CDNet) 2014 [14] is a benchmark dataset that detects changes between video frames. These changes are the moving objects.

The dataset consists of 11 different challenges. Each challenge has a number of videos ranging from 4 to 6, and the number of frames in each video ranges from 1000 to 8000. The total number of videos in the dataset is 53 videos.

ImageNet [15] is a large-scale dataset used as a benchmark for image classification tasks. In this paper, we use the images in the dataset without labels to train the main model to learn the knowledge gained by clients using knowledge distillation.

4.2   Implementation Details

In all experiments, we report the results of five different versions of KDNet. These versions 1) KDNet-base is the proposed model with a single head decoder, 2) KDNet-FL is the proposed model trained with the federated learning settings. In this version, the dataset is into sub-datasets. Then, a client is instantiated to learn from each sub-dataset. After that, the multi-heads of the main model learn from all clients using knowledge distillation loss function without the regularization term in Eq. (1). 3) KDNet-CL is the same as KDNet-FL, but the main model learns directly from the sub-datasets instead of learning from the trained clients. The loss function used is a mean squared error (MSE) with the regularization term in Eq. (1). 4) KDNet-FL-CL is the combination of both federated learning and continual learning. The loss function used in this version is the proposed function in Eq. (1). 5) KDNet-FL-CL-U is the same as KDNet-FL-CL, but the knowledge distillation between the main model and the clients is applied using a completely different unseen dataset (ImageNet) from the one used to train the clients. The point of adding the last version is to show that the proposed work does not need to access the datasets used in training the clients (data privacy).

During the training of KDNet, if the training data is a single dataset, the dataset is randomly split into five groups of videos to simulate multiple dataset training. In this case, the main model has five heads, each one responsible for learning from one of the five groups of videos. On the other hand, if the training data is multiple datasets, then the number of heads of the main model will be the same as the number of different datasets.

In the testing phase, for all versions of KDNet with multi-head, we use one labeled frame for each video to find which head is suitable for segmenting this video. We do this by feeding the frame as an input to the model. Then, the f-measure of each head of KDNet is calculated. The head with the highest f-measure is used to segment foreground objects from all frames of this video.

4.3   Traditional Foreground Segmentation Experiment

This experiment evaluates KDNet using two datasets, DAVIS16 and SegTrackV2. The model is trained and tested using each dataset individually. For this experiment, we show the results of the five versions of KDNet mentioned in the previous subsection. The reported metric for all experiments is the f-measure $(\mathcal{F})$.

Table 1. Traditional foreground segmentation results of KDNet compared with state-of-the-art models on the DAVIS16 dataset. The number inside the circle defines the order of the model performance concerning each evaluation metric.

Model	$\mathcal{F}$
STM [16]	0.901
MHP-VOS [17]	0.895
CFBI [18]	0.905
CFBI+ [18]	0.911
FgSegNet [19]	0.847
CascadeCNN [7]	0.814
STCN [2]	**0.930** ①
REFNet [1]	0.883
TransBlast [9]	0.863
KDNet-base	0.891
KDNet-FL	0.909
KDNet-CL	0.897
KDNet-FL-CL	0.924 ②
KDNet-FL-CL-U	0.921 ③

Table 2. Traditional foreground segmentation results of KDNet compared with state-of-the-art models on the SegTrackV2 dataset. The number inside the circle defines the order of the model performance concerning the evaluation metric.

Model	$\mathcal{F}$
DSRFCN3D [20]	0.878
GDHF [21]	0.868
UFO [22]	0.863
PDB [23]	0.864
STRCF [24]	0.899
FgSegNet [19]	0.880
CascadeCNN [7]	0.867
REFNet [1]	0.904
TransBlast [9]	0.902
KDNet-base	0.905
KDNet-FL	0.911 ③
KDNet-CL	0.909
KDNet-FL-CL	**0.920** ①
KDNet-FL-CL-U	0.914 ②

Table 1 shows the results of KDNet against state-of-the-art foreground segmentation models. The results show that KDNet is in second place by a small gap of 0.06% in f-measure less than the top-performing model.

For the SegTrackV2 dataset, Table 2 shows the results of KDNet against other foreground segmentation models using the SegTrackV2 dataset. As shown in Table 2, the performance of three versions of KDNet is in the top places. KDNet outperforms the second-best model (REFNet) in literature by 1.8%. While the second version of KDNet outperforms REFNet by 1.2%. These tables show the effectiveness of the proposed work in learning from individual datasets, even though the proposed work is mainly designed to learn effectively from multiple datasets.

4.4   Domain Generalization Experiment

To highlight the effectiveness of the proposed work, we conducted multi-domain experiments. The model is trained in these experiments using three benchmark datasets: CDNet, DAVIS16, and SegTrackV2. We show the results of two training procedures. The first training procedure is Joint training, where the models are trained using the three datasets simultaneously as if they are one large dataset. The second training procedure is Fine-tuning, where the models are fine-tuned using one dataset after the other (sequentially). After training is done in both scenarios, the model is evaluated using the testing set of all three datasets.

The results are compared with state-of-the-art foreground segmentation models. Four models with their source code publicly available from the previous experiment are selected to compare KDNet's generalization against them. These models are REFNet, sEnDec, FgSegNetV2, and CascadeCNN.

Tables 3 and 4 show the results of the models when trained using multiple datasets either simultaneously or sequentially. In these tables, it is clear that all models degraded in performance tremendously compared to their performance in the separated training. For example, REFNet has an average of 26.3% drop in performance when trained using multiple datasets. In Table 3, most of the models have higher performance in the first dataset (CDNet) as it is the largest dataset, which made the models biased toward it. However, our model solves this problem by using isolated parameters for each dataset (multi-head decoder). The performance gain in our model is 14.1% compared to REFNet, which is a massive gain in performance. In Table 4, the performance of all models in the last dataset is the highest. This is because the models tend to forget the knowledge gained by previous datasets due to sequential training (catastrophic forgetting). However, our proposed model overcomes this problem by the isolated parameters and the continual learning regularization term in the loss function. Hence, the performance of our proposed model is 13% higher than the second-best model.

Table 3. Comparison of KDNet against state-of-the-art methods when trained using the three datasets CDNet, DAVIS16, SegTrackV2 jointly (i.e., all three datasets are combined and considered as one large dataset). The values in the table represent the F-measure.

Training	Model	CDNet	DAVIS16	SegTrackV2	Average
Joint	sEnDec [25]	0.657	0.571	0.526	0.584
	FgSegNetV2 [19]	0.639	0.567	0.495	0.567
	CascadeCNN [7]	0.582	0.535	0.460	0.525
	REFNet [1]	**0.737**	0.630	0.505	0.624
	KDNet-base	0.627	0.706	0.580	0.637
	KDNet-FL	0.649	0.735	0.721	0.701
	KDNet-CL	0.633	0.719	0.658	0.670
	KDNet-FL-CL	0.662	**0.756**	**0.867**	**0.765**
	KDNet-FL-CL-U	0.659	0.751	0.816	0.742

To show the output of the trained model using some example videos from the three datasets, some visual results from this experiment are shown in Fig. 3.

The effectiveness of the proposed federated learning technique is shown in Fig. 2. In this figure, the average loss of all clients gets lower and converges faster after each federated cycle. Hence, the trained server has good knowledge of different domains and can adapt agilely to new domains.

Table 4. Comparison of KDNet against state-of-the-art methods when trained using the three datasets CDNet, DAVIS16, SegTrackV2 sequentially (i.e., the models are fine-tuned on datasets sequentially. After the model is trained using the last dataset, it is evaluated using the last dataset and all previous ones). The values in the table represent the F-measure.

Training	Model	CDNet	DAVIS16	SegTrackV2	Average
Fine-tuning (Sequential)	sEnDec [25]	0.451	0.562	0.829	0.614
	FgSegNetV2 [19]	0.419	0.518	0.755	0.564
	CascadeCNN [7]	0.398	0.503	0.746	0.549
	REFNet [1]	0.422	0.529	**0.917**	0.622
	KDNet-base	0.421	0.590	0.858	0.620
	KDNet-FL	0.476	0.643	0.872	0.664
	KDNet-CL	0.638	0.716	0.874	0.743
	KDNet-FL-CL	**0.655**	**0.721**	0.880	**0.752**
	KDNet-FL-CL-U	0.647	0.716	0.876	0.746

4.5   Few-Shot Experiment

We conducted a few-shot learning experiment to prove the trained KDNet's versatility and agility to learn new domains with limited data. In this experiment, the KDNet trained using CDNet, SegTrackV2, and DAVIS16 is fine-tuned using a few labeled frames from the DAVIS17 dataset. The number of labeled frames per video is either 1 or 5 frames, which is the default configuration for few-shot learning. Other models are trained jointly using the same three datasets and fine-tuned using the labeled frames from DAVIS17. In Table 5, KDNet (Server) is fine-tuning the jointly trained model, while KDNet (Server-Client) is fine-tuning the model trained using federated learning. The results show the superiority of the KDNet trained with federated learning in the few-shot learning performance. In 1-shot (i.e., one labeled frame per video), the performance of the proposed model is around 6.8% above the second model REFNet, which is expected as shown in Fig. 2 the trained KDNet makes the convergence towards a new task faster and easier. Hence, only a few fine-tuning iterations are required for the trained KDNet to converge.

Table 5. Few-shot foreground segmentation results of KDNet compared to state-of-the-art methods on DAVIS17.

Model	1-shot	5-shot
CascadeCNN [7]	0.624	0.661
FgSegNetV2 [19]	0.676	0.742
sEnDec [25]	0.681	0.759
REFNet [1]	0.692	0.767
KDNet-base	0.714	0.785
KDNet-FL-CL	**0.760**[①]	**0.814**[①]

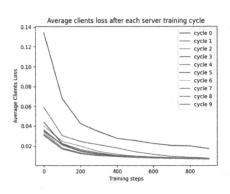

Fig. 2. The average loss of clients of all three datasets after each federated learning cycle.

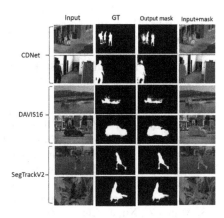

Fig. 3. Sample results of KDNet from domain generalization experiment.

5 Conclusion and Future Work

In this paper, a novel federated learning technique and an encoder-decoder network with multi-heads using multi-domain foreground segmentation datasets. The proposed model is called KDNet. KDNet instantiates a number of clients' networks corresponding to the number of different datasets. Each client is responsible for training using one of the datasets. Then, KDNet learns the knowledge gained by each client using knowledge distillation while minimizing the catastrophic forgetting of knowledge gained by previous clients. The results show that the proposed KDNet outperforms state-of-the-art foreground segmentation models by 1.8% when trained/tested using the SegTrackV2 dataset and in the second place with a small gap of 0.06% using DAVIS16. On the other hand, When the models are trained using multiple datasets to achieve domain generalization, KDNet outperforms other models by a noticeable amount of 14.1% and 13% in Joint training and fine-tuning, respectively. In future work, KDNet will be expanded to be a unified model that simultaneously learns multiple computer vision tasks, such as foreground segmentation, object detection, and image classification.

References

1. Osman, I., Eltantawy, A., Shehata, M.S.: Task-based parameter isolation for foreground segmentation without catastrophic forgetting using multi-scale region and edges fusion network. Image Vision Comput. **113**, 104248 (2021)
2. Cheng, H.K., Tai, Y.-W., Tang, C.-K.: Rethinking space-time networks with improved memory coverage for efficient video object segmentation. Adv. Neural. Inf. Process. Syst. **34**, 11781–11794 (2021)

3. Kairouz, P., et al.: Advances and open problems in federated learning. Found. Trends® Mach. Learn. **14**(1–2), 1–210 (2021)

4. Jain, S.D., Grauman, K.: Supervoxel-consistent foreground propagation in video. In: Fleet, D., Pajdla, T., Schiele, B., Tuytelaars, T. (eds.) ECCV 2014, Part IV. LNCS, vol. 8692, pp. 656–671. Springer, Cham (2014). https://doi.org/10.1007/978-3-319-10593-2_43

5. Fradi, H., Dugelay, J.-L.: Robust foreground segmentation using improved gaussian mixture model and optical flow. In: 2012 International Conference on Informatics, Electronics & Vision (ICIEV), pp. 248–253. IEEE (2012)

6. Lim, L.A., Keles, H.Y.: Foreground segmentation using convolutional neural networks for multiscale feature encoding. Pattern Recogn. Lett. **112**, 256–262 (2018)

7. Wang, Y., Luo, Z., Jodoin, P.-M.: Interactive deep learning method for segmenting moving objects. Pattern Recogn. Lett. **96**, 66–75 (2017)

8. Wang, Z., Xu, J., Liu, L., Zhu, F., Shao, L.: RANet: ranking attention network for fast video object segmentation. In: Proceedings of the IEEE/CVF International Conference on Computer Vision, pp. 3978–3987 (2019)

9. Osman, I., Abdelpakey, M., Shehata, M.S.: TransBlast: self-supervised learning using augmented subspace with transformer for background/foreground separation. In: Proceedings of the IEEE/CVF International Conference on Computer Vision, pp. 215–224 (2021)

10. Wang, Y., Tong, Y., Shi, D., Xu, K.: An efficient approach for cross-silo federated learning to rank. In: 2021 IEEE 37th International Conference on Data Engineering (ICDE), pp. 1128–1139 (2021)

11. ur Rehman, M.H., Dirir, A.M., Salah, K., Damiani, E., Svetinovic, D.: TrustFed: a framework for fair and trustworthy cross-device federated learning in IIoT. IEEE Trans. Industr. Inf. **17**(12), 8485–8494 (2021)

12. Pont-Tuset, J., Perazzi, F., Caelles, S., Arbeláez, P., Sorkine-Hornung, A., Van Gool, L.: The 2017 DAVIS challenge on video object segmentation. arXiv preprint arXiv:1704.00675 (2017)

13. Li, F., Kim, T., Humayun, A., Tsai, D., Rehg, J.M.: Video segmentation by tracking many figure-ground segments. In: Proceedings of the IEEE International Conference on Computer Vision, pp. 2192–2199 (2013)

14. Wang, Y., Jodoin, P.-M., Porikli, F., Konrad, J., Benezeth, Y., Ishwar, P.: CDNet 2014: an expanded change detection benchmark dataset. In: Proceedings of the IEEE Conference on Computer Vision and Pattern Recognition Workshops, pp. 387–394 (2014)

15. Russakovsky, O., et al.: ImageNet large scale visual recognition challenge. Int. J. Comput. Vision **115**(3), 211–252 (2015)

16. Oh, S.W., Lee, J.-Y., Xu, N., Kim, S.J.: Video object segmentation using space-time memory networks. In: Proceedings of the IEEE/CVF International Conference on Computer Vision, pp. 9226–9235 (2019)

17. Xu, S., Liu, D., Bao, L., Liu, W., Zhou, P.: MHP-VOS: multiple hypotheses propagation for video object segmentation. In: Proceedings of the IEEE/CVF Conference on Computer Vision and Pattern Recognition, pp. 314–323 (2019)

18. Yang, Z., Wei, Y., Yang, Y.: Collaborative video object segmentation by foreground-background integration. In: Vedaldi, A., Bischof, H., Brox, T., Frahm, J.-M. (eds.) ECCV 2020. LNCS, vol. 12350, pp. 332–348. Springer, Cham (2020). https://doi.org/10.1007/978-3-030-58558-7_20

19. Lim, L.A., Keles, H.Y.: Learning multi-scale features for foreground segmentation. Pattern Anal. Appl. **23**(3), 1369–1380 (2020)

20. Le, T.-N., Sugimoto, A.: Deeply supervised 3d recurrent FCN for salient object detection in videos. In: BMVC, vol. 1, p. 3 (2017)
21. Le, H., Nguyen, V., Yu, C.-P., Samaras, D.: Geodesic distance histogram feature for video segmentation. In: Lai, S.-H., Lepetit, V., Nishino, K., Sato, Y. (eds.) ACCV 2016. LNCS, vol. 10111, pp. 275–290. Springer, Cham (2017). https://doi.org/10.1007/978-3-319-54181-5_18
22. Su, Y., Deng, J., Sun, R., Lin, G., Wu, Q.: A unified transformer framework for group-based segmentation: co-segmentation, co-saliency detection and video salient object detection. arXiv preprint arXiv:2203.04708 (2022)
23. Song, H., Wang, W., Zhao, S., Shen, J., Lam, K.-M.: Pyramid dilated deeper ConvLSTM for video salient object detection. In: Proceedings of the European Conference on Computer Vision (ECCV), pp. 715–731 (2018)
24. Le, T.-N., Sugimoto, A.: Video salient object detection using spatiotemporal deep features. IEEE Trans. Image Process. **27**(10), 5002–5015 (2018)
25. Akilan, T., Jonathan Wu, Q.M.: sEnDec: an improved image to image CNN for foreground localization. IEEE Trans. Intell. Transp. Syst. **21**(10), 4435–4443 (2019)

Probabilistic Local Equivalence
Certification for Robustness Evaluation

Jacob Bond$^{(\boxtimes)}$, Siddhartha Gupta, and Thanura Elvitigala

General Motors Company, Warren, MI 48092, USA
{jacob.bond,siddhartha.gupta,thanura.elvitigala}@gm.com

Abstract. To evaluate the robustness of non-classifier models, we propose probabilistic local equivalence, based on the notion of randomized smoothing, as a way to quantitatively evaluate the robustness of an arbitrary function. For a given function f, probabilistic local equivalence evaluates whether, when sampling a normally-distributed point x' in a neighborhood of a point x, there is a probability > 0.5 that $f(x')$ is equivalent to $f(x)$, according to a user-defined notion of equivalence. We use probabilistic local equivalence to evaluate the effect of data augmentation methods for improving robustness, including adversarial training, on a model's performance. We also use probabilistic local equivalence to evaluate the effect on robustness of model architecture, number of parameters, pre-training, quantization, and other model properties.

Keywords: Computer Vision · Robustness · Evaluation

1 Introduction

Research has shown that deep learning models often generalize poorly to data outside of its training distribution, whether intentionally manipulated to be outside of the training distribution [16] or simply the result of common image perturbations [8]. A deep learning model's robustness to input perturbations is an important property of the model, providing insight into both its sensitivity to small changes in its input, as well as its ability to generalize outside of its training data. Model robustness is an important property in safety-critical applications, including advanced driver-assistance systems, as well as socially-impactful applications such as automated interview analysis.

Evaluation of a model's robustness typically focuses on evaluating the performance of the model either relative to the training data distribution or a data distribution consisting entirely of manipulated inputs and comparing the relative difference. However, neither is likely to be representative of a model's ability to generalize to real-world data distributions, particularly in the case of long-tail data distributions likely to encountered by cyber-physical systems that interact with people. There is a need for additional methods for evaluating a model's robustness beyond just its performance on manipulated and unmanipulated inputs from the training distribution.

© The Author(s), under exclusive license to Springer Nature Switzerland AG 2023
G. Bebis et al. (Eds.): ISVC 2023, LNCS 14361, pp. 264–276, 2023.
https://doi.org/10.1007/978-3-031-47969-4_21

To this end, we reformulated randomized smoothing [3] as the robustness metric probabilistic local equivalence. This method focuses on evaluating a model's average-case robustness, rather than the worst-case robustness evaluated by input manipulation attacks such as projected gradient descent [4,11]. In this way, probabilistic local equivalence is more sensitive to changing levels of robustness. Further, probabilistic local equivalence does not rely on back-propagation and uses statistical techniques to determine robustness at varying distances, so to understand a how a model's robustness varies with perturbation magnitude, the evaluation requires less computation than plotting a security curve [6]. In order to analyze the efficacy of the robustness metric, we compared the performance of standardly-trained instance segmentation models to models trained using two different approaches to adversarial training.

We found that the proposed robustness metric was able to differentiate between models trained on a variety of data augmentation techniques aimed at improving robustness. Further, in evaluations of pre-trained image classification and detection models, the proposed robustness metric was showed varying levels of performance among models having a similar number of parameters or similar performance metrics (either top-1 classification accuracy or detection box mean average precision (mAP) scores).

2   Related Work

In computer vision, evaluation of robustness has primarily focused on either input manipulation attacks targeted at the model being evaluated, or static perturbations generated beforehand and reused across evaluations. The former class of perturbations includes white-box attacks, such as Projected Gradient Descent (PGD) [11], with knowledge of a model's parameters and black-box attacks, such as Boundary Attack [2], with no access to a model's parameters. One important parameter for evaluation using PGD is the perturbation bound, which controls the allowable magnitude of the perturbations. To better understand a model's robustness, one can plot a security curve showing the model's performance against a range of across a range of perturbation bounds, as in Adversarial Robustness Toolbox [6]. AutoAttack [4] provides a parameter-free method for evaluating a model's robustness to input manipulations combining an adaptive version of PGD with other white- and black-box attacks to create a suite of input manipulation attacks for evaluation, though it is largely limited to object classification models.

The Common Corruptions benchmark [8] was developed as a repeatable test of a model's performance in the face of a range of standardized input perturbations of varying severity, including addition of noise sampled from different probability distributions, several methods for blurring images, and results of JPEG compression. The 3D Common Corruptions [9] framework provides an additional methodology for robustness evaluation by applying transformation that take scene geometry into account.

The randomized smoothing framework established by Cohen et al. [3] provides an inference framework which allows certifying a model's robustness at a point. During inference, the classifier samples several different perturbations from a normal probability distribution and computes the model's output on application of each perturbation, ultimately returning the most common output from the model. Using this framework for inference permits establishing bounds on a model's robustness around a given input using confidence bounds. Salman et al. [14] then developed an input manipulation attack on smoothed classifiers, using it for adversarial training to improve the provable robustness of these classifiers. While the original randomized smoothing method was restricted to classifiers, the method has since been extended in several directions, including an extension to image segmentation by Fischer et al. [5].

3   Probabilistic Local Equivalence Certification

Comparing the innate robustness of two models is challenging. Evaluating the adversarial robustness of a model is often too aggressive, as any model which hasn't been adversarially trained will receive a score of 0. Formally verifying a model typically requires an analysis limited to a specific architecture. We propose a method based on randomized smoothing certification [3] which is applicable to arbitrary functions while also being more sensitive than evaluation of adversarial robustness.

3.1   Probabilistic Local Equivalence Certification

A function f is robust if small changes to its input result in small changes to its output. To this end, given inputs x and x', we will define a notion of how similar the outputs $f(x)$ and $f(x')$ are. Let $f : X \to Y$ be a function and let $\mathcal{M} : Y \times Y \to [0, 1]$ be a scoring function evaluating how similar two elements $y, y' \in Y$ are to each other. Then $\mathcal{M}$ induces a semipseudometric d on X by

$$d(x, x') = 1 - \mathcal{M}\big(f(x), f(x')\big) \tag{1}$$

and the set $B_d(x, t) := \{x' \in X \mid d(x, x') < t\}$ defines the points $x' \in X$ so that $f(x')$ is close to $f(x)$ relative to $\mathcal{M}$. The robustness threshold t is ultimately an application-specific choice depending on a number of factors, but the goal is to capture the amount of variation in the model's output which will avoid significant changes to any downstream results. An extreme example, as mentioned below, occurs when $\mathcal{M}$ is the accuracy metric, in which case all values of $t \in (0, 1)$ are equivalent.

For d defined as in (1), the points in $B_d(x, t)$ can be considered as being equivalent to x relative to f, $\mathcal{M}$, and t since for suitable t, f gives equivalent outputs at all points of $B_d(x, t)$. Returning to the concept of robustness, f is robust if at all nearby inputs, f gives similar outputs. Translating this into the language introduced above, f is robust at x_0 for radius δ if $B_{L^2}(x_0, \delta) \subseteq B_d(x_0, t)$. While evaluating whether $B_{L^2}(x_0, \delta) \subseteq B_d(x_0, t)$ is difficult, the randomized smoothing framework provides a method for approximating this. Specifically, the framework allows us to determine whether

$$\text{for all } x \in B_{L^2}(x_0, \delta), \quad P_{\varepsilon \sim \mathcal{N}}\big(x + \varepsilon \in B_d(x_0, t)\big) > 0.5,$$

where $\mathcal{N}$ is a normal distribution. In this direction, we have the following definitions.

Definition 1. *Relative to a choice of d, t, and distribution $\mathcal{D}$,*

1. *If $B_{L^2}(x, \delta) \subseteq B_d(x_0, t)$, then f is locally equivalent to $f(x_0)$ at x for radius δ.*
2. *If $P_{\varepsilon \sim \mathcal{D}}\big(x + \varepsilon \in B_d(x_0, t)\big) \geq 0.5$, then f is probabilistically locally equivalent to $f(x_0)$ around x.*

Having defined d as in (1), fix a value of t and for any $x \in X$, let $B_x := B_d(x, t)$. The framework of [3,14] will be applied to the indicator function $\mathbb{1}_{x_0} : x \mapsto \mathbb{1}(x \in B_{x_0})$. Specifically, let $\mathcal{N} := \mathcal{N}(0, \sigma^2 I)$, the normal distribution centered at 0 with standard deviation σ with cumulative distribution function Φ, and consider the smoothed function

$$\widehat{\mathbb{1}_{x_0}}(x) := \mathbb{E}_{\varepsilon \sim \mathcal{N}} \mathbb{1}_{x_0}(x + \varepsilon) = P_{\varepsilon \sim \mathcal{N}}(x + \varepsilon \in B_{x_0}). \tag{2}$$

Then the `Certify` algorithm presented in [3], when applied to $\widehat{\mathbb{1}_{x_0}}$, first determines a lower bound $\underline{p}$ for $\widehat{\mathbb{1}_{x_0}}(x_0)$, which establishes that f is locally equivalent to $f(x_0)$ at x_0 with probability at least $\underline{p}$. However, [14] shows that $\Phi^{-1} \circ \widehat{\mathbb{1}_{x_0}}$ is $1/\sigma$-Lipschitz, so that the value $\widehat{\mathbb{1}_{x_0}}(x_0)$ provides additional information about the surrounding neighborhood. In this direction, the `Certify` algorithm applied to $\widehat{\mathbb{1}_{x_0}}$ is then able to provide a radius R guaranteeing, with probability $1 - \alpha$, that f is probabilistically locally equivalent to $f(x_0)$ around all $x \in B_{L^2}(x_0, R)$. This algorithm is reframed for the current context as `CertifyProbabilisticEquivalence`; see [3] for additional details surrounding the original algorithm.

Definition 2. *Let*

$$\text{ProbLocEquiv}(S, f, r) := \{x_0 \in S \mid$$
$$f \text{ is probabilistically locally equivalent to } f(x_0) \text{ around all } x \in B_{L^2}(x_0, r)\}.$$

Proposition 1. *With probability at least $1 - \alpha$ over the randomness in* `CertifyProbabilisticEquivalence`, *if* `CertifyProbabilisticEquivalence` *returns a radius R, then $x \in \text{ProbLocEquiv}(X, f, R)$.*

For a given radius r and evaluation set E, Proposition 1 can be used to determine the percentage of E which lie in $\text{ProbLocEquiv}(E, f, r)$, giving an indication of the robustness of the model to perturbations with an L^2 norm less than r. A robustness score, relative to a given evaluation set E and choice of hyperparameters, can then be computed for a function f by taking the mean of the certified radii over the set E. As in the case of randomized smoothing certification, labels for the evaluation set E are not required.

Algorithm 1. Certification of probabilistic local equivalence of a function f

1: **function** CERTIFYPROBABILISTICEQUIVALENCE(f, x_0, y, σ, n, α, $\mathcal{M}$, t)
2: $\quad y_0 \leftarrow f(x_0)$
3: $\quad x' \leftarrow n$ samples from $\mathcal{N}(x, \sigma^2 I)$
4: $\quad y' \leftarrow f(x')$
5: **if** y is None
6: $\quad$ num_equivalent $\leftarrow$ COUNTTRUE$\left(1 - \mathcal{M}(y_0, y') < t\right)$
7: **else**
8: $\quad$ num_equivalent $\leftarrow$ COUNTTRUE$\left(1 - \frac{\mathcal{M}(y_0, y)}{\mathcal{M}(y', y)} < t\right)$
9: $\quad \underline{p} \leftarrow$ LOWERCONFBOUND(num_equivalent, n, $1 - \alpha$)
10: **if** $\underline{p} > \frac{1}{2}$ **return** radius $\sigma \Phi^{-1}(\underline{p})$
11: **else return** ABSTAIN

Algorithm 2. Compute a robustness score of the function f

1: **function** ROBUSTNESSSCORE(f, E, σ, n, α, $\mathcal{M}$, t)
2: **radii** $\leftarrow$ []
3: **for** $(x, y) \in E$ **do**
4: $\quad$ radius $\leftarrow$ CERTIFYPROBABILISTICEQUIVALENCE($f, x, y, \sigma, n, \alpha, \mathcal{M}, t$)
5: $\quad$ **if radius** is ABSTAIN **then** Append 0 to **radii**
6: $\quad$ **else** Append **radius** to **radii**
7: **return** MEAN(**radii**)

3.2 When Labels are Available

In the case that ground-truth labels $\{y_i\}$ are available for points $\{x_i\} \subseteq X$, there is an alternative formulation for (1). In this case, rather than simply looking at the similarity between $f(x_1)$ and $f(x_2)$, it may be desirable to determine how these values differ relative to the ground-truth y. When a pair $(x, y) \sim \mathcal{D} = X \times Y$, (1) can be replaced with

$$d_y(x, x') = 1 - \frac{\mathcal{M}(f(x'), y)}{\mathcal{M}(f(x), y)}. \tag{3}$$

The convention $d_y(x, x') = 1$ if $\mathcal{M}(f(x), y) = 0 = \mathcal{M}(f(x'), y)$ and $d_y(x, x') = -\infty$ if $\mathcal{M}(f(x), y) = 0 \neq \mathcal{M}(f(x'), y)$ will be adopted. While d_y is no longer even a semipseudometric, the set $B_{d_y}(x, t)$ contains the points x' so that replacing x by x' does not significantly degrade the model's performance. In particular, note that if $\mathcal{M}(f(x'), y) > \mathcal{M}(f(x), y)$, then $d_y(x, x') < 0$ and $x' \in B_{d_y}(x, t)$.

3.3 The Case of Classification

Importantly, in the case of classifiers, the above measure of robustness reduces to the standard measure of robustness. In this case, $\mathcal{M}$ is the accuracy metric:

$$\mathcal{M}(y_1, y_2) = \begin{cases} 1 & \text{if } y_1 = y_2, \\ 0 & \text{otherwise.} \end{cases}$$

Defining d as in (1),

$$x' \in B_d(x,t) \iff 1 - \mathcal{M}\big(f(x), f(x')\big) < t \iff 1 - t < \mathcal{M}\big(f(x), f(x')\big),$$

so that for $0 < t < 1$, $x' \in B_d(x,t) \iff f(x) = f(x')$.

3.4 The Case of Semantic Instance Segmentation

For semantic instance segmentation evaluation, we use symmetric best dice (SBD) as the score function $\mathcal{M}$ and define d as in (3). Figures 1 and 2 illustrate the situation using a lane line instance segmentation model trained following the approach in [1], showing an equivalent and an inequivalent example. Figure 1 shows the original input, the model's output, and the ground truth label, leading to an SBD score of 0.674. Using a relative threshold of $t = 0.1$ and rearranging (3) results in

$$d_y(x, x') < 0.1 \iff 0.9\mathcal{M}(f(x), y) < \mathcal{M}(f(x'), y) \iff \mathcal{M}(f(x'), y) > 0.60066.$$

In Fig. 2, the first example, using $\sigma = 0.2$, leads to an SBD score of 0.661, indicating that the model f has made an equivalent prediction on the given input. However, the second example, using $\sigma = 0.3$, results in an SBD score 0.573, outside of the threshold considered as equivalent.

Fig. 1. The original input x, the model's prediction y, and the ground truth label, resulting in a symmetric best dice score of 0.674.

4 Experiments

4.1 Impacts of Robust Training Methods on Robustness

To assess the evaluative capabilities of probabilistic local equivalence, as well as understand the impact of various strategies for improving robustness, we evaluate standardly-trained and adversarially-trained models for object classification and semantic instance segmentation, comparing the results of probabilistic local equivalence to the model's performance under an input manipulation attack. In the case of classification, we also evaluate a model trained for Common Corruptions [8] robustness.

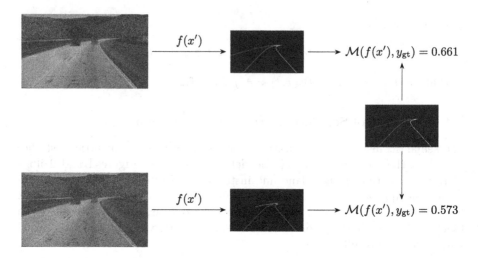

Fig. 2. (Above) An input leading to a symmetric best dice score of 0.661, within the defined permissible threshold of 0.0674 from the original score 0.674. (Below) An input leading to a symmetric best dice score of 0.573, outside of the permissible threshold.

4.2 Classification

For classification, we evaluated three models trained on the CIFAR-100 dataset: a model trained using standard methods, a pre-trained model using the PRIME [12] methodology for improving Common Corruption robustness, and a model using the Fast is Better than Free (FBF) [18] approach to adversarial training.

We applied Algorithm 1 following the approach in Sect. 3.2 with parameters:

- Standard deviation $\sigma = 0.1$,
- Number of perturbed samples per input $n = 64$,
- Significance level $\alpha = 0.05$,
- Metric $\mathcal{M}$ as accuracy metric

$$\mathcal{M}(y_1, y_2) = \begin{cases} 1 & \text{if } y_1 = y_2, \\ 0 & \text{otherwise.} \end{cases}$$

- Equivalence threshold $t = 0.1$. (Note that all $0 < t < 1$ are equivalent.)

We found that probabilistic local equivalence was able to discern different levels of robustness exhibited by the models to randomly sampled perturbations, as shown in Fig. 3a. This is consistent with the expected notion that both adversarial training and PRIME should prevent small perturbations from resulting in significant changes to a model's output. While adversarially-trained models should be robust to any noise distribution, a model trained with PRIME is intended to instead be especially robust to specific classes of perturbations.

In contrast, generating a security curve for these models, as shown in Fig. 3b, is unable to significantly distinguish between the levels of robustness present in the PRIME model and the standardly-trained model due to the worst-case nature of the manipulated inputs.

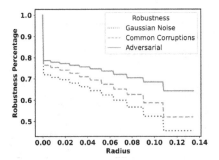

(a) Local equivalence evaluation, with parameters as in Section 4.2, of models trained on the CIFAR-100 dataset

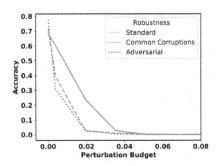

(b) L^∞ security curve for each type of robustness (10 steps of PGD)

Fig. 3. Robustness evaluation of different training methods for CIFAR-100 classification

4.3 Semantic Instance Segmentation

For semantic instance segmentation, we adapted a model from the approach of Neven et al. [13], training the model on the TuSimple lane detection dataset [17]. We trained three versions of the model, one following a standard training methodology, one using FBF adapted for non-classifiers, and one which combined FBF with the TRADES loss [19] as in [1].

To better understand the robustness of the different models, we performed an in-depth analysis of the robustness using the test set. We first performed an analysis of the models' local equivalence robustness following the method in Sect. 3.4 and plotted the results in Fig. 4a, finding that adversarial training improves the robustness of the model to the random perturbations generated in the evaluation. The local equivalence robustness analysis was performed using $\sigma = 0.1$, $\alpha = 0.05$, and $n = 160$ samples per input. Figure 4a shows that local equivalence robustness is able to distinguish between the levels of robustness to normally distributed perturbations present in the standardly-trained and adversarially-trained models, and even between the different adversarially-trained models.

For comparison, we also evaluated the models' adversarial robustness. Although, we weren't able to apply AutoAttack [4], to mitigate the effect of the perturbation budget ε as a hyperparameter, we plotted the security curve for each model, evaluating the model's performance under a 10-step L^∞ PGD manipulation across a range of perturbation budgets in Fig. 4b. As noted in [4], after a few iterations of PGD, the loss function plateaus, so that 10-step PGD results in a good approximation of the optimum, while balancing the computational load required for a thorough sweep of perturbation budgets. For a given budget ε, a step size of $3\varepsilon/(2 \cdot 10)$ was used.

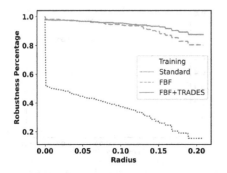 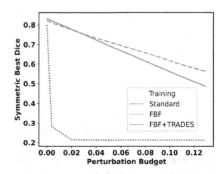

(a) Robustness curve for each training method ($\sigma = 0.1, n = 160$)

(b) L^∞ security curve for each training method (10 steps of PGD)

Fig. 4. Robustness evaluation of the best performing model from each training method

5 Impacts of Model Attributes on Robustness

We evaluated the impact on robustness of a number of model attributes, including quantization use, model size, model width, and accuracy. Using pre-trained image classification and detection models available on the PyTorch Model Zoo, we present a comparison of classification models in Fig. 5 and a comparison of detection models in Fig. 6. The robustness percentage was computed using Algorithm 2 on the ImageNet validation set with $\sigma = 0.1$, $\alpha = 0.05$, $n = 32$ and $t = 0.3$. We found that classification models performing similarly when evaluated for accuracy, can perform significantly differently when evaluated for probabilistic local equivalence. Further, ViT and RegNet models, pre-trained using weakly supervised SWAG strategy [15] before being finetuned on ImageNet, perform best on this metric. Quantized models like MobileNet-V3-Large-Quantized and ResNet50-Quantized and wide models like Wide-ResNet50 and Wide-ResNet101 have higher robustness results than their non-quantized and non-wide counterparts, respectively. We also find that single-stage detection models like RetinaNet-ResNet50-FPN-V2 and FCOS-ResNet50-FPN-V2 have a higher robustness score than the two-stage FasterRCNN-ResNet50-FPN-V2, despite the latter having higher box mean average precision (mAP) and a higher number of parameters. Finally, Fig. 7 illustrates, in the case of a Mask R-CNN pre-trained on the COCO dataset [10] and fine-tuned on the KITTI object detection dataset [7], that as a model is trained across additional epochs, its robustness, as measured by probabilistic local equivalence, decreases.

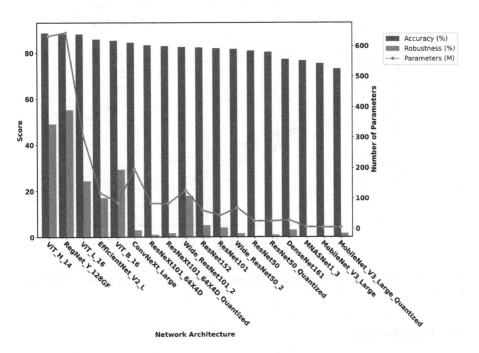

Fig. 5. Robustness and Accuracy comparison of PyTorch image classification models pre-trained on ImageNet dataset

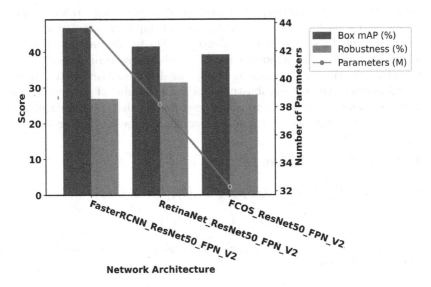

Fig. 6. Robustness and Box mAP comparison of PyTorch object detection models pre-trained on COCO dataset

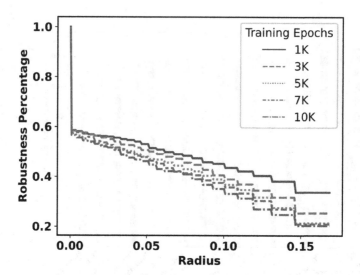

Fig. 7. Robustness evaluation of a model as it is fine-tuned for increasing numbers of epochs

6   Conclusion

We introduced a method based on the theory of randomized smoothing [3] for assessing the robustness of an arbitrary function to randomized input perturbations. By focusing on randomized perturbations, we are able to evaluate a model's robustness from an expected value perspective, rather than the worst-case perspective taken when evaluating against input manipulation attacks. We showed probabilistic local equivalence is able to discriminate between a standardly-trained model, a model trained for robustness against specific classes of perturbations, and an adversarially-trained model. We also evaluated the effect of several model attributes on robustness, including number of parameters, use of quantization, and model width on robustness, finding that quantization, widening, and weakly supervised pretraining all confer improvements to robustness.

A Proof of Proposition 1

Lemma 1 *[14, Appendix A]. Let $f : \mathbb{R}^n \to [0,1]^2$ be defined by*

$$f(x) = \big(f_0(x), f_1(x)\big),$$

with $f_i : \mathbb{R}^n \to [0,1]$ and $f_0(x) + f_1(x) = 1$ for all $x \in \mathbb{R}^n$. Let $\varepsilon \sim \mathcal{N}(0, \sigma^2 I)$. If $\mathbb{E}_\varepsilon f_1(x + \varepsilon) \geq \frac{1}{2}$, then

$$\mathbb{E}_\varepsilon f_1(x + \delta + \varepsilon) \geq \frac{1}{2} \ \text{for all} \ |\delta|_2 < \sigma \Phi^{-1} \circ f_1(x).$$

Proof. Appendix A in [14] shows that the lemma holds for all δ with

$$|\delta|_2 \geq \frac{1}{2}\left(\Phi^{-1} \circ f_1(x) - \Phi^{-1} \circ f_0(x)\right).$$

Noting that $1 - \Phi \circ \Phi^{-1} \circ f_1(x) = \Phi \circ \Phi^{-1}\left(-f_1(x)\right)$,

$$\Phi^{-1} \circ f_0(x) = \Phi^{-1}\left(1 - f_1(x)\right) = \Phi^{-1}\left(1 - \Phi \circ \Phi^{-1} \circ f_1(x)\right)$$
$$= \Phi^{-1} \circ \Phi\left(-\Phi^{-1} \circ f_1(x)\right) = -\Phi^{-1} \circ f_1(x),$$

and the result follows.

Proposition 1. *For any function* $f : \mathbb{R}^n \to [0,1]$ *and* $x \in X \subseteq \mathbb{R}^n$, *with probability at least* $1-\alpha$ *over the randomness in* `CertifyProbabilisticEquivalence`, *if* `CertifyProbabilisticEquivalence` *returns a radius* R, *then*

$$x \in \text{ProbLocEquiv}(X, f, R).$$

Proof. If a radius R is returned by `CertifyProbabilisticEquivalence`, then `LowerConfBound` returned a value $\underline{p} = \Phi(R/\sigma) > 1/2$ and as a lower bound on the probability of success in the Bernoulli trial of being locally equivalent,

$$\underline{p} \leq P_{y'}\left(1 - \mathcal{M}(y_0, y')\right) < t)$$
$$= P_{x'}\left(1 - \mathcal{M}\left(f(x_0), f(x')\right)\right) < t\right)$$
$$= P_{\varepsilon \sim \mathcal{N}}\left(1 - \mathcal{M}\left(f(x_0), f(x_0 + \varepsilon)\right)\right) < t\right)$$
$$= P_{\varepsilon \sim \mathcal{N}}(d(x_0, x_0 + \varepsilon) < t) \qquad \text{(from (1))}$$
$$= P_{\varepsilon \sim \mathcal{N}}\left(x_0 + \varepsilon \in B_d(x_0, t)\right)$$
$$= \widehat{\mathbb{1}_{x_0}}(x_0). \qquad \text{(by (2))}$$

Lemma 1 applied to the function $f = (1 - \mathbb{1}_{x_0}, \mathbb{1}_{x_0})$ then implies that for $x \in B_{L^2}(x_0, R)$, $\widehat{\mathbb{1}_{x_0}}(x) \geq 1/2$ and $x_0 \in \text{ProbLocEquiv}(X, f, R)$.

References

1. Bond, J.: Adversarial training of a lane line instance segmentation model (2023). https://arxiv.org/abs/2206.02539
2. Brendel, W., Rauber, J., Bethge, M.: Decision-based adversarial attacks: reliable attacks against black-box machine learning models. In: 6th International Conference on Learning Representations (ICLR) (2018). https://openreview.net/forum?id=SyZI0GWCZ
3. Cohen, J.M., Rosenfeld, E., Kolter, J.Z.: Certified adversarial robustness via randomized smoothing. In: Proceedings of the 36th International Conference on Machine Learning (ICML), pp. 1310–1320 (2019)

4. Croce, F., Hein, M.: Reliable evaluation of adversarial robustness with an ensemble of diverse parameter-free attacks. In: Proceedings of the 37th International Conference on Machine Learning (ICML), pp. 2206–2216 (2020)
5. Fischer, M., Baader, M., Vechev, M.T.: Scalable certified segmentation via randomized smoothing. In: Proceedings of the 38th International Conference on Machine Learning (ICML), pp. 3340–3351 (2021)
6. Linux Foundation AI & Data Foundation: Adversarial robustness toolbox (2018). https://github.com/Trusted-AI/adversarial-robustness-toolbox
7. Geiger, A., Lenz, P., Urtasun, R.: Are we ready for autonomous driving? The KITTI vision benchmark suite. In: 25th IEEE Conference on Computer Vision and Pattern Recognition (CVPR), pp. 3354–3361. IEEE Computer Society (2012)
8. Hendrycks, D., Dietterich, T.G.: Benchmarking neural network robustness to common corruptions and perturbations. In: 7th International Conference on Learning Representation (ICLR) (2019). https://openreview.net/forum?id=HJz6tiCqYm
9. Kar, O.F., Yeo, T., Atanov, A., Zamir, A.: 3D common corruptions and data augmentation. In: 35th IEEE/CVF Conference on Computer Vision and Pattern Recognition (CVPR), pp. 18941–18952 (2022)
10. Lin, T.-Y., et al.: Microsoft COCO: common objects in context. In: Fleet, D., Pajdla, T., Schiele, B., Tuytelaars, T. (eds.) ECCV 2014. LNCS, vol. 8693, pp. 740–755. Springer, Cham (2014). https://doi.org/10.1007/978-3-319-10602-1_48
11. Mądry, A., Makelov, A., Schmidt, L., Tsipras, D., Vladu, A.: Towards deep learning models resistant to adversarial attacks. In: 6th International Conference on Learning Representations (ICLR) (2018). https://openreview.net/forum?id=rJzIBfZAb
12. Modas, A., Rade, R., Ortiz-Jiménez, G., Moosavi-Dezfooli, S., Frossard, P.: PRIME: a few primitives can boost robustness to common corruptions (2021). https://arxiv.org/abs/2112.13547
13. Neven, D., Brabandere, B.D., Georgoulis, S., Proesmans, M., Gool, L.V.: Towards end-to-end lane detection: an instance segmentation approach. In: 2018 IEEE Intelligent Vehicles Symposium, pp. 286–291. IEEE (2018)
14. Salman, H., et al.: Provably robust deep learning via adversarially trained smoothed classifiers. In: Advances in Neural Information Processing Systems 32 (NeurIPS), pp. 11289–11300 (2019)
15. Singh, M., et al.: Revisiting weakly supervised pre-training of visual perception models. In: 35th IEEE/CVF Conference on Computer Vision and Pattern Recognition (CVPR), pp. 794–804 (2022)
16. Szegedy, C., et al.: Intriguing properties of neural networks. In: 2nd International Conference on Learning Representations (ICLR) (2014). https://openreview.net/forum?id=kklr_MTHMRQjG
17. TuSimple: TuSimple lane detection challenge. Joint Workshop on Computer Vision in Vehicle Technology and Autonomous Driving Challenge (2017). https://github.com/TuSimple/tusimple-benchmark
18. Wong, E., Rice, L., Kolter, J.Z.: Fast is better than free: revisiting adversarial training. In: 8th International Conference on Learning Representations (ICLR) (2020). https://openreview.net/forum?id=BJx040EFvH
19. Zhang, H., Yu, Y., Jiao, J., Xing, E.P., Ghaoui, L.E., Jordan, M.I.: Theoretically principled trade-off between robustness and accuracy. In: Proceedings of the 36th International Conference on Machine Learning (ICML), pp. 7472–7482 (2019)

Challenges of Depth Estimation
for Transparent Objects

Jean-Baptiste Weibel$^{(\boxtimes)}$ [ID], Paolo Sebeto, Stefan Thalhammer[ID],
and Markus Vincze[ID]

Vision for Robotics Laboratory, Automation and Control Institute, TU Wien,
Vienna, Austria
{weibel,sebeto,thalhammer,vincze}@acin.tuwien.ac.at

Abstract. Transparent objects and surfaces are pervasive in man-made
environments and need to be considered in any vision system. Accurate depth data is a key factor for such systems reliability, requiring
transparency to be inferred, due to the sensing challenges. However, the
current state-of-the-art methods to predict the depth of such objects are
not reliable enough to ensure safe operation of robots in arbitrary complex scenes. In order to better understand and improve upon existing
solutions, we evaluate the performance of a variety of depth estimation
methods. Doing so, we disentangle the different factors impacting their
performance. Among our findings, neural radiance fields offer the best
accuracy, but are very sensitive to the number of images used to understand the scene, and do not benefit from any level of object understanding
to help them fill in the gaps.

Keywords: Transparent objects perception · Depth Estimation ·
Depth Completion

1 Introduction

Vision systems need to provide sufficient information for the task and scene at
hand to enable reliable and safe operations, whether in an industrial context, or
when considering a service robot in a household. The COCO and LVIS [4] challenge have demonstrated the very significant progress [5,11,14] made in object
detection and the robustness of such approaches to support scene understanding. An important aspect of that requirement is the ability of vision systems to
reliably understand the geometry of the environment, which becomes necessary
as soon as an agent is expected to act in that environment.

While widely available depth sensors have provided a solid baseline to recover
the scene's geometry, they assume surfaces to be lambertian. Recovering the
shape of transparent objects is therefore still an open challenge. Their appearance strongly depends on the environment in which they are observed for all

Supported by the EU-program EC Horizon 2020 for Research and Innovation under
grant agreement No. 101017089, project TraceBot.

wavelengths commonly used in vision sensors. Either no depth is predicted, preventing any interaction, or the depth of the transparent object's background is estimated, potentially leading to unsafe robot's movement in the scene. Learned methods have been introduced to address this specific problem using the color image to complete the depth [3,12,16], but their generalisation ability when encountering such transparent objects in environments with large scene shift remains to be proven.

This work presents a representative comparison of recent depth completion and NeRF methods for transparent object depth retrieval. The aim is to highlight the advantages and disadvantages of both types of approaches, and to quantitatively evaluate the expected error. We collected diverse data to empirically investigate the reliability of depth estimation methods for transparent objects. By using glass and plastic objects, filled with liquid or empty, properties like opacity and index of refraction are varied. Additionally, scene properties, such as viewing angle, object arrangements and lighting are varied to create diverse evaluation scenarios. In order to provide ground truth depth for evaluation, objects are coated and scanned with a high-quality sensor for creating $3D$ models. Image sets for testing are captured using the uncoated objects. The $6D$ pose annotations are created by registering the object models against the captured images. Ground truth depth is computed using these annotations. Evaluations on these data are provided for a set of methods including monocular depth estimation [15], RGB-D transparent object depth estimation [3,12,16], and neural radiance fields [6] as illustrated in Fig. 1. In summary, our contributions are:

- an in-depth evaluation of the performance of depth estimation methods for transparent objects on common ground.
- a set of principles and recommendations inferred from the requirements of the individual approaches.

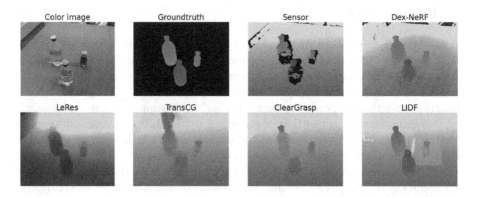

Fig. 1. Visual comparison. Depth prediction examples of the evaluated depth estimation approaches, the sensor and the ground truth.

We now present relevant state-of-the-art methods in Sect. 2, our proposed evaluation scheme in Sect. 3, our experimental results in Sect. 4 before presenting our conclusions in Sect. 5.

2 Related Works

This section introduces the state-of-the-art methods in the field of depth estimation as well as other relevant datasets of transparent objects.

2.1 Depth Estimation

While active depth sensors such as the Microsoft Kinect, the Asus XTion and the Intel Realsense are widely available and provide accurate dense depth maps, none of them provide reliable depth information for transparent objects. Structured light ones tend to provide no depth at all, while active stereo can recover a few points on the edges. In the worst case, such sensor will provide depth values corresponding to the surface behind the transparent object, leading to potentially unsafe motion for a robot.

Another approach is to directly predict the depth from an RGB image using a learned method [1,15]. A major challenge in this context is to predict metric depth, as a single image does not provide information about the absolute scale. In [15], the authors split the task in two steps: first they predict monocular depth, second, they refine the scale and a focal length. A point cloud is created using the initial guess of the camera intrinsics and the estimated depth map and fed to a module that predicts that refinement.

Depth Completion: A few works focused on completing the missing depth maps produced by depth sensors using information from the corresponding RGB image. The first one to do so, ClearGrasp [12], proposed to predict a mask and surface normals of transparent objects, as well as their outline. From this information, an optimisation step would fill in the gap of the sensor depth map. LIDF [16] introduces a new local neural representation from ray-voxels pairs, and use this representation to predict the occupancy of said voxels from which the depth can be inferred. TransCG [3], on the other hand, proposes a more standard but very efficient convolutional neural network designed for depth completion.

Neural Radiance Fields: Neural Radiance fields [9], or NeRF for short, introduced a method to generate novel views of a scene from a set of posed views by learning an implicit representation. A multi-layer perceptron learns to predict density values and emitted colors for every position and direction within the scene the field represents. They are in turn used in a volume rendering scheme to recreate views of the scene. While this process originally took many hours to train on a single scene, improvements introduced by Instant-NGP [10] reduced this to less than 15 min. This speed-up is the result of a more efficient position encoding using a multi-resolution hash encoding combined with more efficient architectures.

In Dex-NeRF [6], the authors noticed that the density values learned by NeRF present small local maxima along rays passing through transparent objects. By setting a low threshold, the distance to the first density value crossing that threshold along the ray is shown to produce depth estimation for transparent objects. In the follow-up work Evo-NeRF [8], optimisation are made to the pipeline to learn the implicit representation faster and predict grasp points directly from a Dex-NeRF predicted depth map. Neural radiance fields have demonstrated their ability to recover scene geometry, even for transparent objects, and are very actively researched.

Transparent Objects Dataset: Transparent object handling has gained considerable momentum, leading to the creation of a number of datasets of varying complexities. Cleargrasp [12] introduced its own synthetic dataset as well as a very small scale real dataset for testing purposes (286 images). LIDF [16] introduced the Omniverse large-scale synthetic dataset but no real counterpart. TransCG [3] introduced a large-scale real dataset focused on bin picking setups, mostly using top views of scenes. Most recently, [7] introduced a dataset comparing different depth sensors, including active and passive stereo, and direct and indirect time-of-flight sensors. This work does include transparent objects but is not focused on them.

The most relevant dataset to our benchmark task, ClearPose [2], introduced a large-scale dataset of scenes containing transparent objects. The annotations are obtained by placing object models in the 3D scene and hand-adjusting their positions based on the reprojection over multiple images. We use a very similar approach that was introduced in 3D-DAT [13], which uses the reconstruction of NeRF to auto-align objects with the scenes. However, ClearPose only considers transparent object with similar index of refraction, without filling. This work utilises more diverse data for evaluation, featuring different materials, containers with and without liquid filling. This allow us to reason about specific properties of objects, as detailed in the Sect. 3.

3   Measuring the Quality of Estimated Depth Maps

This section introduces the methodology to evaluate the quality of depth estimation from a variety of methods, specifically looking into the viewpoint from which scenes are observed, object properties, and scene properties such as background and lighting. Formally, this work is concerned with predicting depth data I_D from a single or multiple color image inputs I_C, and optionally, a sensed and incomplete depth map $\hat{I}_D$. The previous section summarizes methods suited for this task. We choose a representative subset and evaluate them in comparable settings.

3.1   Depth Retrieval in Comparison

Generally, the clear advantages of depth completion approaches [3,12,15,16] is that depth can be predicted from single images without corresponding camera

Table 1. Overview of compared methods. This table presents the inputs and inference parameters for each of the compared ones. For NeRF-based methods, [†] indicate results obtained using an Nvidia RTX 2070 Max-Q.

Method	Multi-view	Input	Inference time (seconds)	Inference resolution
ClearGrasp [12]	✗	RGB-D	4.8	640 × 360
LIDF [16]	✗	RGB-D	0.25	320 × 240
TransCG [3]	✗	RGB-D	0.16	320 × 240
LeRes [15]	✗	RGB	0.06	320 × 240
LeRes [15] (scaled)	✗	RGB	0.06	448 × 448
Dex-Nerf [6]	✓	RGB	14.3/6.25[†]	1280 × 720
Dex-Nerf [6] (half)	✓	RGB		
Dex-NGP [6,10]	✓	RGB	360/219[†] (training)	
NeRF [9] (Expected)	✓	RGB		

pose. This allows broader deployment. Disadvantages are that these approaches need to be trained, and thus inherently contain a bias with respect to the training data, and require preparation time before deployment. NeRF-based approaches [6,9,10] are unbiased with respect to the scene, since models are trained directly on the observed data of the scene of interest. This however, requires availability of multiple views and corresponding camera poses. We present an overview of the input and inference speed (together with the inference resolution) in Table 1. Time were measured using a Nvidia 1080Ti and an Intel i7-7700K, unless mentioned otherwise. We also report timings on a Nvidia RTX 2070 Max-Q for NeRF-based methods since the ray-tracing cores provide significant speed-ups. For those methods, as training has to be performed on every scene, we also report training time. In order to compare the depth retrieval error on a common ground we create a test dataset of transparent objects. The following section outlines this process. The dataset is illustrated in Fig. 2.

Fig. 2. Dataset images. Visualised are different scenes setups and viewing angles.

3.2 Data Collection

The dataset is collected by moving a camera attached to a robot arm around a scene. The same viewpoints are collected for every scene, and the camera poses are obtained through inverse kinematics of the robot arm. We use 3D-DAT [13] for annotation, placing object models in the virtual 3D scene, and manually correcting their poses based on their reprojection error in the different RGB views.

To obtain 3D object models, the physical objects are coated using a mat spray paint after collecting the different scenes. A high-quality depth sensor (Photoneo MotionCam-3D scanner[1]) is used to reconstruct them. The set of objects used in our experiments is illustrated in Fig. 3, and includes plastics and glass objects, filled or empty with a variety of shapes, and a variety of sizes.

A total of 23 scenes is collected using a Intel Realsense D435, saving both the RGB image and the depth image at a resolution of 1280×720 pixels. The robotic arm performs a circular motion around the scene with the camera oriented toward the scene center, placing the camera at four different heights and corresponding polar angles ($68°$, $60°$, $48°$ and $33°$). For each circle, either 16 or 26 views are collecting resulting in a total of 64 or 104 views per scene. The light is uniform and comes from the top of the scene. For four scenes, we add a strong light projector to the side of the scene, producing caustics and other refraction and reflection effects at the interface of transparent objects. Those scenes also have more textured backgrounds, as opposed to the uniform background of the others.

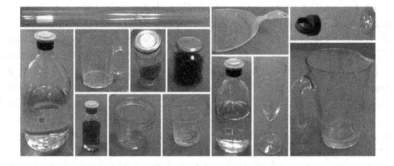

Fig. 3. Object set. Objects used for evaluating depth estimation. Properties are diversified with respect to size, shape, material and filling.

3.3   Evaluation Methodology

We report the same metrics as the ones presented in ClearGrasp [12]. In particular, with GT_p the groundtruth depth at pixel p and D_p^m the depth predicted by method m at pixel p, we consider δ_T the percentage of pixels having a relative depth prediction falling within a threshold T, that is, for P the set of pixels considered:

$$\delta_T = \frac{1}{P} \sum_{p \in P} \begin{cases} 1 & if \max\left(\frac{GT_p}{D_p^m}, \frac{D_p^m}{GT_p}\right) < T \\ 0 & otherwise \end{cases}$$

---

[1] https://www.photoneo.com.

The threshold considered are 5%, 10%, 25%.

With $E_p = GT_p - D_p^m$ the difference at pixel p between the groundtruth depth and the depth predicted by method m, we also report the root mean square error $RMSE = \sqrt{\frac{1}{P} \sum_{p \in P} E_p^2}$, and the mean absolute error $MAE = \frac{1}{P} \sum_{p \in P} |E_p|$.

For all metrics and evaluations only pixels lying on object surfaces are considered, excluding any scene pixel. To provide a common basis for evaluation, given that different methods produce depth maps of different ratios and different sizes, all predicted depths are rescaled using bilinear interpolation, and crop them to fit the $\frac{4}{3}$ ratio (final resolution of 960×720 pixels).

We evaluate Cleargrasp [12], LIDF [16] and TransCG [3], all designed for depth completion for transparent objects from RGB-D pairs. The pre-trained model is used together with the default parameters. In addition to using the results obtained with the original depth sensor capturing the scene as baseline (Intel Realsense D435), the depth maps produced by a monocular depth estimation method (LeRes [15]) are also evaluated. Since LeRes does not have access to any scale information, the results on metric depth prediction are predictably poor. As such, we propose to rescale the predicted depth using the median value of all the ratio $\frac{GT_p}{D_p^{LeRes}}$, giving a sizeable boost to the results and enabling the evaluation of the shape predicted. Except in Table 2, only the rescaled results are presented. Finally, we also present the results of depth maps generated by Neural Radiance Fields. Such approaches use all RGB images of the scene during training, and need to be trained on a per-scene basis, but do not require any depth measurement. Multiple strategies can be used to extract depth maps once trained. We evaluate the results when using the expected depth value obtained from the volume rendering procedure [9], as well as Dex-NeRF depth rendering. To provide a more complete view, we also report the results obtained when training Dex-NeRF with only half of the views collected, meaning that the method never saw half of the views it is evaluated on. We also report the result when combining Dex-NeRF depth rendering with Instant-NGP [10], a neural radiance field using a different position encoding for faster training, that we refer to as Dex-NGP.

4   Results and Findings

We now present our findings regarding the behavior of depth estimation methods. A summary of the results is presented in Table 2. We notice that, while accuracy is underwhelming, all depth completion methods improve over the sensor output, but Dex-NeRF-based methods present the most accurate results, as long as enough views are available. Training with half of the views recorded, that is 32/52 views, seems indeed to be too few views for accurate reconstruction. Indeed RMSE is more strongly affected by incomplete results (missing depth) than the δ_T, which favors ClearGrasp, LIDF and TransCG that all produce "complete" output. We only observe a modest improvement for depth completion methods in $\delta_{1.05}$ values (corresponding to points within a 2.5 cm error at 50 cm, or 5 cm at 1 m) over the sensor output. TransCG, in particular, does not produce very accurate results but its prediction error remains within smaller bounds than others, showing the lowest RMSE value. LIDF produces the most accurate results out of the depth completion methods, that is the highest $\delta_{1.05}$. Finally, LeRes is surprisingly competitive after re-scaling, which is probably due to its access to a much larger training set. It should be emphasized that LeRes predicts a depth from a single RGB image, and is not designed for transparent object depth prediction but general monocular depth prediction. The fact that we use a single scale factor for the entire image suggest that the method is very good at predicting the shape of transparent objects, although not in a metric way.

Table 2. Depth estimation comparison. Results are compared using different metrics. Number are averaged over objects and scenes.

Method	$\delta_{1.05}$ ↑	$\delta_{1.10}$ ↑	$\delta_{1.25}$ ↑	MAE↓	RMSE↓
Sensor (D435)	43.4	57.7	66.1	0.204	0.343
ClearGrasp [12]	46.3	68.1	87.7	0.073	0.109
LIDF [16]	49.7	72.8	92.0	0.055	0.092
TransCG [3]	43.9	68.5	89.5	0.057	**0.071**
LeRes [15]	3.8	7.3	17.3	0.582	0.652
LeRes [15] (scaled)	22.2	36.9	61.5	0.161	0.218
Dex-Nerf [6]	57.5	80.5	**92.6**	0.058	0.088
Dex-Nerf [6] (half)	33.9	51.7	61.3	0.194	0.216
Dex-NGP [6,10]	**78.0**	**86.5**	91.8	**0.054**	0.136
NeRF [9] (Expected)	24.9	51.4	85.7	0.098	0.141

4.1   Impact of the Viewing Angle

As our scenes are captured at four different camera angles, relative to the vertical orientation, Fig. 4 presents the evaluation for each angle. TransCG, and to a lesser extent, Cleargrasp and LIDF, improve the closer the camera gets to a top view. This is a direct manifestation of the training data bias, as TransCG was designed with bin-picking applications in mind. This underlines that none of these learned methods gained a true understanding of transparent objects but are bound by the quality of their training data.

4.2   Impact of the Object Properties

We evaluated the impact of different object properties on the depth estimation methods. We hypothesize, that the more the object impacts the trajectory of the light through refraction and reflection, the more visible it will be. In other words, the stronger the difference of the index of refraction of adjacent mediums and the thicker the medium, the easier it should be to infer the object shape.

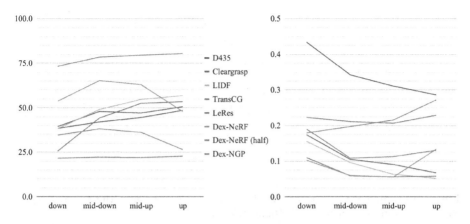

Fig. 4. Influence of the scene viewing angle. Left: Percentage of pixels with predicted depths within 5% of groundtruth ($\delta_{1.05}$). Right: RMSE

The size of transparent objects has a noticeable impact on the results, as illustrated in Fig. 5. We believe this is a subtle manifestation of the impact of the object on the path of the light. Indeed, the strongest light effects happen at the border of objects, while the center tends to be much less noticeable. Larger objects will naturally have a smaller ratio of "border" pixels relative to all the pixels their silhouette covers. This overall trend is slightly weaker for depth completion methods, which can be explained by the fact that these methods benefit from an object prior, having been exposed to many object types during their training. This contrasts with NeRF-based methods that are trained from scratch for every scene. We did not however notice any strong dependency on the material (plastic or glass), or the thickness of the transparent object surfaces. We hypothesize that these effects did not manifest themselves due to the entanglement of the different properties of the chosen objects.

4.3   Impact of the Scene Lighting

In Table 3, the results for different types of scenes are reported. As described in Sect. 3, the additional directional light on the side of the scene leads to stronger refraction and reflection, and the additional scene texture should make the transparent object's distortion of the light path easier to distinguish. These scene changes are positively affecting the RMSE of NeRF-approaches. Conversely, this is detrimental to ClearGrasp and LIDF, but not to TransCG.

ClearGrasp and LIDF are trained from rendered data. It is still challenging to model all the effects of transparent objects using rendering methods. We hypothesize that this is the cause of the bad depth prediction of ClearGrasp and LIDF reflected in the result.

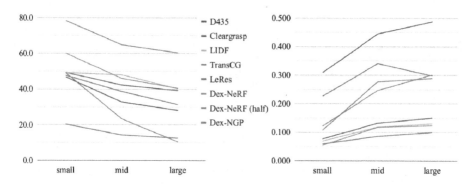

Fig. 5. Influence of the object size. Left: Percentage of pixels with predicted depths within 5% of groundtruth ($\delta_{1.05}$). Right: RMSE

Table 3. Influence of lighting and background First two rows: Percentage of pixels with predicted depths within 5% of groundtruth ($\delta_{1.05}$) per method. Higher is better. Last two rows: RMSE per method.

Scene	D435	Clearg	LIDF	TransCG	LeRes	Dex-NeRF	Dex-NeRF (h.)	Dex-NGP
$\delta_{1.05}$								
Uniform	43.4	48.3	51.9	42.6	20.2	59.3	22.4	**76.2**
Proj.+Clut.	46.0	38.1	39.1	48.0	28.2	57.3	54.5	**86.1**
RMSE								
Uniform	0.357	0.118	0.097	**0.076**	0.243	0.108	0.297	0.161
Proj.+Clut.	0.305	0.097	0.084	0.055	0.137	0.044	0.081	**0.043**

4.4   Discussion

We now succinctly present the main issues facing transparent object depth prediction. As for any learning problem, data is the key to good performance. The training dataset of [3] does not cover every part of the viewing sphere equally and rendered data created as part of [12,16] does not accurately model every light effects induced by transparent objects. This latter statement should however be continuously revised under the light of the progress made in the very active field of computer graphics. Depth completion methods provide more complete but less accurate depth maps, and can do so from a single view, with very short inference time. They indeed benefit from a level of understanding of object shapes implicitly learned during training that helps them to be more robust to varying object's size. Building on the surprisingly good results from [15], larger dataset with high variety seem essential to improve these approaches. The fairly simple but effective architecture presented in [3] also questions the need for architectures designed specifically for transparent objects, as opposed to the more general problem of depth completion.

On the opposite end of the spectrum, NeRF-based methods are the most accurate, and circumvent the issue of training data bias as they perform transductive learning. They also can provide basic guarantees about their convergence. Indeed, as they are designed to render views of the scene, comparing their current rendering to the captured images let us quickly identify the accuracy of the renderings in their close vicinity. Radiance fields are a very recent research direction, and significant progress have already been made in convergence speed, and more are expected. The modeling of transparent objects in [6] is quite simple, and more advanced modeling of light propagation within the learned volume could yield significant improvement in the quality of the recovered geometry, not only for transparent objects, but any scene with complex materials.

5 Conclusion

In this study, we evaluated a large variety of methods for estimating the depth of transparent objects. This includes depth completion methods tailored for transparent objects, general monocular depth estimation methods, as well as neural radiance fields-based methods. We demonstrated that, when possible, NeRF-based methods provide the most accurate results. These methods do not have priors about the scene, which is generally good, but detrimental when it comes to larger objects, where depth far from the border has to be inferred from plausible object shapes. Furthermore, we underlined once again the importance of a high quality, as bias-free as possible, training dataset.

Future work will disambiguate influencing effects on the reconstruction quality more in depth, i.e. clutter, lighting, object fill level, as well as the effect of transparent objects occluding other transparent objects. More detailed analysis on the influence of data distribution shifts will follow, by training depth estimation methods on real and on rendered data, and evaluating the reconstruction quality on transparent objects unseen during training. Furthermore, a natural next step for this work is to investigate the suitability of the depth estimated in the context of down-stream tasks such as object pose estimation. Such an evaluation would help underline how accurately shapes are preserved, as opposed to pixel-level evaluation.

References

1. Chen, W., Fu, Z., Yang, D., Deng, J.: Single-image depth perception in the wild. In: Proceedings of the 30th International Conference on Neural Information Processing Systems, NIPS 2016, Red Hook, NY, USA, pp. 730–738. Curran Associates Inc. (2016)
2. Chen, X., Zhang, H., Yu, Z., Opipari, A., Jenkins, O.C.: ClearPose: large-scale transparent object dataset and benchmark. In: Avidan, S., Brostow, G., Cissé, M., Farinella, G.M., Hassner, T. (eds.) ECCV 2022. LNCS, vol. 13668, pp. 381–396. Springer, Cham (2022). https://doi.org/10.1007/978-3-031-20074-8_22
3. Fang, H., Fang, H.S., Xu, S., Lu, C.: TransCG: a large-scale real-world dataset for transparent object depth completion and a grasping baseline. IEEE Robot. Autom. Lett. 7(3), 7383–7390 (2022). https://doi.org/10.1109/LRA.2022.3183256

4. Gupta, A., Dollar, P., Girshick, R.: LVIS: a dataset for large vocabulary instance segmentation. In: Proceedings of the IEEE Conference on Computer Vision and Pattern Recognition (2019)
5. He, K., Gkioxari, G., Dollár, P., Girshick, R.: Mask R-CNN. In: Proceedings of the IEEE International Conference on Computer Vision, pp. 2961–2969 (2017)
6. Ichnowski, J., Avigal, Y., Kerr, J., Goldberg, K.: Dex-NeRF: using a neural radiance field to grasp transparent objects. In: Conference on Robot Learning (CoRL) (2021)
7. Jung, H., et al.: On the importance of accurate geometry data for dense 3D vision tasks. In: Proceedings of the IEEE/CVF Conference on Computer Vision and Pattern Recognition (CVPR), pp. 780–791 (2023)
8. Kerr, J., et al.: Evo-NeRF: evolving nerf for sequential robot grasping of transparent objects. In: Liu, K., Kulic, D., Ichnowski, J. (eds.) Proceedings of the 6th Conference on Robot Learning. Proceedings of Machine Learning Research, vol. 205, pp. 353–367. PMLR, 14–18 December 2023. https://proceedings.mlr.press/v205/kerr23a.html
9. Mildenhall, B., Srinivasan, P.P., Tancik, M., Barron, J.T., Ramamoorthi, R., Ng, R.: NeRF: representing scenes as neural radiance fields for view synthesis. In: Vedaldi, A., Bischof, H., Brox, T., Frahm, J.-M. (eds.) ECCV 2020. LNCS, vol. 12346, pp. 405–421. Springer, Cham (2020). https://doi.org/10.1007/978-3-030-58452-8_24
10. Müller, T., Evans, A., Schied, C., Keller, A.: Instant neural graphics primitives with a multiresolution hash encoding. ACM Trans. Graph. **41**(4), 1–15 (2022). https://doi.org/10.1145/3528223.3530127
11. Ren, S., He, K., Girshick, R., Sun, J.: Faster R-CNN: towards real-time object detection with region proposal networks. In: Advances in Neural Information Processing Systems, vol. 28 (2015)
12. Sajjan, S., et al.: Clear grasp: 3D shape estimation of transparent objects for manipulation. In: 2020 IEEE International Conference on Robotics and Automation (ICRA), pp. 3634–3642 (2020). https://doi.org/10.1109/ICRA40945.2020.9197518
13. Suchi, M., Neuberger, B., Salykov, A., Weibel, J.B., Patten, T., Vincze, M.: 3D-DAT: 3D-dataset annotation toolkit for robotic vision. In: 2023 IEEE International Conference on Robotics and Automation (ICRA) (2023)
14. Tian, Z., Shen, C., Chen, H., He, T.: FCOS: fully convolutional one-stage object detection. In: Proceedings of the IEEE/CVF International Conference on Computer Vision, pp. 9627–9636 (2019)
15. Yin, W., et al.: Learning to recover 3D scene shape from a single image. In: Proceedings of the IEEE Conference on Computer Vision and Pattern Recognition (CVPR) (2021)
16. Zhu, L., et al.: RGB-D local implicit function for depth completion of transparent objects. In: 2021 IEEE/CVF Conference on Computer Vision and Pattern Recognition (CVPR), pp. 4647–4656 (2021). https://doi.org/10.1109/CVPR46437.2021.00462

Volumetric Body Composition Through Cross-Domain Consistency Training for Unsupervised Domain Adaptation

Shahzad Ali[1]([✉]) [ID], Yu Rim Lee[2] [ID], Soo Young Park[2] [ID], Won Young Tak[2] [ID], and Soon Ki Jung[1] [ID]

[1] School of Computer Science and Engineering, Kyungpook National University, Daegu, South Korea
{shahzadali,skjung}@knu.ac.kr
[2] Department of Internal Medicine, College of Medicine, Kyungpook National University, Kyungpook National University Hospital, Daegu, South Korea

Abstract. Computed tomography (CT) scans of the abdomen have emerged as a robust, precise, and dependable means of determining body composition. The accurate prediction of skeletal muscle volume (SMV) using slices of CT scans holds critical importance in facilitating subsequent diagnosis and prognosis. A significant proportion of research in the field of abdominal image analysis is primarily focused on the third lumbar spine vertebra (L3), owing to two prominent factors. Firstly, L3 is a large vertebra situated in the middle of the lumbar spine, rendering it less susceptible to degenerative changes in comparison to other lumbar vertebrae, making it a stable landmark. Secondly, the slice labeling in a CT volume is an intricate and time-consuming process, demanding significant human efforts, whereas labeling a single slice from a specific vertebral level is comparatively simpler. This study leverages labeled L3 slices i.e., *source domain* to reliably predict unlabeled lumbar region slices other than L3 i.e., *target domain*. We use Cross-Domain Consistency Training (CDCT) to extend network's current knowledge, acquired through segmenting a source domain, by learning to label a target domain. A consistency is enforced between the predictions from two segmentation networks with identical lightweight architecture but have different weight initialization points. The training objective consists of supervised loss terms for the source domain data and unsupervised loss terms for the target domain data. Remarkably, our trained network exhibits a marked enhancement in performance when applied to the target domain, indicating domain invariant feature learning through cross-domain consistency training could significantly enhance a network's generalization capability.

Keywords: Volumetric Body Composition · Skeletal Muscle Volume · Unsupervised Domain Adaptation · Abdominal CT Segmentation

© The Author(s), under exclusive license to Springer Nature Switzerland AG 2023
G. Bebis et al. (Eds.): ISVC 2023, LNCS 14361, pp. 289–299, 2023.
https://doi.org/10.1007/978-3-031-47969-4_23

1   Introduction

Computed tomography (CT) is a frequently employed medical imaging modality that offers intricate insights into the internal anatomical structures of the human body. Owing to its widespread clinical utilization, a vast reservoir of CT data is readily accessible for a variety of research and analytical purposes. However, the acquisition cost of CT labels is substantial, resulting in the proposal of several alternative approaches in the literature to address the annotation burden. Semi-supervised learning (SSL) is one such approach that utilizes unlabeled data along with the partially labeled data while the unsupervised learning (UL) approach has no access to the image labels at all. Alternatively, transfer learning leverages data and models from analogous domains. Deep learning algorithms are predominantly dependent on the assumption of *independent and identically distributed* (i.i.d) data, implying that the training and testing datasets are independent and exhibit identical characteristics. However, the presence of diverse factors such as variations in imaging devices, cohort studies, demographics of patients across medical centers can lead to substantial differences in the distributions of training and testing datasets. This scenario is commonly known as *domain shift* and can pose a challenge for real-world clinical applications. The related yet dissimilar nature of these domains impedes the effectiveness of traditional supervised learning approaches in the target domain due to the violation of i.i.d assumption.

Domain adaptation (DA) has emerged as a promising approach to mitigate the issues with unseen, heterogeneous, and unlabeled medical data [5,15]. This approach has gained significant attention by the medical research community as it seeks to reduce the distribution gap between related domains. It is a form of transfer learning (TL) aimed at building a classifier capable of performing well on data from previously unseen domains. A *domain* is characterized as a probability distribution from which samples are drawn. Typically, a collection of samples i.e., *dataset* can be categorized either as source domain or a target domain. A classifier must be able to generalize to a new target domain without any prior pre-training or fine-tuning. If the similarity between training domains and a target domain is too low, the classifier's performance may suffer on the target domain.

In this work we extended the idea of cross consistency training [12] to make a network generalize well across domains and propose *cross-domain consistency training* (CDCT) [3] as an *unsupervised domain adaptation* (UDA) method for semantic segmentation [10]. The source domain comprises labeled L3 slices, while the target domain consists of unlabeled non-L3 slices. The primary objective of this approach is to ensure that predictions are invariant across networks that are initialized with different weights. This helps to ensure that the resulting network is robust to domain shifts. To achieve this, we enforce consistency between the predictions of two autoencoders, and use additional training signals that are extracted from unlabeled data to enhance the feature representations. To keep the number of trainable parameters within reasonable limits, we utilize dual lightweight autoencoder. Moreover, during inference, we only use the one

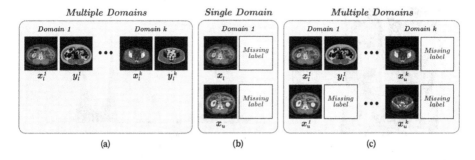

Fig. 1. Illustration of similar tasks i.e., (a) Domain adaptation, (b) Unsupervised learning, and (c) Unsupervised domain adaptation. The labeled and unlabeled data is shown as (x_l^k, y_l^k) and (x_u^k, y_u^k) for $k = \{1, 2, ..., k\}$ domains.

autoencoder, which helps to reduce the computational overhead. Figure 1 displays the aforementioned three related tasks i.e., DA, UL, and UDA, respectively. It has been observed in a recent study [4] that network consistency tends to decrease when the training data is contaminated with noisy labels, leading to network overfitting. In order to address this issue and regularize the network, we propose the use of Jensen-Shannon divergence loss. This loss function promotes consistency across multiple distributions spanning different domains, thereby enhancing the network's resilience to noise.

The proposed method is characterized by its simplicity and efficiency, while also exhibiting flexibility in its ability to seamlessly integrate labeled and unlabeled CT data within the framework of unsupervised domain adaptation. Our approach was validated on an in-house abdominal CT dataset, demonstrating its competitive performance across various domains. We present our contributions as follows:

- We introduce a novel method called cross-domain consistency training (CDCT) as an unsupervised domain adaptation technique (UDA) for semantic segmentation of CT data. CDCT enforces consistency of predictions across dual networks with different initialization points, ensuring invariance of the segmentation results.
- We leverage unsupervised training signals extracted from unlabeled CT data and jointly train the segmentation network across various domains. This allows for a comprehensive and robust training process, incorporating cross-domain information.
- We present the effectiveness of our method through comprehensive experimentation, which includes a comparative analysis with the supervised equivalent.

2   Method

The performance of a segmentation network, trained on L3 vertebra area slices only, severely degrades when encountering *out-of-distribution* (OOD) data i.e.,

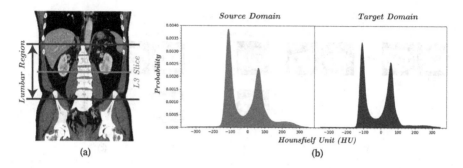

Fig. 2. Overview of the domains. (a) Coronal view of a male patient's CT scan, highlighting the position of the third lumbar vertebra $L3$ (in green), along with the entire lumbar region i.e., $L1, L2, L4, L5$ (excluding $L3$; represented by a blue line). (b) Histograms of the source and target domains. The highest peak on the right represents the adipose tissue class (-110 HU), and the peak immediately to its right corresponds to the muscle class (65 HU). These peaks illustrate a clear domain shift between the source and target domains. (Color figure online)

slices from other positions within the lumbar spine region. Figure 2(a) highlights the L3 position within the lumbar region in the coronal view of the CT scan of a male patient. In this paper, we aim to get reliable predictions for unlabeled slices of non-L3 lumbar spine vertebrae region provided the labeled slices for L3 vertebra region only. A grayscale CT image is formed by reconstructing the absorption/attenuation coefficient of radiation in tissues. The Hounsfield unit is obtained through a linear transformation of the measured attenuation coefficient. In Fig. 2(b), the variations in the distributions of Hounsfield unit (HU) for both domains are illustrated. The highest peak on the left corresponds to adipose tissues, while the second-highest peak adjacent to it represents muscle. The variation between the source and target domains, often referred to as the domain shift problem, can be addressed by employing the proposed CDCT technique, which serves as an unsupervised domain adaptation approach.

2.1   Problem Formulation

Let $D_S = \{(x_i, y_i)\}_{i=1}^m$ represent the source domain with labeled data, and $D_T = \{x_i\}_{i=1}^n$ the target domain with unlabeled data. Here, m and n are the total numbers of slices in the source and target domains. Each $x \in \mathbb{R}^{H \times W}$ is a 2D slice, and its corresponding pixel-level label is denoted by $y \in \mathbb{R}^{C \times H \times W}$, where C is the number of classes. In the context of Unsupervised Domain Adaptation (UDA), the goal is to improve network's generalization ability by leveraging both domains D_S and D_T for the semantic segmentation task. The objective is to learn a function f that can effectively map input CT slices to the label space, i.e., $f : x \rightarrow y$. This function operates on slices drawn from any of the K source domains $D_S = \{D^1, ..., D^K\}$ or the target domain D_T. Importantly, in this scenario, $|D_T| \gg |D_S|$, indicating that the amount of unlabeled data in the target domain is significantly larger than the labeled data in the source domains.

Jensen-Shannon Divergence (JSD). Jensen-Shannon Divergence (JSD) has demonstrated remarkable effectiveness in learning feature representations from noisy labels, combating underfitting, and encouraging consistency regularization [4]. It is a symmetric and smoothed version of the Kullback-Leibler Divergence (KLD) also known as relative entropy. JSD measures similarity between two probability distributions, denoted by y and p and is defined as:

$$L_{jsd_{(y\|p)}} = \frac{1}{2}KLD(y \parallel m) + \frac{1}{2}KLD(p \parallel m), \tag{1}$$

where $m = \frac{1}{2}(y + p)$ is the midpoint distribution, and $KLD(y \parallel p)$ is the KLD between distributions y and p, defined as:

$$KLD(y \parallel p) = \sum_x y(x) \log\left(\frac{y(x)}{p(x)}\right), \tag{2}$$

JSD ranges between 0 and 1, where 0 means the two distributions are identical, and 1 means they are completely dissimilar.

Cross-Domain Consistency Training (CDCT). To obtain additional training signal from the unlabeled domain D_T, we ensure consistency between the outputs of two parallel autoencoders, namely $f(x; \theta_1)$ and $f(x; \theta_2)$, where θ represents the set of learning parameters. Each autoencoder produces a prediction map for a given input. For labeled input slices, we compute a supervised loss term. In the absence of input labels, the probability maps are turned into the pseudo target labels to calculate the unsupervised loss terms [2]

$$L_{dsc} = 1 - \frac{2\sum_i^N y_{1i} \cdot \tilde{y}_{1i}}{\sum_i^N y_{1i} + \sum_i^N \tilde{y}_{1i}}, \tag{3}$$

where y_{1i} and $\tilde{y}_{1i}$ are the target and prediction masks for x_l from $f(x; \theta_1)$ and N is the total number of pixels in a given image. For an input without a target label, the outputs of both autoencoders serve as pseudo target labels for the missing input label, as $y_{1i} \approx \tilde{y}_{2i}$ and $y_{2i} \approx \tilde{y}_{1i}$. L_{jsd} is used as an unsupervised loss and calculated for both the labeled and unlabeled inputs.

Loss Weighing Through Task-Dependent Uncertainty. The total CDCT loss, denoted as L_{cdct}, is a combination of all loss terms, as given in Eq. (1) and Eq. (3), written as:

$$L_{cdct} = \sum_{L_\tau \in \mathbb{T}} \omega_\tau L_\tau. \tag{4}$$

Here, $\mathbb{T}$ is the set of loss functions and ω denotes the weight assigned to each loss term. It is not appropriate to weigh these losses uniformly, i.e., $\{1, 1, ..., 1\}$ or

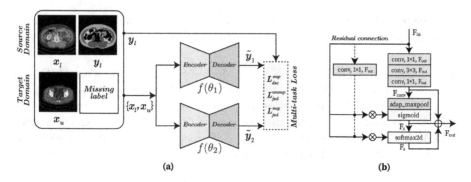

Fig. 3. Proposed CDCT-based UDA for abdominal CT semantic segmentation. (a) The method involves dual autoencoders, denoted by $f(\theta_1)$ and $f(\theta_2)$, where supervised loss is calculated for the source domain D_S slices using the labels y. For slices from the target domain D_T, an unsupervised loss term is calculated using the predictions by both autoencoders $\tilde{y}_1$ and $\tilde{y}_2$ as pseudo target labels. (b) *Res-Conv*, the building block of each encoder-decoder, with spatial and channel attentions. The residual connection is indicated by a dotted path and is used only when the number of input channels is different from the number of output channels.

$\{\frac{1}{|T|}, \frac{1}{|T|}, ..., \frac{1}{|T|}\}$, or non-uniformly, i.e., $\{1, 2, 3, 5, ...\}$. Instead, a dynamic weighting scheme is needed that exploits task-specific uncertainties that vary across T. We adopt an idea similar to that first proposed by [7] and further refined by [9], which enforces positive regularization values. Assuming that each loss is a task, an aggregated loss function in Eq. 4 becomes:

$$L_{cdct} = \sum_{L_\tau \in \mathbb{T}} \frac{1}{2\omega_\tau^2} L_\tau + ln(1 + \omega_\tau^2). \tag{5}$$

2.2   Network Architecture

A lightweight autoencoder inspired by U-Net [14] and ResNet [6] architectures was selected to create a pair of networks. The decision to employ a network with a small number of trainable parameters, as opposed to deeper or wider networks commonly available, was made in order to train two similar networks without sacrificing original image resolution and available memory. Furthermore, this lightweight autoencoder has already demonstrated its efficacy in segmenting foot ulcer wounds in previous research [1]. The encoder of each autoencoder contains 11 Res-Conv blocks and 5 MaxPool layers, while the decoder comprises 4 Res-Conv blocks and 5 ConvTranspose layers. The architecture of the Res-Conv block is illustrated in Fig. 3b. It applies spatial and channel attentions, F_s and F_c, to the input and extracted feature maps, F_{in} and F_{conv}, respectively, and combines them element-wise to produce the block output, F_{out}. These attention weights are learned during network training. The final prediction is obtained

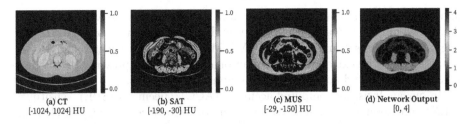

Fig. 4. The network input is composed of three channels, namely (a) CT, (b) SAT, and (c) MUS. The input is formed by windowing raw CT pixels within specific Hounsfield Unit (HU) value ranges i.e., $[-1024, 1024]$, $[-190, -30]$, and $[-29, -150]$, respectively. Subsequently, all values were rescaled to fit within the range of $[0, 1]$. (d) The network output comprises five channels, denoted as 0 to 4, representing BKG, IMAT, SAT, MUS, and VAT, respectively.

from a 1×1 convolutional layer, followed by a softmax layer. Each pixel's class label is determined based on the highest probability value above 0.5.

2.3 Preprocessing

Following [13], the initial step involves thresholding the raw DICOM slice intensity values. Specifically, the thresholding is carried out to constrain the values within the Hounsfield Units (HU) range of $[-1024, 1024]$, $[-190, -30]$, and $[-29, 150]$ for the CT, SAT, and MUS channels, respectively. The outcome of thresholding reflect the distinct features highlighted in each channel. The resulting thresholded values are used to form a three-channel input network, as illustrated in Fig. 4.

3   Experiments and Results

3.1   Dataset and Evaluation Metrics

The proposed method was trained and evaluated on two-dimensional axial CT image labeled slices at the position L3, which served as the source domain. Unlabeled slices from other locations in the lumbar region comprised the target domain. The dataset, provided by Kyungpook National University Hospital (KNUH) in Daegu, South Korea, consisted of 731 retrospectively obtained CT scans from patients who visited hospital in 2020 and 2021[1]. The L3 slices were extracted and then manually annotated by a radiologist, who identified five classes in each slice, under the supervision of a highly experienced radiologist to ensure the quality of the labeling process. For this work, a subset of annotated data was used as a source domain and it was divided randomly into training

---

[1] Public release of the dataset is subject to the approval from the Institutional Review Board/Ethics Committee of the Kyungpook National University Hospital and Kyungpook National University.

and validation sets, consisting of 256 and 200 slices, respectively. The target domain comprised 275 unlabeled images with a fixed resolution of 512Œ512 and five labeled classes, namely IMAT, SAT, MUS, VAT, and background. Down-sampling or patch extraction was intentionally avoided to preserve the original image resolution and achieve superior segmentation results.

In our analysis, we computed accuracy (ACC), specificity (SPE), sensitivity (SEN), precision (PRE), mean Dice Similarity Coefficient (DSC), and mean Intersection over Union (IoU) as the performance metrics defined as:

$$ACC = \frac{TN + TP}{TN + FP + FN + TP}, \tag{6}$$

$$SPE = \frac{TN}{TN + FP}, \tag{7}$$

$$SEN = \frac{TP}{TP + FN}, \tag{8}$$

$$PRE = \frac{TP}{TP + FP}, \tag{9}$$

$$DSC = \frac{2TP}{2TP + FP + FN}, \text{ and} \tag{10}$$

$$IoU = \frac{TP}{TP + FP + FN}. \tag{11}$$

The computation of these metrics relies on true positive (TP), false negative (FN), true negative (TN), and false positive (FP) values. It is important to note that the output range of these measures is between 0 to 1, with a higher score indicating better performance.

3.2   Implementation Details

Training Settings. The network was trained from the ground up for 100 epochs, and a batch size of 1 per GPU was used due to limitations in available memory. At a specified instant, a labeled and unlabeled image pair is sequentially presented to the dual autoencoders, following which the total loss is computed. The experiments did not involve pre-training, transfer learning, or using the encoders from existing trained networks. The learning rate was kept fixed at 0.001 and AdamW optimizer was used for its scale invariance property [8] and better generalization performance [11]. This was essential since the total loss obtained through task-dependent uncertainty was of a greater magnitude than the individual losses. All experiments were carried out on four NVIDIA TITAN X GPUs using PyTorch v1.13.1, an open-source machine learning framework.

Inference Settings. During the inference phase, the batch size is 1 used, and only the prediction generated by a single autoencoder is utilized.

Table 1. Network trained on the data from both domains (D_S, D_T) and tested on the source D_S and target domains D_T, respectively. All values are reported in the form of percentages.

	MUS		IMAT		SAT		VAT		AVG	
	D_S	D_T	D_S	D_T	D_S	D_T	D_S	D_T	D_S	D_T
ACC	99.25	99.29	99.13	99.54	99.80	99.90	99.60	99.72	99.45	99.61
SPE	99.43	99.71	99.83	99.79	99.87	99.97	99.75	99.74	99.72	99.80
SEN	97.39	95.46	64.19	82.07	99.06	98.83	98.05	99.47	89.67	93.96
PRE	93.97	97.39	88.00	84.44	98.67	99.60	97.37	96.43	94.50	94.46
DSC	95.65	96.42	74.23	83.24	98.87	99.21	97.71	97.92	91.62	94.20
IoU	91.66	93.08	59.02	71.28	97.76	98.44	95.52	95.93	86.00	89.69

3.3 Unsupervised Domain Adaptation Setting

Our neural network was trained on both domains, following which we evaluated its performance independently for each of the source and target domains. The outcomes, as depicted in Table 1, indicate that our network performs remarkably well in both domains, with a notable performance in the target domain. The results are given as percentages, and the average is calculated for all foreground classes. Our network exhibits promising results in terms of generalization capability, as evidenced by the improvement in average Dice Similarity Coefficient (DSC) and Intersection over Union (IoU) scores for the test domain. Specifically,

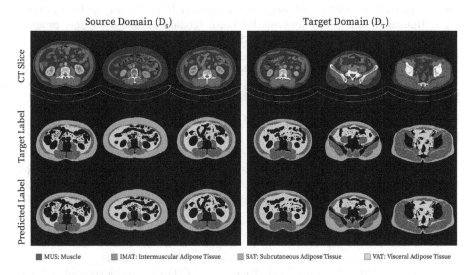

■ MUS: Muscle   ■ IMAT: Intermuscular Adipose Tissue   ■ SAT: Subcutaneous Adipose Tissue   □ VAT: Visceral Adipose Tissue

Fig. 5. Qualitative results for randomly selected CT scans. Target masks are the output of semi-manual labeling, whereas predicted masks are produced by the proposed network.

the test domain saw a 2.6% improvement in average DSC and a 3.7% improvement in average IoU. The most notable enhancement was observed in the minority class of the dataset, which achieved a remarkable 9.0% and 12.3% increase in average DSC and IoU, respectively. These findings demonstrate that our network not only exhibits strong generalization across domains, but also across classes. Figure 5 presents the qualitative outcomes for a selection of images chosen at random from both the source and target domain datasets. The majority of the images exhibited high-quality segmentation results, however, several instances were observed where the network incorrectly classified the assigned class (e.g., misclassification of IMAT as VAT). In a few other cases, the VAT class was segmented within the spine. This could be attributed to the similarities between the pixel values in the Hounsfield Unit domain.

4   Conclusion

The unsupervised domain adaptation, based on cross-domain consistency training, offers promising results for producing detailed predicted masks for MUS, SAT, and VAT classes, while exhibiting reasonable outcomes for the IMAT class. This methodology is particularly useful in cases where data is limited or subject to noise, as the generated pseudo-labels can be used as substitutes and expand the labeled training set. The obtained results suggest that the proposed network could be integrated into a semi-manual CT slice labeling workflow.

Acknowledgments. This study was supported by the AI-based CT Analysis Software Development project funded by AI Plus Healthcare Co., Ltd., Daegu, Korea (202300510000), the MSIT (Ministry of Science and ICT), Korea, under the Innovative Human Resource Development for Local Intellectualization support program (IITP-2022-RS-2022-00156389) supervised by the IITP (Institute of Information & Communications Technology Planning & Evaluation), and the BK21 FOUR project (AI-driven Convergence Software Education Research Program) funded by the MOE (Ministry of Education), School of Computer Science and Engineering, Kyungpook National University, Korea (4199990214394).

References

1. Ali, S., Mahmood, A., Jung, S.K.: Lightweight encoder-decoder architecture for foot ulcer segmentation. In: Sumi, K., Na, I.S., Kaneko, N. (eds.) IW-FCV 2022. CCIS, vol. 1578, pp. 242–253. Springer, Cham (2022). https://doi.org/10.1007/978-3-031-06381-7_17
2. Chen, X., Yuan, Y., Zeng, G., Wang, J.: Semi-supervised semantic segmentation with cross pseudo supervision. In: Proceedings of the IEEE/CVF Conference on Computer Vision and Pattern Recognition, pp. 2613–2622 (2021)
3. Chen, Y.C., Lin, Y.Y., Yang, M.H., Huang, J.B.: CrDoCo: pixel-level domain transfer with cross-domain consistency. In: Proceedings of the IEEE/CVF Conference on Computer Vision and Pattern Recognition, pp. 1791–1800 (2019)

4. Englesson, E., Azizpour, H.: Generalized Jensen-Shannon divergence loss for learning with noisy labels. In: Advances in Neural Information Processing Systems 34, pp. 30284–30297 (2021)
5. Guan, H., Liu, M.: Domain adaptation for medical image analysis: a survey. IEEE Trans. Biomed. Eng. **69**(3), 1173–1185 (2021)
6. He, K., Zhang, X., Ren, S., Sun, J.: Deep residual learning for image recognition. In: Proceedings of the IEEE Conference on Computer Vision and Pattern Recognition, pp. 770–778 (2016)
7. Kendall, A., Gal, Y., Cipolla, R.: Multi-task learning using uncertainty to weigh losses for scene geometry and semantics, pp. 7482–7491 (2018)
8. Kingma, D.P., Ba, J.: Adam: a method for stochastic optimization. arXiv preprint arXiv:1412.6980 (2014)
9. Liebel, L., Körner, M.: Auxiliary tasks in multi-task learning. arXiv preprint arXiv:1805.06334, May 2018
10. Liu, X., et al.: Deep unsupervised domain adaptation: a review of recent advances and perspectives. APSIPA Trans. Signal Inf. Process. **11**(1) (2022)
11. Loshchilov, I., Hutter, F.: Decoupled weight decay regularization. arXiv preprint arXiv:1711.05101 (2017)
12. Ouali, Y., Hudelot, C., Tami, M.: Semi-supervised semantic segmentation with cross-consistency training. In: Proceedings of the IEEE/CVF Conference on Computer Vision and Pattern Recognition, pp. 12674–12684 (2020)
13. Paris, M.T., et al.: Automated body composition analysis of clinically acquired computed tomography scans using neural networks. Clin. Nutr. **39**, 3049–3055 (2020)
14. Ronneberger, O., Fischer, P., Brox, T.: U-Net: convolutional networks for biomedical image segmentation. In: Navab, N., Hornegger, J., Wells, W.M., Frangi, A.F. (eds.) MICCAI 2015. LNCS, vol. 9351, pp. 234–241. Springer, Cham (2015). https://doi.org/10.1007/978-3-319-24574-4_28
15. Zhou, K., Loy, C.C., Liu, Z.: Semi-supervised domain generalization with stochastic stylematch. arXiv preprint arXiv:2106.00592 (2021)

Computer Graphics

Water Animation Using Coupled SPH and Wave Equation

Varun Ramakrishnan and Tim McGraw[✉]

Purdue University, West Lafayette, IN 47907, USA
tmcgraw@purdue.edu

Abstract. This project addresses the need for interactive, real-time water animation techniques that can reproduce convincing effects such as splashes and breaking waves while being computationally inexpensive. Our method couples smoothed-particle hydrodynamics (SPH) and a wave equation solver in a one-way manner to animate the behavior of water in real-time, leveraging compute shaders for interactive performance. In this paper, we present a review of related literature on real-time simulation and animation of fluids, describe our hybrid algorithm, and present a comparison of images and computational costs between SPH, wave equation solution, and our coupled approach. Our approach is faster than a pure SPH solution, but requires fewer particles to achieve a similar appearance. In this work, however, we do not address the problem of water rendering.

Keywords: Water · Animation · Simulation

1 Introduction

Water animation has been a challenging task and an active area of research for many years, due to its popularity and frequent use in special effects for feature films, TV, and video games [1]. A wide range of methods have been developed to animate water, including particle-based techniques, wave equation techniques, lattice-Boltzmann methods, and hybrid approaches that combine multiple methods. Some techniques are volumetric, while others, such as those based on the wave equation only simulate the water surface. However, each method has its own limitations and strengths. No single method can efficiently capture all the complex phenomena that occur in water.

Simulations attempt to accurately model physical phenomena and the properties that give rise to them. On the other hand, *animation* of water is used to produce a visually convincing representation of it. Each approach has pros and cons and generally animation techniques are faster, but less physically accurate. Different approaches can be combined to leverage the benefits of each.

Smoothed Particle Hydrodynamics (SPH) [2] and the wave equation are two widely used methods for water simulation and animation. SPH has the advantage of being highly versatile and capable of modeling a wide range of water behaviors,

G. Bebis et al. (Eds.): ISVC 2023, LNCS 14361, pp. 303–314, 2023.
https://doi.org/10.1007/978-3-031-47969-4_24

including splashes and breaking waves. The wave equation, on the other hand, is based on a mathematical model of waves propagating on a surface. SPH simulation involves computing the pairwise interactions between large numbers of particles representing local physical properties. As such, a data structure to perform spatial queries is very important for maintaining efficiency. In this work, we use a simple uniform grid for spatial queries, implemented in a compute shader. This permits our entire simulation/animation pipeline to remain on the GPU without requiring any time-consuming communication between CPU and GPU.

This work is based on the observation that in an SPH simulation of deep water, particles far below the surface do not contribute directly to the behaviour of particles near the surface. In this paper, we will demonstrate that our coupled technique is able to reproduce effects such as breaking waves, boat wakes, and splashes while being computationally less expensive than a pure SPH implementation. In our approach, the wave equation is used to compute the approximate behavior of a body of water below the surface, while SPH particles which interact with the wave are used to model the fluid dynamics of the water at the surface. This coupling allows for the creation of visually convincing water animations that are interactive, computationally efficient, and behaviorally plausible while requiring fewer particles than a pure SPH implementation.

2   Related Work

Realistic water animation and rendering was a lofty goal in the early days of computer graphics. It was desirable feature of video games, movies, and scientific simulations. Initially, water bodies were used as simple environment entities in games but are now becoming an interactive aspect of gameplay, especially in open-world games. Games like *Assassin's Creed: Origins*, and *Sea of Thieves* were recognized for the quality of their water and how it responds to the user interacting with it [3]. With each new generation of graphics hardware and game console, the expectations for realistic environmental interactions increases.

2.1   Water Simulation Using SPH

Simulating the behavior of water in computer graphics is a challenging task due to its complexity and variety of behaviors. The SPH method is one approach used for water animation as it can handle complex behaviors such as splashes and breaking waves, and variations on the original technique can model effects like turbulence and surface tension [4]. However, achieving real-time interactive frame rates for large-scale simulations is still a challenge, and simplification of complex calculations is necessary.

One approach to simplification is splitting the water body into different areas for different simulations. Lee and Han [5] propose a 2D particle-based approach for simulating water surface behaviors, while Wang et al. [6] use video reconstruction to create water animations. Although both approaches aim to reduce computational complexity, they have limitations in accuracy and usability. Lee and Han reduce the problem to 2D surface interactions which makes splashes and breaking waves impossible to model, while Wang et al. require a source video for the simulation, making it difficult to use in interactive applications.

In summary, simulating water behavior in computer graphics remains a complex and challenging task, with various approaches and limitations. While the SPH method and other physically-based simulations show promise, further research is needed to achieve the performance needed in real-time interactive applications.

2.2   Water Animation Using Wave Equation

An alternative to 3D volumetric or particle-based water simulation is to simulate the water surface using the wave equation. This makes it possible to compute the velocity and height of waves at each point in a 2D domain, which can approximate the motion of the water surface.

The 2D wave equation is second-order partial differential equation given by

$$\frac{\partial^2 z}{\partial t^2} = c^2 \nabla^2 z, \tag{1}$$

where ∇^2 is the Laplacian operator, $z(x, y, t)$ is the wave height as a function of position and time, and c is a constant which depends on surface tension and density. This equation can be discretized and is easily numerically iterated. Shallow water wave equations, which take into account water depth can also be used, and will result in different wave shapes. Since the shape of our wave will also be influenced by SPH particles, we use the wave equation given in Eq. 1.

Jeschke and Wojtan [7] proposed a new method for animating water waves by interpolating parameters across wavefronts, allowing the creation of a wide variety of wave shapes and behaviors. However, this approach may not be suitable for all types of water simulations, particularly those that require a high degree of physical accuracy. On the other hand, the wave equation method is well-suited for simulating large bodies of water and can produce visually appealing results. Gouin et al. [8] introduced the spectral method, which allows for efficient simulation of waves with different frequencies and amplitudes.

Simulating water waves for a large expanse of water is computationally expensive, but Schreck et al. [9] introduced a novel approach for water wave animation using fundamental solutions. The fundamental solutions, which are analytic solutions of the wave equation, are precomputed and used to compute the water surface height and velocity in real-time. The authors presented a technique to construct a library of fundamental solutions that is both efficient to compute and of high quality. The method has several advantages over traditional approaches, including the ability to handle complex geometries and the ability to simulate waves at high resolutions. However, the method has some disadvantages, such as being limited to small-amplitude waves.

Jeschke et al. [10] present a new method for simulating water surface waves that enables the efficient creation of complex and visually appealing wave patterns. The method is based on a wavelet decomposition of the water surface, which breaks down the surface into multiple levels of detail that can be simulated and rendered separately. This approach allows for the efficient computation of large-scale wave patterns while still capturing small-scale details. They also show how their approach can be used to create interactive applications, such as a virtual fountain that responds to user input in real-time. This new approach to water simulation offers significant advantages in terms of both efficiency and visual fidelity.

Overall, the methods based on solving wave equations suffer due to the topological constraints inherent in the nature of the water representation. They solve for vertical displacement of a wave surface over a 2D domain, and so cannot represent splashes and breaking waves. Chentanez and Müller [12] overcame this limitation by adding particles for splashes and sprays, but the particles are simply kinematic and do not interact with each other.

Huang et al. [11] present a novel method for simulating the interaction of large-scale ocean waves with moving ships, specifically focusing on the generation of splashes and wakes. Their method utilizes a combination of a mesh-based fluid simulation – the boundary element method (BEM), and a particle-based method – namely, the fluid implicit particle (FLIP) method. The BEM aspect simulates the large-scale motion of the waves, and the FLIP method captures small-scale details, like splashes. Additionally, the authors introduce a technique for dynamically adapting the simulation resolution based on the ship's position, ensuring that the simulation remains accurate and efficient even for large-scale environments. The results are capable of capturing the plausible complex interactions between ships, waves, and splashes. This approach is similar to ours - we also couple a surface simulation with a particle simulation, but Huang et al. are focused on high resolution offline animations taking on the order of seconds per frame to compute. Our method, based on SPH and wave equation with one-way coupling is capable of hundreds of frames per second.

3   Methods

This section describes the implementation of our technique, including our uniform grid compute shader implementation. This project was implemented using C++, and OpenGL version 4.6. To show the visual and computational differences of the coupled approach, we will compare with standard SPH implementation, and with pure wave equation animation. The coupling in our technique is one-way. The wave surface affects the SPH particles but the SPH particles do not affect the wave surface.

Given the nature of the SPH method, it has good scalability and is inherently parallelizable. These two characteristics make graphical processing units (GPUs), and compute shaders good ways to implement them. A compute shader is a type of GPU shader stage that is primarily used for general-purpose parallel computations, rather than rendering graphics. Although it is capable of generating images, its primary use is to perform tasks that are unrelated to rasterization, such as physics simulations, and data processing. In SPH, each particle has the following properties—position, velocity, acceleration, density, and pressure. These properties are used by the compute shader to proceed from one timestep to the next during simulation.

3.1   Data Structures

The project uses a simple data structure for the particles, which contains all the necessary attributes SPH calculations. In the OpenGL shading language (glsl) the SPH particle is represented as

```
struct Particle
{
    vec4 pos; // .xyz = position, .w = radius
    vec4 vel; // .xyz = velocity, .w = pressure
    vec4 acc; // .xyz = acceleration, .w = density
};
```

This structure packs scalar properties into the w-component of each vector to avoid memory alignment issues. Using vec3s, which are aligned to 16-byte boundaries would have added padding to the structure and increased the memory footprint. With this implementation, each SPH particle will occupy 48 bytes. The following table shows the total memory needed for different particle counts when using this structure (Table 1):

Table 1. Memory needed for different SPH particle counts

Particle Count	Size (MB)
4k (4096)	0.1875
8k (8192)	0.375
16k (16,384)	0.75
64k (65,536)	3.0

These sizes are well within the size limit for shader storage buffers on modern graphics hardware, which is on the order of 2 GB.

Textures provide a way to efficiently store and access large amounts of data, such as heightmaps, they can also be easily loaded and manipulated using various OpenGL functions, allowing for dynamic updates and real-time rendering. For the wave, we use a floating-point texture to store wave heights over a discretized 2D domain. A wave equation compute shader updates the texture to simulate the wave.

For both the particle and the wave data stores (buffers and textures), we use ping-pong buffers to avoid read-write conflicts. This means that each compute shader reads from one data store and writes to a different data store. After each iteration the input and output data stores are swapped (ping-ponged). So the actual memory usage is double what might be expected.

The SPH solver in this project takes advantage of the height of the wave from the wave equation and integrates it such that water effects like splashes, and breaking waves can be animated with ease. This coupling of equations tries to approximate the properties of water in a visually convincing manner.

The uniform grid structure, shown in Fig. 1, is a structure which decomposes space into equal-sized cells to accelerate spatial queries. Each point in the structure is associated with a single cell. To determine which points are within a given distance, d, of another point, q, we first determine which cells are within distance, d, of q, then return all points in those cells. If the queries will always involve the same distance, d, then the grid can be optimized by making the cell size d in each dimension. Then the query result will be points within the $3 \times 3 \times 3$ neighborhood of the cell q is in. Queries of other sizes can be performed by determining which cells a query bounding box overlaps.

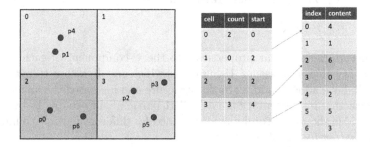

Fig. 1. Uniform grid containing 7 points

Our uniform grid is implemented like a sparse matrix. Empty cells have minimal overhead. On the other hand, cells may have an arbitrary number of points in them. The benefits of the uniform grid break down when there are a large number of points in a few cells, but this tends not to be a problem in SPH since the pressure forces between particles tend to push them apart from each other.

A difficulty with maintaining a uniform grid entirely within a compute shader is that the compute shader cannot allocate memory, so we cannot use per-cell lists which grow and shrink as particles move in and out. As shown in Fig. 1, our uniform grid representation consists of 3 arrays: count, start and contents. We keep a count and starting index for each cell, which determines where in the content array the cell contents (particle indices) are stored. For example, cell 1 contains 2 points, and their indices starts at index 0 in the content array. Cell 1 is empty, and occupies no space in the content array. The total size of this structure remains constant, as long as the number of cells in the grid and the number of particles remain constant. The content array holds point indices, not actual point coordinates, to minimize the amount of data moved when building the grid.

We build the uniform grid in 3 compute shader passes, one for each of the 3 arrays that make up the uniform grid structure.

1. **Count**: For each particle, determine the cell index, and atomic increment the count of that cell
2. **Start**: Compute the start array as the parallel prefix sum of count values
3. **Contents**: Insert points into the contents array by finding the correct location using start and count. Set the contents value to the particle integer index

During step 3, a new running count array is used, initially zero, for insertion into the contents array. Unlike dynamic spatial hashing techniques which can be memory intensive, this collision detection approach only requires 8 bytes per cell plus 4 bytes per particle.

3.2 Ghost Particles for SPH-Wave Coupling and Solid Object Interaction

We use the idea of ghost particles for interaction between SPH particles and solid barriers, and also for the coupling between the wave and the SPH particles. Our implementation uses a cubic spline smoothing kernel for which the kernel support radius and smoothing radius are the same, so we will refer only to the support radius, h.

For solid barriers, the ghost particles typically have zero velocity and a high rest density and are positioned so that they fill the barrier. For wave-coupling ghost particles, the particle density equals water rest density and the velocity is the vertical velocity of the wave as determined using finite differences from the two time steps stored in the wave texture ping-pong buffer.

Note that ghost particles, shown in Fig. 2, are not actually instantiated and are not inserted into the uniform grid, so they do not occupy any memory. SPH particles will have no interaction with wave ghost particles when the SPH height above the wave is greater than h. For an SPH particle with position x, y, z the possible wave ghost particle positions x_g, y_g, z_g are at

$$\begin{bmatrix} x_g \\ y_g \\ z_g \end{bmatrix} = \begin{bmatrix} x + i*r \\ y + j*r \\ w(x+ir, y+jr) - kr \end{bmatrix} \tag{2}$$

where r is the particle radius, i, j are integers, k is a non-negative integer and $w()$ is the wave height function which is linearly interpolated from the wave height texture.

Interactions between SPH particles and wave ghost particles use the same density and force equations as SPH-SPH particle interactions, and will occur when

$$\left\| \begin{bmatrix} x_g \\ y_g \\ z_g \end{bmatrix} - \begin{bmatrix} x \\ y \\ z \end{bmatrix} \right\| < h. \tag{3}$$

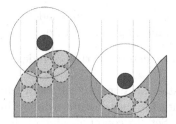

Fig. 2. SPH particles above the wave surface, and corresponding ghost particles beneath the wave surface.

In addition, we add a cohesion force, using the formulation given by suggested by Becker and Teschner [14], between SPH particles and wave ghost particles. This force is usually used to model surface tension and other small scale effects, but we add it here to keep SPH particles near the wave surface instead of being repelled by pressure forces when the wave is moving quickly.

3.3   Implementation

The coupled SPH-wave animation method proceeds in multiple compute shader passes at each timestep, as follows

1. Build uniform grid based on current SPH particle positions
2. Update wave height texture by solving one timestep of the wave equation
3. SPH density and pressure update including wave ghost particles
4. SPH force calculation including wave ghost particles
5. SPH kinematic update based on forces, velocities

Compared to a standard SPH implementation, our approach adds step 2, solution of the wave equations, and augments steps 3 and 4, incorporating density, viscosity and pressure from the wave ghost particles.

3.4   Animated Interactions

To interact with the pure SPH system we apply external forces to the particles, in addition to the gravitational force that is always applied. For example, to create a splash, such as might be observed when an object falls into the water, we add a downward force in the area of impact for a short time and let the simulation proceed.

For the wave equation and coupled wave-SPH system, we instead apply displacements to the wave and allow the wave equation solver to proceed. In the coupled system this displaces the ghost particles which then interact with the SPH particles. Applying instantaneous displacements such as these to the pure SPH system can result in unrealistically high reaction velocities. Since the manner of interaction between the two systems is fundamentally different, it is difficult to get an exact match in visual results between the two systems.

4   Results

In this section we show the visual results of SPH-wave coupling and describe the performance of the technique compared to pure SPH and wave equation approaches. Note that we don't address the problem of SPH rendering in this work, but it is an active area of research. Approaches include isosurface extraction and raycasting the interpolated fluid density field [13]. To visually inspect the behavior of the system we simply render the SPH particles as spheres.

The following table shows a visual comparison of fluid phenomena modelled using pure SPH, the wave equation, and our hybrid method (Table 2).

Table 2. Visual comparison of animations

	SPH	Wave Equation	Coupled SPH/Wave
Splash			
Breaking Wave			
Boat Wake			

4.1   Performance

We implemented our methods in OpenGL and C++ on a PC with Nvidia RTX 4070 (12 GB VRAM) and Intel Core i7-8700K 3.7 GHz and 32 GB RAM. Maximum compute work group invocations, the number of compute shader threads that can run simultaneously, is 1024 on the video card. The following tables show the time taken by various computations in our implementation. Keep in mind that the total time budget per frame is 33.3 ms at 30 frames per second, and 16.67 ms at 60 frames per second. However, in most applications that entire budget cannot be spent on animating water.

Table 3. Wave equation computation time per frame

Wave Texture Resolution	Time (ms)
256 × 256	0.009
512 × 512	0.015
1024 × 1024	0.057

The computation time of the wave equation solution shown in Table 3 is very low and practically negligible when compared to the SPH computations shown in Table 4.

Table 4. SPH computation time per frame

Particle Count	Uniform Grid Time (ms)	SPH Time (ms)	Coupled SPH/Wave Time (ms)
8192	0.091	0.34	0.32
16384	0.093	0.42	0.43
32768	0.096	0.91	0.98
65536	0.102	2.40	2.72

A crucial factor in the computation cost of the uniform grid is the grid size. The number of cells in our grid must be a power-of-two due to the divide and conquer algorithm we use for parallel prefix sum. The results in Table 4 used a grid size of 32 × 32 × 32, which we empirically determined to be optimal by testing a range of grid sizes.

The SPH times shown in the last two columns of Table 4 are for complete SPH implementations, both with and without wave-SPH coupling. These times include uniform grid creation. Although there is some computational overhead associated with the coupling, we can achieve similar visual results with fewer particles by using the coupling approach.

Figures 3 and 4 are visual comparisons of wave and splash animations with varying numbers of particles. With 16k particles, there are not enough particles to form a wave with SPH alone, but with the coupled approach we get more displacement and a breaking wave. In the splash results, at 16k particles there may be a resulting void at the impact location. With the coupled approach, the void will not happen since the wave surface and/or the wave ghost particles can be used during rendering.

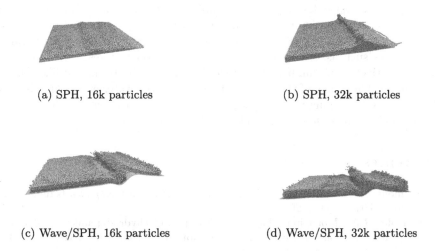

(a) SPH, 16k particles   (b) SPH, 32k particles

(c) Wave/SPH, 16k particles   (d) Wave/SPH, 32k particles

Fig. 3. Wave animations, SPH and coupled Wave/SPH approach comparison

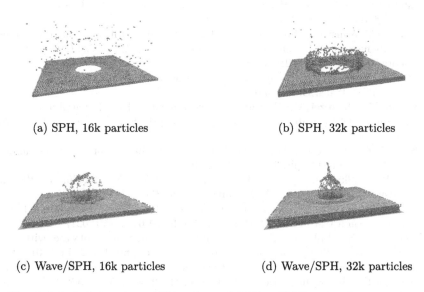

(a) SPH, 16k particles   (b) SPH, 32k particles

(c) Wave/SPH, 16k particles   (d) Wave/SPH, 32k particles

Fig. 4. Splash Animations, SPH and coupled Wave/SPH approach comparison

5   Conclusion

In this paper we have described a new coupled wave equation/SPH approach for real-time water animation effects. The wave surface governs the motion of ghost SPH particles which interact with layers of SPH particles above. This permits water effects such as breaking waves, splashes and boat wakes to be animated with a relatively low number of particles. Although the technique likely lacks the numerical accuracy of the pure SPH technique, the water effects are visually plausible. By leveraging the parallel processing power of modern GPUs, we are able to achieve times suitable for interactive applications.

References

1. Seymour, M.: The science of fluid sims. fxguide (2011). https://www.fxguide.com/fxfeatured/the-science-of-fluid-sims/
2. Gingold, R.A., Monaghan, J.J.: Smoothed particle hydrodynamics: theory and application to non-spherical stars. Mon. Not. R. Astron. Soc. **181**(3), 375–389 (1977)
3. Gilroy, J.: Why the Water in 'Sea of Thieves' Is So Mesmerizing. Fandom (2018). https://www.fandom.com/articles/sea-of-thieves-water
4. Koschier, D., Bender, J., Solenthaler, B., Teschner, M: A survey on SPH methods in computer graphics. In: Computer Graphics Forum, vol. 41, no. 2, pp. 737–760 (2022)
5. Lee, H., Han, S.: Solving the shallow water equations using 2D SPH particles for interactive applications. Vis. Comput. **26**(6), 865–872 (2010). https://doi.org/10.1007/s00371-010-0439-9
6. Wang, C., Wang, C., Qin, H., Zhang, T.Y.: Video-based fluid reconstruction and its coupling with SPH simulation. Vis. Comput. **33**(9), 1211–1224 (2017). https://doi.org/10.1007/s00371-016-1284-2
7. Jeschke, S., Wojtan, C.: Water wave animation via wavefront parameter interpolation. ACM Trans. Graph. **34**(3), 1–14 (2015)
8. Gouin, M., Ducrozet, G., Ferrant, P.: Development and validation of a non-linear spectral model for water waves over variable depth. Eur. J. Mech.-B/Fluids **57**, 115–128 (2016)
9. Schreck, C., Hafner, C., Wojtan, C.: Fundamental solutions for water wave animation. ACM Trans. Graph. **38**(4), 1–14 (2019)
10. Jeschke, S., Skřivan, T., Müller-Fischer, M., Chentanez, N., Macklin, M., Wojtan, C.: Water surface wavelets. ACM Trans. Graph. **37**(4), 1–13 (2018)
11. Huang, L., Qu, Z., Tan, X., Zhang, X., Michels, D.L., Jiang, C.: Ships, splashes, and waves on a vast ocean. ACM Trans. Graph. **40**(6), 1–15 (2021)
12. Chentanez, N., Müller, M.: Real-time simulation of large bodies of water with small scale details. In: Symposium on Computer Animation, pp. 197–206 (2010)
13. Xiao, X., Zhang, S., Yang, X.: Real-time high-quality surface rendering for large scale particle-based fluids. In: Proceedings of the 21st ACM SIGGRAPH Symposium on Interactive 3D Graphics and Games, pp. 1–8 (2017)
14. Becker, M., Teschner, M.: Weakly compressible SPH for free surface flows. In: Proceedings of the 2007 ACM SIGGRAPH/Eurographics Symposium on Computer Animation, pp. 209–217 (2007)

UniTorch - Integrating Neural Rendering into Unity

Laura Fink[1,2]([envelope]) [ID], Daniel Keitel[1,2] [ID], Marc Stamminger[1] [ID],
and Joachim Keinert[2] [ID]

[1] Friedrich-Alexander-Universität Erlangen-Nürnberg, Erlangen, Germany
laura.fink@fau.de
[2] Fraunhofer IIS, Erlangen, Germany

Abstract. Neural rendering techniques have gained significant attention in recent years for their ability to generate highly realistic and immersive visual content. This paper discusses the current state of game engines regarding their ability to integrate neural modules within their pipelines. We exemplarily chose the popular game engine Unity and the deep learning library LibTorch. As we found a severe gap between commonly used auto-diff, deployment and rendering frameworks regarding interoperability and performance, we designed *UniTorch*, a plug-in that allows native access from Unity to Torch. We explore the practical integration of neural rendering methods by faithfully reimplementing and extending state-of-the-art methods. We provide detailed implementation guidelines and use it as means to reveal the mentioned gaps through extensive benchmarking experiments.

1 Introduction

Compared to hand-crafted computer vision algorithms, neural rendering [33] and 3D reconstruction [15] provide impressive photo-realism and rendering quality. These systems are typically designed and trained using sophisticated deep learning frameworks such as PyTorch or TensorFlow [37]. However, practical application of the trained algorithms is still limited, as the results obtained from the deep learning frameworks cannot be easily integrated into computer graphics software widely used for content generation.

In this context, game engines play a crucial role because of their capabilities to render complex scenes in real-time. Applications include games, movie production [1], simulations [28,32] and data set generation with perfect ground truth [29,30]. The image formation process of game engines transforms a scene description, possibly including light and material information, into a 2D image by applying a camera model. It involves several stages, including visibility tests, illumination calculations, and finally displaying the rendered scene [23].

To leverage the benefits of neural rendering, we need to incorporate or replace certain components of the render pipeline with neural networks. This establishes a novel rendering ecosystem where machine learning and render pipelines necessitate to cooperate smoothly. While this sounds simple, it often is not, because on

G. Bebis et al. (Eds.): ISVC 2023, LNCS 14361, pp. 315–328, 2023.
https://doi.org/10.1007/978-3-031-47969-4_25

the one hand, render pipelines of game engines are highly optimized to balance both simplicity, performance and quality. For instance, the game engine *Unity* already offers three different render pipelines [35]. On the other hand, different neural rendering algorithms require different interfaces, ranging from a single pixel color lookup [12] to region based correction of the object geometry [34]. Moreover, neural rendering by itself is computational intensive, requiring an efficient implementation.

Contributions. Our paper bridges the gap between neural rendering and application development using game-engines by providing the following contributions. It (i) analyzes the challenges occurring when integrating neural rendering into game engines, (ii) discusses general interface requirements and (iii) describes an architecture for efficient neural network inference by directly plugging the deep learning library *Torch* [5] into Unity. Its efficacy is demonstrated by showcasing and benchmarking the integration of different state-of-the-art neural rendering applications.

2   Related Work

Neural Network Inference in Game Engines. In recent years, the desire to utilize deep learning methods increased the importance of neural network inference capabilities in game engines. *Unity* provides support for neural network inference through a lightweight cross-platform inference library *Barracuda* [7]. According to the current release notes [7], *Barracuda* is still in the preview development stage except for machine learning (ML) agents and a limited number of other network architectures. Recently, further optimization has been announced in form of *Unity Sentis* [3]. More details on the *Barracuda* pipeline and performed optimizations have been summarized in [24]. It shows practical implications on memory layout, which we also detail in Sect. 3.4. By avoiding inter-device communication, it achieves an efficient style transfer implementation [31] at HD resolution with 30 fps on a PS4Pro console.

The release of *Unreal Engine 5.0* in April 2022 [10] and its introduction of neural network inference [2] provided an alternative solution. Besides ML-agents [9], the general availability of documentation is relatively sparse, indicating that the adoption of neural networks is still in its early stages. In respect to neural rendering, there are a few community tutorials for simple style transfer [8,13]. However, these example implementations rely on external dependencies like OpenCV needing expensive tensor copies between CPU and GPU for each frame.

Unreal Engine as well as *Unity* build upon ONNX [4] as an intermediary format for deployment of neural networks in game engines [9,24]. ONNX enables the interchange of models between different frameworks and offers cross-platform compatibility. However, as ONNX only covers a subset of operations from each deep learning framework, it often represents a functionality bottleneck.

There also exist other community projects that aim to provide a native interface to Torch, but they do not cover the on-the-device data transfer and make a detour via the CPU RAM to implement communication between the software modules [16, 26, 36].

Community Extensions for NeRFs and Alike. The emergence of Neural Radiance Fields (NeRFs) [25] and its successors [15] has sparked a revolution in 3D reconstruction. This caused a growing interest in integrating neural volumetric representations into game engines. They can be represented as an explicit voxel grid [14], implicitly by a neural field [15], or a mixture thereof [27]. However, in all cases their rendering is challenging, as game engines are mostly optimized for polygon rasterization, while the rendering of volumetric representations relies on ray marching. Nevertheless, there is a growing trend to support volume rendering in game engines. *Unreal Engine*, for example, recently added volume rendering to its core functionalities [6], while a popular community plug-in exists for *Unity* [21]. Implicit representations can be very costly as the network has to be inferred several times along each camera ray. This led to hybrid representations that are more compatible with traditional rendering pipelines. Based on such methods, a growing number of community projects make promising steps towards the integration of neural rendering into engines. A VR specialized implementation of instant neural graphics primitives [27] was implemented by Li et al. [22] for Unity. The Unity Viewer [20] for SNeRG [17] bakes an implicit representation into multiple explicit volumes to encode albedo, normals etc. This circumvents the expensive evaluation of implicit neural functions at the price of high memory consumption due to the baked volumetric data.

MobileNeRF [12] and its Unity implementation [19] follow a different path. It discretizes the volume into triangulated planes, resorting to rasterization again. Visual fidelity is enhanced by a deferred neural network pass which translates neural features to colors. Bozic et al. [11] demonstrate more complex scene interaction with neural objects within a game engine like shadows, collision and level of detail (LOD). Shadows and collisions are enabled by a proxy mesh of the volume representation; 3D MIP-mapping is used for LOD. The game engine used is not described in detail, though.

3   UniTorch

3.1   The Software Ecosystem

We identified four main steps to develop and use a neural rendering application, namely (i) *optimization* of the network weights, (ii) (optional) transform into a deployment format, (iii) *inference*, and (iv) use in a *rendering* engine, see Fig. 1: *Optimization* starts the lifecycle - the network's architecture is designed and its weights are optimized. *Deployment* provides im- and export functionalities. If the same framework is used for optimization and inference, usually the full feature set is supported. Optionally, a standardized format for a network's control flow and weights can be used for sharing between frameworks, adding an abstraction layer, potentially limiting the feature set. *Inference* executes a neural network with strong emphasis on performance. It can be optimized down to hardware level and trained weights. *Rendering* is usually performed in a game engine. The latter encapsulates the application and provides inputs for the neural network and consumes its output. The engine defines the main control flow; it triggers initialization and invokes the inference.

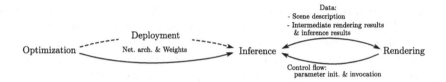

Fig. 1. Relationships and information exchange between frameworks.

The context of neural rendering draws the focus of this work naturally on the interplay of *inference* and *rendering*. For inference, we use Torch [5], same for optimization and deployment. Unity [35] is our choice for rendering. In order to combine these sophisticated frameworks and engines, an interface should consider the following design goals: (i) simple to use, (ii) agnostic to memory layout, (iii) feature-rich to support of various neural network architectures, (iv) avoidant of unnecessary CPU and GPU communication, (v) highly performant and efficient. Additionally, control flow (the render engine calls the inference engine) and data exchange (in both directions) have to be taken into account.

Because of this relationship, it is particularly important to have a well understanding of the rendering engine's control flow in order to correctly incorporate neural components. This knowledge about Unity's specifics, needed for the applications shown in Sect. 4, is introduced in the following.

3.2   Unity's Structure and Control Flow

The Unity render engine constitutes the skeleton for any game or graphical application that is created with it, and thus determines the main control flow and render logic, represented by the main render loop. Figure 2 shows a simplified version of Unity's internal operation and render pipeline illustrating the execution order of important event functions.

Depending on the use case, Unity provides different render pipeline architectures [35]. The (default) built-in render pipeline is easy-to-use and pre-configured, but rather rigid. Alternatively, different specializations are made available by scriptable render pipelines. For the sake of readability, we restrict our introduction to the default pipeline.

Unity scenes are structured by scene graphs with cameras, lights, or meshes as nodes. Attached scripts inheriting from *MonoBehavior*, Unity's base scene object class, may implement pre-declared event functions in C# which are executed in a pre-defined order. Additionally to *MonoBehavior* events, *CameraEvents* and

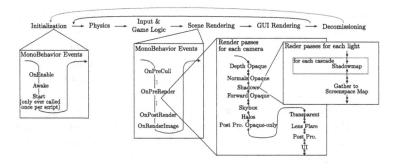

Fig. 2. Excerpt of Unity's main loop detailing on resource initialization and scene rendering. Camera and light events happening before a render pass are indicated as red dot, after events as blue dots. (Color figure online)

LightEvents serve as insertion points for so called *CommandBuffers* to extend the pipeline with additional render or plug-in calls. *CommandBuffers* are created in *MonoBehavior* events and can be explicitly executed there as well. All these events are the gateway to initialize, invoke and communicate with any neural module (with or without *CommandBuffers*). Choosing the right event avoids accidental interference with any inherent rendering logic.

3.3   Usage of UniTorch to Leverage Neural Rendering in Unity

Neural rendering can be integrated into Unity by simple calls to UniTorch, which follow the structure of the Barracuda API. This is exemplified with the following code snippet for style transfer. A network is evaluated on the conventionally rendered RGB image, right before it would have been displayed.

```
// style transfer script is attached to the camera
public class StyleTransferCamera : MonoBehaviour {
  private Module module; // UniTorch interface for neural nets
  private TextureTensor ioTensor; // UniTorch interfaces for tensors
  private TextureTensor styleTensor; // UniTorch interfaces for tensors

  void Start() { <Init variables> } // only called once

  // called every frame after scene rendering
  void OnRenderImage(RenderTexture src, RenderTexture dest) {
    // copy to tensor, infer, copy back (copies resolve memory layout)
    ioTensor.ReadFromTexture(src, 3);
    module.Execute( /*input*/ new TensorProxy[]{ioTensor, styleTensor},
                    /*output*/ ioTensor, /*16 bit float*/ True);
    ioTensor.BlitIntoTexture(dest, 3);
  }
}
```

3.4   Implementation of UniTorch

While Unity is mostly programmed in C#, we design a Unity plug-in to access Torch's C++ API. It implements an interface from a render to an inference engine according to our design goals from Sect. 3.1 as follows.

Data Transfer. Tensors are multi-dimensional data buffers of arbitrary size, used as in- and output for neural networks. Torch implements tensors using CUDA buffers, allowing for efficient data exchange with OpenGL and DirectX, the backbones of Unity. This interface can thus be used to implement the low-level data transfer between LibTorch tensors and Unity compute buffers. However, the default memory layouts of graphics applications and inference engines usually do not match [24], which would be required to achieve optimal performance of the data transfer. These differences may need custom copy operations to match the layout. For these reasons we prefer Unity's compute buffers over textures to manage the memory inside of Unity. Additionally, tensors may well exceed the 4 channel limit of textures and may even be composed from multiple intermediate render buffers. Thus, it is beneficial to implement copy operations in custom compute shaders on user-level which are tailored for the respective application.

Control Flow. In general, it is possible to call UniTorch functions from any script in Unity. However, Unity scripts are executed by parallel child threads which may lead to race conditions when the GPU resources for tensors and networks are accessed or altered. Consequently, such accesses should only be done via Unity's main render thread. In order to enforce this behavior, we define C++ functions in our plug-in that can be called from command buffers. These are always executed by the main render thread. Usage of command buffers becomes especially important for network invocations in camera or light events for more complex neural rendering methods (see Sect. 4). It has the beneficial side effect, that users can insert network inferences wherever Unity allows the execution of command buffers, exceeding the functionality of Barracuda at the time of writing. As these C++ functions are not allowed to return any value and only get a single integer as input parameter, we resort to getter- and setter functions to transfer in- and outputs under the hood.

3.5 Performance Optimization

For high performance, the execution of neural networks should be restricted to relevant image regions. In practice, executing networks on varying resolutions is tricky, as just-in-time compilers initialize networks for a fixed resolution and any new resolution requires a heavy warm-up time of up to multiple seconds. We thus pre-initialize networks for a number of resolutions in advance, and use the next largest resolution at run-time, see Sect. 4.2 for details.

Lastly, we highly recommend to only use 16-bit floating point precision during inference, wherever possible. This has high influence on compute time with minimal influence on quality, as we show in Sect. 4.1. It allows to best leverage tensor cores where many only run on 16-bit precision.

4 Neural Rendering Use Cases

Considering literature, we identified two classes of neural rendering that are promising to be integrated within game engines: *neural image processing* and *neural assets*. *Neural image processing* uses neural networks to alter a rendered image in a desirable way. As an example, we use **Style Transfer** as first use case. *Neural assets* are scene objects that need a neural network to evaluate its appearance. In this paper, we consider two methods: **Baked Volumes**, inspired by MobileNeRFs [12], as well as **Neural Textures**, as used in Neural Deferred Shading [34]. Neural assets might be reconstructed from real-world photographs, so material information and detailed normals might not be available. Thus, lighting calculations on the object may not be trivially inferred from the proxy, but need network evaluation. Furthermore, the geometry may be an approximate proxy, the silhouette of which is refined by a neural post-process on the rendered image. The same is true, when such an object is considered as a shadow caster in a shadow map. This can have large impact on the pipeline integration and we detail on this throughout this section, an overview is given in Fig. 3.

For each use case, we provide short descriptions and benchmarks. All three use cases have been implemented using UniTorch and use a deferred screen-space pass. Thus, neural network inference is mostly done on intermediate render results. Note, that for practical reasons, we refrain from the usage of complex pixel shaders that include (large) neural networks. All benchmarks of this section (including the ones of Barracuda) were done on the same machine equipped with an Intel Core i9-7940x and an Nvidia RTX 2080 Ti.

4.1 Style Transfer

This use cases is simple to integrate: It applies a convolutional neural network to encode the style image and the content image, transfers the style to the content, and outputs the stylized image. Thus, the final previously rendered RGB image can be simply fed into the network, e.g. in OnRenderImage, as shown in Sect. 3.3.

Figure 4 shows benchmarks results. We used a publicly available implementation [18]. UniTorch only needs 60 % of the time required by Barracuda. On top, using 16-bit floating point precision only, reduces time to 25 % of the time used by Barracuda. Even though the example only needs two transfers of an HD RGB texture for the in- and output of the network, such transfer already adds another 22 ms to the frame time.

4.2 Texture-Based Neural Rendering

Our next use case is "Deferred Neural Rendering" [34]. A *neural texture* and a CNN (U-Net) that evaluates the final RGB color, are trained in conjunction based on ground truth training images for every single asset. Thies et al. propose a pipeline where an (inaccurate) proxy mesh is rasterized to output a screen-space UV-map. This map is used to sample a neural texture, which contains multi-dimensional neural descriptors instead of RGB colors, resulting in a neural

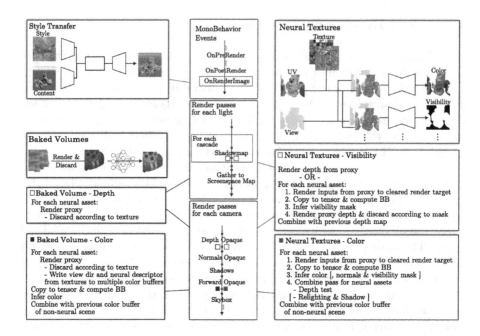

Fig. 3. Integration of neural rendering methods within the Unity built-in pipeline. Black boxes refer to parts of the Unity render loop (see Sect. 3.2). Boxes of the one color indicate the integration of the same method. Green boxes refer to neural textures (see Sect. 4.2), violet to baked volumes and brown to style transfer (see Sect. 4.3 and 4.1). (Color figure online)

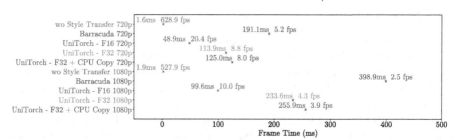

Fig. 4. Style transfer benchmarks.

image. Finally, the CNN converts this neural image to the final RGB result. We extended this work to enable multi-object scenes, shadows, and simple relighting.

Similar to surface light fields, neural textures can encode complex material appearance including view dependent effects. Thus, the appearance of complex materials can be captured from photographs or CGI software like *Blender* and directly be used in the engine. This circumvents the laborious process of remodeling the material using the engine's material system. Figure 5 shows this use case for a car model. Despite of some artifacts like smoothed details (head light) and imperfect specular highlights, appearance is faithfully reproduced.

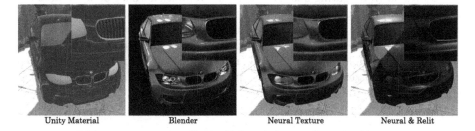

| Unity Material | Blender | Neural Texture | Neural & Relit |

Fig. 5. Renderings of a car model in Unity. From left to right: Asset rendered using Unity materials created by a non-professional. Asset rendered in Blender. Neural asset in Unity. Neural asset including relighting (green scene light) and shadows. (Color figure online)

To achieve seamless blending of neural assets within the rest of the scene, we need to relight our objects appropriately, without having an explicit material description. To this end, we extended the neural texture by a glossiness parameter, coarsely approximated from the variance of the view-dependent color over the training images. Combined with the mesh normals, we can perform basic relighting by mixing the neural color with the light color.

When only coarse, approximate proxy geometry is known, a screen-space visibility mask as an extra output to the pipeline allows us to correct silhouettes and thus refine visibility. The effectiveness of this extension is shown in Fig. 6 for an obelisk model: despite the coarse proxy geometry, the silhouette appearance closely resembles the ground truth shape.

| Neural Texture | Neural Texture & Neural Visibility | Silhouette Difference |

Fig. 6. Renderings of a 3D-reconstructed obelisk model juxtaposing neural rendering with and without silhouette correction.

Furthermore, if only coarse proxy geometry is available, shadows need extra attention. If the proxy is used for the shadow map, the shadow mismatches can become obtrusive. For instance, obvious halos may occur because Unity merges cascaded shadow maps into screen space maps. We thus have to apply the silhouette refinement also in the shadow map rendering passes.

Additionally, relighting quality suffers, when proxy normals do not match the object appearance. In such cases, the neural pipeline must also provide explicit normals, what we implemented by adding another CNN.

In Fig. 7, we illustrate the described effects. We constructed a small scene consisting of multiple objects which share UV space and can thus be considered a single neural asset. To construct a proxy mesh, the original geometry was enlarged and smoothed.

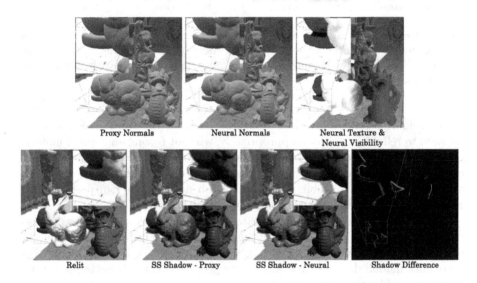

Proxy Normals   Neural Normals   Neural Texture & Neural Visibility

Relit   SS Shadow - Proxy   SS Shadow - Neural   Shadow Difference

Fig. 7. Renderings of single neural asset consisting of multiple objects. Top to bottom, left to right: Normal of the proxy mesh and from a neural output. Rendering without adaptations to neural color output. Neural asset relit by an orange light. Rendering with shadows form screen space (SS) shadow map which was rendered using the proxy geometry or the neural visibility. Difference of shadow results. (Color figure online)

Figure 8 shows the benchmarks for our Neural Texture integration. The major part of the frame time is network inference. In our simple implementation, we added another network of same architecture for each output feature. Thus, runtime complexity is nearly independent from scene complexity and can be approximated by #neural assets × #output features × inference time + scene rendering; if shadows would be calculated based on neural visibility each light source adds additional inference passes for every cascade to the frame time.

We also evaluated the effectiveness of the optimization, where inference is restricted to the object bounding boxes, as mentioned in Sect. 4.2. Thus, computation time can be aggressively lowered which is shown in Fig. 9.

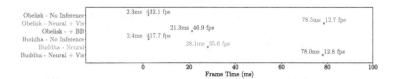

Fig. 8. Benchmarks for scenes of Figs. 7 and 6 at 1080p using 16-bit precision, averaged over 1000 frames. +Vis indicates an additional network for a neural visibility, +BB indicates the use of the optimization shown in Fig. 9.

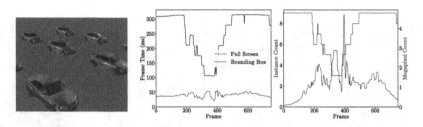

Fig. 9. Benchmarks for the scene depicted on the left (BBs overlayed red) with a camera animation at 1080p. If network inference is restricted to the bounding boxes, inference time, and thus frame time, scales with pixel count (red) instead of scaling with the number of visible neural assets, denoted as instance count (blue). (Color figure online)

4.3 Baked Volumes

Another variant of neural assets is MobileNeRF by Chen et al. [12]. We refer to it as baked volumes as it relies on a NeRF backbone during training, but is baked to explicit geometry for inference. The authors propose stacks of axis-aligned, triangulated planes as proxy in combination with neural textures. Similar to binary alpha maps, fragments are discarded during rasterization based on texture values (without an additional network being involved) to approximate the actual silhouette of the object. Using discard implies that the proxy geometry has to conservatively embrace the actual pixel footprint of the object. In our implementation, a deferred pass translates descriptors from the neural textures and view directions to RGB values using a multi-layer perceptron (MLP).

Figure 10 shows renderings of the proxy geometry and the output rendering of our implementation. The renderings show that opaque neural assets can be integrated into scenes that contain conventional transparent objects. Compatibility is no issue as long as the neural asset is rendered at a camera event prior to the transparent render passes (same holds for Neural Textures). The combination of transparent conventional objects and transparent neural assets in one scene is not possible using the Unity built-in pipeline though, as we cannot place custom commands within its internal transparent render passes. However, transparent neural assets without other transparent objects in the scene can be correctly rendered with custom commands.

Regarding shadows, correct visibility tests do not rely on additional network inferences for this method. However, the approximation of geometry may lead to self-shadowing artifacts due to the layers. These artifacts can be mitigated by carefully tweaking the shadow bias parameter.

Again, relighting is non-trivial due to the missing explicit material description and the proxy's crude normals. The method as proposed misses an additional output to provide realistic normals, similar to our extension of texture-based neural rendering.

| Proxy Geometry | Rendered | with Shadow | Wrong Shadow Bias |

Fig. 10. Renderings of a toy car using a baked volumetric representation.

Table 1. Benchmarks given as frame per second, averaged over 1000 frames.

Resolution/precision	32-bit	16-bit
1080p	20	24
720p	45	54

Table 1 indicates frame times. No bounding box optimizations or shadows were applied. We noted that the layered scene representation lead to heavy overdraw. Frame times of our implementation are higher than the original ones because of a bigger MLP. Specifically, a frequency encoder for the view direction and three fully connected layers with width of 128 + non-linearity were used.

Eventually, we want to share one remark about the usage of CNNs versus MLPs. This comparison shows two clear disadvantages of CNNs: (i) the convolutions of CNNs process multiple neighboring pixels as input. If CNNs, that are overfitted to single assets, are used, each neural asset requires distinct render and inference passes, so that the CNN never sees unknown descriptors from other assets. While this issue could be solved by having a generalized network for all assets within the scene, (ii) the dependence on neighboring pixels remains. Thus, any ray-based evaluation of appearance is impossible.

5 Conclusion

In general, the official integration of neural networks into game engines, particularly for neural rendering, is still in its early stages. The available functionality in game engines for network inference lags behind that of dedicated optimization and deployment frameworks. Game engines place a strong emphasis on cross-platform support and optimization, but this focus can come at the cost of flexibility, smooth integration, and performance, as we showed in the previous section. The limited availability of resources and tutorials highlights the nascent state of neural rendering in game engines, indicating the potential for further advancements. Yet, it is worth noting that there is growing interest and momentum in this direction within the game development community. This increased focus is expected to drive advancements and innovations, as researchers and developers continue to explore and experiment with such techniques. It is highly promising that game engines will catch up and provide more robust and efficient support for neural network inference. The fast progress signifies a bright future for the integration of deep learning and game engines, ultimately leading to more immersive virtual worlds.

References

1. Game On: Game-Engine Technology Expands Filmmaking Horizons - The American Society of Cinematographers (en-US). https://tinyurl.com/2txhdvac
2. NeuralNetworkInference: Unreal Engine Doc. https://tinyurl.com/aa2ryfej
3. Official - Introducing Unity Muse and Unity Sentis, AI-Powered Creativity. https://tinyurl.com/35c8eev8
4. ONNX. https://onnx.ai/
5. Torch—PyTorch 2.0 documentation. https://pytorch.org/docs/stable/torch.html
6. Unreal Engine 5.2 Release Notes. https://tinyurl.com/yx5e6ba3
7. Unity Barracuda. Unity Technologies (2021)
8. PyTorch Realtime Style Transfer Model in Unreal Engine 5 with ONNX Runtime (2022)
9. Neural Network Engine (NNE). Course (2023). https://tinyurl.com/fejs7pem
10. Unreal Engine. Wikipedia (2023)
11. Božič, A., Gladkov, D., Doukakis, L., Lassner, C.: Neural assets: volumetric object capture and rendering for interactive environments (2022)
12. Chen, Z., Funkhouser, T., Hedman, P., Tagliasacchi, A.: MobileNeRF: exploiting the polygon rasterization pipeline for efficient neural field rendering on mobile architectures. In: Proceedings of the IEEE/CVF Conference on Computer Vision and Pattern Recognition, pp. 16569–16578 (2023)
13. Frames, W.: Bringing Deep Learning to Unreal Engine 5—Pt. 2 (2022)
14. Fridovich-Keil, S., Yu, A., Tancik, M., Chen, Q., Recht, B., Kanazawa, A.: Plenoxels: radiance fields without neural networks. In: Proceedings of the IEEE/CVF Conference on Computer Vision and Pattern Recognition, pp. 5501–5510 (2022)
15. Gao, K., Gao, Y., He, H., Lu, D., Xu, L., Li, J.: NeRF: neural radiance field in 3D vision, a comprehensive review (2022)
16. Guttenberg, N.: Neural networks in unity using native libraries. https://www.goodai.com/neural-networks-in-unity-using-native-libraries/
17. Hedman, P., Srinivasan, P.P., Mildenhall, B., Barron, J.T., Debevec, P.: Baking neural radiance fields for real-time view synthesis. In: IEEE/CVF International Conference on Computer Vision (ICCV), Virtual, pp. 5875–5884 (2021)
18. Huang, X., Belongie, S.: Arbitrary style transfer in real-time with adaptive instance normalization. In: ICCV (2017)
19. Kipp, J.: MobileNeRF in Unity (2022). https://t.co/SslORxUbFJ

20. Kipp, J.: SNeRG Unity Viewer (2023). https://github.com/julienkay/SNeRG-Unity-Viewer
21. Lavik, M.: UnityVolumeRendering (2023). https://tinyurl.com/bdf8vhp3
22. Li, K., et al.: Bringing instant neural graphics primitives to immersive virtual reality. In: 2023 IEEE Conference on Virtual Reality and 3D User Interfaces Abstracts and Workshops (VRW), Shanghai, China, pp. 739–740. IEEE (2023)
23. Marschner, S., Shirley, P.: Fundamentals of Computer Graphics. CRC Press, Taylor & Francis Group (2022)
24. Marshall, C.S.: Practical machine learning for rendering: from research to deployment. In: ACM SIGGRAPH 2021 Courses, Virtual Event, USA, pp. 1–239. ACM (2021)
25. Mildenhall, B., Srinivasan, P.P., Tancik, M., Barron, J.T., Ramamoorthi, R., Ng, R.: NeRF: representing scenes as neural radiance fields for view synthesis. In: Vedaldi, A., Bischof, H., Brox, T., Frahm, J.-M. (eds.) ECCV 2020. LNCS, vol. 12346, pp. 405–421. Springer, Cham (2020). https://doi.org/10.1007/978-3-030-58452-8_24
26. Mills, C.: Create a libtorch plugin for unity. https://christianjmills.com/posts/fastai-libtorch-unity-tutorial/part-1/
27. Müller, T., Evans, A., Schied, C., Keller, A.: Instant neural graphics primitives with a multiresolution hash encoding. ACM Trans. Graph. **41**(4), 1–15 (2022)
28. Pokhrel, C., Khatiwada, A.: Deep Q-learning for intelligent non-playable characters in combat games (2023)
29. Qiu, W., Yuille, A.: UnrealCV: connecting computer vision to unreal engine. In: Hua, G., Jégou, H. (eds.) ECCV 2016. LNCS, vol. 9915, pp. 909–916. Springer, Cham (2016). https://doi.org/10.1007/978-3-319-49409-8_75
30. Richter, S.R., Vineet, V., Roth, S., Koltun, V.: Playing for data: ground truth from computer games. In: Leibe, B., Matas, J., Sebe, N., Welling, M. (eds.) ECCV 2016. LNCS, vol. 9906, pp. 102–118. Springer, Cham (2016). https://doi.org/10.1007/978-3-319-46475-6_7
31. Saint-Denis, A., Vanhoey, K., Deliot, T.: Multi-stylization of video-games in real-time guided by G-buffer information. In: High Performance Graphics 2019, Strasbourg, France (2019)
32. Szlęg, P., Barczyk, P., Maruszczak, B., Zieliński, S., Szymańska, E.: Simulation environment for underwater vehicles testing and training in Unity3D. In: Petrovic, I., Menegatti, E., Marković, I. (eds.) IAS 2022. LNNS, vol. 577, pp. 844–853. Springer, Cham (2023). https://doi.org/10.1007/978-3-031-22216-0_56
33. Tewari, A., et al.: State of the art on neural rendering. In: Computer Graphics Forum, vol. 39, no. 2, pp. 701–727 (2020)
34. Thies, J., Zollhöfer, M., Nießner, M.: Deferred neural rendering: image synthesis using neural textures. ACM Trans. Graph. **38**(4), 1–12 (2019)
35. Unity Technologies: Manual: Render pipelines. https://docs.unity3d.com/Manual/render-pipelines.html
36. NeuralVFX: basic libtorch dll. https://github.com/NeuralVFX/basic-libtorch-dll
37. Yuan, L.: A Brief History of Deep Learning Frameworks (2021). https://tinyurl.com/46zb9yfm

Virtual Home Staging: Inverse Rendering and Editing an Indoor Panorama under Natural Illumination

Guanzhou Ji[(⊠)] [iD], Azadeh O. Sawyer[iD], and Srinivasa G. Narasimhan[iD]

Carnegie Mellon University, Pittsburgh, PA 15213, USA
{gji,asawyer,srinivas}@andrew.cmu.edu

Abstract. We propose a novel inverse rendering method that enables the transformation of existing indoor panoramas with new indoor furniture layouts under natural illumination. To achieve this, we captured indoor HDR panoramas along with real-time outdoor hemispherical HDR photographs. Indoor and outdoor HDR images were linearly calibrated with measured absolute luminance values for accurate scene relighting. Our method consists of three key components: (1) panoramic furniture detection and removal, (2) automatic floor layout design, and (3) global rendering incorporating scene geometry, new furniture objects, and real-time outdoor photograph. We demonstrate the effectiveness of our workflow in rendering indoor scenes under different outdoor illumination conditions. Additionally, we contribute a new calibrated HDR (Cali-HDR) dataset that consists of 137 calibrated indoor panoramas and their associated outdoor photographs.

Keywords: HDR Photography · Photometric Calibration · Furniture Removal · Panoramic Rendering · Global Illumination

1 Introduction

The increasing popularity of omnidirectional cameras has driven significant research interest in panoramic photography during recent years. A panoramic photograph provides a complete representation of the surrounding context and enables 360° rendering. The global rendering method proposed by Debevec [7] offers a High Dynamic Range (HDR) image-based rendering model for relighting virtual objects within a realistic scene context.

Previous studies have focused on estimating 360° HDR environment map directly from Low Dynamic Range (LDR) images for scene relighting and object insertion [11,12,15]. However, these data-driven approaches often assume linear proportionality between pixel values and scene radiance without considering photometric calibration. The actual brightness of a scene, measured in luminance (cd/m^2), accurately reflects the light properties in the real world. Bolduc et al. [2] recently conducted a study that calibrated an existing panoramic HDR dataset with approximate scene luminance levels. In our work, we take this a step

© The Author(s), under exclusive license to Springer Nature Switzerland AG 2023
G. Bebis et al. (Eds.): ISVC 2023, LNCS 14361, pp. 329–342, 2023.
https://doi.org/10.1007/978-3-031-47969-4_26

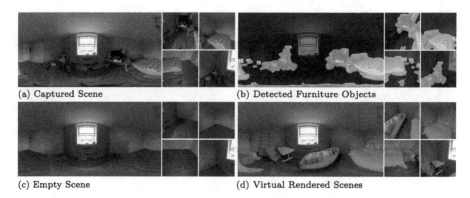

(a) Captured Scene   (b) Detected Furniture Objects

(c) Empty Scene   (d) Virtual Rendered Scenes

Fig. 1. Illustration of Proposed Rendering Pipeline: The captured scene (a) is filled with furniture objects. Detected furniture objects (b) are removed from the scene, and an empty scene (c) is restored. (d) New furniture objects [10] are inserted and rendered with real-time outdoor illumination.

further by calibrating the captured HDR panoramas using absolute luminance value (in SI units) measured in each scene. This calibration ensures that our HDR images accurately represent realistic spatially varying lighting conditions, distinguishing them from existing indoor panorama datasets [6,40,48].

Panoramic images introduce unique challenges for 2D scene understanding tasks, due to the distortion caused by equirectangular projection. When dealing with scenes that contain furniture objects, the complexities of 3D scene reconstruction are further amplified. Existing image segmentation methods are primarily prepared for understanding 2D perspective images [50], limiting their applicability in panoramic images. Recent studies on indoor furniture inpainting focus on furniture removal from 2D perspective images [25,36]. Directly applying these inpainting techniques to furnished panoramas can result in geometric inconsistencies within indoor surfaces. Therefore, our research focuses on furniture removal tasks within panorama images and provides a restored empty room for scene editing.

Indoor global illumination is influenced by various factors, including scene geometry, material properties, and real-time outdoor illumination. In this work, we take an existing indoor panorama and an outdoor photograph as inputs and render photo-realistic renderings featuring a new indoor furniture layout. Our rendering pipeline allows the reconstruction of global illumination between the scene and the newly inserted furniture objects (Fig. 2). In summary, this work presents the first demonstration of furniture removal, furniture insertion, and panoramic rendering for real-world indoor scenes (Fig. 1). To achieve this, our work makes the following technical contributions:

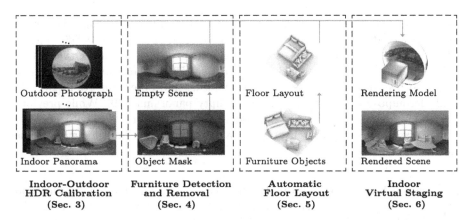

Fig. 2. Our rendering pipeline consists of four modules: Indoor-Outdoor HDR Calibration (Sect. 3) calibrates the captured indoor and outdoor HDR photographs with measured absolute luminance values. Furniture Detection and Removal (Sect. 4) identifies and removes the target furniture objects from the scene. Automatic Floor Layout (Sect. 5) allows the automatic placement of multiple furniture objects. Indoor Virtual Staging (Sect. 6) achieves high-quality indoor virtual staging for furnished and empty scenes.

(1). An approach for calibrating indoor-outdoor HDR photographs and the creation of a new calibrated HDR (Cali-HDR) dataset comprising 137 scenes.

(2). An image inpainting method that detects and removes furniture objects from a panorama.

(3). A rule-based layout design for positioning multiple furniture objects on the floor based on spatial parameters.

2   Related Work

HDR and Photometric Calibration. The dynamic range of radiances in a real-world scene spans from 10^{-3} cd/m^2 (starlight) to 10^5 cd/m^2 (sunlight) [33]. In the context of a 2D perspective image, some studies have focused on predicting panoramic HDR environment maps [12], lighting representation [11], and estimating HDR panoramas from LDR images [15]. Considering that HDR images reflect the relative luminance values from the real world, absolute luminance measurement is required for on-site HDR photography to recover scene radiance [9]. To display the absolute luminance value, the captured HDR image requires photometric calibration, which is a means of radiometric self-calibration [30]. Reference planes, such as matte color checkers or gray cards, should be positioned within the scene for luminance measurement [31].

Indoor Light Estimation. Previous studies on indoor lighting estimation have explored indoor lighting editing [28], material property estimation [43], and the recovery of spatially-varying lighting [13,27,34] from a 2D image. Following the global rendering method [8], some studies aim to estimate a 360° indoor HDR environment map from a 2D image and subsequently render the virtual objects [12,26]. User inputs, such as annotating indoor planes and light sources, have also been utilized to assist scene relighting and object insertion [23]. Zhi et al. decompose the light effects in the empty panoramas [49]. While previous studies have extensively focused on global light estimation and 3D object insertion, there is limited research on panoramic global rendering under real-time outdoor illumination.

Panoramic Furniture Removal. The conventional image inpainting method assumes a nearly planar background around the target object, making it unsuitable for indoor scenes with complex 3D room structures. For the case of indoor scenes, even state-of-the-art inpainting models, such as LaMa [35], cannot recognize the global structure, including the boundaries of walls, ceilings, and floors. Several approaches have been attempted to address this challenge: (1) utilizing lighting and geometry constraints [47], (2) using planar surfaces to approximate contextual geometry [18,24,25], and (3) estimating an empty 3D room geometry from furnished scenes [46]. These studies have primarily focused on furniture detection and inpainting tasks for 2D perspective images. Panoramic scene understanding includes object detection [17] and spherical semantic segmentation [45]. Although the recent studies [14,16] have started furniture removal tasks in panoramas, it is primarily centered around virtually rendered scenes rather than real-world scenes.

3D Layout Estimation. Estimating a 3D room layout from a single image is a common task for indoor scene understanding. While indoor panorama can be converted into a cubic map [4,38], the actual 3D layout is oversimplified. Building on this cube map approach, other studies [37,38] focus on panorama depth estimation using 3D point clouds. Moreover, under the Manhattan world assumption [5], a 360° room layout with separated planar surfaces can be segmented from a single panorama [39,42,48,51]. Moving beyond 3D room layout, detailed scene and furniture geometry can be reconstructed from 2D perspective images [19,22,32]. Additionally, when provided with a 2D floor plan image, indoor space semantics and topology representations can be generated to create a 3D model [41] and recognize elements in floor layouts [44]. An accurate room geometry allows new furniture objects to be inserted precisely into the existing scene.

3   Indoor-Outdoor HDR Calibration

Indoor HDR Calibration. For indoor scenes, a Ricoh Theta Z1 camera was positioned in the room to capture panoramic HDR photographs. The camera settings were configured as follows: White Balance (Daylight 6500), ISO (100),

Aperture (F/5.6), Image Size (6720 × 3360), and Shutter Speed (4, 1, 1/4, 1/15, 1/60, 1/250, 1/1000, 1/4000, 1/8000). To ensure consistency and avoid motion blur during photography, the camera was fixed on a tripod at a height of 1.6m. We placed a Konica Minolta LS-160 luminance meter next to the camera to measure the target luminance on a white matte board. Each HDR photograph needs per-pixel calibration to accurately display luminance values for the scene. The measured absolute luminance value at the selected point is recorded in SI unit (cd/m^2). The measured luminance value and displayed luminance value from the original HDR image are used for calculating the calibration factor (k_1). According to the study by Inanici [21], given R, G, and B values in the captured indoor HDR image, indoor scene luminance (L_i) is expressed as:

$$L_i = k_1 \cdot (0.2127 \cdot R + 0.7151 \cdot G + 0.0722 \cdot B)(cd/m^2) \quad (1)$$

Outdoor HDR Calibration. To capture outdoor scenes, a Canon EF 8–15 mm f/4L fisheye lens was installed on Canon EOS 5D Mark II Full Frame DSLR Camera, and a 3.0 Natural Density (ND) filter was utilized for capturing direct sunlight with HDR technique [35]. The camera settings were configured as follows: White Balance (Daylight 6500), ISO (200), Aperture (F/16), Image Size (5616 × 3744), and Shutter Speed (4, 1, 1/4, 1/15, 1/60, 1/250, 1/1000, 1/4000, 1/8000). Due to the diverse outdoor contexts, it is impractical to place a target plane to measure target luminance values. Each camera has its own fixed camera response curve to merge multiple images with varying exposures into one single HDR image. Rather than performing a separate calibration process for outdoor HDR, our objective is to determine a fixed calibration factor between two distinct cameras and calibrate the outdoor HDR images with indoor luminance measurement.

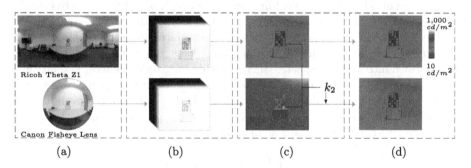

Fig. 3. Calibration Process: (a) Photographs from two cameras. (b) Cropped target regions. (c) Original luminance maps. (d) Luminance maps after HDR image captured by fisheye lens is scaled with k_2.

As shown in Fig. 3, we positioned two cameras in an enclosed room under consistent electrical lighting. Following the camera settings of indoor and outdoor HDR photography (Sect. 3), we captured the target checkboard from two cameras, respectively. Then, 2D perspective images displaying the same target were cropped from the original images. After merging the two sets of images into HDR photographs, we calculated the difference ratio (k_2) between the target pixel region (white patch) on the HDR photographs obtained from the two cameras. Ultimately, the HDR image captured by Canon EOS 5D Camera was linearly calibrated with the computed constant value (k_2), and the HDR photographs from the two cameras were calibrated to display the same luminance range. k_2 is a fixed constant when the two camera settings stay the same. Given R, G, and B values in the captured outdoor HDR image, outdoor scene luminance (L_o) is expressed as:

$$L_o = k_1 \cdot k_2 \cdot (0.2127 \cdot R + 0.7151 \cdot G + 0.0722 \cdot B)(cd/m^2) \qquad (2)$$

where k_1 is the calibration factor determined by the measured luminance target value and displayed luminance value in the captured indoor HDR image, and k_2 is the computed constant for scaling the outdoor hemispherical image into the indoor panorama.

After linear rescaling, the outdoor HDR photographs are processed through the following steps: (1) vignetting correction that compensates for the light loss in the periphery area caused by the fisheye lens [21], (2) color correction for chromatic changes introduced by ND filter [35], and (3) geometric transformation from equi-distant to hemispherical fisheye image for environment mapping [20].

4   Furniture Detection and Removal

Panoramic Furniture Detection. A single panorama displayed in 2D image coordinates can be transformed into a 3D spherical representation [1,39], and this process can also be inverted. Building on this concept, our objective is to convert a panorama into a list of 2D images for scene segmentation. Subsequently, we aim to reconstruct the panorama where target furniture objects are highlighted. The selected region on the input panorama I_p is geometrically cropped and transformed into a 2D perspective image, within longitude angle (θ) and latitude angle (ϕ). $\theta \in (-\pi, +\pi)$ and $\phi \in (-0.5\pi, +0.5\pi)$. With the fixed field of view (FOV) and the image dimension of height (h) by width (w), we obtain 2D perspective image set I $= \{I_1, I_2, I_3, \ldots, I_i\}$, and the process of equirectangular-to-perspective can be expressed as mapping function S:

$$I_i = S(I_p; FOV, \theta, \phi, h, w) \qquad (3)$$

After scene segmentation for 2D perspective images, a set of processed images I$' = \{I'_1, I'_2, I'_3, \ldots, I'_i\}$ is stitched back to reconstruct a new panorama according to annotated θ and ϕ. The invertible mapping process enables image transformation between equirectangular and 2D perspective representations. As shown in Fig. 4, one single panorama is segmented into a set of 2D perspective images and segmented per color scheme in semantic segmentation classes [50]. Given a furnished panorama (Fig. 4(a)), a 3D layout is estimated with separated planer surfaces of the ceiling, wall, and floor textures. The rendering model generates an indoor mask to distinguish the floor and other interior surfaces, and the result highlights the furniture object placed on the floor (Fig. 4(b)).

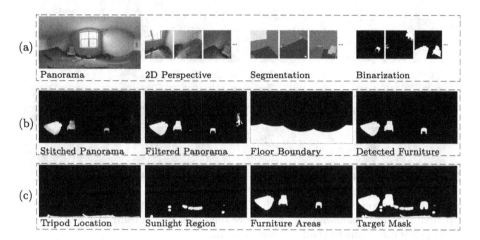

Fig. 4. Panoramic Scene Segmentation: (a) A single panorama is segmented into a set of 2D perspective images, and target furniture objects are detected. (b) The stitched panorama is processed to display furniture contours, and the rendered floor boundary is utilized to filter out solid contours that are not attached to the floor area. (c) Estimated tripod location [49], direct sunlight region, and the detected furniture areas are combined as the target mask.

Furniture Removal. For furnished panoramas, we first estimate the 3D room geometry [39] and utilize the indoor planar information in the panoramas to guide the inpainting process. As shown in Fig. 5, our method allows for image inpainting on the original furnished panoramas with surrounding context, while utilizing the floor boundary as a guiding reference to preserve clear indoor boundaries. One challenge in inpainting the floor texture is when the masked region is distant from nearby pixels, leading to blurring and noise. Unlike walls and ceilings, the floor texture often exhibits a strong pattern with various textures. Thus, we address this issue by treating the floor texture in the indoor scenes as a Near-Periodic Pattern (NPP). Compared to LaMa [36], which is trained on existing 2D image datasets, the NPP model developed by Chen et al. [3] learns the masked region from the provided image. This results in outputs that are optimized based on the content of the input image itself. As demonstrated in Fig. 5, our approach, combined with the LaMa [36] and NPP models [3], effectively recovers the scene context around the detected furniture area. The restored indoor textures, including ceiling, wall and floors, will be incorporated into the 3D rendering model.

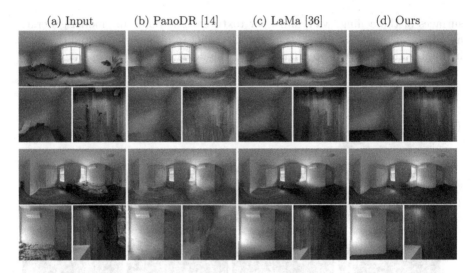

Fig. 5. Comparison of Image Inpainting Methods: The target mask (from Fig. 4 (c)) is paired with input panorama (a) to remove the target region using PanoDR [14] (b), LaMa [36] (c), and our method (d), respectively.

5   Automatic Floor Layout

The rendering model comprises 3D room geometry, allowing precise placement of multiple furniture objects with different orientations and positions. The floor layout follows a series of spatial parameters and rules for furniture arrangements. We segment the floor mesh from the panorama and the orientation of each object is determined based on whether it faces the window or indoor walls. For the translation distance, we normalize the distance between the object's dimension and the floor boundary to a range between 0 and 1. This normalization allows the object to be precisely positioned along the wall and window side. Different spatial parameters and orientation combinations can express alternative floor layouts. The rule-based method adapts to various layout rules by recognizing different floor boundaries and placing target objects accordingly within different indoor scenes.

Within the 3D coordinate system, the segmented floor mesh and furniture objects are positioned on the xy plane (Fig. 6). Each furniture object can be represented as a set of point clouds. The task of floor layout design is subject to the constraint of the floor boundary. Each furniture object rotates around the z axis by an angle θ to align with the target floor edge and translates itself to the designated position, denoted by the distances t_x and t_y. We transform the 3D point set $\mathbf{x_i}$ to its corresponding transformed point $\mathbf{x_i}'$ in the xy plane, by applying the rotation matrix and the translation matrix: $\mathbf{x_i}' = R_z(\theta)\mathbf{x_i} + t$, where $t = [t_x\ t_y\ 0]^T$.

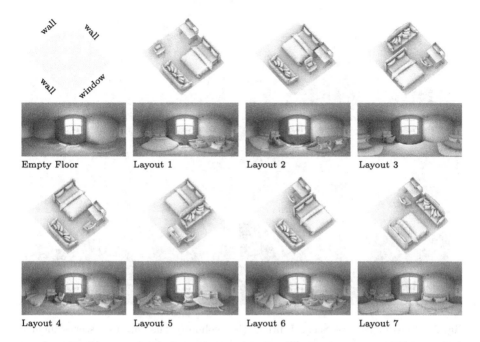

Fig. 6. Furniture Layout Alternatives: Given an empty floor mesh, multiple furniture objects are placed on the floor with predefined positions and orientations.

6   Indoor Virtual Staging

We tested our methodology in various real-world scenes and refurnished the existing scenes with virtual furniture objects (Fig. 7). The new virtual scenes are rendered under real-time outdoor illumination. Compared to previous scene relighting and object insertion approaches [12,27,49], our proposed rendering method integrates complete 3D scene geometry (including both room geometry and furniture objects), outdoor environment map, and material textures. This rendering setup allows the new furniture objects to be virtually rendered within the scene.

By using the real-time outdoor HDR image as the light source, we achieve realistic global illumination within the indoor space and reconstruct the indoor scenes with corresponding outdoor lighting conditions (Fig. 8). The proposed rendering approach not only accurately renders the virtual furniture objects but also reconstructs the inter-reflection between the scene and newly inserted objects. It is important to note that as the scene geometry is approximated into individual planar surfaces, certain indoor details such as curtains or window frames are simplified in the rendering model. Overall, our rendering pipeline effectively generates high-quality indoor panoramas while preserving the essential characteristics of the real-world scenes.

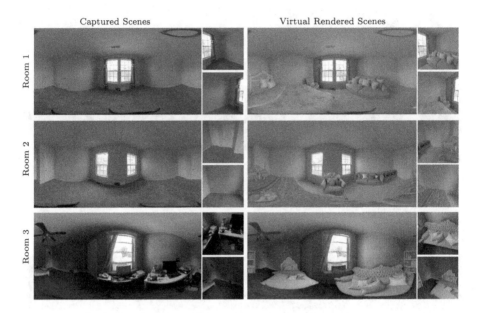

Fig. 7. Photo Gallery of Scene Editing: (left column) The captured scenes include empty and furnished rooms. (right column). The existing rooms are virtually rendered with new furniture objects [10].

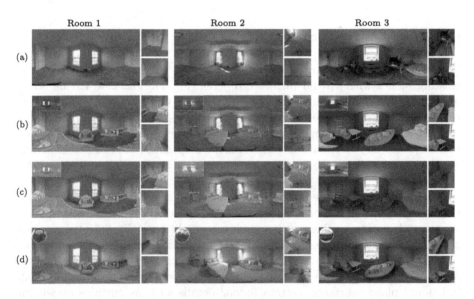

Fig. 8. Comparison of Different Rendering Methods: LDR Input panoramas (a) are used to generate HDR panorama (b) by Liu et al.'s method [29] and render furniture objects. Furniture objects are rendered by our calibrated indoor HDR panoramas (c) and scene rendered by our proposed method (d).

7 Conclusion and Limitation

In this paper, we presented a complete rendering framework that effectively transforms an existing panorama into a new furnished scene, providing high-quality virtual panoramas for 360° virtual staging. Additionally, we introduce a parametric modeling method for placing multiple furniture objects within the scene, which improves the flexibility of floor layout design. The global rendering framework offers a robust solution for realistic virtual home staging and contributes new indoor rendering techniques.

Some limitations exist in our study. The current implementation of the automatic floor layout does not account for the presence of doors in the scene. This means that the generated floor layouts may not fully account for the locations of the doors, potentially leading to impractical furniture arrangements. Furthermore, our research was limited to a fixed view position to match the captured panorama. To expand on these findings, future work will investigate varying view positions within the indoor space and explore human's visual perception under different illumination conditions.

Acknowledgement. This work was partially supported by a gift from Zillow Group, USA.

References

1. Araújo, A.B.: Drawing equirectangular VR panoramas with ruler, compass, and protractor. J. Sci. Technol. Arts **10**(1), 15–27 (2018)
2. Bolduc, C., Giroux, J., Hébert, M., Demers, C., Lalonde, J.F.: Beyond the pixel: a photometrically calibrated HDR dataset for luminance and color temperature prediction. arXiv preprint arXiv:2304.12372 (2023)
3. Chen, B., Zhi, T., Hebert, M., Narasimhan, S.G.: Learning continuous implicit representation for near-periodic patterns. In: Avidan, S., Brostow, G., Cissé, M., Farinella, G.M., Hassner, T. (eds.) ECCV 2022. LNCS, vol. 13675, pp. 529–546. Springer, Cham (2022). https://doi.org/10.1007/978-3-031-19784-0_31
4. Cheng, H.T., Chao, C.H., Dong, J.D., Wen, H.K., Liu, T.L., Sun, M.: Cube padding for weakly-supervised saliency prediction in 360 videos. In: Proceedings of the IEEE Conference on Computer Vision and Pattern Recognition, pp. 1420–1429 (2018)
5. Coughlan, J.M., Yuille, A.L.: Manhattan world: compass direction from a single image by Bayesian inference. In: Proceedings of the Seventh IEEE International Conference on Computer Vision, vol. 2, pp. 941–947. IEEE (1999)
6. Cruz, S., Hutchcroft, W., Li, Y., Khosravan, N., Boyadzhiev, I., Kang, S.B.: Zillow indoor dataset: annotated floor plans with 360deg panoramas and 3D room layouts. In: Proceedings of the IEEE/CVF Conference on Computer Vision and Pattern Recognition, pp. 2133–2143 (2021)
7. Debevec, P.: Image-based lighting. In: ACM SIGGRAPH 2006 Courses, pp. 4–es (2006)
8. Debevec, P.: Rendering synthetic objects into real scenes: bridging traditional and image-based graphics with global illumination and high dynamic range photography. In: SIGGRAPH 2008 Classes, pp. 1–10. ACM (2008)

9. Debevec, P.E., Malik, J.: Recovering high dynamic range radiance maps from photographs. In: SIGGRAPH 2008 classes, pp. 1–10. ACM (2008)

10. Fu, H., et al.: 3D-future: 3D furniture shape with texture. Int. J. Comput. Vis. **129**, 3313–3337 (2021)

11. Gardner, M.A., Hold-Geoffroy, Y., Sunkavalli, K., Gagné, C., Lalonde, J.F.: Deep parametric indoor lighting estimation. In: Proceedings of the IEEE/CVF International Conference on Computer Vision, pp. 7175–7183 (2019)

12. Gardner, M.A., et al.: Learning to predict indoor illumination from a single image. arXiv preprint arXiv:1704.00090 (2017)

13. Garon, M., Sunkavalli, K., Hadap, S., Carr, N., Lalonde, J.F.: Fast spatially-varying indoor lighting estimation. In: Proceedings of the IEEE/CVF Conference on Computer Vision and Pattern Recognition, pp. 6908–6917 (2019)

14. Gkitsas, V., Sterzentsenko, V., Zioulis, N., Albanis, G., Zarpalas, D.: PanoDR: spherical panorama diminished reality for indoor scenes. In: Proceedings of the IEEE/CVF Conference on Computer Vision and Pattern Recognition, pp. 3716–3726 (2021)

15. Gkitsas, V., Zioulis, N., Alvarez, F., Zarpalas, D., Daras, P.: Deep lighting environment map estimation from spherical panoramas. In: Proceedings of the IEEE/CVF Conference on Computer Vision and Pattern Recognition Workshops, pp. 640–641 (2020)

16. Gkitsas, V., Zioulis, N., Sterzentsenko, V., Doumanoglou, A., Zarpalas, D.: Towards full-to-empty room generation with structure-aware feature encoding and soft semantic region-adaptive normalization. arXiv preprint arXiv:2112.05396 (2021)

17. Guerrero-Viu, J., Fernandez-Labrador, C., Demonceaux, C., Guerrero, J.J.: What's in my room? object recognition on indoor panoramic images. In: 2020 IEEE International Conference on Robotics and Automation (ICRA), pp. 567–573. IEEE (2020)

18. Huang, J.B., Kang, S.B., Ahuja, N., Kopf, J.: Image completion using planar structure guidance. ACM Trans. Graph. (TOG) **33**(4), 1–10 (2014)

19. Huang, S., Qi, S., Zhu, Y., Xiao, Y., Xu, Y., Zhu, S.C.: Holistic 3D scene parsing and reconstruction from a single RGB image. In: Proceedings of the European Conference on Computer Vision (ECCV), pp. 187–203 (2018)

20. Inanici, M.: Evalution of high dynamic range image-based sky models in lighting simulation. Leukos **7**(2), 69–84 (2010)

21. Inanici, M.N.: Evaluation of high dynamic range photography as a luminance data acquisition system. Lighting Res. Technol. **38**(2), 123–134 (2006)

22. Izadinia, H., Shan, Q., Seitz, S.M.: IM2CAD. In: Proceedings of the IEEE Conference on Computer Vision and Pattern Recognition, pp. 5134–5143 (2017)

23. Karsch, K., Hedau, V., Forsyth, D., Hoiem, D.: Rendering synthetic objects into legacy photographs. ACM Trans. Graph. (TOG) **30**(6), 1–12 (2011)

24. Kawai, N., Sato, T., Yokoya, N.: Diminished reality based on image inpainting considering background geometry. IEEE Trans. Visual Comput. Graphics **22**(3), 1236–1247 (2015)

25. Kulshreshtha, P., Lianos, N., Pugh, B., Jiddi, S.: Layout aware inpainting for automated furniture removal in indoor scenes. In: 2022 IEEE International Symposium on Mixed and Augmented Reality Adjunct (ISMAR-Adjunct), pp. 839–844. IEEE (2022)

26. LeGendre, C., et al.: DeepLight: learning illumination for unconstrained mobile mixed reality. In: Proceedings of the IEEE/CVF Conference on Computer Vision and Pattern Recognition, pp. 5918–5928 (2019)

27. Li, Z., Shafiei, M., Ramamoorthi, R., Sunkavalli, K., Chandraker, M.: Inverse rendering for complex indoor scenes: shape, spatially-varying lighting and SVBRDF from a single image. In: Proceedings of the IEEE/CVF Conference on Computer Vision and Pattern Recognition, pp. 2475–2484 (2020)
28. Li, Z., et al.: Physically-based editing of indoor scene lighting from a single image. In: Avidan, S., Brostow, G., Cissé, M., Farinella, G.M., Hassner, T. (eds.) ECCV 2022. LNCS, vol. 13666, pp. 555–572. Springer, Cham (2022). https://doi.org/10.1007/978-3-031-20068-7_32
29. Liu, Y.L., et al.: Single-image HDR reconstruction by learning to reverse the camera pipeline. In: Proceedings of the IEEE/CVF Conference on Computer Vision and Pattern Recognition, pp. 1651–1660 (2020)
30. Mitsunaga, T., Nayar, S.K.: Radiometric self calibration. In: Proceedings. 1999 IEEE Computer Society Conference on Computer Vision and Pattern Recognition (Cat. No PR00149), vol. 1, pp. 374–380. IEEE (1999)
31. Moeck, M.: Accuracy of luminance maps obtained from high dynamic range images. Leukos 4(2), 99–112 (2007)
32. Nie, Y., Han, X., Guo, S., Zheng, Y., Chang, J., Zhang, J.J.: Total3DUnderstanding: joint layout, object pose and mesh reconstruction for indoor scenes from a single image. In: Proceedings of the IEEE/CVF Conference on Computer Vision and Pattern Recognition, pp. 55–64 (2020)
33. Reinhard, E., Heidrich, W., Debevec, P., Pattanaik, S., Ward, G., Myszkowski, K.: High Dynamic Range Imaging: Acquisition, Display, and Image-based Lighting. Morgan Kaufmann, Burlington (2010)
34. Srinivasan, P.P., Mildenhall, B., Tancik, M., Barron, J.T., Tucker, R., Snavely, N.: Lighthouse: predicting lighting volumes for spatially-coherent illumination. In: Proceedings of the IEEE/CVF Conference on Computer Vision and Pattern Recognition, pp. 8080–8089 (2020)
35. Stumpfel, J., Jones, A., Wenger, A., Tchou, C., Hawkins, T., Debevec, P.: Direct HDR capture of the sun and sky. In: SIGGRAPH 2006 Courses, pp. 5-es. ACM (2006)
36. Suvorov, R., et al.: Resolution-robust large mask inpainting with Fourier convolutions. In: Proceedings of the IEEE/CVF Winter Conference on Applications of Computer Vision, pp. 2149–2159 (2022)
37. Wang, F.-E., et al.: Self-supervised learning of depth and camera motion from 360° videos. In: Jawahar, C.V., Li, H., Mori, G., Schindler, K. (eds.) ACCV 2018. LNCS, vol. 11365, pp. 53–68. Springer, Cham (2019). https://doi.org/10.1007/978-3-030-20873-8_4
38. Wang, F.E., Yeh, Y.H., Sun, M., Chiu, W.C., Tsai, Y.H.: BiFuse: monocular 360 depth estimation via bi-projection fusion. In: The IEEE/CVF Conference on Computer Vision and Pattern Recognition (CVPR) (2020)
39. Wang, F.E., Yeh, Y.H., Sun, M., Chiu, W.C., Tsai, Y.H.: LED2-Net: monocular 360° layout estimation via differentiable depth rendering. In: Proceedings of the IEEE/CVF Conference on Computer Vision and Pattern Recognition, pp. 12956–12965 (2021)
40. Xiao, J., Ehinger, K.A., Oliva, A., Torralba, A.: Recognizing scene viewpoint using panoramic place representation. In: 2012 IEEE Conference on Computer Vision and Pattern Recognition, pp. 2695–2702. IEEE (2012)
41. Yang, B., Jiang, T., Wu, W., Zhou, Y., Dai, L.: Automated semantics and topology representation of residential-building space using floor-plan raster maps. IEEE J. Sel. Top. Appl. Earth Observations Remote Sens. 15, 7809–7825 (2022)

42. Yang, S.T., Wang, F.E., Peng, C.H., Wonka, P., Sun, M., Chu, H.K.: DuLa-Net: a dual-projection network for estimating room layouts from a single RGB panorama. In: Proceedings of the IEEE/CVF Conference on Computer Vision and Pattern Recognition, pp. 3363–3372 (2019)

43. Yeh, Y.Y., et al.: PhotoScene: photorealistic material and lighting transfer for indoor scenes. In: Proceedings of the IEEE/CVF Conference on Computer Vision and Pattern Recognition, pp. 18562–18571 (2022)

44. Zeng, Z., Li, X., Yu, Y.K., Fu, C.W.: Deep floor plan recognition using a multi-task network with room-boundary-guided attention. In: Proceedings of the IEEE/CVF International Conference on Computer Vision, pp. 9096–9104 (2019)

45. Zhang, C., Liwicki, S., Smith, W., Cipolla, R.: Orientation-aware semantic segmentation on icosahedron spheres. In: Proceedings of the IEEE/CVF International Conference on Computer Vision, pp. 3533–3541 (2019)

46. Zhang, E., Cohen, M.F., Curless, B.: Emptying, refurnishing, and relighting indoor spaces. ACM Trans. Graph. (TOG) **35**(6), 1–14 (2016)

47. Zhang, E., Martin-Brualla, R., Kontkanen, J., Curless, B.L.: No shadow left behind: removing objects and their shadows using approximate lighting and geometry. In: Proceedings of the IEEE/CVF Conference on Computer Vision and Pattern Recognition, pp. 16397–16406 (2021)

48. Zhang, Y., Song, S., Tan, P., Xiao, J.: PanoContext: a whole-room 3D context model for panoramic scene understanding. In: Fleet, D., Pajdla, T., Schiele, B., Tuytelaars, T. (eds.) ECCV 2014. LNCS, vol. 8694, pp. 668–686. Springer, Cham (2014). https://doi.org/10.1007/978-3-319-10599-4_43

49. Zhi, T., Chen, B., Boyadzhiev, I., Kang, S.B., Hebert, M., Narasimhan, S.G.: Semantically supervised appearance decomposition for virtual staging from a single panorama. ACM Transa. Graph. (TOG) **41**(4), 1–15 (2022)

50. Zhou, B., et al.: Semantic understanding of scenes through the ADE20K dataset. Int. J. Comput. Vis. **127**, 302–321 (2018)

51. Zou, C., Colburn, A., Shan, Q., Hoiem, D.: LayoutNet: reconstructing the 3D room layout from a single RGB image. In: Proceedings of the IEEE Conference on Computer Vision and Pattern Recognition, pp. 2051–2059 (2018)

SwarmCurves: Evolutionary Curve Reconstruction

Alexander Komar[(⊠)] and Ursula Augsdörfer

Institute of Computer Graphics and Knowledge Visualisation,
Graz University of Technology, Graz, Austria
a.komar@cgv.tugraz.at

Abstract. The problem of recovering the shape of a curve given partial information about it is a fundamental problem in many applications in visual computing. Which types of curves are fitted to a given input data depends on the application and varies from piece-wise linear approximation to parametric splines. The choice of approximation method depends on the context of the problem, the nature of the data, and the desired level of accuracy and complexity.

In this paper we introduce SWARMCURVES, a curve reconstruction approach based on particle swarm optimization. For given input data SWARMCURVES offers a range of solutions, from linear polygons to rational B-Splines with various degrees of freedom. The algorithm works on dense, sparse or noisy, 2D or 3D input data. We demonstrate the performance of SWARMCURVES, on a number of examples.

Keywords: Curve Reconstruction · Evolutionary Optimization · B-Splines

1 Introduction

To recover the shape of a curve from data points is a challenging problem that appears frequently in a wide range of applications such as computer-aided design, virtual reality and computer graphics, data visualization and medical imaging. Depending on the available information about the curve and the application, qualitatively different approaches can be formulated in order to solve this problem.

Curve fitting aims to find a curve which best represents a given set of possibly noisy or sparse data points. In most applications of computer graphics and geometric modelling it refers to fitting low degree curves to input data. Curve fitting is also used in data analysis, to identify trends and patterns in data [23]. It is closely related to *curve approximation*, which aims to reduce the amount of data required to represent a curve, thereby reducing storage and processing requirements. It involves fitting a mathematical function to an input curve or data set. The goal of *curve reconstruction* is to derive a compact representation for (possibly partial) data at high accuracy, while ensuring that the resulting

© The Author(s), under exclusive license to Springer Nature Switzerland AG 2023
G. Bebis et al. (Eds.): ISVC 2023, LNCS 14361, pp. 343–354, 2023.
https://doi.org/10.1007/978-3-031-47969-4_27

curve is smooth and has no sharp corners or discontinuities. It aims at deriving a smooth and visually appealing curve which is highly relevant in fields such as geometric modelling and computer-aided design/manufacturing (CAD/CAM). In this context B-Splines are the widely preferred approximating functions due to their powerful mathematical properties and their wide support by CAD/CAM systems. Curve reconstruction has become a fundamental tool in reverse engineering, where dense data acquired from physical objects is converted to a digital model of such objects [29].

A combined approach for fitting, approximating and reconstructing arbitrary degree curves from ordered data is to our knowledge still an open problem.

In this paper we introduce SWARMCURVES, a curve reconstruction approach based on particle swarm optimisation, which is general and makes no assumption other than the initial input be a set of ordered data points, 2D or 3D. The output are a set of open or closed curves of arbitrary degree. SWARMCURVES may be applied in reverse engineering to reconstruct curves from very dense data typically obtained from scanner devices. However, SWARMCURVES can also handle sparse and noisy data, which may be collected through other means, for example in context of visual analytics, where curve fitting is used to identify trends. SWARMCURVES, does not require any additional pre- or post-processing and offers various types of fitting solutions: from simple polygons to rational B-Splines with various degrees of freedoms in form of control points. SWARM-CURVES performs well regardless of whether the data comes from curves which are polynomial, rational or belong to any other family of functions and provides solutions even for sparse input data. In the reported examples, the mean error from the output curve to the input data points is usually below 0.35% of the bounding box diagonal.

2   Related Work

Reconstructing smooth curves from point data has been a research topic for decades and numerous approach have been put forward.

2.1   Curve Reconstruction

Curve fitting, approximation and reconstruction are closely related and solve common problems in many fields of research [1,13,17,18].

To reconstruct smooth curves a common representation are NURBS [8] which are given by $C(t) = \sum_{j=1}^{n} \frac{N_{j,d}(t)\omega_j P_j}{N_{j,d}(t)\omega_j}$, where N_j are the B-Spline functions of degree d defined on a knot vector. The resulting B-Spline curve is smooth and approximates its n control points P_j. Although knots can be distributed non-uniformly over the parametric domain, they are often uniform in a modelling context except for multiplicities where interpolation of the control polygon is required.

Reconstructing B-Splines from input data was introduced by de Boor and Rice [5], first for a fixed knot vector and later also for variable knot vectors [4].

The researchers proposed a least squares approximation method for approximating the control points for the spline curves and their knot vectors.

Park [25] presented an error-bound method for B-Spline curve approximation to a given planar input curve. He focused both on accuracy control and data reduction to derive a B-Spline curve with fewer control points while keeping the distance between the given curve and the B-Spline curve smaller than a specified tolerance. The fitting was achieved by first approximating a polygon to the data and then fitting a B-Spline curve to the polygon.

Park and Lee [24] fitted B-Spline curves to a set of ordered points by selecting points called dominant points to achieve a better curve approximation. They adaptively refined a B-Spline curve by selecting fewer dominant points at flat regions but more at complex regions. For the same number of control points, their approach could generate a B-Spline curve with less deviation than previous approaches.

In order to reconstruct cubic B-Spline curves Ebrahimi and Loghmani [6] used the Broyden-Fletcher-Goldfarb-Shanno algorithm [3] to improve the non-linear least squares optimization problem. As initialization for their optimization method, they use a uniformly spaced knot vector and then solve a linear system of equations for the initial control point positions. They optimised the fit by inserting additional control points until the approximation error does not decrease significantly in one iteration.

Recent approaches employ Neural Networks for curve reconstruction [15,19, 20,30,32]. Different input modalities have been used for neural networks, e.g. Point clouds [15,30], depth images [20] and 2D images [32].

In the approach presented in this paper we assume the knot vector fixed and focus on optimising the number of control points, their positions P_j and their corresponding weights ω_j. While for closed curves the knot vector is set to be uniform, open curves are reconstructed using a clamped knot vector, so that first and last control points are interpolated. We evaluate our algorithm by comparing it to a number of examples typically used to assess the quality of the reconstruction.

2.2 Evolutionary Algorithms for Curve and Surface Fitting

Evolutionary optimization has been used in many applications [2,7,11,14,21,28, 31,33], including curve fitting [9,13,27]. Various types of evolutionary optimisation methods exist.

Sun, Liu and Ge [28] are fitting B-Spline curves to a sampled pointset of the outline of a ship using an adapted Hungry Predation Optimization Algorithm. Galvez et al. [10] used a Genetic Algorithm for surface and curve reconstruction. They encoded the parameter values in a genome and used the mean squared error as an error measure for a found solution. They extended their approach and used particle swarm optimisation to fit Bézier surfaces to 3D point clouds [9].

Particle Swarm Optimization (PSO) was first introduced by Kennedy and Eberhart [16] in 1995. It uses an evolutionary approach to optimization in order to eliminate the need for a derivative of the error function. With PSO a swarm

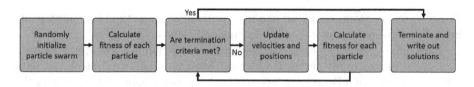

Fig. 1. Particle Swarm Optimization Pipeline

of particles is initially uniformly distributed over the n-dimensional space of possible solutions. Additionally every particle has a velocity with which it travels through this space. Every member of the swarm knows the best global solution and the best solution reached by its local neighbors. Using this information, every particle updates its position and its velocity. This is repeated until a stopping criterion is met or a limit on the number of iterations is reached. For a comprehensive overview on applications and current theory of PSO we refer the reader to two recent survey papers in this field given by Houssein et al. [12] and Shami et al. [26].

An application of PSO to the problem of curve fitting was proposed by Song et al. [27]. The authors adapted the classical PSO algorithm in order to better escape local minima. With this improved algorithm the researchers found paths through partially obstructed workspaces using Bézier curves.

Iglesias et al. [13] introduced a method for B-Spline curve reconstruction using a multilayer embedded bat algorithm (ME-BAT). This algorithm is modelled after the behaviour and communication of bats and, similar to PSO tries to find a globally optimal solution to a given problem. Contrary to our approach the researchers fixed the number of control points before executing the algorithm and do not state a method on how to find the optimal number of control points.

In this paper we propose SWARMCURVES, a novel approached to fit polygons, B-Splines, or rational B-Splines to an ordered set of points. SWARMCURVES is based on PSO, which is better able to solve floating point problems, compared to genetic algorithms for example. SWARMCURVES is able to reconstruct parametric curves of arbitrary degree and various number of control points. We can handle noisy and sparse data.

3   Methodology

We employ the PSO to find the control points of a B-Spline curve which best fits the input data. A single particle of the swarm consists of a list of ordered control point positions in 3D, $P_j = (x_j, y_j, z_j)$. Each position is associated with a velocity, which determines the distance and direction this control point will move in the next iteration. A key element of any evolutionary approach is the fitness of a solution. In context of curve reconstruction the fitness is related to the distance between a given set of data points and the reconstructing B-Spline curve C, computed with the set of control points derived by a single particle. If the data points are sampled from a curve T, then the distance between the target curve

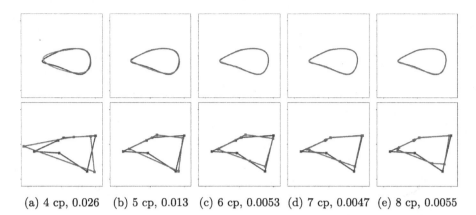

(a) 4 cp, 0.026   (b) 5 cp, 0.013   (c) 6 cp, 0.0053   (d) 7 cp, 0.0047   (e) 8 cp, 0.0055

Fig. 2. An example of a single output provided by SWARMCURVES. Top: Input data points (blue) are shown together with the reconstructed curve colored in the Euclidean distance, where red indicates a close approximation. Below: The reconstructed control polygon (red) is shown together with the control polygon of the original curve (blue). From left to right the number of control points of the solution of the curve reconstruction is increasing, from 4 to 8 control points. The captions also list the error of the solution. (Color figure online)

T that we want to reconstruct, and the B-Spline curve C, defined by a particle's set of control points, P_j, is defined by the error measure $err(c) = d_{avg}(C,T)$. where $d_{avg}()$ is the average Euclidean distance between the sampled curve C to the sampled target curve T.

We restrict the reconstruction in our approach to a uniform knot distribution for closed curves and place knot multiplicities at end points of open curves in order to interpolate the first and last control point positions of the reconstructed B-Splines curve.

A visualization of the PSO Pipeline can be seen in Fig. 1. The swarm is initialized randomly with the number of particles specified by the user. Each particle is initialized with a $3n$-dimensional random position inside a bounding box of normalized data points $[-1, 1]$. Then the local (one particle) and global (over the whole swarm) best position and error are determined. The position of each particle is denoted q_{local}, the optimal position over the whole swarm as q_{global}. Then the iteration loop starts. With each iteration the velocity of each particle is updated according to $v_{i+1} = v_i\psi + (q_{local} - q_i)r_q\phi_q + (q_{global} - q_i)r_g\phi_g$ where v_i is the current velocity, ψ is the inertia weight, q_{local} is the best found solution by the particle, q_i is the current position of the particle, r_q is a random number in the interval $[0, 1]$ and ϕ_q is the weight of influence for the local best position. Further, q_{global} is the globally best position of the swarm, r_g is another random number in the interval $[0, 1]$ and ϕ_g is the weight of influence for the global best position. The position is updated according to $q_{i+1} = q_i + v_{i+1}$. Finally, the error of each particle is updated and the local and global best position

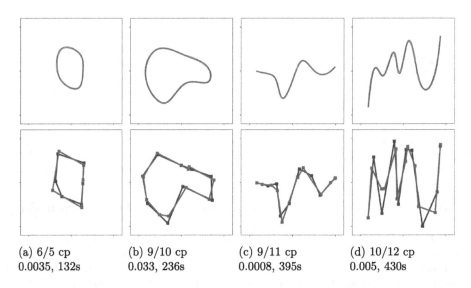

(a) 6/5 cp   (b) 9/10 cp   (c) 9/11 cp   (d) 10/12 cp
0.0035, 132s   0.033, 236s   0.0008, 395s   0.005, 430s

Fig. 3. Reconstruction of randomly generated closed and open B-Spline curves of degree 3. The top row is the target data points in blue and the reconstructed B-Spline curve colored according to the Euclidean distance. Bottom row is the target control polygon in blue and the output control polygon in red. Each caption lists the number of control points of the target B-Spline curve/the number of control points for the reconstructed B-Spline curve/the mean error/the execution time. (Color figure online)

are re-evaluated. The iteration terminates if either the approximation error lies below a predefined threshold or a predefined limit of iteration is reached.

With the start of the algorithm multiple swarms of particles are launched independently, each swarm with a fixed number of control points. The user can choose either the most accurate reconstruction or choose the reconstruction which provides the desired number of control points. Additionally, SWARM-CURVES can provide a number of different degree B-Splines simultaneously. Which degree of smoothness is required for the reconstruction will depend on the context of the application.

4   Results

In this section we present the results of the SWARMCURVES reconstruction algorithm. Although in the previous section the algorithm was described for a setting in 3D, results are shown for 2D for easy visibility. We show results using different benchmarks from related work that demonstrate different abilities of our algorithm. All curves were normalized to fit inside the range of $[-1, 1]$. Multiple swarms of particles are launched for each example and each swarm has an iteration limit (2000). Each swarm provides a range of solutions. The final choice is either made by the system or by the user based on preferences. Out of the range of solutions, the user may be interested in e.g. the sparsest control polygon or the closest approximation.

4.1 Reconstructing B-Splines from Point Data Sampled from Arbitrary B-Spline Curves

Data sampled of closed and open B-Splines and rational B-Splines and non-rational curves may be reconstructed using SWARMCURVES. While for closed curves the knot vector is set to be uniform, open curves are reconstructed using a clamped knot vector, so that the first and last control points are interpolated. All optimizations were run for 2000 iterations.

An example output of five SWARMCURVES can be seen in Fig. 2. The result shows the reconstruction of a B-Spline from data points sampled from a cubic B-Spline originally derived using six control points. The best approximation is given by SWARMCURVES solution shown in Fig. 2(d).

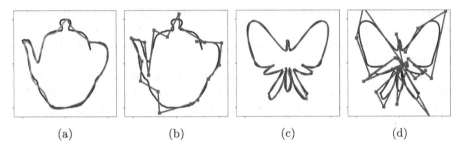

(a)   (b)   (c)   (d)

Fig. 4. Results from reconstructing a benchmark curve (blue) [22] (a) and [13] (c), with its corresponding control polygon (red) in (b) and (d). (Color figure online)

As is clear from the example shown in Fig. 2, the closest approximating SWARMCURVES do not necessarily have the same number of control points as the target curve. This is also evident in Fig. 3, where we show further examples of SWARMCURVES reconstructions of arbitrary closed and open B-Spline curves (top) and their corresponding control polygons. Each reconstruction as been selected for best accuracy from a selection of seven solutions using different number of control points. Calculating a large number of SWARMCURVES does not slow down the reconstructions significantly, since all solutions are derived in parallel.

Even more complex examples are shown in Fig. 4. Figure 4(a) shows the SWARMCURVES fitting of cubic B-Spline to a data point example taken from a benchmark dataset proposed by Ohrhallinger et al. [22]. Although the overall shape is approximated well, small details like the handle on the top lacks almost entirely. This means that it is difficult for the algorithm to reconstruct rather small features. Figure 4(b) shows a SWARMCURVES fitting to the data sampled

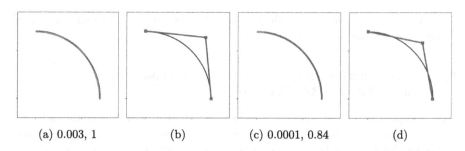

(a) 0.003, 1   (b)   (c) 0.0001, 0.84   (d)

Fig. 5. Approximated circle segment. (a) and (c) show the curve segment (target curve, blue) together with the SWARMCURVES coloured wrt to Euclidean distance. (c) and (d) are the target curve (blue) and control polygon of a fitted rational B-Spline. Captions state the error of the reconstruction and the weight of the center vertex. (Color figure online)

from the closed NURBS curve "Butterfly" presented as a benchmark by Iglesias et al. [13]. While the butterfly has been reconstructed closely, the control polygon provided by SWARMCURVES is not useful for further manipulation of its shape by a designer. Both examples in Fig. 4 clearly show the limitations of SWARMCURVES.

SWARMCURVES can also reconstruct conic sections as can be seen in Fig. 5, where a curve segment has been approximated with a rational B-Spline. The weights, ω_j, of the rational B-Spline are optimised to fit a circle segment.

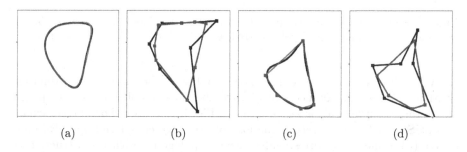

(a)   (b)   (c)   (d)

Fig. 6. (a) A degree five B-Spline curve in blue is reconstructed by a cubic B-Spline curve in red. (b) The control polygon of the target curve (blue) is shown together with the control polygon of the reconstruction. (c) A cubic B-Spline curve in blue is approximated by a polygon in red. (d) The polygon approximation is compared to the control polygon of the target curve. (Color figure online)

SWARMCURVES also offer the possibility to choose the degree of the reconstruct curve from a set of solutions. Figure 6(a) shows the reconstruction of a cubic B-Spline from points sampled from a degree 5 B-Spline. Figure 6(b) shows

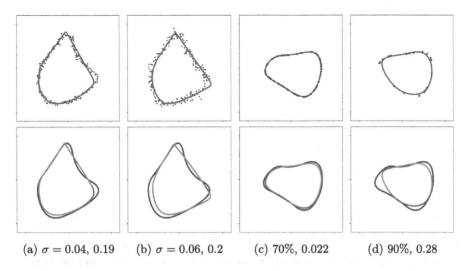

(a) $\sigma = 0.04, 0.19$ (b) $\sigma = 0.06, 0.2$ (c) 70%, 0.022   (d) 90%, 0.28

Fig. 7. Examples show the ability of our algorithm to fit curves (red) to noisy (a),(b) and sparse data (c),(d). Standard deviation (σ) and reduction (in percentage) are stated together with the mean error to the original curve (blue) without noise from which the samples are taken. (Color figure online)

the result of fitting a polygon (linear B-Spline) to data sampled from a cubic B-Spline.

4.2 Reconstructing B-Splines from Noisy or Sparse Data Points Sampled from B-Splines

The robustness against noisy and sparse data is demonstrated in the Fig. 7. The noisy data was generated by sampling from a B-Spline curve and adding a Gaussian noise offset to the curve data in the normal direction. The Gaussian distribution had a mean $\mu = 0$ and standard deviation $\sigma \in \{0.04, 0.06\}$. The cubic B-Spline curve from which the noisy data was created was reconstructed reliably, although more control points where required for a good approximation.

The sparse data was created by randomly removing points from a densely sampled curve until the desired reduction percentage is reached. As can be seen in Fig. 7(c)-(d), the original cubic B-Spline curve was reconstructed even for sparse data samples which was non-uniformly distributed along the original curve.

4.3 Reconstructing B-Splines from Point Data Sampled from Non-parametric Curves

Sun, Liu and Ge [28] proposed a set of analytic curves for testing their B-Spline fitting algorithm. The formulas can be seen in Eqs. 1 through 5, all curves were normalized in the range of $[-1,1]$. The results of fitting B-Splines to those curves using SWARMCURVES can be seen in Fig. 8. The error distribution leads to the

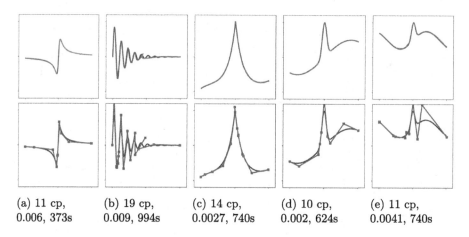

(a) 11 cp,   (b) 19 cp,   (c) 14 cp,   (d) 10 cp,   (e) 11 cp,
0.006, 373s   0.009, 994s   0.0027, 740s   0.002, 624s   0.0041, 740s

Fig. 8. The fitted curves to the benchmark curves from [28]. Top: the fitted curves colored according to the Euclidean distance and the input point cloud in blue. Bottom the fitted control polygon (red) and the input point cloud (blue). The captions list the number of control points used in the fitting, the mean error of the result and the execution time. All fitted curves are B-Splines. (Color figure online)

conclusion that the algorithm has more difficulty fitting a curve to segments with higher curvature.

$$f_1(2x) = \frac{10x}{(1 + 100x^2)} \tag{1}$$

$$f_2(2(x+1)\pi) = e^{-0.5x} \sin(5x) \tag{2}$$

$$f_3\left(\frac{x+1}{2}\right) = \frac{100}{55e^{|10x-5|}} + \frac{(10x-5)^5}{27500} - 0.8 \tag{3}$$

$$f_4(2x) = 0.5\sin(x) + e^{-30x^2} \tag{4}$$

$$f_5(2x) = 0.5\sin(2x) + e^{-36x^2} + 1 \tag{5}$$

5   Conclusion and Future Work

We presented SWARMCURVES, an algorithm based on Particle Swarm Optimization that is able to reconstruct a range of B-Spline curves, from linear polygons to rational B-Splines with various degrees of freedom, from ordered point sets. The user may select a B-Spline curve from a list of different types and numbers of control points and an error value of the reconstruction. We evaluated the reconstruction capabilities by comparing the results to common benchmarks. The algorithm works on dense, sparse or noisy, 2D or 3D input data. We demonstrate the performance of SWARMCURVES, on a number of examples.

Table 1. A table showing the number of control points (cp) and error between the original curve and the B-Spline reconstruction. Note, that for Equation (4) and (5) SWARMCURVES is able to derive a more accurate reconstruction despite using considerable fewer control points as used by Sun et al. [28].

	Eq	(1)	(2)	(3)	(4)	(5)
Sun et al	cp	57	81	44	50	41
	err	$6.32 \cdot 10^{-7}$	$2.31 \cdot 10^{-6}$	$7.5 \cdot 10^{-5}$	$1,38 \cdot 10^{-4}$	$4.18 \cdot 10^{-4}$
SWARMCURVES	cp	11	19	14	10	11
	err	$5.2 \cdot 10^{-3}$	$4.5 \cdot 10^{-4}$	$9.7 \cdot 10^{-2}$	$1.98 \cdot 10^{-5}$	$1.3 \cdot 10^{-4}$

For future work SWARMCURVES may be extended to support the optimisation of non-uniform knot vectors during the reconstruction. This means that the algorithm would be able to reconstruct even more features and sharper features. Further, to reduce the time of reconstruction future version of SWARM-CURVES will be implement partially on the GPU.

References

1. Chen, L., Ghosh, S.K.: Uncertainty quantification and estimation of closed curves based on noisy data. Comput. Stat. **36**, 2161–2176 (2021)
2. Chiong, R., Weise, T., Michalewicz, Z.: Variants of Evolutionary Algorithms for Real-World Applications. Springer, Heidelberg (2011). https://doi.org/10.1007/978-3-642-23424-8
3. Cipolla, S., Di Fiore, C., Tudisco, F., Zellini, P.: Adaptive matrix algebras in unconstrained minimization. Linear Algebra Appl. **471**, 544–568 (2015)
4. De Boor, C., Rice, J.R.: Least squares cubic spline approximation i-fixed knots. International Mathematical and Statistical Libraries (1968)
5. De Boor, C., Rice, J.R.: Least squares cubic spline approximation, ii-variable knots. International Mathematical and Statistical Libraries (1968)
6. Ebrahimi, A., Loghmani, G.B.: B-spline curve fitting by diagonal approximation BFGS methods. Iran. J. Sci. Technol. Trans. A Sci. **43**, 947–958 (2019)
7. Faramarzi, A., Heidarinejad, M., Mirjalili, S., Gandomi, A.H.: Marine predators algorithm: a nature-inspired metaheuristic. Expert Syst. Appl. **152**, 113377 (2021)
8. Farin, G.: Curves and Surfaces for CAGD. Morgan Kaufmann, San Fransisco (2002)
9. Gálvez, A., Cobo, A., Puig-Pey, J., Iglesias, A.: Particle swarm optimization for Bézier surface reconstruction. In: Bubak, M., van Albada, G.D., Dongarra, J., Sloot, P.M.A. (eds.) ICCS 2008. LNCS, vol. 5102, pp. 116–125. Springer, Heidelberg (2008). https://doi.org/10.1007/978-3-540-69387-1_13
10. Gálvez, A., Iglesias, A., Cobo, A., Puig-Pey, J., Espinola, J.: Bézier curve and surface fitting of 3D point clouds through genetic algorithms, functional networks and least-squares approximation. In: Gervasi, O., Gavrilova, M.L. (eds.) ICCSA 2007. LNCS, vol. 4706, pp. 680–693. Springer, Heidelberg (2007). https://doi.org/10.1007/978-3-540-74477-1_62
11. Gandomi, A.H., Alavi, A.H.: Krill herd: a new bio-inspired optimization algorithm. Commun. Nonlinear Sci. Numer. Simul. **17**(12), 4831–4845 (2012)

12. Houssein, E.H., Gad, A.G., Hussain, K., Suganthan, P.N.: Major advances in particle swarm optimization: theory, analysis, and application. Swarm Evol. Comput. **63**, 100868 (2021)

13. Iglesias, A., Gálvez, A., Collantes, M.: Multilayer embedded bat algorithm for B-spline curve reconstruction. Integr. Comput.-Aided Eng. **24**(4), 385–399 (2017)

14. Kaveh, A., Dadras Eslamlou, A.: Water strider algorithm: a new metaheuristic and applications. Structures **25**, 520–541 (2020)

15. Kavita, K., Navin, R., Madan, A.S.: Piecewise feature extraction and artificial neural networks: an approach towards curve reconstruction. Indian J. Sci. Technol. **9**(28), 121–134 (2016)

16. Kennedy, J., Eberhart, R.: Particle swarm optimization. In: Proceedings of ICNN'95-International Conference on Neural Networks, vol. 4, pp. 1942–1948. IEEE (1995)

17. Lee, I.K.: Curve reconstruction from unorganized points. Comput. Aided Geom. Des. **17**(2), 161–177 (2000)

18. Lin, H., Chen, W., Wang, G.: Curve reconstruction based on an interval B-spline curve. Vis. Comput. **21**, 418–427 (2005)

19. Liu, Y., D'Aronco, S., Schindler, K., Wegner, J.D.: PC2WF: 3D wireframe reconstruction from raw point clouds. arXiv preprint arXiv:2103.02766 (2021)

20. Matveev, A., et al.: DEF: Deep estimation of sharp geometric features in 3D shapes. ACM Trans. Graph. **41**(4) (2022)

21. Mirjalili, S., Lewis, A.: The whale optimization algorithm. Adv. Eng. Softw. **95**, 51–67 (2016)

22. Ohrhallinger, S., Peethambaran, J., Parakkat, A.D., Dey, T.K., Muthuganapathy, R.: 2D points curve reconstruction survey and benchmark. In: Computer Graphics Forum, vol. 40, pp. 611–632. Wiley Online Library (2021)

23. Ostertagová, E.: Modelling using polynomial regression. Procedia Eng. **48**, 500–506 (2012). Modelling of Mechanical and Mechatronics Systems

24. Park, H., Lee, J.: B-spline curve fitting based on adaptive curve refinement using dominant points. Comput. Aided Des. **39**, 439–451 (2007)

25. Park, H.: An error-bounded approximate method for representing planar curves in B-splines. Comput. Aided Geom. Des. **21**, 479–497 (2004)

26. Shami, T.M., El-Saleh, A.A., Alswaitti, M., Al-Tashi, Q., Summakieh, M.A., Mirjalili, S.: Particle swarm optimization: a comprehensive survey. IEEE Access **10**, 10031–10061 (2022)

27. Song, B., Wang, Z., Zou, L.: An improved PSO algorithm for smooth path planning of mobile robots using continuous high-degree Bezier curve. Appl. Soft Comput. **100**, 106960 (2021)

28. Sun, C., Liu, M., Ge, S.: B-spline curve fitting of hungry predation optimization on ship line design. Appl. Sci. **12**(19), 9465 (2022)

29. Varady, T., Martin, R., Cox, J.: Reverse engineering of geometric models - an introduction. Comput. Aided Des. **29**(4), 255–268 (1997)

30. Wang, X., et al.: PIE-NET: parametric inference of point cloud edges. In: Advances in Neural Information Processing Systems, vol. 33, pp. 20167–20178. Curran Associates, Inc. (2020)

31. Yazdani, M., Jolai, F.: Lion optimization algorithm (LOA): a nature-inspired metaheuristic algorithm. J. Comput. Des. Eng. **3**(1), 24–36 (2015)

32. Ye, Y., Yi, R., Gao, Z., Zhu, C., Cai, Z., Xu, K.: NEF: neural edge fields for 3D parametric curve reconstruction from multi-view images (2023)

33. Yilmaz, S., Sen, S.: Electric fish optimization: a new heuristic algorithm inspired by electrolocation. Neural Comput. Appl. **32**(15), 11543–11578 (2020)

Medical Image Analysis

Brain Cortical Surface Registration with Anatomical Atlas Constraints

Wei Zeng[1(✉)], Xuebin Chang[1], Liqun Yang[2], Muhammad Razib[3], Zhong-Lin Lu[4], and Yi-Jun Yang[1]

[1] Xi'an Jiaotong University, Xi'an, China
wz@xjtu.edu.cn
[2] China Nanhu Academy of Electronics and Information Technology, Jiaxing, China
[3] Florida International University, Miami, FL, USA
[4] New York University, New York, NY, USA

Abstract. This work presents a novel cortical surface registration framework by using the whole anatomical atlas structures as correspondence constraints, which are extracted as atlas graphs (nodes are the junctions and edges are the intersecting curves of regions). The focus of this work is on the geometric registration category of cortical surfaces, i.e., brains are registered only using structural information without any functional information. We aim to innovate the geometric registration framework by utilizing the prominent anatomical features, atlas, to drive the registration. Intuitively, we convert the 3D cortical surfaces to 2D disks by special geometric mappings, where the curvy atlas regions become straight and convex polygonal regions; then registration is achieved between 2D domains such that curvy constrains become linear constraints and are solvable in linear time. The mappings generated are intrinsic and have theoretic guarantee of existence, uniqueness and optimality in terms of constrained harmonic energy. It differs from the literature geometric approaches using brain curves or point features. To the best of our knowledge, it is the first work of using atlas graph constraints in geometric registration. Our experiments on various brain data sets demonstrate the efficiency and efficacy for brain registration and the practicability of the proposed framework for brain disease classification.

Keywords: Surface registration · anatomical altas · geometric approaches · graph constraints

1 Introduction

Medical image registration has been widely used in image-guided interventions, patient response to treatment, and morphometric analysis. Cortical registration is important since the role of the cerebral cortex in higher-order cognitive function [2]. To ensure the accuracy of surface alignment, landmarks representing distinctive features of the surface are often used to guide the alignment, e.g. curves or points.

There have been a lot of researches on cortical geometric registration (see [3] for a survey). Existing geometric registration methods usually use sulci curves or points as constraints. The challenge is how to guarantee diffeomorphism under these constraints.

© The Author(s), under exclusive license to Springer Nature Switzerland AG 2023
G. Bebis et al. (Eds.): ISVC 2023, LNCS 14361, pp. 357–369, 2023.
https://doi.org/10.1007/978-3-031-47969-4_28

1) Point-constrained methods. Some progresses have been made recently toward solving that. The geodesic flows [12] generate diffeomorphisms along the deformation process. The hyperbolic orbifold model [22] guarantee a diffeomorphism with the exact landmark point alignment. 2) Curve-constrained methods. Most works discretize curves to points [4], but cannot guarantee the alignment of point intervals. Rigorous methods to handle curve constraints have been presented based on the hyperbolic harmonic map [19] and the quasiconformal map [24].

Moreover, the atlas graph's intrinsic curvature and pronounced non-linearity present substantial hurdles when striving for diffeomorphic registration. Taking inspiration from Tutte graph embedding, a technique ensuring convexity for each graph face, we introduce an intrinsic method for convex subdivision mapping applied to 3D surfaces. This novel approach facilitates atlas-based registration while circumventing the need for graph embedding, effectively transforming the 3D curvilinear graph constraints into linear straight-line constraints.

In summary, we present a novel cortical geometric registration framework using anatomical atlas structure as constraints. The major contributions of the proposed brain registration method are as follows:

1. The registration based on intrinsic convex subdivision harmonic map respects intrinsic surface and landmark geometry. It exists and is globally optimal, unique and diffeomorphic. Importantly, the registration achieves more accuracy.
2. The proposed registration with consistent feature graphs (if not consistent, then the graphs are made consistent with graph refinement strategy) has been proved to be globally optimal, unique and diffeomorphic.

Additionally, we have two strategies to validate that: (1) We evaluated the accuracy of the proposed registration by the comparison to the results using only common atlas graphs (without atlas refinement) and FreeSurfer results. (2) We then applied the shape metrics obtained from the registration to the brain classification between Alzheimer's disease (AD) group and healthy control (CTL) group. The classification accuracy is 88% with our method which is better than that using Freesurfer registration [5].

2   Approach Overview

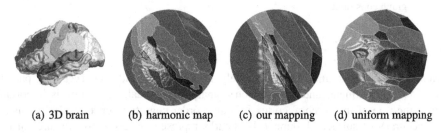

(a) 3D brain   (b) harmonic map   (c) our mapping   (d) uniform mapping

Fig. 1. Cortical surface mappings, where atlas regions are color encoded.

The overall solution is based on the proposed intrinsic graph-driven harmonic map along with graph modification and mapping relaxation techniques. Without considering graph constraint, the harmonic map is intrinsic, but the graph appears highly curvy on the planar domain (see Fig. 1a–b), which cannot be used directly as constraint. In our intrinsic convex harmonic map, boundary vertices are prescribed onto the unit circle using arc length weight, the positions of mesh vertices on atlas graph (including graph nodes) are automatically computed using the weight on their adjacent mesh edges on graph, and the positions of other interior mesh vertices are computed automatically. This setting ensures that the atlas graph is straightened to be convex (see Fig. 1c). The positions computed is intrinsically determined by the surface and graph geometry. In contrast, in the uniform convex mapping [14] (see Fig. 1d), the positions of the graph nodes are given by the uniform Tutte embedding, which are not intrinsic without considering graph geometry.

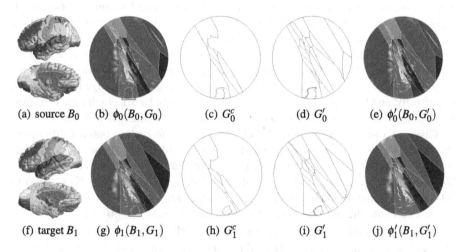

(a) source B_0 (b) $\phi_0(B_0, G_0)$ (c) G_0^c (d) G_0' (e) $\phi_0'(B_0, G_0')$

(f) target B_1 (g) $\phi_1(B_1, G_1)$ (h) G_1^c (i) G_1' (j) $\phi_1'(B_1, G_1')$

Fig. 2. The pipeline of the registration for cortical surfaces. (a)–(e) represents the processing of a convex graph based on cerebral cortex B_0 from the original graph G_0 to the refined graph G_0'; (f)–(g) represents the processing of a convex graph based on cerebral cortex B_1 from the original graph G_1 to the refined graph G_1'. G_k^c: maximal common subgraphs, G_k': consistent refined graphs (red rectangles highlights two-edged regions), ϕ_k: convex map with original graph, ϕ_k': convex map with refined graph and $k = 0, 1$. (Color figure online)

Given the source and target cortical surfaces to be registered, *first*, we check the atlas graph consistency and perform minimal changes to make graphs 3-connected (i.e., node degree ≥ 3, required in convex embedding [7]) and isomorphic. *Then*, we construct the registration over the intrinsic convex subdivision domains by a harmonic map constrained with the linear convex subdivision constraint. *Finally*, we perform a relaxation process to minimize the distortions introduced by graph modification. The resulted registration is guaranteed to be unique and diffeomorphic based on the generalized Radó theorem [17] and Floater's convex combination theorem [7]. The method is linear, implemented by solving sparse linear systems. Figure 2 illustrates the pipeline of the registration for cortical surfaces B_0, B_1. The atlas graphs are inconsistent, but with common subgraphs. The graphs are locally modified around unmatched edges and two-edged regions (as shown in the red rectangles). We can observe that the two-edged regions become three-edged regions and the graphs are mapped to convex subdivisions. In the graph-driven harmonic mapping method, the weights are specially set for the triangle edges on the atlas graph curves, so that the result respects the geometry intrinsically and is proven to be a diffeomorphism based on the Floater's convex combination theorem [7]. Experiments were performed on Mindboggle [10] and LPBA40 [18] and data sets with manual atlas labels to verify atlas inconsistency and to evaluate the algorithm performance.

3   Computational Algorithms

The major steps for registration include: 1) check atlas consistency and refine atlas graph if inconsistent; 2) compute intrinsic atlas-constrained harmonic maps; and 3) register the two harmonic map domains and relax the mapping due to atlas modification.

The cortical surface is represented as a triangular mesh of genus zero with a single boundary (the back-side unknown region is cut off), denoted as $M = (V, E, F)$, where V, E, F represent vertex, edge and face sets, respectively. The atlas graph is denoted as $G = (V_G, E_G, F_G, V_{E_G})$, where V_G, E_G, F_G represent graph node, edge and face sets, respectively, and V_{E_G} represents all mesh vertices on graph. Here a graph edge is formed by a chain of vertices. We use (M, G) to denote an atlas-constrained surface.

Given two surfaces (M_1, G_1), (M_2, G_2), the goal is to find an optimal diffeomorphism $f : (M_1, G_1) \to (M_2, G_2)$, such that atlases G_1 and G_2 are aligned as constraint. If G_1, G_2 are not consistent, we modify them as little as possible to be consistent, i.e., $G_1' \sim G_2'$. The registration employs the 3D-to-2D strategy, which maps 3D surfaces to 2D canonical domains and then simplifies 3D surface registration problems to 2D ones. We first compute the intrinsic graph-driven harmonic maps $\phi_k : (M_k, G_k') \to (D_k, \hat{G}_k')$, where G_k' are canonicalized to be planar convex subdivisions $\hat{G}_k'$ on the unit disk D_k. Then we compute the mapping $h : (D_1, \hat{G}_1') \to (D_2, \hat{G}_2')$ via a constrained harmonic map, followed by an operation η to relax the distortions introduced by atlas modification. Therefore, the registration $f = \phi_2^{-1} \circ \eta \circ h \circ \phi_1$, as shown in Diagram (3). For simplicity, due to the property of convex harmonic map, the registration can also be computed as:

$$
\begin{array}{ccc}
(M_1, G_1) & \xrightarrow{\;f\;} & (M_2, G_2) \\
\phi_1 \downarrow & & \downarrow \phi_2 \\
(D_1, \hat{G}_1) & \xrightarrow{\;h\;} & (D_2, \hat{G}_2)
\end{array}
$$

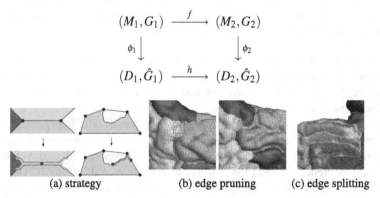

(a) strategy   (b) edge pruning   (c) edge splitting

Fig. 3. Atlas refinement: illustration (a) and examples of edge pruning (b, source vs. target) and edge splitting (c).

3.1 Atlas Consistency Check and Refinement

We first check whether the two atlas graphs are consistent or not. Two nodes are matched (consistent) if they have exactly the same surrounding regions. If all nodes are matched, then $G_1 \sim G_2$. Otherwise, we perform refinement operations (see Fig. 3a), as follows:

1. Refine unmatched edges by edge pruning (see Fig. 3b). Two graph edges in both atlases are matched, if they have the same left and right neighboring regions. We remove the unmatched edge by moving two nodes to the middle. The original graph edge is then divided into two segments. Each segment is shifted to every side by one triangle away from the original position. Repeat edge pruning until there is no unmatched edge. This operation won't introduce new connectivity between regions.
2. Refine two-edged regions by edge splitting. These regions have only two graph nodes and edges (see Fig. 2a,b,f,g, Fig. 3c), and need to be refined as 3-connected (degree ≥ 3), required in convex embedding. We first split the interior edge at the middle vertex to segments and then perturb one segment by one triangle away from the original. Thus the region becomes three sided. The selections of the interior edge for splitting and the segment for perturbing are remembered for consistent operation over atlases.

3.2 Intrinsic Graph-Driven Harmonic Map

We map the cortical surface M onto the convex subdivision domain D, $\phi : (M, G') \to (D, \hat{G}')$, by minimizing harmonic energy (stretches) with the atlas graph conditions. The critical point of harmonic energy is a harmonic map. The energy is formulated as

$$\min\{E(\phi(v_i)) = \Sigma_{[v_i,v_j] \in E} w_{ij}(\phi(v_i) - \phi(v_j))^2, \forall v_i \in V\}, \tag{1}$$

where w_{ij} is the edge weight; in our method, we use the mean value coordinates [14] as edge weights.

 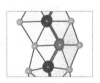 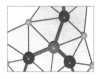

(a)   graph   edge,   (b) zoomed   view   (c) zoomed view of   (d) intrinsic map
graph node   of graph edge   graph node

Fig. 4. Adaptive mean value coordinate. (a) shows graph edge on the top box and graph node on the bottom box, (b) and (c) show the zoomed in view of graph edge and graph node. The blue points are the *one-ring graph neighborhood* of the green ones. (Color figure online)

We map the outer boundary of the brain surface to the unit circle. We employ special handling to automatically and intrinsically map the curvy graph G' as a convex subdivision on the unit disk. To achieve this without graph embedding, we modify the mean value coordinate adaptively according to the atlas graph such that the convex combination map defined in Eq. (1) satisfies the Circumferential Mean Value Theorem [6] at every interior vertex, and it straightens the feature graph to the convex subdivision. In detail, for a vertex on the atlas graph, we define its *one-ring graph neighborhood* as its adjacent vertices lying on the graph (see Fig. 4). For the vertices on the feature graph, we utilize their one-ring graph neighborhood during the computation of the adaptive mean value coordinate, and the interior points of the graph curves will move to the linear interpolation of their two adjacent graph neighbors on the feature curves instead, which will result in a convex subdivision in the canonical domain (see Fig. 2e, j). In detail, to compute the intrinsic harmonic map of graph constrained surfaces, we compute the harmonic weights adaptively as follows (see Fig. 4). If the vertex v_0 is

1. not on the graph, then we utilize the mean value coordinate as the weight.
2. lying inside the interior of graph edge, then the barycentric coordinate is applied to its one-ring graph neighborhood instead. Let v_1 and v_2 denote its two adjacent neighboring vertices on the graph. The adaptive harmonic weight is defined as $w_1 = \frac{|v_2-v_0|}{|v_2-v_0|+|v_1-v_0|}$ and $w_2 = \frac{|v_1-v_0|}{|v_2-v_0|+|v_1-v_0|}$.
3. the graph node, then the Circumferential Mean Value Theorem is applied to its one-ring graph neighborhood to compute the adaptive harmonic weight.

In our construction, each vertex of the surface is a convex combination of neighbors. The resulted mapping is guaranteed to be unique and diffeomorphic and a convex subdivision based on Radó theorem [17] and Floater's convex combination theorem [7].

3.3   Diffeomorphic Graph-Constrained Registration

With the refined consistent atlas graphs, the source (M_1, G'_1) and target (M_2, G'_2) are mapped onto the disk domains with interior convex subdivision by the above intrinsic harmonic map. We then register the two planar domains, $h : (D_1, \hat{G}'_1) \rightarrow (D_2, \hat{G}'_2)$, by minimizing the harmonic energy. We specify the positions of the boundary vertices (by interpolation) and the graph nodes as the corresponding ones on the target, and set the combinations for the vertices on graph edge only using adjacent edges on graph. The resulted mapping is diffeomorphic.

The virtual curve by atlas refinement may introduce fake alignment. Thus we relax the mapping h to lower the distortions.

We first set $\eta = h$. At each step, we compute the gradient of vertex $v_i \in V_1$, $\triangle \eta(v_i) = \sum_{[v_i,v_j] \in E} w_{ij}(\eta(v_i) - \eta(v_j))$, and update $\eta(v_i) \leftarrow \eta(v_i) - \lambda(v_i)d\eta(v_i)$, where $\lambda \in [0,1]$ is a movement scalar function. In detail, (1) for the graph nodes which are on both original and refined graphs of M_1 and boundary vertices, we set $\lambda = 0$ (i.e., exactly aligned by h and fixed); (2) for the vertices which are on virtual curves, we set $\lambda = 1$. To further smoothen the mapping at the end areas of virtual curves, we set $\lambda = \frac{d}{r}$ for the vertices inside, where d is the distance to endpoint, r is the radius of the range; and (3) for the resting mesh vertices, we set $\lambda = 1$ (i.e., with full movement).

The size of local range needs to be carefully selected, depending on the length of the virtual curve. We have flipping check during the relaxation procedure, and reduce movement scalar or stop moving if the movement produces flip. In this relaxation, each

Table 1. Statistics on atlas graphs: G - original graph, G^c - maximum common subgraph, and G' - refined consistent graph over all brains.

Data (left hemisphere)	G-#v/e/f	G^c-#v/e/f	G'-#v/e/f	#unmatched e	#two-edged f	#triangle, time
Mindboggle	59–71/89–103/31	0/0/0	25/47/23	25.10	0	293k, 50 s
LPBA40	46–48/68–72/25	0/0/0	19/40/22	25.85	1.175	131k, 20 s

step reduces the constrained harmonic energy, and therefore this iterative process converges. The composed mapping $\eta \circ h$ gives a diffeomorphism. Along with the ϕ_k, we can generate the diffeomorphic registration f between the 3D atlas-constrained cortical surfaces, under the optimality criterion of minimizing stretches.

4   Experiments

The proposed algorithms underwent validation using publicly available human brain datasets that included manual atlas labels. Specifically, we used a dataset comprising 40 brains from LPBA40 [18] (processed through BrainSuite) and another dataset containing 95 brains from Mindboggle [10]. Notably, these two databases adhere to different protocols for human cortical labeling, resulting in the creation of distinct atlases. Therefore, we conducted registration independently within each database.

To further assess the effectiveness of our method, we applied it to the Alzheimer's Disease Neuroimaging Initiative (ADNI) dataset [9] for Alzheimer's disease classification. All experiments were conducted on a workstation equipped with a 3.7GHz CPU and 16GB of RAM. Our algorithm was implemented in C++, with Matlab serving as the solver for sparse linear systems. It's worth noting that all computations were executed automatically, ensuring stability and robustness without the need for manual intervention.

4.1   Atlas Consistency Analysis and Refinement

Under the same labeling protocol, brains have consistent cortical regions, but no consideration on the junctions (graph nodes) of anatomical regions among brains.

We have done the statistics on the two data sets, as follows: (1) all atlas graphs are embedded on the hemispherical cortical surfaces and are intrinsically planar; (2) LBPA40 data has at most 2 two-edged regions, violating "3-connected" property, and Mindboggle data has no; and (3) atlas graphs are not consistent (isomorphic) among brains, and there is no common subgraphs in each data set, therefore the connection types at junctions are diverse. Furthermore, by comparing the number of triangle edges of unmatched graph edges over brains, the differences of atlas graphs are restricted to a local range (less than 10 in most cases). By graph refinement, the original regions won't disappear. For example, in Fig. 2, the consistent refined graph for brain pair (B_0, B_1) has 45 nodes, 70 edges, and 26 faces (same as the original). Table 1 gives the statistics for all brains in each data set.

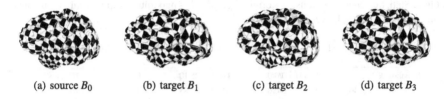

(a) source B_0 (b) target B_1 (c) target B_2 (d) target B_3

Fig. 5. Registration **I** by refining atlases for each pair $<B_0, B_k>, k = 1, 2, 3$ separately.

4.2 Atlas-Based Brain Registration

We applied our registration framework within each data set. Table 1 gives the averaged running time for registering one pair of cortical surfaces. The computational algorithm is efficient and practical. In each data set, we select a brain B_0 (as a reference) to register every other brain, to achieve the co-registration among all brains. Here, for illustration, we show four brains' registration results, $(B_0, G_0), (B_1, G_1), (B_2, G_2), (B_3, G_3)$. Two ways of atlas refinement are as follows: **I.** Refine atlases to be consistent for each pair separately. **II.** Refine atlases to be consistent for 4 brains together. We found out the unmatched edges among all atlases and prune them iteratively. Figures 5 and 6 show the registration results, respectively.

By the registration, we transferred the texture coordinates (e.g., using disk harmonic map parameters in Fig. 1b) of B_0 to all other brains, then the one-to-one registrations can be visualized by the consistent texture mappings (see blue circle areas in Fig. 5). Numerically, we computed the registration accuracy metric as the *dice coefficient* to measure the overlap between regions of M_k^i, defined as $D_c(M_1, M_2) = 2 * \dfrac{\Sigma_i A(M_1^i \cap M_2^i)}{A(M_1) + A(M_2)}$,

where A is the area function. The larger value indicates more accuracy. We performed the following experiments to evaluate the accuracy of the proposed registration method:

For the pair (B_0, B_1), we evaluated the performance under two cases of graph constraints: 1) the maximum common subgraph, and 2) the consistent refined graphs, with the registration accuracy $D_c = 0.88324, 0.9589$ (without relaxation), respectively. This shows that the refined graph registration performs better and verifies the intuition. We tested different smoothness levels in relaxation by selecting 1-ring (no interior vertices, no control on smoothness), 2-ring and 3-ring local ranges, with $D_c = 0.9590, 0.9589, 0.9589$, respectively. The results are similar, but the 1-ring gives the highest result due to less restriction to the movement. Registration with relaxation shows better results than the initial one. We chose 2-ring one to balance smoothness and accuracy.

We made comparisons with the FreeSurfer registration [5], which is computed by running the FreeSurfer software using the parameter "Mri_cvs_register". We have done the evaluation on both registration accuracy and efficiency on three databases including Mindboggle (95 brains), LPBA40 (40 brains), and ADNI (100 brains). The Dice measure on the registration results [23] showed our method performs better than FreeSurfer. With the curvature metric [16], our tests show that our method has 9% higher accuracy on average. In addition, our method is computed by solving sparse linear systems

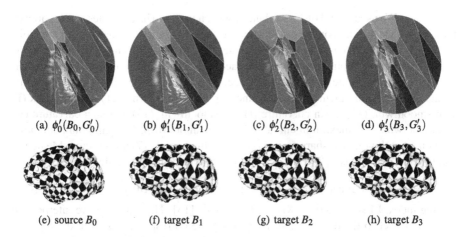

(a) $\phi_0'(B_0, G_0')$	(b) $\phi_1'(B_1, G_1')$	(c) $\phi_2'(B_2, G_2')$	(d) $\phi_3'(B_3, G_3')$
(e) source B_0	(f) target B_1	(g) target B_2	(h) target B_3

Fig. 6. Registration **II** by refining atlas for multiple brains together. Top: the intrinsic harmonic maps with consistent refined graphs, $\phi_i' : (B_i, G_i') \rightarrow (D_i, \hat{G}_i'), i = 0, 1, 2, 3$. Row 2: the one-to-one registration visualized by consistent texture mappings.

and is more efficient and much faster than the nonlinear FreeSurfer method [5], which has been verified in the practical experiments. As an illustration, for the three pairs $(B_0, B_k), k = 1, 2, 3$, we compared the registration results under the two graph refinement strategies **I**, **II** with the FreeSurfer results [15]. The registration accuracy D_c (FreeSurfer, **I**, **II**) is (0.8123, 0.9589, 0.9595) for (B_0, B_1), (0.8825, 0.9611, 0.9560) for (B_0, B_2), and (0.8838, 0.9628, 0.9612) for (B_0, B_3). Our method has higher accuracy.

4.3   Application to AD Classification

Accordingly, the proposed registration framework also produces more accurate shape metrics, which is evaluated by the efficiency of using the obtained shape metrics to classify brains with neudegenerative disease, e.g., AD. The criterion is the classification accuracy. To perform this, we applied the proposed registration method on ADNI data set to classify AD patients, and compared that with FreeSurfer shape metric for the same data.

Participants. Structural brain magnetic resonance imaging (MRI) scans were obtained from ADNI database (adni.loni.usc.edu). For up-to-date information, see www.adni-info.org. A total of 100 brains with 50 age-matched AD brains and 50 CTL brains (Age: AD: 56.5–86.7, CTL: 59.9–89.6; Mini-Mental State Examination score: AD: 20–27, CTL: 26–30) were considered in this study. The cross-sectional study was approved by the Local Ethical Committee on human studies and written informed consent from subjects was obtained prior to their enrolment.

Data Processing. All the brains were processed by Freesurfer's (version 5.1) automated pipeline using the command *recon-all* with default parameters to generate parcellated surfaces. For registration, we randomly select one brain as the source, and register that to all other 99 brains. After the registration, all the brains have one-to-one vertex correspondence. Consider that cortical atrophy is a valid biomarker of AD-related neurodegeneration. We used a total of 17 attributes for each vertex. The attributes are, (1) area on the pial surface, (2) area on the mid cortical surface, (3) gaussian curvature on the white surface, (4) gaussian curvature on the pial surface, (5) average curvature on the white surface, (6) sulcul depth on the white surface, (7) cortical thickness on the white surface, (8) cortical volume on the white surface, (9) bending energy (BE) on smooth white matter surface (smoothwm), (10) curvedness (C) on smoothwm, (11) folding index (FI) on smoothwm, (12) mean curvature (H) on smoothwm, (13) gaussian curvature (K) on smoothwm, (14) maximum curvature (K_1) on smoothwm, (15) minimum curvature (K_2) on smoothwm, (16) sharpness (S) on smoothwm, and (17) atlas region. Mean curvature, H is defined as $1/2 \times (K_1 + K_2)$; Gaussian curvature, K is defined as $K_1 \times K_2$; Curvedness, C is defined as, $\sqrt{\dfrac{K_1^2 + K_2^2}{2}}$; bending energy, BE is defined as $K_1^2 + K_2^2$; folding index, FI is defined as $|K_1| \times (|K_1| - |K_2|)$ [13]. The attributes are interpolated from the target to the deformed surfaces using the correspondence from the registration process. Most current AD classifications only mention indicators such as cortical curvature and volume without detailed feature extraction from the cerebral cortex, and we also believe that refined brain features are more reflective of changes in the cerebral cortex, thus providing a reference for diagnosis.

We computed the distance between the source and the deformed source (registered to target) for all the 17 attributes for each region (total 35 regions excluding the black/unknown region, as obtained by Freesurfer) and used those as the features for the classification. For the attribute region, we assign 0 for the similarity and 1 otherwise; for all other attributes we used the Euclidean distance. Therefore, we get a total of $35 \times 17 = 595$ features for the 35 regions. To detect the important features for classification, we used forward sequential feature selection algorithm [11], and selected a total of 200 features out of these 595 features. After that, we searched over the 200 features incrementally to identify the best combination of features for the classification.

Classification. We used two classification algorithms, (1) Support Vector Machine (SVM) and (2) K Nearest Neighbor (K-NN), with 10-fold cross validation. We used Matlab implementation of both the algorithms. For the SVM algorithm, Gaussian radial basis kernel function (rbf) was used with a scaling factor of 3.63 and box constraint of 2.71. The optimal scaling factor and box constraint were obtained by using the bayesian hyper parameters optimization [21] process. For K-NN algorithm, we used K = 5. We searched incrementally over the features for both SVM and K-NN (see Fig. 7a). The classification accuracy for SVM is 86.0% with false positive rate (FPR) = 8.0% and false negative rate (FNR) = 20.0%, and accuracy for K-NN is 88.0% with FPR = 6.0% and FNR = 18.0% (see Table 2). Both algorithms achieved the best accuracy with 98 features. To visualize the trade-off between the true positive rate (TPR) and FNR, we used Receiver Operating Characteristic (ROC). Figure 7b shows the ROC curve for SVM and K-NN; area under curve (AUC) value for SVM is 0.856, and for K-NN is 0.882.

Table 2. AD classification accuracy with SVM and K-NN.

Algorithms	Sensitivity	Specificity	AUC	Accuary (Ours)	Accuary (FreeSurfer)
SVM	92.0%	80.0%	0.856	86.0%	82.0%
K-NN	94.0%	82.0%	0.882	88.0%	78.0%

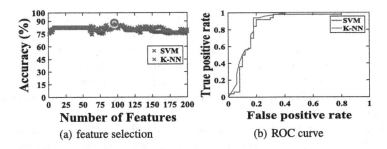

Fig. 7. Classification. (a) The accuracy using different number of features obtained by FSFS algorithm for SVM and K-NN. (b) The ROC curve for SVM and K-NN.

We evaluated our method with the shape metrics with FreeSurfer's registration method. We used the same setting for both SVM and K-NN, and used the same number of features with same number of anatomical atlas regions (excluding the black/unknown region as before). Using the same 98 features, classification accuracy using FreeSurfer registration is 82.0% with SVM, and 78.0% with K-NN (see Table 2). For both algorithms, our registration results perform better as they provide more accurate alignment of the corresponding atlas regions with similar shapes in the registration process and accordingly more accurate shape metrics among them.

5   Discussion

The proposed registration method achieves a delicate equilibrium by aligning atlases to their fullest extent while simultaneously minimizing harmonic energy, thereby preserving local shapes within defined constraints. It is crucial to acknowledge that achieving a flawless registration for cortical surfaces characterized by inherently inconsistent atlases is a formidable challenge. Our approach is meticulously designed to confine alterations primarily to local regions.

Our methodology introduces one-triangle-wide pieces, the smallest units within a triangular mesh, which serve to significantly reduce distortions from the original atlas. This innovative technique preserves the original atlas geometry on the cortical surface to an impressive degree. Additionally, the relaxation procedure further mitigates these distortions. Notably, our method is renowned for its rigor, intrinsic nature, and linearity, as it leverages the classical harmonic map with convex subdivision constraints, offering assurances of uniqueness and diffeomorphism [7].

What truly sets our work apart is our pioneering use of entire cortical atlases as constraints, intrinsically mapping cortical surfaces with atlas graphs onto a convex subdivision domain. Moreover, we have harnessed mean value coordinates to align regions of interest within the cerebral cortex, streamlining the process of atlas alignment across diverse brains. We emphasize that public databases like Mindboggle and LPBA40 predominantly provide structural MRI data paired with manually labeled atlases. Our geometric registration methodology's shape representations and metrics can be seamlessly integrated with fMRI or dMRI data, forming the foundation for a comprehensive multimodal cortical surface registration framework. To guide this integration, we plan to follow the established pipeline proposed in the Multimodal Surface Matching works [16], systematically evaluating the fusion of multiple data modalities.

Our future initiatives entail the incorporation of functional information into our framework, thus enriching our registration approach for a more comprehensive biological interpretation in diverse brain applications. Additionally, we will conduct comparative analyses with CAT12 [8] and ANTs [1], using the same dataset, further expanding the scope of our research.

Within this overarching framework, we anticipate the exploration of more sophisticated methodologies, such as bijective maps designed to minimize distortion metrics without confining graph boundaries to fixed shapes [20]. Furthermore, we aim to incorporate optimization criteria, including minimizing angle or area distortions, to further enhance our registration capabilities.

6 Conclusion

This work presents a novel geometric method to register cortical surfaces with structural atlas constraints. We first perform atlas consistency check and refinement, then convert surfaces to 2D convex subdivision domains by the intrinsic graph-driven harmonic maps, and finally compute the registration over the 2D domains, followed by a relaxation procedure. The mapping is unique and diffeomorphic. The whole process is automatic. Experiments on co-registering brains in two public databases, and the application to Alzheimer's Disease classification have demonstrated the efficiency and practicality of the algorithms. We will further explore the proposed framework by integrating multimodal information and apply that to large-scale brain morphometry analysis and medical and cognitive problems in future works.

Acknowledgment. This work was supported by National Key R&D Program of China (Grant No. 2021YFA1003002) and NSFC (Grant No. 12090021). Data collection and sharing for this project was funded by the Alzheimer's Disease Neuroimaging Initiative (ADNI) (National Institutes of Health Grant U01 AG024904) and DOD ADNI (Department of Defense award number W81XWH-12-2-0012).

References

1. Avants, B.B., Tustison, N., Song, G., et al.: Advanced normalization tools (ANTs). Insight J. **2**(365), 1–35 (2009)
2. Che, T., et al.: AMNet: adaptive multi-level network for deformable registration of 3D brain MR images. Med. Image Anal. **85**, 102740 (2023)
3. Cheng, J., Dalca, A.V., Fischl, B., Zöllei, L., Initiative, A.D.N., et al.: Cortical surface registration using unsupervised learning. Neuroimage **221**, 117161 (2020)
4. Choi, P.T., Lam, K.C., Lui, L.M.: FLASH: fast landmark aligned spherical harmonic parameterization for genus-0 closed brain surfaces. SIAM J. Imaging Sci. **8**(1), 67–94 (2015)
5. Fischl, B., Sereno, M., Dale, A.: Cortical surface-based analysis II: inflation, flattening, and a surface-based coordinate system. Neuroimage **9**(2), 195–207 (1999)
6. Floater, M.S.: Mean value coordinates. Comput. Aided Geom. Design **20**(1), 19–27 (2003)

7. Floater, M.S.: One-to-one piecewise linear mappings over triangulations. Math. Comput. **72**(242), 685–696 (2003)
8. Gaser, C., Dahnke, R., Thompson, P.M., Kurth, F., Luders, E., Initiative, A.D.N.: CAT-a computational anatomy toolbox for the analysis of structural MRI data. biorxiv, pp. 2022–06 (2022)
9. Jack, C.R., et al.: The Alzheimer's disease neuroimaging initiative (ADNI): MRI methods. J. Magn. Reson. Imaging **27**(4), 685–691 (2008)
10. Klein, A., Tourville, J.: 101 labeled brain images and a consistent human cortical labeling protocol. Front. Brain Imaging Methods **6**(171) (2012)
11. Kohavi, R., John, G.H.: Wrappers for feature subset selection. Artif. Intell. **97**(1–2), 273–324 (1997)
12. Kurtek, S., Srivastava, A., Klassen, E., Laga, H.: Landmark-guided elastic shape analysis of spherically-parameterized surfaces. Comput. Graphics Forum **32**(2), 429–438 (2013)
13. Pienaar, R., Fischl, B., Caviness, V., Makris, N., Grant, P.E.: A methodology for analyzing curvature in the developing brain from preterm to adult. Int. J. Imaging Syst. Technol. **18**(1), 42–68 (2008)
14. Razib, M., Lu, Z.L., Zeng, W.: Structural brain mapping. In: International Conference on Medical Image Computing and Computer Assisted Intervention (2015)
15. Reuter, M., Rosas, H., Fischl, B.: Highly accurate inverse consistent registration: a robust approach. Neuroimage **53**(4), 1181–1196 (2010)
16. Robinson, E.C., et al.: MSM: a new flexible framework for multimodal surface matching. Neuroimage **100**, 414–426 (2014)
17. Schoen, R., Yau, S.T.: Lectures on Harmonic Maps. International Press (1997)
18. Shattuck, D.W., et al.: Construction of a 3D probabilistic atlas of human cortical structures. NeuroImage **39**, 1064–1080 (2007)
19. Shi, R., et al.: Hyperbolic harmonic brain surface registration with curvature-based landmark matching. In: Gee, J.C., Joshi, S., Pohl, K.M., Wells, W.M., Zöllei, L. (eds.) IPMI 2013. LNCS, vol. 7917, pp. 159–170. Springer, Heidelberg (2013). https://doi.org/10.1007/978-3-642-38868-2_14
20. Smith, J., Schaefer, S.: Bijective parameterization with free boundaries. ACM Trans. Graphics **34**(4CD), 70.1-70.9 (2015)
21. Snoek, J., Larochelle, H., Adams, R.P.: Practical Bayesian optimization of machine learning algorithms. In: Advances in Neural Information Processing Systems, pp. 2951–2959 (2012)
22. Tsui, A., et al.: Globally optimal cortical surface matching with exact landmark correspondence. In: Gee, J.C., Joshi, S., Pohl, K.M., Wells, W.M., Zöllei, L. (eds.) IPMI 2013. LNCS, vol. 7917, pp. 487–498. Springer, Heidelberg (2013). https://doi.org/10.1007/978-3-642-38868-2_41
23. Yeo, B.T., Sabuncu, M.R., Vercauteren, T., Ayache, N., Fischl, B., Golland, P.: Spherical demons: fast diffeomorphic landmark-free surface registration. IEEE Trans. Med. Imaging **29**(3), 650–668 (2010)
24. Zeng, W., Yang, Y.-J.: Surface matching and registration by landmark curve-driven canonical quasiconformal mapping. In: Fleet, D., Pajdla, T., Schiele, B., Tuytelaars, T. (eds.) ECCV 2014. LNCS, vol. 8689, pp. 710–724. Springer, Cham (2014). https://doi.org/10.1007/978-3-319-10590-1_46

When System Model Meets Image Prior: An Unsupervised Deep Learning Architecture for Accelerated Magnetic Resonance Imaging

Ibsa Jalata$^{(\boxtimes)}$ and Ukash Nakarmi

University of Arkansas, Fayetteville, AR 72701, USA
{ikjalata,unakarmi}@uark.edu

Abstract. Magnetic Resonance Imaging (MRI) is typically a slow process because of its sequential data acquisition. To speed up this process, MR acquisition is often accelerated by undersampling k-space signals and solving an ill-posed problem through a constrained optimization process. While traditional methods use image priors as constraints, modern deep learning methods use supervised learning with ground truth images to learn image features and priors. However, in some cases, ground truth images are not available, making supervised learning impractical. To address this issue, we propose an unsupervised deep learning framework for accelerated MRI that does not require ground truth images for training. Our framework combines a system prior derived from the MR acquisition model with generic image priors to build a more effective unsupervised deep learning framework. The system prior enforces data consistency while the generic image priors regulate the neural network parameters. Our experimental results demonstrate that our proposed unsupervised method outperforms state-of-the-art unsupervised methods and achieves performance comparable to that of supervised methods that require ground truth images for training.

Keywords: Unrolled generator · Wavelets · Unsupervised

1 Introduction

The MRI technique is a potent non-invasive imaging method that provides superior soft tissue contrast compared to computed tomography (CT) without exposing the patient to radiation. However, the slow data acquisition process, caused by low spin polarization, leads to a decreased signal-to-noise ratio (SNR) and necessitates lengthy exams. Moreover, the prolonged MRI acquisition procedure induces patient discomfort, reduces efficiency, and incurs extra economic expenses. Thus, reconstructing high-resolution Magnetic Resonance Imaging from undersampled k-space measurements is the primary objective of the MRI community. The current mainstream methods for achieving this goal

© The Author(s), under exclusive license to Springer Nature Switzerland AG 2023
G. Bebis et al. (Eds.): ISVC 2023, LNCS 14361, pp. 370–381, 2023.
https://doi.org/10.1007/978-3-031-47969-4_29

are MR image reconstruction and super-resolution (SR). The former focuses on removing aliasing artifacts caused by undersampling [4–6], while the latter improves the image resolution.

To speed up MRI acquisition, many MRI reconstructions methods involve undersampling data in the k-space. However, this violates the Nyquist sampling theorem and can result in aliasing artefacts in the image domain. To overcome this, images can be reconstructed through an optimization process that incorporates assumptions about the underlying data, such as its smoothness, sparsity, or spatial redundancy. Previous research has shown that utilizing spatial redundancy using parallel imaging hardware [18] can significantly enhance image reconstruction. Due to the difficulty of choosing the right regularisation function for a specific problem at hand researcher adopt another compressed sensing theory to MRI reconstruction focused on applying sparsifying transforms. Even combining parallel imaging and Compressed Sensing Magnetic Resonance Imaging (CS-MRI) is studied to maximize the acceleration of acquisition [3].

With recent surge of deep learning (DL) techniques in heavily data dependent application, there is an increasing interest in DL from MR acceleration community. Unlike the classical approach that exhibit poor robustness at test time when exposed to noisy perturbations, and poor reconstruction results, DL frameworks [19] have shown superior reconstruction quality and speed. This supervised DL models consider MR acceleration and reconstruction problem as a task of finding an appropriate mapping function $f(\mathring{u})$ parameterized by some neural network parameters that maps undersampled corrupted MR images to fully sampled ground truth images. Although these supervised DL models have shown a good result for many application, it doesn't generalize very well for testing data that differs with training data largely. In addition, in majority of MR Imaging application the fully sampled data is not provided for supervised model to use the paired data for training. To address this challenges, some researchers proposed unsupervised model that does not require the fully sampled data. The models capture the MRI prior using generative model [5]. The joint usage of imaging prior with MRI prior during inference on test data improved generalization against deviations in the imaging operator.

We have developed an unsupervised deep learning framework that combines the advantages of both data-driven deep learning models that enforce system priors and model-based approaches, such as TV and wavelet, which enhance generalization against deviations in the imaging operator. This approach enables us to fully exploit the benefits of both worlds.

Generally, MRI reconstruction can be categorized into two: model based model and data driven models. The model based model [2,3] reconstruct the high quality images by capitalizing on the $l1$ normalization of the inputs. In medical imaging, there is scarcity of MRI images. Therefore, supervised approaches is not viable without the ground truth value. Unsupervised model come to seen to tackle the problem. Previous method [17] proposed unsupervised model using wavelet and TV loss but the method is limited to a single coil k-space data. Our method used unrolled architecture internally and wavelet loss and TV loss.

The rest of the paper is organized as follows. Section 2 covers the related methods. Section 3 outlines the proposed method, including an overview of the fundamental principle behind accelerated MRI with undersampled data. In Sect. 4, we present the experiments and results. Section 5 discusses the limitations, and finally, Sect. 6 provides the paper's conclusion.

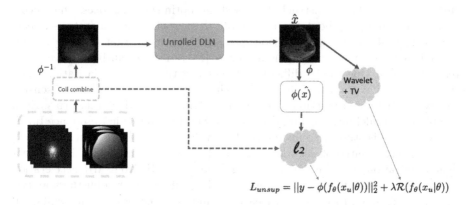

Fig. 1. Overview of the pipeline of our approach. The input image is created by inverse FFT of the coil combine of undersampled k-space data. The unroll deep learning framework consisting Resblock and data consistency (DC) is unrolled K times. Finally, the classical techniques are applied on the output.

2   Related Work

MRI reconstruction methods can typically be classified into two main categories: model-based approaches and data-driven approaches. Model-based approaches leverage techniques such as sparsifying transformations, dictionaries, and sparse coding. On the other hand, data-driven approaches employ advanced neural networks to capture important features for the purposes of learning.

Traditional methods for CS-MRI reconstruction have been designed to utilize signal sparsity by employing widely used sparsifying transforms, such as Fourier transform, Total Variation (TV) [1], and Wavelets [12]. Additionally, they aim to take advantage of spatio-temporal correlations. However, these sparsity-based CS-MRI methods often require solving computationally expensive non-linear $l1$ minimization problems, resulting in significant computational overhead during the reconstruction process. To address this, researchers proposed low-rank matrix completion and nuclear norm techniques for CS-MRI. In addition, they have developed efficient numerical algorithms and implemented parallel computing hardware to accelerate computation time. Dictionary learning-based methods [7] exploits the sparsity of the MRI input signal in a transformed domain. The learned dictionary transform the signal to sparse representation while the undersampled measurements are used to constrain the reconstruction process.

Compared with traditional algorithms, data-driven approaches, such as methods based on deep learning can make full use of the inherent characteristics of images contained in a large amount of training data. One of the earliest and most popular deep learning-based methods for MRI reconstruction is the physics-guided deep learning reconstruction (PG-DLR) approaches have gained interest due to their robustness and improved reconstruction quality [9]. The method uses unrolling algorithm [11] to explicitly incorporate the physics of the data acquisition system into the neural network. Another successful supervised deep learning approach applied for MRI reconstruction includes recurrent CNNs [10,11], residual CNN [14], recurrent CNN [10,11], variational networks and generative adversarial networks (GANs) [12,16]. While supervised model improved reconstruction quality and they are the state-of-the-art, acquisition of large datasets is non-trivial. Furthermore, supervised models often require retraining to cope with deviations in the imaging operator and also it may brings concerns about generalization [15].

Generally, generating high-quality dataset with sufficient size can be challenging in certain MRI applications that involve time-varying physiological processes. This is because dynamic information, such as contrast-related uptake, signal change time courses, may vary considerably between subjects. Thus, unsupervised MRI reconstruction has gained increasing attention, as it offers a promising way to reconstruct high-quality MRI images without the need for large amounts of labeled data. Recently, various significant techniques have been suggested to minimize the need for supervision. One set of studies has reduced the requirement for explicit supervision with respect to the raw data by proposing models trained using datasets where the input and output are unpaired [16,17] or from undersampled measurements [5,6]. However, these models involve implicit supervision related to the imaging operator and are trained for a particular coil-array configuration and k-space sampling density, which is assumed to be uniform across both the training and test datasets.

3   Methods

3.1   General CS-MRI

The data acquisition in accelerated Magnetic Resonance Imaging (MRI) [4] could be expressed as

$$y = \phi(x) \tag{1}$$

where $y \in \mathbb{R}^{1 \times M}$ is the vectorized undersampled k-space measurement, ϕ is forward operator representing partial Fourier operation and coil sensitivities, and vectorization, $x \in \mathbb{R}^{1 \times N}$ is the unobserved desired image which consists of $\sqrt{N} \times \sqrt{N}$ pixels formatted as a column vector. Since there are limited number of measurements compared to the actual requirement to reconstruct the ideal image, i.e., $(M << N)$, the system of the equation is ill-posed. To solve this ill-posed problem and reconstruct x from y, the classical reconstruction frameworks

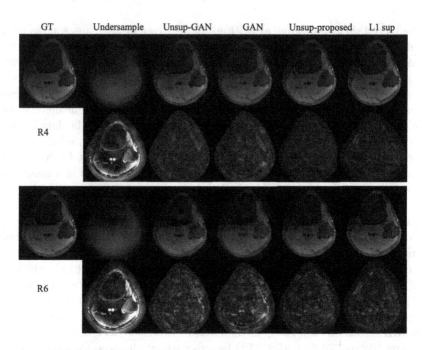

Fig. 2. Representative reconstruction spatial results and error map comparison for reduction factor 4 and 6. For each reduction factor, the top row shows the reconstruction output from contemporary methods and the proposed unsupervised method. The bottom row shows the reconstruction errors amplified by 5×.

pose it as a constrained optimization problem [5,6] such that:

$$x^* = argmin_x ||y - \phi(x)||_2^2 + \lambda \mathcal{R}(x) \qquad (2)$$

Where $||y - \phi(x)||^2$ ensures data consistency with measured data and $\mathcal{R}(\cdot)$ is a regularization term which enforces image priors. λ is a constant term used to balance the data consistency and the regularization term. In classical model-based approach, the data regularizer is enforced via common image priors such as dictionary [7], total variation (TV) [1], 2D wavelet [12]. Typically, the function represented by Eq. 2 is non-convex. Therefore, the variable splitting technique is commonly used to separate the fidelity and regularisation terms. To accomplish this, an auxiliary variable z is introduced, which is constrained to match x. Using the penalty method, Eq. 2 can be reformulated as a cost function that minimizes the following:

$$x^* = argmin_x ||y - \phi(x)||_2^2 + \mu ||x - z||_2^2 + \lambda \mathcal{R}(z) \qquad (3)$$

Here μ is a penalty parameter. When μ is large, the solutions of Eq. 3 are an approximation of the solutions of Eq. 2 . To solve this variable splitting technique iteratively, an alternating minimization algorithm can be utilized via the following iterative procedures:

$$z^{(i+1)} = argmin_{xz}\mu||x^i - z||_2^2 + \lambda\mathcal{R}(z) \tag{4}$$

$$x^{(i+1)} = argmin_x||y - \phi(x)||_2^2 + \mu||x - z^{(i+1)}||_2^2 \tag{5}$$

In MRI reconstruction, Eq. 5 is commonly considered a data consistency (DC) step, with $x(0) = xu = FuHy$ serving as the zero-filled reconstruction initialization and z as an intermediate state in the optimization process. A closed-form solution [9] can be obtained by utilizing this step.

$$x^{(i+1)} = F^H \wedge F z^{(i)} + \frac{\lambda}{\mu + \lambda} F_u^H y, \tag{6a}$$

$$\wedge = \begin{cases} 1 & \text{if } k \in \Omega \\ \frac{\mu}{\lambda + \mu} & \text{if } k \in \Omega \end{cases} \tag{6b}$$

where Ω is an index set of the acquired k-space samples, $\wedge$ is a diagonal matrix. F is the full Fourier encoding matrix, H represents the Hermitian transpose operation. $F_u^H y$ is the reconstruction from the zero-filled undersampled k-space measurements.

In supervised deep learning (DL) framework, the image priors are learned using convolutional neural network (CNN) [6,19–23] such that $\mathcal{R}(x) \rightarrow \mathcal{R}_{CNN}(x)$ by minimizing some loss function $\mathcal{L}(\hat{x}, x)$ for a given training data set $x_i^u, x_i, i = 1, 2, 3, ...T$ of image pairs; aliased undersampled image x^u and fully sampled desired images x. Some examples of popular loss function $\mathcal{L}(\cdot)$ in the supervised framework are l_1 norm, l_2 norm, and mean squared error. For example, the supervised deep learning model approach can be represented as:

$$argmin_{x,\theta}||y - \phi(x)||^2 + \lambda||x - f_\theta(x_u|\theta)||_2^2 \tag{7}$$

Where f_θ is the forward network parameterised by θ, which takes an undersampled image and produces an estimation $\hat{x}$ of fully sampled desired image x, such that $\hat{x} = f_\theta(x_u|\theta)$.

3.2   Proposed Method

The first term in Eq. 6 enforces the data consistency and acquisition system priors such as coil sensitivities and acquisition model [24]. During supervised training, the term is represented with the "Unrolled Deep Learning" model [4]. However, in many cases, the fully sampled images x are not available so the second term of Eq. 3 cannot be computed. The parameters θ learned by such unsupervised deep learning frameworks are not regularized and the image reconstructed is not efficient. In [8] the authors opted to utilize the GAN loss instead of matched high-dose data to match probability distribution, but their approach is not without limitations. Due to the generative nature of GAN, the network can be highly sensitive and may generate spurious artifacts if not trained with caution.

In [6] authors use image priors to regulate deep learning parameters in an unsupervised fashion for image denoising and single-channel accelerated reconstruction. To exploit the benefits of both unrolled optimization that enforces system priors such as multi-coil images, and sensitivity maps, and the benefits of general image priors such as TV, wavelet, we build a combined Unsupervised DL framework that integrates the unrolled optimization and image priors as shown in Fig. 1. For our unsupervised model, the reference image is not provided, so we formulated the loss in our model as:

$$L_{unsup} = ||y - \phi(f_\theta(x_u|\theta))||_2^2 + \lambda \mathcal{R}(f_\theta(x_u|\theta)) \tag{8}$$

$\mathcal{R}(\cdot)$ represents the combination of the l_1 norm of the Wavelet transform of the output $\hat{x}$ from the unrolled network, as well as the Total Variation of the output $\hat{x}$. This combination captures both the sparsity and the smoothness properties of the output, allowing for a comprehensive characterization of its structure.

When using wavelet-based estimation, the image can be transformed into an orthogonal wavelet expansion, resulting in a sparse representation with only a few large coefficients and many small ones. The vector of wavelet coefficients are obtained through the discrete wavelet transform (DWT) and its inverse.

$$T(x) = ||Wx||_1 \tag{9}$$

where T is the l_1 norm of the wavelet transform of the output $\hat{x}$ from the unrolled network. Small high-frequency oscillatory artifacts can occur in wavelet-based compressed sensing reconstructions due to the incorrect detection of fine-scale wavelet components. To reduce these artifacts, we include a minor TV penalty, denoted as $(V(x))$, alongside the wavelet penalty. This requirement can be seen as enforcing sparsity in both wavelet and finite difference transforms of the image.

$$\mathcal{R}(x) = T(x) + \alpha V(x) \tag{10}$$

4   Experiments

In this section, we present the results of our proposed framework on the Knee dataset. We demonstrate how our method performs as the size of the data increases.

4.1   Datasets

We utilized fully-sampled 3T knee images from [25]. Each subject's data is a $320 \times 320 \times 256$ complex-valued volume of knee images, split into 320×256 axial slices. The data is collected by performing MRI exams on 22 consecutive subjects (11 males and 11 females) using a 3T whole body scanner [25]. A fully sampled sagittal 3D FSE CUBE sequence with proton density weighting is acquired with fat saturation and saved the raw k-space data. Each subject's knee is positioned

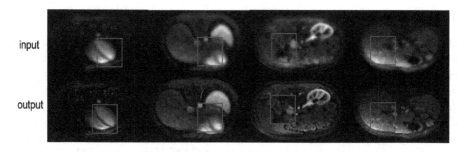

Fig. 3. Representative reconstruction spatial results for DCE datasets.

in an 8-channel HD knee coil and placed it vertically straight anterior to posterior within $+/-$ 10° to isocenter. We generated undersampled k-space data as input using Poisson-disc masks from BART [26]. Coil sensitivity maps were created using the SENSE [24] method.

The second dataset utilized for this study involved dynamic contrast enhanced (DCE) acquisitions of the abdomen, which were obtained through a fat-suppressed butterfly-navigated free-breathing SPGR acquisition [2]. The training dataset consisted of 886 subjects, while the testing dataset consisted of 50 subjects. Due to the fast dynamics of the intravenously injected contrast, it was not possible to obtain fully-sampled data for DCE using the imaging hardware. Each scan acquired a volumetric image with dimensions of $192 \times 180 \times 80$. To compress the raw data from 32 channels to 6 virtual channels, a singular-value-decomposition-based compression algorithm was employed [2].

4.2   Implementation Details

First, we trained our proposed method on a set of knee scans, and compare the reconstruction performance with zero reconstruction and supervised methods. For each knee scan, we utilized a 20×20 fully sampled calibration region in the center of k-space. To determine image quality, we evaluated the peak signal-to-noise ratio (PSNR), structural similarity index (SSIM), and average normalized root-mean-square error (NRMSE), between the reconstructed image and the fully sampled ground truth on test datasets. The Resnet block of our unrolled deep learning framework has 128 feature maps, 4 residual blocks, and 4 iterations, as depicted in Fig. 1. Subsequently, we evaluated the reconstruction performance of our approach on the knee scans set as a function of the acceleration factor of the training datasets. Figure 2 shows the qualitative results of our method and the supervised approach. From Fig. 3 and 4, we can conclude that our proposed method outperforms the existing l_1 supervised methods.

All networks were trained with Adam optimization with a learning rate of 0.001 and batch size of 8. Our work is implemented in Pytorch, the experiments are conducted using NVIDIA GeForce RTX 3090 with 24 GB RAM.

4.3   Result

During training, the training data consisted only of multi-coiled undersampled k-space data at an undersampling rates of 2, 3, 4, 6, 8, and 9. A total of 4800 undersampled data was used during training. No fully sampled images were used in the proposed method and Unsupervised GAN method training. Test data sets with an undersampling factor of 2, 3, 4, 6, 8, and 9 were also created. Each test set consisted of 1100 undersampled k-space data with corresponding undersampling rates. In addition to our method, we have conducted experiments on contemporary methods, such as supervised GAN, Unsupervised GAN [5], and supervised unrolled CNN using l_1 loss [4]. Figure 2 and 4 show two representative reconstructed images for reduction factors 4 and 6 each. From the figure, we can see the proposed unsupervised method has a better performance than all other methods except for the supervised l_1 method. The proposed unsupervised method still has comparable results to the supervised l_1 method, if not better. Figures 4, 5, 6 present and compare quantitative error and performance metrics NRMSE, PSNR, and SSIM respectively for all test data sets and all reduction factors. The quantitative results also show that the proposed unsupervised method performs better than all other contemporary methods and has comparable results to the supervised unrolled l_1 method which requires ground truth images for training.

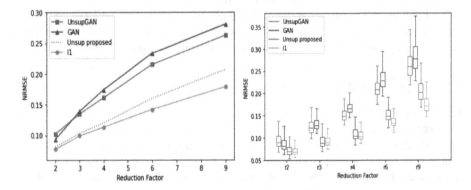

Fig. 4. NRMSE comparison of proposed unsupervised approach with contemporary methods. Left: Average NRMSE for test data, Right: Box plot of NRMSE for test data.

5   Discussion

In this paper, we have showed that the proposed method is capable of generating high quality images from undersampled data without the use of fully sampled data. Comparing to CS reconstruction and unsupervised methods [5] our method shows superior results on the given dataset. Among the supervised method we have tested in this work, our method performs better than the supervised GAN

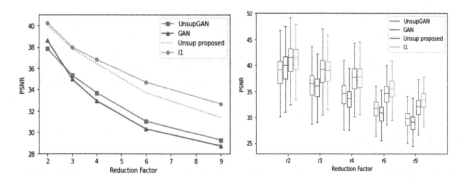

Fig. 5. PSNR comparison of proposed unsupervised approach with contemporary methods. Left: Average PSNR for test data, Right: Box plot of PSNR for test data.

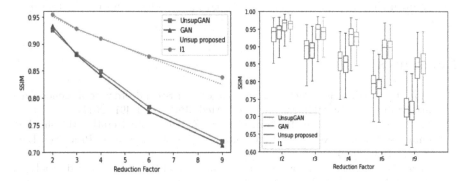

Fig. 6. SSIM comparison of proposed unsupervised approach with contemporary methods. Left: Average SSIM for test data, Right: Box plot of SSIM for test data.

[8] for the dataset with reduction factor 2–9. However, for reduction factor 2, the supervised GAN shows better results. The supervised l_1 methods yields better results than our proposed unsupervised method for test data undersampled by all reduction factors. This outcome is unsurprising as the supervised methods has the advantage of accessing fully-sampled data, which provides the network with a more robust prior.

As the acceleration factor of the training knee datasets increases, the reconstruction performance of the proposed unsupervised method, l_1 supervised model, GAN, unsupGAN and the zero filled reconstruction data deteriorates, as indicated by declining PSNR, NRMSE, and SSIM metrics. This trend is expected because the methods has access to a smaller range of sampled k-space as the acceleration factor increases.

Through our results, we have demonstrated that when fully- sampled data is available, supervised training should still be used for best reconstruction quality. However, in the situations where fully-sampled data is not available for training a reconstruction model, our unsupervised method can still produce reconstructions which are comparable to a supervised counterpart and better than CS.

Limitations: Since fully-sampled data was unavailable for our DCE dataset, it was challenging to perform quantitative validation of the experimental outcomes. We intend to validate these results against clinically significant measures in the future.

6   Conclusion

We proposed an unsupervised deep learning framework for accelerated magnetic resonance imaging. Our proposed technique integrates system priors and classical image priors to train DL frameworks for accelerated MRI without the ground truth. The proposed method has better performance than all contemporary unsupervised models and has comparable results to unrolled supervised model.

References

1. Knoll, F., Bredies, K., Pock, T., Stollberger, R.: Second order total generalized variation (TGV) for MRI. Magn. Reson. Med. **65**(2), 480–491 (2011)
2. Qu, X., Zhang, W., Guo, D., Cai, C., Cai, S., Chen, Z.: Iterative thresholding compressed sensing MRI based on contourlet transform. Inverse Prob. Sci. Eng. **18**, 737–758 (2010)
3. Goldstein, T., Osher, S.: The split Bregman method for L1-regularized problems. SIAM J. Imag. Sci. **2**(2), 323–343 (2009)
4. Wang, S., et al.: Accelerating magnetic resonance imaging via deep learning. In: 2016 IEEE 13th International Symposium on Biomedical Imaging (ISBI), pp. 514–517. IEEE (2016)
5. Cole, E.K., Pauly, J.M., Vasanawala, S.S., Ong, F.: Unsupervised MRI reconstruction with generative adversarial networks. arXiv preprint arXiv:2008.13065 (2020)
6. Wang, A.Q., Dalca, A.V., Sabuncu, M.R.: Neural network-based reconstruction in compressed sensing MRI without fully-sampled training data. In: Deeba, F., Johnson, P., Würfl, T., Ye, J.C. (eds.) MLMIR 2020. LNCS, vol. 12450, pp. 27–37. Springer, Cham (2020). https://doi.org/10.1007/978-3-030-61598-7_3
7. Zhan, Z., Cai, J.-F., Guo, D., Liu, Y., Chen, Z., Xiaobo, Q.: Fast multiclass dictionaries learning with geometrical directions in MRI reconstruction. IEEE Trans. Biomed. Eng. **63**(9), 1850–1861 (2015)
8. Yi, Z., Zhang, H., Tan, P., Gong, M.: Dual-GAN: unsupervised dual learning for image-to-image translation. In: ICCV (2017)
9. Aggarwal, H.K., Mani, M.P., Jacob, M.: MoDL: model-based deep learning architecture for inverse problems. IEEE Trans. Med. Imaging **38**, 394–405 (2019)
10. Qin, C., Schlemper, J., Caballero, J., Price, A.N., Hajnal, J.V., Rueckert, D.: Convolutional recurrent neural networks for dynamic MR image reconstruction. IEEE Trans. Med. Imaging **38**(1), 280–290 (2019)
11. Hosseini, S.A.H., Yaman, B., Moeller, S., Hong, M., Akçakaya, M.: Dense recurrent neural networks for accelerated MRI: history-cognizant unrolling of optimization algorithms. IEEE J. Sel. Top. Sig. Process. **14**(6), 1280–1291 (2020)

12. Chen, Y., Firmin, D., Yang, G.: Wavelet improved GAN for MRI reconstruction. In: Proceedings of SPIE, vol. 11595, p. 1159513 (2021)
13. Mardani, M., Monajemi, H., Papyan, V., Vasanawala, S., Donoho, D., Pauly, J.: Recurrent generative adversarial networks for proximal learning and automated compressive image recovery. arXiv:1711.10046 (2017)
14. Lee, D., Yoo, J., Tak, S., Ye, J.C.: Deep residual learning for accelerated MRI using magnitude and phase networks. IEEE Trans. Biomed. Eng. 65(9), 1985–1995 (2018)
15. Eldar, Y.C., et al.: Challenges and open problems in signal processing: panel discussion summary from ICASSP 2017. IEEE Signal Process. Mag. 34, 8–23 (2017)
16. Oh, G., Sim, B., Chung, H., Sunwoo, L., Ye, J.C.: Unpaired deep learning for accelerated MRI using optimal transport driven cycleGAN. IEEE Trans. Comput. Imaging 6, 1285–1296 (2020)
17. Eun, D.-I., Jang, R., Ha, W.S., Lee, H., Jung, S.C., Kim, N.: Deep-learning-based image quality enhancement of compressed sensing magnetic resonance imaging of vessel wall: comparison of self-supervised and unsupervised approaches. Sci. Rep. 10(1), 13950 (2020)
18. Heidemann, R.M., et al.: A brief review of parallel magnetic resonance imaging. Eur. Radiol. 13, 2323–2337 (2003)
19. Cheng, J.Y., Chen, F., Alley, M.T., Pauly, J.M., Vasanawala, S.S.: Highly scalable image reconstruction using deep neural networks with bandpass filtering. arXiv preprint arXiv:1805.03300 (2018)
20. Alaba, S.Y., Ball, J.E.: WCNN3D: wavelet convolutional neural network-based 3D object detection for autonomous driving. Sensors 22(18), 7010 (2022)
21. Jalata, I.K., Truong, T.D., Allen, J.L., Seo, H.S., Luu, K.: Movement analysis for neurological and musculoskeletal disorders using graph convolutional neural network. Future Internet 13(8), 194 (2021)
22. Alaba, S.Y., Ball, J.E.: Deep learning-based image 3D object detection for autonomous driving. IEEE Sens. J. 23, 3378–3394 (2023)
23. Jalata, I., Chappa, N.V.S.R., Truong, T.D., Helton, P., Rainwater, C., Luu, K.: EQAdap: equipollent domain adaptation approach to image deblurring. IEEE Access 10, 93203–93211 (2022)
24. Pruessmann, K.P., Weiger, M., Scheidegger, M.B., Boesiger, P.: SENSE: sensitivity encoding for fast MRI. Magn. Reson. Med. Official J. Int. Soc. Magn. Reson. Med. 42(5), 952–962 (1999)
25. FSE'XL, C. U. B. E., PD PD, FAT FAT: Creation of fully sampled MR data repository for compressed sensing of the knee. SMRT 22nd Annual Meeting, Salt Lake City, Utah, USA (2013)
26. Luo, G., Blumenthal, M., Uecker, M.: Using data-driven image priors for image reconstruction with BART. In: Proceedings of the International Society for Magnetic Resonance in Medicine, vol. 29, p. 3768 (2021)

3D Reconstruction from 2D Cerebral Angiograms as a Volumetric Denoising Problem

Sean Wu[1]([✉]), Naoki Kaneko[2], Steve Mendoza[1], David S. Liebeskind[3], and Fabien Scalzo[1,3]

[1] Keck Data Science Institute, Pepperdine University, Malibu, CA 90265, USA
sean.wu@pepperdine.edu
[2] Department of Interventional Neuroradiology, UCLA, Los Angeles, CA 90095, USA
[3] Department of Neurology, UCLA, Los Angeles, CA 90095, USA

Abstract. Accurately capturing the 3D geometry of the brain's blood vessels is critical in helping neuro-interventionalists to identify and treat neurovascular disorders, such as stroke and aneurysms. Currently, the gold standard for obtaining a 3D representation of angiograms is through the process of 3D rotational angiography, a timely process requiring expensive machinery, which is also associated with high radiation exposure to the patient. In this research, we propose a new technique for reconstructing 3D volumes from 2D angiographic images, thereby reducing harmful X-ray radiation exposure. Our approach involves parameterizing the input data as a back-projected noisy volume from the images, which is then fed into a 3D denoising autoencoder. Through this method, we have achieved clinically relevant reconstructions with varying amounts of 2D projections from 49 patients. Additionally, our 3D denoising autoencoder outperformed previous generative models in biplane reconstruction by 15.51% for intersection over union (IOU) and 3.5% in pixel accuracy due to keeping a semi-accurate input with back projection. This research highlights the significant role of back-projection in achieving relative visual correspondence in the input space to reconstruct 3D volumes from 2D angiograms. This approach has the potential to be deployed in future neurovascular surgery, where 3D volumes of the patient's brain blood vessels can be visualized with less X-ray radiation exposure time.

Keywords: 3D Reconstruction · Deep Learning · Denoising Autoencoder · Rotational Angiography · Cerebral Angiograms

1 Introduction

Digital subtraction angiography (DSA) is a medical imaging technique that gives clinicians insightful information regarding the blood vessels in a patient's brain. DSA operates by injecting a contrast agent into the patient's bloodstream and acquiring an X-ray scan to obtain a clear image of the blood vessels after digital subtraction [1]. DSA is typically used to monitor the blood flow in the brain and

G. Bebis et al. (Eds.): ISVC 2023, LNCS 14361, pp. 382–393, 2023.
https://doi.org/10.1007/978-3-031-47969-4_30

allows for radiologists to have a stronger understanding of certain cerebral disorders such as ischemic stroke and brain aneurysms [2]. 3D rotational angiography remains the gold standard for cerebral aneurysms and other diseases [3] and extends the concept of DSA to a volumetric visualization of the brain's blood vessels. Rotational angiography generates a 3D mesh of the brain's blood vessels by using a C-arm to capture the brain at different angles in a time series while the contrast agent is flowing through it [4].

While 3D rotational angiography provides crucial information regarding the blood flow in the brain in an interpretable modality, acquiring these volumetric meshes cannot be done during surgical procedures due to large machinery and lengthy procedures. Additionally, there may be safety concerns regarding the long acquisition times that could expose patients to high radiation levels for extended periods of time. While X-rays can provide highly detailed insights into bone and vessel structure, the ionizing radiation emitted from X-Ray beams can be so harmful that when passed through the body, they may cause mutations in cells and molecules, potentially causing cancer and other diseases [5]. This is precisely why we are interested in creating a deep-learning pipeline that can accurately reconstruct the three-dimensional CT angiogram from fewer two-dimensional images to reduce the X-Ray exposure time for patients and also to help radiologists evaluate neurovascular properties given these sparse viewpoints. By performing 3D reconstruction, we also hope to eventually be able to visualize blood flow properties in the patient that cannot usually be interpreted from a 2D DSA acquisition. This paper also discusses the minimum number of viewpoints that provide a clinically relevant 3D reconstruction for future model training.

1.1 Related Works

3D object reconstruction from 2D images has been a popular field in computer vision for many years and exploded in popularity with the release of ShapeNet in 2015, where thousands of everyday objects were being reconstructed with various algorithms [6]. Many works have solved the single and multi-view reconstructive problems with high precision on real-world landscapes and commodities all around us such as airplanes, clothing, and even people [7,8]. Some papers deal with the 3D reconstruction of images through an implicit encoder-decoder-like architecture, where the encoder learns to embed the features of the 2D image to a lower dimensional space, then transforms it to a 3D surface through the decoder layers. An amazing breakthrough in 2020 was the neural radiance field paper (NeRF) [9] that aimed to reconstruct a scene's positional depth, lightning, and geometry from arbitrary camera angles. NeRF, at a high level, is mapping the 3D scene as a 5D continuous function in which both a 3D coordinate and a 2D camera angle are taken as input in tandem to generate a volume and color.

One method for 3D reconstruction has been a spherical deformation technique, where a Convolutional Neural Network (CNN) outputs the vertex offset for each point and edits the original sphere based on its predictions [10]. Although 3D reconstruction is a well-researched field with many new contributions each year, there have been few studies applying deep 3D reconstruction algorithms to specific medical tasks such as angiographic data because of expensive medical machinery and sensitive patient data. There have been attempts at this task, such as a contour-interpolation [11], and even self-supervised deep learning approaches [12] that have solved the 3D reconstruction task with 4–12 projections. The self-supervised paper [12] created a 2D to 3D reconstruction pipeline of angiographic images by leveraging the input digital subtracted angiogram images as a learning objective, meaning they took a 2D acquisition from the predicted 3D volume and compared it to the original input image. We present a supervised 2D to 3D reconstruction algorithm because we had access to high-quality volumetric 3D data obtained from a university medical center, which gives our model a clear learning objective. There have been few works researched in angiogram reconstruction because of the difficulties to obtain high-quality volumetric datasets from medical centers. Other papers [13] have attempted this challenging task by implementing a generative adversarial network [14] to generate angiographic slices. However, due to the nature of this generative approach, this resulted in a significant amount of noise and inaccurate geometry in the reconstructed volumes. In order to tackle this challenging problem, we first consider the 2D to 3D reconstruction task using different numbers of projections to observe how many projections are needed for a non-generative model to converge. Additionally, we attempt to tackle the biplane problem by creating a deep-learning model capable of performing the reconstruction task with just two projections.

1.2   Problem Definition

We define our research as creating a deep learning algorithm to perform 3D reconstruction from 2D projections of the brain's blood vessels. One reason we chose the angiogram medium for our study is the high-quality images captured by the X-ray machine. Reconstructing the blood vessels in the brain is a problem that is difficult due to the complexity and intricacy of finer blood vessels. However, we show that our proposed method of a deep learning algorithm can solve this complex task due to the nature of the high-quality images, and registration within angiographic images. Researchers are commonly interested in either explicit reconstruction, where convolutional layers are utilized to output a volume or implicit reconstruction is utilized, where every point in space is sampled to be either inside or outside of the mesh. In our case, we use explicit 3D reconstruction because sampling every point in space with an implicit decoder [15] for a $384 \times 384 \times 384$ volume can take roughly 56 million passes, which can make the model slow on inference time.

In this paper, we discover the minimum number of projections needed to reconstruct the 3D geometry of the brain's blood vessels accurately, and also present an interesting 2D to 3D reconstruction methodology that exploits the properties of computed tomography angiogram acquisitions to learn the input-output mapping function between a sets of angiographic images and the corresponding 3D CT volume. This project contains two primary steps. Firstly, the data is pre-processed to ensure exact visual correspondence between the input and output, eliminating the use of separate images, which poses an inherently ambiguous problem. Secondly,

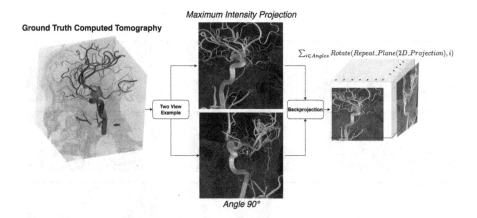

Fig. 1. Illustration of the pre-processing pipeline. We start with the given patient volume (1), then we take a maximum intensity projection (2) for all n viewpoints, then finally, we use back-projection to get a noisy volume (3).

we proceed to train a 3D denoising autoencoder to acquire a semi-photorealistic volume.

2D to a 3D reconstruction poses an inherent challenge due to the limited depth information available from a small number of views and the absence of visual correspondence between the input images and the ground truth volume. Without a perfect visual correspondence where the predicted volume is in spatial alignment with the original CT volume, it is difficult to compute a loss comparing the prediction with the ground truth for training deep learning models. In this paper, we present our methodology for transforming this ill-defined problem [16] into a 3D denoising autoencoder encoder [17]. Our objective is to achieve relative visual correspondence in the model's input space, enabling the network to primarily focus on learning the volume-to-volume translation process.

2 Methodology

To address this intricate problem, we implemented a back-projection technique utilizing angiographic images to obtain a "noisy" three-dimensional volume that matches with relative visual correspondence with the ground truth. This allowed us to obtain a voxel-based representation of the blood vessels, enabling us to apply convolutional operations on the 3D volumes using deep neural networks (Fig. 2).

2.1 Data Pre-processing

For this dataset, we acquired high-quality computed tomographic volumes in the form of DICOM files using [18] from 49 patients who were screened for various neurovascular conditions, including stroke and aneurysms in a clinical database at a university medical center. These CT scans are of size (384,384,384) and have

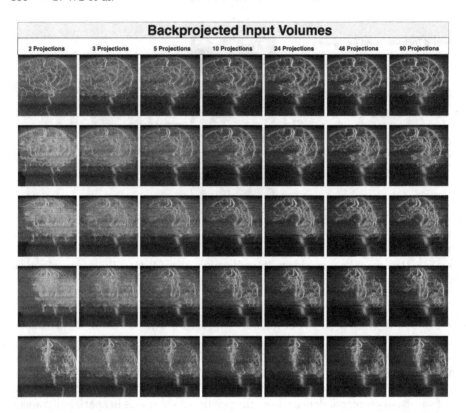

Fig. 2. Depiction of a max-projection at various angles (0,22.5,45,67.5,90) for the back-projected volumes at different viewpoints. The quality of the projection becomes visually worse with fewer than 5 projections.

already been pre-computed with a CT machine and contain information not only about the vessels but also about the skull and other elements in the patient's head. To obtain the 2D acquisitions from this pre-computed ground truth volume, we employed a max-projection technique with [19]. This involved taking the maximum value along the second dimension of an (x, y, z) volume, essentially collapsing the volume and providing us with a clear two-dimensional image of the blood vessels from that angle. We repeated this procedure 90 times for each patient so each patient held a total of 90 projections that we sampled from and utilized for training. In this study, we analyzed 2D to 3D reconstruction from 90, 46, 24, 10, 5, 3, and 2 projections to visualize how many projections are needed to obtain an accurate 3D reconstruction. In all cases, we used the first (0°) and last (90°) projections as input, alongside the other viewpoints obtained by looping through the 90 projections and evenly sampling images depending on how many projections we used. For example, to sample 46 images, we utilized every other angle from 0° to 89° while ensuring the first and last projections are always used.

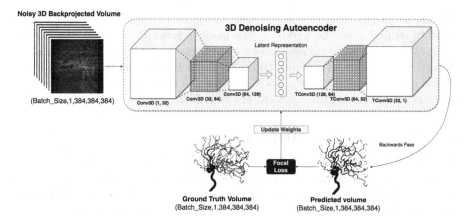

Fig. 3. End to end representation of the forward and backward passes of our 3D denoising autoencoder. (Real example from testing set)

To obtain input volumes, we apply a simple back-projection summation algorithm from n 2D projections by first initializing an empty volume of (384, 384, 384). Then we take each 2D image and repeat that image 384 times to get a volume (384, 384, 384). Finally, we rotate volume based on what projection the 2D image was taken at and sum it to the initialized volume (Fig. 1). By doing this, we ensure that the blood vessels will have larger numbers in the summation, therefore giving us some visual corespondence in the input space. We follow this process where for 90, 46, 24, 10, 5, 3, and 2 projections. Finally, we standardized each volume to hold voxel values between 0 and 1. To obtain ground truth binary data, we appy Otsu's segmentation model [20] from the scikit-learn package [21] to all of the original .dcm files to obtain 3D binary masks as a learning objective. Given the limited availability of data, we adopt an approximate 0.9/0.1 training/testing split, omitting a separate validation set. There are no overlap between patient ids in the training and testing set. The testing set contains 5 unique patients. This decision ensures that we have a larger amount of data for training purposes (Fig. 3).

2.2   Deep Learning Methods

After obtaining the ground truth, we created a standard 3D denoising autoencoder to encode the features into a smaller latent feature tensor. We then used transposed convolution to reconstruct the volume into a denoised representation of it. Our model consists of three 3D convolutional layers. The first layer encoded from one channel to 32 channels, the second layer encoded from 32 channels to 64, and the third layer encoded from 64 channels to 128 output channels. After each convolutional layer, we included a 3D batch normalization layer to standardize the distribution of parameters to have zero mean and standard deviation of one. We also included the ReLU nonlinear activation function after each batch normalization layer to introduce nonlinearity to the network. In addition, we included a

3D max pooling layer after the first two convolutional layers to perform dimensionality reduction on the tensors in the model's forward pass. Our 3D decoder was created in a similar fashion, where we utilized the transposed convolution in PyTorch [22] with kernel size and stride of 2. Our network consists of 360,481 training parameters, each input size is 226.49 (MB), the forward/backwards pass size is 43.034 (GB), and the estimated total size is 43.261 (GB).

2.3   Model Training and Hyper-parameters

To train our 3D denoising autoencoder, we set the batch size to just 1 to stay within the computational limits of our RTX A6000 GPU and set the learning rate to $1e-3$ with the Adam optimizer [23]. We chose the focal loss function [24], primarily used for semantic segmentation, as the criterion for our models.

$$\text{Focal Loss(pred)} = -\alpha(1 - pred)^\gamma \log(pred)$$

This function assigns weights and gives greater attention to data samples that are misclassified, emphasizing more on challenging tasks. The variable "pred" represents the probability of the binary prediction, assuming that it has already been passed through a sigmoid or equivalent activation function (in this case, BCE with logits). The parameter α correlates to the balance between precision and recall of positive class errors, while γ determines the tradeoff for penalizing hard-to-classify data versus non-hard-to-classify data. In our case, we left the α and γ parameters to their default values of 0.5 and 0.2, respectively. Finally, we utilized mixed precision training [25] to train our 3D denoising autoencoder due to the massive size of the (384,384,384) input tensors to our network. This allows us to keep the quality of the original angiographic data, while still having enough GPU memory to compute the forward and backwards passes of the model. Mixed precision training leverages both float16 (half-float precision) and float32/float64 (full and double precision) during network training to significantly reduce the training time by nearly half.

3   Results

In this paper, five unique patients were in the testing set to evaluate how well our 3D denoising autoencoder can generalize on unseen data. For precise analysis, we test each volume with the mean squared error (MSE), mean absolute error (MAE), and intersection over union (IoU) [26], which is a commonly used metric for semantic segmentation tasks. We can use metrics such as this because we are confident that the predicted volumes have an extremely close spatial orientation to the ground truth volumes as a result of our back-projecting technique. The output of our denoising autoencoder is a volume of shape (384, 384, 384) of probabilities, $>= 0.5$ being in the surface and < 0.5 being part of the background. To test the model, we first thresholded each predicted volume to be binary based on these criteria, then computed the metrics to score the prediction based on IoU, MSE, and MAE.

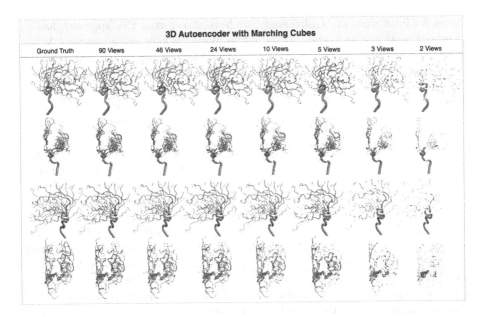

Fig. 4. Visualization of the predicted angiographic volumes from a few different viewpoints of one of the samples in our testing set. The left column represents the ground truth, and the remaining columns are the model outputs at various projections.

The results of our experiments are as expected, with 90, 46, 24, and 10 projections all performing similarly in terms of IoU. While there is a slight decrease in IoU from 90 to 10 views, the fluctuation of IoU in 90, 46, and 24 projections can be accounted for with the random weight initialization (Table 1). To visualize our final outputs, we used the marching cubes [27] surface reconstruction algorithm to extract vertices and faces of the numpy volumes. In this study, we compare our findings with a similar paper by [13], which is one of the only similar papers we could find on the task of biplane 2D to 3D reconstruction. This previous work utilized a 2D conditional generative adversarial network to generate the volume slice-wise. Our 3D denoising algorithm reports a pixel accuracy of 0.9985 and an IoU score of 0.2683 (Table 2), significantly improving both metrics from the previous works.

4   Discussion

In this paper, we have presented a novel technique of supervised 2D to 3D reconstruction given angiographic images by back-projecting the viewpoints into a noisy volume to keep visual correspondence in the input and ground truth, then we train a 3D denoising autoencoder to learn the correct volume translation to the binary ground truth. Our results show that it is possible to train a clinically accurate 3D reconstruction from 90, 46, 24, 10, and even 5 2D projections. However less projections (3, 2) fail to reconstruct fine vessels (Fig. 4), and demonstrates large rooms for improvement. Additionally, we have shown that this approach has an improved pixel accuracy and IoU score than previous generative methods. While there are a few possible reasons for this improvement, it is possible that a generative model is not ideal for this case due to it "guessing" the unseen vessels based on the information learned during training. However, in this case, that may mean generating realistic vessels that do not actually match the geometry of the input images, meaning scarce vessels will have a higher IoU score than incorrectly predicted vessels.

The results of our paper have some implications for future work on reconstructing 3D geometry from fewer projections, such as two or three views. Rather than combating the ill-defined 2D to 3D reconstruction task, we transformed the problem into a 3D to 3D denoising problem, allowing us to keep relative geometry between the two orthogonal images. This may mean that with cleaner data/more computational power, the results may be convincing enough to be deployed in clinical practice. Despite the successes of outperforming previous generative models in a similar 2D to 3D reconstruction task of angiographic images, some limitations to our research are important to discuss. Firstly having only 49 patients may affect our model's generalizability because each CT volume has a different zooming factor, and the vessel structures are highly variant.

Additionally, we did not apply data augmentations in this study due to the computational time required to rotate or transform a 3D volume of (384, 384, 384) for every batch in our training data. Another limitation to discuss is the batch size of the one used for this research. To prevent a loss of information for the intricate and fine details of the blood vessels, we decided to keep the original quality of the data (384, 384, 384) volumes for training. However, because of this, we were required to set the batch size to one to match the memory requirements of our GPU. Some issue that may have arisen from the small batch size is noisy gradients, the gradient computed for each volume may be noisy and not be explanative of the dataset as a whole. While this paper shows a solid proof of concept for this method of 2D to 3D reconstruction transformed as a denoising problem, some

Table 1. Table representing the error and intersection of union (IoU) scores for each model.

Number of Projections	IoU	MSE	MAE
Ninety	56.81%	0.00124	0.0196
Forty-Six	57.06%	0.00103	0.0153
Twenty-Four	56.43%	0.001396	0.0197
Ten	52.22%	0.00173	0.0241
Five	45.35%	0.00277	0.0275
Three	32.17%	0.00224	0.0256
Two	26.83%	0.00264	0.02516

Table 2. Depiction of our biplane (two-view) reconstruction results where we surpass previous generative methods.

Biplane (Two-Projection) Analysis				
Model Type	Pixel Accuracy	IoU	MSE	MAE
ConditionalGan [13]	0.9631	0.0726	N/A	N/A
L1 + ConditionalGAN [13]	0.9587	0.1132	N/A	N/A
3D Denoising (Ours)	0.9985	0.2683	0.0026	0.0251

significant areas and methods can improve the reconstruction to get a watertight volume almost indistinguishable from the ground truth.

In this study, it is evident that the biplane reconstruction task has not been solved. There is naturally a loss of information when back projecting two orthogonal viewpoints into one volume. This loss of information on the 180° angle from the images is due to the binary thresholding. One possible improvement to our pipeline to mitigate this loss is to include another input channel for the original grayscale angiographic images. This additional channel would retain depth and fine detail for all of the vessels. Previous studies, specifically [12] have shown remarkable results for reconstructing the 3D volume from 4+ viewpoints. One interesting method for future research is generating the 2D straight angle (180°) given a single angiographic image. By doing this successfully, it is possible to have two natural and two artificial viewpoints for a new deep-learning model, and we expect the results to be much improved. For clinically relevant medical, the geometry of the reconstructed vessels must match what is possible in the physical realm. Therefore for future projects, we hope to constrain the predictions of the network with a physical-based loss function to our model to penalize predicted vessels that deviate from the dictionary of valid vessel geometries.

5 Conclusion

This paper presents a new methodology for performing 2D to 3D reconstruction of angiographic images by utilizing the properties of the 2D max-projected images and transforming the 2D to 3D problem into a 3D to 3D denoising task. We also conclude that without a generative model, at least three projections at approximately (0, 45, 90) degrees should be utilized to obtain a reasonable 3D reconstruction. Although preliminary, our network may be utilized for future works where more high-quality data, better computational resources, and additional input channels are obtained to produce higher-quality reconstructions where more depth information is recovered. This research utilized a max-projected angiographic image from the ground truth computed tomography volumes. However, due to the nature of our back-projection algorithm, our pipeline should also be compatible with digital subtraction angiograms or other mediums where vessel information is captured in a rotational fashion. With further improvements to the network in future iterations of the project, the problem of 2D to 3D reconstruction of angiographic images will have major impacts by decreasing radiation exposure and the need for expensive machinery in neurological procedures. This will help neurosurgeons better visualize many disorders such as aneurysms, blood clots, and strokes.

Acknowledgements. We would like to thank the Keck Foundation for their grant to Pepperdine University to support our Data Science program and this research.

References

1. Scalzo, F., Liebeskind, D.S., et al.: Perfusion angiography in acute ischemic stroke. Comput. Math. Methods Med. **2016** (2016)
2. Cieściński, J., Serafin, Z., Strześniewski, P., Lasek, W., Beuth, W.: DSA volumetric 3D reconstructions of intracranial aneurysms: a pictorial essay. Pol. J. Radiol. **77**, 47 (2012)
3. van Rooij, W.J., Sprengers, M., de Gast, A.N., Peluso, J., Sluzewski, M.: 3D rotational angiography: the new gold standard in the detection of additional intracranial aneurysms. Am. J. Neuroradiol. **29**, 976–979 (2008)
4. Ishihara, S., Ross, I., Piotin, M., Weill, A., Aerts, H., Moret, J.: 3D rotational angiography: recent experience in the evaluation of cerebral aneurysms for treatment. Interv. Neuroradiol. **6**, 85–94 (2000)
5. Frenz, M., Mee, A.: Diagnostic radiation exposure and cancer risk. Gut **54**, 889–890 (2005)
6. Chang, A.X., et al.: Shapenet: An information-rich 3D model repository. arXiv preprint arXiv:1512.03012 (2015)
7. Saito, S., Huang, Z., Natsume, R., Morishima, S., Kanazawa, A., Li, H.: PIFu: pixel-aligned implicit function for high-resolution clothed human digitization. In: Proceedings of the IEEE/CVF International Conference on Computer Vision, pp. 2304–2314 (2019)
8. Wang, N., Zhang, Y., Li, Z., Fu, Y., Liu, W., Jiang, Y.G.: Pixel2mesh: generating 3d mesh models from single RGB images. In: Proceedings of the European Conference on Computer Vision (ECCV), pp. 52–67 (2018)
9. Mildenhall, B., Srinivasan, P.P., Tancik, M., Barron, J.T., Ramamoorthi, R., Ng, R.: NeRF: representing scenes as neural radiance fields for view synthesis. Commun. ACM **65**, 99–106 (2021)
10. Kato, H., Ushiku, Y., Harada, T.: Neural 3D mesh renderer. In: Proceedings of the IEEE Conference on Computer Vision and Pattern Recognition, pp. 3707–3916 (2018)
11. Galassi, F., et al.: 3D reconstruction of coronary arteries from 2D angiographic projections using non-uniform rational basis splines (NURBS) for accurate modelling of coronary stenoses. PLoS ONE **13**, e0190650 (2018)
12. Zhao, H., et al.: Self-supervised learning enables 3D digital subtraction angiography reconstruction from ultra-sparse 2D projection views: a multicenter study. Cell Rep. Med. **3**, 100775 (2022)
13. Zuo, J.: 2D to 3D neurovascular reconstruction from biplane view via deep learning. In: 2021 2nd International Conference on Computing and Data Science (CDS), pp. 383–387. IEEE (2021)
14. Goodfellow, I.J., et al.: Generative adversarial networks (2014)

15. Chen, Z., Zhang, H.: Learning implicit fields for generative shape modeling. In: Proceedings of the IEEE/CVF Conference on Computer Vision and Pattern Recognition, pp. 5939–5948 (2019)
16. Pontes, J.K., Kong, C., Eriksson, A., Fookes, C., Sridharan, S., Lucey, S.: Compact model representation for 3D reconstruction. arXiv preprint arXiv:1707.07360 (2017)
17. Venkataraman, P.: Image denoising using convolutional autoencoder. arXiv preprint arXiv:2207.11771 (2022)
18. Mason, D.: SU-E-T-33: pydicom: an open source DICOM library. Med. Phys. **38**, 3493–3493 (2011)
19. Harris, C.R., et al.: Array programming with NumPy. Nature **585**, 357–362 (2020)
20. Otsu, N.: A threshold selection method from gray-level histograms. IEEE Trans. Syst. Man Cybern. **9**, 62–66 (1979)
21. Pedregosa, F., et al.: Scikit-learn: machine learning in python. J. Mach. Learn. Res. **12**, 2825–2830 (2011)
22. Paszke, A., et al.: Automatic differentiation in pytorch (2017)
23. Kingma, D.P., Ba, J.: Adam: a method for stochastic optimization. arXiv preprint arXiv:1412.6980 (2014)
24. Lin, T.Y., Goyal, P., Girshick, R., He, K., Dollár, P.: Focal loss for dense object detection. In: Proceedings of the IEEE International Conference on Computer Vision, pp. 2980–2988 (2017)
25. Micikevicius, P., et al.: Mixed precision training. arXiv preprint arXiv:1710.03740 (2017)
26. Rezatofighi, H., Tsoi, N., Gwak, J., Sadeghian, A., Reid, I., Savarese, S.: Generalized intersection over union: a metric and a loss for bounding box regression. In: Proceedings of the IEEE/CVF Conference on Computer Vision and Pattern Recognition, pp. 658–666 (2019)
27. Lorensen, W.E., Cline, H.E.: Marching cubes: a high resolution 3D surface construction algorithm. In: Seminal Graphics: Pioneering Efforts that Shaped the Field, pp. 347–353 (1998)

An Integrated Shape-Texture Descriptor for Modeling Whole-Organism Phenotypes in Drug Screening

Jiadong Yu[1] and Rahul Singh[1,2(✉)]

[1] Department of Computer Science, University of Iowa, Iowa City, Iowa 52242-1419, USA
rahul-singh@uiowa.edu
[2] Center for Discovery and Innovation in Parasitic Diseases, UC San Diego, CA 92093, USA

Abstract. Schistosomiasis is a parasitic disease with global health and socio-economic impacts. The World Health Organization (WHO) and National Institutes of Health (NIH) list it among diseases for which new treatments are urgently required. Drug discovery for Schistosomiasis typically involves whole-organism phenotypic screening. In such an approach, the parasites are exposed to different chemical compounds, and systemic phenotypic effects captured via microscopy (video or still images) are analyzed to identify promising molecules. Changes in parasite phenotypes tend to be multidimensional, involving changes in shape, appearance and behavior, and time-varying. In many image representation frameworks, shape and appearance are measured independently and their inter-correlation can be lost. In this paper, we propose an integrated shape-texture descriptor called the *skeleton-constrained shortest band* (SCSB) that extends the family of shape context descriptors well known in computer vision. We examine how SCSB can be used to measure temporally varying shape and appearance changes occurring as a consequence of chemical action and compare its performance with other members of the shape context family.

Keywords: Shape Context · biological imaging · microscopy · parasitic diseases · whole-organism screening · drug discovery

1 Introduction

1.1 Background

Schistosomiasis is a parasitic disease with global health and socio-economic impacts. It is estimated that over 200 million people are currently infected and more than 700 million are at risk across 78 countries. Treatment is largely based on the drug praziquantel (PZQ). However, it is primarily effective during the adult stage of the worm life cycle [1] and resistance to the drug has been observed [2]. Thus, the World Health Organization (WHO) and National Institutes of Health (NIH) list schistosomiasis among diseases for which new treatments are urgently required.

G. Bebis et al. (Eds.): ISVC 2023, LNCS 14361, pp. 394–405, 2023.
https://doi.org/10.1007/978-3-031-47969-4_31

Drug discovery for Schistosomiasis (and other helminthic diseases) typically involves whole organism phenotypic screening. In this process, parasite(s) are exposed to different compounds and the resultant multidimensional and systemic phenotypic changes are recorded and analyzed to determine the efficacy of the compounds and identify putative novel drugs. Starting with the pioneering work in [3], the development of phenotype-analysis methods for this area has attracted significant interest. Within this context, one of the key technical challenges lies in the development of image representation-comparison frameworks that can capture the wide variety of correlated shape-appearance changes exhibited by the parasites causing schistosomiasis.

1.2 Problem Formulation

In order to precisely measure complex parasite phenotypes, the representation must be accurate, robust, and invariant to the following characteristics: (1) Euclidean and scale invariance, (2) significant deformations that occur as the parasites move, and (3) a range of imaging conditions. Furthermore, shape and appearance changes are not only two of the most important aspects of parasite phenotypic responses, but they can also be correlated. For example, as the shape of the parasite deforms during motion, its body texture changes in a coupled manner. Consequently, integrated shape-texture descriptors are required since measuring these attributes independently may fail to capture their interrelationship.

The example in Fig. 1 illustrates these characteristics. In it, a group of parasites exposed to the antipsychotic drug acepromazine are followed across 10 non-consecutive frames. It is easy to note that the illumination changes over the recording time. More importantly, we can observe that the parasite at the bottom left of the top row underwent significant changes in both shape and texture due to its movements. The reader may also

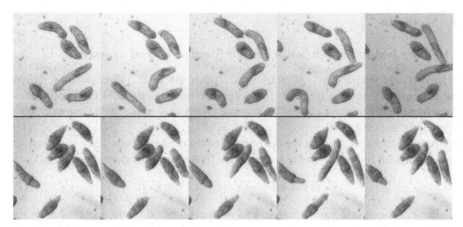

Fig. 1. Depiction of shape and appearance changes over time: top-row due to parasite motion and across top-and bottom row due to chemical action. The top row shows 6 parasites in 5 frames exposed to acepromazine (10 μM and one day of exposure to the compound). The bottom row shows 5 frames with the parasites also exposed to acepromazine (10 μM, , four days after exposure to the compound).

note the temporally evolving systemic degradation suffered by the parasites (bottom row) when compared with the top row, as a result of chemical action.

2   Prior Work

The first attempt to describe the complex phenotypes of Schistosomiasis using algorithmic image analysis was made by Singh *et al.* [3]. In this work the problems of segmentation, appearance encoding, and phenotype classifications were addressed by analyzing parasites exposed to a select set of compounds. The description of the shape and appearance relied on measurements of eccentricity, entropy, and local pixel range. Nevertheless, eccentricity alone is insufficient to fully encompass all of the intricate deformation-driven alterations in the parasite shape. In a significant advancement thereafter, a public webserver called QDREC [4] for automatically determining dose-response characteristics and IC_{50} values from microscopy images was developed. In QDREC, 71 image-based features were used to describe the shape and appearance. As mentioned above, many these features were calculated independently for shape-appearance changes that are coupled and any interrelationships were, at best, reflected implicitly in QDREC. Method development reported by us in this paper is motivated by the shape-context family of representations. The progenitor of this family of methods, the shape context (SC) representation [5], is known to be a robust shape descriptor that is invariant to translation, rotation, and scale. Its generalization, called the inner distance shape context (IDSC), and a combined descriptor using IDSC and intensity gradient directions called the shortest path texture context (SPTC) were proposed later [6]. However, we have found (and demonstrate in this paper) that IDSC can be sensitive to inconsequential shape variations. Furthermore, intensity gradient directions may be too simplistic to describe complex texture changes.

3   Methods

3.1   Integrated Representation of Parasite Morphology and Appearance

In this section, we start by summarizing the shape context (SC) representation. Given the contours of a parasite $P|P \in R^2$, , the shape context descriptor $SC(P)$ is defined as the relative distribution of each of the contour points of P to the other contour points. That is, for the contour $P = \{c_1, \ldots, c_n\}$, , $SC(P) = \{d_1, d_2, \ldots, d_n\}$, where d_m is a log-polar histogram capturing the distribution of the contour points $\{c_j \neq c_m\}$ relative to c_m as defined in Eq. (1), where k indexes the bins of the histogram (See Fig. 2a).

$$d_m(k) = \#\{(c_j - c_m) \in bin(k), m \neq j\} \tag{1}$$

Each histogram d_m can be rotated and positioned based on the tangent line at c_m to obtain rotation invariance. SC is also invariant to Euclidean transformations and is known to be highly noise tolerant. Scale-invariance can be obtained if the radius of the log-polar histogram is calculated using the mean distance between all the points pairs.
   In the IDSC, the geodesic distance *i.e.,* the shortest path between a pair of points that is completely contained inside the shape is used to construct the log-polar histogram

(Fig. 2b). Due to its use of inter-point geodesics, IDSC is invariant to shape articulations. The reader is referred to the original SC and IDSC papers for a detailed technical explanation underlying the characteristics of SC and IDSC methods. However, the geodesic distance uses other points as bridge points if the Euclidean distance between a pair of points doesn't entirely lie within the shape, and as we have found, it is particularly sensitive to small changes on the contour under these conditions.

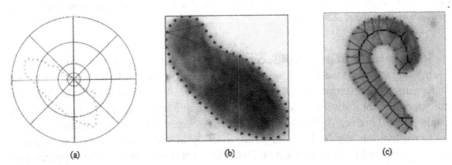

(a)   (b)   (c)

Fig. 2. A figure caption is always placed below the illustration. Short captions are centered, while long ones are justified. The macro button chooses the correct format automatically.

Such sensitivity is of course highly undesirable, since in such cases, the geodesic distance may fluctuate unpredictably for small local changes in the contour. As an alternative we propose a descriptor which constrains the geodesic distances between an arbitrary pair of contour points to pass through the shape skeleton (Fig. 2c). The incorporation of the shape skeleton leads to more robust descriptor that is also sensitive to shape articulations when compared to SC and IDSC.

We define the skeleton-constrained inner distance (SCID) for object O with contour P and skeleton $S = \{s_1, \ldots, s_t\}$ as follows:

$$\alpha(c_i, c_j; O) = \alpha(c_i, s_i; O) + \alpha(s_i, s_j; S) + \alpha(s_j, c_j; O) \tag{2}$$

$$\alpha(c_i, s_i; O) = min\{\alpha(c_i, s_j; O), c_i \in P \text{ and } \forall s_j \in S\} \tag{3}$$

In Eq. (2) and (3), $\alpha(c_i, c_j; O)$ is the skeleton-constraint inner distance from $c_i \in P$ to $c_j \in P$, $\alpha(c_i, s_i; O)$ is the shortest (in the least square) sense path from the contour point c_i to the $s_i \in S$ which contained inside the object O, $\alpha(s_j, c_j; O)$ is the shortest (in the least square) sense path between $s_j \in S$ and $c_j \in P$, and $\alpha(s_i, s_j; S)$ is the path from s_i to s_j along the skeleton S. Typically, the skeleton is computed using the media axis transformation and can be sensitive to contour variations leading to unnecessary branching of the skeleton. To improve the robustness, a pruning step is applied to the skeleton. Specifically, the skeleton S is first divided into the main branch S_a and side branches S_i such that:

$$S = S_a \cup \{\bigcup_i S_i\} \text{ and } S_a \cap S_i = \varnothing, \forall i \tag{4}$$

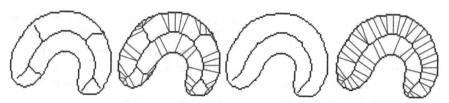

Fig. 3. Skeleton and their skeleton-constrained shortest paths before and after the pruning step. The left two images represent the unpruned version, and the right two images represent the pruned version with only the main branch left.

Subsequently, a proportion of S_i can be pruned based on its characteristics (Fig. 3). The pruning is done as the following: (1) The main branch and side branches are identified by measuring the distance along the skeleton between all its endpoints, (2) side branches are ordered by their distance, and (3) the shortest side branches are pruned based on a pruning ratio which can either be user-specified or determined automatically.

To explain our approach to the joint modeling of shape and texture, we begin by noting that in the SPTC by the shape information captured by the IDSC is supplemented by measuring the distributions of (weighted) relative orientation through the shortest paths. The relative orientation is obtained by measuring the angles between intensity gradient directions and shortest path direction, and the weight is gradient magnitudes. The SPTC is a 3-D histogram where the inner-distance and the inner-angle used as the first two dimensions are the same as IDSC. The third dimension is binned normalized histogram of weighted relative orientation.

Our approach combines shape and appearance through similarly but uses a different texture descriptor called dominant rotated local binary pattern (DRLBP) [7]. DRLBP is a rotation invariant texture descriptor that builds on top of the local binary pattern (LBP), where the central pixel of a local circular region is compared with its neighbors.

$$LBP_{R,B} = \sum_{b=0}^{B-1} s(p_b - p_c) \cdot 2^b \qquad (5)$$

In Eq. (5), p_c and p_b denote the gray level intensity of the central pixel and its neighbors, R is the radius of the circular neighborhood, B the number of neighbors, and s is an indicator function where its value is 0 if the neighbor pixel is less than the central pixel, 1 otherwise. A dominant direction is then defined (Eq. (6)), which can be used to rotate the LBP and thereby achieve rotational invariance (Eq. (7)).

$$DIR = \text{argmax}_{b \in (0,1,...,B-1)} |p_b - p_c| \qquad (6)$$

$$DRLBP_{R,B} = \sum_{b=0}^{B-1} s(p_b - p_c) \cdot 2^{mod(b-DIR,B)} \qquad (7)$$

DRLBP is invariant to illumination due to the indicator function. It is also a more flexible and informative texture descriptor as a broader range of neighborhood pixels can be considered with the radius parameter (Fig. 4). To distinguish darker parasites

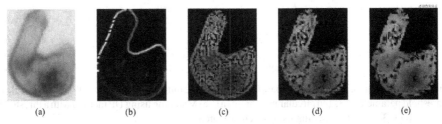

Fig. 4. Appearance and texture of a parasite using relative orientation and DRLBP. (a) Original parasite, (b) Weighted relative orientation. (c)(d)(e) Weighted Rotated Local Binary Pattern (WRLBP) with radii 1, 2, 3, respectively.

from lighter ones, even when they are similarly textured, we can weigh the RLBP as the following:

$$WRLBP_{R,B} = DRLBP_{R,B} \cdot \frac{p_c}{2^B} \tag{8}$$

Finally, to obtain the integrated shape-appearance description of an object O with contour P, which we shall call the skeleton-constrained shortest band (SCSB), $\alpha(c_m, c_j; O)$ is the shortest path between the contour point c_m and c_j of P as defined above. The new k^{th} bins of the 3D-histogram can be formulated as the following:

$$d_m(k) = \#\{p_i \in bin(k), p_i \in \alpha(c_m, c_j; WRLBP_{R,B}(O))\} \tag{9}$$

where $WRLBP_{R,B}(O)$ is the appearance of object O and p_i are the pixels along the SCID inside $WRLBP_{R,B}(O)$.

To match two objects with their histograms, we must find the point correspondences and compute the dissimilarity score between them. The dissimilarity between the contour points from one object to another is calculated as the χ^2 distance between their corresponding histograms:

$$cost\left(c_i^P, c_j^Q\right) = \chi^2\left(d_i^P, d_j^Q\right) = \frac{1}{2}\sum_{k=1}^{K} \frac{[d_i^P(k) - d_j^Q(k)]^2}{d_i^P(k) + d_j^Q(k) + \varepsilon} \tag{10}$$

In Eq. (10), d_i^P represents the histogram computed at point c_i of an object with contour P and $cost\left(c_i^P, c_j^Q\right)$ represents the dissimilarity in terms of χ^2 distance between histograms d_i^P and d_j^Q.

Given a set of $cost\left(c_i^P, c_j^Q\right)$ of all the points between two objects, the final dissimilarity score and correspondences can be computed by obtaining correspondences between pairs of contour points. Such a correspondence can be obtained either by using the Hungarian algorithm with additional "dummy" points used by Belongie et al. [5] or by dynamic programming (DP), as proposed by Ling et al.[6]. However, both approaches are problematic. The Hungarian algorithm computes the optimal cost between two objects but doesn't consider the connectivity constraints between contour points leading

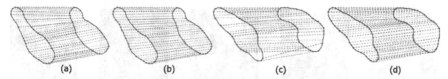

(a)	(b)	(c)	(d)

Fig. 5. Matching of two pairs of parasites using the Hungarian methods, DP method with a threshold parameter 0.3, and circular matching: (a), (c) Matching using DP method with a threshold parameter 0.3. (b), (d) Matching using circular matching.

to non-monotonic matching of point pairs. The "dummy" points introduce a constant cost and can be treated as a threshold parameter to filter out the pairs of points with high-cost scores. However, this doesn't consider the non-monotonic matching with low-cost scores. In our case, this parameter is hard to choose as large deformation can result in a higher cost score while small deformation can result in a lower cost score and the final dissimilarity score could be inconsistent due to the choice of the threshold parameter. See Fig. 5a and 5c, the correspondences for the same threshold 0.3 works very differently when large and medium deformation appears. Therefore, we use a similar approach to the DP method but enforce all matching without the threshold parameter as this is better at presenting dissimilarity score involving large deformation, and we call this circular matching (CM) (Fig. 5b and 5d).

Table 1. Statistical summary of the dataset

	Dataset
Total parasites	175
The size of parasites	2314–6668
Perimeter of parasites	166–390
Proportion of the bbox filled	19%–79%
Grayscale mean intensity	108–196
Exposure time in days	1, 2, 3, 4, 7
Concentration in μM	0*, 0.01, 0.1, 1, 10
Compounds	Acepromazine, Alimemazine, Amitriptyline, Chlorophenothiazine, Clomipramine, Cyclobenzaprine, Desipramine, Hycanthone, Imipramine, K777, Methiothepin Mesylate, Mevastatin, Niclosamide, Pravastatin, Praziquantel (PZQ), Promazine, Promethazine, Rosuvastatin, Simvastatin, Triflupromazine, Control*

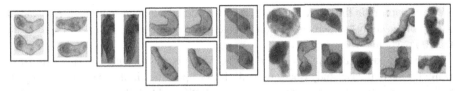

Fig. 6. The comprehensive datasets. Left are examples from the 50 paired parasites. Right are examples from the 75 unique parasites.

4 Experiments

The proposed methods are evaluated with a comprehensive chemical-phenotype dataset that was reported in [8]. It contains 50 paired parasites from consecutive frames of the same video include small, medium and large deformations, and 75 parasites with unique phenotypes (Fig. 6). A summary of the dataset is provided in Table 1.

Now we describe the parameter used through all the experiments. We use n to denote the number of sample points on the outer contour of the shapes. As n gets large, is the contour representation becomes more accurate but less efficient. For the size of histograms, n_r, n_t, and n_i are used for the number of bins for log-distance on the radius, the number of bins for the angles, and the number of bins for the intensity levels, respectively. For the pruning fraction used to prune branches of the skeleton, f is used. In our work, a typical setting for these parameters was $n_r = 5$, $n_t = 12$, $n_i = 16$, $f = 0.25$ and are used through all the experiments in this paper.

4.1 Shape Retrieval in Terms of Deformation

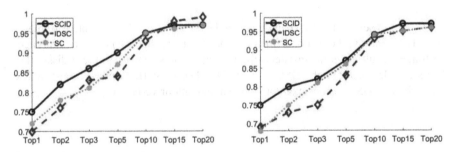

Fig. 7. Two case studies on shape retrieval in terms of deformation. (a) Case study one with 100 parasites. (b) Case study two with 175 parasites.

Although SCID does not explicitly factor-in deformation, it is relatively robust for deformable shape retrieval when compared to SC and IDSC. The 50 pairs of parasites from consecutive frames show a variety of cases when small, medium, and large deformations are observed to occur in the Dataset (see Fig. 6). We designed two case studies to compare SCID, IDSC, and SC. Both the case studies go through the same step. For each of the 100 parasites (50 pairs), if the desired shape (the other parasite in the pair) appears in the top K retrievals, it is considered a hit (the parameter K is varied as part of the study). A percentage can be calculated based on the number of hits for all the 100 parasites.

The first case study query uses only the 50 pairs of the parasites (total of 100), while the second case study query uses all the 175 parasites in the Dataset. See Fig. 7. SCID shows better shape retrieval compared to IDSC and SC. Both case studies lead to similar conclusions, *i.e.*, SCID is better at shape retrieval when deformation are presents, especially when $K \leq 10$ corresponding to the requirement of high precision in the retrievals.

4.2 Robustness and Sensitivity

In this section, we compare the sensitivity of SCID and IDSC. We have noted that IDSC may be sensitive to small changes on the contour while SCID is not. An example is shown in Fig. 8.

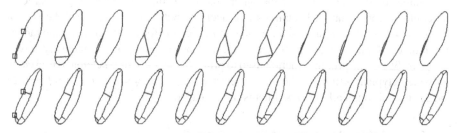

Fig. 8. Fluctuations in the IDSC (top row, showing the shortest paths) and SCID between the same two points of the same parasite taken from 11 consecutive frames.

We can observe that the shape changes between these 11 consecutive frames are small. However, the shortest path inner distance fluctuates between the two points across the frames resulting in inconsistent dissimilarity scores. In Fig. 9, these dissimilarity scores are shown for both IDSC and SCID. Clearly, SCID is more robust and less sensitive than IDSC for this example with small contour variations.

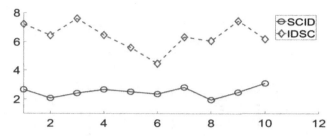

Fig. 9. Dissimilarity scores between 11 parasites in successive frames using both SCID and IDSC. Unlike the SCID curve, the IDSC curve shows large fluctuation even when parasite shapes show small changes.

For significant deformations, the fluctuations in the geodesic distance used in IDSC are greater as compared to the SCID. To demonstrate this, consider the following five parasites across 11 consecutive frames (Fig. 10).

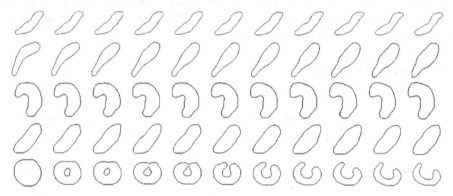

Fig. 10. 5 parasite contours across 11 consecutive frames exhibiting significant shape deformations.

Instead of determining the shortest path using IDSC and SCID between two specific points of these parasites as in the previous experiment, we compute a more holistic statistic obtained by determining the variances of the shortest path distances between all paired points across the 11 frames for these two methods. For each of the five parasites, a pair of boxplots is used to present a side-by-side comparison of the variances in Fig. 11.

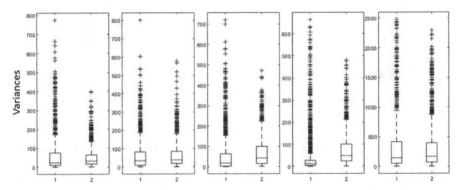

Fig. 11. The boxplots from left to right correspond to the parasites (and their deformations) shown from top to bottom in Fig. 10. The label 1 in each boxplot denotes the variance of IDSC while the label 2 denotes the variances of SCID.

The reader may note that both IDSC and SCID show large variances for large shape deformations. However, the variances in SCID measurements are always less than the corresponding variances in the IDSC measurements. These two experiments demonstrate the robustness of the SCID representation.

4.3 Phenotype Retrieval

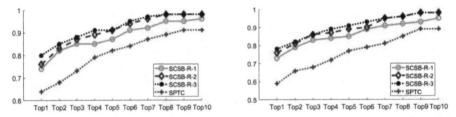

Fig. 12. Two case studies on shape retrieval in terms of deformation: (left) Case study with 100 parasites. (right) Case study with the set of 175 parasites.

In the previous section, we showed how SCID compared with SC and IDSC. Using the same experimental settings we compare the SPTC with the SCSB (using radii of 1, 2, and 3). In Fig. 12, the retrieval performances are shown for the top-K hits ($K \leq 10$). SCSB is found to consistently perform better than SPTC across all the values of K with the best results obtained with the radius value of 3.

5 Conclusion

This paper describes a novel shape-texture descriptor based on a new inner-distance formulation called skeleton-constraint inner distance and compares it to prior shape context formulations. Preliminary results on phenotypic screening data underline the robustness and promise of the proposed approach for shape and appearance matching.

Acknowledgements. The authors thank Conor R. Caffrey for the screening data reported in [8]. This work was funded by NSF (IIS 1817239) and NIH (AI146719).

References

1. Vale, N., Gouveia, M.J., Rinaldi, G., Brindley, P.J., Gärtner, F., Correia Da Costa, J.M.: Praziquantel for schistosomiasis: single-drug metabolism revisited, mode of action, and resistance. Antimicrob. Agents Chemother. **61**, e02582–16 (2017). https://doi.org/10.1128/AAC.02582-16

2. Fallon, P.G.: Schistosome resistance to praziquantel. Drug Resist. Updates **1**, 236–241 (1998). https://doi.org/10.1016/S1368-7646(98)80004-6

3. Singh, R., Pittas, M., Heskia, I., Xu, F., McKerrow, J., Caffrey, C.R.: Automated image-based phenotypic screening for high-throughput drug discovery. In: 22nd IEEE International Symposium on Computer-Based Medical Systems, pp. 1–8. IEEE, Albuquerque, NM, USA (2009)

4. Asarnow, D., Rojo-Arreola, L., Suzuki, B.M., Caffrey, C.R., Singh, R.: The QDREC web server: determining dose–response characteristics of complex macroparasites in phenotypic drug screens. Bioinformatics **31**, 1515–1518 (2015). https://doi.org/10.1093/bioinformatics/btu831

5. Belongie, S., Malik, J., Puzicha, J.: Shape matching and object recognition using shape contexts. IEEE Trans. Pattern Anal. Mach. Intell. **24**, 509–522 (2002). https://doi.org/10.1109/34.993558

6. Ling, H., Jacobs, D.W.: Shape classification using the inner-distance. IEEE Trans. Pattern Anal. Mach. Intell. **29**, 286–299 (2007). https://doi.org/10.1109/TPAMI.2007.41

7. Mehta, R., Egiazarian, K.: Dominant rotated local binary patterns (DRLBP) for texture classification. Pattern Recogn. Lett. **71**, 16–22 (2016). https://doi.org/10.1016/j.patrec.2015.11.019

8. Lee, H., et al.: Quantification and clustering of phenotypic screening data using time-series analysis for chemotherapy of schistosomiasis. BMC Genomics **13**, S4 (2012). https://doi.org/10.1186/1471-2164-13-S1-S4

Enhancing Image Reconstruction via Phase-Constrained Data in an Iterative Process

Alan Okinaka[1], Gulfam Saju[2], and Yuchou Chang[2(✉)]

[1] Physics Department, Ursinus College, 601 E Main St, Collegeville, PA 19426, USA
[2] Computer and Information Science Department, University of Massachusetts Dartmouth, 285 Old Westport Road, Dartmouth, MA 02747, USA
ychang1@umassd.edu

Abstract. This paper proposes an innovative approach to improve residual artifacts in image-based parallel magnetic resonance imaging (MRI) reconstruction. Despite its superior signal-to-noise ratio (SNR) over the conventional Sensitivity Encoding (SENSE) method, SENSE is hindered by persisting residual artifacts, causing it to be less effective in image-based parallel MRI reconstruction. We propose a joint estimation of actual and virtual coil sensitivity maps, along with the reconstructed image. Inspired by the principles of the Joint Sensitivity Encoding (JSENSE) method, the proposed approach employs an iterative optimization process via phase-constrained data of virtual conjugate coils, progressively refining these integral components to achieve superior image quality. Experimental results show that the proposed method not only enhances MRI image quality by suppressing residual artifacts but also paves the way for future research into the potential of virtual conjugate coils in image-based MRI reconstruction. Different from the phase-constrained data for enhancing k-space-based parallel MRI, the method shows that the phase-constrained data also improve image-based parallel MRI reconstruction.

Keywords: Magnetic Resonance Imaging · Virtual Conjugate Coil · Phase-Constrained Reconstruction

1 Introduction

Virtual Conjugate Coil (VCC) [1, 2] has undeniably brought about significant improvements in the quality of parallel Magnetic Resonance Imaging (MRI) reconstructions and deep network-based methods. Renowned techniques such as VCC-GRAPPA [2], VCC-LORAKS [3], and VCC-ESPIRIT [4] along with newer approaches like virtual coil augmentation for MR coil extrapolation via deep learning [11], have showcased their efficacy in suppressing residual artifacts in reconstructed images and enhancing the Signal-to-Noise Ratio (SNR).

Virtual Conjugate Coil Sensitivity Encoding (VCC-SENSE) [2], a technique that has gained significant attention in the field, has demonstrated a superior SNR compared to the

© The Author(s), under exclusive license to Springer Nature Switzerland AG 2023
G. Bebis et al. (Eds.): ISVC 2023, LNCS 14361, pp. 406–414, 2023.
https://doi.org/10.1007/978-3-031-47969-4_32

conventional Sensitivity Encoding (SENSE) [5] approach. However, this approach is not without its flaws. Residual artifacts, lingering remnants from the reconstruction process that interfere with the interpretation of the final image, continue to persist in VCC-SENSE reconstructions. This shortcoming has led to VCC being less studied in the realm of image-based parallel MRI reconstruction compared to k-space-based reconstruction [2–4].

In this context, it becomes imperative to devise innovative strategies that focus on the reduction and potential elimination of these residual artifacts. In this paper, our primary goal is to improve these residuals in SENSE reconstructions. Our approach involves solving an iterative optimization problem, a strategy that has proven successful in various computational tasks. Motivated by the principles of Joint Sensitivity Encoding (JSENSE) [8], we propose a joint estimation of actual coil sensitivity maps, virtual coil sensitivity maps, and the reconstructed image. This is not a straightforward approach, as it involves iteratively enhancing and refining these three integral components to achieve superior image quality. The coil sensitivity maps – both actual and virtual – along with the image to be reconstructed, undergo a series of improvements, progressively refining the final output.

The iterative optimization process offers a systematic and guided approach to improve the quality of the reconstructed image. The idea is to start with an initial estimation for each of the three components and iteratively refine them, with each iteration offering an improvement over the last. The process continues until an optimal or near-optimal solution is found. The joint estimation approach provides a mechanism for the system to learn from the residuals, enabling it to correct and suppress these artifacts. The suppression of these residuals can significantly improve the quality of the reconstructed images. By addressing one of the major shortcomings of the SENSE-related techniques, we aim to bring VCC to image-based MRI reconstruction and provide an improved approach that balances both SNR and the minimization of residual artifacts. In this paper, the first and the second sections of this paper present an introduction and background. The proposed method is given in the third part. Experimental results and conclusions are provided in the fourth and fifth sections.

2   Background

Joint Sensitivity Encoding (JSENSE) [8] is a magnetic resonance imaging (MRI) technique designed to overcome certain limitations of conventional SENSE [5] method, which rely heavily on precise estimations of coil sensitivity maps for image reconstruction. The conventional SENSE method can suffer from inaccuracies in these initial estimates, leading to degraded image quality. JSENSE adopts an iterative approach optimizing both coil sensitivity maps and the image concurrently. This innovative strategy allows for the refinement of the actual coil image sensitivity profile during the image reconstruction process, thus potentially yielding higher-quality images. Despite the computational demands of this iterative process making JSENSE more resource-intensive than conventional SENSE methods, ongoing research including the application of deep learning methods is focused on enhancing the performance and efficiency of JSENSE, particularly in situations where initial coil sensitivity profiles are inaccurate or change during MRI scan.

Efforts to improve calibration accuracy in MRI reconstruction have necessitated mining valuable data within the restricted auto-calibration signal (ACS) lines, where a notable strategy involves the application of the VCC concept. The VCC enhances encoding power, effectively bolstering the reconstruction performance of numerous methodologies such as SENSE [2], GRAPPA [2], ESPIRiT [4], KerNL [6], iterative RAKI [9], nonlinear GRAPPA [7], even multi-contrast data [10], and PROPELLER [13]. Additionally, the VCC method introduces extra equations into the inverse reconstruction matrix by incorporating additional phase information, augmenting the precision of the reconstructed images. In the context of machine learning, VCC serves as an effective data augmentation technique, contributing to the enhanced performance of learning models [6]. However, while VCC improves the reconstruction quality, it results in increased computational costs due to the doubling of channels in the k-space data used in the process. For instance, a dataset involving a 32-coil k-space would necessitate a total of 64 coils for reconstruction, including the original 32 and an added 32 virtual coils, making the procedure more computationally demanding.

3 Proposed Method

3.1 The Proposed Framework

The proposed methodology framework is illustrated in Fig. 1. Phase-constrained data are generated as VCC signals. Both physical coil data and VCC data are used in JSENSE-like iterative reconstruction.

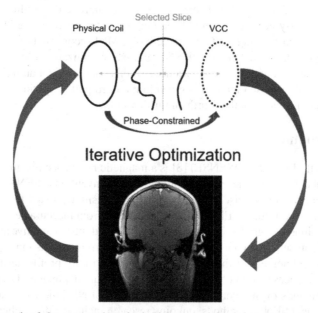

Fig. 1. Framework of the proposed method. Phase-constrained data are incorporated into the iterative reconstruction process, which is supported by JSENSE-like method.

3.2 Generating Phase-Constrained Data

In parallel MRI, one coil's k-space data denotes the Fourier Transform (FT) of the distribution of the spatial spins combined with the coil sensitivities. Furthermore, in practical imaging, background phase effects caused by B0 field inhomogeneity, flow, and pulse sequence also exist in the effective coil sensitivities. The coil k-space data can be represented as [1]

$$S_j(\mathbf{p}) = \text{FT}\Big(\rho(\mathbf{x}) \cdot e^{i\varphi(\mathbf{x})} \cdot C_j(\mathbf{x})\Big), \tag{1}$$

where $\rho(\mathbf{x})$ represents the spin distribution, $e^{i\varphi(\mathbf{x})}$ denotes background phase, $C_j(\mathbf{x})$ is the coil sensitivities of the jth coil, $\mathbf{p}$ is the k-space data vector, and $\mathbf{x}$ represents the vector in the image domain. The symmetric complex-conjugate k-space data can be represented as [1]

$$S_j^*(\mathbf{p}) = \text{FT}\Big[\rho(\mathbf{x}) \cdot e^{-i\varphi(\mathbf{x})} \cdot C_j^*(\mathbf{x})\Big], \tag{2}$$

where $*$ is the complex-conjugate operator. Additional phase information is provided in the VCC, although the magnitude sensitivities are the same between actual and virtual coils.

Additional equations are added in the VCC-based reconstruction, and reconstructed image quality is improved due to the additional encoding power from VCC. The explicit knowledge of the background phase information is not required when VCC is combined with GRAPPA reconstruction [1] for improving the quality. Encoding power is significantly improved by using the phase variations in the complex coil sensitivities. On the other hand, insufficient phase variations and inaccurate knowledge of spatial phase information cause artifacts [1].

3.3 Iterative JSENSE Reconstruction Using VCC Data

The SENSE technique takes advantage of the spatial sensitivity variations of multiple surface receiver coils. It's a parallel imaging method that helps reduce scan times by acquiring less k-space data, thus speeding up the imaging process. SENSE uses an array of multiple receiver coils. Each of these coils has a different spatial sensitivity pattern, which means they pick up signals with varying strength depending on their position relative to the body. As a result, each coil can provide a unique "view" of the body, which contains spatial encoding information in addition to the signal data. The SENSE technique then uses these unique views to fill in the gaps in the undersampled k-space data, thus allowing for a reduction in the number of phase-encoding steps and consequently faster image acquisition. It is important to note that the accuracy of the reconstructed image depends on the correct estimation of the coil sensitivity profiles. Misestimation could lead to errors known as aliasing artifacts. For the SENSE imaging formulation,

$$\mathbf{Ef} = \mathbf{d}, \tag{3}$$

where **d** represents the acquired k-space data from all actual coils, the encoding matrix **E** contains the product of Fourier encoding with undersampled k-space and coil-specific sensitivity modulation over the image, and **f** is the unknown image to be reconstructed.

For JSENSE, the imaging equation becomes

$$E(a)f = d, \tag{4}$$

where **a** represents unknown actual coil sensitivities. In our study, we are introducing a method where we propose a simultaneous estimation of actual coil sensitivity maps, virtual coil sensitivity maps, and the reconstructed image. The traditional approach usually treats these aspects independently, but our method acknowledges their interconnected nature and leverages this relationship for a more accurate and effective reconstruction process. By jointly estimating these factors, we can address challenges in MRI reconstruction and improve the quality of the resultant image. In particular, the actual coil sensitivity maps are key to accounting for the distinct signal reception profiles of different coils. On the other hand, the virtual coil sensitivity maps introduce extra equations to the inverse reconstruction matrix by incorporating additional phase information. Furthermore, the reconstructed image integrates these considerations to result in improved final output. Overall, our proposed method aims to enhance MRI image reconstruction by comprehensively considering all the key contributing factors in a unified estimation process. So, the image equation is

$$E\left(a, a'\right)f = d, \tag{5}$$

where a' denotes the unknown virtual coil sensitivities. We apply iterative optimization to solve the Eq. (5). In phase-constrained reconstruction, actual and virtual coils are harmoniously combined. They are fed into the reconstruction procedures without separating them, resulting in a unified input. This integrated approach is also maintained during the iterative optimization process, where both coil types are jointly involved. Therefore, the actual and virtual coils coexist throughout the iterations, contributing to the overall solution.

Specifically, the cost function is alternatively minimized for

$$\left\{\left[a, a'\right], f\right\} = \arg \min_{[a,a'],f} U\left(\left[a, a'\right], f\right). \tag{6}$$

In each computational cycle of the reconstruction process, the image that is being restructured is integrated with actual and virtual coil sensitivity maps—computational representations of the coil's sensitivities. This integration results in two unique images, an actual coil image and a virtual coil image, which facilitate a more accurate image reconstruction. The coil sensitivity maps are initially generated through a self-calibration process, establishing a foundation for the iterations to improve the image. After all the iterations are completed, a final reconstructed image is produced. This image is then assessed for its clarity, detail, and fidelity compared to the original image. This evaluation process gauges the effectiveness of the reconstruction process and identifies potential enhancements for future iterations, with the final image demonstrating the success of the applied method.

4   Experimental Results

4.1   Datasets and Evaluation Metrics

Two datasets are used to evaluate the reconstruction performance of the proposed random feature method. The first dataset of axial brain images was acquired on a 3T scanner (SIEMENS AG, Erlangen, German) with a 32-channel head coil using a 2D gradient echo sequence (TE/TR = 2.29/100 ms, flip angle = 25°, matrix size = 256 × 256, slice thickness = 3 mm, and FOV = 24 × 24 cm^2). The second set of coronary brain data was acquired using a 2D gradient echo sequence (slice thickness = 3.0 mm, matrix size = 256 × 256, FOV = 24 × 24 cm^2, and TE/TR = 2.29/100 ms). The k-space data was subject to undersampling by a reduction factor, with the count of the ACS lines is set as 32. The reconstruction algorithm was executed in MATLAB, a high-level programming language developed by MathWorks based in Natick, Massachusetts. All image reconstruction was carried out on a laptop equipped with an i7 processor and 32GB of RAM. Given that the proposed technique does not apply deep learning, there was no requirement for a graphics processing unit (GPU).

In addition to the subjective evaluation, the suggested technique is also benchmarked against alternative methods employing two quantifiable evaluation standards. These standards encompass the normalized mean square error (NMSE), which measures the magnitude of error, and the structural similarity index measurement (SSIM), a method that gauges image quality by comparing changes in structural information.

4.2   Reconstruction Results

For the first dataset of axial brain, k-space is undersampled with 32 ACS lines and the outer reduction factor of 4. The fully sampled k-spaced data are inversely Fourier transformed to image space and all coil images are combined to generate the final image. Missing k-space data are recovered by CG-SENSE [12], JSENSE [8], and the proposed JSENSE-VCC methods. A region-of-interest (ROI) is extracted for comparing the details of reconstructed images. In Fig. 2, it is seen that the proposed method can suppress aliasing artifacts and noise in the reconstructed image. In contrast, CG-SENSE image has typical aliasing artifacts and JSENSE also have artifacts and noise. The proposed method has the closest appearance of image content to the reference image. In addition, SSIM values are presented in Fig. 2. It is seen that the proposed JSENSE-VCC method has the highest SSIM value 0.9303 in all three images reconstructed from undersampled k-space data.

For the second dataset of the coronary brain, 32 ACS lines and the outer reduction factors of 2, 4, and 8 are used to undersample k-space data, respectively. The fully sampled k-spaced data are inversely Fourier transformed to image space and all coil images are combined to generate the final image. Missing k-space data are recovered by CG-SENSE, JSENSE, and the proposed JSENSE-VCC methods. A ROI is extracted for comparing the details of reconstructed images. In Fig. 3, it is seen that the proposed method can suppress aliasing artifacts and noise in the reconstructed image. CG-SENSE image has typical aliasing artifacts and noise, and JSENSE reconstruction also has noise. The proposed method has the closest appearance of image content to the reference image.

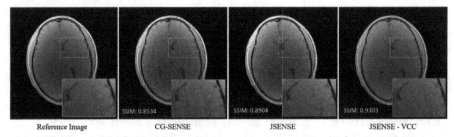

Fig. 2. For the axial brain data, reconstruction performance comparison among the reference image, CG-SENSE, JSENSE, and the proposed JSENSE-VCC method. The reference image is fully sampled. The proposed method can suppress aliasing artifacts in comparison to CG-SENSE. In comparison to the conventional JSENSE, JSENSE-VCC can restore more details. The proposed method has the highest SSIM value.

In addition, SSIM and NMSE values are presented in Fig. 3. It is seen that the proposed JSENSE-VCC method has the highest SSIM value 0.9706 and the lowest NMSE value 0.003022 in all three images reconstructed from undersampled k-space data. Besides the JSENSE-VCC, feature selection-based reconstruction [14], dual-interpolator-based reconstruction [16], and broad learning reconstruction [15] may also be combined with VCC concept for further improvement of performance.

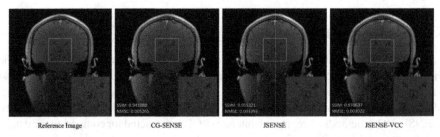

Fig. 3. For the coronary brain data, reconstruction performance comparison (outer reduction factor 4) among the reference image, CG-SENSE, JSENSE, and the proposed JSENSE-VCC method. The reference image is fully sampled. The proposed method can suppress aliasing artifacts in comparison to CG-SENSE. In comparison to the conventional JSENSE, JSENSE-VCC can restore more details. The proposed method has the highest SSIM and the lowest NMSE values.

To quantitatively evaluate the reconstruction performance, the undersampled k-space data of the coronary brain are reconstructed by CG-SENSE, JSENSE, and JSENSE-VCC, respectively. Quantitative results are shown in Table 1.

It is seen that the proposed JSENSE-VCC method has the highest SSIM values for images reconstructed at the outer reduction factor 2, 4, and 8, respectively.

Table 1. Quantitative Metric Values for Evaluating Reconstruction Performance of Coronary Brain Data.

	R2		R4		R8	
	SSIM	NMSE	SSIM	NMSE	SSIM	NMSE
CG-SENSE	0.943532	0.002597	0.941088	0.005265	0.794037	0.021442
JSENSE	0.963015	0.003143	0.955321	0.003393	0.829628	0.015490
JSENSE-VCC	**0.971696**	**0.002107**	**0.970637**	**0.003022**	**0.921765**	**0.007200**

5 Conclusion

In conclusion, the study presented an innovative approach to improve the quality of image-based MRI reconstruction. Our methodology leverages an iterative optimization process that jointly estimates actual and virtual coil sensitivity maps, along with the image to be reconstructed. Each iteration refines these three components and enhances the final output. The proposed method notably elevates the quality of reconstructed images through suppressing residual artifacts. The results not only bolster the promise of image-based MRI reconstruction but also highlight the potential of this approach in improving both SNR and minimizing residual artifacts.

Acknowledgment. This work was supported by the National Science Foundation under Grant No. 2050972.

References

1. Blaimer, M., Gutberlet, M., Kellman, P., Breuer, F.A., Köstler, H., Griswold, M.A.: Virtual coil concept for improved parallel MRI employing conjugate symmetric signals. Magn. Reson. Med. **61**(1), 93–102 (2009)
2. Blaimer, M., Heim, M., Neumann, D., Jakob, P.M., Kannengiesser, S., Breuer, F.A.: Comparison of phase-constrained parallel MRI approaches: analogies and differences. Magn. Reson. Med. **75**(3), 1086–1099 (2016)
3. Kim, T.H., Bilgic, B., Polak, D., Setsompop, K., Haldar, J.P.: Wave-LORAKS: combining wave encoding with structured low-rank matrix modeling for more highly accelerated 3D imaging. Magn. Reson. Med. **81**(3), 1620–1633 (2019)
4. Uecker, M., Lustig, M.: Estimating absolute-phase maps using ESPIRiT and virtual conjugate coils. Magn. Reson. Med. **77**(3), 1201–1207 (2017)
5. Pruessmann, K.P., Weiger, M., Scheidegger, M.B., Boesiger, P.: SENSE: sensitivity encoding for fast MRI. Magn. Reson. Med. **42**(5), 952–962 (1999)
6. Chang, Y., Zhang, J., Pham, H.A., Li, Z., Lyu, J.: Virtual conjugate coil for improving KerNL reconstruction. In: The 44th Annual International Conference of the IEEE Engineering in Medicine and Biology Society (EMBC), Glasgow (2022)
7. Wang, H., et al.: Improving GRAPPA reconstruction using joint nonlinear kernel mapped and phase conjugated virtual coils. Phys. Med. Biol. **64**(14), 14NT01 (2019)
8. Ying, L., Sheng, J.: Joint image reconstruction and sensitivity estimation in SENSE (JSENSE). Magn. Reson. Med. **57**(6), 1196–1202 (2007)

9. Dawood, P., et al.: Iterative RAKI with complex-valued convolution for improved image reconstruction with limited scan-specific training samples. arXiv:2201.03560 (2022)
10. Bilgic, B., et al.: Improving parallel imaging by jointly reconstructing multi-contrast data. Magn. Reson. Med. **80**(2), 619–632 (2018)
11. Yang, C., Liao, X., Wang, Y., Zhang, M., Liu, Q.: Virtual coil augmentation technology for MRI via deep learning. arXiv:2201.07540 (2022)
12. Maier, O., et al.: CG-SENSE revisited: results from the first ISMRM reproducibility challenge. Magn. Reson. Med. **85**(4), 1821–1839 (2021)
13. Chang, Y., Saju, G., Yu, J., Abiri, R., Liu, T., Li, Z.: Phase-constrained reconstruction for enhancing PROPELLER SNR. In: The 31st Annual Meeting in International Society of Magnetic Resonance in Medicine (ISMRM), Toronto (2023)
14. Chang, Y., Saritac, M.: Group feature selection for enhancing information gain in MRI reconstruction. Phys. Med. Biol. **67**(4), 045011 (2022)
15. Chang, Y., Nakarmi, U.: Parallel MRI reconstruction using broad learning system. In: 43rd Annual International Conference of the IEEE Engineering in Medicine and Biology Society (EMBC), Online, Oct. 31 - Nov. 4 (2021)
16. Chang, Y., Pham, H.A., Li, Z.: A dual-interpolator method for improving parallel MRI reconstruction. Magn. Reson. Imaging **92**, 108–119 (2022)

Biometrics

I Got Your Emotion: Emotion Preserving Face De-identification Using Injection-Based Generative Adversarial Networks

Md Shopon[✉] and Marina L. Gavrilova

Department of Computer Science, University of Calgary, Calgary, AB, Canada
md.shopon@ucalgary.ca

Abstract. Traditional visual information concealing methods involve blurring or pixelating the face, which can obscure emotional expression and lead to misunderstandings and misinterpretations. This research proposes the very first end-to-end emotion-preserving de-identification method that employs an end-to-end Generative Adversarial Network (GAN) for producing natural-looking de-identified images. The proposed method is based on the StyleGAN architecture to generate a synthetic face image dataset for proxy face images, followed by using the DeepFace model to classify the gender of the target image and selecting a representative image with the same gender for face swapping. An enhanced SimSwap framework is proposed to improve the emotion preservation quality of the de-identification. A new loss function is introduced specifically to preserve emotional expressions. The deep face model is used to classify the original image's emotional expression, and then the same model is used to recognize the emotional expression of the de-identified swapped image. Emotional expressions are explicitly preserved during face-swapping by minimizing attribute preservation loss. The proposed method outperformed the most recent face de-identification method in terms of accuracy and emotion-preserving capabilities.

Keywords: Facial images · Facial emotions · Privacy · De-identification · Injection-based GANs · Deep learning · Biometrics

1 Introduction

In recent years, privacy concerns have become increasingly prevalent as the amount of personal data generated and collected has skyrocketed. With the recent advancement of deep learning, biometric data such as facial images, voice, and gait, are easily mined to collect additional information for commercial and business purposes [25]. Recent years have also seen many high-profile data breaches and security incidents [5]. Biometric data, in particular, is considered some of the most sensitive personal information that can be collected. Once

© The Author(s), under exclusive license to Springer Nature Switzerland AG 2023
G. Bebis et al. (Eds.): ISVC 2023, LNCS 14361, pp. 417–430, 2023.
https://doi.org/10.1007/978-3-031-47969-4_33

compromised, it can lead to irreversible harm, and its misuse can have severe consequences [20]. The current solutions for protecting biometric data have several limitations. Traditional encryption methods are not enough to safeguard biometric data because it needs to be stored in a readable format for authentication purposes. Additionally, existing cancellability approaches, while removing identifying information, often are difficult to implement and are not practical [16].

De-identification is becoming an increasingly important technique in the protection of personal data, alongside other techniques such as encryption and cancelability [15]. It refers to removing identifying information from data sets while preserving their utility for analysis [20]. The de-identification of biometric data is necessary to protect privacy and ensure that the data can be used for research and other applications without violating ethical and legal regulations. Facial images are unique and can be used to identify individuals accurately [13]. However, facial data is often publicly available, making it easier for malicious actors to misuse it. On another hand, de-identifying facial images can lead to losing critical attributes such as gender, age, and ethnicity. Therefore, preserving selected attributes can enable much-needed flexibility while still maintaining the privacy of individuals. Moreover, preserving the emotional content of biometric data can be more beneficial than merely de-identifying it, especially in fields such as psychology, psychiatry, and neuroscience [14]. Emotions play crucial role in these fields, and provide valuable insights into a patient's mental state. Moreover, emotional content can enable the use of facial images in training machine learning models, which can further aid in data analysis.

Traditional de-identification techniques, such as blurring or pixelating an individual's face, can protect privacy, but they frequently result in losing vital information, such as emotions, age, gender, and facial expressions [24]. This loss of information can be especially troublesome in circumstances where biometric attributes are crucial, such as in law enforcement and healthcare. Only a handful of methods that used machine learning for de-identification were proposed recently [1,10]. However, these methods do not preserve emotional content crucial in specific applications. This paper introduces a novel GAN-based approach to generating realistic images that preserve the original image's emotional content while protecting an individual's privacy. To the best of our knowledge, this is the first end-to-end emotion-preserving face de-identification method. Here, "end-to-end" means a comprehensive and seamless approach that encompasses the entire process of emotion-preserving face de-identification without the need for external interventions.

This research develops a novel de-identification system capable of preserving emotions while safeguarding an individual's privacy. The following are the main contributions:

- The first end-to-end emotion-preserving de-identification system that utilizes deep learning without any intermediary processing steps is proposed.
- A novel method for emotion-preserving de-identification using Generative Adversarial Networks (GANs), which can accurately and seamlessly generate a high-fidelity de-identified version of a face while unequivocally preserving the subject's emotions, is introduced.

- A novel attention-based identity injection module is proposed for producing natural-looking de-identified images.
- The StyleGAN architecture is utilized to generate a synthetic face image dataset for proxy face images, which can increase the diversity of images available for training the GAN.
- A novel attribute-preserving loss function is introduced to preserve the subject's emotions during de-identification.
- The proposed enhanced SimSwap architecture is capable of handling non-frontal views and wearable accessories of subjects.

The developed system is particularly important in applications where the recognition and interpretation of facial expressions and emotions are critical, such as in healthcare or psychology. The proposed method was trained using the VGGFace2 dataset and validated on CELEB-A and LFW datasets.

2   Literature Review

Emotion-preserving face de-identification is an emerging research, that is gaining an increased amount of attention due to the widespread use of facial recognition technology in various domains, from unlocking smartphones to surveillance in public spaces. With the growing concerns about personal privacy and the potential misuse of biometric data, de-identification techniques have been proposed to mitigate these concerns. However, traditional de-identification methods often result in losing essential attributes, such as emotions, which play a fundamental role in human behavior and have significant implications in psychology, psychiatry, and neuroscience. Traditional de-identification methods can be broadly categorized into complete de-identification, soft biometrics de-identification, and traditional biometric preserving de-identification [21]. In recent years, neural network-based systems have gained popularity in face de-identification research. These approaches utilize machine learning algorithms, such as Convolutional Neural Networks (CNNs) and Generative Adversarial Networks (GANs), to automatically generate de-identified faces by learning from large datasets. CNNs can be trained to predict facial attributes, such as emotions, and then used to generate de-identified faces by modifying the predicted attributes.

Traditional face de-identification methods employ blurring [7], warping [22], and pixelation [11] techniques to protect individuals' privacy in images or videos. These methods aim to alter or obscure facial features while retaining the overall appearance of a face, making it difficult for unauthorized individuals to identify individuals from visual content. They often result in a loss of visual quality, making the de-identified faces look unnatural or distorted. Furthermore, they lose soft biometric attributes which are essential for biometric analysis.

Several recent works have proposed neural network-based methods for face de-identification, leveraging the power of deep learning to achieve effective de-identification performance. These methods incorporate various techniques to ensure that the generated images protect the identity of individuals while preserving the emotional content. In [2], the authors employed a method combining a Gaussian Mixture Modelling (GMM) based background subtraction algorithm and an improved version of the GrabCut algorithm to find and segment pedestrians. Faces are detected separately using a standard face detector. The neural art algorithm is then applied, utilizing the responses of a deep neural network to obfuscate the detected faces through style mixing with reference images. Sun et al. [23] utilized a head inpainting technique for privacy protection in personal photos shared online. This method generates realistic person images by leveraging facial landmarks from image context. Ren et al. [17] introduced an adversarial training-based approach for video face anonymization to address privacy concerns in computer vision devices. This method utilizes an adversarial training setting to modify the original videos by removing privacy-sensitive information from individuals' faces while maintaining spatial action detection performance. Khorzooghi et al. [10] employed a style mixing approach with generative adversarial networks. The authors reported emotion preservation accuracy using CIAGAN and Deep Privacy was 52% and 60% respectively. Shahbaz et al. [19] employed a image processing method for emotion-preserving de-identification. The authors used a proxy set of faces generated using StyleGAN and later used those proxy faces to obfuscate the target face.

This work introduces a new method for emotion-preserving de-identification method using generative adversarial networks (GANs). Existing methods for face de-identification have limitations in preserving facial emotion and struggle with non-frontal face images or occlusions. The proposed approach utilizes a proxy set of anonymous faces generated through StyleGAN. By mapping an input face to a corresponding face in the proxy setting with similar emotions, the method achieves excellent performance and flexibility in preserving emotional expressions during de-identification. Advantages include the use of StyleGAN to generate a realistic and diverse synthetic face image dataset, and a new loss function that explicitly preserves emotional expressions. This method can handle non-frontal views and subjects with wearable accessories effectively.

3   Proposed Method

This research proposes a novel methodology for emotion-preserving face de-identification using Generative Adversarial Networks (GANs). This proposed method involves several steps. First, the StyleGAN [9] architecture was utilized to generate a synthetic face image dataset for proxy face images. Next, the Deep-Face [18] model was used to classify the gender of the target image and select a proxy image with the same gender for face swapping. Then, the Enhanced SimSwap architecture was applied to transform the original image into a de-identified version while preserving the subject's emotions. The overall flow of the proposed method is depicted in Fig. 1.

3.1   SimSwap Architecture

SimSwap [4] is a state-of-the-art face-swapping framework that enables high-fidelity face swapping while preserving target face attributes. Its architecture

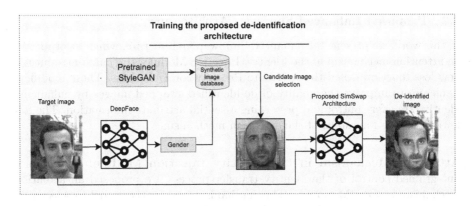

Fig. 1. The proposed emotion preserving face de-identification system.

consists of an encoder, a decoder, and a discriminator. The encoder extracts facial features from the original image using convolutional layers and activation functions. These features are passed to the Identity Injection Module (IIM), which transfers the identity of a source face to an arbitrary target face while maintaining attribute information. IIM comprises identity extraction and embedding parts using modified residual blocks with adaptive instance normalization (AdaIN) to inject identity information. The decoder takes the output of IIM to generate the final de-identified swapped image, resembling the proxy face image in terms of identity and attributes, while preserving the original image's emotional expressions. The discriminator distinguishes real and fake images. Overall, SimSwap achieves high-quality arbitrary face swapping with identity preservation. The discriminator plays an essential role in adversarial training by distinguishing results with apparent errors using the patchGAN algorithm.

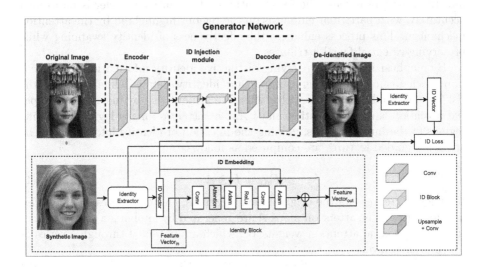

Fig. 2. The generator architecture of the proposed system.

3.2   Proposed Enhanced SimSwap Architecture

In this work, we present the enhanced SimSwap architecture, which incorporates an attention mechanism in the Identity Injection Module (IIM) and introduces a new loss function called the Attribute Preservation (AP) Loss. These modifications aim to improve the quality of de-identified swapped images by enhancing identity transfer control and preserving essential attribute information. The following are the four steps of the attention mechanism.

Attention Mechanism in the Identity Injection Module. To enhance fine-grained control of the identity transfer process, we proposed an attention mechanism-based IIM module. This mechanism enables the model to selectively focus on crucial regions of the facial features during identity injection. The Identity Injection Module (IIM) is a novel component that offers several advantages for face de-identification. It enables selective and accurate injection of identity features from a source face to a target face, enhancing the fidelity and realism of the de-identified swapped image. The IIM also incorporates an attribute preservation loss function, ensuring the retention of non-identity attributes such as emotional expressions. With its flexibility and adaptability, the IIM module contributes to improved privacy protection by generating high-quality, emotion-preserving de-identified images. The attention mechanism plays a crucial role in the Identity Injection Module. It generates attention maps that highlight significant regions in both the source and target faces, indicating the relevance of each spatial location. These attention maps are then used to calculate weights for each location in the feature maps through a softmax function, ensuring proper weighting of different facial regions. The calculated weights are applied to fuse the features from the source and target faces, emphasizing the regions considered more important. By injecting the identity information from the source face into the target face using the fused features, the identity transfer is performed accurately, with particular emphasis on the regions highlighted by the attention mechanism. This process enhances the effectiveness of identity swapping while preserving essential facial attributes.

By emphasizing regions carrying distinctive identity information, the attention mechanism helps preserve important identity details while reducing the risk of unwanted artifacts or distortions. We achieve this by incorporating spatial attention through attention maps A. The attention maps highlight specific regions of the input features, guiding the injection of identity information. The attention-guided features are computed as follows:

$$F_{att} = F \otimes A \tag{1}$$

where F represents the original facial features, and $\otimes$ denotes element-wise multiplication. The attention maps A are generated by applying a softmax function on the spatial attention weights W, which are obtained through a series of convolutional layers:

$$W = \text{softmax}(W_{conv}(F)) \tag{2}$$

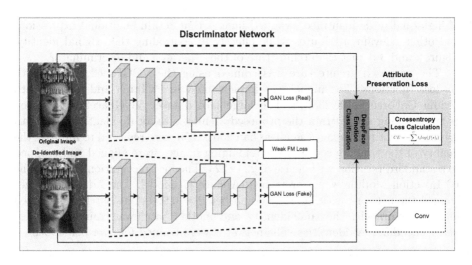

Fig. 3. The discriminator architecture of the proposed GAN.

Attribute Preservation Loss. The attribute preservation loss can be defined as the difference between the original and de-identified image classification loss. This proposed loss function is incorporated with the five loss function that was originally used in the SimSwap architecture. This loss encourages the de-identified image to retain the same attribute information as the original image while removing or altering the identity information. To compute this loss, both the original and de-identified images are passed through the DeepFace retained, and compute the classification loss (e.g. cross-entropy loss) is between the predicted emotional expression and the ground truth emotional expression for each image.

$$L_{attr} = \sum_{i=1}^{N_{attr}} [H(y_i, f_i(\hat{x})) - H(y_i, f_i(x))] \tag{3}$$

where N_{attr} is the number of attributes being preserved, y_i is the ground truth label for attribute i, x is the original image, $\hat{x}$ is the de-identified image, $f_i(\cdot)$ is the classifier for attribute i, and $H(\cdot)$ is the cross-entropy loss. The square brackets indicate that the difference between the two cross-entropy terms is summed over all preserved attributes. By minimizing the Attribute Preservation Loss, we encourage the de-identified images to preserve the same attribute information as the originals, such as emotional expressions, while ensuring the removal or alteration of identity-related features.

By incorporating the attention mechanism and the Attribute Preservation Loss, our enhanced SimSwap architecture provides improved control over identity transfer and better preservation of attribute information. The attention mechanism enables selective focus on crucial facial regions, preserving important identity details, while the Attribute Preservation Loss ensures the retention of desired attributes. These enhancements collectively contribute to the generation of high-quality de-identified swapped images that retain emotional expressions and other relevant attributes while effectively concealing the original identity. Figure 2 and 3 depict the architecture of the generator and discriminator.

The proposed architecture was trained using the VGGFace2 dataset with six loss functions. The model was implemented in PyTorch and trained with Nvidia GeForce GTX-2080Ti. The large face dataset VGGFace2 was chosen as the training set to train the proposed architecture for de-identification with arbitrary identities. Images smaller than 250×250 were removed to improve the quality of the training set, and the remaining images were aligned and cropped to a standard position with a size of 224×224. The face recognition model in the ID Injection Module was a pretrained Arcface [6] model. The Adam optimizer trained the network with beta1 = 0 and beta2 = 0.999. One batch was trained for image pairs with the same identity, and another batch was trained for image pairs with different identities. The networks were trained for over 500 epochs.

Table 1. De-identification Accuracy of CELEB-A and LFW Datasets

Dataset	Number of Images	De-identification Accuracy
CELEB-A	202,599	93.37%
LFW	13,000	96.89%

4   Experimental Results

4.1   Dataset

Three different datasets were used for training and validation. VGGFace2 [3] dataset was used for training the proposed architecture. It is a large-scale face recognition dataset containing over 3.31 million images of 9131 subjects. The images covered a wide range of poses, ages, and ethnicity. Celeb-A [12] dataset was used for evaluating the proposed model. This is a large-scale face attribute dataset containing over 200,000 images of celebrities with 40 different attribute annotations per image. The attributes include hair color, facial hair, age, gender, etc. Labeled faces in the wild [8] dataset was used to aid further evaluation. This is a popular benchmark dataset for face recognition algorithms. It contains over 13,000 images of faces collected from the web, each labeled with the person's name.

The CELEB-A and Labeled Faces in the Wild dataset were used to evaluate the proposed architecture's performance. The evaluation was carried out in two parts: the first was evaluating the de-identification accuracy, and the second was evaluating the emotion preservation accuracy. A candidate image was passed into the trained model to evaluate the de-identification accuracy, and the de-identified result was produced. The performance was measured using accuracy

Table 2. Emotion Preservation Accuracy of CELEB-A and LFW Datasets

Dataset	Number of Images	Emotion Preservation Accuracy (Rank-1)	Emotion Preservation Accuracy (Rank-2)
CELEB-A	202,599	72.32%	86.44%
LFW	13,000	78.18%	90.31%

as the evaluation metric. For evaluating the emotion preservation accuracy, the Deepface library was used, which extracts facial features containing identity and attribute information and produces an emotion. The produced result was used to evaluate the accuracy of the emotion preservation. The proposed method is compared with the baseline SimSwap architecture. The results demonstrate the effectiveness of the attribute preservation loss function presented in this work.

The goal was to measure the ability of the proposed architecture to correctly de-identify and preserve emotions. A test set was created using all the images in the CELEB-A and Labeled Faces in the Wild dataset.

Fig. 4. Generated de-identified faces preserving original emotions.

4.2   Experimentation and Analysis

De-identification accuracy refers to the effectiveness of a method in removing personally identifiable information from an image. The higher the accuracy, the better the method is. Table 1 demonstrates the de-identification accuracy of two popular face recognition datasets, CELEB-A and LFW. CELEB-A dataset has 202,599 images with a de-identification accuracy of 93.37%, whereas LFW dataset has 13,000 images with a de-identification accuracy of 96.89.

Emotion preservation accuracy measures how well a system can maintain the emotional expression of a person's face, even when subjected to various transformations or distortions. The higher the accuracy, the better the system is at preserving the original emotional expression of the individual in the image. Table 2 shows the emotion preservation accuracy of the CELEB-A dataset, which contains 202,599 facial images. The emotion preservation accuracy is reported for the top two ranks, with the accuracy for Rank-1 being 72.32% and for Rank-2 being 86.44%.

Figure 4 displays three images side by side: the original image, a synthetic image generated using StyleGAN to replace the person's face, and the de-identified image with identifying features removed. The de-identified images look natural and effectively preserve the original face's structure while concealing the person's identity. The proposed method's effectiveness extends to non-frontal face views and situations with accessories, as shown in Fig. 5. The results demonstrate the approach's robustness in preserving emotional expressions and privacy in challenging scenarios. This versatility makes it suitable for real-world applications, enhancing privacy protection without compromising emotional expression preservation.

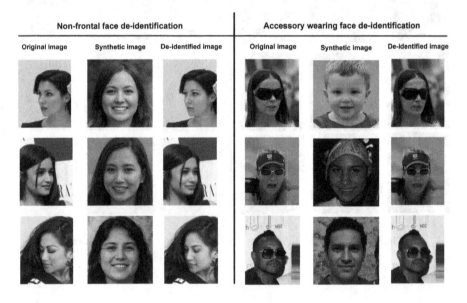

Fig. 5. Generated non-frontal and accessory-wearing face de-identification.

To demonstrate the superiority of the attribute preservation loss of the proposed method, we compared our work with the baseline architecture. Figure 6 depicts a comparison of both de-identification and emotion preservation accuracy. Based on the results, it can be seen that the proposed method attained

Table 3. Comparison of results using LightFace pre-trained model

Method	De-identification Accuracy	Emotion Preservation Accuracy
EPIC [19]	97.36	57.00
Proposed architecture	97.54	78.32

higher de-identification accuracy on CELEB-A and LFW datasets. Moreover, the proposed method achieved 9.44% higher Rank-1 accuracy than the baseline architecture and 16.29% higher Rank-2 accuracy for CELEB-A dataset. The proposed method attained 11.84% higher Rank-1 accuracy and 11.34% higher Rank-2 accuracy for the LFW dataset compared to the baseline architecture. The results show that the proposed attribute preservation loss performs extremely well.

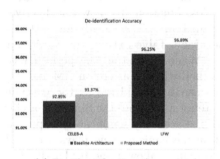

(a) De-identification Accuracy.

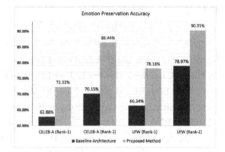

(b) Emotion Preservation Accuracy.

Fig. 6. De-identification and Emotion preservation accuracy compared to the baseline architecture.

We also have compared our method with the state-of-the-art recent facial de-identification system EPIC [19] (see Table 3). Both methods were evaluated using the LightFace pre-trained model. For de-identification accuracy, our proposed method achieved a slightly higher accuracy of 97.54%. However, our method significantly outperformed EPIC in terms of emotion preservation accuracy, achieving 78.32% instead of 57% reported by their method. This substantial improvement in emotion preservation underscores the importance of our attention-guided Identity Injection Module (IIM) and attribute preservation loss function, both of which contribute to better emotion retention during the de-identification process. The results indicate that our proposed method achieves superior emotion preservation, making it well-suited for privacy-sensitive applications that require maintaining the emotional expressions of individuals in de-identified images.

Table 4. Ablation study to demonstrate the effectiveness of attention IIM and attribute preservation loss function for de-identification and emotion-preservation.

Dataset	Method	De-identification accuracy			Emotion-preservation accuracy		
		Components			Components		
CELEB-A	SimSwap	✓	✓	✓	✓	✓	✓
	Attention IIM	x	✓	✓	x	✓	✓
	AP Loss	x	x	✓	x	x	✓
	Accuracy	81.26%	93.21%	93.37%	48.41%	52.17%	72.32%
LFW	SimSwap	✓	✓	✓	✓	✓	✓
	Attention IIM	x	✓	✓	x	✓	✓
	AP Loss	x	x	✓	x	x	✓
	Accuracy	83.95%	95.75%	96.89%	51.63%	54.87%	78.18%

4.3 Ablation Study

Two novel components that were proposed in this work are the attention-based IIM module and the attribute preservation loss function. To show the effectiveness of the two components we have performed an ablation study for both de-identification and emotion preservation accuracy. Table 4 shows the results for de-identification and emotion-preservation. When evaluating the performance on the CELEB-A dataset, the proposed method without attention IIM and AP loss achieved an accuracy of 81.26%. This can be considered as the baseline performance. Next, by incorporating the attention IIM into the SimSwap architecture while keeping the AP loss disabled, the accuracy significantly improved to 93.21%. This indicates that the attention mechanism alone plays a crucial role in enhancing the de-identification performance, allowing better handling of non-frontal face views and accessories. Furthermore, when incorporating both the attention IIM and the AP loss function, the accuracy further increased to 93.37%. This demonstrates the complementary effect of both components, where the attention mechanism improves the handling of non-frontal face views and accessories, while the AP loss function helps preserve the attribute information during the de-identification process. From Table 4 it can be observed that, for the CELEB-A dataset, the baseline performance of the proposed method achieved an accuracy of 48.41%. By incorporating the attention IIM alone into the SimSwap architecture, the accuracy improved to 52.17%. Furthermore, when incorporating both the attention IIM and the AP loss function, the accuracy increased to 72.32%. This indicates that the combination of the attention mechanism and the AP loss function leads to a substantial improvement in emotion preservation. The attention mechanism helps capture important facial cues related to emotions, while the AP loss function ensures that the de-identified images retain the emotional expressions of the original faces. For LFW dataset a similar pattern can be observed. It can be concluded that the novel components of the proposed method have a strong impact on the performance and accuracy of the proposed de-identification system.

5   Conclusion

This paper proposed a novel method for emotion-preserving face de-identification using GANs. The proposed method utilizes the StyleGAN architecture to generate synthetic face images for proxy face images and the DeepFace model to classify the gender of the target image for face swapping. The Enhanced Sim-Swap architecture is then used to de-identify the original image while preserving the subject's emotions. The new loss function introduced in the SimSwap framework allows for improving the emotion preservation quality of the face-swapping process and preserving emotional expressions. Experimental results on various datasets demonstrate that the proposed method can be applied to both frontal and side images, can handle facial occlusions, and attains a high degree of de-identification while generating realistically looking de-identified facial images while preserving original emotions. The proposed architecture can be applied in various areas that require face de-identification while preserving emotional expressions, such as law enforcement, medical research, and social media. While the proposed method aims to preserve the subject's emotions during de-identification, future research will consider the preservation of other critical identity-related features such as age and gender.

Acknowledgement. The authors acknowledge the Natural Sciences and Engineering Research Council (NSERC) Discovery Grant funding, the Innovation for Defense Excellence and Security Network (IDEaS) and the UCalgary Research Excellence Chair Program for the partial funding of this project.

References

1. Agarwal, A., Chattopadhyay, P., Wang, L.: Privacy preservation through facial de-identification with simultaneous emotion preservation. Signal Image Video Process. **15**, 951–958 (2021)
2. Brkić, K., Hrkać, T., Sikirić, I., Kalafatić, Z.: Towards neural art-based face de-identification in video data. In: 2016 First International Workshop on Sensing, Processing and Learning for Intelligent Machines (SPLINE), pp. 1–5. IEEE (2016)
3. Cao, Q., Shen, L., Xie, W., Parkhi, O.M., Zisserman, A.: VGGFace2: a dataset for recognising faces across pose and age. In: 2018 13th IEEE International Conference on Automatic Face & Gesture Recognition (FG 2018), pp. 67–74. IEEE (2018)
4. Chen, R., Chen, X., Ni, B., Ge, Y.: SimSwap: an efficient framework for high fidelity face swapping. In: Proceedings of the 28th ACM International Conference on Multimedia, pp. 2003–2011 (2020)
5. Datta, P., Bhardwaj, S., Panda, S.N., Tanwar, S., Badotra, S.: Survey of security and privacy issues on biometric system. In: Gupta, B.B., Perez, G.M., Agrawal, D.P., Gupta, D. (eds.) Handbook of Computer Networks and Cyber Security, pp. 763–776. Springer, Cham (2020). https://doi.org/10.1007/978-3-030-22277-2_30
6. Deng, J., Guo, J., Xue, N., Zafeiriou, S.: ArcFace: additive angular margin loss for deep face recognition. In: Proceedings of the IEEE/CVF Conference on Computer Vision and Pattern Recognition, pp. 4690–4699 (2019)
7. Frome, A., et al.: Large-scale privacy protection in google street view. In: IEEE 12th Int. Conference on Computer Vision, pp. 2373–2380 (2009)

8. Huang, G.B., Mattar, M., Berg, T., Learned-Miller, E.: Labeled faces in the wild: a database for studying face recognition in unconstrained environments. In: Workshop on Faces in 'Real-Life' Images: Detection, Alignment, and Recognition (2008)

9. Karras, T., Laine, S., Aila, T.: A style-based generator architecture for generative adversarial networks. In: Proceedings of the IEEE/CVF Conference on Computer Vision and Pattern Recognition, pp. 4401–4410 (2019)

10. Khorzooghi, S.M.S.M., Nilizadeh, S.: StyleGAN as a utility-preserving face de-identification method. arXiv preprint arXiv:2212.02611 (2022)

11. Korshunov, P., Cai, S., Ebrahimi, T.: Crowdsourcing approach for evaluation of privacy filters in video surveillance. In: Proceedings of the ACM Multimedia 2012 Workshop on Crowdsourcing for Multimedia, pp. 35–40 (2012)

12. Liu, Z., Luo, P., Wang, X., Tang, X.: Large-scale celeb faces attributes (CELEBA) dataset. Retrieved August 15(2018), 11 (2018)

13. Luo, Y., Gavrilova, M.L., Wang, P.S.: Facial metamorphosis using geometrical methods for biometric applications. Int. J. Pattern Recognit. Artif. Intell. 22(03), 555–584 (2008)

14. Marcó-García, S., Ferrer-Quintero, M., Usall, J., Ochoa, S., Del Cacho, N., Huerta-Ramos, E.: Facial emotion recognition in neurological disorders: a narrative review. Rev. Neurol. 69(5), 207–219 (2019)

15. Paul, P.P., Gavrilova, M., Klimenko, S.: Situation awareness of cancelable biometric system. Vis. Comput. 30, 1059–1067 (2014)

16. Punithavathi, P., Subbiah, G.: Can cancellable biometrics preserve privacy? Biomet. Technol. Today 2017(7), 8–11 (2017)

17. Ren, Z., Lee, Y.J., Ryoo, M.S.: Learning to anonymize faces for privacy preserving action detection. In: Proceedings of the European Conference on Computer Vision (ECCV), pp. 620–636 (2018)

18. Serengil, S.I., Ozpinar, A.: Hyperextended lightface: a facial attribute analysis framework. In: 2021 International Conference on Engineering and Emerging Technologies (ICEET), pp. 1–4. IEEE (2021)

19. Shahbaz Nejad, B., Roch, P., Handte, M., Marrón, P.J.: Enhancing privacy in computer vision applications: an emotion preserving approach to obfuscate faces. In: Bebis, G., et al. (eds.) ISVC 2022. LNCS, vol. 13599, pp. 80–90. Springer, Cham (2022). https://doi.org/10.1007/978-3-031-20716-7_7

20. Shopon, M., et al.: Biometric system de-identification: concepts, applications, and open problems. In: Lim, C.-P., Chen, Y.-W., Vaidya, A., Mahorkar, C., Jain, L.C. (eds.) Handbook of Artificial Intelligence in Healthcare. ISRL, vol. 212, pp. 393–422. Springer, Cham (2022). https://doi.org/10.1007/978-3-030-83620-7_17

21. Shopon, M., Tumpa, S.N., Bhatia, Y., Kumar, K.P., Gavrilova, M.L.: Biometric systems de-identification: current advancements and future directions. J. Cybersecur. Priv. 1(3), 470–495 (2021)

22. Sohn, H., De Neve, W., Ro, Y.M.: Privacy protection in video surveillance systems: analysis of subband-adaptive scrambling in jpeg xr. IEEE Trans. Circuits Syst. Video Technol. 21(2), 170–177 (2011)

23. Sun, Q., Ma, L., Oh, S.J., Van Gool, L., Schiele, B., Fritz, M.: Natural and effective obfuscation by head inpainting. In: Proceedings of the IEEE Conference on Computer Vision and Pattern Recognition, pp. 5050–5059 (2018)

24. Wu, Y., Yang, F., Xu, Y., Ling, H.: Privacy-protective-GAN for privacy preserving face de-identification. Comput. Sci. Technol. 34, 47–60 (2019)

25. Yanushkevich, S.N., Stoica, A., Srihari, S.N., Shmerko, V.P., Gavrilova, M.: Simulation of biometric information: the new generation of biometric systems. In: Int. Workshop Modeling and Simulation in Biometric Technology, pp. 87–98 (2004)

DoppelVer: A Benchmark for Face Verification

Nathan Thom[(⊠)], Andrew DeBolt, Lyssie Brown, and Emily M. Hand

University of Nevada, Reno, Reno, NV 89557, USA
{nthom,adebolt,abrown}@nevada.unr.edu, emhand@unr.edu
https://www.machineperceptionlab.com

Abstract. The field of automated face verification has become saturated in recent years, with state-of-the-art methods outperforming humans on all benchmarks. Many researchers would say that face verification is close to being a solved problem. We argue that evaluation datasets are not challenging enough, and that there is still significant room for improvement in automated face verification techniques. This paper introduces the DoppelVer dataset, a challenging face verification dataset consisting of doppelganger pairs. Doppelgangers are pairs of individuals that are extremely visually similar, oftentimes mistaken for one another. With this dataset, we introduce two challenging protocols: doppelganger and Visual Similarity from Embeddings (ViSE). The doppelganger protocol utilizes doppelganger pairs as negative verification samples. The ViSE protocol selects negative pairs by isolating image samples that are very close together in a particular embedding space. In order to demonstrate the challenge that the DoppelVer dataset poses, we evaluate a state-of-the-art face verification method on the dataset. Our experiments demonstrate that the DoppelVer dataset is significantly more challenging than its predecessors, indicating that there is still room for improvement in face verification technology.

Keywords: face verification · datasets · negative pair selection

1 Introduction

The task of face recognition has received considerable attention from computer vision and pattern recognition researchers in the past 20 years. This is because face identification has significant utility in the fields of biometrics, visual search, and socially assistive technologies [1,11]. Additionally, compute equipment capable of running increasingly powerful algorithms has become relatively cheap and widely available. Face recognition technologies have significant impact on society with a market share of $5.69 billion worldwide in 2023 and a projected $12.05 billion by 2028 [18].

Work in face recognition and verification is dataset motivated. Every time a new dataset is released, there are significant improvements in face verification technology. Over the last several decades, there have been many datasets which

© The Author(s), under exclusive license to Springer Nature Switzerland AG 2023
G. Bebis et al. (Eds.): ISVC 2023, LNCS 14361, pp. 431–444, 2023.
https://doi.org/10.1007/978-3-031-47969-4_34

have challenged the state-of-the-art (SOTA) face verification methods, such as Labeled Faces in the Wild (LFW), IARPA Janus Benchmarks A, B, and C (IJB-{A,B,C}), etc. [8,10,17,24]. With the release of these datasets came a renewed interest in the field. Over the last few years, however, face identification on these datasets has reached a saturation point. For example, many methods achieve over 99% accuracy on the LFW benchmark. With such high accuracies we are able to visually inspect the samples that are incorrectly classified. In many cases these incorrectly classified samples are mislabeled meaning there is really no room for improvement on these datasets. In addition, face identification datasets are often collected with a focus on quantity, neglecting other important attributes. These problems provide the motivation for the proposed work.

This report introduces a new dataset – *DoppelVer* – consisting of unconstrained face images of doppelgangers – that is, individuals who look very similar and are often mistaken for each other. The purpose of DoppelVer is to challenge current SOTA facial feature extraction and face verification and identification methods. Although a plethora of datasets have been published to this end in the past decade, many of them are either unavailable or have been nearly solved. DoppelVer offers a specific challenge for modern face recognition methods, specifically the task of differentiating individuals who could pass for each other. To the best of our knowledge DoppelVer is the first dataset to increase face classification difficulty by increasing inter-class similarity rather than decreasing intra-class similarity. Upon publication of this paper, DoppelVer will be made publicly available.

Here we detail the highlights of the DoppelVer dataset, which will be expanded upon in the remainder of this work.

- DoppelVer contains 390 unique identities, each with at least one corresponding doppelganger pair.
- We provide the unaltered source images along with cropped, aligned, and centered (CCA) images.
- There is an average of 72 CCA samples per identity, with a minimum of 11 and a maximum of 98.
- For the CCA images we provide two evaluation protocols: doppelganger and **V**isual **S**imilarity from **E**mbeddings (ViSE). Under the doppelganger protocol negative samples are select images depicting an identity's doppelganger. The ViSE protocol uses a generalized image embedding model to select negative images that are highly visually similar to the current image sample.
- Both protocols are divided into 10 cross validation splits which are distinct across identities. The doppelganger protocol's cross validation splits are made up of 14,000 image pairs while ViSE's splits contain 3,500 image samples.

The remainder of the paper is organized as follows: in Sect. 2 we provide background to the field of face recognition, with a focus on feature extraction and face classification methods. Section 2 also details similar datasets and the novelty of DoppelVer. Section 3 contains a more detailed description of the DoppelVer dataset including data collection, pre-processing, labeling, and the generation of the evaluation protocols. In Sect. 4 we provide results of our experimentation comparing the performance of SOTA facial recognition pipelines on existing benchmark datasets and DoppelVer.

2   Related Work

2.1   Background

Face recognition is separated into three well-defined steps: (1) face detection and localization, (2) extraction of features from the detected face, and (3) classification (verification or identification) [11]. The first task is to decide whether or not there are faces in an image. If there are one or more faces, then the system identifies bounding boxes for each face. The feature extraction step generates a feature vector from the localized face. This feature vector should be discriminative enough to separate images of one identity from images of other identities. Lastly, there is the classification step. This is separated into two classes of techniques: identification and verification. In the identification scenario the system is aware of a finite number of identities and it should learn to match each image sample to one identity class. For the verification task the model is only provided with supervision in the form of a binary label which represents either same or different, and so pairs of images are compared at each step.

Any face recognition system that is meant to be deployed in "the wild" will need to perform all three of these steps. That being said, each step is commonly considered an active research topic. The intended purpose of the DoppelVer dataset is to contribute towards improvements in the final two steps. In this work, we devote our efforts towards the feature extraction and classification tasks. This is because most modern methods employ deep learning techniques, which combine feature extraction and classification into a single system. Additionally, research has seemingly slowed in these areas.

One might suggest that the field of face classification is reaching its maturity, citing results on the well-known benchmarks such as LFW, AgeDB, or IJB-{A,B,C} [8,10,17,19,24]. Rather than assuming that the reported metrics are due to the techniques solving the task of visually recognizing faces, we hypothesize that the modern techniques have improved beyond the level of difficulty provided by the current benchmarks. For example, in 2015 Liu et al. published a result of 99.77% accuracy on the LFW benchmark [13]. The dataset's evaluation protocol contains only 6000 images. This means that for nearly a decade methods have been attempting to show improvements on a method that mis-classifies only 14 images, five of which are known to be incorrectly labeled.

Other methods have emerged with the intent of contributing to the issue of increasing unconstrained face recognition benchmark difficulty [19,21,28,29]. These methods primarily focus on increasing difficulty of the classification task with highly varied pose and age. These features essentially decrease the intraclass similarity (i.e. selecting images of the same identity that are visually different).

Our DoppelVer dataset increases classification difficulty by increasing inter-class similarity (i.e. selecting images of different identities that are visually similar). We accomplish this goal in two distinct ways. First, we aggregate doppelganger pairs. A doppelganger pair is simply two individuals who have similar facial features. This protocol is constructed by human labelers selecting visually similar identities. Second, for a given image we mine a negative sample which is highly visually similar. This is accomplished by generating an embedding or latent vector for all images in the dataset. We search for pairs of images whose embeddings are near one another in the latent space. By these two methods we produce two protocols that we have named doppelganger and **Vi**sual **S**imilarity from **E**mbeddings (ViSE).

2.2 Existing Datasets

There are a large number of datasets collected and presented for the purpose of facial feature extraction and classification. Many of these datasets are designed either for training or evaluation. Here we describe the major datasets that already exist for the purpose of model evaluation and benchmarking and compare them with the proposed DoppelVer dataset.

Labeled Faces in the Wild (LFW) [8]: The LFW dataset was created by Huang et al. in 2007. At the time of publishing, many face recognition datasets were collected by small teams of researchers with the intent of collecting facial images in constrained settings. LFW however was meant for studying the problem of recognizing faces in unconstrained settings. The dataset contains 13,233 images and 7,549 identities. The researchers behind LFW contributed significantly to the field by presenting a dataset organization that focused on the honest reporting of results for the task of open-set face recognition. Their dataset contains a development view and an evaluation view as well as splits for 10 fold cross-validation. The current SOTA accuracy on LFW is 99.8% ($\pm$0.2001) [2].

AgeDB [19]: This dataset was introduced in 2017, with a focus on accurate hand-labeling of age. This is a useful database when performing tasks such as age-invariant face verification, age estimation, and face age progression. The database contains 16,488 images of 568 identities with accurate-to-the-year age labels. The average number of images per individual is 29, with an age range of 1 to 101 years old, the average age for an individual being 50.3 years. AgeDB provides four face verification protocols, each split into 10 folds following LFW's process. These four protocols restrict the age variance across sample pairs. The provided protocols cap age range to 5, 10, 20 and 30 years respectively. The current SOTA accuracy on AgeDB 30 is 98.7% [3].

Cross-Age LFW (CA-LFW) [29]: The authors of this database posit that methods reporting accuracy on LFW's benchmark are optimistic. To show this, CA-LFW has both positive and negative pairs which depict a large age gap, while also providing negative pairs which are of the same race and gender. These visually similar negative pairs emphasize the effect of age difference on classifier performance. This dataset contains the same identifies as LFW with 6,000 image pairs. The current SOTA accuracy on CA-LFW is 95.87% [5].

Cross-Pose LFW (CP-LFW) [28]: CP-LFW was proposed by the same authors as CA-LFW and was released one year later. This publication shifts focus to the important task of face verification in the presence of extreme pose. They note that nearly all images in LFW are near-frontal, suggesting that results on LFW provide a poor representation of a face recognition method's performance when deployed into a real setting. The current SOTA accuracy on CA-LFW is 92.08% [5].

Each of the databases detailed above provide an important contribution to furthering the field of face recognition. These datasets provide unconstrained images and in the cases of [19, 21, 28, 29] the sample pairs vary along specific axis which were not well represented in LFW. As mentioned previously, these datasets focus on selecting positive pairs which are visually dissimilar to one another. DoppelVer's goal is to expand on a dimension of challenge which has not yet been addressed. This dimension is that of visual similarity among negative samples. This yet unseen challenge will force methods to extract significantly more fine-grained, prominent features from face images. In order to achieve high performance on DoppelVer, techniques will be required to extract those features which uniquely define a given identity.

3   Proposed Method

3.1   Dataset Collection

In order to construct a dataset for which negative samples are analogous to positive samples it is intuitive to begin by aggregating a list of identities which bare visual similarity to human labelers (i.e. doppelgangers). Doppelganger identity pairs were collected through labeler intuition of similar looking identities and lists of doppelgangers publicly available on the Internet. We present a large list of doppelganger identity combinations, totalling 237 pairs and 390 individuals. For each individual, 100 images were scraped from online sources. The average number of images presented in the dataset for each person is approximately 72 due to pruning of noisy samples and duplicates.

3.2   Data Preparation

Data preparation involved two distinct steps: (1) cropping, aligning and centering the images, and (2) hand removal of erroneous samples and duplicate images.

Cropping, Aligning and Centering: The first step in the data preparation is to reduce the original images into cropped, aligned, and centered images. We crop to remove information which is extraneous to the face recognition task. Alignment and centering are performed as they have been recognized as important for achieving competitive face recognition benchmark performance. Alignment involves rotating the image such that the eyes lie on a horizontal line (i.e. the same y-coordinates). The operation of centering moves the face in the frame of the image such that it appears centrally. Centering is accomplished by repeating edge pixels along either the horizontal or vertical borders of the image. The cropping operation relies on a bounding box and centering/alignment rely on facial landmarks. We extract the bounding boxes and facial landmarks for images in DoppelVer with the MTCNN detector [27].

While processing the dataset with MTCNN, three cases may occur: (1) MTCNN does not detect a face, (2) MTCNN detects a single face, and (3) MTCNN detects multiple faces. Images where a face is not detected are pruned from the dataset. Although MTCNN returns a detected face in most images, not all detections contain the target identity or a valid face. Each detection is hand-checked for validity during the cleaning phase of pre-processing. When at least one face is detected, MTCNN returns a bounding box for the image along with five facial landmarks. The landmarks provide the detected location of the centers of the eyes, corners of the mouth, and tip of the nose.

Initially we cropped the source images to the bounding boxes predicted by MTCNN, but found that the crop was too tight. These crops often removed valuable information such as the top of head, ears and most of the neck. We expand MTCNN's detected bounding box width and height by 50%. This produces crops which contain more contextual information. There are cases for which the detected face is near the border of the image, restricting our ability to expand the bounding box. In these cases we simply set the desired bounding box location to the border of the image.

After cropping, we align the images according to the extracted landmark locations. Our alignment rotates the images such that the detected landmark for left and right eyes have the same y-axis coordinate. During the alignment process some image information is lost due to the corners of the image rotating outside of the frame. Following the lead of the CelebA dataset, we reduce the effects of this information loss by performing same padding for any pixels that are lost due to rotation [16].

The last pre-processing step is to center the image so that the center most pixel of the image is within the bounds of the detected face. Centering is performed by computing a landmark which lies at the mid-point between the left and right eye landmarks. Additional pixels are appended to the horizontal and vertical image borders such that the center of the face is equidistant to each border. The appended pixels are simply duplicates of the pixels which are along the border that needs to be expanded.

Removal of Erroneous or Duplicate Images: We remove unsatisfactory images by hand and by automatic detection. In the case of hand labeling, labelers began with the original image set collected from the internet. Their task was to pass over the images and delete any image which contained erroneous detections (e.g. not depicting the correct identity or images not containing a face). The set of images which had complete labeler agreement was accepted. The set of images which did not have agreement were re-labeled. Any remaining images which the labelers did not reach agreement on were pruned from the dataset. The images which achieved hand label agreement were passed to the automatic detection system.

The automatic detection system works by generating embeddings for each face image in the dataset with the dinov2s model [20]. dinov2s is a general purpose image embedding model, built to capture a discriminative representation of input images without finetuning. The cosine similarity is computed between all combinations of input images' embeddings to determine samples which are highly visually similar. To compute the embeddings and cosine similarities efficiently we utilize the fastdup library [12] from Visual Layer. For any image pair that has exact similarity (i.e. duplicate images), one image from the pair is pruned from the dataset. Next, we return all of the image pairs that are above a threshold of 0.92 similarity. We extract these images pairs and provide them to human labelers to find near duplicate images (i.e. images that have been horizontally flipped, color jittered, cropped slightly differently, etc.), which are removed from the dataset.

3.3 Protocol Generation

The DoppelVer dataset contains in total 27,967 carefully curated and processed images. The question that remains is the best way to utilize these images for assessing and benchmarking feature extraction and face classification methods. To answer this question, we introduce two protocols for evaluation using DoppelVer: doppelganger and ViSE. Figure 1 provides example image pairs for each protocol in DoppelVer and Fig. 2 shows samples from CA-LFW and CP-LFW.

Both protocols are made up of positive and negative image pairs. Positive image pairs in both protocols signify instances where both images depict the same identity. In the doppelganger protocol, negative pairs are made up of one image sample depicting the current target identity and one image sample depicting their doppelganger. In the ViSE protocol the negative pairs contain an image sample depicting an identity which does not generally appear as visually similar to the current identity, but in a one-off case is visually similar. Such similarity often arises due to comparable pose, lighting, hair style, clothing, or image background. After generating a large number of image pairs, we divide the dataset into 10 equally sized splits. Each split is divided such that images of an identity are in only a single split. Identities are divided the same in each protocol (e.g. split 0 of the doppelganger protocol depicts the same identities as split 0 of ViSE).

The doppelganger protocol is generated with our curated list of doppelganger pairs. We create the pair instances in the doppelganger protocol as follows. First, we sample 500 image combinations, without replacement, for every pair of doppelgangers and identities with themselves. After generating all pairs following this criteria we separate the samples into 10 splits based on their identities and

Doppelganger Protocol Samples

Fig. 1. Shown above are samples from both protocols of the DoppelVer dataset – doppelganger and ViSE. We note that negative samples from the Doppelganger protocol share facial attributes while the image pairs in ViSE frequently share factors external to the face such as pose, clothing, and background.

Fig. 2. The upper portion of this figure presents samples from the CA-LFW dataset and the lower portion contains samples from CP-LFW. The CA-LFW samples showcase differences in age while CP-LFW's images showcase differences in pose.

pairs such that the same identity never shows up in multiple splits. Approximately 10% of the dataset is placed into each split. Finally, from each split we randomly sample 7,000 positive pairs and 7,000 negative pairs. We do this to follow the procedures laid out by LFW. This protocol has a positive label and negative label ratio of exactly 50%. It has a gender distribution of 44.96% males and 55.04% female samples respectively. Identities in each split have a relatively even representation with an average minimum contribution of 4.31%, average maximum contribution of 19.07%, and an average standard deviation between representation of 5.32%. In total the doppelganger protocol has 140,000 sample pairs.

To generate the ViSE protocol we use a similar approach to the one described in the automatic detection of unsatisfactory images. We begin by generating embeddings for each image in the dataset with the dinov2s model. Next, we compute the cosine similarity between images which do not come from the same identity. We retain all image pairs that have a similarity greater than 0.80. We have found that this form of mining hard pairs image by image rather than individual by individual results in significantly more visual similarity between image pairs. Using the same identities in each split as the doppelganger protocol, we break the protocol into 10 splits with unique identities in each split. This protocol has a positive label and negative label ratio of exactly 50%. It has a gender distribution of 40.36% male and 59.64% female. Identities in each split have a relatively even representation with an average minimum contribution of 2.29%, average maximum contribution of 17.61%, and an average standard deviation between representation of 3.6%. This protocol has 35,000 verification pairs.

3.4 Intended Use

The DoppelVer dataset is intended to provide a new challenge for the research community developing methods in the area of facial recognition. DoppelVer has been designed to act as an evaluation dataset, not a training dataset. In the past decade the most effective methods of facial recognition have utilized large training sets such as CASIA-WebFace, MegaFace, VGGFace2, MS-Celeb-1M [4,7,9,26]. These datasets contain 34.94K, 1.03M, 3.31M, 10M samples respectively. Although an aggregate of visually difficult pairs is attractive for faster convergence time, DoppelVer does not contain enough diversity to effectively and ethically train models.

We provide cross validation splits for both protocols in DoppelVer. The purpose of these splits is two-fold. First, some methods may wish to perform feature extraction prior to face classification. Such extraction methods should pre-train on external sources and infer features for each image in DoppelVer. At evaluation time final-stage classifiers should be iteratively trained from scratch (using their pre-trained feature extraction methods) on nine splits and evaluated on the tenth. Performance should be recorded as an average across the 9 models. We refer to interaction with the dataset in this way as **View 1**. Second, methods that wish to train on external data and perform only evaluation on DoppelVer should use split 0 for algorithm development and validation of results. The model should not be exposed to data in any of the other nine splits until final evaluation. Use of the dataset in this way is called **View 2**.

Taking motivation from the LFW dataset, we suggest that researchers utilizing **View 1** report estimated mean accuracy (EM ACC) and standard error of the mean (SEM). We define these metrics in the following way:

$$\hat{\mu} = \frac{\Sigma_{i=1}^9 p_i}{9}, SEM = \frac{\hat{\sigma}}{\sqrt{9}}, \hat{\sigma} = \sqrt{\frac{\Sigma_{i=1}^9 (p_i - \hat{\mu})^2}{9}}$$

where p_i is the percentage of correct classifications on **View 1** when using the ith split for testing. $\hat{\sigma}$ is the estimate of the standard deviation. As noted by the authors of LFW, it is important that accuracy is computed with parameters and thresholds chosen independently of the test data. Researchers should not simply choose the point on a Precision-Recall curve giving the highest accuracy.

For the methods which utilize **View 2** of DoppelVer, we advocate for the use of accuracy (ACC) and area under the receiver operating characteristic curve (ROC AUC). We elect for the use of ACC and ROC AUC because of the balanced nature of classes in the Doppelganger and ViSE protocols. In addition, the correct classification of true positives is equally important to classification of true negatives.

4   Experiments

In this section, we highlight the challenges posed by the DoppelVer dataset as compared to other existing evaluation datasets. We detail the methods used for evaluation, the training data, and the process employed for training and testing.

4.1   Evaluation Model

To provide an accurate depiction of the challenge posed by DoppelVer, it is important that we evaluate DoppelVer with SOTA face recognition models. Due to ease of implementation and competitive results we have elected to utilize the techniques described by Wen et al. in SphereFace2 [23]. In particular we train the 20 layer SphereFace Network (SFNet-20), initially proposed in [14], with the following loss functions: COCO, SphereFace, CosFace, ArcFace, and SphereFace2. Following Wen et al., we equip SFNet-20 with batch normalization to facilitate model optimization. A complete implementation for training SFNet-20 with the aforementioned loss functions can be found in the OpenSphere GitHub repository [25].

4.2   Training and Evaluation Process

For pre-processing, we crop face images in each dataset with MTCNN, resize images to a size of 112 × 112, and normalize each RGB pixel [0, 255] to the range [-1, 1]. We trained our models on a single Nvidia Geforce RTX 3090 GPU. Each model is trained for 70,000 batches of size 512. The model weights are updated by stochastic gradient descent with a momentum of 0.9 and weight decay of 0.0005. The initial learning rate of 0.1 is reduced by a factor of 0.1 at batches 40,000; 60,000; and 70,000.

We evaluate our dataset and protocols with VGGFace2, MS-Celeb-1M, and CASIA-WebFace [4,7,26]. In each run the VGGFace2 dataset was found to produce the best results on each evaluation dataset. VGGFace2 contains between 80 and 800 images for each identity making it a powerful training dataset for the face verification task. Evaluation of the trained models is performed on LFW, CA-LFW, CP-LFW, AgeDB 30, view 2 of DoppelVer's doppelganger protocol, and view 2 of DoppelVer's ViSE protocol. Our measured accuracy and ROC AUC are provided in Tables 1 and 2 respectively.

Table 1. Average accuracy of face verification for the comparison models trained with VGGFace2 and benchmarked on various datasets.

Method	LFW	CA-LFW	CP-LFW	AgeDB	Doppelganger	ViSE
COCO [15]	99.08	91.25	88.48	89.40	61.14	52.53
SphereFace [14]	99.58	93.15	91.65	93.53	63.48	57.08
CosFace [22]	99.52	93.03	91.37	93.02	63.29	56.93
ArcFace [6]	99.55	93.40	91.18	92.57	63.28	57.70
SphereFace2 [23]	99.53	93.80	90.83	93.38	61.66	55.41
Average	**99.45**	**92.93**	**90.70**	**92.38**	**62.57**	**55.93**

Table 2. Average AUC of face verification for the comparison models trained with VGGFace2 and benchmarked on various datasets.

Method	LFW	CA-LFW	CP-LFW	AgeDB	Doppelganger	ViSE
COCO [15]	99.89	96.56	93.57	96.03	65.13	50.53
SphereFace [14]	99.92	97.44	95.50	98.11	68.65	59.41
CosFace [22]	99.91	97.28	95.64	97.86	67.91	58.58
ArcFace [6]	99.89	96.99	95.46	97.53	68.15	59.79
SphereFace2 [23]	99.89	97.55	95.42	98.02	65.43	55.77
Average	**99.90**	**97.16**	**95.12**	**97.51**	**67.05**	**56.82**

4.3   Discussion of Results

We are satisfied with the performance achieved by the SOTA methods on the existing benchmark datasets. SOTA performance on the LFW dataset is 99.8% accuracy. Our training of SphereFace achieves an accuracy of 99.58%, misclassifying just 25 samples. With this result we can be assured that this baseline is competitive with other SOTA methods. The best published results on the other benchmark datasets are 95.87%, 92.08%, and 98.7% accuracy on CA-LFW, CP-LFW, and AgeDB 30 respectively. Regardless of loss function, the baseline networks struggle significantly more with variations in pose than variations in age. CA-LFW and AgeDB appear to present a similar degree of difficulty to the models.

It is clear from our experiments that the doppelganger and ViSE protocols of DoppelVer are much more difficult for the classifiers than the other datasets. Results are better for the doppelganger protocol than the ViSE protocol. This result aligns with intuition. Two identities that are doppelgangers may in general share facial attributes, but variations in clothing, hair style, lighting, and facial expression are expected when viewing a gallery of images depicting them.

On the other hand, the ViSE protocol contains image pairs which are adversarial in nature. By this we mean that the combinations of samples are those which a deep network is expected to struggle to differentiate. Although we use a different deep convolutional network to select samples which are visually similar than we do for performing facial recognition, one would expect that the visual features which are attended to by deep networks would have some similarity.

We believe that methods which will perform well on the ViSE protocol will need to extract features which are highly specific to the task of facial recognition. In addition, methods will need to not only detect relevant facial features, but discern if the features are prominent/defining to the individual's face.

5   Conclusion

In this work we introduce DoppelVer, a novel evaluation dataset for the tasks of facial feature extraction and face verification. DoppelVer consists of 27,967 carefully curated face images, which are used in two face verification protocols of image pairs: doppelganger and ViSE. We evaluate our methods using several SOTA methods. A near SOTA baseline model is only capable of correctly performing face verification at an accuracy of 62.57% and 55.93% in the doppelganger and ViSE protocols respectively. This indicates that despite impressive results on popular benchmark datasets, there is still work to be done in the field of facial recognition.

Future research should explore improvements to deep vision models to enable accurate classification of visually similar individuals. Additionally, future work might involve the application of the ViSE protocol's adversarial image pair selection to larger selections of facial data to enable the training of deep networks with visually similar negative pairs. Lastly, this data might be used to understand the difference in vision model perceptions between images of identical twins or parents and children at similar times of life.

Acknowledgement. This material is based upon work supported by the National Science Foundation under Grants No. 1909707, 2150394, and 2302187. Standard disclaimers apply.

References

1. Adjabi, I., Ouahabi, A., Benzaoui, A., Taleb-Ahmed, A.: Past, present, and future of face recognition: a review. Electronics **9**(8) (2020). https://doi.org/10.3390/electronics9081188, https://www.mdpi.com/2079-9292/9/8/1188

2. Alansari, M., Hay, O.A., Javed, S., Shoufan, A., Zweiri, Y., Werghi, N.: Ghost-FaceNets: lightweight face recognition model from cheap operations. IEEE Access **11**, 35429–35446 (2023). https://doi.org/10.1109/ACCESS.2023.3266068

3. An, X., et al.: Partial FC: training 10 million identities on a single machine. In: Proceedings of the IEEE/CVF International Conference on Computer Vision, pp. 1445–1449 (2021)

4. Cao, Q., Shen, L., Xie, W., Parkhi, O.M., Zisserman, A.: VGGFace2: a dataset for recognising faces across pose and age. In: 2018 13th IEEE International Conference on Automatic Face & Gesture Recognition (FG 2018), pp. 67–74 (2018). https://doi.org/10.1109/FG.2018.00020

5. Deng, J., Guo, J., Xue, N., Zafeiriou, S.: ArcFace: additive angular margin loss for deep face recognition. In: Proceedings of the IEEE/CVF Conference on Computer Vision and Pattern Recognition, pp. 4690–4699 (2019)

6. Deng, J., Guo, J., Yang, J., Xue, N., Kotsia, I., Zafeiriou, S.: ArcFace: additive angular margin loss for deep face recognition. IEEE Trans. Pattern Anal. Mach. Intell. **44**(10), 5962–5979 (2022). https://doi.org/10.1109/TPAMI.2021.3087709

7. Guo, Y., Zhang, L., Hu, Y., He, X., Gao, J.: MS-Celeb-1M: a dataset and benchmark for large-scale face recognition. In: Leibe, B., Matas, J., Sebe, N., Welling, M. (eds.) ECCV 2016. LNCS, vol. 9907, pp. 87–102. Springer, Cham (2016). https://doi.org/10.1007/978-3-319-46487-9_6

8. Huang, G.B., Ramesh, M., Berg, T., Learned-Miller, E.: Labeled faces in the wild: a database for studying face recognition in unconstrained environments. Technical report 07-49, University of Massachusetts, Amherst (2007)

9. Kemelmacher-Shlizerman, I., Seitz, S.M., Miller, D., Brossard, E.: The MegaFace benchmark: 1 million faces for recognition at scale. In: 2016 IEEE Conference on Computer Vision and Pattern Recognition (CVPR), pp. 4873–4882 (2016). https://doi.org/10.1109/CVPR.2016.527

10. Klare, B.F., et al.: Pushing the frontiers of unconstrained face detection and recognition: IARPA Janus benchmark A. In: 2015 IEEE Conference on Computer Vision and Pattern Recognition (CVPR), pp. 1931–1939 (2015). https://doi.org/10.1109/CVPR.2015.7298803

11. Kortli, Y., Jridi, M., Al Falou, A., Atri, M.: Face recognition systems: a survey. Sensors **20**(2) (2020). https://doi.org/10.3390/s20020342, https://www.mdpi.com/1424-8220/20/2/342

12. Visual layer: fastdup (2023). https://github.com/visual-layer/fastdup

13. Liu, J., Deng, Y., Bai, T., Wei, Z., Huang, C.: Targeting ultimate accuracy: face recognition via deep embedding (2015)

14. Liu, W., Wen, Y., Yu, Z., Li, M., Raj, B., Song, L.: SphereFace: deep hypersphere embedding for face recognition. In: 2017 IEEE Conference on Computer Vision and Pattern Recognition (CVPR), pp. 6738–6746 (2017). https://doi.org/10.1109/CVPR.2017.713

15. Liu, Y., Li, H., Wang, X.: Rethinking feature discrimination and polymerization for large-scale recognition. CoRR abs/1710.00870 (2017). http://arxiv.org/abs/1710.00870

16. Liu, Z., Luo, P., Wang, X., Tang, X.: Deep learning face attributes in the wild. In: 2015 IEEE International Conference on Computer Vision (ICCV), pp. 3730–3738 (2015). https://doi.org/10.1109/ICCV.2015.425

17. Maze, B., et al.: IARPA Janus benchmark - C: face dataset and protocol. In: 2018 International Conference on Biometrics (ICB), pp. 158–165 (2018). https://doi.org/10.1109/ICB2018.2018.00033

18. MordorIntelligence   (2023).   https://www.mordorintelligence.com/industry-reports/facial-recognition-market

19. Moschoglou, S., Papaioannou, A., Sagonas, C., Deng, J., Kotsia, I., Zafeiriou, S.: AgeDB: the first manually collected, in-the-wild age database. In: Proceedings of the IEEE Conference on Computer Vision and Pattern Recognition Workshop, vol. 2, p. 5 (2017)

20. Oquab, M., et al.: DINOv2: learning robust visual features without supervision (2023)

21. Sengupta, S., Chen, J.C., Castillo, C., Patel, V.M., Chellappa, R., Jacobs, D.W.: Frontal to profile face verification in the wild. In: 2016 IEEE Winter Conference on Applications of Computer Vision (WACV), pp. 1–9 (2016). https://doi.org/10.1109/WACV.2016.7477558

22. Wang, H., et al.: CosFace: large margin cosine loss for deep face recognition. In: 2018 IEEE/CVF Conference on Computer Vision and Pattern Recognition, pp. 5265–5274 (2018). https://doi.org/10.1109/CVPR.2018.00552

23. Wen, Y., Liu, W., Weller, A., Raj, B., Singh, R.: SphereFace2: binary classification is all you need for deep face recognition (2022)

24. Whitelam, C., et al.: IARPA Janus benchmark-B face dataset. In: 2017 IEEE Conference on Computer Vision and Pattern Recognition Workshops (CVPRW), pp. 592–600 (2017). https://doi.org/10.1109/CVPRW.2017.87

25. ydwen: Opensphere (2023). https://github.com/ydwen/opensphere

26. Yi, D., Lei, Z., Liao, S., Li, S.Z.: Learning face representation from scratch (2014)

27. Zhang, K., Zhang, Z., Li, Z., Qiao, Y.: Joint face detection and alignment using multitask cascaded convolutional networks. IEEE Signal Process. Lett. **23**(10), 1499–1503 (2016). https://doi.org/10.1109/LSP.2016.2603342

28. Zheng, T., Deng, W.: Cross-pose LFW: a database for studying cross-pose face recognition in unconstrained environments. Technical report 18-01, Beijing University of Posts and Telecommunications (2018)

29. Zheng, T., Deng, W., Hu, J.: Cross-age LFW: a database for studying cross-age face recognition in unconstrained environments. CoRR abs/1708.08197 (2017). http://arxiv.org/abs/1708.08197

Two-Stage Face Detection
and Anti-spoofing

M. Faisal Nurnoby[1] and El-Sayed M. El-Alfy[1,2(✉)]

[1] Information and Computer Science Department, College of Computing
and Mathematics, King Fahd University of Petroleum and Minerals,
Dhahran, Saudi Arabia
`alfy@kfupm.edu.sa`
[2] Fellow SDAIA-KFUPM Joint Research Center for Artificial Intelligence,
Interdisciplinary Research Center of Intelligent Secure Systems, King Fahd University
of Petroleum and Minerals, Dhahran, Saudi Arabia

Abstract. Face recognition is a widely used biometric technique that
has received a lot of attention. It is used to establish and verify the
user's identity, and subsequently grant access for authorized users to
restricted places and electronic devices. However, one of the challenges
is face spoofing or presentation attack allowing fraudsters who attempt
to impersonate a targeted victim by fabricating his/her facial biometric data, e.g., by presenting a photograph, a video, or a mask of the
targeted person. Several approaches have been proposed to counteract
face spoofing known as face anti-spoofing techniques. This paper's major
goals are to examine pertinent literature, and develop and evaluate a two-
stage approach for face detection and anti-spoofing. In the first stage, a
multi-task cascaded convolutional neural network is used to detect the
face region, and in the second stage, a multi-head attention-based transformer is used to detect spoofed faces. On two benchmarking datasets, a
number of experiments are carried out and examined to assess the proposed solution. The results are encouraging, with a very high accuracy,
which encourages further research in this direction to build more robust
face authentication systems.

Keywords: Presentation attack · Biometric authentication · Face
recognition · Face anti-spoofing · Deep learning · Vision Transformer

1 Introduction

Biometric security systems offer a plethora of convenient options for access control and surveillance. One of the most common and frequently utilized biometric
technologies today is face recognition, which is increasingly built into a variety
of devices for various security needs. Additionally, it is more convenient, non-
intrusive, and efficient relative to other biometric traits [12]. It has attracted
growing interest and become among the most active research areas of computer

© The Author(s), under exclusive license to Springer Nature Switzerland AG 2023
G. Bebis et al. (Eds.): ISVC 2023, LNCS 14361, pp. 445–455, 2023.
https://doi.org/10.1007/978-3-031-47969-4_35

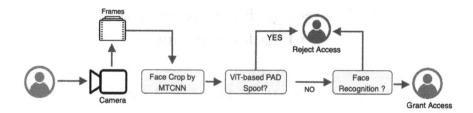

Fig. 1. Presentation Attack Detection System

vision, with numerous applications and commercial systems for access control, authentication of mobile payments, surveillance, human-computer interactions, and forensics. However, most of the face recognition systems are susceptible to assaults like spoofing, also called a face presentation attack [6]. A spoofing attack is a security threat that occurs when someone attempts to bypass a face recognition biometric system by presenting a fake face in front of the camera. A facial image can be simply put on photo paper, or printed on various masks, such as resin and silicon masks, as part of the presentation attack. Sometimes it can even be displayed on very high-resolution hand-held devices, including tablets, mobile phones, and laptops. The faces that are shown can be presented in front of any access control system [14]. Due to the widespread usage of devices that require this type of access, presentation or spoofing attacks have become increasingly sophisticated, posing considerable difficulties for the security of authentication systems.

An insecure face recognition system is always vulnerable to presentation attacks. A presentation attack detection (PAD) system aims to detect and prevent these kinds of attacks. Figure 1 shows an authentication system with PAD. Both impersonation and identity obfuscation are used in presentation spoofing. In an impersonation spoof attack, the attacker attempts to bypass authentication as someone else; in contrast, obfuscation attacks aim to conceal the identity of the attacker [10]. Any object used as a tool for presentation attacks is called spoof presentation assault instrument (PAI) [12]. PAIs include photo printouts, video replays, or 3D masks. In order to detect attacks such as replay and 2D printouts, features including color, texture, motion, and physiological indications, as well as CNN-based techniques, are frequently applied in the literature. Most presentation attack detection techniques found in current research focus on a small range of PAIs, and they are mostly images in the visible spectrum. Any PAD module witnesses a remarkable gain in performance after applying recent deep network models. Yet those methods do not generalize well to more realistic contexts [14]. Several cues can help detect the liveness of a face image and contribute to performance gains. Usually, those cues are able to prevent a particular type of attack, if not all [3]. Convolutional neural network (CNN)-based models are showing comparatively better performances. Nevertheless, those models are mostly 2D and are possibly vulnerable to attacks such as partial and 3D. As a remedy, many researchers moved their focus to the multi-channel approach (such as [17]) to trade accuracy with costs in terms of time and hardware.

In the area of computer vision, the application of self-attention based transformer architecture is still limited, even though it is a state-of-the-art tool for natural language processing tasks. The attention layer is either used in combination with convolutional layers in vision or is used to replace some layers of the convolutional network's constituent parts while maintaining the overall structure of the network. A pure transformer applied directly to sequences of picture patches may successfully perform image classification tasks without the need for CNNs. Besides, transformers are able to perform tasks on test data at a much faster speed compared to vanilla CNN models due to matrix operations and the efficient use of GPUs. Moreover, we aspire to investigate the effectiveness of a PAD when random-patched face images are fed to a ViT-based model. Our hypothesis is that detecting complex presentation attacks with a ViT [8] might bring about a more efficient solution.

Our work employed a fine-tuned Vision Transformer based model for face presentation attack detection. We argue that most of the existing solutions in the area of PAD show overfitting on the training dataset, and do not generalize well towards new and unseen spoofing attack samples. However, due to the patch-based nature of the ViT architecture, it showed more robust behavior when presented with new attacks or benign samples. We performed an ablation study through a series of experiments in order to measure the impacts of different environmental components in the experiments.

2   Related Works

Several approaches have been proposed in the literature for presentation attack detection (PAD). Moreover, a number of datasets have been introduced in the literature for benchmarking such as Replay-Attack, Replay-Mobile, SWAX, NUAA, SiW-M, CASIA-FASD, MSU-MFSD, CASIA-SURF, HiFiMask, WMCA, CelebA-Spoof and OULU-NPU. The majority of the research focus on face PAD, particularly 2D printouts and replay attacks. In this section, we provide a quick overview of recent PAD approaches.

2.1   Feature-Based PAD Systems

One of key findings is that the majority of prior face anti-spoofing research relied on a classifier based on hand-crafted features like motion patterns [2], image quality [9], Local Binary Patterns (LBP) [5], and image distortion measure [21]. It was recommended in [21] to use an image distortion analysis (IDA) face spoof detection method. Four different features, including specular reflection, blurriness. chromatic moment, and color diversity, are extracted to form the IDA feature vector. To differentiate between real (live) and spoof faces, an ensemble classifier made up of various SVM classifiers trained for various face spoof attempts (such as printed images and replayed videos) is employed. The suggested method is expanded to include voting-based multiframe face spoof detection in videos. According to the authors of [22], texture characteristics like

LBP, DoG, or HOG may be employed to differentiate between fake faces and actual faces. Texture-based techniques have been quite successful in the Idiap and CASIA databases.

2.2   CNN-Based PAD Systems

Despite the possibility of a wide range of PA, most of the works in the literature have detected 2D-type attacks such as replays and prints, primarily because such PAIs are simple to produce. However, the majority of the most recent cutting-edge findings come from techniques based on CNN.

The authors in [14] extended their previous work [13] on a deep patch-based CNN model for face PAD. The article argued that a model trained with face image patches can detect spoofs better. One important takeaway from the experiment is that the patch-based approach helps the model avoid memorizing the background of a face image. As the proposed approach leverages image patches, it requires less image data.

In [18], the authors applied a meta-teacher architecture with pixel-wise supervision in order to oversee presentation attack detectors. They demonstrated that, in comparison to teacher-student models and hand-crafted labels, the metateacher model offers better-suited monitoring. They found that the meta-teacher approach offered adequate supervision without the need for pixel-wise class labels when training networks. The article [19], which formulates the PAD issue as problems of both zero-shot learning and few-shot learning. They used live and spoof films, together with a few examples of novel assaults, for training a fine-tuned meta-learner that focuses on identifying hidden face spoof attack types. They demonstrated how their approach can outperform the competition on PAD benchmarks that are already in use.

For recognizing presentation attacks, the authors of [7] suggested a method, known as FaceSpoof Bluster, that combines deep neural networks and inherent visual features. The technique uses a pre-trained CNN model and an SVM classifier to analyze illumination, salience, and depth maps of face images in conjunction with to provide robust and discriminating features. Each of these attributes is identified separately, and then a meta-learning classifier combines them to produce better results.

2.3   Multichannel PAD Systems

The fundamental principle of multichannel approaches is that they use complimentary data acquired from many channels, which makes it very difficult for the adversaries to trick the spoof detection systems. According to the channels employed in the PAD system, an attacker must duplicate the characteristics of a genuine sample to a number of sensing domains; this makes the system harder to compromise [11].

George et al. in [12] argued systems that uses multiple channels, such as color, depth, infra-red, and thermal, might be more useful in addressing this presentation attack problem. They purposed a multi-channel Convolutional Neural

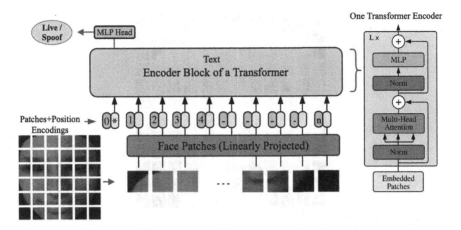

Fig. 2. Proposed face transformer based model

Network (MCCNN)-based PAD method. They also developed a new database for face PAD called Wide Multi-Channel Presentation Attack (WMCA), which comprises a wide range of 2D and 3D presentation assaults for both impersonation and obfuscation attacks. This database is publicly accessible through Idia Research Institute in Switzerland and can be found at[1] and contains 1941 short video recordings of 72 different identities. To enhance the study of facial PAD, data from many channels, including color, depth, near-infrared, and thermal, is present. The suggested methodology outperformed the baselines when compared to feature-based methods, attaining ACER score of 0.3% on the introduced dataset. In [10], the authors readdressed the same problem and presented a new framework to learn a robust PAD system. By adding a unique loss function that requires the network to learn a compact embedding for the legitimate class while being removed from the representation of attacks, the paper further expands the MCCNN technique to a one-class classifier framework. A unique method of learning a strong spoof attack detection system from real and known attack categories is introduced in the presented framework. The usefulness of the suggested method is demonstrated by the higher performance in unseen assault samples in the WMCA database.

Some recent papers on PAD have applied diverse approaches. The work in [16] outlined a video processing method named Temporal Sequence Sampling (TSS) by discarding affine movement and finally encoding the video into a single RGB image. The work applied a CNN with self-supervised learning for automatic labeling. Another approach for PAD based on CNN and background subtraction with ensemble classifiers is presented in [4]. Experiments were conducted for merely three attack types from four datasets in a selective manner. More recently, the authors in [1] used a unified DNN approach for PAD by integrating all the standalone tasks. They applied an ensemble approach with ViT-based features.

---

[1] https://paperswithcode.com/dataset/wmca.

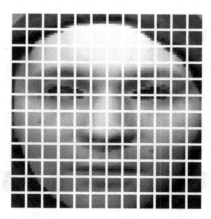

Fig. 3. Sample Face Patches from the SiW dataset

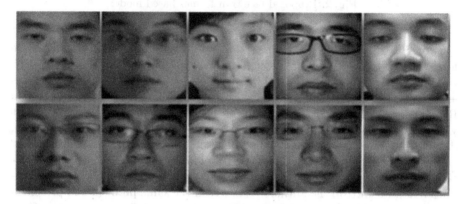

Fig. 4. Samples from the NUAA dataset

3 Methodology

In this study, we developed a transfer-learning model based on a vision transformer for detecting the face presentation attack. The workflow is explained in the following subsections.

3.1 Face Detection

The MTCNN (Multi-Task Cascaded Convolutional Neural Network) is used to recognize faces in the color channel. First, we extract image frames from the video files and take only the 20th frame of the sequence as the videos have very minor facial movements. We crop the faces during the preprocessing stage to remove the influence of the background. The MTCNN algorithm is then used for face detection and landmark localization. The eyes' centers are horizontally aligned on the chosen faces. The photos are then reduced to a resolution of 128 × 128 after this alignment to feed the transformer.

3.2   Anti-spoofing Model Architecture

In our work, we evaluated a vision transformer (ViT) as shown in Fig. 2 to detect presentation attacks on facial images, drawing inspiration from the success of the transformer application in NLP. We applied a pretrained vision transformer as proposed by Alexey Dosovitskiy et al. [8] as the backbone of our network. Without the use of convolution layers, the ViT model applies the Transformer architecture to a sequence of picture patches with self-attention. To handle 2D images, an image is transformed into a series of flattened 2D patches, which also act as the transformer's useful input sequence. The patches are flattened and mapped using a trainable linear projection known as the patch embeddings because the transformer employs a constant latent vector across all of its layers.

3.3   Model Implementation Details and Training

The vision transformer models surpass cutting-edge techniques in several vision benchmarks despite having been trained with a lot of data. A huge model must be completely retrained, which is computationally expensive. On the other hand, fine-tuning may make use of these potent models in settings with little data without necessitating a lot of computing capacity. We used a model trained on 6×6 patches; hence, the length of the input sequence is the same as the patches' number times THE height-width of the input image, which is 72 for both. Therefore, a face image would consist of 144 patches in total (Fig. 3). To keep positional information, a 1D positional embedding is additionally inserted in addition to patch embeddings. For the classification task, an MLP head with a fully connected layer was stacked on top of the transformer layers. To be more specific, we adjusted the model and applied binary cross-entropy loss. Then we replaced the last MLP layer and added a single output layer. We have examined the effect of fine-tuning.

During the training phase, we applied data augmentation using random horizontal flips. A fixed learning rate of 0.001 and a weight decay value of 0.0001 were used to supervise the network. During training, a batch size of 256 was employed. We trained the model on a GPU grid of a Macbook-M1-Pro/32GB-RAM computer for 25 epochs using the common Adam Optimizer. We chose our optimum model considering the lowest loss value in the validation dataset. Keras-Tensorflow was used to implement the architecture.

4   Experimental Work

4.1   Datasets and Performance Measures

Two datasets have been used in our experiments: *Spoof in Wild with Multiple Attack (SiW-M) Database*: This dataset contains a large range of attacks recorded with an RGB camera [15]. It contains 493 subjects with 660 live samples and 968 attack samples. Altogether, they make 1,628 files with a total of 13

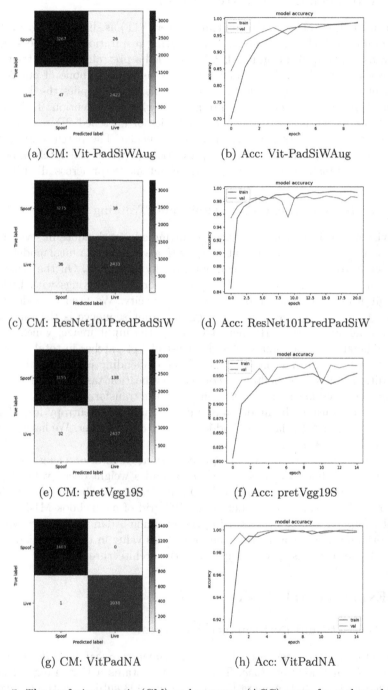

(a) CM: Vit-PadSiWAug   (b) Acc: Vit-PadSiWAug

(c) CM: ResNet101PredPadSiW   (d) Acc: ResNet101PredPadSiW

(e) CM: pretVgg19S   (f) Acc: pretVgg19S

(g) CM: VitPadNA   (h) Acc: VitPadNA

Fig. 5. The confusion matrix (CM) and accuracy (ACC) curve for each model

possible poses, expressions, and lighting variations. The attack samples were generated from multiple sessions. The attacks include a variety of makeups, masks, partials, and 2D presentation assaults.

NUAA Photo Imposter Database: This is a publicly available imposter database created by using a generic WebCam [20]. It has 15 subjects and images were captured in two sessions. Images of both the live subjects and their pictures were taken during each session. Each subject was instructed to look directly into the camera during the capture, maintaining a neutral expression and refraining from any outward motions, such as head movements or blinking eyes. Figure 4 shows some screenshots of the recorded photos.

As per ISO/IEC 30107-3 metrics, we used three performance measures in addition to the accuracy (ACC): Bonafide Presentation Classification Error Rate (BPCER), Attack Presentation Classification Error Rate (APCER), Average Classification Error Rate (ACER).

4.2   Experiments and Results

Three CNN-based baselines have been applied for comparison with the proposed ViT-based approach. We compared our model with other transfer learning-based models that are from two well-known architectures, such as VGG, and ResNet101, as the presented approach is also a transfer learning-based one.

We have conducted a set of six rounds of experiments with the SiW-M and NUAA datasets. In particular, we evaluated the proposed ViT-based PAD model on the two datasets and compared the model with two pretrained models dubbed as pretResNet101S and pretVGG19S. The outcomes of the six experiments are demonstrated in Table 1. The first experiment was on the SiW-M dataset with the proposed model ViTPadS without data augmentation during the training. The model shows a higher APCER score compared to BPCER. However, the same model trained with augmented data shows better scores. The pretrained baseline model, dubbed as pretVGG19PadS, scored lower accuracy, thus having higher scores in both APCER and BPCER. The best performance on the SiW-M dataset was shown by the pretrained ResNet101-based model with the lowest ACER score of 1.0. The experiment we carried out on the NUAA dataset using the proposed model, VitPadNA, scored an ACER score of 0.05. We also record the training and validation accuracy curves of our experiments. The confusion matrix and accuracy curves for each model are shown in Fig. 5. All curves show decent behaviors except for the experiment of the VitPadNA model which was trained and tested on the NUAA dataset. The model seems to converge quickly; it only required two epochs. This is due to the small data size. It is also too much biased for the training dataset. Also, the NUAA dataset has fewer variations in data.

Table 1. Comparison of various models using four performance measures

Model	Dataset	APCER	BPCER	ACER	ACC
ViTPadS	SiW-M	1.9	0.79	1.35	98.7
ViTPadSA	SiW-M	1.46	0.58	1.02	99.01
pretResNet101S	SiW-M	1.46	0.55	1.0	99.10
pretVGG19PadS	SiW-M	1.30	4.19	2.74	97.10
ViTPadNA	NUAA	0.01	0.0	0.05	99.60
ViTPadMulti	SiW-M	–	–	–	97.70

5   Conclusion and Future Work

Face recognition systems are one of the most prominent biometric tools for numerous access control solutions. This paper explores a two-stage approach for face detection and anti-spoofing. Faces are detected using a multi-task cascaded convolutional neural network, and a vision-transformer-based model, dubbed ViTPadS, is developed for face presentation attack detection. Two datasets were used to evaluate the performance of the model with or without data augmentation. The model's performance is also compared to two other pretrained models used as baseline models. The experimental work demonstrated promising results for the proposed ViT-based model. This work can be further improved by conducting an ablation study and fine-tuning. Also, to make the model more robust against any unknown attacks, cross-dataset testing with a zero or few-shot learning architecture can also be considered.

Acknowledgment. The authors would like to thank King Fahd University of Petroleum and Minerals for support under the Interdisciplinary Research Center for Intelligent Secure Systems Grant no. INSS2204.

References

1. Al-Refai, R., Nandakumar, K.: A unified model for face matching and presentation attack detection using an ensemble of vision transformer features. In: Proceedings of the IEEE/CVF Winter Conference on Applications of Computer Vision, pp. 662–671 (2023)
2. Anjos, A., Marcel, S.: Counter-measures to photo attacks in face recognition: a public database and a baseline. In: IEEE International Joint Conference on Biometrics (IJCB), pp. 1–7 (2011)
3. Atoum, Y., Liu, Y., Jourabloo, A., Liu, X.: Face anti-spoofing using patch and depth-based CNNs. In: IEEE International Joint Conference on Biometrics (IJCB), pp. 319–328 (2017)
4. Benlamoudi, A., et al.: Face presentation attack detection using deep background subtraction. Sensors **22**(10), 3760 (2022)
5. Boulkenafet, Z., Komulainen, J., Hadid, A.: Face anti-spoofing based on color texture analysis. In: IEEE International Conference on Image Processing (ICIP), pp. 2636–2640 (2015)

6. Boulkenafet, Z., Komulainen, J., Hadid, A.: Face spoofing detection using colour texture analysis. IEEE Trans. Inf. Forensics Secur. **11**(8), 1818–1830 (2016)

7. Bresan, R., Pinto, A., Rocha, A., Beluzo, C., Carvalho, T.: FaceSpoof buster: a presentation attack detector based on intrinsic image properties and deep learning. arXiv preprint arXiv:1902.02845 (2019)

8. Dosovitskiy, A., et al.: An image is worth 16×16 words: transformers for image recognition at scale. arXiv preprint arXiv:2010.11929 (2020)

9. Galbally, J., Marcel, S., Fierrez, J.: Image quality assessment for fake biometric detection: application to iris, fingerprint, and face recognition. IEEE Trans. Image Process. **23**(2), 710–724 (2013)

10. George, A., Marcel, S.: Multi-channel face presentation attack detection using deep learning. In: Ratha, N.K., Patel, V.M., Chellappa, R. (eds.) Deep Learning-Based Face Analytics. ACVPR, pp. 269–304. Springer, Cham (2021). https://doi.org/10.1007/978-3-030-74697-1_13

11. George, A., Marcel, S.: On the effectiveness of vision transformers for zero-shot face anti-spoofing. In: IEEE International Joint Conference on Biometrics (IJCB), pp. 1–8 (2021)

12. George, A., Mostaani, Z., Geissenbuhler, D., Nikisins, O., Anjos, A., Marcel, S.: Biometric face presentation attack detection with multi-channel convolutional neural network. IEEE Trans. Inf. Forensics Secur. **15**, 42–55 (2019)

13. Kantarcı, A., Dertli, H., Ekenel, H.K.: Shuffled patch-wise supervision for presentation attack detection. In: IEEE International Conference of the Biometrics Special Interest Group (BIOSIG), pp. 1–5 (2021)

14. Kantarcı, A., Dertli, H., Ekenel, H.K.: Deep patch-wise supervision for presentation attack detection. IET Biomet. **11**(5), 396–406 (2022)

15. Liu, Y., Stehouwer, J., Jourabloo, A., Liu, X.: Deep tree learning for zero-shot face anti-spoofing. In: Proceedings of the IEEE/CVF Conference on Computer Vision and Pattern Recognition, pp. 4680–4689 (2019)

16. Muhammad, U., Yu, Z., Komulainen, J.: Self-supervised 2D face presentation attack detection via temporal sequence sampling. Pattern Recogn. Lett. **156**, 15–22 (2022)

17. Nikisins, O., George, A., Marcel, S.: Domain adaptation in multi-channel autoencoder based features for robust face anti-spoofing. In: IEEE International Conference on Biometrics (ICB), pp. 1–8 (2019)

18. Qin, Y., Yu, Z., Yan, L., Wang, Z., Zhao, C., Lei, Z.: Meta-teacher for face anti-spoofing. IEEE Trans. Pattern Anal. Mach. Intell. **44**, 6311–6326 (2021)

19. Qin, Y., et al.: Learning meta model for zero-and few-shot face anti-spoofing. In: Proceedings of the AAAI Conference on Artificial Intelligence, vol. 34, pp. 11916–11923 (2020)

20. Tan, X., Li, Y., Liu, J., Jiang, L.: Face liveness detection from a single image with sparse low rank bilinear discriminative model. In: Daniilidis, K., Maragos, P., Paragios, N. (eds.) ECCV 2010. LNCS, vol. 6316, pp. 504–517. Springer, Heidelberg (2010). https://doi.org/10.1007/978-3-642-15567-3_37

21. Wen, D., Han, H., Jain, A.K.: Face spoof detection with image distortion analysis. IEEE Trans. Inf. Forensics Secur. **10**(4), 746–761 (2015)

22. Yang, J., Lei, Z., Liao, S., Li, S.Z.: Face liveness detection with component dependent descriptor. In: IEEE International Conference on Biometrics (ICB), pp. 1–6 (2013)

Autonomous Anomaly Detection in Images

Driver Anomaly Detection Using Skeleton Images

Radovan Fusek[✉][ORCID], Eduard Sojka, Jan Gaura, and Jakub Halman

Department of Computer Science, Faculty of Electrical Engineering and Computer Science, VSB - Technical University of Ostrava, 17. listopadu 2172/15, 70800 Ostrava, Czech Republic
{radovan.fusek,eduard.sojka,jan.gaura,jakub.halman.st}@vsb.cz

Abstract. Many unexpected situations can occur while driving that may lead to dangerous accidents. Some of them may be caused by sudden health problems (e.g. heart attack, stroke, total collapse) or by driver inattention (e.g. microsleep, visual distraction). This has motivated the need for developing the methods that are able to monitor the driver's state in the first step and to prevent the accidents in the second step (e.g. by activating an acoustic signal, or even by taking over driving). In this paper, we propose a method that can be used for detecting the abnormal driving situations. Our approach is based on two main steps. In the first step, the MNIST-like skeleton images are created with the use of human pose detector. In the second step, an appropriate neural network is used for the final classification. Since we also include the anomalies consisting in an unusual trajectory of a certain body part (not only an unusual shape of body, which can be detected from the isolated images), short sequences of images are examined. The LSTM (long short-term memory) autoencoder is used as a main network architecture. The experiments that are presented show that the proposed method achieves better results than other compared methods.

Keywords: Anomaly detection · Autoencoder · LSTM · Deep learning · CNN · Driver monitoring

1 Introduction

In recent years, we can observe an increasing number of vehicles in the cities. This phenomenon raises various challenges that need to be addressed. As the number of drivers continues to rise, the likelihood of the event that something unexpected may happen while driving also increases. The accidents may be caused by various factors, such as a car fault, a health problem or driver inattention [1,5,16,28]. These problems create the motivation to develop a system that can prevent or avoid these accidents. Obviously, we can use a variety of sensors to analyse driver behaviour in the car, e.g. vision based sensors, microphones or physical sensors attached to the driver's body. Since the recording of audio signals can

G. Bebis et al. (Eds.): ISVC 2023, LNCS 14361, pp. 459–471, 2023.
https://doi.org/10.1007/978-3-031-47969-4_36

be problematic due to privacy concerns and the use of physical sensors may not be convenient for the driver, we present the method using camera images in this paper.

It is clear that a robust dataset is required for testing and training the neural networks. Nowadays, there are several available datasets in the field of driver behaviour: Driving Monitoring Dataset [19], Drive&Act dataset [15], 100-Driver dataset [23], Driver anomaly dataset [8]. Various conditions are recorded in the mentioned datasets, e.g. phone calls, smoking, health problems (coughing, sneezing, total collapse), fatigue, sleep.

In [8], the authors presented an approach (together with the dataset) for the analysis of anomalous states of the driver. The approach is based on the two main steps. In the first step, the driver pose is estimated with the use of Lightweight OpenPose detector [20]. In the second step, the distances between the body parts are assembled into a feature vector. Finally, the distance feature vector is used as an input for the autoencoder network [9] with the LSTM cells. We experimented with this method and we found the areas where the approach could be improved. Firstly, we use the whole 2D images containing the pose instead of a simple distance vector. Secondly, we improved the architecture of the neural network that the authors presented. As will be shown in the subsequent sections, these improvements yield better results on the same dataset. We can conclude that these improvements are the main contributions of this paper.

The rest of the paper is organized as follows. In Sect. 2, the previous methods in this area are mentioned. In Sect. 3, the main ideas of the proposed approach are described. In Sect. 4, the experiments are presented.

2   Related Work

Several studies that address in-vehicle driver analysis have been presented in recent years. These publications can be divided into several categories according to the different data and sensors (e.g. physiological data, cameras, microphones, vehicle-based sensors).

In the area of physiological signals and sensors, the authors presented that ECG data can be used to detect driver inattention (e.g. drowsiness, fatigue) with the use of SVM and KNN classifiers in [18]. In another study [31], the authors presented that EEG signals can also be used to detect the driver's state. Deep learning models (EEG-Conv and EEG-Conv-R) for the classification of driver mental states were proposed in [29]. The driver drowsiness detection method based on heart rate variability (HRV) analysis was proposed in [7]. In [2], the authors used EEG signals and the encoder-decoder model for driver drowsiness detection.

In the area of visual sensors, a lot of useful studies have also been published. In [8], the driver anomaly detection method using skeleton localization and LSTM networks was presented. In that method, the distances between the parts of driver body are used as an input for LSTM networks. As will be shown in the subsequent sections, this method inspired us to create an alternative way to detect anomalous driver behaviour in the car. It is important to note that in the area of anomaly detection, the methods based on the deep learning techniques have been presented in many papers. Especially, the methods based on LSTM networks have become useful and these networks have been used in many different applications [11,14]. In [17], the driver state monitoring system with the use of 3D convolutional neural network was proposed. With the use of Kinect RGB-D sensor, AdaBoost classifier, and Hidden Markov Model, the authors presented an approach for detection and recognition of different types of driver distraction in [6]. In [26], the authors used driver head and body posture information for driving task recognition with the use of artificial neural networks and Kinect sensor. Another image-based approach was proposed in [25]. The authors identified seven driving activities that were divided into two groups; normal (i.e. right mirror checking, rear mirror checking, left mirror checking) and distraction (i.e. using in-vehicle radio device, texting, and answering the mobile phone). Gaussian mixture model is used to extract the area of driver body. In the last step, the three different CNN models were evaluated (AlexNet, GoogLeNet, and ResNet50).

In [30], the author proposed a comprehensive literature survey that address the challenges in the area of human emotions in the automotive context. The authors have reviewed a large number of publications that cover the use of different types of sensors (e.g. cameras, biosensors, microphones, CAN-Bus) and methods (e.g. supervised, unsupervised, and statistical approaches). A study that reviews the methods of driver behaviour analysis was presented in [32]. Several typical machine learning approaches were examined (e.g. random forest, support vector machine, convolutional neural network, recurrent neural network) in that study.

3   Proposed Method

To recognize the driver's activity using the images, it is essential to obtain the information about the position of particular important parts of the driver's body in the first step. We use the Lightweight OpenPose [20] for this purpose (see Fig. 1), which is an optimized variant of the OpenPose [4]. As the authors of the Lightweight OpenPose mention, their method can localize the skeleton very fast even without using modern GPUs. The method is based on the feature extractor using the MobileNet network [10,22].

In the second step, it is necessary to obtain the appropriate features from the positions of the body parts. In [8], the authors used a set of 91 distances between the body parts like nose, neck, eyes, palms, knees, elbows, shoulders, and ears. In this paper, we propose to use a different approach. Instead of measuring the distances between the particular body parts, we use here the whole image containing the visible part of body skeleton (Fig. 2). We use two-level images with white skeleton and black background. (i.e. we extract the information about the body in the form that is similar to the MNIST database of handwritten digits [12]). We believe that this approach has several advantages. Firstly, the

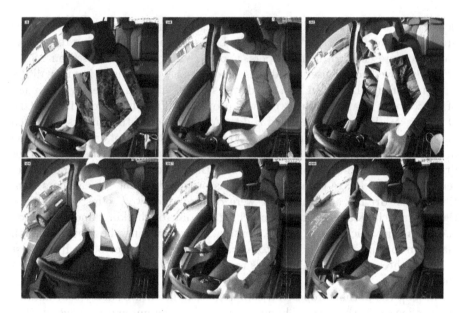

Fig. 1. Several examples of the skeleton detected using the Lightweight OpenPose [20].

information that is not needed for the analysis, e.g. clothing, gender, background image is filtered out in this approach. Secondly, the information is not compressed into a certain number of a priori chosen values only, but we are allowing the network to choose what it considers to be relevant. Moreover, the approach with images easily solves the problem of what to do if some part of driver body is not detected successfully (e.g. hand), which may happen. In the approach with numerical features, a certain artificial value must be used instead of the items that cannot be computed in such a case. In the approach with images, the skeleton can be simply sent to analysis as it was detected, i.e. possibly without a certain missing part.

Fig. 2. An example of training images.

It should be noted that two different types of anomaly situations may be distinguished. (1) The anomalies that can be detected directly from one image, which may be possible if the body shape itself is unusual. (2) The anomalies requiring more images for their detection since the anomaly may also consist in an unusual movement (unusual trajectory) of a body part whereas the body shape itself remains usual in every particular frame. It seems that the anomalies of the first type may probably be more frequent in practice. However, the time should be generally considered, i.e. more frames should be evaluated in the case that the anomalies of the second type should be captured too.

For solving the problem, we have proposed and tested four types of neural networks (we refer to them as Netw1, Netw2, Netw3, and Netw4). We regard Netw1 as a basic solution, Netw2, 3, and 4 are alternative networks whose purpose was to verify some our opinions and hypotheses that might be worth mentioning. All the networks are created as autoencoders, which follows the hypothesis that the reconstruction of the skeleton picture (Fig. 3) can be carried out with a small error only if a similar picture was present in the training set. If not, the reconstruction error is expected to be big, which indicates an anomaly situation. For measuring the reconstruction error, the usual mean-square distance between the input and reconstructed images is used.

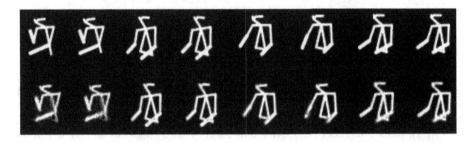

Fig. 3. An example of reconstruction process. The input skeleton images are shown in the first row. The reconstructed skeleton images are shown in the second row. In the first two examples (from the left), it can be seen that the network is not able to reconstruct the whole skeleton image correctly. The images with a big reconstruction error are labeled as anomalous (in this particular case, the images that represent drivers with coughing attacks).

The network Netw1 is characterised by the use of LSTM units both in encoder and decoder (since we consider time), the majority of the remaining layers are 2D convolution and max pooling layers in the encoder, and transposed 2D convolution layers in the decoder. Figure 4 shows the network together with a detailed description of its parameters.

In Netw2, the LSTM layers are replaced by the dense (fully connected) layers. This was motivated by our experiments that have shown that, in the case that the number of different times that should be considered is not too high, this can be done without sacrificing the efficiency (moreover, the training may be faster). The network is depicted and its parameters are specified in Fig. 5.

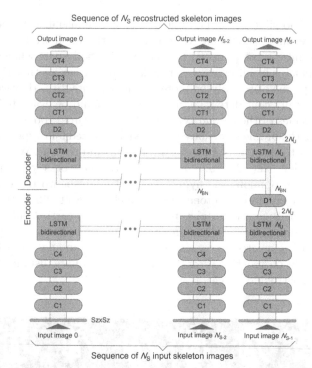

Fig. 4. Basic version (see text) of neural network (Netw1). The network processes N_S images of size 64×64 ($Sz = 64$). C1, C2, C3, C4 are time distributed convolutional layers. C1: $8 \times (7,7)$, $8 \times (7,7)$, ReLU, maxPool $(2,2)$; C2: $32 \times (5,5)$, $32 \times (5,5)$, ReLU, maxPool $(2,2)$; C3: $64 \times (3,3)$, $64 \times (3,3)$, ReLU, maxPool $(2,2)$; C4: $64 \times (3,3)$, $64 \times (3,3)$, ReLU, maxPool $(2,2)$. D1 is a dense layer with N_{BN} cells and no activation (i.e. N_{BN} is the number of variables creating the bottleneck.) D2 is a time distributed dense layer with no activation whose output is reshaped to N_S channels containing $4 \times 4 \times 128$ images. CT1, CT2, CT3, CT4 are transposed 2D convolution layers. CT1: $128 \times (3,3)$, $(2,2)$ strides, $128 \times (3,3)$, $(1,1)$ strides, ReLU; CT2: $64 \times (3,3)$, $(2,2)$ strides, $64 \times (3,3)$, $(1,1)$ strides, ReLU; CT3: $32 \times (5,5)$, $(2,2)$ strides, $32 \times (5,5)$, $(1,1)$ strides, ReLU; CT4: $16 \times (7,7)$, $(2,2)$ strides, $1 \times (7,7)$, $(1,1)$ strides, linear. N_u stands for the number of parameters of LSTM units; LSTM units are bidirectional, their activation function is linear.

Netw3 (Fig. 6) uses LSTM layers again, but the convolution and transposed convolution layers are replaced with the dense layers, which is possible since the images are relatively small and simple. It can also be well understood from the theoretical point of view. Whereas the convolution anticipates only the class of the shift invariant image operators, there is no similar restriction for the image operators realised in the dense layers. The only problem is that the number of parameters is rapidly increasing. For small images, however, the number of parameters remains acceptable, and training the network may be faster than in the case with the convolutional layers. The legitimacy of this approach was

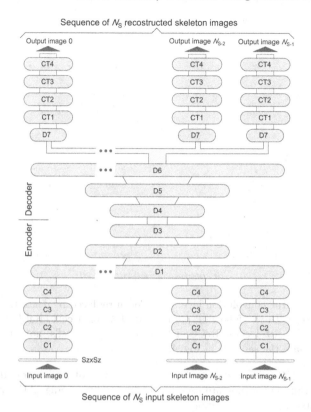

Fig. 5. In Netw2, the LSTM layers have been replaced by the dense layers (see text). The numbers of cell are as follows: $N_S \times 128$ for D1; $2 \times N_{BN}$ for D2; N_{BN} for D3; $2 \times N_{BN}$ for D4; $N_S \times 128$ for D5; $N_S \times 256$ for D6. No activation for all the mentioned layers. The parameters of the remaining layers are the same as in Fig. 4.

also supported experimentally (see Sect. 4). Finally, Netw4 (Fig. 7) uses only the dense layers, which can be understood as a logical consequence of what has been explained for Netw2 and Netw3. The results of testing all the particular networks can be found in the next section.

4   Experiments

In the experiments, we used the video dataset published in [8]. The dataset contains the records of rides of six different drivers. Two types of rides are provided: (1) The rides containing only the normal situations. (2) The rides containing anomalies (e.g. sneeze, cough, telephoning). The anomaly rides are annotated by specifying the type and time of each anomaly situation. A sample image from this dataset is shown in Fig. 1. (We note that in Fig. 1, the body skeleton is added by us, it is not contained in the original dataset.) We also compare our method with several other methods: the method presented in [8] (Fusek at al.), Elliptical

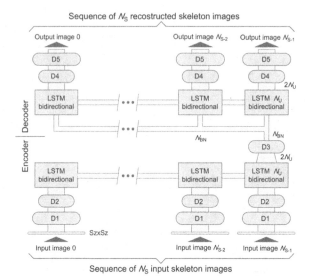

Fig. 6. In Netw3, the convolution layers have been replaced by dense time distributed layers (see text) with the following parameters. D1: 1024 cells, ReLU; D2: 512 cells, no activation; D4: 1024 cells, ReLU, D5: 4096 (Sz × Sz) cells, no activation. Other parameters remain the same as in Fig. 4.

Table 1. The AUC (area under the ROC curve) results of various tested methods for $N_S = 2$ (two frames at a time are used for analysis). The average AUC value for each method is stated in the last column.

	Driver-1	Driver-2	Driver-3	Driver-4	Driver-5	Driver-6	avg.
Netw1	0.9572	0.9651	0.9523	0.9723	0.8926	0.848	0.9313
Netw2	0.9592	0.9656	0.9505	0.97	0.9018	0.8548	0.9337
Netw3	0.9523	0.9715	0.9409	0.969	0.8814	0.8677	0.9305
Netw4	0.9539	0.9691	0.9476	0.9689	0.8816	0.8649	0.931
Fusek at al.	0.9744	0.9535	0.9019	0.9736	0.8643	0.7895	0.9095
EE	0.8397	0.7199	0.7239	0.8443	0.6929	0.6969	0.7529
Forest	0.8745	0.7301	0.7967	0.9339	0.7425	0.7379	0.8026
LOF	0.965	0.9648	0.7401	0.9039	0.7797	0.7205	0.8457
SVM-SGD	0.09022	0.8989	0.7486	0.9142	0.734	0.677	0.8125
SVM	0.9159	0.9422	0.6474	0.8995	0.6697	0.6522	0.7878

Envelope method (EE) [21], Local Outlier Factor method (LOF) [3], classical One-Class SVM method (SVM) with the Radial Basis Function (RBF) kernel, One-Class SVM using a kernel approximation and stochastic gradient descent (SVM-SGD) [24,27], and Isolation Forest method (Forest) [13]. For $N_S = 2$ (two frames at a time are used for analysis), the main results of testing are sum-

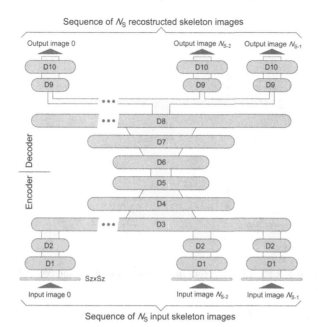

Fig. 7. In Netw4, only the dense layers are used whose parameters are specified in Figs. 5 and 6.

Table 2. The AUC (area under the ROC curve) results of various tested methods for $N_S = 4$ (four frames at a time are used for analysis). The average AUC value for each method is stated in the last column.

	Driver-1	Driver-2	Driver-3	Driver-4	Driver-5	Driver-6	avg.
Netw1	0.9551	0.9665	0.9341	0.9609	0.8732	0.8478	0.9229
Netw2	0.9594	0.9655	0.9477	0.9682	0.8856	0.8671	0.9322
Netw3	0.9509	0.9702	0.93	0.9623	0.8703	0.861	0.9241
Netw4	0.9542	0.9694	0.9428	0.9682	0.8814	0.8742	0.9317
Fusek at al.	0.9738	0.950	0.8997	0.9623	0.807	0.7555	0.8914
EE	0.7898	0.6452	0.7333	0.821	0.641	0.688	0.7197
Forest	0.8797	0.7388	0.7913	0.9322	0.7238	0.714	0.7966
LOF	0.9243	0.9568	0.7259	0.7351	0.7676	0.7009	0.8018
SVM-SGD	0.9017	0.8941	0.7385	0.9068	0.7353	0.6828	0.8099
SVM	0.9132	0.9326	0.6637	0.8926	0.6973	0.6614	0.7935

marised in Fig. 8 containing the resulting ROC curves and also in Table 1. For $N_S = 4$ (four frames), the results are provided in Table 2.

From the tables and the figure, it can be seen that all four networks we have proposed give very similar results. We must admit, however, that we strove to

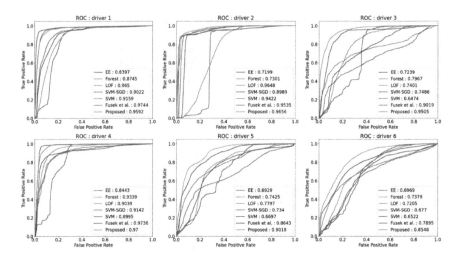

Fig. 8. The results for various drivers and various methods for $N_S = 2$ (two frames at a time are used for analysis).

create the alternative networks Netw2, Netw3, and Netw4 with the goal that this would happen. Netw1 may be regarded as a classical approach if the images and time should be taken into account. The remaining networks (Netw4 especially) might sometimes be preferred for some reasons, e.g. speed of learning and speed of analysis as will be discussed later.

It is important to mention that all the proposed networks achieved better results than the method presented in [8] and also than all the other methods that were used for comparison. We may conclude that the results show that using the images containing a sketch of body, which is proposed here (i.e. something like MNIST images) may be efficient, more straightforward, and more convenient than time-consuming seeking for the best feature vector.

Another interesting fact has been revealed during testing. The times required for learning as well as the times required for analysis were very different for particular networks on our hardware (an i7 computer with GTX 1080 GPU, or without GPU) and for our TensorFlow installation. The networks Netw1 and Netw2 required more than 10 times longer time for learning as well as for analysis. For example, on an i7 computer without GPU (the analysis should be carried out in car, therefore, not too special computers are preferred in this case), the pure times required for analysis ($N_S = 2$) by the particular networks were as follows: 5 ms for Netw1, 4.9 ms for Netw2, 0.25 ms for Netw3, and 0.2 ms for Netw4. (We note that this time does not include detecting the body parts by Lightweight OpenPose, which took approx 20 ms per one image.) Although we are aware of the fact that the speed of learning and recognition depends on many hardware and software details, we do not exclude that it may also become a criterion for choosing the network that is best for a given environment.

5   Conclusion

In this paper, we have focused on developing the methods for detecting the anomalous driver states with the motivation to contribute to reduction of the number of road accidents, e.g. the accidents caused by sudden health problems of drivers. The method we propose is based on the image analysis and machine learning. In the first step, the skeleton images are created with the use of human pose detector. In the second step, the deep learning methods are used for the final classification. Four types of autoencoders processing the skeleton images captured in several different times have been proposed. We show that using the images containing a sketch of body, which is proposed here, may be efficient, more straightforward, and more convenient than seeking for the best feature vector. The results we presented seem to be promising and providing the perspective for the future development of a practical application solving the studied problem.

Acknowledgments. This work is partially supported by Grants of SGS No. SP2023/072, VSB - Technical University of Ostrava, Czech Republic.

References

1. Adanu, E., Jones, S.: Effects of human-centered factors on crash injury severities. J. Adv. Transp. 1–11 **2017** (2017). https://doi.org/10.1155/2017/1208170
2. Arefnezhad, S., et al.: Driver drowsiness estimation using EEG signals with a dynamical encoder-decoder modeling framework. Sci. Rep. **12**, 2650 (2022). https://doi.org/10.1038/s41598-022-05810-x
3. Breunig, M.M., Kriegel, H.P., Ng, R.T., Sander, J.: LOF: identifying density-based local outliers. SIGMOD Rec. **29**(2), 93–104 (2000). https://doi.org/10.1145/335191.335388
4. Cao, Z., Hidalgo, G., Simon, T., Wei, S.E., Sheikh, Y.: Openpose: realtime multi-person 2D pose estimation using part affinity fields (2019)
5. Comi, A., Polimeni, A., Balsamo, C.: Road accident analysis with data mining approach: evidence from Rome. Transp. Res. Procedia **62**, 798–805 (2022) https://doi.org/10.1016/j.trpro.2022.02.099, https://www.sciencedirect.com/science/article/pii/S2352146522002265. 24th Euro Working Group on Transportation Meeting
6. Craye, C., Karray, F.: Driver distraction detection and recognition using RGB-D sensor. CoRR abs/1502.00250 (2015), http://arxiv.org/abs/1502.00250
7. Fujiwara, K., et al.: Heart rate variability-based driver drowsiness detection and its validation with EEG. IEEE Trans. Biomed. Eng. **66**(6), 1769–1778 (2019). https://doi.org/10.1109/TBME.2018.2879346
8. Fusek, R., Sojka, E., Gaura, J., Halman, J.: Driver state detection from in-car camera images. In: Bebis, G., et al. (eds.) ISVC 2022. LNCS, pp. 307–319. Springer, Cham (2022). https://doi.org/10.1007/978-3-031-20716-7_24
9. Hinton, G.E., Salakhutdinov, R.R.: Reducing the dimensionality of data with neural networks. Science **313**(5786), 504–507 (2006). https://doi.org/10.1126/science.1127647, https://www.science.org/doi/abs/10.1126/science.1127647
10. Howard, A.G., et al.: MobileNets: efficient convolutional neural networks for mobile vision applications. CoRR abs/1704.04861 (2017). http://arxiv.org/abs/1704.04861

11. Kingma, D.P., Welling, M.: Auto-encoding variational bayes (2013)
12. LeCun, Y., Cortes, C., Burges, C.: Mnist handwritten digit database. ATT Labs (2010). http://yann.lecun.com/exdb/mnist 2
13. Liu, F.T., Ting, K.M., Zhou, Z.H.: Isolation forest. In: 2008 Eighth IEEE International Conference on Data Mining, pp. 413–422 (2008). https://doi.org/10.1109/ICDM.2008.17
14. Malhotra, P., Ramakrishnan, A., Anand, G., Vig, L., Agarwal, P., Shroff, G.: LSTM-based encoder-decoder for multi-sensor anomaly detection. CoRR abs/1607.00148 (2016). http://arxiv.org/abs/1607.00148
15. Martin, M., et al.: Drive & act: a multi-modal dataset for fine-grained driver behavior recognition in autonomous vehicles. In: The IEEE International Conference on Computer Vision (ICCV) (2019)
16. Martìn-delosReyes, L.M., Lardelli-Claret, P., García-Cuerva, L., Rivera-Izquierdo, M., Jiménez-Mejías, E., Martínez-Ruiz, V.: Effect of periodic vehicle inspection on road crashes and injuries: a systematic review. Int. J. Environ. Res. Public Health 18(12) (2021). https://doi.org/10.3390/ijerph18126476, https://www.mdpi.com/1660-4601/18/12/6476
17. Moslemi, N., Azmi, R., Soryani, M.: Driver distraction recognition using 3D convolutional neural networks. In: 2019 4th International Conference on Pattern Recognition and Image Analysis (IPRIA), pp. 145–151 (2019). https://doi.org/10.1109/PRIA.2019.8786012
18. Murugan, S., Selvaraj, J., Sahayadhas, A.: Detection and analysis: driver state with electrocardiogram (ECG). Phys. Eng. Sci. Med. 43, 525–537 (2020). https://doi.org/10.1007/s13246-020-00853-8
19. Ortega, J.D., et al.: DMD: a large-scale multi-modal driver monitoring dataset for attention and alertness analysis. In: Bartoli, A., Fusiello, A. (eds.) ECCV 2020. LNCS, vol. 12538, pp. 387–405. Springer, Cham (2020). https://doi.org/10.1007/978-3-030-66823-5_23
20. Osokin, D.: Real-time 2d multi-person pose estimation on CPU: lightweight openpose (2018). https://doi.org/10.48550/ARXIV.1811.12004
21. Rousseeuw, P.J., Driessen, K.V.: A fast algorithm for the minimum covariance determinant estimator. Technometrics 41(3), 212–223 (1999). https://doi.org/10.1080/00401706.1999.10485670
22. Sandler, M., Howard, A.G., Zhu, M., Zhmoginov, A., Chen, L.: Inverted residuals and linear bottlenecks: mobile networks for classification, detection and segmentation. CoRR abs/1801.04381 (2018)
23. Wang, J., et al.: 100-driver: a large-scale, diverse dataset for distracted driver classification. In: Under Review (2022)
24. Williams, C., Seeger, M.: Using the nyström method to speed up kernel machines. In: Leen, T., Dietterich, T., Tresp, V. (eds.) Advances in Neural Information Processing Systems. vol. 13. MIT Press (2000)
25. Xing, Y., Lv, C., Wang, H., Cao, D., Velenis, E., Wang, F.Y.: Driver activity recognition for intelligent vehicles: a deep learning approach. IEEE Trans. Veh. Technol. 68(6), 5379–5390 (2019). https://doi.org/10.1109/TVT.2019.2908425
26. Xing, Y., et al.: Identification and analysis of driver postures for in-vehicle driving activities and secondary tasks recognition. IEEE Trans. Comput. Soc. Syst. 5(1), 95–108 (2018). https://doi.org/10.1109/TCSS.2017.2766884
27. Yang, T., Li, Y.F., Mahdavi, M., Jin, R., Zhou, Z.H.: Nyström method vs random Fourier features: a theoretical and empirical comparison. In: Pereira, F., Burges, C., Bottou, L., Weinberger, K. (eds.) Advances in Neural Information Processing Systems, vol. 25. Curran Associates, Inc. (2012)

28. Yeole, M., Jain, R., Menon, R.: Road traffic accident prediction for mixed traffic flow using artificial neural network. Materials Today: Proceedings 77, 832–837 (2023). https://doi.org/10.1016/j.matpr.2022.11.490, https://www.sciencedirect.com/science/article/pii/S2214785322073473. international Conference on 'Innovations in Mechanical and Civil Engineering'

29. Zeng, H., Yang, C., Dai, G., Qin, F., Zhang, J., Kong, W.: EEG classification of driver mental states by deep learning. Cogn. Neurodyn. **12**, 597–606 (2018). https://doi.org/10.1007/s11571-018-9496-y

30. Zepf, S., Hernandez, J., Schmitt, A., Minker, W., Picard, R.W.: Driver emotion recognition for intelligent vehicles: a survey. ACM Comput. Surv. **53**(3), 1–30 (2020). https://doi.org/10.1145/3388790

31. Zhang, T., Wang, H., Chen, J., He, E.: Detecting unfavorable driving states in electroencephalography based on a PCA sample entropy feature and multiple classification algorithms. Entropy **22**(11), 1248 (2020). https://doi.org/10.3390/e22111248, https://www.mdpi.com/1099-4300/22/11/1248

32. Zhao, D., Zhong, Y., Fu, Z., Hou, J.J., Zhao, M.: A review for the driving behavior recognition methods based on vehicle multisensor information. J. Adv. Transp. **2022**, 1–16 (2022). https://doi.org/10.1155/2022/7287511

Future Video Prediction from a Single Frame for Video Anomaly Detection

Mohammad Baradaran$^{(\boxtimes)}$ and Robert Bergevin

Université Laval, 065, avenue de la Medecine, Quebec City, QC G1V 0A6, Canada
mohammad.baradaran.1@ulaval.ca, robert.bergevin@gel.ulaval.ca

Abstract. Video anomaly detection (VAD) is an important but challenging task in computer vision. The main challenge rises due to the rarity of training samples to model all anomaly cases. Hence, semi-supervised anomaly detection methods have gotten more attention, since they focus on modeling normals and they detect anomalies by measuring the deviations from normal patterns. Despite impressive advances of these methods in modeling normal motion and appearance, long-term motion modeling has not been effectively explored so far. Inspired by the abilities of the future frame prediction proxy-task, we introduce the task of future video prediction from a single frame, as a novel proxy-task for video anomaly detection. This proxy-task alleviates the challenges of previous methods in learning longer motion patterns. Moreover, we replace the initial and future raw frames with their corresponding semantic segmentation map, which not only makes the method aware of object class but also makes the prediction task less complex for the model. Extensive experiments on the benchmark datasets (ShanghaiTech, UCSD-Ped1, and UCSD-Ped2) show the effectiveness of the method and the superiority of its performance compared to SOTA prediction-based VAD methods.

Keywords: Video anomaly detection · long-term motion modeling · future video prediction · semi-supervised learning

1 Introduction

Videos are rich sources of information and can be used to extract valuable insights about the world around us. With the widespread availability of cost-effective and high-quality cameras, there has been a surge in the amount of video data being recorded. Video analysis is of great importance for various applications (e.g., security, traffic monitoring, etc.). One crucial piece of information that can be obtained from video streams is the possible presence of abnormal events, as their occurrence often necessitates swift action. Abnormal video events refer to events that deviate significantly from expected patterns (i.e. normals), in a given context.

Many researchers in the field of video anomaly detection have put forth deep-learning-based methods, drawing inspiration from the success of Deep Neural

© The Author(s), under exclusive license to Springer Nature Switzerland AG 2023
G. Bebis et al. (Eds.): ISVC 2023, LNCS 14361, pp. 472–486, 2023.
https://doi.org/10.1007/978-3-031-47969-4_37

Networks (DNN) in numerous computer vision applications such as segmentation and classification. Researchers have endeavored to effectively model and analyze both spatial and temporal features to detect related anomalies. Given the challenge of acquiring enough training samples for anomalies, they have shown a general interest in semi-supervised VAD methods, in which the objective is to fit a normality model on normal events and to detect anomalies by measuring deviations from the learned model. These methods usually leverage unsupervised DNNs aiming to learn a model for a proxy-task on normal data. A proxy task is defined as a task that is not directly linked to the anomaly detection task but can be utilized for anomaly detection by measuring the performance of the model on anomalies if it has been trained solely on normal data. Frame reconstruction and future frame prediction are the most frequently used proxy-tasks for VAD.

While existing state-of-the-art VAD methods have achieved impressive results in modeling normals and detecting related anomalies, they suffer from a common shortcoming: unlike the local short-term motion patterns, long-term motion pattern has not been effectively explored and considered. In essence, exisitng methods take into account instant motion features (e.g., instant speed, instant direction, or motion changes) for anomaly detection. In this paper, we propose a model that can effectively incorporate long-term motion information for video anomaly detection, in addition to short-term motion patterns. The proposed method takes a prediction-based approach, inspired by earlier methods [1–3] that predict the future, based on past data. However, unlike the existing methods, our method predicts future video instead of only the immediate future frame. Additionally, unlike methods such as [4,5], and drawing inspiration from [6], the future video (the next 10 frames) is predicted from an initial frame rather than a sequence of past frames.

Since predicting future frames solely based on a single initial frame may confuse the model in estimating the correct motion direction and lead to incorrect predictions, the proposed method includes the initial motion direction as an additional input, along with the initial frame. Furthermore, prior research [7,8] has demonstrated that deterministic video prediction results in blurry outcomes, which are essentially the mean of all possible outcomes. Therefore, in the proposed method, a separate branch that utilizes a Variational Autoencoder (VAE) is employed, to make the generation task stochastic. In the proposed method, two distinct encoders are utilized for encoding the necessary inputs into a latent space, and a shared decoder is employed to decode them into future frames. In summary, the proposed method introduces the following contributions:

- A video anomaly detection approach that integrates long-term motions for improved anomaly detection.
- The first method to predict semantic future video from an initial semantic frame for video anomaly detection.
- Superior performance in comparison to SOTA prediction-based methods.

2 Related Work

Semi-supervised VAD methods have received significant attention from researchers in the field, as abnormal samples are not always readily available, unlike normal samples. In semi-supervised video anomaly detection methods, one or multiple proxy-tasks are used to train an unsupervised model on normal samples for a given task. The anomaly score is then calculated by measuring the deviation of normal models on each test sample.

One commonly used proxy-task in semi-supervised VAD methods is frame reconstruction [9–13] in which, an unsupervised neural network is trained on normal frames, assuming that the reconstruction error would be comparatively higher for abnormal frames. The main limitation of these methods is the difficulty to effectively incorporate motion information into the anomaly detection decision, mainly due to the dominance of appearance features on temporal ones [14]. Even with the incorporation of motion-aware layers (such as Conv-LSTM-AE) [15,16], motion information is not effectively modeled and considered in these methods. To this end, researchers have proposed two/multi-stream [17,18] methods, where spatial and temporal features are modeled separately, to have an independent effect on the final decision, rather than being dominated by the other one. Anomaly detection in the motion branch is generally accomplished by extracting explicit motion features from frames (such as optical flow maps or temporal gradients of frames) and leveraging CNNs' ability in analyzing spatial data to analyze motion patterns [19].

Neygun et al. [20] utilized a generative adversarial network to map a raw frame to its corresponding optical flow map for motion information modeling. However, predicting motion direction from a single frame is challenging for the network, leading to incorrect predictions. To address the mentioned challenge, Baradaran et al. [21] proposed translating from the raw frame to its corresponding optical flow magnitude map for motion anomaly detection. They also proposed an additional method [22] that utilizes multiple attention networks to incorporate contextual information for more accurate motion modeling.

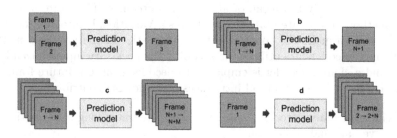

Fig. 1. Different prediction-based VAD methods. (a) Video-to-Frame (2:1). (b) Video-to-Frame (N:1). (c) Video-to-Video (N:N). (d) Frame-to-Video (1:N).

As a proxy-task customized for motion modeling, researchers have proposed future frame prediction [2,3,15,23–30]. Prediction-based models are trained to predict future frames by observing a history of past frames and are expected to encounter difficulties in predicting the location of objects with abnormal motion, in future frames. Baradaran et al. [21] predict the immediate next frame to detect abnormal motions. Other researchers [1–3,26] propose to feed a longer sequence as an input (generally 4 frames) and design sophisticated networks to effectively predict the immediate next frame. However, both groups (i.e., 2:1 and N:1 as in Fig. 1 a,b) have shortcomings; mainly long-term motion is not effectively modeled. Even by increasing the length of historical frames, models tend to consider the last frames for future prediction, due to the high correlation between adjacent frames. To consider longer motion patterns for VAD, [4,5] have proposed Video-to-Video prediction proxy-task (N:N as in Fig. 1 c). Despite showing better results in considering longer motion patterns, they fail in detecting monotonic abnormal motions (such as a car driving in a constant fast motion through frames), since the network can infer the motion pattern from historical frames to predict the future frames, which may result in a precise prediction for anomalies. These methods are not fully explored apparently due to the complexity of the task.

Motivated by the ability of future video prediction task in modeling longer motion patterns, we propose a novel proxy-task for video anomaly detection and introduce the Frame-to-Video prediction task (Fig. 1 d) to video anomaly detection. Moreover, unlike conventional Frame-to-Video applications, we provide the semantic segmentation map of initial frames to predict the semantic map of future frames. Replacing raw frames with corresponding semantic maps not only makes the method aware of the object classes but also addresses the challenges of the model in dealing with the complexity of the background in raw frames.

3   Method

3.1   Overview of the Proposed Method

We propose a novel video anomaly detection method that addresses the challenges of existing methods by incorporating long-term motion patterns, in addition to short-term motions. Our approach is based on predicting future video from a single initial frame, leveraging the semantic map of each frame instead of the raw frame as input and target to reduce prediction task complexity. This is the first work to introduce future video prediction from an initial frame for video anomaly detection. The overview of the proposed method is depicted in Fig. 2.

3.2   Video-to-Video

Previous studies have shown that VAD methods based on predicting the next frame from a sequence of previous frames face a few challenges: 1) They may

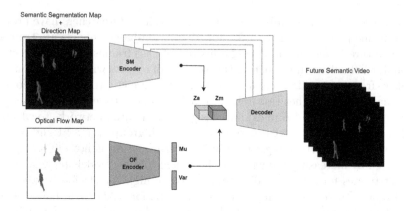

Fig. 2. Overview of the proposed Frame-to-Video prediction based VAD method.

generalize to anomalies due to the high learning capacity of DNNs. 2) Since these methods tend to use the last frame(s) for inference, only short-term motions are considered for VAD. To overcome this challenge, in the first phase of our experiments, we designed a video-to-video prediction-based VAD method. To achieve this goal we leveraged the SimVP (Simpler yet Better Video Prediction) model [31], one of the state-of-the-art video prediction models, that receives a sequence of past raw frames and predicts future raw frames. Consequently, the anomaly score is computed by measuring the difference between the real and the predicted video.

3.3 Frame-to-Video

Experiments on Video-to-Video methods have shown that they suffer from a shortcoming: DNNs can generalize to anomalies, as they can infer the trend of anomalous motions from past frames. In other words, DNNs can formulate the prediction as finding the relation between frames rather than learning patterns. To address this, we formulated our VAD method as Frame-to-Video prediction. Our generative model consists of one convolutional encoder, one convolutional variational encoder, and a shared decoder, and takes an initial frame as input to generate the future video conditioned on initial motion information.

3.4 Stochasticity

To address the challenge of generating sharp video frames, which is a common challenge in deterministic prediction models, we use a variational encoder in our lower branch [8]. This is in line with previous works [7], which have shown that deterministic models can underperform in this task. By adopting a variational encoder, we can model the inherent stochasticity of the problem, capturing multiple possible future motions that are conditioned on the motion information in the initial frame.

3.5   Semantic Maps

Our initial experiments indicated that utilizing raw RGB frames as input and target may contribute to the complexity of the video prediction task. The abundance of spatial details in raw frames requires the predictor to focus on learning and reconstructing these details rather than learning temporal patterns. This becomes more evident when considering backgrounds which usually occupy most of the frame and have no motion, yet consist of many details. To address this, we conducted experiments using semantic maps as input and target. The results showed that utilizing semantic maps makes it easier for the model to converge and learn motion patterns. This also helps address previous challenges, such as the complexity of backgrounds, as semantic colors replace the previous complex information (textures, intensities, shapes, etc.).

Previous studies, such as [6], emphasize the importance of leveraging semantic information for predicting motion. These works argue that different object classes have very distinctive motions, and utilizing semantic information can aid in better modeling these motions. Results from these works demonstrate that with semantic representation as input, the model can learn better motion for dynamic objects compared to not utilizing semantic information.

3.6   Initial Motion Direction

Our experiments also showed that predicting video from a static frame resulted in wrong motion directions, as the model favored the most frequent directions and preferred to predict motions mostly in these directions. To address this issue, we incorporated the initial motion direction along with the initial frame in the prediction process. We introduced the direction information to the model at the lowest layer, by concatenating the frame and the direction map to form the input for the model. This provides exact direction information for each pixel in the frame. The direction of motion was provided through two separate maps representing the Sine and Cosine of the motion angle, which was extracted using a pre-trained optical flow extraction model called Raft [32].

$$Mag, Ang = OF(I_{t-1}, I_t) \tag{1}$$

$$DM = Concatenate(|Cos(Ang)|, |Sin(Ang)|) \tag{2}$$

Where, DM, Mag, and Ang stand for the direction map, magnitude, and angle of motion respectively.

3.7   Network

Our proposed architecture consists of two encoders and a shared decoder, all utilizing 3×3 2D convolutional filters. The first encoder, referred to as the Semantic Map (SM) Encoder in Fig. 2, is a convolutional encoder that takes the concatenation of the initial semantic segmentation map and the initial direction map as input. It encodes these inputs into $512 \times 4 \times 4$ feature maps. The second encoder, known as the Optical Flow (OF) Encoder, is a variational convolutional encoder that encodes the initial optical flow map into a normal distribution. From this distribution, a motion feature map of size $512 \times 4 \times 4$ is sampled. The encoders downsize the feature resolution using 2×2 max pooling.

On the other hand, the shared decoder is a convolutional decoder that receives the concatenated encoded features and decodes them, using transpose convolution layers, to generate future semantic segmentation maps. Skip connections are incorporated between the convolutional encoder and the decoder to facilitate the transfer of information from the encoder to the decoder while preserving the original high-resolution features. Throughout the architecture, Leaky ReLU with a slope of 0.1 is utilized as the activation function for all layers, except for the last layer of the decoder, which employs the sigmoid activation function.

3.8   Loss Functions

To train our proposed Frame-to-Video-based VAD method, we leverage three loss functions. As a primary loss function used in prediction-based methods, we use reconstruction loss, denoted as L_{Rec}. Let $\hat{y}$ be the predicted future video and y the expected future video, we minimize the L2 distance between y and $\hat{y}$ as the reconstruction loss:

$$L_{Rec} = ||y - \hat{y}||_2^2 \tag{3}$$

We also define a temporal gradient loss, to ensure that the evolution between frames (i.e., motion patterns) has been considered for model optimization. This loss function is defined as below:

$$L_{TG} = MAELoss(TG(y), TG(\hat{y})) \tag{4}$$

Where TG is a function that computes the temporal gradient of the video and is defined as below:

$$TG([F_1, F_2, ..., F_N]) = [F_2 - F_1, F_3 - F_2, ..., F_N - F_{N-1}] \tag{5}$$

Where F_t denotes the frames t at different times in the frame sequence. Finally, KL-divergence is also considered as a complementary loss to add regularization to the training while also considering the prior normal distribution for the input optical flow maps to address the stochasticity in future prediction.

Overall, the total training loss for the model is defined below:

$$L_{Total} = L_{Rec} + L_{TG} + \beta * KL \tag{6}$$

In this equation, a controlling hyperparameter named β is added to weigh the KL-divergence in the final loss value.

3.9 Inference

During the inference phase, we use the reconstruction loss value to calculate the anomaly score, assuming that a model trained on normal video clips would generate higher reconstruction loss for anomalous videos compared to normal videos. By setting a threshold for the anomaly score, we can detect anomalous events in the test video.

Considering the frame rate, we can assume that adjacent frames are similar to each other and there are no big changes from one frame to the immediate next frame. However, in our experiments, we observe some big fluctuations in anomaly scores between adjacent frames. Our analysis shows that these jumps can happen mostly due to failures of the semantic segmentation framework. Hence we apply the Savitzky-Golay filter [33] as a temporal relaxing technique. Finally, calculated anomaly scores are normalized to the range of [0,1] using Eq. 7.

$$L_{norm} = \frac{L_{Rec} - Min(L_{Rec})}{Max(L_{Rec}) - Min(L_{Rec})} \tag{7}$$

4 Experiments

4.1 Datasets

The ShanghaiTech Campus [2], UCSD-Ped1, and UCSD-Ped2 datasets [34] are extensively adopted reference in the evaluation of semi-supervised video anomaly detection methods. The training partitions of these datasets exclusively encompass normal frames, in contrast to the testing partitions, which incorporate both normal and abnormal instances. Across all these datasets, normality is characterized by individuals walking on the sidewalk, whereas any encounters with unobserved objects or motion patterns are defined as anomalies. The ShanghaiTech Campus dataset exhibits a higher degree of complexity relative to UCSD-Ped1 and Ped2, featuring 13 different scenes and considerably expanded types of anomalies. However, the UCSD datasets, notably Ped1, present their own distinct complexities owing to their lower resolution and grayscale frames. These features potentially lead to occasional segmentation inaccuracies.

4.2 Evaluation Metric

In order to assess the effectiveness of our proposed approach, we followed prevalent SOTA methods in the field and employed the frame-level Area Under Curve (AUC) metric for evaluation. The AUC curve is constructed by recording various True Positive Rates (TPR) and False Positive Rates (FPR) of the approach, brought about by changing the anomaly score threshold from its minimum to its maximum limit. A higher AUC value signifies a better performance level.

4.3   Implementation Details

Through all stages of our experiments, which encompassed both Video-to-Video and Frame-to-Video methods, we standardized the images to dimensions of 128×128 pixels. For the Video-to-Video based VAD method, which use SimVP as a generator, we followed the guidance provided in the main reference ([31]) for training, also supplying ten frames as input and setting an equal number of frames as targets. During our Frame-to-Video experiment, we employed Mask-RCNN, pre-trained on MS COCO, for the generation of semantic maps for each individual frame. Following the resizing of these maps to 128×128 pixels, a single frame is designated as input and its subsequent ten frames are treated as targets for prediction. For the computation of optical flow maps, we utilized the RAFT optical flow extraction model. We select its basic version to facilitate a swifter processing time. All inputs and corresponding targets are supplied to the model in batches of 16. To facilitate the training of the model, learning rates are set at an initial value of $1-e3$ and were halved at intervals of every 10 epochs. Parameter optimization is carried out using the Adam optimizer. Finally, the best results are obtained for $\beta = 1$.

4.4   Results of Video-to-Video Experiments

Experiments (Table 1) show that formulating VAD as prediction of farther frames boosts the anomaly detection frame-level accuracy, as going far to the future the difference between predictions and expectations (real future frames) grows in anomalies compared to normals.

Table 1. Performance (AUC) of the Video-to-Video prediction-based VAD (with SimVP as predictor) on ShanghaiTech dataset for different prediction time steps in the future.

prediction time step	1	2	3	4	5	6	7	8	9	10
AUC	74.37	76.37	76.9	77.76	78.42	78.43	78.47	78.55	78.73	78.91

However, related qualitative experiments (Fig. 3) also depict that Video-to-Video based VAD methods may infer the anomalous motion patterns from past frames and use them to predict future frames, in which case even by going far to the future, the difference between predictions and expectations does not grow considerably for anomalies (anomalies are highlighted in red boxes in Fig. 3).

4.5   Qualitative Evaluation for Frame-to-Video Method

The qualitative results (Fig. 4: anomaly maps of predictions in different time steps) provide compelling evidence that the proposed method is highly proficient in detecting unfamiliar (novel) objects accurately, primarily from the immediately following frame (Fig. 4, first row). Besides, the method exhibits the ability to identify abnormal motions from the subsequent frames. Overall, the effectiveness of anomaly detection improves as we move further into the future. Row 2

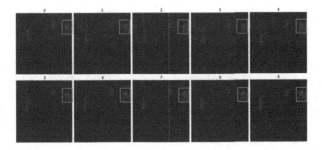

Fig. 3. Anomaly map (difference between predicted future frames and expected (real) future frames) of the Video-to-Video based VAD method for a sample clip from Shang-haiTech, for different time steps in the future.

and 3 in Fig. 4 show some samples, which contain anomalous motion patterns (fighting and chasing here) by normal objects (i.e. humans in green). In this case, the anomaly map activations in the immediate next frame are not distinct for anomalies compared to normals. However, as we go toward the future, the disparity between predictions and expectations grows considerably for anomalies compared to normals. Conversely, when examining normal objects with normal motion (Fig. 4, last row), the anomaly maps display minimal activations through all frames, primarily confined to the boundaries of the objects.

As another example, Fig. 5 exhibits the initial frame in the first column and the future predictions in the next columns. In this figure, the first row shows the predictions of the model, and the second and third rows respectively illustrate the

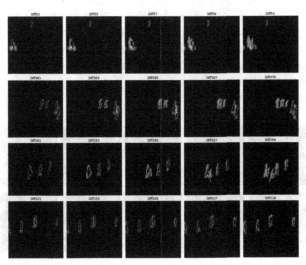

Fig. 4. Anomaly maps of different clips from ShanghaiTech dataset. Each row shows results for different clips and each column shows the anomaly maps for different frames in the future (columns 1, 2, 3, 4, 5 respectively are for the next 1st, 3rd, 5th, 7th, and 10th frames in the future). Different colors refer to different object classes and higher intensities in the anomaly maps indicate higher confidence in anomaly detection. (Color figure online)

corresponding expectations (semantic segmentation of future frames as pseudo-ground-truth) and computed anomaly maps (difference between predictions and expectations) for each time sample. These qualitative results indicate that in the case of abnormal patterns, the disparity between predictions and expectations increases more rapidly when progressing toward future frames compared to normal patterns. Results show that novel objects (a bike in this example: segmented in red in the pseudo-ground-truth) are classified as human (green color) in the predictions, as humans have been frequently observed during the training.

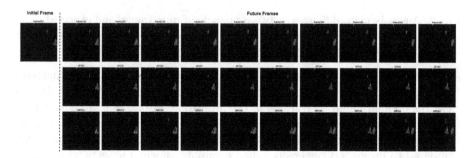

Fig. 5. Qualitative results for a sample clip from the ShanghaiTech dataset. The first, second, and third rows show the model's predictions, expectations, and related anomaly maps (difference between predictions and expectations), respectively. The first column shows the initial semantic frame and the next frame shows future predictions.

Qualitative results show that the proposed Frame-to-Video based method is successful in learning long motion patterns to predict future frame sequences, without generalizing to anomalies (unlike Video-to-Video based methods, which may use motion patterns in the past video to predict future motions). Figure 6 shows similar qualitative results respectively for samples from the UCSD-Ped2 and Ped1.

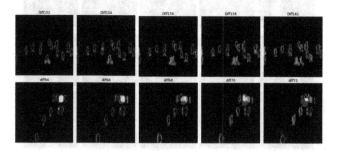

Fig. 6. Anomaly maps of sample clips from the UCSD-PEd2 and Ped1 respectively in the first and the second rows. Each column shows the anomaly maps of predictions for different frames in the future (columns 1, 2, 3, 4, 5 respectively are for the next 1st, 3rd, 5th, 7th, and 10th frames in the future).

4.6   Quantitative Evaluation for Frame-to-Video Method

Table 2 compares the performance of our proposed method, in terms of AUC, with SOTA prediction-based video anomaly detection methods. This table shows the performances for three benchmark datasets (ShanghaiTech, UCSD-Ped1, and UCSD-Ped2 datasets). As shown in the table, our proposed method shows superior performance for ShanghaiTech and UCSD-Ped2 datasets compared to other holistic prediction-based VAD methods.

Table 2. Comparison of performance (AUC) with SOTA work.

Method	ShanghaiTech	UCSD-Ped1	UCSD-Ped2
Dong et al. [1]	73.7	N/A	95.6
Liu et al. [2]	72.8	83.1	95.4
Lu et al. [3]	N/A	**86.2**	96.06
Luo et al. [23]	73.0	84.3	96.2
Morais et al. [5]	75.4	N/A	N/A
Ye et al. [28]	73.6	N/A	96.8
Cai et al. [24]	73.7	N/A	96.6
Hui et al. [25]	73.8	85.1	96.9
Park et al. [13]	70.5	N/A	97.0
Wang et al. [26]	76.6	83.4	96.3
Yang et al. [27]	74.7	N/A	97.6
Ours	**85.25**	84.1	**97.8**

An examination of Table 2 reveals that the performance of the method is lower for the UCSD-Ped1 dataset. Upon analyzing the anomaly maps for video clips in UCSD-Ped1, we identified a significant number of false positives within the anomaly map. These false positives primarily stem from errors in the performance of Mask-RCNN, due to the low resolution of the UCSD-Ped1 dataset.

Table 3. Table 3: Performance (AUC) of the Frame-to-Video prediction-based VAD for different prediction time steps in the future. This performance is evaluated on the ShanghaiTech dataset.

Prediction time step	1	2	3	4	5	6	7	8	9	10	All
AUC	83.49	84.03	85.18	86.00	86.37	86.59	86.80	86.12	85.43	84.51	85.25

As Table 3 exhibits, the performance of the method (AUC) increases as going toward the future. Although higher performance is achieved when using the prediction error for the next 7th frame in the future, here for the ShanghaiTech dataset, the optimal time step is not always the same across all clips or datasets. On the other hand, the total reconstruction error (mean of the loss for all frames) is always stable in terms of being considerably higher than the loss value of the immediate next frame. Hence, we chose to present this number in our comparisons. This loss also considers all motion patterns (short and long-range patterns) for anomaly detection. Considerable performance rise after the first two frames, as supported by quantitative results, is due to the fact that future frame prediction methods detect motion anomalies in farther frames more effectively, compared to the immediate future frames.

5   Conclusion

In this study, we've put forth a new way to detect abnormal patterns in video content, which is based on predicting future video from just one starting frame. To simplify the learning of motion and focus more on the class of objects, we have replaced the original video frames with semantic segmentation maps, which give us a clearer understanding of the objects in the scene. Our experiments have led to two important observations: 1) When we model motion by predicting future video from one frame, we are able to account for longer motions and it is less prone to generalization to anomalies. 2) Predicting video frames further in the future leads to better performance, as shown by a higher AUC. The qualitative results validate our findings, while the quantitative data illustrates the superiority of our proposed method over existing prediction-based VAD methods, particularly when applied to the Shanghaitech and UCSD-Ped2 datasets.

References

1. Dong, F., Zhang, Y., Nie, X.: Dual discriminator generative adversarial network for video anomaly detection. IEEE Access **8**, 88170–88176 (2020)
2. Liu, W., Luo, W., Lian, D., Gao, S.: Future frame prediction for anomaly detection a new baseline. In: CVPR (2018)
3. Lu, Y., Kumar, K.M., Shahabeddin Nabavi, S., Wang, Y.: Future frame prediction using convolutional VRNN for anomaly detection. In: AVSS, pp. 1–8 (2019)
4. Medel, J.R., Savakis, A.: Anomaly detection in video using predictive convolutional long short-term memory networks (2016)
5. Morais, R., Le, V., Tran, T., Saha, B., Mansour, M., Venkatesh, S.: Learning regularity in skeleton trajectories for anomaly detection in videos. In: CVPR (2019)
6. Pan, J., et al.: Video generation from single semantic label map. In: CVPR (2019)
7. Henderson, P., Lampert, C.H., Bickel, B.: Unsupervised video prediction from a single frame by estimating 3d dynamic scene structure. arXiv preprint arXiv:2106.09051 (2021)
8. Franceschi, J.Y., Delasalles, E., Chen, M., Lamprier, S., Gallinari, P.: Stochastic latent residual video prediction. In: Thirty-Seventh International Conference on Machine Learning, International Machine Learning Society (2020)
9. Hasan, M., Choi, J., Neumann, J., Roy-Chowdhury, A.K., Davis, L.S.: Learning temporal regularity in video sequences. In: CVPR, pp. 733–742 (2016)
10. Leroux, S., Li, B., Simoens, P.: Multi-branch neural networks for video anomaly detection in adverse lighting and weather conditions. In: WACV (2022)

11. Abati, D., Porrello, A., Calderara, S., Cucchiara, R.: Latent space autoregression for novelty detection. In: CVPR, pp. 481–490 (2019)
12. Gong, D., et al.: Memorizing normality to detect anomaly: memory augmented deep autoencoder for unsupervised anomaly detection. In: ICCV, pp. 1705–1714 (2019)
13. Park, H., Noh, J., Ham, B.: Learning memory-guided normality for anomaly detection. In: CVPR, pp. 14360–14369 (2020)
14. Baradaran, M., Bergevin, R.: A critical study on the recent deep learning based semisupervised video anomaly detection methods. MTAP (2023)
15. Chen, D., Wang, P., Yue, L., Zhang, Y., Jia, T.: Anomaly detection in surveillance video based on bidirectional prediction. Image Vis. Comput. **98**, 103915 (2020)
16. Luo, W., Liu, W., Gao, S.: Remembering history with convolutional LSTM for anomaly detection. In: ICME, pp. 439–444 (2017)
17. Ionescu, R.T., Khan, F.S., Georgescu, M.I., Shao, L.: Object-centric auto-encoders and dummy anomalies for abnormal event detection in video. In: CVPR, pp. 7834–7843 (2019)
18. Georgescu, M.I., Barbalau, A., Ionescu, R.T., Khan, F.S., Popescu, M., Shah, M.: Anomaly detection in video via self supervised and multi-task learning. In: CVPR, pp. 12742–12752 (2021)
19. Duman, E., Erdem, O.A.: Anomaly detection in videos using optical flow and convolutional autoencoder. IEEE Access **7**, 183914–183923 (2019)
20. Nguyen, K.T., Dinh, D.T., Do, M.N., Tran, M.T.: Anomaly detection in traffic surveillance videos with GAN-based future frame prediction. In: ICMR, pp. 457–463 (2020)
21. Baradaran, M., Bergevin, R.: Object class aware video anomaly detection through image translation. In: 19th CRV Conference (2022)
22. Baradaran, M., Bergevin, R.: Multi-task learning based video anomaly detection with attention. In: CVPRW-VAND (2023)
23. Luo, W., Liu, W., Lian, D., Gao, S.: Future frame prediction network for video anomaly detection. TPAMI **44**(11), 7505–7520 (2021)
24. Cai, R., Zhang, H., Liu, W., Gao, S., Hao, Z.: Appearance-motion memory consistency network for video anomaly detection. In: Proceedings of the AAAI Conference on Artificial Intelligence, vol. 35, pp. 938–946 (2021)
25. Lv, H., Chen, C., Cui, Z., Xu, C., Li, Y., Yang, J.: Learning normal dynamics in videos with meta prototype network. In: CVPR, pp. 15425–15434 (2021)
26. Wang, X., et al.: Robust unsupervised video anomaly detection by multipath frame prediction. IEEE Trans. Neural Netw. Learn. Syst. **33**(6), 2301–2312 (2021)
27. Yang, Z., Wu, P., Liu, J., Liu, X.: Dynamic local aggregation network with adaptive clusterer for anomaly detection. In: Avidan, S., Brostow, G., Cisse, M., Farinella, G.M., Hassner, T. (eds.) ECCV 2022. LNCS, vol. 13664, pp. 404–421. Springer, Cham (2022)
28. Ye, M., Peng, X., Gan, W., Wu, W., Qiao, Y.: Anopcn: video anomaly detection via deep predictive coding network. In: ACM International Conference on Multimedia. Association for Computing Machinery (2019)
29. Vu, T.H., Ambellouis, S., Boonaert, J., Taleb-Ahmed, A.: Anomaly detection in surveillance videos by future appearance-motion prediction. In: Proceedings of the 15th International Joint Conference on Computer Vision, pp. 484–490 (2020)
30. Roy, P.R., Bilodeau, G.-A., Seoud, L.: Local anomaly detection in videos using object-centric adversarial learning. In: Del Bimbo, A., et al. (eds.) ICPR 2021. LNCS, vol. 12664, pp. 219–234. Springer, Cham (2021). https://doi.org/10.1007/978-3-030-68799-1_16

31. Gao, Z., et al.: SimVP: simpler yet better video prediction. In: CVPR (2022)

32. Teed, Z., Deng, J.: RAFT: recurrent all-pairs field transforms for optical flow. In: Vedaldi, A., Bischof, H., Brox, T., Frahm, J.-M. (eds.) ECCV 2020. LNCS, vol. 12347, pp. 402–419. Springer, Cham (2020). https://doi.org/10.1007/978-3-030-58536-5_24

33. Wu, Chongke, Shao, Sicong, Tunc, Cihan, Satam, Pratik, Hariri, Salim: An explainable and efficient deep learning framework for video anomaly detection. Cluster Comput., 1–23 (2021). https://doi.org/10.1007/s10586-021-03439-5

34. Mahadevan, V., Li, W., Bhalodia, V., Vasconcelos, N.: Anomaly detection in crowded scenes. In: CVPR (2010)

Latent Diffusion Based Multi-class Anomaly Detection

Chenxing Wang[✉][iD] and Alireza Tavakkoli[iD]

University of Nevada, Reno, Reno, NV 89512, USA
{chenxingw,tavakkol}@unr.edu

Abstract. The unsupervised anomaly detection problem holds great importance but remains challenging to address due to the myriad of data possibilities in our daily lives. Currently, distinct models are trained for different scenarios. In this work, we introduce a reconstruction-based anomaly detection structure built on the Latent Space Denoising Diffusion Probabilistic Model (LDM). This structure effectively detects anomalies in multi-class situations. When normal data comprises multiple object categories, existing reconstruction models often learn identical patterns. This leads to the successful reconstruction of both normal and anomalous data based on these patterns, resulting in the inability to distinguish anomalous data. To address this limitation, we implemented the LDM model. Its process of adding noise effectively disrupts identical patterns. Additionally, this advanced image generation model can generate images that deviate from the input. We have further proposed a classification model that compares the input with the reconstruction results, tapping into the generative power of the LDM model. Our structure has been tested on the MNIST and CIFAR-10 datasets, where it surpassed the performance of state-of-the-art reconstruction-based anomaly detection models.

Keywords: Anomaly Detection · Diffusion Model

1 Introduction

The field of anomaly detection [2,17] has gained substantial popularity in recent years, as techniques in this domain are increasingly applied across various sectors. The advent of deep learning has significantly enhanced our capacity to represent complex data. This advancement facilitates improved feature representation for high-dimensional, graph, or spatial data in anomaly detection. Currently, we observe the utilization of anomaly detection in areas such as medical data analysis, risk management, and AI safety, to name a few. In most real-world applications, access to anomalous data is not feasible, and normal data often comprises various types of objects. For instance, in invasive species detection, access to anomaly data is limited, and the normal dataset includes different local animal species.

G. Bebis et al. (Eds.): ISVC 2023, LNCS 14361, pp. 487–498, 2023.
https://doi.org/10.1007/978-3-031-47969-4_38

Many contemporary anomaly detection algorithms are designed for one-class anomaly detection. In this approach, the model is trained on samples from a particular class. The model learns a probability density function that captures behavior for that specific class. Samples from other classes are considered anomalies, regardless of whether they belong to normal data or not. For multi-class anomaly detection, a model should learn a probability density function for all classes to delineate the boundaries of all normal data.

In this study, we aim to construct an unsupervised anomaly detection model capable of identifying anomalies across various normal object classes. Specifically, the training data consists of normal samples from several different object categories. During both training and inference processes, we do not have access to the category labels of any samples in the training data.

A commonly adopted methodology in anomaly detection involves the use of image or feature reconstruction. This approach assumes that a well-tuned model can consistently generate normal samples, even in the presence of potential anomalies in the input data. However, many widely used reconstruction networks often fail to meet the stringent requirements of this task. This failure is evidenced by an observed "identity shortcut" pattern. This shortcut leads to the direct replication of the input, potentially allowing for the accurate replication of even anomalous samples and, consequently, hampering their detection.

This challenge becomes more pronounced in contexts where the normal data distribution is inherently complex. When attempting to construct a unified model capable of reconstructing a broad range of objects, the model must endeavor to understand the joint distribution. Resorting to an "identity shortcut" might be a simpler path, but it compromises the model's effectiveness in anomaly detection.

The ever-increasing volume of digital data necessitates the development of sophisticated probabilistic models to handle inherent noise and distortion. Diffusion Denoising Probabilistic Models (DDPM), a unique category within these models, provide an innovative approach to the information bottleneck problem. Trained to systematically de-noise corrupted inputs, these models reshape the strategy for noise management. Unlike traditional models where the bottleneck is an intrinsic property, DDPM views the bottleneck as an externally adjustable feature during model inference. While previous studies have explored DDPMs as autoencoders with externally adjustable bottlenecks, none have harnessed this property for reconstruction-based anomaly detection. This paper aims to fill this void, delving into novel insights and methodologies to leverage DDPMs for enhanced anomaly detection.

In this work, we proposed a multi-class anomaly detection structure based on the LDM model. We examined the use of latent space within the DDPM framework and developed a classification model that utilizes the generative capabilities of the diffusion model. This is to determine whether the input and reconstructed image belong to the same category.

2   Related Work

2.1   Anomaly Detection

The anomaly detection problem has a long research history. Classic anomaly detection techniques include the Gaussian Distribution estimation method [22,26], Mahalanobis distance [13], mixture distribution [7] and nonparametric density estimation [5]. With the advancement of deep learning and machine learning techniques, recent anomaly detection models are now based on deep learning structures. For example, one-class classification-based methods such as v-SVC [21], and Support Vector Data Description (SVDD) [23] train a deep neural network to map a set of data instances into a sphere of minimal volume, assessing whether test samples conform to the training data. Knowledge distillation methods [28,29] assist in understanding the frequency of various underlying patterns in the data.

2.2   Reconstruction Models

The basic idea of reconstruction methods is to learn a model which optimized to reconstruct all normal data instance and detection the anomalous data instance by high reconstruction error.

The objective function of reconstruction models can be shown as $\phi(\theta) : X \rightarrow X$ which is a feature mapping from data to itself. It includes two steps, the encoding step

$$z = \phi_e\left(x; \theta_e\right) \tag{1}$$

and the decoding step

$$\hat{x} = \phi_d\left(z; \theta_d\right) \tag{2}$$

Autoencoder networks are the most frequently used algorithms in reconstruction models. They utilize various types of neural networks to encode the input data and then decode it for recovery. Originally, autoencoders were used for dimension reduction [11,24]. However, nowadays, they have become the most popular algorithms employed in anomaly detection [3,4,32]. The reconstruction loss function is used to learn the parameters of both networks. To represent the low-dimensional feature space, a bottleneck network is typically used.

To minimize the reconstruction error and detect anomalous data, features extracted in the latent space should be highly relevant to normal data instances. Only in this manner will the reconstruction error of an anomalous data instance be significantly higher than the reconstruction error of normal data. Consequently, the reconstruction error can be used as an anomaly score.

Several innovative types of autoencoders have been developed to enhance feature representations. The denoising autoencoder [27] s designed to train on corrupted data instances, making it robust against minor variations. The sparse autoencoder [16] aims to increase sparsity in the hidden layer, retaining only the top K most active units. The contractive autoencoder [18] is proposed to be robust against minor variations around its neighbors.

2.3 GAN Based Models

AnoGAN [20] is an example of the first usage of GAN in anomaly detection. Similar with the autoencoder, the training process is only focus on normal data instance. The main idea is that given input data instances x, try to find out z in the latent feature space of the generative network G in order to make $G(z)$ and x as similar as possible. The training of GAN in only normal data will let the generator learn the underlying distribution of normal data. Once an anomalous image is encoded, the reconstruction result will be a normal image generated by G. The difference between input image and reconstruction image will show the anomalous area.

Many other GAN based anomaly detection methods have been introduced based on different GAN architectures. For example, EBGAN [31] first introduced BiGAN architecture in anomaly detection based on the idea from [10], f-AnoGAN [20] which uses Wasserstein GAN [1] to replace the standard GAN in anomaly detection.

3 Method

3.1 Diffusion Models

The basic design of diffusion models are based on two Markov chains. Given any data $x_0 \sim q(x_0)$, the first Markov chain is called the forward chain, which transfer the data into noise. Standard Gaussian noise is typical choice when using the diffusion model because of its unique properties. The forward Markov chain uses T steps, with Gaussian noise added into the data for each step.

$$q(x_t \mid x_{t-1}) = \mathcal{N}\left(x_t; \sqrt{1 - \beta_t} x_{t-1}, \beta_t I\right) \tag{3}$$

where $t = 1, 2, ..., T$ and $\beta \in [0, 1]$ denotes the noise variance schedule. From the equation above, given data x_0 and step t, we can get the distribution of a noise image

$$q(x_t \mid x_0) = \mathcal{N}\left(x_t; \sqrt{\bar{\alpha}_t} x_0, (1 - \bar{\alpha}_t) I\right) \tag{4}$$

where here we use $\bar{\alpha}_t$ represent $\prod_{s=1}^{t}(1 - \beta_s)$

The other Markov chain represents the reverse process, which begins from the standard Gaussian noise image and keeps adding small amount of noise in order to recover the input data. This process begins at the point

$$p(x_T) = \mathcal{N}(x_T; 0, I) \tag{5}$$

And small amount of Gaussian noise will be added onto the image step by step.

$$p_\theta(x_{t-1} \mid x_t) = \mathcal{N}(x_{t-1}; \mu_\theta(x_t, t), \Sigma_\theta(x_t, t)) \tag{6}$$

where μ_θ and Σ_θ are the mean value and standard variation of the Gaussian noise added in each step. In order to reverse the forward process, we set $\Sigma_\theta(x_t, t) = \beta_t I$ and μ_θ should estimate $\frac{1}{\sqrt{\alpha_t}}\left(x_t - \frac{\beta_t}{\sqrt{1-\bar{\alpha}_t}}\epsilon\right)$, thus we can set

$$\mu_\theta(x_t, t) = \frac{1}{\sqrt{\alpha_t}}\left(x_t - \frac{\beta_t}{\sqrt{1-\bar{\alpha}_t}}\epsilon_\theta(x_t, t)\right) \tag{7}$$

In order to estimate $\epsilon_\theta(x_t, t)$, a U-net is built to minimize the objective function

$$L = E_{t\sim[1-T], x_0 \sim q(x_0), \epsilon \sim N(0,I)}\left[\|\epsilon - \epsilon_\theta(x_t, t)\|^2\right] \tag{8}$$

where $\epsilon \sim \mathcal{N}(0, I)$. From equation above, the U-net model is trained so that, given any input x_t, the output of the U-net model should be equal to $\mathcal{N}(0, I)$ In the inference process we can get

$$x_{t-1} = \frac{1}{\sqrt{\alpha_t}}\left(x_t - \frac{\beta_t}{\sqrt{1-\bar{\alpha}_t}}\epsilon_\theta(x_t, t)\right) + \beta_t z \tag{9}$$

3.2 Architecture with Latent Diffusion Models

As depicted in Fig. 1 our multi-class anomaly detection model comprises three components: a compression model, a diffusion network, and a classification network. The compression model compresses the image into a lower-dimensional space. The diffusion network reconstructs the latent space of normal data, while the classification network determines whether the input and output of the compression model belong to the same class. An anomaly class is detected if the input and output are classified into different classes.

Compression Model. The input of compression model is the original image x, the compression procedure can be expressed as $z = E(x)$, and the decode procedure can be denoted as $x' = D(z)$. The architecture of our compression model, based on work [8], trains an autoencoder considering both perceptual loss and adversarial objectives. Therefore, during the image compression, it accounts for not only pixel-wise information but also the composition of image parts from a codebook constructed by the image.

Utilizing a compression model before the diffusion model in anomaly detection provides several benefits:

i The computational complexity during the training of the diffusion model is reduced since this model operates in the latent space.
ii The latent space prevents the DDPM reconstruction structure from encountering the "identity shortcut" issue, which arises when the network consistently produces a copy of the input data.
iii A compression model allows for flexibility in choosing an appropriate latent space for the DDPM process. Typically, both the input and output of the autoencoder should depict the original image. In this study, however, we've

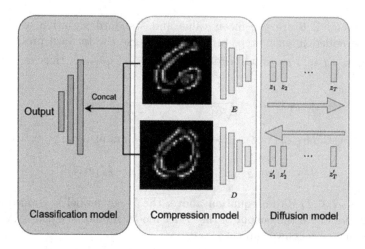

Fig. 1. An overview of our framework, which comprises a compression model, a diffusion model, and a classification model. The compression model constructs an encoder and decoder to create a latent space. The diffusion model continuously adds noise during the forward process and estimates the input latent data in the reverse process. The classification model determines whether the input image and the reversed input image belong to the same class.

also experimented with transforming the autoencoder's output into an edge label, a change that can reduce the propensity for the structure to fall into the "identity shortcut" issue.

Diffusion Model. The input of the diffusion model is the latent space vector z from compression model. Then following the forward process of the DDPM from Eq. 4. Given any time $t \in [0, T]$, the latent space z_t can be calculate by

$$z_t = z_0\sqrt{\bar{\alpha}_t} + \epsilon_t\sqrt{1 - \bar{\alpha}_t} \qquad (10)$$

where $\epsilon_t \sim \mathcal{N}(0, I)$.

With the t becomes larger and larger, more and more Gaussian noise is added into the image and the latent vector z_t loose its original spatial structure and looks near the Gaussian noise. In the reverse process, we can follow the Eq. 9. We need to train the U-net model $\epsilon(x, t)$ in order to let it predict the noise ϵ.

In our anomaly task, the result of DDPM reconstruction should be the same with input latent vector z if it is a latent representation from normal data. In practice, the reconstruction could keep the similarity of input if the reverse process begins from time t. As the choice of t becomes larger, the output would become more random and lose the ability to keep the input similarity even it comes from a normal data instance.

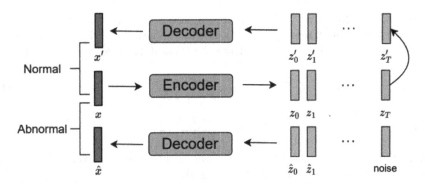

Fig. 2. Illustration of the training process within the classification model. If the reversed input equals the forward diffusion process, the input image and reversed image are considered to belong to the same class. If the reversed input equals random noise, the input image and reversed image are considered to belong to different classes.

Classification Model. As illustrated in Fig. 2 the classification network determines whether the input image and the reconstructed image belong to the same category. The classification network takes in a channel-wise concatenation of the input image x_0 and the reconstruction estimation $\hat{x}_0$. A CNN-based architecture is employed for this classification network. One challenge in this classification is that we only have access to normal data instances, providing us with only positive labels. To obtain negative labels, for each training data input x_0 we reconstruct x_0' by reversing the DDPM process from a random noise latent space.

4   Experiment

4.1   Datasets and Metrics

Datasets. This research primarily employs two datasets: MNIST [14] and CIFAR-10 [12]. MNIST is an extensive database of handwritten digits, ranging from 0 to 9, with images sized at 28×28 pixels. CIFAR-10 is a widely-recognized image classification dataset containing ten distinct object categories, each image being $32 \times 32 \times 3$ in size.

For anomaly detection studies associated with both datasets, the prevalent approach is the one-versus-rest scenario. In this, one object category is treated as normal data, while the others are deemed anomalies. Notably, prior literature hasn't explored the MNIST dataset in a many-versus-one scenario. In this setting, models are trained on nine categories as normal data, with the remaining category considered anomalous. For the CIFAR-10 dataset, Semantic AD [6] has tackled the many-versus-one scenario using transfer learning. Meanwhile, UniAD [30] employed an embedding method in a many-versus-many context.

In our study, we explore the many-versus-one setting for the MNIST dataset and delve into the many-versus-many scenario for the CIFAR-10 dataset, employing a fundamentally distinct approach.

Metrics. In this paper, all the experiments are using the Area Under the Receiver Operating Curve (AUROC) as the evaluation metric. AUROC scored is defined based on False Positive Rate (FPR) and True Positive Rate (TPR).

$$FPR = \frac{FP}{FP + TN} \tag{11}$$

$$TPR = \frac{TP}{TP + FN} \tag{12}$$

where FP represents false positive, TN represents true negative, TP represents true positive and FN represents false negative.

4.2 Reconstruction Selection

Reconstruction-based anomaly detection algorithms are one of the most researched topics in anomaly detection. Numerous studies [15, 20, 27] have been developed in recent years. The primary assumption behind using a reconstruction model is that the reconstruction distribution should closely match the normal distribution. This assumption rarely fails under the one-versus-rest setting because learning the distribution of one category is typically straightforward. However, in a many-versus-one setting or many-versus-many setting, normal data includes different object categories, making the distribution challenging to describe. Often, the reconstruction-based model falls victim to the "identity shortcut" issue, where the output always attempts to replicate the input, regardless of the context.

Diffusion models show immense potential in image generation. Because the forward process of diffusion involves adding noise to the image, the reverse

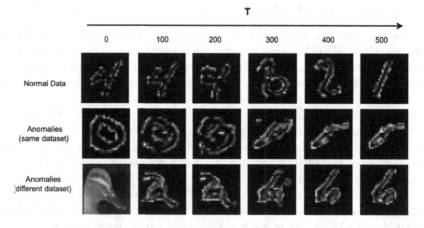

Fig. 3. Reconstructions using our model trained on the MNIST dataset, excluding all instances of the digit '0'. The figure depicts reconstruction results for normal data, anomalies from the same dataset, and anomalies from a different dataset.

process becomes unstable. This instability can be beneficial, as it can prevent the model from taking the "identity shortcut" when evaluating an anomalous instance. However, it can also cause the reconstructed version of normal data to differ from the input. As seen in Fig. 3 the reconstruction results change from timestamps 0 to 500. The stability of the reconstruction of normal data starts deteriorating after the diffusion timestamp 200. Yet, the reconstruction results for anomalies begin to deviate from the input even before the diffusion times-tamp 200. Therefore, we have chosen diffusion timestamp 200 in this study to effectively detect anomalous data.

4.3 Anomaly Detection on MNIST

For our MNIST experiments, we adopted a many-versus-one setting. In each iter-ation, one digit was designated as anomalous data while our model was trained using images of the remaining nine digits. The architecture of the compression and diffusion models is grounded on the Latent Diffusion Model [19]. For the compression model, we employed a 3-layer autoencoder with channel sizes of [64, 128, 256]. This model compresses the image from a size of 32×32 down to a $8 \times 8 \times 3$ latent space, and it also incorporates a VQ-regularization [25] term. Subsequently, the diffusion training is facilitated by a 3-layer U-net model with channel sizes [224, 448, 672]. For classification, we deployed the ResNet-18 model. The input to this classifier is a concatenation of the original and the reconstructed image. As observed from Table 1 when our model is compared to three other reconstruction-based anomaly detection methodologies, our method consistently outperforms the others. Specifically, across all ten experiments, our model ranked as the most effective in nine out of the ten anomaly detection tests.

Table 1. AUROC score of anomaly detection on MNIST dataset

Anomaly digit	0	1	2	3	4	5	6	7	8	9
Autoencoder	53.1	60.2	62.2	57.8	55.2	56.9	56.3	50.3	63.1	51.2
AnnoDDPM	57.0	54.6	57.3	51.0	54.8	57.3	60.9	53.1	58.9	52.1
DDPM [9]	65.0	61.4	67.5	65.8	59.9	65.5	61.5	51.2	61.5	52.1
Our Method	64.9	73.2	72.6	69.7	69.7	68.7	68.0	72.6	71.5	56.3

Table 2. AUROC score of anomaly detection on CIFAR-10 dataset

Anomaly classes	{01234}	{23456}	{45678}	{67890}
Autoencoder	50.4	51.4	60.8	51.2
AnnoDDPM	52.3	56.4	54.7	56.2
DDPM	57.6	51.8	54.6	53.3
Our Method	64.5	60.1	54.0	57.4

4.4   Anomaly Detection on CIFAR-10

For the CIFAR-10 dataset, our experimental approach was grounded in the many-versus-many setting. In each iteration, we designated five distinct classes as the 'normal' dataset and the remaining five as 'anomalous' datasets. To clarify, in Table 2, the numerals 0 through 9 respectively symbolize the classes: airplane, automobile, bird, cat, deer, dog, frog, horse, ship, and truck.

The architectural foundation of our model for the CIFAR-10 dataset remains consistent with that employed for the MNIST dataset. However, our results on the CIFAR-10 were not as promising as those on the MNIST. Even though our model still surpassed other existing reconstruction-based algorithms, the performance decrement can primarily be attributed to the less stable reconstruction results on the CIFAR-10 dataset.

This instability might arise due to CIFAR-10 images being more complex and diverse in content than MNIST's handwritten digits. Thus, while our model demonstrates superiority over other reconstruction-based approaches, there remains a potential for refining and optimizing it further, especially when tackling complex datasets like CIFAR-10.

5   Conclusion

Tackling multi-class anomaly detection is a formidable challenge, given the intricate distribution characterizing normal data. Our approach, anchored in the latent diffusion model, underscores the promise and efficacy of this method for addressing such anomaly detection challenges. Notably, our model presents a remedy to the identity-shortcut predicament that frequently plagues conventional reconstruction-based anomaly detection mechanisms. A promising frontier for ensuing research in this domain is delving deeper into methodologies that can further stabilize the reverse process in diffusion during anomaly detection tasks.

Acknowledgements. Research reported in this publication was supported in part by the National Science Foundation under grant numbers [OAC-2201599] and the National Institute of General Medical Sciences of the National Institutes of Health under grant numbers [P30 GM145646].

References

1. Arjovsky, M., Chintala, S., Bottou, L.: Wasserstein generative adversarial networks. In: International Conference on Machine Learning, pp. 214–223. PMLR (2017)
2. Boukerche, A., Zheng, L., Alfandi, O.: Outlier detection: methods, models, and classification. ACM Comput. Surv. (CSUR) **53**(3), 1–37 (2020)
3. Chalapathy, R., Menon, A.K., Chawla, S.: Robust, deep and inductive anomaly detection. In: Ceci, M., Hollmén, J., Todorovski, L., Vens, C., Džeroski, S. (eds.) ECML PKDD 2017. LNCS (LNAI), vol. 10534, pp. 36–51. Springer, Cham (2017). https://doi.org/10.1007/978-3-319-71249-9_3

4. Chen, J., Sathe, S., Aggarwal, C., Turaga, D.: Outlier detection with autoencoder ensembles. In: Proceedings of the 2017 SIAM International Conference on Data Mining, pp. 90–98. SIAM (2017)
5. Dasgupta, D., Nino, F.: A comparison of negative and positive selection algorithms in novel pattern detection. In: SMC 2000 Conference Proceedings. 2000 IEEE International Conference on Systems, Man and Cybernetics. Cybernetics Evolving to Systems, Humans, Organizations, and their Complex Interactions cat. no. 0, vol. 1, pp. 125–130. IEEE (2000)
6. Deecke, L., Ruff, L., Vandermeulen, R.A., Bilen, H.: Transfer-based semantic anomaly detection. In: International Conference on Machine Learning, pp. 2546–2558. PMLR (2021)
7. Eskin, E.: Anomaly detection over noisy data using learned probability distributions (2000)
8. Esser, P., Rombach, R., Ommer, B.: Taming transformers for high-resolution image synthesis. In: Proceedings of the IEEE/CVF Conference on Computer Vision and Pattern Recognition, pp. 12873–12883 (2021)
9. Graham, M.S., Pinaya, W.H., Tudosiu, P.D., Nachev, P., Ourselin, S., Cardoso, J.: Denoising diffusion models for out-of-distribution detection. In: Proceedings of the IEEE/CVF Conference on Computer Vision and Pattern Recognition, pp. 2947–2956 (2023)
10. Gulrajani, I., Ahmed, F., Arjovsky, M., Dumoulin, V., Courville, A.C.: Improved training of Wasserstein GANs. In: Advances in Neural Information Processing Systems, vol. 30 (2017)
11. Hinton, G.E., Salakhutdinov, R.R.: Reducing the dimensionality of data with neural networks. Science 313(5786), 504–507 (2006)
12. Krizhevsky, A., Hinton, G., et al.: Learning multiple layers of features from tiny images (2009)
13. Laurikkala, J., Juhola, M., Kentala, E., Lavrac, N., Miksch, S., Kavsek, B.: Informal identification of outliers in medical data. In: Fifth International Workshop on Intelligent Data Analysis in Medicine and Pharmacology, vol. 1, pp. 20–24. Citeseer (2000)
14. LeCun, Y., Bottou, L., Bengio, Y., Haffner, P.: Gradient-based learning applied to document recognition. Proc. IEEE 86(11), 2278–2324 (1998)
15. Lu, W., et al.: Unsupervised sequential outlier detection with deep architectures. IEEE Trans. Image Process. 26(9), 4321–4330 (2017)
16. Makhzani, A., Frey, B.: K-sparse autoencoders. arXiv preprint arXiv:1312.5663 (2013)
17. Pang, G., Shen, C., Cao, L., Hengel, A.V.D.: Deep learning for anomaly detection: a review. ACM Comput. Surv. (CSUR) 54(2), 1–38 (2021)
18. Rifai, S., Vincent, P., Muller, X., Glorot, X., Bengio, Y.: Contractive auto-encoders: explicit invariance during feature extraction. In: ICML (2011)
19. Rombach, R., Blattmann, A., Lorenz, D., Esser, P., Ommer, B.: High-resolution image synthesis with latent diffusion models. In: Proceedings of the IEEE/CVF Conference on Computer Vision and Pattern Recognition, pp. 10684–10695 (2022)
20. Schlegl, T., Seeböck, P., Waldstein, S.M., Schmidt-Erfurth, U., Langs, G.: Unsupervised anomaly detection with generative adversarial networks to guide marker discovery. In: Niethammer, M., et al. (eds.) IPMI 2017. LNCS, vol. 10265, pp. 146–157. Springer, Cham (2017). https://doi.org/10.1007/978-3-319-59050-9_12
21. Schölkopf, B., Platt, J.C., Shawe-Taylor, J., Smola, A.J., Williamson, R.C.: Estimating the support of a high-dimensional distribution. Neural Comput. 13(7), 1443–1471 (2001)

22. Shewhart, W.A.: Economic Control of Quality of Manufactured Product. Macmillan And Co Ltd, London (1931)
23. Tax, D.M., Duin, R.P.: Support vector data description. Mach. Learn. **54**(1), 45–66 (2004)
24. Theis, L., Shi, W., Cunningham, A., Huszár, F.: Lossy image compression with compressive autoencoders. arXiv preprint arXiv:1703.00395 (2017)
25. Van Den Oord, A., Vinyals, O., et al.: Neural discrete representation learning. In: Advances in Neural Information Processing Systems, vol. 30 (2017)
26. Velleman, P.F., Hoaglin, D.C.: Applications, Basics, and Computing of Exploratory Data Analysis. Duxbury Press, New York (1981)
27. Vincent, P., Larochelle, H., Lajoie, I., Bengio, Y., Manzagol, P.A., Bottou, L.: Stacked denoising autoencoders: learning useful representations in a deep network with a local denoising criterion. J. Mach. Learn. Res. **11**(12) (2010)
28. Wang, S., Wu, L., Cui, L., Shen, Y.: Glancing at the patch: anomaly localization with global and local feature comparison. In: Proceedings of the IEEE/CVF Conference on Computer Vision and Pattern Recognition, pp. 254–263 (2021)
29. Xia, Y., Zhang, Y., Liu, F., Shen, W., Yuille, A.L.: Synthesize then compare: detecting failures and anomalies for semantic segmentation. In: Vedaldi, A., Bischof, H., Brox, T., Frahm, J.-M. (eds.) ECCV 2020. LNCS, vol. 12346, pp. 145–161. Springer, Cham (2020). https://doi.org/10.1007/978-3-030-58452-8_9
30. You, Z., et al.: A unified model for multi-class anomaly detection. Adv. Neural. Inf. Process. Syst. **35**, 4571–4584 (2022)
31. Zenati, H., Foo, C.S., Lecouat, B., Manek, G., Chandrasekhar, V.R.: Efficient GAN-based anomaly detection. arXiv preprint arXiv:1802.06222 (2018)
32. Zhou, C., Paffenroth, R.C.: Anomaly detection with robust deep autoencoders. In: Proceedings of the 23rd ACM SIGKDD International Conference on Knowledge Discovery and Data Mining, pp. 665–674 (2017)

ST: Artificial Intelligence in Aerial and Orbital Imagery

Investigating the Impact of a Low-Rank Tensor-Based Approach on Deforestation Imagery

Charalampos Zafeiropoulos[1]([✉])[ID], Ioannis N. Tzortzis[1][ID],
Eftychios Protopapadakis[2][ID], Maria Kaselimi[1][ID], Anastasios Doulamis[1][ID],
and Nikolaos Doulamis[1][ID]

[1] National and Technical University of Athens, Athens, Greece
mpampiszafeiropoulos@mail.ntua.gr
[2] University of Macedonia, Thessaloniki, Greece

Abstract. In this work we handle deforestation as a semantic segmentation problem using convolution-free methods, specifically tensor-based neural networks. The methodology follows a two-step process: first, we enhance the identification of deforestation areas through the application of low-level filters. Second, we merge the filter outcomes with the original image to create an object-level tensor representation. We introduce a tensor-based model that effectively identifies and analyzes complex patterns even with limited data availability. To evaluate our model, its outcomes are compared with established state-of-the-art models. The experimental results demonstrate the effectiveness and efficiency of the proposed approach in accurately mapping land cover patterns, particularly in deforestation detection and analysis. Based on the results, Squeezed-Net perform better when more data are available, while Tensor neural network model (TNN) outperformed when limited data are available.

Keywords: Deforestration · Land Cover · Tensor based model · Deep Learning · Limited Data

1 Introduction

Deforestation, the widespread clearing of forests for various purposes such as agriculture, mining, urbanization, and logging, has emerged as a critical environmental issue with devastating consequences over the past few decades [3]. The loss of extensive forested areas worldwide has resulted in far-reaching impacts on the environment, including climate change, soil erosion, biodiversity loss, and disruptions in the water cycle.

The advent of deep learning models and the availability of appropriate datasets have led to significant advancements in land cover detection using optical sensors [6]. A common approach, when handling image data, are the Convolutional neural networks (CNNs), and their variations [7]. Satellite imagery,

G. Bebis et al. (Eds.): ISVC 2023, LNCS 14361, pp. 501–512, 2023.
https://doi.org/10.1007/978-3-031-47969-4_39

particularly high-resolution data from sources like Landsat, Sentinel, or aerial photography, is frequently utilized as input for deep learning models in land cover detection.

Data availability and types play a crucial role in land cover analysis. Multiple studies have utilized various data sources, such as RGB imagery, hyperspectral data, and 3D spatial data obtained through LiDAR technology [2]. Each data type offers unique advantages, but they also come with certain limitations.

RGB images, being a straightforward approach, provide valuable visual information, but their data is limited to three color channels, which may constrain the level of detail in land cover classification. Hyperspectral images, offer rich spectral information, enabling precise discrimination of land cover classes. However, their lower spatial resolution may result in challenges when capturing fine-grained details [15].

In contrast, LiDAR technologies provide a high level of detail in 3D spatial data, allowing for accurate characterization of land surface structures. Nevertheless, LiDAR data acquisition and processing can be more resource-intensive compared to other data sources [18]. Balancing these advantages and limitations is essential for selecting the most suitable data type for specific land cover analysis applications.

In this study, we investigate the performance of an alternative approach compared to established techniques when data availability is limited. We propose a Tensor-based model, which effectively captures complex relationships and patterns in multidimensional data. Tensor-based models have shown great promise in efficiently representing, analyzing, and modeling tensors, making them suitable for various applications involving high-dimensional data [16].

2   Related Work

Prior to proposing any schemes for land cover change detection, researchers need to consider both the data source and the possible decision models to be involved. The former case involves various types of images, including RGB imagery, satellite imagery, and hyperspectral imagery. The latter case, primarily involve, primarily, CNNs or variations, e.g. U-nets, FCNs, but other approaches have also emerged.

Isaienkov et al. [5] applied mulipple segmentation models, mainly based on U-Net architecture variations, to handle deforestation detection as a binary classification problem. Data consist of Sentinel-2 images from the Kharkiv region of Ukraine.

Ortega et al. [14] utilized Early Fusion, Siamese Network (SN), and Convolutional SVM (CSVM) deep learning approaches, over the Amazon and Cerrado biomes in Brazil. The experimental analysis relied on two LANDSAT 8/OLI optical images acquired at dates about one year apart from each other. Four different scenarios were considered, using one, two, three, and four tiles training. The performance of all methods increased with the number of training samples.

Matosak et al. [13] a dataset of Landsat-8 and Sentinel-2 images to train a hybrid deep learning model for mapping deforestation in the Cerrado biome in

Brazil. The model was a combination of two parts: a Long Short-Term Memory (LSTM) network to analyze the time series of satellite images, and a U-Net network to analyze the spatial patterns of the images.

Wang et al. [17] proposed a combination of a Siamese network and an HRNet-OCR network to classify images into different categories, such as deforested, non-deforested, and cloud cover. The application scenario involved pixel-level on 11 provincial regions in the Yangtze River Economic Zone of China, containing a total number of 8330 samples (the size of each sample being 512×512 pixels. The current approach can be applied to two bi-temporal image change detections so far.

A convolution free approach, based on vision transformer models have been introducted by Kaselimi et al. [8]. It was a multiclass classification problem, using as inputs Landsat-8 images. Results cover an area of approximate 100,000 square kilometers in the Brazilian Amazon rainforest. Since the model was convolution-free, it is considered more efficient, to the traditional approaches, and can be trained on smaller datasets.

The recent advancements in deforestation detection, via DL, have shown promising results. Research explored various data sources, including RGB, satellite, and hyperspectral imagery, and multiple detection models to address deforestation detection as a binary or multiclass classification problem.

Additionally, convolution-free approaches, like vision transformer models, have demonstrated potential for efficiency and accuracy, particularly with smaller datasets. In this study we investigate the applicability of convolution free models, based on tensor decomposition, to tackle a common problem of limited available data samples.

3   Problem Formulation

In this work we address the task of mapping deforested areas in Ukrainian forestries, as a semantic segmentation problem. In particular, given an image I, a pixel in position (x, y) is described by an $m \times n \times c$ image patch, say $p_{x,y}$, where m, n are odd numbers, pixel $I_{x,y}$ is located at the center of the patch, and c denotes the number of available channels. The goal is to estimate a predictive function $f(p_{x,y}) \to t$, where t stands for the target class. Although the raw data are RGB images, in this study we have more than 3 channels, as explained in Sect. 3.1.

3.1   Tensor Preparation

Despite the advancements in deep learning models, low-level features still hold relevance and utility in certain scenarios, including land cover analysis. Two key aspects involve interpretability and complementarity. Integrating low-level features as additional inputs to deep learning models can enhance their performance by providing them with valuable preprocessed information, aiding in fine-grained analysis and improving the interpretability of the deep learning-based land cover detection systems.

Multiple image processings filters have been considered for the extraction of low-level features, enhancing the input space, prior to run any deep learning model. In particular, the following filters were considered: Blur, Gabor, Gamma, Gaussian difference, Gaussian blur, Histogram, Laplacian, Median, Sharpen, and Sobel. Additionally, combinations of these features were considered, e.g. Gabor Gaussian (Fig. 1). In our research, the Images are merging into multi-class objects with dimension $48 \times 512 \times 512$. Each object consists of the original image and 15 image filter outputs for each one of the 3 RGB channels.

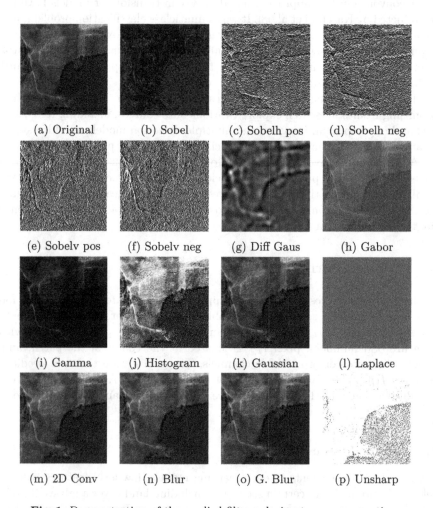

(a) Original   (b) Sobel   (c) Sobelh pos   (d) Sobelh neg

(e) Sobelv pos   (f) Sobelv neg   (g) Diff Gaus   (h) Gabor

(i) Gamma   (j) Histogram   (k) Gaussian   (l) Laplace

(m) 2D Conv   (n) Blur   (o) G. Blur   (p) Unsharp

Fig. 1. Demonstration of the applied filters, during tensor preparation.

3.2 Tensor-Based Models

In this study, a Rank-R FNN model, as the one in [11,12], was consideered as an alternative the convolution based approaches. The TNN is a two-layer neural network that receives as input D-dimensional tensor objects. The inputs are propagated to the hidden layer via a set of weights on which the Canonical-Polyadic (CP) decomposition has been applied. CP decomposition can significantly reduce the number of trainable parameters, making the Rank-R FNN model very efficient for small sample setting problems that involve high dimensional data, like data points in tensor format.

Given an input $\boldsymbol{X} \in \mathbb{R}^{I_1 \times \cdots \times I_D}$, the Rank-R FNN models the weights connecting the input layer with the hidden layer as:

$$\boldsymbol{W}^{(q)} = [\![\boldsymbol{W}_1^{(q)}, \cdots, \boldsymbol{W}_D^{(q)}]\!] \in \mathbb{R}^{I_1 \times \cdots \times I_D}, \tag{1}$$

or else

$$\text{vec}(\boldsymbol{W}^{(q)}) = (\boldsymbol{W}_D^{(q)} \odot \cdots \odot \boldsymbol{W}_1^{(q)}) \boldsymbol{1}_R \in \mathbb{R}^{\prod_{d=1}^{d=D} I_d}, \tag{2}$$

where $\boldsymbol{1}_R$ stands for a vector with R ones, q stands for the number of hidden layer's neurons, and "$\odot$" operator for the Khatri-Rao product. The output of the q-th hidden neuron of the Rank-R FNN is given by

$$u_q = g(\langle \boldsymbol{W}^{(q)}, \boldsymbol{X} \rangle) = \text{trace}\Big(g\big((\boldsymbol{W}_d^{(q)})^T \boldsymbol{Z}_{\neq d}^{(q)}\big)\Big), \tag{3}$$

where $\boldsymbol{W}_d^{(q)} \in \mathbb{R}^{I_d \times R}$, R is the rank for the CP decomposition and

$$\boldsymbol{Z}_{\neq d}^{(q)} = \boldsymbol{X}_{(d)} (\boldsymbol{W}_D^{(q)} \odot \cdots \odot \boldsymbol{W}_{d+1}^{(q)} \odot \boldsymbol{W}_{d-1}^{(q)} \odot \cdots \odot \boldsymbol{W}_1^{(q)}) \tag{4}$$

with $\boldsymbol{X}_{(d)}$ to denote the mode-d matricization of tensor $\boldsymbol{X}$.

After the transformation of the tensor input into a vector at the first hidden layer, the information is propagated to the output layer of the Rank-R FNN. The parameters of the model are estimated based on the available labelled data using an appropriate loss function (e.g., cross-entropy for classification problems of mean squared error for regression), the back-propagation algorithm and gradient-based optimization (for more information about the training procedure, we refer the interested reader to [11]).

In this study, the tensor input embeddings correspond to the output of the hidden layer of the trained Rank-R FNN. In other words, the tensor inputs are represented by q-dimensional vectors that are obtained by the output of the penultimate layer of the Rank-R FNN.

3.3 Convolution-Based Deep Learning Approaches

The adopted semantic segmentation approach consist of a patch first, classify second approach. Therefore, state of the art CNN approaches should be considered for comparison purposes. Towards that direction, two CNN architectures are considered: AlexNet and SqueezeNet.

CNNs are composed of multiple layers, each performing specific operations on the input data. The key layers in a typical CNN architecture include convolutional layers, activation functions, pooling layers, and fully connected layers.

Let X be the input data represented as a 2D image, and W denote the learnable convolutional filters. The convolution operation, denoted by $*$, convolves the filters over the input data, resulting in the computation of feature maps as follows:

$$H = f(\boldsymbol{X} * \boldsymbol{W} + \boldsymbol{b}) \tag{5}$$

where f is an element-wise activation function, and b represents the bias terms. The convolutional layer learns to detect low-level patterns, such as edges and textures, capturing essential visual information that aids in subsequent recognition tasks. The learned features are then passed through additional layers, like activation functions and pooling layers, before ultimately being used in fully connected layers for high-level feature representation and classification.

AlexNet. AlexNet became widely known due to the exceptionally performance achieved on ImageNet dataset back in 2012 [1], catalyzing extensive research advancements and cementing the prominence of deep convolutional neural networks in image classification tasks. The architecture comprises of five convolutional and three fully connected layers. With over 60 million trainable parameters, AlexNet represented a substantial leap in model capacity, enabling the acquisition of intricate hierarchical representations necessary for improved classification accuracy.

AlexNet demonstrated the efficacy of employing rectified linear units (ReLU) as activation functions, effectively overcoming the vanishing gradient problem. Furthermore, the application of dropout regularization within the network mitigated overfitting, enabling robust generalization. The highly performance was, also, attributed to the incorporation of advanced data augmentation techniques, such as horizontal flipping and random cropping, which facilitated enhanced model generalization to previously unseen images.

In our paper, the network consists of five convolutional layers. The first layer takes an input with 48 channels, applies 64 filters of size 11×11, with a stride of 4 and padding of 2. The classifier consists of three fully connected layers (over 50 million parameters). These weights are randomly initialized and adjusted according to training process. Not transfer learning approach is adapted.

SqueezeNet. SqueezeNet is, in its core, a CNN architecture that focused on efficiently reducing the number of parameters compared to traditional deep networks, e.g. AlexNet, for image classification tasks [4]. It employs a unique design strategy to achieve a smaller model size without compromising accuracy, by replacing the conventional 3×3 filters in convolutional layers with 1×1 filters, referred to as "squeeze" layers. This reduction of parameters, due to smaller convolution kernel sizes, enables a significantly smaller model size, i.e. 50 times fewer parameters than AlexNet, while maintaining competitive accuracy levels.

It is worth mentioning that SqueezeNet employs, also, "expand" layers, which are a combination of 1×1 and 3×3 filters to extract local and global information effectively. A combination of introduced "fire modules," consisting of a combination of squeeze and expand layers, known as "fire modules", was strategically designed to strike a balance between model capacity and parameter efficiency.

In this study, the network consists of a sequential module containing the layers responsible for feature extraction. Also, the Fire class represents a specific building block used in SqueezeNet (over 600.000 parameters). Similar to AlexNet, not transfer learning approach is adapted.

4   Experimental Setup

To conduct pixel-wise classification, i.e., to classify each hyperspectral image pixel $I_{x,y}$ at location (x, y) according to the material it depicts, we follow the approach proposed in [9,11]. The performance of the employed Rank-R FNN tensor-based neural network is mainly affected by two hyperparameters: the rank R for the CP decomposition and the number q of neurons placed at the hidden layer. In this study, based on the findings of [10], we set the parameter R equals to 1, and the values for the number of hidden neurons q, equal to 100. We opt for these settings since these values balance the trade-off between high classification performance and computational requirements.

4.1   Dataset Description

The study area was located in the areas of Ukrainian forestries. The dataset was created using PyAutoGui and Google Earth Pro. The dataset consists of 322 RGB images from three different regions. Images contain not only areas with forest or deforestation, but areas with roads, villages located inside the forest, open sources of water like rivers, and ponds. In our case, we will use only images that contain two classes (forest, and deforestation). Images have 512×512 pixels size and are saved with the corresponding masks in Google Cloud Storage. In our paper, we used only 5 images during the training phase and 5 other images during the evaluation phase in order to simulate a limited dataset scenario.

We should note that, for the current dataset, there are limited areas of interest, i.e. deforested, resulting in a highly unbalanced dataset. Therefore, the multichannel images are cropped into smaller objects (patches), using a predefined step. During the sampling phase, we select random samples from the tensor objects to create the training and the test sets. A permutation process is also implemented on the training set to reduce bias effect. We normalize each multichannel image using the min-max normalization to compress the pixels' responses at each band to $[0, 1]$. After normalization, we split each image into patches of dimension s $\times$ s $\times$ 48.

The size of each object depends on the tensor window size (TWS) hyperparameter, exploiting the additional spatial information of the neighborhood. The generated patches of all the available multichannel images are gathered into a single set. From this set, we randomly select a number samples per class for training the DL models, while the rest of the patches are used as a test set for evaluating the defect detection performance.

4.2   Experimental Results

In this section, we present the impact of the patch size and the number of channels on the average performance of the models, in the evaluation dataset. The former case is demonstrated in Fig. 2 and the latter case is demonstrated in Fig. 3. Results showed that increasing the patch size and the number of the channels is beneficial only for the tensor based architecture (TNN). Lastly, Fig. 4 depicts the impact of sample size on the average performance of the proposed models.

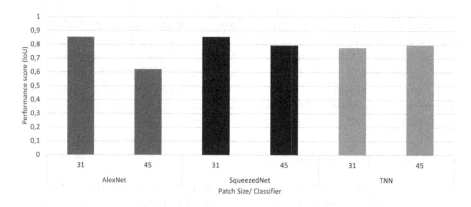

Fig. 2. Patch size performance per classifier

Figure 2 demonstrates how the performance affected when we change the size of the patches. It is intriguing that, for both AlexNet and SqueezedNet approaches, we observed a declining performance while TNN has a minor gain. Towards that, we could say that using greater patches is beneficial.

In Fig. 3 we illustrate the impact of different number of channels given a specific deep learning architecture. When we are use the RGB image as is, i.e. 3 channels, all models have similar performance. Among these, SqueezedNet achieved slightly better Intersection over Union (IoU) score than the other two architectures.

When increasing the number of the channels to 16 channels, AlexNet and SqueezedNet have similar performance, and TNN follows with slightly less score. Nevertheless, at 48 channels both AlexNet and SqueezedNet demonstrate a descending performance, while TNN performs better. Therefore, when increasing the number of channels, the technique with the most gains is the tensor based approach. Given all the above, one last parameter to investigate, is the impact of the available training samples on the performance.

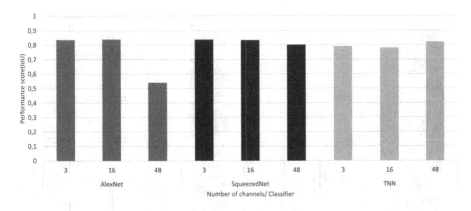

Fig. 3. Number of channels performance per classifier

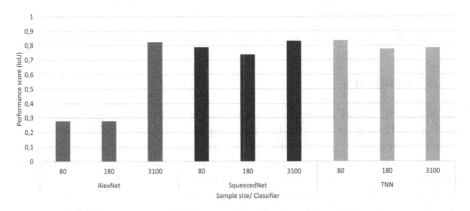

Fig. 4. Sample size performance per classifier

Figure 4 demonstrates how the number of available samples affect the performance of each model architecture, given that we have 45 patch size and 48 channels. In 3100 patches, the best performance score is achieved by SqueezedNet while in 180 patches and 80 patches the greatest IoU score is achieved by TNN. To sum up, when enough training samples are available the other approaches outperform TNN. However, we can see that TNN is the best approach when the number of patches is limited.

Figure 5 presents the output generated image for each model. First column depicts the original satellite image, second column shows the ground truth mask. Each other column represents the corresponding model output. For 3100 patches, AlexNet provided the most accurate image annotation output. For 80 patches, however, AlexNet classified the whole image as deforestated area. SqueedNet provided good results with many false deforestated areas. TNN had better results with small red dots in the real deforestated areas.

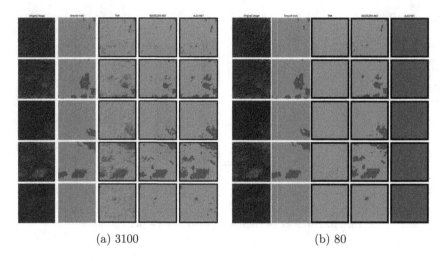

(a) 3100   (b) 80

Fig. 5. Model annotations for different training sizes (Color figure online)

5   Conclusions

In this paper, we try to create a new methodology of identifying deforestation area on RGB satellite images while handling limited data. First, low-level filters were implemented to provide valuable information regarding the region of interest during the preprocessing phase. Next, all filter outcomes are merged into one object creating a tensor. By cropping each tensor into little patches, we create a much bigger dataset which, later, is used to train and validate the performance of 3 state of the art deep learning models. Despite the fact that SqueezedNet and AlexNet perform better on bigger datasets, TNN provide more reliable results when less data are available.

Acknowledgment. This paper is supported by the European Union Funded project "Deployment and Assessment of Predictive modelling, environmentally sustainable and emerging digital technologies and tools for improving the resilience of IWW against Climate change and other extremes" under the HORIZON.2.5 - Climate, Energy and Mobility, grant agreement No. 101069941.

References

1. Han, X., Zhong, Y., Cao, L., Zhang, L.: Pre-trained AlexNet architecture with pyramid pooling and supervision for high spatial resolution remote sensing image scene classification. Remote Sens. **9**(8), 848 (2017)
2. Hänsch, R., Hellwich, O.: Fusion of multispectral lidar, hyperspectral, and RGB data for urban land cover classification. IEEE Geosci. Remote Sens. Lett. **18**(2), 366–370 (2020)
3. Huaranca, L.L., Iribarnegaray, M.A., Albesa, F., Volante, J.N., Brannstrom, C., Seghezzo, L.: Social perspectives on deforestation, land use change, and economic

development in an expanding agricultural frontier in northern Argentina. Ecol. Econ. **165**, 106424 (2019)

4. Iandola, F.N., Han, S., Moskewicz, M.W., Ashraf, K., Dally, W.J., Keutzer, K.: SqueezeNet: AlexNet-level accuracy with 50x fewer parameters and ¡ 0.5 MB model size. arXiv preprint arXiv:1602.07360 (2016)

5. Isaienkov, K., Yushchuk, M., Khramtsov, V., Seliverstov, O.: Deep learning for regular change detection in Ukrainian forest ecosystem with sentinel-2. IEEE J. Sel. Top. Appl. Earth Obs. Remote Sens. **14**, 364–376 (2020)

6. Karra, K., Kontgis, C., Statman-Weil, Z., Mazzariello, J.C., Mathis, M., Brumby, S.P.: Global land use/land cover with sentinel 2 and deep learning. In: 2021 IEEE International Geoscience and Remote Sensing Symposium IGARSS, pp. 4704–4707. IEEE (2021)

7. Kaselimi, M., Doulamis, N., Voulodimos, A., Doulamis, A., Delikaraoglou, D.: Spatio-temporal ionospheric TEC prediction using a deep CNN-GRU model on GNSS measurements. In: 2021 IEEE International Geoscience and Remote Sensing Symposium IGARSS, pp. 8317–8320. IEEE (2021)

8. Kaselimi, M., Voulodimos, A., Daskalopoulos, I., Doulamis, N., Doulamis, A.: A vision transformer model for convolution-free multilabel classification of satellite imagery in deforestation monitoring. IEEE Trans. Neural Netw. Learn. Syst. **34**(7), 3299–3307 (2023)

9. Makantasis, K., Doulamis, A., Doulamis, N., Nikitakis, A., Voulodimos, A.: Tensor-based nonlinear classifier for high-order data analysis. In: 2018 IEEE International Conference on Acoustics, Speech and Signal Processing (ICASSP), pp. 2221–2225. IEEE (2018)

10. Makantasis, K., Doulamis, A.D., Doulamis, N.D., Nikitakis, A.: Tensor-based classification models for hyperspectral data analysis. IEEE Trans. Geosci. Remote Sens. **56**(12), 6884–6898 (2018)

11. Makantasis, K., Georgogiannis, A., Voulodimos, A., Georgoulas, I., Doulamis, A., Doulamis, N.: Rank-R FNN: a tensor-based learning model for high-order data classification. IEEE Access **9**, 58609–58620 (2021)

12. Makantasis, K., Voulodimos, A., Doulamis, A., Doulamis, N., Georgoulas, I.: Hyperspectral image classification with tensor-based rank-R learning models. In: 2019 IEEE International Conference on Image Processing (ICIP), pp. 3148–3125. IEEE (2019)

13. Matosak, B.M., Fonseca, L.M.G., Taquary, E.C., Maretto, R.V., Bendini, H.N., Adami, M.: Mapping deforestation in cerrado based on hybrid deep learning architecture and medium spatial resolution satellite time series. Remote Sens. **14**(1), 209 (2022)

14. Ortega Adarme, M., Queiroz Feitosa, R., Nigri Happ, P., Aparecido De Almeida, C., Rodrigues Gomes, A.: Evaluation of deep learning techniques for deforestation detection in the Brazilian Amazon and cerrado biomes from remote sensing imagery. Remote Sens. **12**(6), 910 (2020)

15. Patro, R.N., Subudhi, S., Biswal, P.K., Dell'acqua, F.: A review of unsupervised band selection techniques: land cover classification for hyperspectral earth observation data. IEEE Geosci. Remote Sens. Mag. **9**(3), 72–111 (2021)

16. Tzortzis, I.N., Rallis, I., Makantasis, K., Doulamis, A., Doulamis, N., Voulodimos, A.: Automatic inspection of cultural monuments using deep and tensor-based learning on hyperspectral imagery. In: 2022 IEEE International Conference on Image Processing (ICIP), pp. 3136–3140. IEEE (2022)

17. Wang, Z., Liu, D., Liao, X., Pu, W., Wang, Z., Zhang, Q.: SiamHRnet-OCR: a novel deforestation detection model with high-resolution imagery and deep learning. Remote Sens. **15**(2), 463 (2023)
18. Yu, Y., et al.: Land cover classification of multispectral lidar data with an efficient self-attention capsule network. IEEE Geosci. Remote Sens. Lett. **19**, 1–5 (2021)

Strategic Incorporation of Synthetic Data for Performance Enhancement in Deep Learning A Case Study on Object Tracking Tasks

Jatin Katyal[✉] and Charalambos Poullis

Immersive and Creative Technologies Lab, Concordia University,
Montreal, QC, Canada
jatinkatyal96@gmail.com

Abstract. Obtaining training data for machine learning models can be challenging. Capturing or gathering the data, followed by its manual labelling, is an expensive and time-consuming process. In cases where there are no publicly accessible datasets, this can significantly hinder progress. In this paper, we analyze the similarity between synthetic and real data. While focusing on an object tracking task, we investigate the quantitative improvement influenced by the concentration of the synthetic data and the variation in the distribution of training samples induced by it. Through examination of three well-known benchmarks, we reveal guidelines that lead to performance gain. We quantify the minimum variation required and demonstrate its efficacy on prominent object-tracking neural network architecture.

Keywords: Synthetic Data · Deep Learning · Multiple Object Tracking

1 Introduction

The process of data collecting is not without challenges, requiring substantial investments of time and resources to obtain labelled samples of high quality. Given the resource and capital costs associated with data acquisition, it is more pragmatic and cost-effective to utilize publicly available datasets that have already been published. In practice, however, straightforward application of such datasets may not always be feasible or effective due to a variety of potential challenges or constraints such as biases. One potential solution to these challenges is utilizing synthetic data as a supplement to real-world datasets. By supplementing real-world data with synthetic data, researchers can overcome the limitations inherent to traditional data sources [1,2], thereby enhancing the overall quality and utility of their datasets.

The utilization of synthetic data has been extensively documented in recent literature, as evidenced by multiple works [30,33,38]. However, much of this prior research has focused on domain adaptation techniques which is adding another

G. Bebis et al. (Eds.): ISVC 2023, LNCS 14361, pp. 513–528, 2023.
https://doi.org/10.1007/978-3-031-47969-4_40

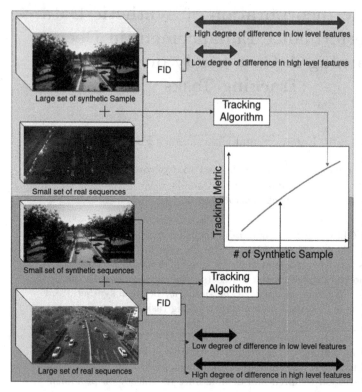

Fig. 1. A combination of synthetic and real datasets with more synthetic samples and higher variance in distribution (top) outperforming another combination with a lower number of synthetic samples and lower variance in distribution (bottom).

computationally expensive step to an already resource-hungry deep learning task. This paper examines the impact of the direct use of synthetic data on the performance of machine learning models. In a preliminary step, we analyze the Frechet Inception Distance (FID) [12] between the synthetic and the real sequences for three benchmark datasets. Building upon the patterns observed, we form clusters for both low and high level features which makes us inquisitive about the impact of these clusters on the performance of the models, if affected then by how much and why? Next, we examine the impact of different concentrations of photo-realistic sequences on training for the three benchmarks and two rendered datasets one of which is generated by us using a game engine. We demonstrate that the use of synthetic images during training can positively affect performance. Also, we discuss instances where the clusters from our preliminary analysis provide an additional stimulus in the form of a gain or drop in performance. We quantify the variation and provide design guidelines for creating synthetic datasets used to train object-tracking models.

The approach we propose is both simple and straightforward, involving the direct utilization of synthetic data without the need for additional domain adaptation steps during training. We justify this approach by viewing the domain adaptation step as a potentially costly and extra procedure when dealing with an already challenging task.

Our proposed strategy aligns with prior studies that have incorporated synthetic data into their training procedures without domain adaptation. However, our approach differs significantly from those studies. For instance, the Virtual KITTI dataset [9] involves a two-step process where pre-training is performed on the virtual data followed by fine-tuning on real data. The MOTSynth challenge [8] encourages training on synthetic data only and testing on real data, without any use of the latter during the training phase.

In contrast, our approach involves fine-tuning models on an amalgamation of both actual and synthetic data, thereby improving tracking performance. To the best of our knowledge, this technique has not been previously explored in the literature.

In this paper, we investigate the efficacy of integrating synthetic data with real data for improving the performance of Multiple Object Tracking. We also conduct a comprehensive analysis of our experimental results and offer insights on the synergistic effects of using synthetic and real data. Drawing from our observations, we formulate a set of general recommendations for the generation and incorporation of synthetic data to enhance model performance.

In the following sections, we conduct a literature review of previous works involving synthetic data and Multiple Object Tracking, followed by an analysis of the similarity between real and synthetic data, our experimentation on different datasets and finally a discussion of the results and conclusions drawn from it.

2   Related Works

This section delves into the various methodologies employed by researchers to generate synthetic data for computer vision tasks. The discussion highlights the value of synthetic data in improving deep learning models' performance through techniques such as domain adaptation and pre-training. Additionally, we examine the different tracking techniques that incorporate various concepts, including behavioural models, graph models, convolutional architectures, and transformers, to achieve robust and accurate tracking performance.

2.1   Synthetic Data

To study the impact of synthetic data, the creation of the dataset is important. [13,24,25,33] use RAGE for generating their corresponding virtual datasets. Detouring [6] was employed in [24] to create synthetic a benchmark from commercial software and evaluate visual perception tasks. In [3] a dataset of virtual human subjects under different illumination conditions was developed using Unreal Engine. In [27], Unity Engine was used to develop a dataset for semantic segmentation. Some of the known publically available virtual datasets include Synthia [27] a collection of synthetic images in an urban environment of a virtual city, MOTSynth [8] a large open-source synthetic dataset for pedestrian detection and tracking, Virtual KITTI dataset [9] a synthetic adaptation of popular KITTI Vision benchmark [10].

Various studies demonstrate the efficacy of using synthetic data for enhancing the performance of deep learning models in various computer vision tasks. In [13] utilized only synthetic images to train their model, which outperformed the model trained on actual images in object classification. Wang et al. [33] simulated a crowd in their GCC dataset and proposed the SSIM Embedding cycle GAN for counting crowds in the wild. Sindagi et al. [30] demonstrated that their Gaussian Process-based framework, which was trained on synthetic data, outperformed other domain adaptation techniques that relied only on real data. H. Zunair and A. Hamza [38], utilized domain adaptation to generate synthetic chest X-ray scans and showed that when used as supplementary data during training, the performance of convolutional architectures for classification improved. In [3] a synthetic dataset was used along domain adaptation to improve the performance of a person re-identification task.

2.2   Multiple Object Tracking

L. Taixé et al. introduced a tracker that uses social and grouping behaviours inside a graph model formulating the tracking as a minimum cost flow optimization problem [14]. H. Nam and B. Han proposed MDNet [20] a multi-domain learning convolutional neural network framework that learns domain-independent features during pretraining and domain-specific information during the tracking.

L. Bertinetto [5] trained a fully convolutional Siamese network to learn a similarity function in an offline manner to be evaluated online during training to locate a template image within the search image using the strong embeddings learned in the offline phase. B. Li [15] proposed a Siamese Region Proposal Network consisting of a template and a detection branch which are trained offline and correlational maps for feature extraction, the tracking is formulated as a local one-shot detection task.

P. Bergman and T. Meinhardt introduced tracktor [4] that exploits bounding box regression of an existing object detector, without any additional training required for tracking objects. Zhou presented a point-based tracking framework called CenterTrack [35] that uses CenterNet [36] detector conditioned on two consecutive frames that also predicts a displacement vector for associating positions of the objects through frames.

Y.Zhang et al. introduced FairMOT [34], also a CenterNet [36] based technique for a multi-task learning approach for detection and re-identification. In this technique, the competition for accuracy between the two tasks was addressed by introducing fairness. This results in an unbiased network which treats both tasks equally thus, it doesn't affect their accuracy adversely.

G. Ning et. al proposed ROLO [21] a recurrent extension of YOLO [22] architecture by adding an LSTM stage, training involves three phases pertaining of convolutional layers, training of object proposal module and training of recurrent LSTM module.

P. Sun et al. introduced TransTrack [31] an attention-based query-key scheme inspired by transformers [32] that uses attention to track objects, their framework generates two sets of queries containing information for new coming objects and information for maintaining tracklets. T. Meinhardt et al. introduced Trackformer [18] following the tracking by attention paradigm for joint detection and tracking, attention is computed between frame features, tracks and object queries to output bounding boxes and identities.

3 Synthetic Dataset and Observations

In this section we touch upon the synthetic dataset that we created and a publically available synthetic dataset for supplementing the real dataset. We also discuss our key observations when comparing these synthetic datasets to real video sequences using Fréchet Inception Distance (FID) [12].

Our experimental setup utilizes synthetic video sequences generated with the AirSim plugin [29] for Unreal engine. Details on the generation of the dataset are discussed in Sect. 4.1. Along with this new dataset, we use two published Unmanned Aerial Vehicle (UAV) benchmarks for the detection and tracking of vehicles, UAVDT benchmark [7] and VisDrone dataset [37] as real sequences. To eliminate bias due to the domain and task, and ensure the generalization of the insights, we additionally use another pair of real and synthetic tracking datasets with people tracking in place of vehicle tracking as the objective. For this purpose, we use MOT17 [19] and MOTSynth [8] as real and synthetic datasets respectively.

Fréchet Inception Distance (FID) is a quality measure first introduced in [12], for capturing the similarity of the images generated by GANs, this metric also correlates with human judgement. FID score for 2 identical images is 0, and for 2 identical sets of images or videos is close to 0. It increases as the visual similarities between the two images or sets of images reduce as depicted in Fig. 2. A synthetic sequence with similar lighting, camera angle and elevation as the real sequence results in a relatively lower FID in contrast to another real sequence that has different lighting, camera angle and elevation. We use it to estimate the degree of similarity between synthetic and real images for each pair of real and synthetic sequences.

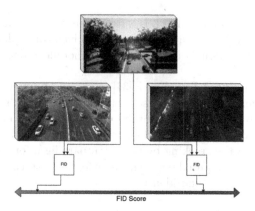

Fig. 2. FID computation example for low level features between AirSim generated video sequence (top) with a similar looking (bottom-left) and a different looking (bottom-right) real video sequence from UAVDT dataset. The computed value towards the green end depicts similarity between the two sequences, and contrary to that towards the red side depicts visual dissimilarity. (Color figure online)

We computed the Fréchet Inception Distance for three combinations of real and synthetic datasets from the first pooling layer features (FID64), the second max pooling features (FID192), the pre-auxiliary classifier features (FID768) and the final average pooling features (FID2048) [28]. The computations from the second max pooling (FID192) and the final average pooling (FID2048) features do not add more information or echoes that the first max pooling features (FID64) and the pre-auxiliary classifier features (FID768) already express. Thus, we only use FID scores obtained from the first max pool layer features and the pre-auxiliary classifier features for the low level features and the high level features respectively. The FIDs for all synthetic and real datasets are plotted as heatmaps in Fig. 3.

In the heatmaps, each row is a real sequence and each column is a synthetic sequence from corresponding real and synthetic dataset pairs. Within the heat maps for low level features 3a, the combination of UAVDT benchmark and AirSim generated dataset shows patterns of higher FID scores for some real sequences while most of the real sequences have a relatively lower FID Score. The other 2 dataset combinations only observe a relatively low FID score for all real and synthetic sequence pairings. Contrasting to this, the heatmaps for high level features 3b, show more patterns of high FID scores for real sequences in all three dataset combinations. Interestingly, a pattern for high FID score is also noticeable for synthetic sequences in the MOT17 and MotSynth datasets pairing. We discuss these patterns further in this section.

These initial observations from the heatmaps motivate us to define rigid clusters based on the FID computations. We cluster sequences under 3 categories namely, lower, moderate or higher degrees of difference in low or high level features. This clustering is required to isolate features on the basis of similarity and measure their impact on the performance of the training process. We later use these clusters in further sections for experimentation and discussion.

For the clustering, we create a range between 0 (the minimum achievable distance) and the maximum calculated FID determined across all datasets plus an additional buffer. In our experiments the max value for low level and high level featres were 45 and 3 with additional buffers of 5 and 0.5. We fit all the sequences to this range and scale them to get a range between 0 and 1. This scale is divided into three parts using 0.3 and 0.6 as the division points. The sequences that fall under the first, the second and the third segment are termed as sequences with lower, moderate or higher degrees of difference respectively. Although this work uses FID as a measure for calculating similarity, the use of other metrics is also encouraged. FID was used because of the demerits of other metrics highlighted in [12].

3.1   FID for Low Level Features

The FIDs obtained after first pooling layer features for the sequences from the UAVDT benchmark and the AirSim generated dataset, sequences with a higher degree of difference have an average of 32.80 ± 2.60, the same for sequences having a moderate degree of difference is 18.93 ± 2.33 and finally the sequences with a lower degree of difference have an average of 7.80 ± 2.93. We observe that all sequences in the VisDrone dataset compared to the synthetic dataset generated using AirSim have a lower degree of difference for low level features with an average of 7.40 ± 2.31. A similar observation is made for the sequences from the MOT17 and the MOTSynth datasets, all the sequences lead to an average of 8.66 ± 3.48 thus falling under a lower degree of difference for low level features. The FIDs for all synthetic and real sequences are visually represented in Fig. 3a, where the green regions represent the lower degree of difference, yellow-orange shades depict the moderate degree of difference and dark orange-red represents the higher degree of difference.

3.2   FID for High Level Features

On the basis of the clustering scheme discussed earlier in this section and the FIDs obtained from the pre-auxiliary classifier features for UAVDT and AirSim generated sequences, we cluster sequences among low, medium or high degrees of difference for high level features among real data. The average values for clusters are 1.60 ± 0.05, 2.13 ± 0.19 and 2.65 ± 0.12 respectively. With the same synthetic dataset when FID values are calculated along the VisDrone dataset the clusters obtained have 1.72 ± 0.01 for lower degree of difference, 2.07 ± 0.22 for a moderate degree of difference and 2.76 ± 0.21 for a higher degree of difference in high level features. When calculating the FIDs with higher level features for MOT17 and MOTSynth datasets, we obtain 1.75, 1.99 ± 0.16 and 2.72 for lower, moderate and higher degrees of differences. Unlike other real and synthetic dataset combinations, we also observe a pattern for synthetic sequences for MOT17 and MOTSynth. The average values for lower, moderate and higher degrees of difference in high level features are 1.57 ± 0.09, 2.01 ± 0.20 and 2.68 ± 0.18 respectively. We visualize these FID computations in the form of a heatmap in Fig. 3b.

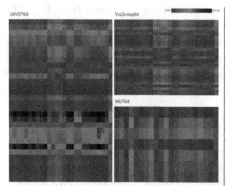 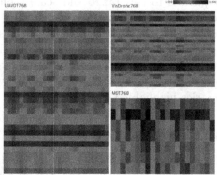

(a) FID64: Fréchet Inception Distance obtained from first pooling features. Left: UAVDT and AirSim, Right-Top: Visdrone and AirSim, Right-Bottom: MOT and MOTSynth. Each row represents a real sequence and each column represents a synthetic sequence.

(b) FID768: FID obtained from pre-auxiliary classifier features. Left: UAVDT and AirSim, Right-Top: Visdrone and AirSim, Right-Bottom: MOT and MOTSynth. Each row represents a real sequence and each column represents a synthetic sequence.

Fig. 3. FIDs heatmaps for low level features (a) and high level features (b). Dark green represents lower degree of difference, dark red represents higher degree of difference, and the shades in between represent moderate degree of difference in lower/higher level features. (Color figure online)

3.3   Objectives

With the derived insights and our objective of impact investigation of synthetic data as a supplement in combination with real data, we aim to answer the following questions:

- How effective is the use of synthetic data when supplementing a real dataset?
- What is the impact of different real-synthetic concentrations on the performance metric?
- What are the characteristics of the synthetic data that drive this change, the concentration, the degree of diversity in information brought by the synthetic samples or both factors?

4   Experiments

In this section, we discuss in detail the synthetic and the real datasets that we use, our strategy to answer the questions that were raised in the previous section and our trials.

4.1 Datasets

As already discussed briefly in Sect. 3, we generate a set of synthetic video sequences using the AirSim plugin in Unreal engine. To generate the simulated video sequences, we load the environment with a simulated drone and dictate its flight trajectory by a set of three-dimensional points in the simulation environment transmitted through APIs. We assimilate input from the camera mounted on the virtual drone and detect vehicles within the field of view of the drone using another pair of APIs to save frames and annotation to a local storage device. We also alter weather conditions across different flight paths to create a diverse set of simulated video sequences. In total, we generated 25 sequences exhibiting different weather conditions, providing a diverse range of scenarios for evaluation.

For the real dataset we use the Unmanned Aerial Vehicle Benchmark [7] (UAVDT) which is a collection of video sequences captured by drones. This benchmark dataset offers sequences with various conditions for illumination, camera viewpoint and elevation. To ensure that our experimentation is not limited to a single dataset, we also conduct tests on another UAV detection and tracking dataset called VisDrone [37]. It contains both city and country environments with annotations for many objects in various weather and lighting conditions. Since our synthetic dataset only had information about vehicles, we rank all the sequences on the most number of vehicles in the scene and only considered the top 30 videos which had the most number of vehicles for our vehicle tracking experiments.

For the extensiveness of our experiments, we use another pair of real and synthetic datasets. MOT17 [19] dataset which is a pedestrian detection and tracking dataset with video sequences having different viewports, camera movements and weather conditions. For the synthetic part, we used the MOTSynth [8] dataset which was created for pedestrian detection, tracking and segmentation and contains frames generated using a rendering game engine. We only required a limited number of sequences according to our experiment setup and a random selection of 21 sequences is used to serve as the training set.

4.2 Strategy

We use models trained only on real datasets as baseline models to compare and evaluate against the results obtained from models discussed further in our training strategy. In our strategy, we keep the total number of real and synthetic training sequences constant, that is the number of real sequences available for training. We then substitute real sequences with synthetic sequences. We focus on the substitution and not on the addition of new data for two reasons. First, additional training data will lead to unfair evaluation as the new dataset will have more training samples when compared to the baseline model. Second, substitution creates an artificial scarcity of data enabling us to evaluate the impact of synthetic data when the actual data is insufficient or missing. For these reasons, we formulate an approach to break down the datasets into different-sized folds such that, a bigger chunk from the real dataset has a complementary smaller fold in the synthetic dataset and vice-versa. The combined dataset always accounts for the same number of total video sequences as originally in the training set for the real dataset. For the vehicle tracking experiments, we use ratios 1:5, 1:2, 1:1, 2:1 and 5:1 between real and synthetic data i.e. when there are 5 real sequences we use 25 synthetic sequences, 10 real and 20 synthetic sequences and so on. For people tracking experiments, we use 1:6, 1:2, 2:1 and 6:1 as the ratios.

We use multiple folds for each concentration of real-synthetic combination to understand the consistency of the change in the tracking metric with the real-to-synthetic data ratio. Within the folds, we vary the number of sequences with lower, moderate and higher degrees of difference for low-level and high-level features as discussed in the previous section. In our experiments, each fold is denoted by a lowercase letter.

4.3   Training

For our experiments, we train FRCNN [23] network for object detection and ResNet50 [11] model for re-identification, together these two models are used in combination as described in the Tracktor [4] technique. The datasets, both real and synthetic are aimed for detection and tracking and not for re-identification. To allow training of re-identification models on these sequences we create a re-identification dataset from the given frames. We crop the frames where bounding boxes are present and use these crops for tracked objects as a re-identification dataset. We use the described setup of an object detector and a re-identifier with different folds of the training set as discussed in Sect. 4.2. Models trained on different folds are evaluated using HOTA [17] and IDF1 [26] as the calculative measures for assessing performance. The metrics IDP and IDR are intermediatory measures that are needed to calculate IDF1 value while DetA and AssA are used to calculate HOTA. The metrics are calculated using trackeval [16]. The results of public detection from different manifestations of the Tracktor on the UAVDT benchmark and the AirSim generated dataset are reported in Fig. 4, on VisDrone dataset and AirSim generated dataset are reported in Fig. 5 and on MOT17 and MOTSynth are reported in Fig. 6. Further, we discuss these results in Sect. 5.

Also, we extend the applicability of synthetic datasets to transformer-based architectures. We select the Transtrack [31] architecture, which is an encoder-decoder framework with a ResNet-50 [11] backbone network. We train the models on MOT17 and MOTSynth datasets, using the same concentrations and folds as used for the Tracktor experiments. Results are reported in Fig. 7 and further discussed in Sect. 5.

5   Discussion

Figures 4 and 6 show a significant increase in performance measure when synthetic data is included in the training set against the benchmark that only contains all real data. The improvement is up to a 14% increase for the UAVDT benchmark and up to a 10% increase for the MOT17 dataset. Also, Fig. 5 shows an increase up to 4% was achieved for the VisDrone dataset. Figure 7 shows an increase up to 7% for the MOT17 dataset on a transformer-based architecture. There is a positive correlation between the percentage of synthetic data in the training set and the performance measure for the UAVDT benchmark and the VisDrone dataset. The performance increase for the MOT17 dataset is moreover constant and is not affected by changes in dataset concentrations on Tracktor but we again observe the correlation between the number of synthetic samples and the tracking metric on transformer-based architecture. We further discuss each dataset individually under the following subsections.

Real Set		Synthetic Set							
Size	Fold	Size	Fold	IDP↑	IDR↑	DetA↑	AssA↑	IDF1↑	HOTA↑
5	a	25	a	84.232	83.500	**77.950**	63.984	83.864	70.489
5	b	25	a	84.877	83.538	75.616	63.979	84.202	69.405
5	c	25	a	78.229	78.535	67.812	59.057	78.382	63.134
5	d	25	a	**90.251**	**87.227**	77.166	**70.266**	**88.713**	**73.504**
5	e	25	a	85.501	84.279	72.327	62.985	84.885	67.313
5	f	25	a	85.632	83.054	76.823	64.676	84.323	70.378
10	g	20	b	86.740	82.318	73.588	67.232	85.409	70.252
10	h	20	b	82.459	81.612	68.126	62.729	82.033	65.235
10	i	20	b	87.303	81.945	69.367	64.190	84.539	66.584
15	j	15	c	90.029	79.524	66.662	66.109	84.451	66.259
15	k	15	c	87.484	80.520	67.165	63.453	83.858	65.163
20	l	10	d	81.393	78.686	64.573	61.158	80.016	62.722
20	m	10	e	89.997	76.785	62.950	65.291	82.868	64.004
20	n	10	f	85.122	75.669	62.724	63.897	80.118	63.146
25	o	5	g	81.287	75.073	60.347	60.683	78.057	60.378
25	p	5	h	82.752	77.801	62.214	61.078	80.200	61.513
25	q	5	i	81.746	78.741	64.828	61.166	80.216	62.832
25	r	5	g	86.904	69.093	54.706	62.014	76.982	58.104
25	s	5	h	83.274	74.501	61.816	62.026	78.644	61.744
25	t	5	i	82.871	78.444	63.305	61.988	80.597	62.432
30	u	0	NA	82.085	75.486	61.183	60.948	78.647	60.921

Real Set		Synthetic Set							
Size	Fold	Size	Fold	IDP↑	IDR↑	DetA↑	AssA↑	IDF1↑	HOTA↑
5	a	25	a	69.957	72.991	64.611	**57.841**	71.442	**60.701**
5	b	25	a	63.117	65.636	63.323	50.193	64.352	55.975
5	c	25	a	68.029	70.809	59.921	54.752	69.391	56.779
5	d	25	a	68.278	70.847	**65.364**	55.616	69.539	59.961
5	e	25	a	65.193	67.949	64.281	52.798	66.543	57.834
5	f	25	a	71.052	74.107	61.694	57.558	72.547	59.241
10	g	20	b	63.448	66.078	63.482	50.621	64.736	56.271
10	h	20	b	69.845	72.378	62.859	56.169	71.089	59.043
10	i	20	b	67.547	70.272	63.569	54.147	68.882	58.307
15	j	15	c	66.078	68.449	61.602	51.998	67.242	56.239
15	k	15	c	67.924	70.180	64.041	54.747	69.034	58.902
20	l	10	d	65.904	67.146	61.679	51.545	66.519	56.053
20	m	10	e	65.603	67.782	64.136	51.997	66.675	57.462
20	n	10	f	67.121	68.683	63.215	53.425	67.893	57.779
25	o	5	g	65.085	65.854	62.107	50.922	65.467	55.953
25	p	5	h	65.430	66.037	61.531	50.750	65.732	55.557
25	q	5	i	65.541	66.822	62.856	51.431	66.176	56.511
25	r	5	g	69.491	67.100	62.294	52.595	68.275	56.943
25	s	5	h	**72.598**	71.483	62.676	55.977	72.036	58.948
25	t	5	i	64.689	65.665	62.643	50.480	65.173	55.885
30	u	0	NA	64.324	64.601	61.910	49.864	64.462	55.252

Fig. 4. Results for Tracktor technique trained on datasets with different concentrations of UAVDT benchmark (real) and AirSim generated dataset (synthetic). Column Size denotes the number of sequences and Fold denotes which fold was used.

Fig. 5. Results for Tracktor technique trained on datasets with different concentrations of Visdrone dataset (real) and AirSim generated dataset (synthetic). Column Size denotes the number of sequences and Fold denotes which fold was used.

5.1 UAVDT

We observe a direct link between the performance measure and the percentage of the synthetic dataset in the overall training set, by increasing the number of synthetic samples we notice an increase in the HOTA metric. It is highest when we use twenty-five synthetic samples and five real ones, and lowest when use twenty-five real and five synthetic samples across a number of folds. Also, among folds comprised of five real and twenty-five synthetic sequences, the HOTA metric is highest when the training set includes sequences with a higher degree of difference for low level features. Additionally, in the folds consisting of twenty-five real and five synthetic sequences, we notice that the HOTA metric reduces when the folds are constituted from sequences with low or moderate degrees of difference for low level features. All experiments are reported in Fig. 4.

5.2 VisDrone

Our findings indicate an increasing trend, albeit with a few deviations for the VisDrone and AirSim datasets. The performance of models trained on different folds generally increases, except for the folds where five sequences are synthetic the models perform worst than the benchmark but the performance increases gradually as the percentage of synthetic data increases. Another deviation is remarked, where models trained on folds with 20 synthetic sequences perform better than the models trained on folds with synthetic data but the latter still outperforms the benchmark model.

With the FIDs analysis for low level features (Sect. 3.1) as the foundation, it is hard to come to conclusions as all sequences for this dataset combination fall under a low degree of difference. Drawing on the insights derived from the FID analysis for high level features (Sect. 3.2), experiments with folds having 5, 10 or 15 real sequences, the fold having the most number of sequences with a lower degree of difference for high level features outperforms the rest of the folds in that category.

Real Set		Synthetic Set							
Size	Fold	Size	Fold	IDP↑	IDR↑	DetA↑	AssA↑	IDF1↑	HOTA↑
3	a	18	a	48.893	63.291	40.617	52.277	55.168	45.904
3	b	18	b	49.996	59.487	41.928	48.766	54.330	45.069
3	c	18	c	53.866	59.708	44.196	49.285	56.636	46.547
3	d	18	d	55.581	62.286	43.842	51.946	58.743	47.559
3	e	18	e	48.792	61.824	41.173	50.731	54.540	45.552
3	f	18	f	50.057	64.044	40.420	53.327	56.193	46.312
3	g	18	g	52.789	61.614	43.340	50.591	56.861	46.726
7	h	14	h	46.250	61.112	39.961	49.537	52.652	44.250
7	i	14	i	52.175	63.552	42.574	52.785	57.304	47.294
7	j	14	j	48.708	62.582	41.035	52.501	54.780	46.313
14	k	7	k	47.634	62.714	40.470	50.411	54.143	45.080
14	l	7	l	49.877	65.935	41.136	56.227	56.793	47.927
14	m	7	m	50.716	63.499	42.412	53.109	56.392	47.333
18	n	3	n	48.730	63.345	40.822	52.392	55.084	46.142
18	o	3	o	50.245	64.282	41.520	53.084	56.403	46.873
18	p	3	p	48.210	63.303	40.821	52.738	54.735	46.289
18	q	3	q	50.598	66.076	41.154	56.023	57.311	47.540
18	r	3	r	49.462	65.915	41.347	55.496	56.515	47.806
18	s	3	s	50.404	65.135	41.934	54.193	56.830	47.570
18	t	3	t	50.398	63.233	41.706	53.768	56.090	47.234
21	u	0	NA	34.597	46.205	40.230	32.198	39.567	35.883

Real Set		Synthetic Set							
Size	Fold	Size	Fold	IDP↑	IDR↑	DetA↑	AssA↑	IDF1↑	HOTA↑
3	a	18	a	62.653	53.443	45.824	49.286	57.683	46.968
3	b	18	b	44.166	72.288	39.513	67.894	54.831	51.514
3	c	18	c	66.111	57.044	47.974	51.432	61.244	49.268
3	d	18	d	67.937	55.626	45.120	53.142	61.168	48.695
3	e	18	e	67.314	64.160	49.847	55.861	65.699	52.523
3	f	18	f	74.162	59.827	51.015	56.889	66.228	53.463
3	g	18	g	62.410	57.089	43.517	53.589	59.631	47.928
7	h	14	h	44.227	73.213	40.035	67.432	55.143	51.738
7	i	14	i	62.208	64.166	48.555	54.669	63.172	51.261
7	j	14	j	63.459	66.120	49.082	58.896	64.762	53.421
14	k	7	k	43.836	78.055	40.616	68.205	56.142	52.385
14	l	7	l	45.196	79.390	41.596	68.821	57.600	53.242
14	m	7	m	60.775	67.998	48.565	59.332	64.184	53.390
18	n	3	n	44.370	78.334	41.759	68.752	56.651	53.378
18	o	3	o	42.178	77.860	40.276	66.858	54.716	51.656
18	p	3	p	44.261	77.375	40.184	69.770	56.311	52.751
18	q	3	q	43.894	78.164	41.590	66.904	56.218	52.510
18	r	3	r	43.388	79.442	40.974	69.318	56.124	53.073
18	s	3	s	60.466	59.020	44.717	56.860	59.734	50.124
18	t	3	t	44.689	81.538	41.186	69.973	57.735	53.523
21	u	0	NA	43.207	79.424	41.177	67.884	55.967	52.633

Fig. 6. Results for Tracktor technique trained on datasets with different concentrations of MOT17 dataset (real) and MOTSynth dataset (synthetic). Column Size denotes the number of sequences and Fold denotes which fold was used.

Fig. 7. Results for TransTrack architecture trained on datasets with different concentrations of MOT17 dataset (real) and MOTSynth dataset (synthetic). Column Size denotes the number of sequences and Fold denotes which fold was used.

5.3 MOT17

We observe up to 10% increase in HOTA metric for supplementing the MOT17 dataset with the MOTSynth dataset. However, unlike the previous two benchmarks where an increasing trend was observed, our examination reveal about a constant increase in performance measure invariant of the real-synthetic concentrations throughout the experiments.

Guided by the FIDs analysis of high level features, amongst the folds with 3 real sequences, the HOTA metric is the least when trained on samples with higher degree of difference for high level features in comparison to when these samples are excluded. The same is observed in folds with 7 real sequences. This phenomenon becomes hazy for folds with 18 real scenarios. Also to note, the performance metric improves when sequences with higher degree of difference are excluded from the folds comprising synthetic data.

Experiments with the TransTrack architecture show a similar result, an almost constant trend for the HOTA metric. However, the trend is clearly visible in the IDF1 metric. The performance of the model is directly correlated with the amount of synthetic data in the training dataset. The fold including the sequences with a higher degree of difference for high-level features, always performs the worst among the folds of the same size.

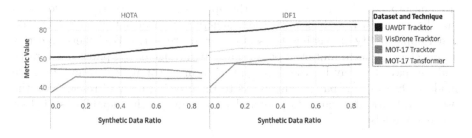

Fig. 8. Change in HOTA and IDF1 measures on increasing the concentration of synthetic samples in the training set for Tracktor on UAVDT benchmark, VisDrone dataset and MOT17 dataset; for TransTrack on MOT17 dataset.

5.4 Guidelines

Considering the key insights derived in this section we can deduce that by using synthetic data, one can increase the performance of a model. We derive the following principles from our experiments.

– When synthetic data is used in orders of magnitudes of real data a performance can be anticipated. In our experiments, the increase in performance was up to 15% when synthetic data accounted five times more than the actual video sequences.
– The performance improvement is higher when the variance in low-level features is high. In our experiments, we clustered sequences with values greater than 0.6 on our scale (FIDs greater than 30 units calculated from first pooling layer features) as a high degree of difference for low-level features. The presence of these sequences resulted in a better performance.
– The increase in performance is limited by the variance in high-level features and is recommended to be kept minimal. Our experiments with sequences with values lower than 0.3 on our scale (under 1.75 units for FIDs calculated from pre-auxiliary classifier features) showed an increased improvement.

6   Conclusion

In this study, we investigated the effectiveness of using synthetic data in combination with real data for Single Camera Multi-Object Tracking tasks. We utilized three different datasets and two different tracking techniques to evaluate the impact of using synthetic data. Our results indicate that the inclusion of synthetic data in the training process of deep learning models improves the performance metrics when compared to using real data alone. Furthermore, we also explored the specific aspects of synthetic data that should be emphasized to further enhance the performance of the models.

Our findings suggest that the combination of real and synthetic data can lead to a new paradigm for training deep learning models. While synthetic data has traditionally been used for pre-training or domain adaptation, our study highlights the potential for a simpler technique to complement real data in the training process. We aim to validate the application of synthetic data for solving challenges such as bias mitigation, generalization of outside datasets, and wider applicability of existing datasets in our future works. We believe that this approach can lead to improved performance in a range of computer vision tasks and can pave the way for the development of more sophisticated and accurate models. Overall, this paper contributes to the growing body of research on the use of synthetic data and its potential for enhancing the capabilities of deep learning models.

Acknowledgement. This work is financially supported by the Natural Sciences and Engineering Research Council of Canada Grants RGPIN-2021-03479 (NSERC DG) and ALLRP 571887 - 2021 (NSERC Alliance). The authors would like to thank Sacha Leprêtre (CAE, formerly Presagis Inc, Canada) and his team for their continued support of this work.

References

1. Adimoolam, Y.K., Chatterjee, B., Poullis, C., Averkiou, M.: Efficient deduplication and leakage detection in large scale image datasets with a focus on the crowdai mapping challenge dataset. arXiv preprint arXiv:2304.02296 (2023)
2. Baek, K., Shim, H.: Commonality in natural images rescues GANs: pretraining GANs with generic and privacy-free synthetic data. In: Proceedings of the IEEE/CVF CVPR, pp. 7854–7864 (2022)
3. Bak, S., Carr, P., Lalonde, J.: Domain adaptation through synthesis for unsupervised person re-identification. CoRR abs/1804.10094 (2018). http://arxiv.org/abs/1804.10094
4. Bergmann, P., Meinhardt, T., Leal-Taixé, L.: Tracking without bells and whistles. In: ICCV (2019)
5. Bertinetto, L., Valmadre, J., Henriques, J.F., Vedaldi, A., Torr, P.H.S.: Fully-convolutional siamese networks for object tracking. CoRR abs/1606.09549 (2016). http://arxiv.org/abs/1606.09549
6. Brubacher, D.: Detours: Binary interception of win32 functions. In: Windows NT 3rd Symposium (Windows NT 3rd Symposium). USENIX Association, Seattle, WA (1999)

7. Du, D., et al.: The unmanned aerial vehicle benchmark: object detection and tracking. In: ECCV (2018)
8. Fabbri, M., et al.: Motsynth: how can synthetic data help pedestrian detection and tracking? In: Proceedings of the IEEE/CVF International Conference on Computer Vision, pp. 10849–10859 (2021)
9. Gaidon, A., Wang, Q., Cabon, Y., Vig, E.: Virtual worlds as proxy for multi-object tracking analysis. CoRR abs/1605.06457 (2016). http://arxiv.org/abs/1605.06457
10. Geiger, A., Lenz, P., Urtasun, R.: Are we ready for autonomous driving? the kitti vision benchmark suite. In: CVPR (2012)
11. He, K., Zhang, X., Ren, S., Sun, J.: Deep residual learning for image recognition. CoRR abs/1512.03385 (2015). http://arxiv.org/abs/1512.03385
12. Heusel, M., Ramsauer, H., Unterthiner, T., Nessler, B., Hochreiter, S.: GANs trained by a two time-scale update rule converge to a local nash equilibrium. NeurIPS (2017)
13. Johnson-Roberson, M., Barto, C., Mehta, R., Sridhar, S.N., Vasudevan, R.: Driving in the matrix: Can virtual worlds replace human-generated annotations for real world tasks? CoRR abs/1610.01983 (2016). http://arxiv.org/abs/1610.01983
14. Leal-Taixé, L., Pons-Moll, G., Rosenhahn, B.: Everybody needs somebody: modeling social and grouping behavior on a linear programming multiple people tracker. In: ICCV Workshops, pp. 120–127 (2011). https://doi.org/10.1109/ICCVW.2011.6130233
15. Li, B., Yan, J., Wu, W., Zhu, Z., Hu, X.: High performance visual tracking with siamese region proposal network. In: 2018 IEEE/CVF CVPR, pp. 8971–8980 (2018). https://doi.org/10.1109/CVPR.2018.00935
16. Luiten, J., Hoffhues, A.: Trackeval (2020). https://github.com/JonathonLuiten/TrackEval
17. Luiten, J., et al.: Hota: a higher order metric for evaluating multi-object tracking. Int. J. Comput. Vis. **129**, 1–31 (2020)
18. Meinhardt, T., Kirillov, A., Leal-Taixe, L., Feichtenhofer, C.: Trackformer: multi-object tracking with transformers. In: IEEE CVPR (2022)
19. Milan, A., Leal-Taixé, L., Reid, I., Roth, S., Schindler, K.: MOT16: a benchmark for multi-object tracking. arXiv:1603.00831 [cs] (2016), http://arxiv.org/abs/1603.00831, arXiv: 1603.00831
20. Nam, H., Han, B.: Learning multi-domain convolutional neural networks for visual tracking. CoRR abs/1510.07945 (2015), http://arxiv.org/abs/1510.07945
21. Ning, G., et al.: Spatially supervised recurrent convolutional neural networks for visual object tracking. In: 2017 IEEE ISCAS, pp. 1–4. IEEE (2017)
22. Redmon, J., Divvala, S., Girshick, R., Farhadi, A.: You only look once: Unified, real-time object detection. In: Proceedings of the IEEE Conference on Computer Vision and Pattern Recognition, pp. 779–788 (2016)
23. Ren, S., He, K., Girshick, R.B., Sun, J.: Faster R-CNN: towards real-time object detection with region proposal networks. CoRR abs/1506.01497 (2015). http://arxiv.org/abs/1506.01497
24. Richter, S.R., Hayder, Z., Koltun, V.: Playing for benchmarks. CoRR abs/1709.07322 (2017). http://arxiv.org/abs/1709.07322
25. Richter, S.R., Vineet, V., Roth, S., Koltun, V.: Playing for data: ground truth from computer games. CoRR abs/1608.02192 (2016). http://arxiv.org/abs/1608.02192
26. Ristani, E., Solera, F., Zou, R., Cucchiara, R., Tomasi, C.: Performance measures and a data set for multi-target, multi-camera tracking. In: Hua, G., Jégou, H. (eds.) ECCV 2016. LNCS, vol. 9914, pp. 17–35. Springer, Cham (2016). https://doi.org/10.1007/978-3-319-48881-3_2

27. Ros, G., Sellart, L., Materzynska, J., Vazquez, D., Lopez, A.M.: The synthia dataset: a large collection of synthetic images for semantic segmentation of urban scenes. In: CVPR, pp. 3234–3243 (2016). https://doi.org/10.1109/CVPR.2016.352
28. Seitzer, M.: pytorch-fid: FID Score for PyTorch (2020). https://github.com/mseitzer/pytorch-fid
29. Shah, S., Dey, D., Lovett, C., Kapoor, A.: Airsim: high-fidelity visual and physical simulation for autonomous vehicles. In: Field and Service Robotics (2017). https://arxiv.org/abs/1705.05065
30. Sindagi, V.A., Yasarla, R., Babu, D.S., Babu, R.V., Patel, V.M.: Learning to count in the crowd from limited labeled data. In: Vedaldi, A., Bischof, H., Brox, T., Frahm, J.-M. (eds.) ECCV 2020. LNCS, vol. 12356, pp. 212–229. Springer, Cham (2020). https://doi.org/10.1007/978-3-030-58621-8_13
31. Sun, P., et al.: Transtrack: multiple-object tracking with transformer. arXiv preprint arXiv: 2012.15460 (2020)
32. Vaswani, A., et al.: Attention is all you need. In: NeurIPS, 30 (2017)
33. Wang, Q., Gao, J., Lin, W., Yuan, Y.: Learning from synthetic data for crowd counting in the wild. In: IEEE CVPR, pp. 8198–8207 (2019)
34. Zhang, Y., Wang, C., Wang, X., Zeng, W., Liu, W.: Fairmot: on the fairness of detection and re-identification in multiple object tracking. Int. J. Comput. Vision **129**, 3069–3087 (2021)
35. Zhou, X., Koltun, V., Krähenbühl, P.: Tracking objects as points. In: Vedaldi, A., Bischof, H., Brox, T., Frahm, J.-M. (eds.) ECCV 2020. LNCS, vol. 12349, pp. 474–490. Springer, Cham (2020). https://doi.org/10.1007/978-3-030-58548-8_28
36. Zhou, X., Wang, D., Krähenbühl, P.: Objects as points. arXiv preprint arXiv:1904.07850 (2019)
37. Zhu, P., et al.: Detection and tracking meet drones challenge. IEEE TPAMI **44**, 1–1 (2021). https://doi.org/10.1109/TPAMI.2021.3119563
38. Zunair, H., Hamza, A.B.: Synthesis of covid-19 chest x-rays using unpaired image-to-image translation. Soc. Netw. Anal. Min. **11**, 1–12 (2021)

Autonomous Navigation via a Cascading CNN Framework Leveraging Synthetic Terrain Images

Abigail Rolen$^{(\boxtimes)}$ and Sandeep Singh

Advanced Space Concepts Lab (ASCLab), Rensselaer Polytechnic Institute,
Troy, NY 12180, USA
{rolena,sandes5}@rpi.edu
http://www.asclabrpi.com

Abstract. The expansion of human spaceflight to include more planetary bodies and intricate mission architectures demands the advancement of autonomous navigation algorithms, especially for the powered descent phase. The advent of machine learning presents an entirely new paradigm for autonomous, closed-loop control systems, offering promising solutions to guidance, navigation and control (GNC) problems. In this research, a novel cascading architecture is proposed to train a series of convolutional neural networks (CNN) to localize segmented images within a larger domain. This approach leverages image information to effectively determine the relative location of a target area, which provides necessary information for determining the state of a spacecraft and an optimal course correction maneuver. The proposed methodology has been implemented using the lunar surface as a case study in this work by generating a synthetic dataset using a digital terrain map (DTM) from the Lunar Reconnaissance Orbiter (LRO) data and Blender's ray-tracing renderer, Cycles.

Keywords: convolutional neural network (CNN) · cascading architecture · machine learning (ML) · image processing · artificial dataset

1 Introduction

The next major milestone in human space exploration is establishing a sustainable human presence on the Moon and Mars. A major challenge pertaining to landing on our near-neighbors and other celestial bodies is achieving autonomy. Historically, during the Apollo era, landing rovers on the lunar terrain was designed as a "human in loop" activity. This led to significantly exaggerated errors, with the final landing location missing the target location by a few kilometers. Autonomy for planetary landing has since been studied by researchers

Supported by New York Space Grant.

and Terrain Relative Navigation (TRN) has been identified as a key component. The premise of TRN is to use optical sensors and feature identification and tracking to accurately localize the spacecraft by matching features of the current scene to known images of the planetary terrain. While the lunar surface has been imaged with a sub-meter per pixel resolution, images captured by the Mars Reconnaissance Orbiter (MRO) have a resolution of about one meter per pixel [7]. The future Europa Imaging System (EIS) will "image certain areas of Europa at half a meter per pixel," according to Lynnae Quick of the EIS team [6].

The first instance of using TRN for a "real" space mission was the Mars 2020 rover depositing the Perseverance rover to the martian surface, achieving a high precision landing (about 40m) [8,13]. With the advent of advanced on-board computation capabilities, the boundaries of autonomy are being redefined. Future robotic missions are planned by NASA for Europa, which includes a lander also expected to land with 100 m accuracy on terrain that may be more harsh than any explored to date [16]. In order to replicate the level of precision of the Mars 2020 mission, the approaching spacecraft will need to perform course correction autonomously, as communication with Earth will be limited due to the distance. Furthermore, the localization algorithm and learning models need robustness. This becomes increasingly relevant for unmapped planets and moons due to the availability of sparse data.

The current state of the art image-based TRN usually relies on feature matching techniques. Downes et. al. [5] used a neural network to detect craters in LRO images and match them to a known crater database. Feature-matching computer vision approaches to TRN problems are known to be extremely sensitive to changes in illumination conditions, camera angle, and other slight variations that are likely to occur in a real mission scenario. Mourikis et. al. [12] also used mapped features and a matching algorithm to this end, with similar sensitivity to changes in lighting. Landmarks selection algorithms have been developed which help improve the accuracy of feature-matching based TRN systems, such as the one developed by Steiner et. al. [15]. Christian et. al. [4] used visual odometry to estimate attitude changes without the need for a catalogue of the lunar surface. Their methods also proved to be robust against changes in lighting conditions and terrain roughness. An important development in visual odometry was the framework introduced by McCabe et. al. [11] for measuring error from image data for use in TRN applications. Mancini et. al. [10] proposed a comparative siamese neural network architecture to generate a similarity map for visual odometry. Their system improves upon previous systems by demonstrating robustness against changes in lighting conditions and perturbations to camera conditions, and relies on a convolutional neural network schema similar to the one explored in this paper.

The current research aims to 1) generate accurate, artificial images in Blender from known lunar terrain images by changing the illumination conditions (i.e., sun angle) in order to build the entire dataset 2) split a larger image of an "area of interest" on the lunar terrain (e.g. the lunar south pole craters) into smaller sub-images and segregate into training and testing datasets 3) train a series of CNNs to perform 2D classification to localize a new sub-image in the larger "original image". If the images are assumed to be perfectly nadir pointed, this effort will solve the navigation problem for the spacecraft and help localize the spacecraft states. Performance in the presence of uncertain camera angles and illumination conditions have also been evaluated and demonstrate satisfactory robustness.

1.1 Problem Formulation

Campbell et. al. [9] used part of the Lunar Reconnaissance Orbiter Camera (LROC) digital terrain map (DTM) of the Apollo 16 landing site, taking a strip from the DTM that was 1024 pixels across, and further dividing it into 128×128 pixel images, taking an image every 8 pixels. The CNN was trained to classify the images into 1024 separate classes, one for each pixel in the length of the strip, where the center pixel determines the class. As stated previously, a significant challenge in using deep learning for landing GNC is the scarcity of data. Classification tasks using deep learning techniques require several thousand images per class as the training dataset. Therefore, the authors generated more images artificially, using ray-tracing software (Blender) to generate realistic renders of the selected region for several sun-angles in order to simulate realistic lunar lighting conditions and upscale the training dataset. The CNN was trained on less than 2500 images, which is extremely sparse and may result in poor classification accuracy and robustness. Unsurprisingly, the classification accuracy achieved by their trained model was not up to the standards needed for realistic missions. Additionally, the fact that the classification was one-dimensional means that the results are merely academic and need gross updating to reach the desired technology readiness. This research extends upon their developments, expanding the classification into 2 dimensions, correctly localizing the unknown image in both the x and y directions of the image plane associated with the larger image.

The proposed research ultimately aims to develop a robust and accurate methodology for determining a spacecraft's location relative to the sparsely mapped planetary terrain using a cascading Convolutional Neural Network framework. This method is anticipated to be useful for future missions to Mars, Europa, and other celestial bodies, allowing for safer and more precise spacecraft landings. The expanded dataset and improved neural network architecture will also make the model more robust and reliable in realistic, mission-ready scenarios. The use of realistic images, even for the synthetic dataset means the research will adhere to the technological readiness plan and expand the applicability of TRN based on trained CNNs in future missions.

2 Methodology

Due to the aforementioned data scarcity, it is imperative to append "realistic" synthetic data to the available data and pre-train the neural networks, which can then be uploaded to a spacecraft with the aim of performing GNC tasks. For the sake of tractability, it is assumed that the spacecraft will be equipped with

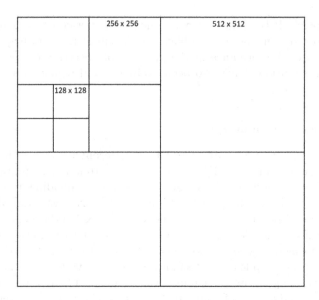

Fig. 1. Visualization of the quadrant division cascading structure.

a camera which takes images of a consistent resolution. These images can then be scaled down to the specific meter-per-pixel resolution needed for the network. A scenario is envisioned where a descending spacecraft captures an image, uses the first overall neural network to determine which quadrant contains the area of interest. The onboard guidance system uses the navigation input to maneuver the spacecraft to the center of the selected quadrant, before the next navigation input is sought. The next image will need to be reduced in resolution to match the resolution of the training data, approximately half the resolution of the first network. This approach has been schematically represented in Fig. 1; where the original 1024×1024 image is segmented into quadrants of 512×512 images and the same architecture is carried forward until the quadrant resolution reaches 128×128.

2.1   Artificial Dataset Generation

The LROC DTM [1] and a ray-tracing software (Blender [3]) are used to create a height map, simulating the terrain of the moon as it appears in the images. The DTM is a geoTIFF file, from which a 6000×6000 pixel subimage, shown in Fig. 3, is taken as the region of interest. Using Blender, this 6000×6000 image is imported applied to a plane as a texture with a displacement modifier, as shown in Fig. 2. Blender is used to render images of this area that are 1024×1024 pixels, with the sun rotated to different angles to simulate possible angles of the sun hitting the moon over the course of one revolution about the moon's axis. Table 1 provides the parameters used to render the synthetic images in the Blender environment.

Table 1. Synthetic Image Generation Parameters (Blender)

Displacement	
Lowest real-world elevation	$-168\,\mathrm{m}$
Highest real-world elevation	$771\,\mathrm{m}$
Strength parameter (displacement modifier)	0.178913738
DTM resolution	$2\,\mathrm{m/px}$
Lighting Conditions	
Sun angle	$0.5314604081°$
Sun 'Strength'	1.37
Sun rotation X [max, min]	$[3.08535, -3.13255]\,\mathrm{rad}$
Sun rotation Y [max, min]	$[1.29956, -1.29950]\,\mathrm{rad}$
Sun rotation Z [max, min]	$[1.29957, -1.29957]\,\mathrm{rad}$
Camera Parameters	
Focal Length	$50\,\mathrm{mm}$
Z Location (elevation)	$250\,\mathrm{m}$

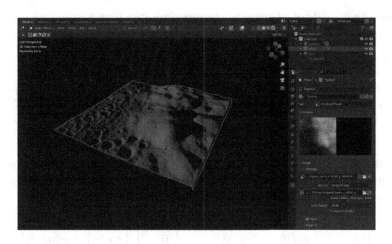

Fig. 2. The DTM in the blender environment.

Sun Angles. To determine realistic sun angles, the latitude and longitude of the selected patch of the lunar surface are required. The selected area is between $\phi \in [15.14,\ 15.94]°$(latitude), and $\theta \in [-9.65, -8.61]°$(longitude) [1]. Taking ϕ_c to be the center latitude (in radians):

$$\phi_c = \frac{(15.94 + 15.14)}{2} \cdot \frac{\pi}{180} \tag{1}$$

Taking θ_c to be the center longitude of the selected patch of the lunar surface:

$$\theta_c = \frac{(9.65 + 8.61)}{2} \cdot \frac{\pi}{180} \tag{2}$$

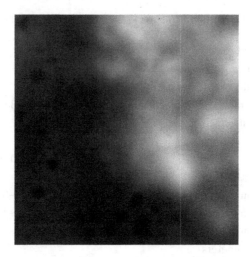

Fig. 3. The selected 6000 × 6000 pixel patch of the LRO DTM.

The longitude angle, θ, changes as the moon rotates. Considering one revolution of the moon around its axis, the range of possible longitude angles is:

$$\theta \in [0, 2\pi] - \theta_c \tag{3}$$

Let α represent the angle the moon's equator makes with the ecliptic plane in radians. The moon has an obliquity of 6.68°, and an inclination of 5.15°. This results in an alpha of:

$$\alpha = (6.688 - 5.15) \cdot \frac{\pi}{180} \tag{4}$$

Resulting in $\alpha = 1.538°$, as shown in Fig. 4. The following rotation matrix is computed to find the possible Euler Angle sequence that characterize of the sun's rays hitting the selected patch of the moon's surface:

$$R = \begin{bmatrix} sin(\phi)\cos(\theta) & sin(\phi)sin(\theta) & -cos(\phi) \\ -sin(\theta) & cos(\theta) & 0 \\ cos(\phi)cos(\theta) & cos(\phi)sin(\theta) & sin(\phi) \end{bmatrix} \begin{bmatrix} cos(\alpha) & -sin(\alpha) & 0 \\ sin(\alpha) & cos(\alpha) & 0 \\ 0 & 0 & 1 \end{bmatrix} \tag{5}$$

Afterwards, angle sequences where the illumination conditions are too dark are removed from the dataset, leaving angles between approximately $-\frac{\pi}{2}$ and $\frac{\pi}{2}$. Eventually, the final dataset comprises 193 possible Euler Angle sets to position the sun relative to the lunar terrain. Figure 5 shows an example of the same 128 × 128 pixel region under different lighting conditions characterized by the Euler Angle sequence.

2.2   Image Splitting

Once all of the 1024 × 1024 images are generated, they were segmented into sub-images of different sizes at each level. As the quadrants/classification areas

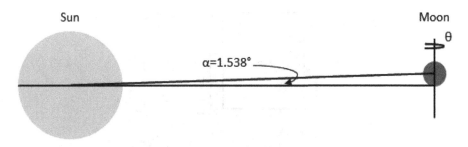

Fig. 4. Diagram of the sun and moon

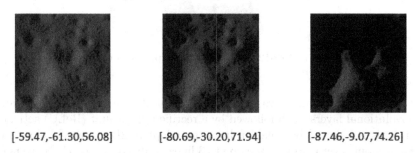

| [-59.47,-61.30,56.08] | [-80.69,-30.20,71.94] | [-87.46,-9.07,74.26] |

Fig. 5. Effect of sun illumination on synthetic images (Sun Euler Angles given, in degrees).

shrink in size, the dataset becomes more refined by decreasing the amount of shift between images in the dataset. Three datasets were crafted from the 1024×1024 pixel images. The first was created by segmenting the images into 512×512 images, each shifted 64 pixels from the last location, as illustrated in Fig. 6. The second set comprises 256×256 images shifted by 32 pixels, and the last is 128×128 images every 16 pixels. Once all images are segmented, any images that have an average pixel value less than 3 are removed, as they are too dark to provide discernible features. This results in unequal dataset sizes for the different CNNs. The number of images in each dataset is given in Table 3.

2.3 Cascading Architecture

To expand the classification in 2 dimensions, a cascading CNN architecture was developed. Using center pixels as labels would result in 1048576 possible categories for a 1024×1024 image plane, resulting in immense computational overhead. To address this, a novel CNN architecture is implemented which categorizes the images into quadrants of the original image, then quadrants of the selected quadrant and so on. For this paper, images were categorized down to a range of 128×128 pixels rather than down to the specific center pixel as a proof of concept, as described by Fig. 1.

The cascading architecture requires models to be trained at each level; thereby resulting in 21 CNNs trained overall. CNNs follow the same architecture

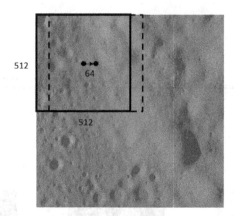

Fig. 6. 512 × 512 image shifting 64 pixels to the right

and the hyperparameters have been listed in Table 2. The images are fed through 3 convolutional layers, each followed by a rectified linear unit (ReLU) activation layer. This is followed by a flatten layer, an adaptive 2D average pooling layer, and a dropout layer before passing on to 3 linear fully connected (FC) layers (see Fig. 7). The first two FC layers use ReLU, and the final FC layer uses a softmax classifier to sort the images into their final categories.

Table 2. CNN hyperparameters

Parameter	Value
batch size	128
epochs	100
learning rate	0.001
momentum	0.9
dropout	0.7
stride (conv. layers)	3
optimizer	Stochastic Gradient Descent (SGD)
loss	Negative Log Likelihood (NLL)

Figure 8 shows example images at each level, as an example of the flow of categorization. The 128 × 128 pixel image on the right represents an example target region. The series of CNNs would classify the target region within the largest subimage, and if correct, continue classifying down to the 128 × 128 pixel region. Labels are assigned to the quadrants according to convention, with quadrant one on the top right, and the rest following counter-clockwise. Therefore, in Fig. 8, the correct labels for each image would be 3, 3, 4 from left to right.

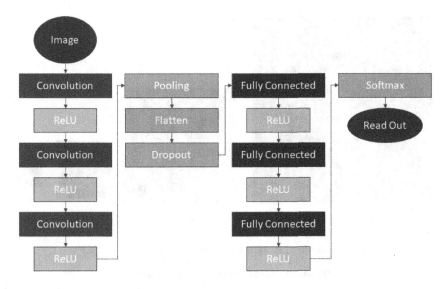

Fig. 7. CNN architecture.

3   Results

The accuracy of the CNNs are shown in Table 3. The test set used to get the accuracies in column 5 is 25% of the generated training data. The validation set in column 6 is composed of images generated in blender with the blender "camera" held at different angles. The camera was rotated about the x and y axes, at a random combination of 0, $+/-$ 2.5, or $+/-$ 5°, excluding the possibility of 0 and 0 together. The illumination conditions of the "camera angles" set were randomly selected sun angles available in the training set. The validation set in column 7 is composed partially of images with illumination conditions outside the training set. Twelve sets of extra sun angles were selected, the overall images segmented, and the generated images are integrated into a set of randomly selected images from the training set to maintain a consistent test set size. These additional illumination conditions are unrealistic for the Sun-Moon system, and are used here only to test the robustness of the CNNs. The images integrated from the training dataset are randomly selected 10 times, and the accuracies recorded in Table 3 are averaged over the 10 random draws of data to perform an unbiased testing of the model. The CNNs in Table 3 have an average test accuracy of 99.30%. This is reduced to 79.02% when tested on the camera rotated set, and 80.49% on the set with extraneous sun angles. The probability of success of the overall system can be calculated using the formula for the probability of all three independent classification events occurring:

$$P_{Success} = P(A) \cdot P(B) \cdot P(C) \tag{6}$$

Where A, B , and C represent the probability of correct classification (accuracy) of the CNNs at the three different levels. This calculation is performed on

Fig. 8. Example of images that were categorized at each level

Table 3. Table of CNN accuracy results

Image size	Label 1	Label 2	Dataset Size	Test Accuracy	Validation Accuracy (Camera angles)	Validation Accuracy (Sun angles)
512 × 512	None	None	15552	99.33	98.10	87.17
256 × 256	1	None	32448	99.19	92.69	87.44
256 × 256	2	None	29952	96.27	74.86	72.27
256 × 256	3	None	27648	98.64	82.22	79.71
256 × 256	4	None	29952	99.87	88.17	90.11
128 × 128	1	1	19676	99.51	83.24	77.71
128 × 128	1	2	24008	99.68	78.16	82.31
128 × 128	1	3	30464	99.49	73.10	80.23
128 × 128	1	4	21390	99.84	76.79	74.64
128 × 128	2	1	22469	99.66	68.95	81.82
128 × 128	2	2	17318	97.97	68.11	79.42
128 × 128	2	3	22277	99.89	72.74	81.60
128 × 128	2	4	29669	99.50	68.60	81.14
128 × 128	3	1	29266	99.11	82.69	79.40
128 × 128	3	2	20636	99.77	82.75	77.78
128 × 128	3	3	15110	99.89	78.97	79.79
128 × 128	3	4	22505	99.45	87.91	81.05
128 × 128	4	1	23637	99.51	75.29	78.02
128 × 128	4	2	30330	99.79	77.54	78.93
128 × 128	4	3	22164	99.95	75.95	80.64
128 × 128	4	4	16735	99.04	72.62	79.20

each of the three test sets, and the results are recorded in Table 4. The average probability of mission success is 97.35% using the test set similar to the training data. The probability of mission success is lowered to 69.53% when the camera is not perfectly nadir-pointed, and 60.68% when unseen illumination conditions are introduced.

Table 4. Probability of Mission Success

Label 1	Label 2	Probability of Success	Probability of Success (Camera angles)	Probability of Success (Sun angles)
1	1	98.04	75.69	59.22
1	2	98.21	71.07	62.73
1	3	98.02	66.47	61.15
1	4	98.37	69.82	56.89
2	1	95.30	62.70	62.36
2	2	93.68	61.93	60.53
2	3	95.52	66.14	62.19
2	4	95.15	62.38	61.85
3	1	97.11	75.19	60.52
3	2	97.75	75.24	58.29
3	3	97.87	71.81	60.82
3	4	97.44	79.94	61.78
4	1	98.71	68.46	59.47
4	2	98.99	70.51	60.16
4	3	99.15	69.06	61.47
4	4	98.25	66.03	60.37

4   Conclusions

Our cascading deep learning architecture shows promising results for TRN applications, with high accuracy at each level of classification, as well as a very high probability of success of the overall framework under ideal conditions. The main contribution of this paper is introducing a novel framework to classify images in two dimensions for the purpose of TRN using synthetic images. The results also illustrate the robustness of the architecture in the presence of near-nadir pointing scenarios and unseen illumination conditions.

Acknowledgements. Thanks to the New York Space Grant for funding this research.

References

1. Apollo 16 landing site DTM - digital terrain model (32-bit geotiff). https://wms.lroc.asu.edu/lroc/view_rdr_product/NAC_DTM_APOLLO16
2. Eric Berger - 17 Nov 2015 2:00 pm UTC: Attempt no landing there? yeah right-were going to Europa. https://arstechnica.com/science/2015/11/attempt-no-landing-there-yeah-right-were-going-to-europa/
3. Blender Homepage. https://www.blender.org/

4. Christian, J.A., et al.: Image-based lunar terrain relative navigation without a map: measurements. **58**(1), 164–181 (2021). https://doi.org/10.2514/1.A34875

5. Downes, L.M., et al.: Lunar terrain relative navigation using a convolutional neural network for visual crater detection. In: 2020 American Control Conference (ACC), pp. 4448–4453. IEEE (2020)

6. EIS. https://europa.nasa.gov/spacecraft/instruments/eis/

7. High Resolution Imaging Science Experiment, HiRISE. https://hirise.lpl.arizona.edu/

8. Johnson, A.E., et al.: Real-time terrain relative navigation test results from a relevant environment for Mars Landing. In: AIAA Guidance, Navigation, and Control Conference, p. 0851 (2015)

9. Campbell, T. et al.: A deep learning approach for optical autonomous planetary relative terrain navigation. In: 27th AAS/AIAA Spaceflight Mechanics Meeting, pp. 3293–3302 (2017)

10. Mancini, P., et al.: Deep learning for asteroids autonomous terrain relative navigation. Adv. Space Res. **71**(9), 3748–3760 (2023). https://doi.org/10.1016/j.asr.2022.04.020

11. McCabe, J.S., DeMars, K.J.: Anonymous feature-based terrain relative navigation. J. Guid. Control. Dyn. **43**(3), 410–421 (2020)

12. Mourikis, A.I., et al.: Vision-aided inertial navigation for spacecraft entry, descent, and landing. IEEE Trans. Rob. **25**(2), 264–280 (2009)

13. NASA: Mars Technologies. https://mars.nasa.gov/mars2020/mission/technology/

14. NASA: PDS Image Atlas. https://pds-imaging.jpl.nasa.gov/search/?fq=-ATLAS_THUMBNAIL_URL%3Abrwsnotavail.jpg&q=%2A%3A%2A

15. Steiner, T.J., et al.: Graph-based terrain relative navigation with optimal landmark database selection. In: 2015 IEEE Aerospace Conference (2015)

16. Tan-Wang, G., Sell, S.: Europa Lander Mission Concept Overview. Astrobiology Science Conference, 26 June 2019, Bellevue WA. https://d2pn8kiwq2w21t.cloudfront.net/documents/02-AbsSciCon-Mission-Overview-13Jun2019-no-BU.pdf

ST: Data Gathering, Curation, and Generation for Computer Vision and Robotics in Precision Agriculture

Synthetically Labeled Images for Maize Plant Detection in UAS Images

Piyush Pandey⬤, Norman B. Best⬤, and Jacob D. Washburn[✉]⬤

United States Department of Agriculture - Agricultural Research Service, Plant Genetics Research Unit, Columbia, MO 65211, USA

jacob.washburn@usda.gov

Abstract. The detection of individual plants within field images is critical for many applications in precision agriculture and research. Computer vision models for object detection, while often highly accurate, require large amounts of labeled data for training, something that is not readily available for most plants. To address the challenge of creating large datasets with accurate labels, we used indoor images of maize plants to create synthetic field images with automatically derived bounding box labels, enabling the generation of thousands of synthetic images without any manual labeling. Training an object detection model (Faster R-CNN) exclusively on synthetic images led to a mean average precision (mAP) value of 0.533 when the model was evaluated on pre-processed real plot images. When fine-tuned with a small number of real plot images, the model pre-trained on the synthetic images (mAP = 0.884) outperformed the model that was not pre-trained.

Keywords: Plant detection · Synthetic data · Computer vision in agriculture

1 Introduction

In the past decade, the use of Unoccupied Aerial Systems (UAS) has become widespread in precision agriculture, plant breeding, and agricultural research studies. Image data acquired using UAS technology have been used to address a variety of agricultural problems including the estimation of plant growth rate [32], detection of disease [25] and pests [31], and prediction of yield [9]. In using UAS image data, the general process starts with the acquisition of a large number of aerial images of a field followed by the creation of an orthomosaic image using one of several available software tools [4,26]. The orthomosaic image is then partitioned into smaller units of interest (such as a single plot), generally by manual delineation of boundaries. Although this process is slow and laborious, it is manageable in cases where the unit of interest is a single plot or a single field. However, using this method for the extraction of features at the level of smaller units such as an individual plant is untenable. If a practical solution were to be available, the ability to extract plant features at the individual level would be

G. Bebis et al. (Eds.): ISVC 2023, LNCS 14361, pp. 543–556, 2023.
https://doi.org/10.1007/978-3-031-47969-4_42

advantageous for several applications including heterozygous population trials or experiments for screening mutants that are segregating in a population that is common in forward genetics studies. Additionally, in research as well as in agricultural operations, the detection of individual plants can facilitate rapid and accurate stand counts and the discrimination of crop species from weeds. The latter is an important step for automated operations in precision agriculture; for example, a robotic weeding or spraying machine relies on the successful identification of weed species at the single plant level.

Supervised machine learning models using Convolutional Neural Networks (CNNs) are the current standard tools for object detection in images [2] and most of the published studies addressing individual plant detection have used these models [8,13,19]. While newer deep learning architectures incorporating Vision Transformers have shown excellent performance in recent years, this performance has been limited to problems where extremely large datasets are available [12]. Before the popularity of deep learning models, a number of techniques based on spectral and spatial features had been devised for detecting individual plants. The general steps in using these non-deep learning models involves the extraction of carefully selected image features followed by the creation of a downstream model using these features [3,5]. CNN models have been found to be generally more accurate compared to this traditional approach, and the extraction of features is implicitly conducted within the CNN model thereby removing the need for expert judgment when creating the subset of features to be used. The superior performance of a CNN model comes with several caveats. The primary requirement for the training of an accurate model is a large amount of labeled data. The performance of the model depends on the quality of the annotated data which should ideally belong to the same distribution as the test data (or the data that the model will encounter when deployed). This can be challenging because labeling thousands of images is a laborious, time-consuming process. We propose to address this problem by creating synthetic, labeled images using indoor images from the greenhouse. Since these images are acquired in controlled indoor environments with a consistent background and lighting, the segmentation of plant pixels is less challenging than it is for field images due to the presence of shadows, weeds, and artifacts on the soil surface. Once the plant pixels are segmented from the background, the location of the plant in the images can be calculated accurately and consistently using traditional computer vision techniques. As a result, these images can be algorithmically transformed into training images for a CNN model to be deployed for detecting plants in outdoor field images.

Indoor images differ from field UAS images in several ways including in resolution and illumination, and if a model is trained directly using the greenhouse images, we cannot expect good accuracy when it is used to detect plants in outdoor images. To address this problem, we can first "transform" the indoor images so that they resemble outdoor images in terms of color and illumination [17]. Even if the transformed images are not identical to the outdoor target images, the model can still be expected to learn useful features (although it will not be an accurate model). The principle of transfer learning informs us that a pre-trained model with tuned parameters performs well with minimal training even if the pre-training was conducted with data from a different distribution [35]. The creation of a model trained on a large dataset of synthetic images can reduce the total amount of labeling effort required in training a new model. We evaluated this hypothesis by using real field images to fine-tune the synthetic data model which is then evaluated on independent real field images.

In this paper, we present a case study of a maize (Corn, *Zea mays* L.) plant detection model trained on synthetic field images. We also evaluate the usefulness of the synthetic data by comparing the accuracy of the synthetic data model fine-tuned with limited real images against the accuracy of a model fine-tuned with the same limited set but not pre-trained with the synthetic images. We used images of maize plants because it is one of the most economically important crops in the world and both the indoor and outdoor images needed were readily available publicly and/or within our research program. We expect that this same framework could be applied to other crops and plants with similar results.

2 Related Work

Several studies using deep learning with plant images have reported the augmentation of training data using synthetic images [1,6,16–18,24,28,33,34]. As identified by Gomes et al. (2020) [28], the generation of synthetic images in these studies can be categorized into one of three approaches: 1. Graphical generation of plant images (often with procedural modeling) 2. "Cut and paste" where a plant image patch is pasted onto different background images 3. Using generative networks. Training image data is often augmented by adding noise to the images and by applying image transformations (such as rotations and cropping); these images are not generally considered synthetic images.

The procedural modeling approach has been successfully used in case of leaf counting with CNNs [24,33]. Since a complete three-dimensional plant structure can be computationally generated, this approach shows great promise for the creation of synthetic image data. The utility of the images depends on the match between the fidelity of the available model and the requirement of the application. As an example of a realistic image generation system, Cieslak et al. [7] have used L-systems [29] to generate synthetic images calibrated using actual greenhouse images of maize and canola *(Brassica napus)* plants.

The "cut and paste" approach is arguably the simplest method of creating synthetic images based on existing images. This approach does require the availability of original images from which the plant patch can be easily extracted, preferably using an algorithmic method. Krosney et. al (2022) [17] used laboratory images taken in a controlled environment with a uniform background to obtain the plant patches that were then placed on background images of the field to create composite images. They additionally used a Generative Adversarial Network (GAN) [11] to create additional image patches based on the indoor images. Using a YOLOv5 nano object detection model [15], they reported a mean average precision (mAP) score of 0.454 for the model trained on the composite images and a mAP score of 0.479 for the model trained on GAN images. The model trained on the merged dataset with synthetic images from both sources had a mAP score of 0.528.

In our study, we used the "cut and paste" approach with indoor images and created synthetic images replicating the distribution of plants in outdoor field rows. We present a novel method for the creation of synthetic field images where plant features are derived from indoor images and plant distribution is derived from actual UAS-acquired field images. Unlike the previous studies above, we also evaluated the accuracy of the model trained on synthetic images when it is fine-tuned with a limited number of actual images. This is a more practical approach to using synthetic images for model training because of the discrepancy between the synthetic and actual images.

3   Methods

3.1   Image Acquisition

Greenhouse Images were obtained from a Cyverse commons dataset [20] that has been previously described by Liang et al. [21]. We refer the reader to this publication for more information on the image acquisition system used in the greenhouse. The published dataset includes hyperspectral, infrared, and fluorescent images along with RGB images acquired from multiple perspectives. For the current study, only the top view RGB images were used. A total of 5,448 top view images were processed to create the synthetic plot images (see Figs. 1 and 2).

Field Images used in this study were collected by the authors in June 2021 in a maize field in Columbia, MO two weeks after planting. The RGB images of dimension 5472×3648 pixels were acquired using the UAS DJI Mavic 2 Pro (SZ DJI Technology Co., Ltd., Shenzhen, China) from an elevation of 20 m ensuring an 85% overlap between images both laterally and in the direction of flight. Opendronemap [26] was used to create the orthomosaic of the field with a resolution of 5 mm per pixel. The 242 plots on the orthomosaic were manually labeled and rectangular image sections were extracted to create single plot images.

3.2   Synthetic Image Creation

Segmentation of Greenhouse Images. The segmentation of plant pixels from the background was the first step in the creation of synthetic plot images. The segmentation of plant pixels was based on thresholding the "greenness value" of each pixel. Here, we use an index calculated at each pixel location as shown in Eq. 1.

$$G_{i,j} = \frac{2 \times I_{i,j,1}}{I_{i,j,0} + I_{i,j,2}} \qquad (1)$$

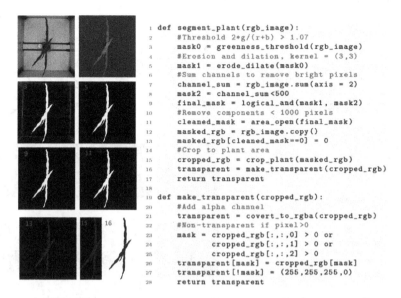

```
 1  def segment_plant(rgb_image):
 2      #Threshold 2*g/(r+b) > 1.07
 3      mask0 = greenness_threshold(rgb_image)
 4      #Erosion and dilation, kernel = (3,3)
 5      mask1 = erode_dilate(mask0)
 6      #Sum channels to remove bright pixels
 7      channel_sum = rgb_image.sum(axis = 2)
 8      mask2 = channel_sum<500
 9      final_mask = logical_and(mask1, mask2)
10      #Remove components < 1000 pixels
11      cleaned_mask = area_open(final_mask)
12      masked_rgb = rgb_image.copy()
13      masked_rgb[cleaned_mask==0] = 0
14      #Crop to plant area
15      cropped_rgb = crop_plant(masked_rgb)
16      transparent = make_transparent(cropped_rgb)
17      return transparent
18
19  def make_transparent(cropped_rgb):
20      #Add alpha channel
21      transparent = covert_to_rgba(cropped_rgb)
22      #Non-transparent if pixel>0
23      mask = cropped_rgb[:,:,0] > 0 or
24             cropped_rgb[:,:,1] > 0 or
25             cropped_rgb[:,:,2] > 0
26      transparent[mask] = cropped_rgb[mask]
27      transparent[!mask] = (255,255,255,0)
28      return transparent
```

Fig. 1. Left: The steps from a greenhouse RGB image to a plant patch with a transparent background. The numbers on the images represent the line number on the pseudocode to the right that produces the image. Right: Pseudo-code for greenhouse image segmentation

Where I is the original RGB (or BGR) image and G is the single-channel greenness index.

This index enhances the green vegetation pixels since the green channel of the original image is doubled and divided by the sum of the red and blue channels. Using an empirically derived threshold value of 1.07, a binary mask for the green vegetation is obtained. Two successive morphological operations, erosion followed by dilation with a kernel size of 3×3, were used to remove small wrongly segmented areas in the binary image. After this step, it was observed that the remaining falsely segmented pixels consisted mostly of white background pixels in the RGB image. Thus, another empirical threshold value of 500 was used with the sum of all three channels in the RGB image to remove the white background pixels. This was followed by morphological area opening with a threshold of 1,000 pixels.

Next, the bounding rectangle circumscribing the segmented plant pixels was calculated and the non-plant pixels were rendered transparent by adding an alpha channel to the RGB image (RGBA). At this point, the plant image was ready for being placed on any random background image. This process is illustrated with images and Python-like pseudocode in Fig. 1.

Creation of Synthetic Plot Images. For the creation of synthetic plot images, the following variables needed to be controlled: 1. Image size 2. Number of plants in the image 3. Location of each plant in the image 4. Size of each

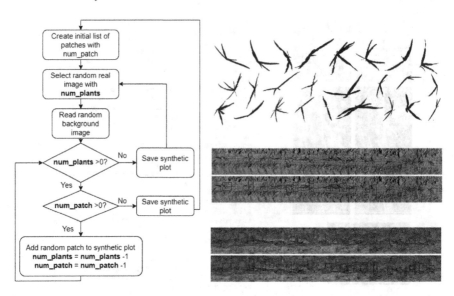

Fig. 2. Left: Flowchart showing one iteration through the plant patches for creating synthetic plot images. Right: Example plant patches with transparent background (top), Real plot image with and without manually labeled bounding boxes for plants (middle), Synthetic plot image with algorithmically derived bounding boxes (bottom).

plant. To create a realistic distribution of plants, these variables were derived from actual plot images (cropped from the orthomosaic image, see Sect. 3.1). The distribution of plants in the synthetic images was based on 242 plot images derived from the orthomosaic image. Five complete iterations with the entire set of 5,448 images were completed to create 2,001 synthetic plots. Figure 2 shows one complete iteration through the images along with example plant patches and the resulting synthetic plots. Although the same plant image was used for five different plot images, the randomness in the selection of background image, the random size and location of the plant within the synthetic image, and the variation introduced by illumination correction ensured that sufficient variation existed among repeated instances of the same plant image.

The size of each synthetic image was fixed at twice the size of the original plot images to obtain higher-resolution images. Similarly, plant locations were fixed based on the bounding boxes drawn on the original plot images (with appropriate scaling). In order to avoid multiple images with the bounding boxes repeated at the same location, random noise was added to both the x and y location of the bounding boxes. This was achieved by adding a randomly selected integer between -10 and $+10$ to each of the location coordinates. Additionally, the dimension of the plant area was increased by 20% for each odd-numbered iteration to ensure variation in the size of plants. In some cases, this increase in size led to the creation of overlapping plants that contributed to the variety of images in the training set.

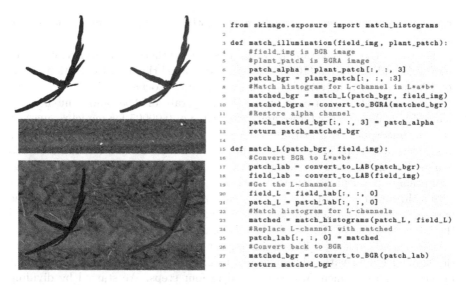

```
 1  from skimage.exposure import match_histograms
 2
 3  def match_illumination(field_img, plant_patch):
 4      #field_img is BGR image
 5      #plant_patch is BGRA image
 6      patch_alpha = plant_patch[:, :, 3]
 7      patch_bgr = plant_patch[:, :, :3]
 8      #Match histogram for L-channel in L*a*b*
 9      matched_bgr = match_L(patch_bgr, field_img)
10      matched_bgra = convert_to_BGRA(matched_bgr)
11      #Restore alpha channel
12      patch_matched_bgr[:, :, 3] = patch_alpha
13      return patch_matched_bgr
14
15  def match_L(patch_bgr, field_img):
16      #Convert BGR to L*a*b*
17      patch_lab = convert_to_LAB(patch_bgr)
18      field_lab = convert_to_LAB(field_img)
19      #Get the L-channels
20      field_L = field_lab[:, :, 0]
21      patch_L = patch_lab[:, :, 0]
22      #Match histogram for L-channels
23      matched = match_histograms(patch_L, field_L)
24      #Replace L-channel with matched
25      patch_lab[:, :, 0] = matched
26      #Convert back to BGR
27      matched_bgr = convert_to_BGR(patch_lab)
28      return matched_bgr
```

Fig. 3. Illumination correction for plant patches based on histogram equalization. Left: An example image of a plant that is matched to the illumination of a field background image. The original image with low illumination and the final image after illumination correction are shown. Right: Python-like pseudocode for illumination correction.

Illumination Correction. Since the indoor plant images were used to create synthetic plot images, a clear difference in illumination could be observed between indoor images and outdoor field images. To ensure better fidelity of our synthetic images in terms of illumination, we processed the plant image patch using histogram matching. The histogram matching operation transforms a given image into a new image such that the histogram of the new image matches a specified histogram [10]. In our case, the matching operation was limited to the perceptual lightness channel (L) of the CIELAB (L*a*b*) image. The plant patch, as well as the field image, were first converted to the L*a*b* color space, and the histogram matching algorithm was then used to transform the L channel of the plant patch to match the histogram of the L channel of the field image. The resulting L*a*b image of the plant patch was converted back to the RGBA color space before being placed onto the background field image to create synthetic plot images. The process used for illumination correction is illustrated with example images and Python-like pseudocode in Fig. 3.

3.3 Object Detection

Training. For our experiment with the synthetic data, we used Faster R-CNN [30], a two-stage object detection model. We used the Pytorch [27] implementation of the model with a Resnet-50 [14] backbone and a Feature Pyramid Network (FPN) [22] to extract features at multiple spatial scales. We used model weights obtained by pre-training on the Microsoft common objects in context (COCO) dataset [23].

For the initial model training, we divided the synthetic plot images into training (90%) and validation (10%) datasets and trained the object detection model for 50 epochs with a training batch size of four. Stochastic Gradient Descent (SGD) optimization was used with a learning rate of 0.05, and a momentum value of 0.9. We also used a weight decay value of 0.00005 for model regularization and incorporated a learning rate decay with a multiplicative factor of 0.7 after every five steps in the training process. This model was evaluated on 188 real plot images in their raw form and after segmenting the plant pixels. The segmentation of plant pixels followed the same process as described in Sect. 3.2 but with a threshold value of 1.04 for the greenness index as this value produced the best segmentation on field images. The masked background pixels were assigned the intensity value of 120 for all three channels creating a gray background.

Next, we conducted a fine-tuning experiment to observe the performance of the trained model with additional fine-tuning on a small number of real plot images. This experiment was conducted in four steps. We started by dividing the real plot images into a fine-tuning set and a test set. The fine-tuning set contained 42 images whereas the test set contained 188 images. We fine-tuned the model first with ten images for 50 epochs followed by 20, 30, and 42 images. Each fine-tuning run was followed by running the model to detect plants on the 188 test images. In all cases described in the results, the test set images were derived from UAS images over an actual maize field (not synthetic images) that had not previously been used for training that model.

Finally, we trained the original model not trained with the synthetic dataset (but pre-trained on the COCO images) on the small number of images in our fine-tuning dataset. The same procedure was used for the fine-tuning with 10, 20, 30, and 42 images used for training and 188 images used for evaluation.

Evaluation Metric. The mAP values were used to evaluate model performance on the test images. This metric is calculated as the area under the precision-recall curve, and thus represents the precision value averaged across a range of recall values corresponding to different confidence thresholds.

Since the object detection model predicts a bounding box (and not a classification label), a threshold intersection over union (IoU) value is selected to classify true and false predictions. In calculating precision and recall values, we used an IoU threshold of 0.5. The mAP values were calculated using the COCO API in Python [23].

4   Results and Discussion

4.1   Model Trained only on Synthetic Images

Table 1 shows the mAP values for evaluation with the test set images. The mAP value for the raw plot images without segmentation is 0.278. When the segmented

Table 1. Test mAP for raw plot images and segmented plot images

Test images	mAP
Raw plot images	0.278
Segmented plot images	0.533

plant images with a gray background are used for evaluation, the mAP value increased to 0.533. The motivation for using segmented images resulted from our observation that the model trained on synthetic images tends to make false positive predictions for non-plant image artifacts including shadows and soil contours. This is a predictable outcome since the synthetic images lack additional features such as shadows. We tried to address this by segmenting out the plant pixels from the background such that all other artifacts are removed. The difference in these two approaches is illustrated in Fig. 4. The mAP value of 0.278 that we obtained for raw images is lower than the value reported by Krosney et al. (2022). However, the mAP value for the segmented images (0.533) is comparable to the best accuracy (0.528) reported by Krosney et al. (2022) when using a mixture of composite and GAN images for training.

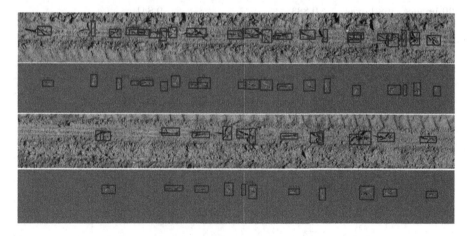

Fig. 4. Two plot images and their corresponding segmented versions with the bounding boxes predicted by the model trained entirely on synthetic images. Segmentation of the plant pixels improves the accuracy of the prediction model by removing shadows and other artifacts.

4.2   Fine-Tuned Model Performance

The mAP values for the evaluation of fine-tuned models are shown in Table 2 and in Fig. 5. The mAP value of 0.278 obtained from the model trained only on synthetic images gradually increased as we fine-tuned this model with additional real images. Training with only ten images (including 98 instances of labeled maize plants) increased the mAP value to 0.805. The mAP values for 20, 30, and 42 images showed an increasing trend, although the gain in prediction accuracy appeared to plateau after 30 images. In the case of the original model not pre-trained with the synthetic data, a similar trend in increasing accuracy of detection was observed starting with 0.565 mAP for training with 10 images. We could see that using the model pre-trained with synthetic data provided an advantage if labeled images are limited (which is almost always the case in our experience with agricultural data). As we increased the number of images used for fine-tuning, the difference in mAP values between the two models showed a decreasing trend. Figure 6 shows an example image with the predicted bounding box from the fine-tuned model.

Table 2. Test mAP(IoU = 0.5) with and without pre-training on synthetic images

Training data	Pre-trained	Not pre-trained
Synthetic only	0.278	–
10 images, 98 boxes	0.805	0.565
20 images, 243 boxes	0.870	0.754
30 images, 398 boxes	0.883	0.841
42 images, 563 boxes	0.884	0.834

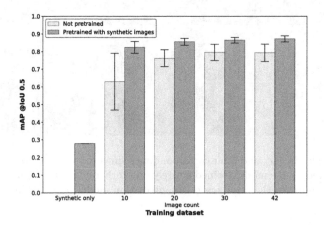

Fig. 5. Test mAP(IoU = 0.5) values with and without fine-tuning the model with real images. Error bars show 95% confidence interval obtained by bootstrapping.

As mentioned in Sect. 2, the model trained on synthetic images is not presented as a tool to be directly implemented for plant detection. The value of the

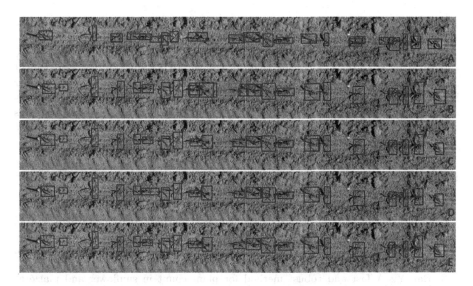

Fig. 6. Bounding box predictions on a sample image showing the performance of the fine-tuned model. The top image (A) shows the predictions of the model trained solely on synthetic images. Images B, C, D, and E show the bounding box predictions from the model fine-tuned with 10, 20, 30, and 42 images respectively.

synthetic images is in creating a baseline model with tuned features that can be quickly fine-tuned with a limited number of images from the required application. We demonstrated the usefulness of this purpose and showed that the accuracy of an object detection model can be quickly increased with a limited number of training examples if the model was pre-trained with a large number of synthetic images. In the future, training a model (or an ensemble of models) on a much larger set of synthetic images will be an important step towards creating an initial model that can be used by researchers and practitioners as a starting point to save the time and resources required for acquisition and labeling of image data.

5   Conclusion

In this article, we presented a case study in using synthetic field images created from indoor images for training an object detection model. The object detection model trained entirely on automatically labeled synthetic images led to an mAP of 0.533 when tested on segmented images of real plot images. When fine-tuned with a limited number of real plot images, the mAP value increased up to a value of 0.884. After fine-tuning with a small number of images, the performance of the model pre-trained on synthetic images was superior to that of the model not pre-trained on synthetic images.

Acknowledgements. This research was supported in part by an appointment to the Agricultural Research Service (ARS) Research Participation Program administered by the Oak Ridge Institute for Science and Education (ORISE) through an interagency agreement between the U.S. Department of Energy (DOE) and the U.S. Department of Agriculture (USDA). ORISE is managed by ORAU under DOE contract number DE-SC0014664. Funding was provided by the United States Department of Agriculture, Agricultural Research Service, SCINet Postdoctoral Fellows Program. All opinions expressed in this publication are the author's and do not necessarily reflect the policies and views of USDA, DOE, or ORAU/ORISE.

References

1. Abbas, A., Jain, S., Gour, M., Vankudothu, S.: Tomato plant disease detection using transfer learning with C-GAN synthetic images. Comput. Electron. Agric. **187**, 106279 (2021)
2. Amit, Y., Felzenszwalb, P., Girshick, R.: Object detection. In: Computer Vision: A Reference Guide, pp. 1–9 (2020)
3. Bai, Y.: A fast and robust method for plant count in sunflower and maize at different seedling stages using high-resolution UAV RGB imagery. Precision Agric. (2022). https://doi.org/10.1007/s11119-022-09907-1, mAG ID: 4281983142
4. Brach, M., Chan, J.W., Szymanski, P.: Accuracy assessment of different photogrammetric software for processing data from low-cost UAV platforms in forest conditions. iForest-Biogeosciences For. **12**(5), 435 (2019)
5. Calvario, G., Alarcón, T.E., Dalmau, O., Sierra, B., Hernandez, C.: An agave counting methodology based on mathematical morphology and images acquired through unmanned aerial vehicles. Sensors **20**(21), 6247 (2020)
6. Chen, J., Wang, W., Zhang, D., Zeb, A., Nanehkaran, Y.A.: Attention embedded lightweight network for maize disease recognition. Plant. Pathol. **70**(3), 630–642 (2021)
7. Cieslak, M., et al.: L-system models for image-based phenomics: case studies of maize and canola. Silico Plants **4**(1), diab039 (2022). https://doi.org/10.1093/insilicoplants/diab039
8. David, E., et al.: Plant detection and counting from high-resolution RGB images acquired from UAVs: comparison between deep-learning and handcrafted methods with application to maize, sugar beet, and sunflower (2022). https://doi.org/10.1101/2021.04.27.441631
9. Gilliot, J.M., Michelin, J., Hadjard, D., Houot, S.: An accurate method for predicting spatial variability of maize yield from UAV-based plant height estimation: A tool for monitoring agronomic field experiments. Precision Agric. **22**(3), 897–921 (2021)
10. Gonzalez, R.C., Woods, R.E.: Digital Image Processing, Prentice Hall. Upper Saddle River, NJ (2008)
11. Goodfellow, I., et al.: Generative adversarial nets. In: Advances in Neural Information Processing Systems, vol. 27 (2014)
12. Han, K., et al.: A survey on vision transformer. IEEE Trans. Pattern Anal. Mach. Intell. **45**(1), 87–110 (2022)
13. Pathak, H., Igathinathane, C., Zhang, Z., Archer, D., Hendrickson, J.: A review of unmanned aerial vehicle-based methods for plant stand count evaluation in row crops. Comput. Electron. Agric. **198**, 107064–107064 (2022). https://doi.org/10.1016/j.compag.2022.107064, mAG ID: 4281551313

14. He, K., Zhang, X., Ren, S., Sun, J.: Deep residual learning for image recognition. In: Proceedings of the IEEE Conference on Computer Vision and Pattern Recognition, pp. 770–778 (2016)
15. Jocher, G., et al.: ultralytics/yolov5: v6. 1-tensorrt, tensorflow edge TPU and openvino export and inference. Zenodo (2022)
16. Klein, J., Waller, R.E., Pirk, S., Palubicki, W., Tester, M., Michels, D.: Synthetic Data at Scale: A Paradigm to Efficiently Leverage Machine Learning in Agriculture (2023)
17. Krosney, A.E., Sotoodeh, P., Henry, C.J., Beck, M.A., Bidinosti, C.P.: Inside out: transforming images of lab-grown plants for machine learning applications in agriculture (2022). http://arxiv.org/abs/2211.02972, arXiv:2211.02972 [cs]
18. Kuznichov, D., Zvirin, A., Honen, Y., Kimmel, R.: Data augmentation for leaf segmentation and counting tasks in rosette plants (2019)
19. Li, H., Wang, P., Huang, C.: Comparison of deep learning methods for detecting and counting sorghum heads in UAV imagery. Remote Sens. **14**(13), 3143–3143 (2022). https://doi.org/10.3390/rs14133143, mAG ID: 4283765418
20. Liang, Z., Schnable, J.: Maize diversity phenotype map. CyVerse Data Commons (2017)
21. Liang, Z., et al.: Conventional and hyperspectral time-series imaging of maize lines widely used in field trials. Gigascience **7**(2), gix117 (2018)
22. Lin, T.Y., Dollár, P., Girshick, R., He, K., Hariharan, B., Belongie, S.: Feature pyramid networks for object detection. In: Proceedings of the IEEE Conference on Computer Vision and Pattern Recognition, pp. 2117–2125 (2017)
23. Lin, T.-Y., et al.: Microsoft COCO: common objects in context. In: Fleet, D., Pajdla, T., Schiele, B., Tuytelaars, T. (eds.) ECCV 2014. LNCS, vol. 8693, pp. 740–755. Springer, Cham (2014). https://doi.org/10.1007/978-3-319-10602-1_48
24. Miao, C., et al.: Simulated plant images improve maize leaf counting accuracy. BioRxiv, 706994 (2019)
25. de Oliveira Dias, F., Magalhães Valente, D.S., Oliveira, C.T., Dariva, F.D., Copati, M.G.F., Nick, C.: Remote sensing and machine learning techniques for high throughput phenotyping of late blight-resistant tomato plants in open field trials. Int. J. Remote Sens. **44**(6), 1900–1921 (2023)
26. OpenDroneMap Authors: ODM - a command line toolkit to generate maps, point clouds, 3D models and DEMs from drone, balloon or kite images (2020). https://github.com/OpenDroneMap/ODM
27. Paszke, A., et al.: Pytorch: an imperative style, high-performance deep learning library. In: Advances in Neural Information Processing Systems, vol. 32 (2019)
28. Gomes, D.P.S., Zheng, L.: Recent data augmentation strategies for deep learning in plant phenotyping and their significance. In: 2020 Digital Image Computing: Techniques and Applications (DICTA), pp. 1–8 (2020). https://doi.org/10.1109/DICTA51227.2020.9363383
29. Prusinkiewicz, P., Cieslak, M., Ferraro, P., Hanan, J.: Modeling plant development with L-systems. In: Morris, R.J. (ed.) Mathematical Modelling in Plant Biology, pp. 139–169. Springer, Cham (2018). https://doi.org/10.1007/978-3-319-99070-5_8
30. Ren, S., He, K., Girshick, R., Sun, J.: Faster R-CNN: towards real-time object detection with region proposal networks. In: Advances in Neural Information Processing Systems, vol. 28 (2015)
31. Tetila, E.C., et al.: Detection and classification of soybean pests using deep learning with UAV images. Comput. Electron. Agric. **179**, 105836 (2020)

32. Tirado, S.B., Hirsch, C.N., Springer, N.M.: UAV-based imaging platform for monitoring maize growth throughout development. Plant Direct **4**(6), e00230 (2020)

33. Ubbens, J., Cieslak, M., Prusinkiewicz, P., Stavness, I.: The use of plant models in deep learning: an application to leaf counting in rosette plants. Plant Meth. **14**, 1–10 (2018)

34. Velumani, K., et al.: Estimates of maize plant density from UAV RGB Images using faster-RCNN detection model: impact of the spatial resolution. Plant Phenomics 2021, 2021/9824843 (2021). https://doi.org/10.34133/2021/9824843

35. Weiss, K., Khoshgoftaar, T.M., Wang, D.: A survey of transfer learning. J. Big Data **3**(1), 1–40 (2016)

An Open Source Simulation Toolbox for Annotation of Images and Point Clouds in Agricultural Scenarios

Dario Guevara[1(✉)], Amogh Joshi[2], Pranav Raja[2], Elisabeth Forrestel[1], Brian Bailey[3], and Mason Earles[1,2]

[1] Department of Viticulture and Enology, University of California, Davis, USA
dguevara@ucdavis.edu
[2] Department of Biological and Agricultural Engineering, University of California, Davis, USA
[3] Department of Plant Sciences, University of California, Davis, USA

Abstract. In recent years, the utilization of RGB cameras and LiDAR sensors in agricultural settings has surged, leading to an expanded application of machine learning techniques. Nonetheless, many machine learning challenges in agriculture are hampered by the laborious and cost-intensive process of data labeling, a task made particularly complex by the variability of crops and the sparse nature of point cloud information derived from LiDAR data. Moreover, training datasets are typically site-specific, encompassing factors such as light conditions and time of day, and often capture only a single point in a crop growing season. This specificity complicates the development of models that can generalize across different crop types, cultivars, management practices, seasons, and other variables. To address these issues, this article presents an open-source simulation toolbox designed for the easy generation of synthetic labeled data for both RGB imagery and point cloud information, applicable to a wide array of cultivars. We demonstrate how this toolbox can generate a variety of datasets with custom annotations and conditions, and we provide a straightforward pipeline for integrating this data with numerous machine learning models, specifically for this manuscript we applied an image object detection and a semantic segmentation point cloud model. This approach paves the way for a broad range of potential applications in the field of agriculture.

Keywords: Simulation · sensors · annotations · images · point cloud

1 Introduction

The agricultural sector is swiftly responding to escalating food demand, a trend fueled by climate change, global conflicts, and pandemics. Current technological advances provide us with a wealth of diverse data types - including RGB, multispectral, thermal, and point clouds - available at varying spatial-temporal

© The Author(s), under exclusive license to Springer Nature Switzerland AG 2023
G. Bebis et al. (Eds.): ISVC 2023, LNCS 14361, pp. 557–570, 2023.
https://doi.org/10.1007/978-3-031-47969-4_43

resolutions, such as satellite, aerial, and terrestrial. However, the task of managing this vast data volume is far from straightforward, and becomes even more complex when accounting for the variety of crops and applications, including aspects like water potential, nitrogen supply, disease detection, stress assessment, and yield prediction. Within this challenging landscape, machine learning has emerged as a crucial tool, assisting farmers in effectively managing this data deluge and generating valuable insights at various stages of the crop season.

A primary hurdle for the practical application of machine learning is the time-intensive nature of data annotation, which often impedes the rapid deployment of more accurate models. While labels for some applications can be crowdsourced effectively [13], this approach falls short when expert knowledge is required for annotation, necessitating the involvement of specialists [5]. Despite the availability of tools designed to streamline the process, such as CVAT[1] and Label-box[2], the annotation process remains labor-intensive and often results in small datasets. Various strategies are being investigated to facilitate the creation of larger, more reliable datasets [10,16]. For instance, [8] propose a robotic system that can autonomously generate and label extensive datasets of plant images. However, despite its potential for creating reliable datasets, the system utility is constrained by its setup and data processing requirements, limiting its applicability across a broad range of specialty crops and applications.

Regarding point cloud information, there are some tools that can facilitate the process of annotating 3D point clouds[3,4], but they are less common than the image annotation tools. Unfortunately, even with such tools, identifying the different parts of the plants within such an amount of data is not trivial due to the variability of the crops and the sparse nature of the point cloud information. As a consequence, datasets are usually small and plant specific [4,11]. For example, in [4], the authors label manually the fruits of eleven Fuji apple trees in a 3D point cloud reconstruction. To accelerate this process, for example, in [11] it was presented Label3DMaize an annotation toolkit for maize shoots used to achieve semi-automatic point cloud segmentation and annotation at different growth stages. This tool, however, is still designed for specific usage and can not be extended to other crops or conditions.

To overcome the above-mentioned challenges, domain adaptation is gaining traction in the machine learning community, as it could potentially yield a large number of labeled images through simulations. However, in the agricultural context, there is a lack of tools that allow to obtain a simulated environment with object labels in specialty crops [7]. Thus, specialized and sophisticated tools are needed to obtain fast and accurate annotations in RGB imagery and point clouds in agriculture environments. The latter is the main issue this work faces: a synthetic data module for generating imagery and point cloud data in diverse

---

[1] https://cvat.org/.

[2] https://labelbox.com/.

[3] https://segments.ai/point-cloud-labeling.

[4] https://github.com/supervisely-ecosystem/pointcloud-labeling-tool.

scenarios, complete with annotations, to enhance machine learning applications in agriculture environments.

2   Related Work

As previously mentioned, the simulation of imagery and point cloud data is a viable candidate for solving the labeling issue. This have been widely explored in trees for forestry applications [6,18]. For imagery, for example, the authors in [6] used a simulated forest environment to automatically generate pixel-level annotations on thousands of synthetic images, and then use them to train deep learning algorithms for tree detection. With respect to point clouds, [18] presents SimTreeLS (Simulated Tree Laser Scans), an open-source simulator for generating a simulated scanning of trees with user-defined parameters. SimTreeLS is a great option for label trunks, branches, and leaves in synthetic forests. A more in detail simulator is the one presented in [2], where the users can create their plant, and label all the elements on it. This, however, still requires a certain level of detail provided by the user for generating a new plant each time and it is only focus on point cloud generation. Other types of simulators are plant-specific. For example, in [15], the authors use a synthetic dataset of roses to train, validate and test the performance of semantic segmentation algorithms in rosebush 3D point cloud data.

In this work, we present a toolbox for an easy generation of synthetic label imagery and point cloud data that can be used with a great variety of specialty crops. To the best of our knowledge, a simulation toolbox that can generate synthetic custom-label RGB images and point clouds in specialty crops has not been presented yet. The contributions of this paper are: (i) a pipeline for generation and custom labeling of RGB synthetic imagery in a variety of specialty crops, and (ii) a pipeline for generation and point-level labeling of synthetic point clouds in a variety of specialty crops.

3   Methodology

The simulation toolbox presented in this manuscript has been included as part of Helios plugins[5] and the AgML[6] project. The AgML project is a python-based open-source comprehensive library for agricultural machine learning, it contains a great number of public datasets for common agricultural tasks, and agriculture-specific machine learning functionality related to data, training, and evaluation [9]. To facilitate the adoption of our described methods, this paper presents the procedures of synthetic label data generation within the pipeline of AgML.

---

[5] https://baileylab.ucdavis.edu/software/helios/_plug_ins.html.
[6] https://github.com/Project-AgML/AgML.

3.1   Simulation Environment

As previously mentioned, the annotation toolbox has been included as part of Helios [1] plugins. Helios serves as the core of the simulation environment for AgML. Helios, a three-dimensional plant and environmental modeling framework, operates through a C++ application programming interface (API). It includes several plugins and functionalities such as *lidar, canopy generator*, and *synthetic annotation*. The API offers multiple functions for reading and writing to standard file formats, specifically XML, PLY, and OBJ formats. XML files, based on a convention specific to Helios, are employed to read and write simulation data. The usage of these files is elaborated upon in the Helios documentation (refer to Helios documentation[7] for more details). Importantly, the XML files facilitate interaction between Helios and all its plugins (e.g., canopy generator, synthetic data, lidar), as well as the AgML pipeline. While Helios can simulate various types of sensors, this manuscript will focus solely on two: the RGB camera and the LiDAR sensor.

The *canopy generator* in the simulation environment is designed to create 3D models of various types of crops, as shown in Fig. 1. The current range of available crops includes four types of vines (i.e., goblet, unilateral, split, and VSP), sourghum, walnut, strawberry, and tomatoes. By modifying geometric parameters specified in the XML file, users can create customized crops. The Helios framework generates semi-random tree geometries using the procedural tree generation algorithm [17]. In this context, Helios assigns a unique universal identifier (UUID) to each element of the canopies. This UUID can then be referenced and utilized to label the element, applicable to both the LiDAR sensor and the RGB camera.

Fig. 1. All the crops available in Helios software (up to this date). Four different type of vines are available, namely, (a) unilateral, (b) goblet, (c) split, and (d) VSP. In addition, Helios has available (e) sorghum, (f) walnut, (g) strawberry, and (h) tomato.

For RGB imagery, Helios employs OpenGL [1], which enables users to generate RGB images from any perspective within the scene (e.g., terrestrial, aerial).

---

[7] https://baileylab.ucdavis.edu/software/helios/.

From these images, three types of annotations can be created for any element (i.e., leaves, trunk, branches, fruits): (i) object detection, (ii) semantic segmentation, and (iii) instance segmentation. The procedure for generating these annotations is included in the *synthetic annotation* plugin in Helios.

Additionally, the *LiDAR* plugin operates a set of algorithms concurrently on the GPU, thereby enabling the generation of point clouds that can be directly integrated into the Helios context [1]. Depending on the specified parameters, the generated point cloud can be either *discrete* or *full-waveform*. Moreover, each LiDAR scan can encompass a point-level label based on the annotated UUID.

3.2 AgML: Synthetic Data Generation

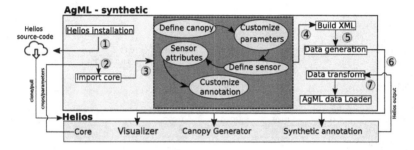

Fig. 2. Pipeline of the simulation toolbox. From AgML the user can specify several input parameters that will compile the Helios simulation using the lidar, canopy generator, and synthetic annotation plugins. As a result, AgML can provide an output of the synthetic data, annotations, and also the ability to visualize the data.

Figure 2 showcases the structured flow of the simulation toolbox, wherein Helios [1] operates as the central component of the simulation environment. The *synthetic* module takes on the task of synthetic data generation and establishes communication with the Helios API to accomplish this task. The operational steps of the *synthetic* module are as follows: (1) The presence of Helios is initially checked by the module. If Helios is not found to be installed, the system proceeds to download it. If it is already installed, the system ensures it is updated to its latest version. (2)The core of Helios and its corresponding dependencies are then installed. (3) Subsequently, customization of the environment, sensors, and annotations is carried out. (4) Post customization, an XML file is crafted. (5) With the XML file in place, the system moves to the data generation phase. (6) Following data generation, the newly created data is subjected to transformation. (7) Finally, the AgML data loader is engaged to manage the produced data. Once all data is inside AgML, it can be used within all available models.

Crop Parameters. The *synthetic* module is designed to offer the user flexibility by enabling access to and modification of all parameters associated with each crop type. These parameters, while variable depending on the crop, generally include factors like the number of plants, the spacing between plants, and the spacing between rows. These parameters and their default values are comprehensively detailed in Table 1. It is important to note that not all parameters are applicable to every crop type, and default values can differ between crops. Further customization is allowed through the ability to modify the texture file of any crop element, including leaves, trunks, branches, and fruits.

Table 1. Detail of properties for different crops

Property of plants	Unilateral	Goblet	Split	VSP	Walnut	Strawberry	Tomato
Leaf Width	0.18	0.18	0.18	0.18			
Leaf Length					0.15	0.1	0.2
Leaf Subdivisions	(1,1)	(1,1)	(1,1)	(1,1)	(1,2)	(4,4)	(4,3)
Steam Subdivision						10	
Steam Radius						0.005	
Plant Height						0.4	1.0
Stems Per Plant						50	
Trunk Height	0.7	0.7	1.3	0.7	4		
Trunk Radius	0.05	0.05	0.05	0.05	0.15		
Branch Length					(4.0,0.75,0.75)		
Cordon Height	0.9	0.9	1.5	0.9			
Cordon Radius	0.02	0.02	0.02	0.02			
Cordon Spacing	-	-	1.0				
Shoot Length	0.9	0.9	1.2	0.9			
Shoot Radius	0.005	0.005	0.005	0.005			
Shoots per Cordon	20	10	10	20			
Shoot subdivision							10
Shoots Tip Angle	$0.4\,\pi$	$0.4\,\pi$	$0.4\,\pi$	$0.4\,\pi$			
Leaf Spacing Fraction	0.6	0.6	0.6	0.6			
Fruit Radius	0.0075	0.0075	0.0075	0.0075	0.04	0.025	0.03
Cluster Per Steam						0.6	
Cluster Radius	0.03	0.03	0.3	0.03			
Fruit Color	(0.18,0.2,0.25)	(0.18,0.2,0.25)	(0.18,0.2,0.25)	(0.18,0.2,0.25)			(0.7,0.28,0.2)
Fruit Subdivisions	8	8	8	8	16	12	8
Property of canopy	Unilateral	Goblet	Split	VSP	Walnut	Strawberry	Tomato
Plant spacing	2	2	2	2	6	0.5	2
Row Spacing	2	2	4	2	8	1.5	2
Plant Count	(3,3)	(3,3)	(3,3)	(3,3)	(4,2)	(4,2)	
Canopy Origin	(0,0,0)	(0,0,0)	(0,0,0)	(0,0,0)	(0,0,0)	(0,0,0)	(0,0,0)
Canopy Rotation	0	0	0	0	0	0	0

In Fig. 3, we demonstrate the effect of parameter variation in a walnut canopy and a unilateral vine. The walnut canopy, presented in Fig. 3(a), displays variations in *leaf width* of 0.15, 0.1, and 0.05 in., transitioning from left to right. This transition emulates the progression from the blooming period through to the end of the season. Conversely, for the unilateral vine showcased in Fig. 3(b), we observe an increase in the *leaf width* and *cluster size* from left to right. This manipulation provides a visual representation of the stages of a season, moving from the dormant phase to the flowering stage, and ultimately, to the veraison stage.

RGB Camera. Generating images from 3D-rendered crops provides the distinct advantage of potentially infinite image production from a diverse array of

Fig. 3. Parameters can be customize in all crops. For example, we can simulate a walnut canopy from blooming to the end of the season or, on the other side, we can simulate a vine in the dormant, flowering and veraison stages by modifying the parameters of the fruits and leaves.

perspectives. To navigate within this simulated environment, users simply specify three parameters: the camera position, orientation, and image resolution. To simplify the potentially complex task of defining the camera orientation relative to the crop position, users only need to designate the desired viewpoint. The system will automatically compute the necessary rotations. Table 2 lists the RGB camera parameters. Each view requires its unique position and look-at vector, but the resolution is a singular specification for all views.

As an example, one can create multiple views from either a terrestrial or aerial perspective for a single plant, which would necessitate various position and look-at vectors. The resolution of the images can be freely defined, ranging from low to high, as shown in Fig. 4. All generated images and annotations can be directly exported for user convenience, or seamlessly loaded into the AgML pipeline to train existing machine learning architectures. Further details can be found in the AgML documentation[8].

Table 2. Detail of camera properties

Parameters	Input
Position	(x,y,z)
Look at	(x,y,z)
Resolution	(Width, Height)

---

[8] https://github.com/Project-AgML/AgML/examples.

Fig. 4. The resolution of the image can be customized. It can be seen an example of three different resolutions, a low-resolution (256 × 256 pixels), medium-resolution (2512 × 512 pixels), and a high resolution (1080 × 720 pixels) image.

LiDAR. Multiple LiDAR scans can be generated simultaneously, and the resulting point clouds can be merged into a global reference frame. As illustrated in Fig. 5, the LiDAR point cloud reconstruction and annotations of a single 'vine' are accomplished through the employment of four LiDAR sensors. A color-coding system is used to differentiate between elements: blue corresponds to points linked with the trunk, orange to points linked with fruits, light blue to points linked with the cordon and branches, and green to points linked with leaves. The adaptable design of the toolbox allows for the setting of both the position and orientation of the LiDAR sensor. The customizable parameters of the simulated LiDAR sensor are detailed in 3.

Table 3. Detail of LiDAR properties

Parameters	Input
Origin	(x,y,z)
Size	Number of points in zenithal and azimuthal angles
θ_{min}	0°
θ_{max}	180°
ϕ_{min}	0°
ϕ_{max}	360°
Translation	No translation
Rotation	No rotation
Beam exit diameter (meters)	0 (discrete return)
Beam divergence angle (rad)	0
ASCII file column format	x y z r g b intensity label

This provides an opportunity to personalize the pose and field of view of the sensor. Notably, beyond the label for each 3-tuple of points - x, y, z - there is

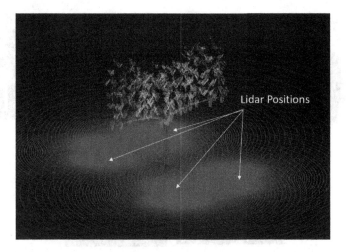

Fig. 5. Annotate point cloud generated using AgML, where trunk is label in blue color, leafs are green fruits are orange, and branches are yellow. Four LiDARs located around the vine were used and their data was merged in the generation of the synthetic point cloud.

also access to RGB information and LiDAR intensity values. Additional details about how intensity is simulated can be found in the Helios documentation. The toolbox also provides the ability to export the point cloud in a variety of formats, including PCD, PLY, and XYZ, and even offers the option for users to convert the input file to their preferred extension. Additionally, AgML includes 3D visualization tools, granting users the flexibility to plot individual scans or, alternatively, to combine all scans into a comprehensive global map.

4   Simulation Results

The validation of the experiments encompassed a range of crops. For RGB annotation, Fig. 6 demonstrated all the available labeling formats: object detection, semantic segmentation, and instance segmentation. Specifically, Fig. 6(a) displayed fruit detection using rectangular labels for an entire sorghum field. Figure 6(b) presented semantic segmentation of fruits, leaves, and trunks in a Goblet vineyard. Meanwhile, Fig. 6(c) showcased fruit detection with instance segmentation in a strawberry plant. It was noted that in the case of rectangular labeling, all objects within the camera view were marked, even those that were barely noticeable. However, if desired, labels of minimally visible, small objects could easily have been removed in a post-processing stage. During the process of semantic segmentation, only the visible pixels of the target object were marked. Conversely, in instance segmentation, all preferred elements were labeled, even if the object was partially hidden, as demonstrated with the strawberries in Fig. 6(c).

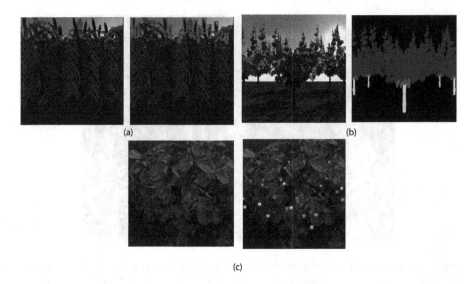

Fig. 6. Different annotations are available for RGB images, as (a) fruit detection for Sorghum, (b) leaves, trunks, and fruits semantic segmentation for Goblet vine, and (c) fruit instance segmentation for a strawberry plant.

In the LiDAR case, a single *tomato* plant with default parameters was mapped with four LiDARs, situated as in the example shown in Fig. 5. In this setup, each LiDAR was configured to be discrete with no rotation, covering $0 < \phi < 360°$ and $0 < \phi < 180°$, and contained 250 and 450 points for zenith and azimuth angles, respectively. Once all the point clouds were merged into a global reference frame, the resulting point cloud could be seen in Fig. 7. Given that four sensors were used for the reconstruction, a very dense point cloud with a high level of detail in the features was observed. Moreover, as previously mentioned, data could be color-mapped based on label, intensity, and RGB information.

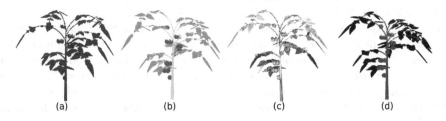

Fig. 7. Point cloud reconstruction of a tomato plant (a), colored based on (b) labels, (c) intensity, and (d) RGB values.

5   Applications

As part of AgML, we have provided a set of models that can be used in a variety of tasks, such as object detection, semantic segmentation and instance segmentation. To date, AgML has focuses only on RGB image analysis, thus all the available pre-trained models correspond to image-based tasks. In this section, we will show how a pre-trained model can performed on synthetic data generated with the toolbox. Regarding the point cloud data, we illustrate an application in walnut branch-leaf segmentation, training a model only with synthetic data and testing the model with a real point cloud.

5.1   Cluster Detection with Pre-trained Model

By using a pre-trained *EfficientDetD4* [14] model, we evaluated a dataset generated using the toolbox presented in this study. This demonstration illustrates the ease with which the generated data can be integrated into any model. The dataset comprises images of a *VSP Grapevine* tree, generated with default parameters and captured from a static camera positioned at the fruit level. We generated a total of 100 images, each with a resolution of 512×512 pixels. These images were divided into training (80%), validation (10%), and testing (10%) sets. Figure 8 illustrates an example of inference obtained from this dataset.

Fig. 8. Single scan from the dataset, where only *fruits* were labelled, in (a) the ground-truth data and in (b) the predictions of the model.

When comparing the inference results with the ground-truth annotations, we observed that by fine-tuning the pre-trained model we can achieve a mean average precision (mAP) of 0.81 at an intersection over union (IoU) threshold of 0.5. This experiment demonstrates one way in which the generated data can be utilized. Apart from this, synthetic data can also serve as a valuable resource for training and fine-tuning models to enhance performance on real images. Techniques such as domain adaptation, as previously demonstrated in our work [3], can be effectively employed for this purpose.

5.2   Walnut Leaf-Branch Point Cloud Semantic Segmentation

We generated data based on a Walnut tree, using its default parameters. Our labels distinguished between leaf and non-leaf elements. Four LiDARs were used, each one was configured to be discrete with no rotation, covering $0 < \phi < 360°$ and $0 < \phi < 180°$, and contained 250 and 450 points for zenith and azimuth angles, respectively. This configuration allow us to obtain a relative dense point cloud of around 130,000 points per canopy. The generated dataset contains a total of 200 point clouds of Walnut canopies, which are divided in 80% for training, 10% for validation and 10% for testing. For the purpose of this manuscript, we have selected PointNet++ [12] as our model for development. PointNet++ takes an unordered set of points in a 3D point cloud as its input and assigns a class label to each one of those points as output. We downsampled the data to 10,000 points. As a result we have obtained a mAP of 0.84 when considering only the geometric information.

For the context of this manuscript, the real data is a single scan of a Walnut orchard obtained using a static RIEGL VZ-1000. As a consequence, the point cloud exhibits denser data on one side. The original point cloud comprises approximately 3 million points. Given that our model was trained with a resolution capped at 10,000 points, we downsampled the point cloud in a manner consistent with the processing of the synthetic data. Figure 9 illustrates the ground truth for one Walnut in the test dataset alongside its model-predicted output with a point count of 10,000. Adjacent to this, the models output is presented. As it can be noted in the synthetic data, most of the miss-classified points correspond to the branches that have lower point cloud resolution, as in the top of the canopy. It is evident that the model adeptly identifies the core of the trunk and several branches on the denser side (left). However, on the right, mirroring the effect of low-point cloud resolution, there is a limited estimation of non-leaf points.

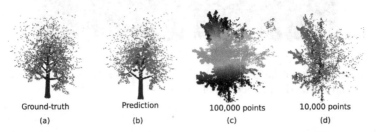

Fig. 9. Walnut point cloud data, where (a) ground-truth synthetic data, (b) prediction on synthetic data, (c) real walnut point cloud data sub-sampled to 100,000 points and colored by height, and (d) prediction on real data downsampled to 10,000 points.

6   Conclusions and Future Work

Data labeling poses a significant challenge in deploying machine learning applications, especially in the agriculture sector. Addressing this, our study unveils an open-source simulation toolbox, which serves as a comprehensive solution for generating synthetic labeled images and point cloud data in agricultural contexts. Our findings suggest that synthetic data can not only augment existing machine learning applications in agriculture but also pave the way for a myriad of new opportunities. In this manuscript, we have demonstrated two applications: one that validates the utility of synthetic data in current object detection models, and another that illustrates the potential of synthetic point cloud data for complex labeling tasks, such as branch-leaf segmentation.

Despite offering significant flexibility in customizing annotations for various crops, the developed toolbox has certain limitations. Currently, it does not support independent modification of parameters within objects of the same category, precluding tasks like altering the texture file (color) of individual strawberries on a plant. Additionally, while capable of creating agricultural environments of any size and capturing data at any resolution, a trade-off exists between accuracy and computational resources. Users must carefully weigh this balance to optimize the tool's efficiency and effectiveness.

AgML is an open-source library that is continuously being updated with new models and functionalities. At present, the focus of AgML lies predominantly in image analysis. However, the authors future work aims to incorporate machine learning functionalities specifically tailored for point cloud data in agricultural contexts. This addition is intended to facilitate easy benchmarking of models for the broader community.

References

1. Bailey, B.N.: Helios: a scalable 3D plant and environmental biophysical modeling framework. Front. Plant Sci. **10**, 1185 (2019). https://doi.org/10.3389/FPLS.2019. 01185/BIBTEX
2. Chaudhury, A., Boudon, F., Godin, C.: 3D plant phenotyping: all you need is labelled point cloud data, pp. 1–17 (2020). https://doi.org/10.3389/FPLS.2019. 01185/BIBTEX
3. Fei, Z., Olenskyj, A., Bailey, B.N., Earles, M.: Enlisting 3D crop models and GANs for more data efficient and generalizable fruit detection
4. Gené-Mola, J., et al.: Fruit detection, yield prediction and canopy geometric characterization using lidar with forced air flow. Comput. Electron. Agric. **168**, 105121 (2020). https://doi.org/10.1016/J.COMPAG.2019.105121
5. Giuffrida, M.V., Chen, F., Scharr, H., Tsaftaris, S.A.: Citizen crowds and experts: observer variability in image-based plant phenotyping. Plant Meth. **14**, 1–14 (2018). https://doi.org/10.1186/S13007-018-0278-7/TABLES/4
6. Grondin, V., Pomerleau, F., Giguère, P.: Training deep learning algorithms on synthetic forest images for tree detection. https://github.com/norlab-ulaval/ PercepTreeV1

7. Hartley, Z.K., French, A.P.: Domain adaptation of synthetic images for wheat head detection. Plants (Basel, Switzerland) **10** (2021). https://doi.org/10.3390/PLANTS10122633, https://pubmed.ncbi.nlm.nih.gov/34961104/

8. Id, M.A.B., Liu, C.Y., Bidinosti, C.P., Id, C.J.H., Godee, C.M., Ajmani, M.: An embedded system for the automated generation of labeled plant images to enable machine learning applications in agriculture (2020)

9. Joshi, A., Guevara, D., Earles, M.: Standardizing and centralizing datasets for efficient training of agricultural deep learning models. Plant Phenomics **5** (2023). https://doi.org/10.34133/PLANTPHENOMICS.0084

10. Ldchen, J.W., Rzanny, M., Seeland, M., Mäder, P.: Automated plant species identification-trends and future directions (2018)

11. Miao, T., Wen, W., Li, Y., Wu, S., Zhu, C., Guo, X.: Label3dmaize: toolkit for 3D point cloud data annotation of maize shoots. GigaScience **10**, 1–15 (2021). https://doi.org/10.1093/GIGASCIENCE/GIAB031, https://academic.oup.com/gigascience/article/10/5/giab031/6272094

12. Qi, C.R., Yi, L., Su, H., Guibas, L.J.: Pointnet++: deep hierarchical feature learning on point sets in a metric space. In: Advances in Neural Information Processing Systems 2017-December, pp. 5100–5109 (2017). https://doi.org/10.48550/arxiv.1706.02413, https://arxiv.org/abs/1706.02413v1

13. Singh, A., Ganapathysubramanian, B., Singh, A.K., Sarkar, S.: Feature review machine learning for high-throughput stress phenotyping in plants. Trends Plant Sci. **21** (2016). https://doi.org/10.1016/j.tplants.2015.10.015

14. Tan, M., Pang, R., Le, Q.V.: EfficientDet: scalable and efficient object detection (2020). https://github.com/google/

15. Turgut, K., Dutagaci, H., Galopin, G., Rousseau, D.: Segmentation of structural parts of rosebush plants with 3D point-based deep learning methods. Plant Meth. **18**, 1–23 (2022). https://doi.org/10.1186/S13007-022-00857-3/TABLES/11

16. Ubbens, J., Cieslak, M., Prusinkiewicz, P., Stavness, I.: The use of plant models in deep learning: an application to leaf counting in rosette plants. Plant Meth. **14**, 1–10 (2018). https://doi.org/10.1186/S13007-018-0273-Z/FIGURES/6

17. Weber, J., Penn, J.: Creation and rendering of realistic trees "from such small beginnings-a mere grain of dust, as it were-do mighty trees take their rise". Henry David Thoreau from "Faith in a Seed"

18. Westling, F., Bryson, M., Underwood, J.: SimTreeLS: simulating aerial and terrestrial laser scans of trees. Comput. Electron. Agric. **187**, 106277 (2021). https://doi.org/10.1016/J.COMPAG.2021.106277

Multimodal Dataset for Localization, Mapping and Crop Monitoring in Citrus Tree Farms

Hanzhe Teng, Yipeng Wang, Xiaoao Song, and Konstantinos Karydis$^{(\boxtimes)}$

University of California Riverside, Riverside, CA 92521, USA
{hteng007,ywang1040,xsong036,karydis}@ucr.edu

Abstract. In this work we introduce the CitrusFarm dataset, a comprehensive multimodal sensory dataset collected by a wheeled mobile robot operating in agricultural fields. The dataset offers stereo RGB images with depth information, as well as monochrome, near-infrared and thermal images, presenting diverse spectral responses crucial for agricultural research. Furthermore, it provides a range of navigational sensor data encompassing wheel odometry, LiDAR, inertial measurement unit (IMU), and GNSS with Real-Time Kinematic (RTK) as the centimeter-level positioning ground truth. The dataset comprises seven sequences collected in three fields of citrus trees, featuring various tree species at different growth stages, distinctive planting patterns, as well as varying daylight conditions. It spans a total operation time of 1.7 h, covers a distance of 7.5 km, and constitutes 1.3 TB of data. We anticipate that this dataset can facilitate the development of autonomous robot systems operating in agricultural tree environments, especially for localization, mapping and crop monitoring tasks. Moreover, the rich sensing modalities offered in this dataset can also support research in a range of robotics and computer vision tasks, such as place recognition, scene understanding, object detection and segmentation, and multimodal learning. The dataset, in conjunction with related tools and resources, is made publicly available at https://github.com/UCR-Robotics/Citrus-Farm-Dataset.

Keywords: Datasets · Agricultural Robotics · Precision Agriculture · Crop Monitoring · Localization and Mapping · Multimodal Perception

1 Introduction

Crop monitoring is an essential and critical component in precision agriculture. Its value is that it can provide growers and agronomists with different pieces of information that are useful for determining a range of indicators, such as plant growth [10], water stress level and health condition [17], to name a few. This can lead to more informed future decisions on irrigation, disease prevention, pest control, fruit harvesting and ultimately higher yields [16]. Given the dynamic nature of changes that happen in the field, crop monitoring tasks need to be

© The Author(s), under exclusive license to Springer Nature Switzerland AG 2023
G. Bebis et al. (Eds.): ISVC 2023, LNCS 14361, pp. 571–582, 2023.
https://doi.org/10.1007/978-3-031-47969-4_44

performed regularly, a process that can quickly become time- and labor-intensive and scale poorly both spatially and temporally [2]. These challenges can be addressed to a certain extend by automating parts of the overall process with mobile robots.

Datasets are an essential tool to help develop autonomous robot systems in agricultural environments. Navigational sensor data is crucial for the development of accurate localization and mapping algorithms, which can enable a range of fully automated tasks such as soil conductivity measurement [5] and physical sample retrieval [4]. On the other hand, multispectral images are particularly valuable in agricultural research, as they can provide informative measurements for computing domain-specific indices. For example, the Normalized Difference Vegetation Index (NDVI) can be computed from red and near-infrared spectral channels and serves as an indicator of plant health [17]. If both sensing modalities are available, a detailed and accurate map with multimodal data (e.g., thermal, NDVI) can be constructed by an automated mobile robot for crop monitoring on a regular basis. However, there currently exist limited public datasets that provide *both multispectral images and navigational sensor data* to facilitate the development of such autonomous robot systems.

To this end, we present the CitrusFarm dataset, a comprehensive multi-sensor dataset in the citrus tree farms. The dataset comprises seven sequences collected in three fields of citrus trees, featuring various tree species at different growth stages, distinctive planting patterns, as well as varying daylight conditions. The dataset offers stereo RGB images with depth information, as well as monochrome, near-infrared and thermal images, presenting diverse spectral responses crucial for agricultural research. Furthermore, it provides a range of navigational sensor data encompassing wheel odometry, LiDAR, inertial measurement unit (IMU), and GNSS with Real-Time Kinematic (RTK) as the centimeter-level positioning ground truth. In comparison to related works, our CitrusFarm dataset provides a total of nine sensing modalities, thus enabling significant potential for multimodal and crossmodal research in the robotics and computer vision community.

We anticipate that this dataset can facilitate the development of autonomous robot systems operating in agricultural tree environments, primarily for localization, mapping and navigation tasks. With both multispectral and navigational data, automated multimodal mapping becomes possible for crop monitoring on a regular basis. Given the rich sensing modalities, sensor fusion can be conducted with any combination of sensing sources of interest. This can advance the research on localization in challenging unstructured agricultural environments, and enable a full range of automated agricultural operations contingent on accurate localization. Lastly, this dataset can serve as the training and testing data in machine learning tasks, and support research in a variety of robotics and computer vision applications, such as scene understanding, segmentation, object detection, place recognition and multimodal learning.

2   Related Works

Agricultural robotics datasets that provide both multispectral images and navigational sensor data are scarce. Lu and Young reviewed public agricultural image datasets for weed control, fruit detection and miscellaneous applications, without navigational sensors involved [11]. In the following, *we focus on public datasets that contain both images and navigational data.* Overall, such datasets can be categorized into two broad types.

Datasets Recorded Following the Same Route Over Time: Chebrolu et al. recorded the dataset on a sugar beet farm over a period of three months, aiming to advance research on plant classification, localization and mapping [6]. Bender et al. presented a multimodal dataset that contains weekly scans of cauliflower and broccoli covering a ten-week growth cycle from transplant to harvest using the Ladybird agricultural robot [3]. In addition, that dataset also provides physical characteristics of the crop, soil sensor data and environmental data from a weather station. Polvara et al. collected multi-sensor data following the same route in a vineyard environment over a time span of six months; the resulting dataset can be used for long-term localization and mapping, phenotyping and crop mapping tasks [13].

Datasets Collected in a Variety of Scenes: Pire et al. collected six sequences of multi-sensor data on soybean fields, with the focus being on visual localization and mapping under various challenging situations [12]. Güldenring et al. focused on the problem of weed control using vision-equipped robots and presented the RumexWeeds dataset that comprises color images with annotations and navigational sensing data associated with each image frame [9]. Ali et al. recorded the dataset in a forest environment in various seasons and daylight conditions using a sensor rig mounted on a car vehicle [1].

Our work fits into the second category, and aims to diversify the data collection process in the citrus tree environments. We collected seven sequences in three agricultural fields featuring various tree species at different growth stages, distinctive planting patterns, as well as varying daylight conditions, all while following various routes in the fields. More details about our data collection process are to be discussed in Sect. 5.

Moreover, in comparison to related works, our CitrusFarm dataset provides a total of nine sensing modalities, thereby unlocking vast potential for multimodal research in robotics and computer vision. Among the nine modalities, the presence of LiDAR data distinguishes this work from the offering geo-referenced images alone, and multispectral images further provide with a unique perceptual perspective. A detailed overview of the sensing modalities encompassed within each dataset is presented in Table 1.

3   Mobile Robot Setup

We employ the Clearpath Jackal wheeled mobile robot to collect multi-sensor data in the agricultural fields. Jackal is a differential-drive robot that follows

Table 1. Summary of Available Sensing Modalities in Related Public Datasets and Comparison with Our Developed Dataset.

Dataset	Mono	RGB	Depth	NIR	Thermal	LiDAR	Wheel-Odom	IMU	GPS(-RTK)
Chebrolu et al. [6]		✓	✓	✓		✓	✓		✓
Bender et al. [3]	✓	✓		✓	✓			✓	✓
Polvara et al. [13]		✓	✓			✓	✓	✓	✓
Pire et al. [12]		✓					✓	✓	✓
Güldenring et al. [9]		✓					✓	✓	✓
Ali et al. [1]		✓						✓	✓
Ours	✓	✓	✓	✓	✓	✓	✓	✓	✓

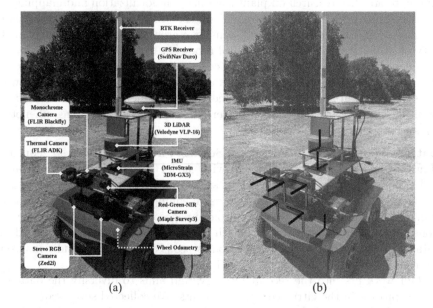

(a) (b)

Fig. 1. a) The Clearpath Jackal mobile robot with a variety of sensors mounted onboard, ready to collect data in the field. (b) The corresponding reference frames of five camera lenses, IMU, LiDAR and wheel odometry superimposed on the Jackal robot. Relative poses between frames are real parameters after extrinsic calibration. Red, green and blue bars denote x, y and z axes respectively. (Color figure online)

the unicycle kinematic model, which can take linear and angular velocities as the control input. It can support in-place turns and a maximum linear speed of 2 m/s. The onboard computer installed on the robot is a Jetson Xavier AGX, with 32 GB RAM, 2 TB storage and Ubuntu 18.04 operating system. The Robot Operating System (ROS) is utilized as the middleware to connect with all sensors and record data.

On top of the robot base, we designed and manufactured several mounting parts to secure a variety of sensors onboard. Figure 1 illustrates the sensor setup on the robot. We discuss the specification and configuration of each sensing modality in detail as follows.

Monochrome Camera: We use the FLIR Blackfly BFS-U3-16S2M-CS camera to capture monochrome images. It is equipped with a Computar A4Z2812CS-MPIR lens, with an adjustable focal length and aperture. This monochrome modality can reflect the overall light intensity in the visible spectrum, and is useful for both multimodal perception and vision-based autonomous navigation (e.g., visual odometry [14]).

Stereo RGB Camera: We employ the Stereolabs Zed2i camera to capture color images in visible spectrum. This camera possesses two high-resolution RGB lenses, and depth images can be computed from stereo images in real-time by leveraging the GPU of the Xavier onboard computer. Furthermore, we also include the internal IMU data and the poses computed by the Zed camera driver in our data collection process.

Red-Green-NIR Camera: We use the Mapir Survey3 camera to capture images with three channels: Red, Green, and Near-InfraRed (NIR). The merit of this multispectral configuration is the capability to compute domain-specific indices directly from a single image. For instance, the Normalized Difference Vegetation Index (NDVI) can be derived from the Red and NIR channels, via the equation $NDVI = \frac{NIR-Red}{NIR+Red}$. Such indices can enable growers and agronomists to keep track of the health status of plants (e.g., [17]).

Thermal Camera: We consider the FLIR ADK thermal camera to capture images in the Long-Wave InfraRed (LWIR) range (around 8–14 micrometers). This thermal modality can effectively detect humans and animals, as well as facilitate the understanding of plant health condition (e.g., water stress level, disease prevention, pest control). Furthermore, a thermal modality can also enhance navigation tasks in degenerated environments (e.g., [7]).

A summary of the different cameras used in our robot is provided in Table 2.

Table 2. Summary of Camera Specification and Configuration.

Camera	Modality	Shutter	Rate	Resolution	HFOV	Bit/Channel
FLIR Blackfly	Monochrome	Global	10 Hz	1440 × 1080	72°	8 × 1
FLIR ADK	Thermal	Global	10 Hz	640 × 512	65°	8 × 1
Stereolabs Zed2i	Stereo RGB	Rolling	10 Hz	1280 × 720	102°	8 × 3 × 2
Stereolabs Zed2i	Depth	Rolling	10 Hz	1280 × 720	102°	32 × 1
Mapir Survey3	Red-Green-NIR	Rolling	10 Hz	1280 × 720	85°	8 × 3

Note: Although most cameras can support up to 30 Hz or 60 Hz frame rate, we operate them at 10 Hz to match the LiDAR's operating frequency.

3D LiDAR: We utilize a Velodyne VLP-16 LiDAR for 3D mapping. It comprises 16 scan lines (constituting 30° vertical FOV) and each line contains 1800 points (constituting 360° horizontal FOV), providing a total of 28800 points per point cloud at a rate of 10 Hz. The maximum measurement distance extends to 100 m, with an accuracy of ±3 cm.

IMU: A MicroStrain 3DM-GX5-AHRS IMU is installed underneath the LiDAR to collect linear acceleration and angular velocity data for inertial navigation. It comes equipped with built-in complementary filter and Extended Kalman Filter (EKF) algorithms that operate ahead of output, at a maximum frequency of 1000 Hz. In our configuration, we adjust its rate to 200 Hz. The internal reference frames of the accelerometer and gyroscope are treated as identical.

Wheel Odometry: We record the wheel odometry data provided by the Jackal mobile robot software, computed from its wheel encoders at a rate of 50 Hz. However, this measurement can drift over time and requires fusion with other sensors for accurate estimation. The reference frame of this sensing modality is located at the bottom center of the robot base.

GPS-RTK: We utilize the SwiftNav Duro GPS system to function as the positioning ground truth. By leveraging Real Time Kinematic (RTK) technology, it is possible to acquire centimeter-level positioning accuracy of the robot at a rate of 10 Hz. The raw measurements, denoted as (latitude, longitude, altitude), are transformed to a path aligned with the origin as per the WGS84 standard, utilizing a Python script.

4   Sensor Calibration

The calibration of all sensors is conducted in three steps: 1) calibration of both intrinsic and extrinsic parameters of all cameras, 2) calibration of the extrinsic parameter between the IMU and one selected camera, and 3) calibration of the extrinsic parameter between the LiDAR and one selected camera. We elaborate on each step in the following subsections, and provide a summary discussion at the end of this section.

| (a) | (b) | (c) |

Fig. 2. Sample images of the calibration target with checkerboard pattern in (a) monochrome modality, (b) thermal modality, and (c) thermal modality with grayscale values inverted. Images are captured under direct sunlight.

4.1 Multi-camera Calibration

We use the Kalibr [8] toolbox to calibrate four cameras at once. A 24-inch square calibration target with a checkerboard pattern (Fig. 2(a)) is placed at multiple locations under direct sunlight, to cover most of the field of view of all cameras. Pinhole camera model and radtan (radial-tangential) distortion model are applied in the optimization. Results comprise the intrinsics (including distortion coefficients) of each camera lens, and a chain of transformation matrices from the first to the last camera lens.

One notable challenge we addressed in this process is the recognition of the checkerboard pattern in the thermal modality. In a typical indoor environment, the checkerboard pattern cannot be captured by the thermal camera, since the temperature of the calibration target at each point is almost the same. Considering that black areas absorb more heat than white areas, we placed the calibration target outdoor under direct sunlight instead. The resulting pattern being captured by the thermal camera is illustrated in Fig. 2(b). We then invert its grayscale values to make it consistent with other checkerboard patterns for use in the Kalibr toolbox (see Fig. 2(c)).

During calibration, the checkerboard pattern in thermal images may become blurry as the heat transfers from black cells to white cells. To alleviate this effect, a foam board was placed in between the poster paper (with the checkerboard pattern printed on it) and the medium density fiberboard (MDF) in the back to reduce heat transmission. Furthermore, the calibration can be conducted in the afternoon when sunlight is not very intense, and a fan can be used to cool down the calibration target when needed.

4.2 IMU-Camera Calibration

We use again the Kalibr [8] toolbox to calibrate the extrinsic parameter for the IMU and the FLIR Blackfly monochrome camera. A 24-inch square calibration target with an aprilgrid pattern is placed on the ground statically. With the pattern being captured by the camera all the time, we first collected a recording of about ten seconds when the robot is static, and then moved the robot (with both sensors rigidly mounted) towards x, y, z, roll, pitch and yaw directions, respectively, each lasting a few seconds. The final transformation matrix is obtained by optimizing the joint observations from the IMU and the camera.

In this process, the intrinsics of both sensors are required. We calibrate the noise density and random walk of the IMU by the Allan variance method beforehand.[1] The intrinsic parameters of the camera are taken from the results of multi-camera calibration.

4.3 LiDAR-Camera Calibration

We use the ACFR LiDAR-Camera calibration toolbox [15] to estimate the transformation between the LiDAR and the FLIR Blackfly monochrome camera. The

---

[1] https://github.com/ori-drs/allan_variance_ros.

24-in. square calibration target with a checkerboard pattern is reused herein, and is placed at multiple locations within the field of view of both sensors. One additional requirement is that the target has to be placed in a tilted position (e.g., 45-degree) in mid-air, such that the LiDAR point cloud of this target can be segmented out and square edges can be detected. In this way, the calibration program can align the center of the calibration target in both modalities.

Table 3. Summary of Calibrated Extrinsic Parameters.

Parent Frame	Child Frame	x[m]	y[m]	z[m]	q_x	q_y	q_z	q_w
base_link	velodyne_lidar	0.0400	0.0000	0.3787	0.0000	0.0000	0.0000	1.0000
velodyne_lidar	gps_rtk	−0.2200	0.0000	0.1530	0.0000	0.0000	0.0000	1.0000
velodyne_lidar	flir_blackfly	0.2178	0.0049	−0.0645	0.5076	−0.4989	0.4960	−0.4974
flir_blackfly	imu_link	−0.0061	0.0157	−0.1895	0.4987	0.5050	−0.4987	0.4977
flir_blackfly	zed2i_rgb_left	−0.0663	0.0956	−0.0161	0.0020	−0.0081	0.0031	1.0000
zed2i_rgb_left	zed2i_rgb_right	0.1198	−0.0003	−0.0046	0.0013	0.0013	0.0000	1.0000
zed2i_rgb_right	flir_adk	0.0251	−0.0948	−0.0203	0.0026	−0.0032	0.0059	1.0000
flir_adk	mapir	−0.1608	−0.0046	−0.0138	0.0028	0.0186	−0.0094	0.9998

4.4   Summary

After completing the calibration in these three steps, we can obtain the extrinsic parameters for seven modalities. The remaining two modalities are wheel odometry and GPS-RTK. Their extrinsic parameters are represented with respect to the LiDAR sensor, and can be measured and computed from the computer-aided design (CAD) models of the robot base, LiDAR and our mounting plates.

A summary of calibrated extrinsic parameters of all sensors is available in Table 3. The seven parameters detailed as $(x, y, z, q_x, q_y, q_z, q_w)$ indicate the translation measured in meters and the orientation presented in quaternions. Collectively, these variables define the transformation of a child reference frame with respect to a parent reference frame. The corresponding visualization of all sensor frames using these extrinsic parameters is shown in Fig. 1(b).

5   Data Collection in Citrus Tree Farms

We collected the CitrusFarm dataset in the Agricultural Experimental Station at the University of California, Riverside in the summer of 2023. Three fields of citrus trees were selected in the experiments, owing to their variety in tree species, growth stages and planting patterns. Composite sample images of the three fields are shown in Fig. 3.

During data collection in each field, the robot was remotely piloted and followed by a human operator to travel through various paths. The GPS-RTK

Fig. 3. The composite satellite image and sample photos of the three fields of citrus trees, covering various planting environments.

Table 4. Key Characteristics of Our Developed Dataset.

Field	Planting Pattern	Seq	Distance (m)	Duration (min:sec)	Time of Day	Motion	Loop or Retrace
One	sparse, uniform	01	1533.96	21:26	3 pm	lawn-mower	No
		02	524.60	07:24	5 pm	every-fifth-row	No
		03	2035.21	28:27	7 pm	every-other-row	Yes
Two	semi-dense, in-row	04	896.15	12:49	4 pm	square-spiral	Yes
		05	865.33	12:39	6 pm	lawn-mower	Yes
Three	dense, in-row	06	356.57	05:02	4 pm	every-other-row	No
		07	1212.74	16:53	6 pm	lawn-mower	Yes

base station, affixed to a tripod, was positioned in the center of the field to maintain proximity to the robot. By leveraging high-gain antennas for both the base station and the rover receiver on the robot, the reliable communication range can be increased to 150 m, with trees interposed. Notably, no instances of signal loss were observed throughout the experiments.

In total, we collected seven sequences in the three fields. These sequences span a total operation time of 1.7 h, cover a total distance of 7.5 km, and constitute a total of 1.3 TB of data. Key characteristics of the dataset are summarized in Table 4. The dataset offers a total of nine sensing modalities. Figure 4 depicts sample images from five camera modalities, and one instance of a domain-specific

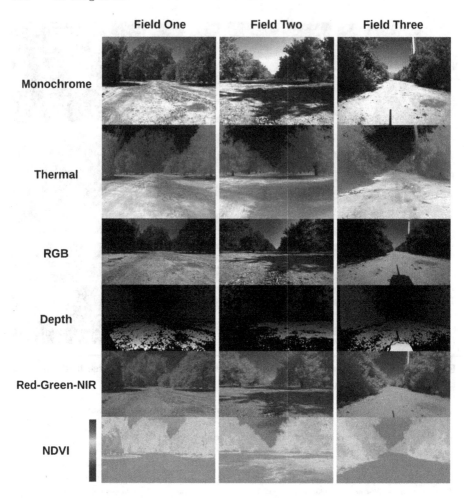

Fig. 4. Sample images collected in the three fields in various modalities, where depth images are computed from stereo RGB images, and NDVI images are computed from the Red and NIR channels of the Red-Green-NIR images. (Color figure online)

index computed from multispectral images (i.e. NDVI). Figure 5 provides sample trajectories of selected sequences.

The primary data format we used in data collection is ROS bags. To simplify data storage and transfer, we split recorded data into blocks of 4 GB, and categorized them based on their respective modalities. This categorization allows users to selectively download the subsets that are of their interest. To utilize the dataset, users need to only place the downloaded subsets in a common folder and initiate data playback; ROS will then automatically arrange the data across all bags and sequence the playback according to timestamps. Additional details on how to utilize the dataset, along with some highlighted use cases, are provided in the open-source repository for this work.

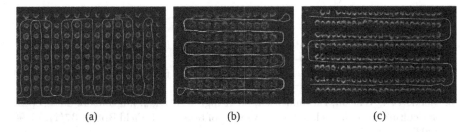

Fig. 5. Sample point cloud maps reconstructed from 3D LiDAR data, superimposed with GPS-RTK trajectories, for (a) sequence 03, (b) sequence 05, and (c) sequence 06 (sequence details are listed in Table 4).

Further, to accommodate diverse use cases, we also provide Python scripts to extract data from ROS bags into files, organized in different levels of folders. These comprise images of five modalities, point clouds obtained from 3D LiDAR, CSV files for IMU readings, wheel odometry readings, and ground-truth paths from the GPS-RTK data. Moreover, raw data collected during the calibration process and the computed calibration parameters are also included as part of the dataset to be released.

6 Conclusion

In this work we presented the CitrusFarm dataset, a comprehensive multi-sensor data collection in the citrus tree farms. The dataset comprises seven sequences collected in three fields of citrus trees, featuring various tree species at different growth stages, distinctive planting patterns, as well as varying daylight conditions. Furthermore, it provides a total of nine sensing modalities: monochrome, stereo RGB, depth, near-infrared and thermal images, as well as wheel odometry, LiDAR, IMU and GPS-RTK data.

We anticipate that this dataset can facilitate the development of autonomous robot systems operating in agricultural tree environments, primarily for localization, mapping and navigation tasks. The rich sensing modalities provided in this dataset can promote a wide range of research in robotics and computer vision, such as sensor fusion and multimodal machine learning.

Future works based on this dataset can include the development of a multimodal mapping framework for crop monitoring, sensor fusion for localization in unstructured agricultural tree environments, and the integration of localization and mapping algorithms into fully automated agricultural operations.

Acknowledgments. We gratefully acknowledge the support of NSF CMMI-2046270, USDA-NIFA 2021-67022-33453, ONR N00014-18-1-2252 and Univ. of California UC-MRPI M21PR3417. Any opinions, findings, and conclusions or recommendations expressed in this material are those of the authors and do not necessarily reflect the views of the funding agencies.

References

1. Ali, I., et al.: Finnforest dataset: a forest landscape for visual slam. Robot. Auton. Syst. **132**, 103610 (2020)
2. Bechar, A., Vigneault, C.: Agricultural robots for field operations: concepts and components. Biosyst. Eng. **149**, 94–111 (2016)
3. Bender, A., Whelan, B., Sukkarieh, S.: A high-resolution, multimodal data set for agricultural robotics: a ladybird's-eye view of brassica. J. Field Robot. **37**(1), 73–96 (2020)
4. Campbell, M., Dechemi, A., Karydis, K.: An integrated actuation-perception framework for robotic leaf retrieval: detection, localization, and cutting. In: IEEE/RSJ International Conference on Intelligent Robots and Systems (IROS), pp. 9210–9216 (2022)
5. Campbell, M., Ye, K., Scudiero, E., Karydis, K.: A portable agricultural robot for continuous apparent soil electrical conductivity measurements to improve irrigation practices. In: IEEE International Conference on Automation Science and Engineering (CASE), pp. 2228–2234 (2021)
6. Chebrolu, N., Lottes, P., Schaefer, A., Winterhalter, W., Burgard, W., Stachniss, C.: Agricultural robot dataset for plant classification, localization and mapping on sugar beet fields. Int. J. Robot. Res. **36**(10), 1045–1052 (2017)
7. Chen, L., Sun, L., Yang, T., Fan, L., Huang, K., Xuanyuan, Z.: RGB-T SLAM: a flexible SLAM framework by combining appearance and thermal information. In: IEEE International Conference on Robotics and Automation (ICRA), pp. 5682–5687 (2017)
8. Furgale, P., Rehder, J., Siegwart, R.: Unified temporal and spatial calibration for multi-sensor systems. In: IEEE/RSJ International Conference on Intelligent Robots and Systems (IROS), pp. 1280–1286 (2013)
9. Güldenring, R., Van Evert, F.K., Nalpantidis, L.: Rumexweeds: a grassland dataset for agricultural robotics. J. Field Robot. **40**(6), 1639–1656 (2023)
10. Kim, W.S., Lee, D.H., Kim, Y.J., Kim, T., Lee, W.S., Choi, C.H.: Stereo-vision-based crop height estimation for agricultural robots. Comput. Electron. Agric. **181**, 105937 (2021)
11. Lu, Y., Young, S.: A survey of public datasets for computer vision tasks in precision agriculture. Comput. Electron. Agric. **178**, 105760 (2020)
12. Pire, T., Mujica, M., Civera, J., Kofman, E.: The Rosario dataset: multisensor data for localization and mapping in agricultural environments. Int. J. Robot. Res. **38**(6), 633–641 (2019)
13. Polvara, R., et al.: Bacchus long-term (BLT) data set: acquisition of the agricultural multimodal BLT data set with automated robot deployment. J. Field Robot. (2023)
14. Qin, T., Li, P., Shen, S.: VINS-Mono: a robust and versatile monocular visual-inertial state estimator. IEEE Trans. Rob. **34**(4), 1004–1020 (2018)
15. Tsai, D., Worrall, S., Shan, M., Lohr, A., Nebot, E.: Optimising the selection of samples for robust lidar camera calibration. In: IEEE International Intelligent Transportation Systems Conference (ITSC), pp. 2631–2638 (2021)
16. Vougioukas, S.G.: Annual review of control, robotics, and autonomous systems. Agric. Robot. **2**(1), 365–392 (2019)
17. Zhao, T., Stark, B., Chen, Y., Ray, A.L., Doll, D.: A detailed field study of direct correlations between ground truth crop water stress and normalized difference vegetation index (NDVI) from small unmanned aerial system (sUAS). In: IEEE International Conference on Unmanned Aircraft Systems (ICUAS), pp. 520–525 (2015)

Identification of Abnormality in Maize Plants from UAV Images Using Deep Learning Approaches

Aminul Huq[1] , Dimitris Zermas[2] , and George Bebis[1]([✉])

[1] University of Nevada Reno, Reno, NV 89512, USA
aminul.huq@nevada.unr.edu, bebis@unr.edu
[2] Sentera, Saint Paul, USA
dimitris.zermas@sentera.com

Abstract. Early identification of abnormalities in plants is an important task for ensuring proper growth and achieving high yields from crops. Precision agriculture can significantly benefit from modern computer vision tools to make farming strategies addressing these issues efficient and effective. As farming lands are typically quite large, farmers have to manually check vast areas to determine the status of the plants and apply proper treatments. In this work, we consider the problem of automatically identifying abnormal regions in maize plants from images captured by a UAV. Using deep learning techniques, we have developed a methodology which can detect different levels of abnormality (i.e., low, medium, high or no abnormality) in maize plants independently of their growth stage. The primary goal is to identify anomalies at the earliest possible stage in order to maximize the effectiveness of potential treatments. At the same time, the proposed system can provide valuable information to human annotators for ground truth data collection by helping them to focus their attention on a much smaller set of images only. We have experimented with two different but complimentary approaches, the first considering abnormality detection as a classification problem and the second considering it as a regression problem. Both approaches can be generalized to different types of abnormalities and do not make any assumption about the abnormality occurring at an early plant growth stage which might be easier to detect due to the plants being smaller and easier to separate. As a case study, we have considered a publicly available data set which exhibits mostly Nitrogen deficiency in maize plants of various growth stages. We are reporting promising preliminary results with an 88.89% detection accuracy of low abnormality and 100% detection accuracy of no abnormality.

Keywords: Precision Agriculture · Deep Learning · Computer Vision · Maize Plants · Abnormality Detection

G. Bebis et al. (Eds.): ISVC 2023, LNCS 14361, pp. 583–596, 2023.
https://doi.org/10.1007/978-3-031-47969-4_45

1   Introduction

The negative impact of climate change and it's repercussions related to the agricultural sector and the environment is increasing at an alarming rate. Additionally, with the increased demand of food because of the ever-increasing population, the agricultural sector faces huge problems in the future. With the help of artificial intelligence and different methodological approaches, these problems may be handled to some extend. Automation of different agricultural tasks reduces human effort, increases food production and mitigates the adverse effects on the environment to some extend. Since most of the agricultural farms encompass a vast amount of land and produce, using sophisticated technological approaches has a significant impact in providing ease to human efforts and the environment. Machine learning and its applications have aided in various research and practical problems. Many times, machine learning approaches have surpassed human performance. Examples include face recognition, question answering, medical image analysis, speech recognition and others [1–4]. It's application in the field of precision agriculture is also noteworthy [5,6].

In order to ensure food security and economic stability for the U.S., production of corn plays a vital role. The U.S. is one of the major corn producers in the world. According to the data collected from the United States Department of Agriculture (USDA) in 2022, corn farmers of the U.S. produced about 13.7 billion bushels of corn at 79.2 million acres of land [7]. Apart from using this commodity as a food source, it is also used as a bio-fuel and other industrial applications. Proper inspection for any abnormalities in the plant leaves and subsequent treatment have a huge impact on the yield of maize plants. In the initial phase of an abnormality, the leaves of the plants usually turn from healthy green to different shades of yellow. There are various reasons for this like a disease or nutrient deficiency. There are also cases where the leaves turn yellow due to changes of weather, lack of water or other reasons. In general, manual assessment of the plants and their leaves is required from an expert who traverses the whole area where the plants are cultivated. This is a tedious process which needs to be done multiple times during the lifetime of the plants.

There have been several attempts to automate these processes, however, a general approach irrespective of the growth stage of the plants or type of abnormality is still under investigation. Past challenges include low resolution images, inefficient data collection approach, and problem-depended methodology based on specific deficiencies, viruses, insects [8–10]. Lack of a large set of properly labelled data is also another major limitation which prevents researchers from training effective deep learning models.

Using powerful sensors, Unmanned Aerial Vehicles (UAVs) are capable of taking high resolution images from a large area of a maize field leading to an efficient data collection approach for abnormality inspection purposes but also for collecting large amounts of data for training deep learning models [11]. The goal of this research work is to develop a system which can identify and quantify the level of abnormality from images irrespective of the abnormality type or level (i.e., low, medium, high or none). There are two main benefits behind the proposed system. First, it can provide useful information to farmers in terms of potential plant abnormalities and their quantification. Second, it can provide valuable assistance to human annotators for ground truth collection by focusing their attention on a subset of images instead of examining all the images captured in a UAV data collection flight. The main contributions of this research work can be summarized as follows:

– A methodology which can be used to identify and quantify abnormalities in maize plants. The proposed methodology can be extended to different types of plants.
– A customized EfficientNet-B0 is used as a baseline model in this study. Comparison with other models are shown, demonstrating the superiority of the baseline model.
– The labelled images with annotations which have been created for this research work are released of the benefit for the research community[1].

The rest of the paper is organized as follows: Sect. 2 provides a review of related works. Details about the data set and how it was prepared is mentioned in Sect. 3. The proposed methodology, and the baseline deep learning architecture can be found in Sect. 4. Section 5 presents the experiments performed and discusses our results. Finally, Sect. 6 provides our conclusions and directions for future research.

2   Background

Identifying nutrient deficiencies and abnormalities is a major concern in precision agriculture research. There are some interesting research works that have been performed in the past. Chore and Thankachan [12] attempted to identify Potassium, Nitrogen, Copper, Zinc and Phosphorus deficiencies from the leaves of orange, cotton, apple, banana, mango, litchi, henna, gooseberry, and okra plants. The plant leaves were manually collected from the fields using a multi-frequency visible light leaf scanning approach. Using multi-frequency analysis coupled with image processing, 16 features were used to train a deep learning model. The proposed approach involved a four step lengthy process, however, the results reported were quite high. The collected data was not made publicly available.

Rahadiyan et al. [13] performed similar work on Chilli plants. In particular, they extracted texture and color based feature and used a Multi-Layer Perceptron model to identify seven classes namely healthy, Phosphor, Magnesium, Sulfur, Calcium, Magnesium-Sulfur, and Multi-deficiency. However, the size of the total dataset was only 817. Moreover, the dataset included only images of individual plant leaves which were picked and placed on a white background rather than the whole plant in the field. Using the combination of RGB, Greyscale and LBP features the authors were able to achieve only 79.67% of accuracy.

---

[1] https://github.com/aminul-huq/Abnormality-Corn-ISVC-23.

To figure out the stress caused to plants by drought, Tejasri et al. [14] used a UAV to capture aerial RGB images of maize plants and utilized an ensemble model based on U-Net and U-Net++ where ResNet34 was used as the backbone of the model. The UAV device captured images of the whole maize field from where the authors extracted 150 samples of healthy and stressed crops. The authors created a segmentation mask using Otsu's method and a naive thresholding approach. They were able to improve overall performance by stacking and averaging the performance of U-Net and U-Net++ models. The final mIoU score of the ensemble model was 0.7163. As the segmentation mask or the ground truth was based on the Otsu's and naive thresholding method it can be assumed that the ground truth was not fine tuned enough to capture all the details in the images. A polygon based method may improve the ground truth collection process and the segmentation models performance. Using image processing techniques for detecting Nitrogen deficiency in rice plant leaves, Yuan et al. [15] experimented with various color based features like normalized RGB, HSV, and Dark Green Color Index. Their objective was to establish a correlation between these features and the amount of chlorophyll present in the rice plant leaves with the help of a SPAD-502 meter. The SPAD-502 meter is a hand held device which can be used to get an accurate measure of leaf chlorophyll concentration. One of the setbacks of this method is that, the authors used only three positions to collect data for the SPAD-502 meter. If they had considered more number of positions then the measurement would have been more accurate.

To assist human annotators quickly identify Nitrogen deficiencies in maize plants, Zermas et al. [11] proposed a solution based on Support Vector Machines(SVMs). Three different SVMs were used: the first one was used to separate green pixels from the rest (i.e., yellow and soil colored ones). The second one performed another classification to separate yellow pixels from the rest; finally, the third SVM determined whether a particular pixel was yellow due to Nitrogen deficiency. The proposed approach was shown to be much faster than human annotators in creating image data sets for Nitrogen deficiency classification. Additionally, the authors presented an approach which utilized the dataset to build a model which determined whether there was Nitrogen deficiency in the images.

Unfortunately, most of past published research work does not address the issue of early identification of abnormalities. Moreover, apart from a few examples, most of them focus on examining individual leaves or plants, instead of considering a larger area of plants. Data collection is also manual using handheld instruments which limits generality and large scale deployment of the proposed approaches. Many previous methodologies are also abnormality-depended which limits their effectiveness to different types of abnormalities. Our goal is to develop a general-purpose abnormality detection system which leverages modern technologies for data collection and can detect different types of abnormalities as early as possible from a large area of plants of various growth stages.

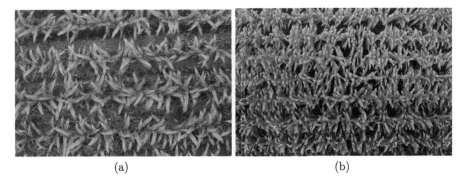

(a)   (b)

Fig. 1. Illustration of abnormalities in large scale images for (a) V8 and (b) V12 growth stages.

3 Dataset

We have experimented with a publicly available data set which contains images of maize plants of various growth stages exhibiting mostly Nitrogen deficiency but also abnormalities due to other types of nutrient deficiency and dryness [11]. The data set contains high resolution RGB images captured by a UAV at two different locations. For the purpose of this study, we used images from the V8 and V12 growth stages from the Becker field. Here, V stands for vegetative stage and the number associated with it represent how many leaves are present in the plant. It should be noted that although the labels of the data set indicate that the plants come from the V8 and V12 growth stages, there are several images in each category which contain maize plants from different growth stages. Moreover, although nutrient deficiencies typically start at an early growth stage, this is not always the case as we have confirmed from the images provided in the data set. The image resolution for V8 and V12 images are $4000 \times 6000 \times 3$ and $6000 \times 4000 \times 3$ respectively. With the help of an annotation tool named Label Studio [16], 44 images from the V8 stage and 46 images from the V12 stage were annotated using a bounding box to specify areas of abnormality (ground truth). Any yellow leaves on the ground were excluded from ground truth labeling.

Figure 1 shows two representative annotated images from the V8 and V12 growth stages. For training purposes, we selected 36 images from V8 and 36 images from V12 (we refer to this as set A); the rest, 8 images from V8 and 10 images from V12, were selected for testing purposes (we refer to this as set B). Based on the annotations, three separate data sets were created, one for training and two for testing. The training set was created by randomly cropping $250 \times 250 \times 3$ sub-images from set A as we wanted to build a general purpose abnormality detector which can perform well on any part of the field. To evaluate the performance of the abnormality detector (i.e., EfficientNet-B0), the first test data set was created in the same way (i.e., randomly cropped sub-images) using set B. To evaluate abnormality quantification, the second test data set

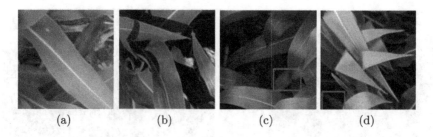

(a)   (b)   (c)   (d)

Fig. 2. Illustration of normal (a) & (b) and abnormal (c) & (d) samples.

was created from set B again but now using a non-overlapping sliding window approach to make sure that the whole image is covered.

A particular sub-image was labelled as abnormal if it completely contained at least one bounding box. A total of 4966 randomly selected abnormal sub-images and 4966 randomly selected normal sub-images were extracted for training. Normal samples did not include any part of a bounding box. For validation purposes, 10% of the training data was used. The first test set was built by selecting a total of 1211 abnormal and 1211 normal randomly cropped sub-images. Figure 2 shows some representative normal and abnormal sub-images. Since the UAV captures a big portion of the field which might contain 100–120 maize plants, it was determined that this area might be too big to be labeled as abnormal or normal. Therefore, each large scale test image was partitioned in 4 quarters, yielding 72 quarter scale images, each containing an average of 25–30 maize plants. The second test set was created from the quarter scale images using a sliding-window approach yielding a total of 6912 sub-images; each sub-image in this case was labelled as abnormal if it contained any part of a bounding box and normal otherwise.

4   Methodology

The proposed approach assumes that high resolution maize images have been collected by a UAV. The goal is to analyze each image collected to determine whether the plants exhibit low, medium, high or no abnormality. Our system does not currently perform any abnormality localization but we plan to include this feature in future versions of the system.

Two approaches have been considered to quantify the level of abnormality in a test image. In the first approach, we consider all non-overlapping sliding windows in the image where each sliding window is classified as normal or abnormal using a deep learning classifier as discussed later. To quantify the level of abnormality in the whole image, we take the ratio of abnormal sliding windows over the total number of sliding windows; we refer to this ratio as the abnormal window probability and represents a coarse estimate of the amount of abnormality present in an image. We have empirically divided the window probability in several intervals as shown in Table 1 in order to quantify the amount of abnormality

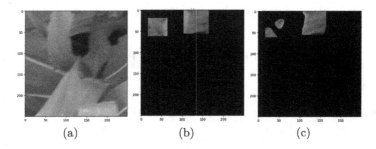

(a)   (b)   (c)

Fig. 3. (a) A representative abnormal image (b) bounding boxes focusing on abnormality (c) abnormal pixels using color segmentation.

as low, medium, high and no abnormality. In practice, these thresholds should be set up with the help of an expert.

In the second approach, we consider all non-overlapping sliding windows again in a test image and count all abnormal pixels in each sliding window based on the bounding boxes which are inside the window. We then add the abnormal pixels from all sliding windows and divide the sum by the total number of pixels in the image. We refer to this ratio as the abnormal pixel probability and represents a finer estimate of the amount of abnormality present in the image. Typically, computing the abnormal pixel probability requires segmenting the area of abnormality within the bounding boxes. Here, we have used a simple color segmentation scheme to roughly estimate the abnormal area within each bounding box. This was performed using simple thresholding in the HSV color space to extract yellow colored pixels inside any bounding boxes present in the image. Figure 3 illustrates the color segmentation task for a representative abnormal image.

Using a Pearson correlation we verified a high positive correlation between the abnormal window and pixels probabilities. To quantify the amount of abnormality present in an image, we chose the thresholds for the abnormal pixel probability based on the thresholds of the abnormal window probability such that the number of test images in each category between the two approaches remains the same. However, there is no guarantee that the same exactly images belong to the same category for each method. This is because there are some borderline cases where the image is considered of low abnormality using the window probability but of medium abnormality using the pixel probability; this is also the case for the medium and high abnormality categories. Apart from this, there might be a bounding box in the computation of the window probability which falls into multiple neighboring sliding windows; as a result, the window probability can be overestimated. This is not the case when computing the abnormal pixel probability, however, the computation of the abnormal pixel probability suffers from possible segmentation errors due to using a rather simple color segmentation scheme. In the future, we plan to compute both probabilities more accurately.

Table 1. Quantification of different abnormalities (probability x is scaled in the range [0–100] for both methods)

	Abnormal Window Probability	Abnormal Pixel Probability	No. of Images
None	0	0	7
Low	$0 <x<5$	$0<x<0.0415$	9
Medium	$5<x<20$	$0.0415<x<0.80$	19
High	$x>20$	$x>0.80$	37

Table 1 shows the corresponding thresholds for the abnormal pixel probability as well as the number of quarter scale test images in each category.

4.1   Custom EfficientNet-B0 Classifier

EfficientNet-B0 architecture is a light weight model which is capable of performing classification tasks very well which is the main reason for choosing this network in our study. Later versions of this network does perform slightly better but those require more time to train as they have significantly larger parameters. We have modified this model to better suit it in the context of our application. Generally, it is considered that any classification deep neural network has two parts. The first one is the feature extraction part which contains the convolutional, maxpooling, normalization layers etc. The second part is the classification layer which takes the features from the previous layers, performs average pooling, and feeds the results to a few fully-connected (FC) layers. Here, we have removed the classification part and have inserted in its place several convolutional, batch normalization and self attention layers. The reason for including self-attention layers is that abnormalities occupy only a small area in the image; therefore, the model is expected to perform better if it focuses on a small region only. Additionally, a skip connection was introduced to retain both information and gradients that could potentially be lost during the training process. Following the inclusions of these layers, three FC layers we used for performing classification. Figure 4 provides a visual illustration of the customized model used in this study.

4.2   Abnormality Quantification Using Window Probability

To quantify the amount of abnormality in a test image using the window probability, each sliding window in the test image must be classified as normal or abnormal. We have experimented with two different classifiers and their fusion: the customized EfficientNet-B0 described earlier and a Support Vector Machine (SVM) classifier [17,18]. The fusion model predicted an image as abnormal if either one of the above classifiers predicted it as abnormal. We decided to fuse a traditional machine learning model with a deep learning model since their solutions would be rather different which typically benefits fusion schemes most.

Both the customized EfficientNet-B0 model and the SVM model were trained on the same training data and optimized using the validation data. During testing, each model was evaluated using the randomly cropped test set. As the training and test images were $250 \times 250 \times 3$, Principal Component Analysis(PCA) followed by Linear Discriminant Analysis (LDA) were performed in the case of SVM to help it find more powerful features. For the deep learning model, various data augmentation approaches (e.g., random vertical and horizontal flips) were performed. After the classification of each sliding window as normal or abnormal, the window probability was computed and the test image was assigned to an abnormality category or to the normal category using the thresholds shown in Table 1. Finally, the accuracy was calculated based on the original and predicted labels. An illustration of the training and testing phases is shown in Fig. 5.

4.3 Abnormal Quantification Using Pixel Probability

In order to predict the abnormal pixel probability of a test image, a regression model, namely Histogram-based Gradient Boosting Regression Tree, was applied to each sliding window in the test image [19]. This is a faster version of the Gradient Boosting Regression Tree [20]. The regression model was trained on the randomly cropped abnormal samples only (i.e., it wasn't trained on the whole data set because of the zero inflation problem [21]). Since the dimension of each sliding window is $250 \times 250 \times 3$, which is rather big for the regression model, PCA was used to reduce the dimension by preserving 99% of the variance in the data, leading to 3394 features. The abnormal pixel probability for each small scale test image was computed by summing up the predicted pixel probabilities for all sliding windows. Each test image was then assigned to the appropriate abnormal category using the thresholds shown in Table 1. Finally, the accuracy was calculated based on the original and predicted labels.

5   Results and Discussion

In this section a short description about the parameters of the models and results obtained from the experimentations are discussed.

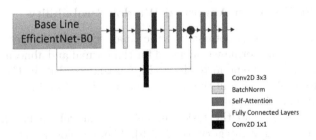

Fig. 4. Proposed customized EfficientNet-B0.

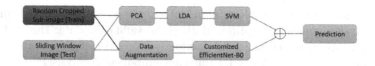

Fig. 5. Training and testing phases for predicting the abnormal window probability.

Table 2. Performance comparison of different models

	Training Accuracy(%)	Validation Accuracy(%)	Test Accuracy(%)
ResNet152	93.75	94.06	92.36
DenseNet201	95.00	93.06	92.90
EfficientNet-B0	94.69	93.96	92.69
Customized EfficientNet-B0	99.97	93.26	**93.15**

5.1 Experimental Setup

The randomly cropped data sets described in Sect. 3 were used to train and test the classification and regression models. EfficientNet-B0 was trained for 200 epochs using SGD optimizer with a learning rate of 0.0001. Additionally, one-cyclic learning rate was used for updating the learning rate in each epoch [22]. In order to train the SVM model, we used an RBF kernel; the value of C was set to 1. The regression model was trained for 750 iterations using the squared loss, a max depth value of 7, and the L2 regularization value set to 3. Other parameter values were experimented as well but for these values provided the best results.

5.2 Abnormal vs Normal Classification

Table 2 compares the performance of the customized EfficientNet-B0 with the original EfficientNet-B0 as well as with DenseNet-201 and ResNet-152 using the randomly cropped data set. As it can be observed from the results, the customized EfficientNet-B0 model outperformed all other models, including the original EfficientNet-B0 model.

5.3 Results Based on Abnormal Window Probability

Table 3 shows the results obtained on the small scale test images. The rows of the table show the performance achieved for the normal and abnormal categories while the columns correspond to the SVM, Customized EfficientNet-B0 mdoels and their fusion. As shown in the table, the model based on fusion out-performs the other two models.

To better understand the fusion model (best model), a bar plot was created for each abnormal category (see Fig. 6). The bar plot depicts a side by side comparison between the original and predicted window probability values for each image in each category. In the plots, the x-axis represents the ID numbers

Table 3. Performance on sliding window test set for abnormal window probability

	SVM(%)	Customized EfficientNet-B0(%)	Fusion Model(%)
None	100	100	100
Low	55.56	77.78	88.89
Medium	63.16	68.42	84.21
High	51.35	94.59	100

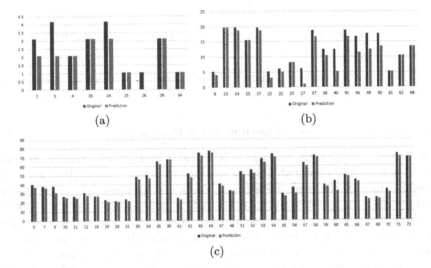

(a)

(b)

(c)

Fig. 6. Performance comparison between the original and predicted window probabilities for (a) low (b) medium and (c) high abnormal categories.

of the individual test images and the y-axis represents the window probability (scaled in the interval [1–100]). The model miss-classified 1 out of 9 test images and 3 out of 19 images for low and medium abnormality category. For the low abnormality category, the model was not able to correctly predict any abnormal window for a particular test image. A detailed analysis revealed that the particular test image (i.e., #26) had only one abnormal sliding window out of 96 sliding windows. That particular window had a very small amount of abnormal pixels. It appears that this window was too difficult for the model to be classified correctly. In case of the medium abnormality category, it can be observed from Fig. 6(b) that the test images miss-classified (i.e., images #8, #21 and #61) had abnormal window probability values slightly over 5% which was the threshold between the low and medium abnormality categories. For hard thresholds, like in this study, the number of similar errors would increase with more categories. Figure 7 shows several test images which have been labelled as normal by the classifier but are in fact abnormal images as shown by the red bounding box. As

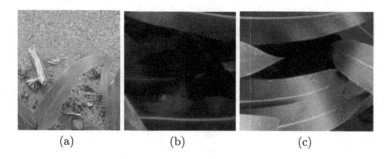

(a)   (b)   (c)

Fig. 7. Sample images that are classified wrongly by the classifier.

it can be observed, occlusion, lighting, small region of interest are some of the factors that hamper the performance of the model.

5.4   Results Based on Abnormal Pixel Probability

With the help of the regression model 100%, 66.67%, 100% and 89.19% accuracy for the abnormal pixel probability was obtained for None, Low, Medium and High category through the experimentations. As it can be observed, the regression model performs very well for normal and medium abnormality category; however, its performance is lower on the low and high abnormality categories. A bar plot was created again to better understand the results obtained in this case (see Fig. 8). As it can be observed, the regression model predicted a zero abnormal pixel probability for two images in this category (i.e., images #21 and #26).

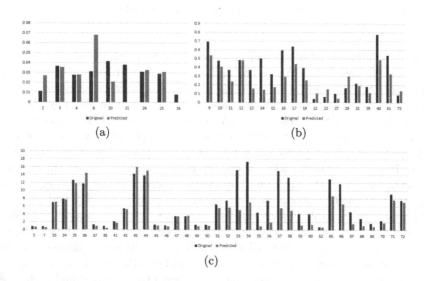

Fig. 8. Performance comparison between the original value and predicted value for (a) low (b) medium and (c) high abnormal pixel probability.

Image #26 is the same image mistaken by the window probability approach. A detailed analysis on image #21 revealed that there were only two windows which contained abnormalities and due to illumination and occlusion issues the model was not able to provide any regression values. There were also four test images which were not correctly categorized in the high abnormality category (i.e., images #5,#7#38 and #62). These had predicted values which were very close to the threshold while the original values were just above the threshold for the high abnormality category. There are more factor that have contributed to errors using abnormal pixel probability such as inaccurate estimation of these probabilities in the training set and dried yellowish leaves on the ground.

6 Conclusions

Detection of abnormalities in maize plants in early stages is extremely crucial. However, even in cases when the abnormality has progressed to some extend, certain actions can still be taken in order to ensure proper growth and yields. This research work focused on identifying abnormalities using UAV images to detect whether a particular area contains low, medium, high or no abnormality which mitigates the aforementioned problem. Abnormal window probability and abnormal pixel probability approaches were considered to quantify potential abnormalities in the field. We have reported promising preliminary results using a publicly available data set. We plan to estimate the pixel probability more accurately as well as fuse the window and pixel probabilities to improve abnormality quantification. Since the original data was not collected by us we could not recommend ideal UAV heights, camera view, optimal illumination conditions etc. In the future, we plan to experiment with more data including data from different growth stages, different locations, and exhibiting different types of abnormalities. Finally, we plan to incorporate abnormality localization capabilities to better assist human annotators to create larger data sets for training deep learning models.

Acknowledgement. : This work was supported by the National Institute of Food and Agriculture/USDA, Award No. 2020-67021-30754.

References

1. Du, H., et al.: The elements of end-to-end deep face recognition: a survey of recent advances. ACM Comput. Surv. (CSUR) **54**(10s), 1–42 (2022)
2. Hao, T., et al.: Recent progress in leveraging deep learning methods for question answering. Neural Comput. Appl. **34**, 2765–2783 (2022)
3. He, K., et al.: Transformers in medical image analysis: a review. Intell. Med. **3**, 59–78 (2022)
4. Fendji, J., et al.: Automatic speech recognition using limited vocabulary: a survey. Appl. Artif. Intell. **36**(1), 2095039 (2022)

5. Shaikh, T.A., Rasool, T., Lone, F.R.: Towards leveraging the role of machine learning and artificial intelligence in precision agriculture and smart farming. Comput. Electron. Agric. **198**, 107119 (2022)
6. Coulibaly, S., et al.: Deep learning for precision agriculture: a bibliometric analysis. Intell. Syst. Appl. **16**, 200102 (2022)
7. Nseir, A., Honig, L.: Corn and Soybean Production down in 2022, USDA Reports Corn Stocks down, Soybean Stocks down from Year Earlier Winter Wheat Seedings up for 2023, United States Department of Agriculture, 12 January 2023. https://www.nass.usda.gov/Newsroom/2023/01-12-2023.php
8. Barbedo, A., Garcia, J.: Digital image processing techniques for detecting, quantifying and classifying plant diseases. Springerplus **2**(1), 1–12 (2013)
9. Romualdo, L.M., et al.: Use of artificial vision techniques for diagnostic of nitrogen nutritional status in maize plants. Comput. Electron. Agric. **104**, 63–70 (2014)
10. Sethy, P.K., et al.: Nitrogen deficiency prediction of rice crop based on convolutional neural network. J. Ambient. Intell. Humaniz. Comput. **11**, 5703–5711 (2020)
11. Zermas D., et al.: A methodology for the detection of nitrogen deficiency in corn fields using high-resolution RGB imagery. IEEE Trans. Autom. Sci. Eng. **18**(4), 1879–1891 (2021)
12. Chore, A., Thankachan, D.: Nutrient defect detection in plant leaf imaging analysis using incremental learning approach with multifrequency visible light approach. J. Electr. Eng. Technol. **18**(2), 1369–1387 (2023)
13. Rahadiyan, D., et al.: Classification of chili plant condition based on color and texture features. In: Seventh International Conference on Informatics and Computing (ICIC), Denpasar, Bali, Indonesia, pp. 01–07 (2022)
14. Tejasri, N., et al.: Drought stress segmentation on drone captured maize using ensemble U-Net framework. In: 2022 IEEE 5th International Conference on Image Processing Applications and Systems (IPAS), Genova, Italy, pp. 1–6 (2022)
15. Yuan, Y., et al.: Diagnosis of nitrogen nutrition of rice based on image processing of visible light. In: 2016 IEEE International Conference on Functional-Structural Plant Growth Modeling, Simulation, Visualization and Applications (FSPMA), pp. 228–232 (2016)
16. Tkachenko, M., et al.: Label studio: data labeling software (2020–22). https://github.com/heartexlabs/label-studio
17. Cortes, C., Vapnik, V.: Support-vector networks. Mach. Learn. **20**, 273–297. Springer (1995)
18. Tan, M., Le, Q.: Efficientnet: rethinking model scaling for convolutional neural networks. In: International Conference on Machine Learning, pp. 6105–6114. PMLR (2019)
19. Ke, G., et al.: Lightgbm: a highly efficient gradient boosting decision tree. Adv. Neural Inf. Process. Syst. **30**, 3146–3154 (2017)
20. Friedman, J.H.: Stochastic gradient boosting. Comput. Stat. Data Anal. **38**(4), 367–378 (2002)
21. Heilbron, D.C.: Zero-altered and other regression models for count data with added zeros. Biom. J. **36**(5), 531–547 (1994)
22. Smith, L.N., Topin, N.: Super-convergence: very fast training of neural networks using large learning rates. In: Artificial Intelligence and Machine Learning for Multi-Domain Operations Applications, vol. 11006, pp. 369–386 (2019)

Deep Learning for Super Resolution of Sugarcane Crop Line Imagery from Unmanned Aerial Vehicles

Emília A. Nogueira[1], Juliana Paula Felix[1], Afonso Ueslei Fonseca[1], Gabriel Vieira[1], Julio Cesar Ferreira[3], Deborah S. A. Fernandes[1], Bruna M. Oliveira[2], and Fabrizzio Soares[1](✉)

[1] Institute of Computing, Federal University of Goias, Goiânia, GO, Brazil
emilia@discente.ufg.br, afonso@inf.ufg.br,
gabriel.vieira@ifgoiano.edu.br, fabrizzio@ufg.br
[2] Agronomy School, Federal University of Goias, Goiânia, GO, Brazil
mendesbruna@ufg.br
[3] Federal Institute of Education, Science and Technology of Goiás, Urutaí, GO, Brazil
julio.ferreira@ifgoiano.edu.br

Abstract. Improving resolution of sugarcane crop images is crucial for extracting valuable information related to productivity, diseases, and water stress. With the rise of remote sensing technologies like Unmanned Aerial Vehicles (UAVs), the number of images available has grown exponentially. In this study, we aim to enhance image resolution using deep learning techniques, namely MuLUT, LeRF, and Real-ESRGAN, to optimize extraction of sugarcane agronomic characteristics. Although these models were initially designed for landscapes, people, cars, and anime images, our experiments with agricultural images show promising results, outperforming classic upsampling algorithms by an impressive 482.81%. Visually, the image quality improvement is significant, making our approach an attractive alternative for extracting crucial information about the crop. This research has the potential to revolutionize the analysis of sugarcane crops, opening new possibilities for precision agriculture and improved agricultural decision-making.

Keywords: Super-Resolution · Sugarcane · Unmanned Aerial Vehicle · Deep learning

1 Introduction

Brazil's sugarcane production is a prominent and leading sector, making the country the world's largest crop producer. According to FAOSTAT [1], Brazil accounted a remarkable 40.5% of global production. Sugarcane thrives in tropical and subtropical regions, and Brazil's favorable climate provides the ideal conditions for its cultivation. The crop's semi-evergreen nature allows for multiple harvests over several years, contributing significantly to its high productivity

[2]. On the global stage of agricultural production, sugarcane plays a pivotal role. Between 2000 and 2018, sugarcane represented approximately 20% of the world's agricultural production, almost twice as much compared to which is corn the second most cultivated crop worldwide during that period [3]. These statistics highlight the importance of sugarcane production in Brazil, not only in terms of volume but also in its economic and energy impact. Consequently, genetic improvement programs are of paramount importance to boost sugarcane productivity without the need for expanding the planted area. However, one of the main challenges lies in phenotyping, which involves evaluating a large number of plants to identify the best possible combinations [4].

Phenotyping techniques play a crucial role in characterizing and quantifying essential phenotypic traits in sugarcane. This process involves measurement and analysis of observable characteristics, such as plant height, stem diameter (a type of stem found in grasses like sugarcane and bamboo), number of tillers, stem mass, biomass production, and other attributes used for sugarcane production and genetic improvement [5,6]. By employing phenotyping in sugarcane, specific varieties with desired traits can be identified, aiding in the development of more productive cultivars [7]. In the past, traditional phenotyping methods involved destructive measurements, where crops were harvested at specific growth stages for genetic testing and mapping of agronomic characteristics [8]. However, this approach proved to be costly and time-consuming for genetic improvement programs, as requires repeated experimental trials to determine the most relevant traits of interest. Nowadays, computational tools have been employed to accelerate the phenotyping process. However, the number of analyzed plants remained relatively small, limiting the scope and accuracy of the assessment [9].

To effectively study phenotypes, the volume of data to be analyzed is substantial, necessitating the expansion of research for High-Throughput Phenotyping (HTP) [10]. HTP aims to reduce time, costs, and labor involved in character analysis by utilizing non-invasive image capture and processing techniques. However, in the case of sugarcane, there remains a dearth of studies on HTP, mainly due to the plant's inherent complexity in evaluating agronomic characteristics, which is directly proportional to the size of the plantation [11]. The HTP has proven to be a valuable tool in the assessment of sugarcane, enabling efficient, accurate, and non-destructive evaluation of numerous samples. Leveraging technologies like satellite imagery, Unmanned Aircraft Systems (UAV), remote sensors, multispectral cameras, and large-scale data analysis, HTP offers cost-effective platforms for data collection [12]. However, given the specific traits of sugarcane and the necessity to gather a substantial amount of information, UAV flights need to be at an altitude of around 400 feet for good results [13,14]. Imagery obtained from high-altitude UAVs poses several challenges, such as blurred images, low resolution, and small targets, leading to subpar performance in existing object detection algorithms [15]. Additionally, these images may not adequately represent the essential agronomic characteristics required for sugarcane HTP.

More in-depth studies on this topic are needed. For instance, in Fig. 1, traditional interpolation techniques (Nearest Neighbor [16] method) (a), were

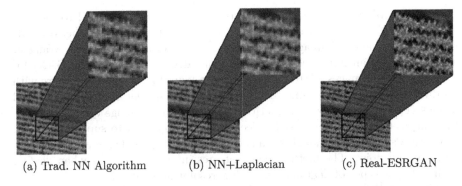

(a) Trad. NN Algorithm   (b) NN+Laplacian   (c) Real-ESRGAN

Fig. 1. Visual comparison between interpolation techniques and deep learning.

attempted to improve image resolution. However, it often results in serrated images. To mitigate this effect, smoothing techniques (b) was applied, but it led to blurry result, which does not happen with Real-ESRGAN [17] that managed to provide a less jagged and sharper image (c) even without the smoothing filter. Development of a more effective and specialized image processing techniques is crucial to enhance the quality and accuracy of UAV-acquired imagery for sugarcane HTP. To address these challenges, this study aimed to enhance the resolution of sugarcane culture images using advanced deep learning techniques, specifically MuLUT [18], LeRF [19], and Real-ESRGAN [17].

The goal was to improve post-flight image processing, thereby facilitating a more accurate extraction of essential agronomic characteristics from sugarcane crops. This work is organized as follows: Sect. 2 provides related work overview. Section 3 details this research methods and materials. In Sect. 4, the experimental design is outlined. Results and discussions are presented in Sect. 5. Finally, the study concludes with insights into future work in Sect. 6.

2   Related Work

Image scaling plays a crucial role in image processing and finds extensive applications in various fields, including aviation, medicine, communication, meteorology, remote sensing, animation production, film compositing, and military applications [20]. The image quality can be enhanced through hardware-based scaling, but it is costly. Thus, improving visual image appearance through software-based scaling, achieved by employing interpolation techniques[1], becomes essential.

Interpolation methods are generally classified into two main categories: linear and non-linear. In this study, our focus lies on non-linear interpolation methods, including Nearest Neighbor interpolation, bilinear interpolation, and bicubic interpolation. These techniques hold significance in achieving superior results when scaling digital images and enhancing their overall visual appeal.

---

[1] Interpolation is the process of estimating pixel values in an image when reconstructing or resizing it.

In image processing, non-linear interpolation methods are used to increase image resolution images, restore damaged or corrupted images, perform 3D reconstruction and fill image gaps captured by sensors or cameras. Wang et al. [21] propose an improved adversarial generative neural network (GAN) for super resolution images. ESRGAN uses a deep neural network architecture with residual attention mechanisms to improve quality and detail of super-resolved images. The method shows competitive results in many image quality metrics. In, Zhang et al. [22] is proposed a deep learning approach to super resolution, in which a single CNN model is trained to handle various degradations such as blurring and noise. The method demonstrates interesting results when dealing with different types of degradations in low resolution images.

Lim et al. [23] propose an approach to improve deep residual networks for the task of image super resolution. They introduce a residual attention mechanism that allows the network to focus on important parts of the image during the reconstruction process. The method demonstrates promising improvements in terms of visual quality and reconstruction accuracy. Recently, Batuhan Bilecen and Ayazoglu [24] create an improved bicubic (Bicubic++), aiming to improve image resolution obtained through the traditional Bicubic method. Bicubic++ won the NTIRE 2023 RTSR Track 2×3 SR competition, and is the fastest of all methods that competed. This is, almost as fast as the standard Bicubic upsampling method. These studies focus on enhancing images by altering their spatial resolution through interpolation algorithms. However, none have been specifically applied to the context of sugarcane. To address this gap, a thorough literature search was conducted in four prominent scientific databases, namely Scopus[2], IEEE Xplore[3], ACM Library[4], and Engineering Village[5] The goal was to identify works that discussed super-resolution techniques applied to images obtained from sugarcane UAVs. The search string was: sugarcane and computer vision and (upsampling OR Super-resolution OR Superresolution OR Super resolution OR Image reconstruction OR High quality images OR Visual qualities). Unfortunately, no relevant articles on this topic have been found so far.

3   Methods and Materials

Image interpolation is a method used to artificially increase the number of pixels in an image, and it finds various applications, including facial reconstructions and image super-resolution. Amongst traditional methods used in super resolution, interpolation techniques play a significant role, and the literature offers several options for performing interpolation. In the field of nonlinear interpolation for images, three widely used techniques are Nearest Neighbor, bilinear, and bicubic interpolation. These methods are highly valuable in enhancing image visualization quality, and their descriptions are provided below [25, 26]:

---

[2] Scopus: www.scopus.com.
[3] IEEE Xplore: ieeexplore.ieee.org/Xplore/home.jsp.
[4] ACM Library: dl.acm.org/.
[5] Engineering Village: www.engineeringvillage.com.

Nearest Neighbor. The Nearest Neighbor interpolation involves replicating pixels. While it is a basic method, it can prove useful in certain situations, especially when processing speed is critical or when preserving critical point characteristics in the interpolated data is essential [16].

Bilinear. Bilinear interpolation is another technique based on a weighted average of pixels. It calculates the value of a new point by taking the weighted average of the four Nearest Neighbor data points that form a square or rectangle around the point to be interpolated. The weights assigned to each data point depend on the distance between the new point and its neighboring data points. Although computationally more demanding than Nearest Neighbor, bilinear interpolation is expected to yield more favorable results [27].

Bicubic. Unlike bilinear interpolation, which relies on a weighted average of the four Nearest Neighbor data points, bicubic interpolation considers a 4×4 matrix of neighboring data points to calculate the interpolated value. This approach allows for a more accurate estimate by incorporating a larger area of neighboring data. Although more complex and time-consuming compared to the previous two methods, bicubic interpolation can yield superior results in certain cases [26].

In addition to these traditional interpolation algorithms, we also applied deep learning techniques to our dataset. Specifically, we tested the effectiveness of MuLUT [18], LeRF [19], and Real-ESRGAN [17] in improving post-flight processing for better extraction of sugarcane agronomic characteristics. More details are presented in the following sections.

3.1 MuLUT

SR-LUT emerged due to the demand for methods aimed at image super-resolution (SR) using the look-up table (LUT) with learning-based SR method. However, the size of a single LUT grows exponentially with the increase of its indexing capacity. Consequently, the receptive field of a single LUT is restricted, resulting in inferior performance. To address this issue, they extend SR-LUT by enabling the cooperation of Multiple LUTs, termed MuLUT [18].

3.2 Real-ESRGAN

The authors have extended ESRGAN [21] for practical and fast restoration application (Real-ESRGAN [17]), which is trained with pure synthetic data. Authors proposes 1) a high-order degradation process to model practical degradations, using sinc filters to model common ringing and overshoot artifacts. 2) Employ several essential modifications (e.g., U-Net discriminator with spectral normalization) to increase discriminator capability and stabilize the training dynamics. 3) Real-ESRGAN trained with pure synthetic data is able to restore most real-world images and achieve. According to the authors, is the better visual performance than previous works, making it more practical in real-world applications. In the first part of the training, authors will perform 1000k iterations.

3.3 LeRF

This work proposes a novel method of Learning Resampling Function (LeRF [19]), which takes advantage of both structural priors learned by deep neural networks (DNNs) and locally continuous assumption of interpolation methods. Specifically, LeRF assigns spatially-varying steerable resampling functions to input image pixels and learns to predict hyper-parameters that determine the orientations of these resampling functions with a neural network. To achieve highly efficient inference, they adopt look-up tables (LUTs) to accelerate the inference of a learned neural network. Furthermore, they design a directional ensemble strategy and edge-sensitive indexing patterns to better capture local structures. However, it is not available for training a new model with our database. We were only able to use the pre-trained model provided by the authors.

3.4 Dataset

Images were collected by our research group for sugarcane crop line detetection and can also be applied in the context of super-resolution [13], in the state of Goiás, Brazil, with latitude $18°36'16.15''$ S and longitude $50°27'27.99''$ W. To perform the mapping, a UAV was used, model BATMAP I[6], at an altitude of 400 feet to capture images, equipped with a RGB camera with 24.3-MP resolution.

4 Experimental Settings

Training Details with 40 Images. For model training, the dataset described in Sect. 3.4 was utilized. In this initial stage, only 40 images were used as part of preliminary testing. The training was conducted on a 48 GB NVIDIA V100 GPU. MuLUT and Real-ESRNet were trained for 1k iterations. To create the Low-Resolution (LR) base, high-resolution (HR) images underwent Downsampling at 3 scales ($4\times$, $3\times$, $2\times$). Data augmentation techniques, such as random image cropping and rotation, were employed to create a diverse and heterogeneous database. Once the models were trained, the testing phase commenced [28].

Details of Tests with 40 Images. In the testing stage, images of size 300×300 pixels were used. These images were resized (Downsampling) at $4\times$, $3\times$, and $2\times$ scales, resulting in low-resolution images of 75×75 pixels, 100×100 pixels, and 150×150 pixels, respectively. For these reduced images, the Nearest Neighbor, Bilinear, Bicubic, MuLUT, LeRF and Real-ESRGAN methods were applied, aiming to upscale the tested images to scales of $2\times$, $3\times$, and $4\times$. The scale applied to the images during both training and testing directly impacts the results. The influence of scale variations on the methods can be observed in Fig. 2.

Details Training with 500 Images. The same dataset described in Sect. 3.4 was used for training the models in this second stage, but this time, we employed

---

[6] http://nuvemuav.com/batmap.

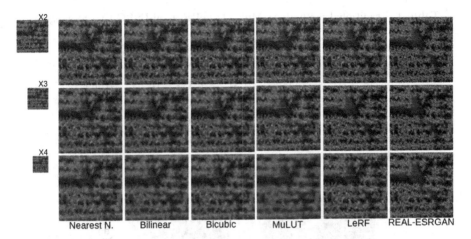

Fig. 2. Sample for visualization comparison in different scales and algorithms.

500 images. The computer settings remained consistent with the 40-image experiment, and we trained MuLUT and Real-ESRNet for 10k iterations. Additionally, the data augmentation technique was applied to enhance model performance. Once the models were trained, we proceeded to conduct the tests.

Details of Tests with 500 Images To ensure a fair comparison between the experiments involving models trained with 40 and 500 images in the subsequent sections, we maintained the same test configurations for both experiments. To compare the results across different tested methods, the metrics described in Sect. 5.1 were calculated to determine the similarity between the High-Resolution (HR) image and the synthetic image obtained through the resolution enhancement techniques. The subsequent sections elaborate on these results.

5 Results and Discussion

This section presents a quantitative assessment based on the methodology developed by Zhang et al. [29] and a visual inspection of the results.

5.1 Quantitative Assessment

The evaluation was conducted using 5 metrics: (1) Euclid [30], (2) Mean Squared Error (MSE) [31], (3) Peak Signal-to-Noise Ratio (PSNR) [32], (4) Structural Similarity Index Measure (SSIM) [33], and (5) Learned Perceptual Image Patch Similarity (LPIPS) [29]. The first four metrics primarily focus on image fidelity rather than visual quality. In contrast, LPIPS aims to determine the similarity between images based on human visual perception [29]. The results obtained for each tested method with these metrics applied to both the 40-image database and the 500-image database can be found in Table 1 and Table 2, respectively.

Table 1. Traditional methods vs MuLUT; LeRF; Real-ESRGAN (40 images).

Algorithm	Euclid ↓	MSE ↓	PSNR ↑	SSIM ↑	LPIPS ↓
Nearest Neighbor	9.000	70.20%	25.043	0.775	0.730
Bilinear	15.906	67.37%	26.342	0.804	0.269
Bicubic	14.453	62.31%	27.415	0.848	0.227
MuLUT	11.094	52.81%	28.980	0.897	0.146
LeRF	12.961	54.38%	28.457	0.894	0.123
Real ESRGAN	15.586	69.13%	26.294	0.847	0.190

↑ The higher the better; ↓ The lower the better

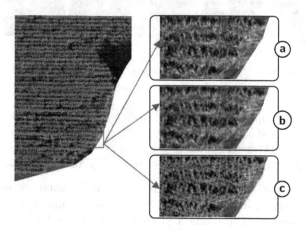

Fig. 3. Sample of Algorithm comparison in same region (in red): (a) HR image captured by the UAV; (b) Image after MuLUT; (c) Image after Real-ESRGAN. (Color figure online)

Table 1 displays results from Fig. 4. It is evident that deep learning methods analyzed achieved remarkable improvements compared to traditional methods, with gains reaching up to 233.61% for MuLUT compared to Nearest Neighbor using the MSE metric. Thus, it can be stated that deep learning-based methods are highly effective in enhancing the resolution of sugarcane images.

Table 2 presents the results obtained from Fig. 5. Both deep learning methods achieved satisfactory results, with gains reaching up to 482.81% when comparing LeRF to Nearest Neighbor using the LPIPS metric, except for Real-ESRGAN. The unsatisfactory results for Real-ESRGAN are attributed to the artifacts generated during the upsampling process. When the High-Resolution (HR) image is analyzed and compared with the results of Real-ESRGAN and MuLUT techniques on a 5x scale (Fig. 3), it is evident that Real-ESRGAN produces an image that differs from the target image.

Table 2. Traditional methods vs MuLUT; LeRF; Real-ESRGAN (500 images).

Algorithm	Euclid ↓	MSE ↓	PSNR ↑	SSIM ↑	LPIPS ↓
Nearest Neighbor	13.672	61.28%	26.134	0.791	0.746
Bilinear	12.203	54.93%	27.519	0.830	0.242
Bicubic	13.453	48.86%	28.492	0.867	0.247
MuLUT	10.195	41.81%	29.637	0.904	0.178
LeRF	8.430	84.21%	22.325	0.668	0.413
Real ESRGAN	13.641	43.39%	29.251	0.901	0.128

↑ The higher the better; ↓ The lower the better

5.2 Quality Assessment

Figure 4 provides a summary of the experiments conducted after training the super-resolution models with 40 images. It is evident that, visually, the deep learning techniques yield sharper images, even with the training dataset containing only 40 images. Figure 5 illustrates the experiments performed after the models were trained using the database with 500 images. It is possible to visually observe that the Real-ESRGAN technique results in a sharper image. In Fig. 6, two images from the test database containing trees were utilized. These images were downsampled by 4×, resulting in low-resolution (LR) images. For each LR image, the interpolation techniques were applied. We focused on zooming in on just the treetops to assess the sharpness of these cutouts, and once again, Real-ESRGAN demonstrates superior visual results.

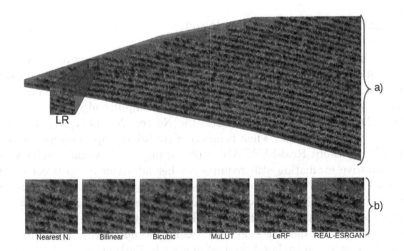

Fig. 4. Comparison of results from training images. a) Database image reduced for testing purposes. b) Results after upsampling techniques in LR image.

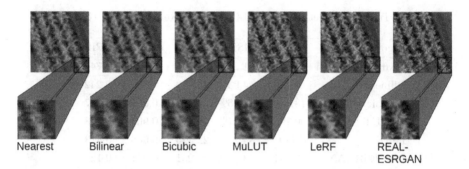

Nearest　　Bilinear　　Bicubic　　MuLUT　　LeRF　　REAL-
　　　　　　　　　　　　　　　　　　　　　　　　　　　ESRGAN

Fig. 5. Sample results after applying upsampling techniques.

MuLUT　　　　　　　　LeRF　　　　　　　Real-ESRGAN

Fig. 6. Images interpolated via deep learning algorithms.

6　Conclusion and Future Work

In this work, we conducted tests using various methods to improve the resolution of sugarcane images captured via UAV. The experimental results demonstrated substantial gains of 482.81% (Nearest Neighbor), 89.06% (Bilinear), and 92.97% (Bicubic) when comparing some traditional upsampling algorithms to LeRF. Additionally, we observed gains of 319.10% (Nearest Neighbor), 35.96% (Bilinear), and 38.76% (Bicubic) when comparing traditional upsampling algorithms to MuLUT. Notably, Real-ESRGAN displayed impressive visual results, though its quantitative evaluation still requires further adjustments to become a reliable tool for upsampling UAV images. Despite these peculiarities, these methods have shown potential in addressing resolution issues in UAV images, especially for sugarcane applications. As future work, we aim to enhance this approach by training on different databases and increasing the number of iterations during training to match the authors' original approach. Furthermore, we plan to test this method on satellite images and compare it with more complex algorithms that utilize neural networks, such as Bicubic++. These steps will contribute to further improving the effectiveness and versatility of the resolution enhancement techniques for various imaging applications.

Acknowledgments. The authors of this study would like to acknowledge the support of the Fundação de Amparo á Pesquisa do Estado de Goiás (FAPEG) - 18/2020, Process no. 202110267000772, and for the support of the Coordenação de Aperfeiçoamento de Pessoal de Nível Superior (CAPES) - Financing Code #001.

References

1. Food, FAO et al.: Faostat statistical database. Rome: Food and Agriculture Organisation of the United Nations (2020)
2. Mulyono, S., et al.: Identifying sugarcane plantation using LANDSAT-8 images with support vector machines. In: IOP Conference Series: Earth and Environmental Science, vol. 47, p. 012008. IOP Publishing (2016)
3. Food FAOSTAT. Agriculture organization of the united nations FAO statistical database, p. 40 (2023). https://www.fao.org/. Accessed June 2023
4. Crossa, J., et al.: The modern plant breeding triangle: optimizing the use of genomics, phenomics, and enviromics data. Front. Plant Sci. **12**, 651480 (2021)
5. Nogueira, E., Oliveira, B., Bulcão-Neto, R., Soares, F.: A systematic review of the literature on machine learning methods applied to high throughput phenotyping in agricultural production. IEEE Lat. Am. Trans. **21**(7), 783–796 (2023)
6. Sun, J., et al.: High-throughput phenotyping platforms enhance genomic selection for wheat grain yield across populations and cycles in early stage. Theor. Appl. Genet. **132**, 1705–1720 (2019)
7. Yang, W., et al.: Crop phenomics and high-throughput phenotyping: past decades, current challenges, and future perspectives. Mol. Plant **13**(2), 187–214 (2020)
8. Furbank, R.T., Tester, M.: Phenomics-technologies to relieve the phenotyping bottleneck. Trends Plant Sci. **16**(12), 635–644 (2011)
9. Mota, L.F.M., et al.: Evaluating the performance of machine learning methods and variable selection methods for predicting difficult-to-measure traits in Holstein dairy cattle using milk infrared spectral data. J. Dairy Sci. **104**(7), 8107–8121 (2021)
10. Araus, J.L., Cairns, J.E.: Field high-throughput phenotyping: the new crop breeding frontier. Trends Plant Sci. **19**(1), 52–61 (2014)
11. Gebremedhin, A., Badenhorst, P.E., Wang, J., Spangenberg, G.C., Smith, K.F.: Prospects for measurement of dry matter yield in forage breeding programs using sensor technologies. Agronomy **9**(2), 65 (2019). https://doi.org/10.3390/agronomy9020065. https://www.mdpi.com/2073-4395/9/2/65
12. Araus, J.L., Kefauver, S.C., Zaman-Allah, M., Olsen, M.S., Cairns, J.E.: Translating high-throughput phenotyping into genetic gain. Trends Plant Sci. **23**(5), 451–466 (2018)
13. Rocha, B., et al.: Skew angle detection and correction in text images using RGB gradient. In: Sclaroff, S., Distante, C., Leo, M., Farinella, G.M., Tombari, F. (eds.) Image Analysis and Processing – ICIAP 2022. ICIAP 2022. LNCS, vol. 13232, pp. 249–262. Springer, Cham (2022). https://doi.org/10.1007/978-3-031-06430-2_21
14. Demirel, M., Kaya, Y., Polat, N.: Investigation of the effect of UAV flight altitude in map production. Intercont. Geoinf. Days **4**, 21–24 (2022)

15. Chang, Y., Li, D., Gao, Y., Yun, S., Jia, X.: An improved yolo model for UAV fuzzy small target image detection. Appl. Sci. **13**(9), 5409 (2023)
16. Rosenfeld, A.: Digital Picture Processing. Academic Press, Cambridge (1976)
17. Wang, X., Xie, L., Dong, C., Shan, Y.: Real-ESRGAN: training real-world blind super-resolution with pure synthetic data. In: Proceedings of the CVF International Conference on Computer Vision, vol. 2021-October (2021)
18. Li, J., Chen, C., Cheng, Z., Xiong, Z.: MuLUT: cooperating multiple look-up tables for efficient image super-resolution. In: Avidan, S., Brostow, G., Cisse, M., Farinella, G.M., Hassner, T. (eds.) Computer Vision – ECCV 2022. ECCV 2022. LNCS, vol. 13678, pp. 238–256. Springer, Cham (2022). https://doi.org/10.1007/978-3-031-19797-0_14
19. Li, J., et al.: Learning steerable function for efficient image resampling. In: Proceedings of the IEEE/CVF Conference on Computer Vision and Pattern Recognition, pp. 5866–5875 (2023)
20. Panagiotopoulou, A., et al.: Super-resolution techniques in photogrammetric 3D reconstruction from close-range UAV imagery. Heritage **6**(3), 2701–2715 (2023)
21. Wang, X., et al.: ESRGAN: enhanced super-resolution generative adversarial networks. In: Proceedings of the European Conference on Computer Vision (ECCV) Workshops (2018)
22. Zhang, K., Zuo, W., Zhang, L.: Learning a single convolutional super-resolution network for multiple degradations. In: Proceedings of the IEEE Conference on Computer Vision and Pattern Recognition, pp. 3262–3271 (2018)
23. Lim, B., Son, S., Kim, H., Nah, S., Mu Lee, K.: Enhanced deep residual networks for single image super-resolution. In: Proceedings of the IEEE Conference on Computer Vision and Pattern Recognition Workshops (2017)
24. Bilecen, B.B., Ayazoglu, M.: Bicubic++: slim, slimmer, slimmest-designing an industry-grade super-resolution network. In: Proceedings of the IEEE/CVF Conference on Computer Vision and Pattern Recognition, pp. 1623–1632 (2023)
25. Singh, A., Singh, J.: Review and comparative analysis of various image interpolation techniques. In: 2019 2nd International Conference on Intelligent Computing, Instrumentation and Control Technologies (ICICICT), vol. 1, pp. 1214–1218. IEEE (2019)
26. Keys, R.: Cubic convolution interpolation for digital image processing. IEEE Trans. Acoust. Speech Signal Process. **29**(6), 1153–1160 (1981)
27. Rosenfeld, A.: Picture processing by computer. ACM Comput. Surv. (CSUR) **1**(3), 147–176 (1969)
28. Nogueira, E.A., et al.: Upsampling of unmanned aerial vehicle images of sugarcane crop lines with a Real-ESRGAN. In: 2023 IEEE Canadian Conference on Electrical and Computer Engineering (CCECE), pp. 1–4. IEEE (2023)
29. Zhang, R., Isola, P., Efros, A. A., Shechtman, E., Wang, O.: The unreasonable effectiveness of deep features as a perceptual metric. In: Proceedings of the IEEE Conference on Computer Vision and Pattern Recognition (2018)
30. Bishop, C.M.: Pattern recognition and machine learning. In: Jordan, M., Kleinberg, J., Schölkopf, B. (eds.) Pattern Recognition. Information Science and Statistics, vol. 4, no. 4, pp. 738. Springer (2006). https://doi.org/10.1117/1.2819119. http://www.library.wisc.edu/selectedtocs/bg0137.pdf
31. Das, K., Jiang, J., Rao, J.N.K.: Mean squared error of empirical predictor. Ann. Stat. **32**(2), 818–840 (2004). https://doi.org/10.1214/009053604000000201

32. Korhonen, J., You, J.: Peak signal-to-noise ratio revisited: is simple beautiful? In: 2012 Fourth International Workshop on Quality of Multimedia Experience, pp. 37–38. IEEE (2012)
33. Wang, Z., Bovik, A.C., Sheikh, H.R., Simoncelli, E.P.: Image quality assessment: from error visibility to structural similarity. IEEE Trans. Image Process. **13**(4), 600–612 (2004)